Alan R. Gitelson, *Loyola University of Chicago*
Robert L. Dudley, *George Mason University*
Melvin J. Dubnick, *University of New Hampshire*

Q **When you wrote this book, what did you hope it would do for students?**

A In developing *American Government: Myths and Realities,* we were also driven by the need for an affordable paperback textbook that filled the void between texts that relied too much on a particular framework that offered a narrow view of government and those designed to provide a comprehensive introduction to political science through the study of American government. We believe that most students who enroll in the basic American government course are not interested in some ideological perspective on politics, nor are they necessarily on track to become political scientists. Rather, we believe most students are just attempting to come to terms with what they regard as an often baffling political system. Our goal is to help them make sense of American government by playing off of those widespread myths and beliefs shared by many Americans.

Q **What has your experience been in teaching the American government course?**

A During the 1990s, each of us became active in the movement to enhance civic education, and our work in that effort also influenced our revisions of the textbook. We were especially interested in efforts by the American Political Science Association to adapt the American government course to a new generation of Internet-connected students who required new pedagogical approaches. While maintaining the textbook's core approach, we have always been open to adjusting to generational shifts in beliefs and attitudes about the U.S. political system—and constantly adapting to the new realities of American government that have taken root in the 21st century.

The "Myths and Realities" theme is incorporated clearly and distinctively into each chapter

Demonstrates to students that the myths surrounding our governmental and political life play an important role in how we make sense of the baffling and complex realities that we hear and read about each day

Provides a resource that helps students make sense of their government in light of constantly evolving myths and realities

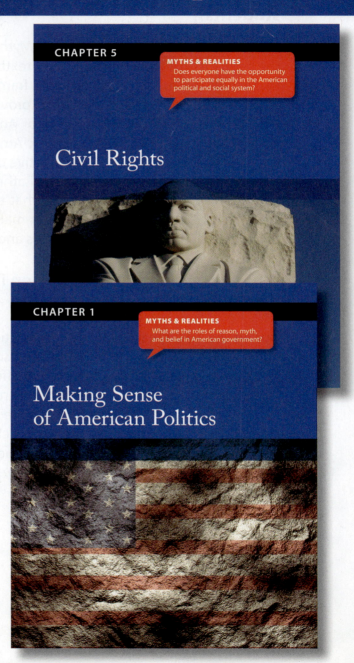

CHAPTER 5

MYTHS & REALITIES
Does everyone have the opportunity to participate equally in the American political and social system?

Civil Rights

CHAPTER 1

MYTHS & REALITIES
What are the roles of reason, myth, and belief in American government?

Making Sense of American Politics

New "Policy Connection" features at the end of each chapter present domestic and foreign policy within the context of chapter topics, integrating policy coverage throughout. This approach capitalizes on student interest and allows professors to bring the material into the course in a more contextualized fashion.

Policy Connection

What is the relationship between American domestic policies and U.S. foreign policy?

DOMESTIC AND FOREIGN POLICY

The Policy Challenge

Among the major challenges facing those who shape and direct American foreign policy is how to reconcile what they do on the international stage with the realities of how the United States handles many of its toughest domestic issues. Similarly, those who work on domestic policy problems can hardly ignore that, in a sense, the whole world is watching how America deals with important issues, especially those related to the treatment of minority populations.

In this Policy Connection we consider those policy dilemmas, highlighting the post–World War II struggles to advance civil rights that we discussed in Chapter 5.

The Whole World Was Watching

In Septe...
sent a tho...
sion to pr...
ing to ent...
School. I...
order that...
of forced...

The image of students being escorted to and from Little Rock Central High School 1957 was the cause of considerable embarrassment for U.S. foreign-policy makers and diplomats.

176

Policy Connection

How can the government maintain its commitment to civil liberties while minimizing the nation's vulnerability to attack?

FOREIGN POLICY

The Policy Challenge

In the years following the attacks of September 11, 2001, Americans were confronted with a major policy challenge. As important as it is for the government to generate and maintain the support of the American people during a national security crisis, the social controls and intrusions into their private lives that might have to take place—actions that they would find unacceptable during peacetime—may require a reconsideration of those basic constitutional liberties we Americans hold so dear.

In this Policy Connection we consider the various policy approaches that the government has applied under conditions related to our national security or other national emergencies, especially those that seem to threaten our civil liberties, as we have discussed in Chapter 4.

President George W. Bush is informed of the attacks of September 11, 2001, by Andrew Card, his chief of staff.

"We Are Going to War"

Bob Woodward, one of America's best-known journalists, wrote of the moment that President George W. Bush learned of the attacks of September 11, 2001:

A photo of that moment is etched for history. The president's hands are folded formally in his lap, his head turned to hear [Andrew] Card's words. His face has a distant sober look, almost frozen, edging on bewilderment. Bush remembers exactly what he was thinking: "They had declared war on us, and I made up my mind at that moment that we are going to war."[1]

The decision to commit the United States to any war effort has obvious policy implications, and the War on Terror initiated in response to 9/11 was no different. Not only do armies and navies have to be mobilized on behalf of the war effort, but so too do

145

Rich pedagogy reflects the needs and demands of today's students

Each chapter opens with an outline and focus questions that introduce the main points covered in that chapter

Review questions help students measure their understanding of the key concepts covered in each chapter

"Asked & Answered" boxes employ a question-and-answer format in order to examine various political issues, such as "How knowledgeable are U.S. students about their government?" and "Shouldn't we have more than just two party options on the ballot?"

Marginal key terms, accompanied by definitions, highlight key concepts in each chapter

The Crime of "Driving or Shopping While Black"

On August 17, 1988, a New Jersey state trooper pulled over, for speeding, a Porsche driven by an African American male. Although the trooper did not use a radar gun to clock the speed of the vehicle, she observed that the late-model sports car was traveling "faster than the flow of traffic." As the trooper approached the vehicle, the driver made "furtive movements" toward the passenger side of the car—movements that she considered suspicious. The trooper later admitted that the driver was cooperative and polite and had complied with all requests. Nevertheless, she asked him to exit the car; she conducted a pat-down, and in a subsequent search of the vehicle she found a fully loaded handgun on the passenger side rear floor. She asked the driver if he had a gun permit as required by New Jersey state law. He did not, and the trooper placed him under arrest, charging him with possessing an unregistered dan-

CHAPTER OUTLINE AND FOCUS QUESTIONS

The Continuing Struggle Against Racism

> What have been the breakthroughs in the movement toward racial justice in America?

Sex Discrimination

> How have the rights of women evolved?

Sexual Orientation

> How has the legal status of gays, lesbians, and transgender people changed?

Equality and Citizenship Status

> What constitutional rights do noncitizens have?

Review Questions

1. Write an essay in which you discuss how the level of scrutiny applied in cases involving racial discrimination differs from the level used in cases concerning discrimination based on gender.
2. Write an essay in which you discuss the progress that gays and lesbians have made in advancing their claims for equality.

ASKED & ANSWERED

ASKED: What do we mean by *Jim Crow*?

ANSWERED: Between 1877 and 1965, many state and local governments, particularly those of the former Confederacy, sought to enshrine racial segregation in their communities by constructing often elaborate legal codes that prohibited consorting among the races. These laws and the social norms surrounding this era came to be called "Jim Crow," the stage name of Thomas Dartmouth Rice, a white minstrel performer (1808–1860). With his blackened face and grotesque manner, Rice became famous for his extravagant and demeaning caricatures of slaves. Although it is not certain how the minstrel character came to symbolize a regime of apartheid, they both demeaned African Americans and furthered the separation the races.

Jim Crow is best known for the laws requiring segregated schools, drinking fountains, restrooms, restaurants, and transportation services. But these were

Of course, the most common Jim Crow law was the absolute prohibition of intermarriages. But miscegenation laws were not limited to former confederate states. States as far flung as California, Connecticut, Indiana, Montana, and North Dakota had at some point, during this period, prohibited interracial marriages. Likewise, laws requiring segregation in public schools were not limited to the South. After all, the schools in the nation's capital were segregated by race. Even Wyoming specified that schools should be segregated anytime there were fifteen or more African American children in the district.

Legal codes, however, were only one part of the Jim Crow era. Jim Crow was also about attitudes and unwritten codes of behavior. As the author and folklorist Stetson Kennedy noted, African Americans were expected to show deference to whites at all times. No African American could ever imply that a white person was lying or dishonest. Nor could an African American man comment on the appearance of

Racial profiling A practice in which decisions about whether to enforce a law are based on the race or ethnicity of an individual rather than on any suspicious or illegal act.

searches and seizures. In the Barneys incident, the issue is false arrest.

Ask members of the African American community, however, and they will tell you that what was involved in both instances has more to do with civil rights—that is, protection against discrimination and unequal treatment under the law—than civil liberties. The 1988 case made news across the country because the driver of the Porsche was Charles Barkley, at the time a well-known professional basketball player with the Philadelphia 76ers. Although not brought up in court at the time, questions were raised as to whether the traffic stop was really an example of **racial profiling**—a practice in which decisions about whether to enforce a law are based on the race or ethnicity of an individual rather than on any suspicious or illegal act. A secret internal study conducted by the state police a few years later indicated that the practice of racial profiling was pervasive among the troopers who patrolled the New Jersey Turnpike. Finally, in 1999 the state attorney general issued a public report that noted that African Americans were "routinely targeted" for traffic stops. The practice was so common that African Americans claimed that the only reason they were stopped was for the crime of "driving while black."

The 2013 Barneys case made headlines when the New York media

Support to help you teach

Ancillary Resource Center

The Ancillary Resource Center (ARC) provides access to all of the up-to-date teaching resources for this text—at any time—while guaranteeing the security of grade-significant resources. It also allows OUP to keep instructors informed when new content becomes available. Register for access and create your individual user account by clicking on the Instructor's Resources link on the book's Companion Website, **www.oup.com/us/gitelson**. The ARC for *American Government: Myths and Realities* includes the Instructor's Resource Manual with Test Bank, a Computerized Test Bank, and PowerPoint-Based Slides.

Instructor's Resource Manual with Test Bank

Available on the Ancillary Resource Center, the Instructor's Resource Manual includes chapter objectives, detailed chapter outlines, lecture suggestions and activities, discussion questions, video resources, and Web resources. The Test Item File includes multiple-choice, short-answer, and essay questions. Questions are identified as factual, conceptual, or applied, and correct answers are keyed to the text pages where the concepts are presented.

Computerized Test Bank

Using the test authoring and management tool Diploma, the Computerized Test Bank that accompanies this text is designed for both novice and advanced users. Diploma enables instructors to create and edit questions, create randomized quizzes and tests with an easy-to-use drag-and-drop tool, publish quizzes and tests to online courses, and print quizzes and tests for paper-based assessments. It is available on the Ancillary Resource Center or in the form of a **Course Cartridge**.

PowerPoint-Based Slides

Each chapter's slide deck includes a succinct chapter outline and incorporates relevant chapter graphics. The slides are available on the Ancillary Resource Center.

CNN Videos (978-0-19-021620-7)

Offering recent clips on timely topics, this DVD provides fifteen films tied to the chapter topics in the text. Each clip is approximately 5–10 minutes in length, offering a great way to launch your lectures. Contact your local OUP sales representative for details.

Course Cartridges

Course cartridges are available for Blackboard, WebCT, Angel, D2L, or whatever course management system you prefer.

For access to the instructor's resources, please contact your Oxford University Press representative or call 800.280.0280.

Support to help your students succeed

Companion Website (www.oup.com/us/gitelson)

This **free** and **open-access** site includes a number of study tools for students, including learning objectives, key-concept summaries, quizzes and essay questions, web activities, and web links.

 Dashboard

Online homework made easy! Tired of learning management systems that promise the world but are too difficult to use? Oxford offers you Dashboard, a simple, nationally hosted, online learning course—including study, review, interactive, and assessment materials—in an easy-to-use system that requires less than fifteen minutes to master. Assignment and assessment results flow into a straightforward, color-coded gradebook, allowing you a clear view into your students' progress. The system works on every major platform and device, including mobile devices.

For the best experience teaching and learning American government, this Dashboard offers quizzes, exams, and essay questions correlating to chapter learning objectives; CNN videos with corresponding test items; and web links for additional resources. In addition, a new simulation series invites students to "learn by doing" with media activities that integrate learning across chapters, with assessment scores that report to the color-coded gradebook. The five simulations are *Comprehensive Immigration Reform, Managing a Congressional Election, Advocating for a New Warship, Playing President on Foreign Policy,* and *All the Way to the Supreme Court.*

Only $5 with the price of a new book! Also available for sale on its own.

Contact your local OUP representative to order *American Government: Myths and Realities* and the Access Code Card for Dashboard. Please use package ISBN 978-0-19-023375-4 to order.

Now Playing: Learning American Government Through Film

Through documentaries, feature films, and YouTube videos, *Now Playing: Learning American Government Through Film* provides video examples of course concepts to demonstrate real-world relevance. It is available in both a student and instructor edition and can be packaged with *American Government: Myths and Realities* for free.

E-Book

Available through CourseSmart for $39.95.

AMERICAN GOVERNMENT

AMERICAN GOVERNMENT

MYTHS AND REALITIES

2014 Election Edition

Alan R. Gitelson

Loyola University of Chicago

Robert L. Dudley

George Mason University

Melvin J. Dubnick

University of New Hampshire

New York Oxford
Oxford University Press

Oxford University Press is a department of the University of Oxford.
It furthers the University's objective of excellence in research,
scholarship, and education by publishing worldwide.

Oxford   New York
Auckland   Cape Town   Dar es Salaam   Hong Kong   Karachi
Kuala Lumpur   Madrid   Melbourne   Mexico City   Nairobi
New Delhi   Shanghai   Taipei   Toronto

With offices in
Argentina   Austria   Brazil   Chile   Czech Republic   France   Greece
Guatemala   Hungary   Italy   Japan   Poland   Portugal   Singapore
South Korea   Switzerland   Thailand   Turkey   Ukraine   Vietnam

For titles covered by Section 112 of the US Higher Education
Opportunity Act, please visit www.oup.com/us/he for the
latest information about pricing and alternate formats.

Published in the United States of America by
Oxford University Press
198 Madison Avenue, New York, NY 10016
http://www.oup.com

Oxford is a registered trademark of Oxford University Press.

Library of Congress Cataloging-in-Publication Data

Gitelson, Alan R.
   American government: myths and realities / Alan R. Gitelson, Loyola University
of Chicago, Robert L. Dudley, George Mason University, Melvin J. Dubnick,
University of New Hampshire.—2014 election edition.
      pages cm
   ISBN 978-0-19-937422-9
   1. United States—Politics and government—Textbooks. I. Dudley, Robert L.
II. Dubnick, Melvin J. III. Title.
   JK276.G58 2016
   320.473—dc23
                                                                    2014035171

Printing number: 9 8 7 6 5 4 3 2 1

Printed in the United States of America
on acid-free paper

To Idy, Laura, Rachel, Doug, Josh, Eli, Jonah, Zoe, and Daniel . . .
who make life so much sweeter.

A. R. G.

As always, to Judy, Patrick, and Michael, but also to Catherine for
making Patrick so happy.

R. L. D.

To Randi, Heather, and PD—and the students at UNH who make it
very difficult to remain cynical about the future of American
government.

M. J. D.

Brief Contents

Contents

In addition to the unique Policy Connection essays in each chapter, instructors interested in providing more traditional coverage of domestic and foreign policies can refer students to Chapters 15 and 16, located on the companion website at **www.oup.com/us/gitelson**.

Preface

It would be an understatement to say that we live in interesting times, for it is likely that every American has been touched in some way by the major economic, social, and political upheavals of the past quarter-century.

When we began work on the first edition of *American Government* in 1986, Ronald Reagan was president and the economy was growing at a moderate rate, continuing a recovery from the downturn attributed to "stagflation" of the late 1970s. Internationally, the Cold War continued to be waged with the Soviet Union. At home, desktop computers using "floppy disks" were starting to replace typewriters in offices and movie theaters featured "Ferris Bueller's Day Off" and "Top Gun."

Writing this edition, we three authors cannot help but reflect on how much things have changed. Barack Obama, an African-American who was working as a community organizer in Chicago when Reagan was in office, now sits in the Oval Office. The economy is still in recovery mode, but this time emerging from the Great Recession of 2008–2009 triggered by a collapse of financial markets. The Cold War came to an end with the collapse of the Soviet Union in 1991, but relationships are at times as tense between Russia and the United States as they were in the 1980s, although the issues are more often about Moscow's influence over neighboring states than the spread of Soviet Communism. Floppy disks have been replaced by Internet-based "cloud computing" and desktops by tablets and smart phones with considerably more power than the larger computers they replaced. As for "Ferris Bueller's Day Off" and "Top Gun," they are now "classics" that can be "streamed" at anytime—and anyplace—you can access your Netflix or Amazon accounts. The one thing that has been constant over the years has been change.

Each edition of our textbook that followed that first publication reflected the events that altered the political landscape of the time. Throughout, however, we remained committed to providing a resource that helped students make sense of their government in light of constantly evolving myths and realities. As will be evident to those instructors who assigned any of those previous editions, that commitment remains strong and continues to provide the anchor for this edition.

However, we began the revision for this edition well aware that a good deal of the conventional "textbook" wisdom about American government and politics is undergoing a major transformation even as students read this latest edition. The political and constitutional landscape is constantly changing, often in ways that is difficult to predict. Moreover, some of the changes raise questions about the effectiveness and long term stability of the U.S. political system. Two widely respected observers of American politics, Thomas E. Mann of the Brookings Institution and Norman Ornstein of the American Enterprise Institute, captured the state of affairs in the title of their 2012 book, *It's Even Worse Than It Looks: How the American Constitutional System Collided with the New Politics of Extremism*. Other analysts have wondered if the "new normal" for American government is to operate from crisis to crisis, striking short-term bargains that satisfy no one and make potential long-term solutions more costly—and less probable.

Faced with these changes and challenges to the operations of American government, the role of myths, ideologies, and beliefs described in Chapter 1 seems even more significant than in the past. These intellectual devices for "making sense" of American government and politics are playing a central role in how Americans frame their political world, and in the process they alter the realities of political life. In response to the myth of party irrelevance (Chapter 7), for example, political scientists in the past would note that the very real differences between the parties were often covered over by the search for the middle ground in efforts to win elections by appealing to the "median voter." Today, however, political scientists are focused on the role those differences play in exacerbating the "partisan polarization" that has characterized policy gridlock during the Obama Administration. And while the political implications of judicial decisions have become even more evident in recent years with decisions on a range of issues from same-sex marriage to campaign finance reform, the myth that emphasizes the Court's role as the ultimate "objective" authority regarding what is (or is not) constitutional (Chapter 14) remains a powerful force in shaping the public's view of how our government ought to operate.

While remaining focused on the myths and realities of American government, this edition is different from earlier versions in several key respects. We are pleased that *American Government: Myths and Realities* is now published by Oxford University Press (OUP). The move to OUP has provided us an opportunity to rethink the traditional structure of the typical American government textbook and to work with new approaches to content and pedagogy reflecting the needs and demands of today's students. Additionally, in an era where prices of textbooks are skyrocketing, we are extremely pleased to be working with a publisher who is committed to producing quality scholarship at the best possible price.

What Students Tell Us

Students tell us they want a textbook that reflects the way they actually learn and study at a price they can afford. *American Government: Myths and Realities* meets students' primary goals: a price-conscious text presented in a way that makes the learning process more interesting. We know that different students learn in different ways. Some learn best by reading, whereas others are more visually oriented. The ideal textbook gets to the point quickly, is easy to understand, has shorter chapters, has pedagogical materials designed to reinforce key concepts, has strong supporting ancillaries for quizzing, testing, and assessment, and provides them with real value for their dollar.

American Government: Myths and Realities provides exactly what students want and need pedagogically in a textbook. It does this by:

• Being concise

• Keeping material current

• Highlighting and boldfacing key concepts and information

• Incorporating review questions into each chapter for self-testing

• Providing students with a product that is price-sensitive and therefore a true value

Bringing Currency to Your Classroom

While we continue to make use of familiar historical narratives to introduce students to many of the basic concepts and institutions of American government, each chapter of *American Government: Myths and Realities* has been updated to provide coverage of major events that have shaped our nation in recent years, providing students with a unique lens through which to examine the current state of American government and politics. The updates are also informed by the latest political science research on American government. Past users of *American Government: Myths and Realities* will also notice major changes in the text's organization. Key updates include:

• A new full color design complete with updated photos and figures, which give further examples and emphasize student interest, at a great price point.

• Fourteen chapters rather than fifteen, a change that reflects the realities of the typical semester calendar.

• Two distinct chapters to cover civil liberties (Chapter 4) and civil rights (Chapter 5).

• Coverage of a range of policy topics has been integrated into the "Policy Connection" features that follow each chapter. We offer details about these changes below.

• The content covered in Chapters 14 (domestic policies) and 15 (foreign and defense policies) of previous editions have been moved to the text's companion website.

• Coverage of the 2014 midterm congressional elections and Supreme Court decisions.

- Coverage of the 2012 and 2014 Supreme Court decisions regarding the Affordable Care Act, DOMA, and the Voting Rights Act.

- Updated coverage regarding same-sex marriage, immigration, and affirmative action.

- New data regarding PACs and Super-PACs and limits on contributions.

- Updated coverage concerning media and politics and the impact of social media.

- Updated coverage of government surveillance in light of the disclosures made by Edward Snowden and the National Security Administration.

- Chapter opening vignettes and Asked & Answered feature content have been updated for currency.

The Approach of This Book: Myths and Realities

As active classroom teachers committed as much to engaging students as to informing them, we have always found that highlighting and contrasting the complex myths and realities of American government facilitated student understanding and appreciation of the subject. Underpinning the attraction of the myths and realities theme was the intent of demonstrating to students that the myths surrounding our governmental and political life play an important role in how we make sense of the baffling and complex realities we hear and read about each day. We continue to believe that this is an effective approach to introducing students to the study and appreciation of American government. We are constantly reminded of the "broken branch myth" (Chapter 11) when we read about public opinion polls that that show that congressional job approval is at only 15 percent, while Barack Obama learned quite early in his first term that in reality it is impossible to live up to expectations that come along with the myth of the "all-powerful presidency" (Chapter 12).

One of the benefits of this approach has been its flexibility in the face of cultural and technological changes. For many of us, the traditional classroom provided the opportunity to isolate students from the outside world for an hour or so while we lectured or engaged them in focused discussions. In the wireless environments of most university campuses, we can no longer think of the classroom as the only or most effective means for focusing the attention of our students. With laptops, mobile devices, and access to the Internet, the outside world is a constant and competing classroom presence that offers a previously unfathomable range of sense-making approaches from the paranoiac (e.g., conspiracy theory blogs) to the satirical (e.g., *The Daily Show with Jon Stewart*) and the partisan (e.g., Fox News and MSNBC). These are the new media outlets through which old and new myths about American government and politics are developed and sustained. Rather than regard these alternative perspectives as threats to a better understanding and appreciation of our civic life, *American Government: Myths And Realities* accepts the role that they play and seeks to have students take a more reflective and critical view of how they and others perceive American government.

Policy Connection Essays

Introductory courses in American government are typically focused on core institutions and political dynamics, and this has been reflected in the structure of traditional American government textbooks. In many cases, public policy—that is, how government responds to public problems—is relegated to one or two chapters at the end of the traditional textbook. This approach often makes it difficult for students to appreciate the complex connections among government institutions, partisan politics, and the public policies that affect their daily lives.

In *American Government: Myths and Realities*, we deal with this problem by introducing a Policy Connection essay at the end of each chapter. Each essay addresses a particular issue that connects the subject of the preceding chapter with a domestic or foreign policy-related question. Among the questions addressed in these essays are:

- What role does "federalism" play in your education? (Policy Connection 3)

- When it comes to economic policy, does it really matter which party is in power? (Policy Connection 7)

• Are special interest groups really able to control public policy? (Policy Connection 9)

• How has government policy shaped the media landscape? (Policy Connection 10)

• Does the president of the United States really control American foreign policy? (Policy Connection 12)

As distinct units within the textbook, each essay is designed to be used in a number of ways. Each can be treated as an extension of the preceding chapter or used as material to stimulate classroom or online discussion in conjunction with class lectures. Instructors can select certain Policy Connection essays as the basis for creating a special topic that can be added to the general syllabus. Students can be assigned one or more essays to explore on their own as research paper topics or for extra credit assignments.

In addition to the unique use of the Policy Connection essays in each chapter, those faculty interested in providing more traditional coverage of domestic and foreign policies can refer students to chapters 15 and 16 provided on the companion website.

Features

American Government: Myths and Realities includes a number of helpful pedagogical features.

• Each chapter includes an "Asked & Answered" feature, which uses an accessible question-and-answer format to take a closer look at political issues of interest to students. Topics include:

> So you want to change the Constitution? (Chapter 2)

> Why can't we reduce the role of money in elections as other nations do? (Chapter 8)

> Why are there so few women serving in legislative bodies? (Chapter 11)

• The "Politics & Popular Culture" feature, referenced in each of the text chapters, appears on the text's companion website. This feature examines how popular culture reflects and influences government and politics. Topics include:

> HBO's Favorite Founding Father (Chapter 2)

> Twitter Campaigning in the Digital Age (Chapter 8)

> Hollywood Bureaucrats and Other Myths (Chapter 13)

Chapter-Opening Vignettes

Each chapter opens with an introductory vignette, all of which are new. Among the new and updated topics covered in this edition are:

• Constitutional Trade-Off: New York City and Stop-and-Frisk (Chapter 2)

• Driving and Shopping While Black (racial profiling) (Chapter 5)

• The Impact of *War of the Worlds* (Chapter 10)

Skills-Focused Pedagogical Features

Carefully structured to enhance student learning, each chapter:

• Opens with a preview outline and focus questions correlated to each major section of the chapter

• Introduces the myths and realities to be discussed in the chapter.

• Includes boldfaced key terms, whose definitions appear in the margins of the chapter where the terms first appear

• Closes with a Conclusion presenting a retrospective glance at the highlighted myths in light of the whole chapter discussion

• Reviews the chapter materials with "Focus Questions Review," a point-by-point summary of the chapter's main ideas that includes a recap of, and answers to, the focus questions

Appendices

Appearing at the end of the text are the Declaration of Independence and The Constitution of the United States of America (annotated as to those paragraphs no longer in effect).

Ensuring Student Success

Oxford University Press offers instructors and students a comprehensive ancillary package for qualified adopters of *American Government: Myths and Realities.*

- **Dashboard**

  Online homework made easy! Tired of learning management systems that promise the world but are too difficult to use? Oxford offers you Dashboard, a simple, nationally hosted, online learning course—including study, review, interactive, and assessment materials—in an easy-to-use system that requires less than fifteen minutes to master. Assignment and assessment results flow into a straightforward, color-coded gradebook, allowing you a clear view into your students' progress. The system works on every major platform and device, including mobile devices. For the best experience teaching and learning American government, this Dashboard offers quizzes, exams, and essay questions correlating to chapter learning objectives; CNN videos with corresponding test items; and web links for additional resources. In addition, a new simulation series invites students to "learn by doing" with media activities that integrate learning across chapters, with assessment scores that report to the color-coded gradebook. The five simulations are *Comprehensive Immigration Reform, Managing a Congressional Election, Advocating for a New Warship, Playing President on Foreign Policy,* and *All the Way to the Supreme Court.*

  Only $5 with the price of a new book! Also available for sale on its own. Contact your local OUP representative to order *American Government: Myths and Realities* and the Access Code Card for Dashboard. Please use package ISBN 978-0-19-023375-4 to order.

- **Ancillary Resource Center**

  This convenient, instructor-focused website provides access to all of the up-to-date teaching resources for this text—at any time—while guaranteeing the security of grade-significant resources. In addition, it allows OUP to keep instructors informed when new content becomes available. Register for access and create your individual user account by clicking on the Instructor's Resources link at www.oup.com/us/gitelson. Available on the ARC:

  > **Instructor's Manual:** The Instructor's Resource Manual includes chapter objectives, a detailed chapter outline, lecture suggestions and activities, discussion questions, video resources, and web resources.

  > **Test Item File:** This resource includes nearly 1,800 test items, including multiple choice, short answer, and essay questions. Questions are identified as factual, conceptual, or applied, and correct answers are keyed to the text pages where the concepts are presented.

  > **Computerized Test Bank:** Using the test authoring and management tool Diploma, the computerized test bank that accompanies this text is designed for both novice and advanced users. Diploma enables instructors to create and edit questions, create randomized quizzes and tests with an easy-to-use drag-and-drop tool, publish quizzes and tests to online courses, and print quizzes and tests for paper-based assessments.

  > **PowerPoint Presentations:** Each chapter's slide deck includes a succinct chapter outline and incorporates relevant chapter graphics.

- **Companion Website at www.oup.com/us/gitelson**

  > This open access companion website includes a number of learning tools to help students study and review key concepts presented in the text including learning objectives, key-concept summaries, quizzes, essay questions, web activities, and web links.

- *Now Playing: Learning American Government Through Film*

  > Through documentaries, feature films, and YouTube videos, *Now Playing: Learning American Government Through Film* provides video examples of course concepts to demonstrate real-world relevance. Each video is accompanied by a brief summary and discussion questions.

- **CNN Videos**
  - > Offering recent clips on timely topics, this DVD provides 15 films tied to the chapter topics in the text. Each clip is approximately 5-10 minutes in length, offering a great way to launch your lectures. Contact your local OUP sale representative for details.
- **E-Book**
  - > Available through CourseSmart.
- **Course Cartridges**
  - > To order course cartridges, please contact your local OUP sales representative.

Packaging Options

Adopters of *American Government: Myths and Realities* can package *any* Oxford University Press book with the text for a twenty percent savings off the total package price. See our many trade and scholarly offerings at www.oup.com, then contact your local OUP sales representative to request a package ISBN. In addition, the following items can be packaged with the text for free:

Now Playing: Learning American Government Through Film (ISBN 9780190233341)
Williams, *Research and Writing Guide for Political Science* (ISBN 9780190243357)
Dashboard (ISBN 9780190233754)

We also encourage the following texts for packaging:

Very Short Introduction Series

Valelly, *American Politics*
Crick, *Democracy*
Boyer, *American History*

Other titles recommended for packaging:

Lindsay, *Investigating American Democracy: Readings on Core Questions*
Miethe/Gauthier, *Simple Statistics: Applications in Social Research*
Niven, *Barack Obama: A Pocket Biography of Our 44th President*
Wilkins, *Questioning Numbers: How to Read and Critique Research*

Acknowledgments

Many people contribute to the success of a textbook, and such is the case with *American Government: Myths and Realities*. We gratefully acknowledge the many helpful comments of the following reviewers:

Gerard P. Clock
Borough of Manhattan Community College

Matthew A. Childers
University of Georgia

Martin Cohen
James Madison University

Amy Shriver Dreussi
University of Akron

Maurice Moshe Eisenstein
Purdue University Calumet

Brian L. Fife
Indiana University–Purdue University Fort Wayne

Megan Francis
Pepperdine University

George David Garson
North Carolina State University

George A. Gonzalez
University of Miami

John Hanley
Duquesne University

Jillian J. Hartley
Arkansas Northeastern College

Jennifer J. Hora
Valparaiso University

Mark S. Jendrysik
University of North Dakota

Aubrey Jewett
University of Central Florida

Joon S. Kil
Irvine Valley College

Melvin C. Laracey
University of Texas at San Antonio

Angela K. Lewis
University of Alabama at Birmingham

Chris Malone
Pace University

George Martinez
Pace University

Paul A. Mego
University of Memphis–Lambuth

Steven P. Millies
University of South Carolina Aiken

Kenneth W. Moffett
Southern Illinois University Edwardsville

Paul Nolette
Marquette University

John Barry Ryan
Stony Brook University

Jennifer Sacco
Quinnipiac University

Robert Saldin
University of Montana

Shawn Erik Schooley
Auburn University

Zack Sullivan
Metro State University
Inver Hills Community College

Troy Manuel Vidal
Columbus State University

Whit Waide
Mississippi State University

Winn W. Wasson
University of Wisconsin–Washington County

Matthew Wright
American University

In a venture of this magnitude, authors realize that the success of a textbook is closely tied to the editors associated with the project. We have been fortunate enough to work with a dedicated, creative, and sensitive editorial staff at Oxford University Press. For this edition, we are indebted to Jennifer Carpenter, Executive Editor; Thom Holmes, Development Manager; Barbara A. Conover, Freelance Development Editor; Maegan Sherlock, Development Editor; Barbara Mathieu, Senior Production Editor; Matthew Rohal, Editorial Assistant; and Laura Wilmot, Copyeditor.

As always, we welcome comments and feedback from readers of this book. All comments and inquiries should be sent to the authors at the following email addresses:

Alan R. Gitelson: AGITELS@luc.edu
Robert L. Dudley: rdudley@gmu.edu
Melvin J. Dubnick: amgov@dubnick.net

If you have any suggestions for future editions, or find any errors or omissions, please let us know.

We also want to give an unqualified thanks, with love, to Idy, Laura, Rachel, Doug, Josh, Eli, Jonah, Zoe, and Daniel; to Randi, Heather, and PD; and to Judy, Patrick, and Michael, and also to Catherine for making Patrick so happy.

When this team was brought together, it was Alan Gitelson who assumed the role of "front man" for the team, while a "flip of the coin" determined the order of Bob Dudley and Mel Dubnick. As with any writing project that has gone through multiple editions, responsibilities for individual chapters and various features have shifted over the years, but throughout there was no junior partner in this joint venture. The identity of the book has never changed from "the Gitelson text."

A. R. G.
R. L. D.
M. J. D.

About the Authors

ALAN GITELSON is Professor of Political Science and former Assistant Provost and Chair of the Department of Political Science at Loyola University of Chicago. He received his Ph.D. from the Maxwell School, Syracuse University. In addition to numerous scholarly articles, his books include *American Political Parties: Stability and Change* (with M. Margaret Conway and Frank Feigert), *Public Policy and Economic Institutions* (with Melvin Dubnick), and *American Elections: The Rules Matter* (with Robert L. Dudley). Dr. Gitelson is a former member of the American Political Science Association Standing Committee on Education and Professional Development. He is a frequent guest commentator on radio and television, speaking on topics including campaigns and elections, campaign financing, political parties, the media, and interest groups.

Dr. Gitelson has been designated as a Master Teacher by the College of Arts and Sciences at Loyola University Chicago. He also received the Outstanding Faculty Member of the Year Award from Loyola University Chicago and the Edward T. and Vivijeanne F. Sujack Award for Teaching Excellence. When not teaching, reading, or writing, Alan enjoys music, travel, and sailing with his wife, Idy; his daughters, Laura and Rachel; his sons-in-law Doug and Josh; and all of his wonderful grandchildren.

ROBERT L. DUDLEY is Professor of Government and Politics in the School of Policy, Government, and International Affairs at George Mason University. A native of Illinois, he received his Ph.D. from Northern Illinois University and was, prior to joining the faculty at George Mason University, on the faculties at Loyola University in Chicago and Colorado State University. Trained in American politics with a specialization in judicial politics, Dr. Dudley has contributed articles to several professional journals, including the *American Journal of Political Science*, *American Politics Quarterly*, *Journal of Politics*, and *Political Research Quarterly*.

MELVIN DUBNICK is Professor of Political Science at the University of New Hampshire and Professor Emeritus at Rutgers University. He received his Ph.D. from the University of Colorado–Boulder in 1974, and he has held positions at Emporia State University, Loyola University of Chicago, the University of Kansas, Baruch College/City University of New York, and Rutgers University–Newark. He was also affiliated with the Institute of Governance at Queen's University, Belfast (Northern Ireland), where he served as a Fulbright Distinguished Fellow and Senior Fellow from 2003 to 2005. He has held adjunct appointments at Columbia University and the University of Oklahoma and has taught courses in Japan, Korea, Panama, and Colombia. In addition to *American Government*, Dr. Dubnick has coauthored textbooks on public policy analysis and American public administration. He has served as managing editor of *Public Administration Review*, as well as co-editor-in-chief of *Policy Studies Journal*. A Fellow of the National Academy of Public Administration, he currently focuses his research on issues related to accountability, corporate governance, government regulation, and the reform of financial markets.

Dr. Dubnick has been actively engaged in efforts to improve and advance political science education. He was cochair of the American Political Science Association's Task Force on Civic Education in the Next Century and managed APSA-CIVED, a listserv focused on issues related to civic education. He is currently experimenting with innovative grading methods, distance learning technologies, and the integration of the Internet into the political science classroom.

Where to Find Policy Content

Policy Topic	Page References	Key Concepts
Defining public policy	Chapter 1 PC: 32–34	Public policy; public goods; guns-or-butter
Policymaking	Chapters 2, 8, and 13 PCs	
The policymaking process	Chapter 2 PC: 70–73	Lawmaking; policy stages; issue identification; agenda setting; policy formulation, adoption, implementation, and evaluation
Decision making models	Chapter 2 PC: 73–74	Rational choice; incrementalism; bargaining and compromise
Democratic policymaking	Chapter 2 PC: 74–75 Chapter 8 PC: 284–289	Democratic, elite, and pluralist policymaking; initiative and referenda
Policy implementation	Chapter 13 PC: 455–459 Chapter 14 PC: 489–495	Administrative efficiency, reform, and discretion
Criminal justice policies	Chapter 14 PC: 489–495	Police and prosecutorial discretion
Economic policies	Chapters 7, 10, and 11 PCs	
Role of government in economy	Chapter 7 PC: 243–244 Chapter 10 PC: 347–349	Hamiltonian and Jeffersonian approaches; antitrust policies and enforcement; corporate regulation
Macroeconomic policies	Chapter 7 PC: 244–247	Monetary and fiscal policies; Keynesian economics; the "Fed"
Economic development policies	Chapter 7 PC: 247–248	Free trade; balance of trade; globalization; tax incentives; industrial polices; supply-side economics
Regulatory and antitrust policies	Chapter 10 PC: 347–350	Media; conglomerates; mergers
Education policies	Chapter 3 PC: 107–110	Access to education; funding; curriculum; quality and accountability
Environmental policies	Chapter 6 PC: 212–216	Public attitudes; climate change; land management; conservation; protection, ecology, clean water and air; EPA; Earth Day; issue-attention cycle
Foreign policy	Chapters 4, 5, and 12 PCs	
National security policies	Chapter 4 PC: 146–149	War on Terror; homeland security; Patriot Act; Garrison State; temporary-state-of-war approach; glass firewall; enemy-with approach; NSA
Post-World War II policies	Chapter 5 PC: 176–179; Chapter 12 PC: 416–420	Cold War; isolationism; unilateralism; containment; Marshall Plan; massive retaliation; flexible response; détente; balance of power; new world order; post-containment; human rights; NAFTA; WTO; War on Terror; Iraq and Afghanistan wars
Historical approaches and domestic influences	Chapter 5 PC: 176–181	American Exceptionalism; Wilsonian, Hamiltonian, Jeffersonian, and Jacksonian visions
Presidential role in foreign policy	Chapter 12 PC: 420–421	Grand strategies; Monroe Doctrine; Bush Doctrine
Health care policy	Chapter 9 PC: 314–319	National health insurance; lobbying; Medicare; Medicaid; Affordable Care Act
Social welfare policies	Chapter 3 PC: 110–113	General, work, and categorical assistance; welfare reform; Social Security; Supplemental Security Income; food stamps; Medicaid, Federal Poverty Level; Affordable Care Act

AMERICAN GOVERNMENT

CHAPTER 1

MYTHS & REALITIES
What are the roles of reason, myth, and belief in American government?

Making Sense
of American Politics

"It Just Makes No Sense!"

The events we read about or hear on the daily news often seem confusing and defy explanation. Indeed, many of us have trouble figuring out how our political system operates. Consider the following:

- In the presidential election of 2000, the Democratic Party candidate, Al Gore, received the most popular votes nationwide; nevertheless, the Republican candidate, George W. Bush, won the election. For many Americans this was a baffling outcome. It just made no sense.

- On December 12, 2012, twenty first-grade students and six adults were murdered at Sandy Hook Elementary School in Connecticut. A little more than four months later, on April 17 of 2013, with many relatives of the slain looking on from the chamber gallery, the U.S. Senate voted 54–46 *in support of* legislation that would expand background checks on firearm purchases at gun shows. Despite that favorable majority vote, the media would report to the nation that the bill was effectively defeated. For the average American, the news made no sense. How could a majority vote in favor of a bill end up being reported as a defeat?

- In 2003, he was a self-described "skinny kid with a funny name" serving in the Illinois state senate, a relative unknown on the national political scene. Five years later, Barack Obama won the presidency of the United States—and thus became the first African American to hold that post. Most experts and media pundits were astonished at Obama's

< Flags are like other symbols, and how people treat them indicates their attitudes toward what they represent. Despite the negative view of government that many American express in everyday conversation and opinion polls, their level of respect for the political system itself is apparent in their positive reaction to the American flag.

CHAPTER OUTLINE
AND FOCUS QUESTIONS

The Nature and Role of Government and Politics

> How do we define government and politics? What has been the role of government in American history?

What Are the Fundamental Issues of Government and Politics?

> How does the U.S. political system deal with the issues of who should govern and where authority should be vested?

Understanding American Government and Politics

> How do we understand and make sense of our political system and government? What are the roles of myths, reason, beliefs, and ideologies in that effort?

meteoric rise; given what they knew and assumed about U.S. politics and voters, this should not have happened. Obama's reelection in 2012 was also a surprise to many political observers who believed that the depressed state of the U.S. economy would make it difficult for him to win reelection to a second term. Nevertheless, he not only won that second term but did so by a four-point margin over his Republican rival, Mitt Romney.

- According to pollsters who monitor public attitudes toward Congress, between 1980 and 2008 "approval ratings" averaged slightly more than 43 percent. But in recent years the ratings became decidedly more negative, with some polls indicating approval ratings of 10 percent and below. The Gallup Poll, which has been tracking public opinion about Congress since 1974, characterized the low approval scores as "dismal" and "historical."[1] Yet, over that same period of four decades, *no less than 85 percent* of the members of the U.S. House of Representative were reelected—and often by large margins.[2] Why do voters continue to elect the same representatives time and time again despite their relative displeasure with Congress's overall performance? This, too, just doesn't make any sense.

These are just a few examples of the many things about American government and politics that often baffle and confuse those of us who are trying to understand our complex political system and how it operates. It doesn't matter whether you are a professional political pundit or just a casual observer of political life; surprising and puzzling events are common.

Although few of us will admit it to even our closest friends, most of us share uneasiness about our lack of understanding about politics and government. After all, this is a democracy where citizens are expected to be well informed as well as active participants in the political system. Somewhat embarrassed, many of us avoid discussing politics, tuning out rather than engaging in the civic lives of our communities.

But that civic life is impossible to avoid in this day and age. Government and the policies it generates are a pervasive fact of modern life. From the light switch at our bedside when we awaken and the roads we ride to work on to the critical decisions we make about whether (and whom) to marry and where to live, we are constantly connected to the actions that take place in the political arena.

Myths Those stories, proverbial sayings, pervasive attitudes, and other narratives that we use to help us think about the world around us.

Dealing with these facts means that we cannot avoid the challenge of making sense of that baffling world, and we often do so by relying on **myths**—that is, those stories and narratives we tell ourselves or share with friends and family that help us better comprehend our surroundings. Unlike novels, short stories, and the plots of movies, these sense-making tales are not the product of creative writers who design their work to entertain or generate some aesthetic response. Nor are they the journalistic reports we read daily that are designed to tell us the "who, what, when, where and why" of some newsworthy event. Rather, these myths are the tales and narratives we tell ourselves when confronted with things that initially make little or no sense. Myths are, in the words of critic Mark Schorer, "the instruments by which we continually struggle to make our experience intelligible to ourselves."[3] Moreover, they are instruments we apply to help us deal with many different aspects of our lives, from politics to sports and from science to religion.[4]

The stories we tell ourselves are more often than not drawn from those we learn while growing up (see the discussion of political socialization in Chapter 6). Over time we come to question many of those stories. In fact, because many of the stories and narratives we hear and read seem to play fast and loose with the facts, it is commonplace for us to think of myths as synonymous with lies and falsehoods. But equating myths with lies ignores the fact that storytelling plays an important role in our lives. Although they may involve some partial truths or even outright falsehoods, myths also contain what comedian Stephen Colbert has called "truthiness"—"truth that comes from the gut, not books."[5]

Many of the myths we learn as children contain moral lessons. For example, throughout most of the nineteenth century and well into the twentieth, the elementary schoolbook "readers" used by American schoolchildren included the parable of a young George Washington who could not tell a lie, or the tale of a young store clerk named Abe Lincoln who walked miles to repay a customer whom he had inadvertently shortchanged by a few pennies. Later in life we find ourselves relying on stories to make sense of events that, at the moment they occur, seem unfathomable or inexplicable. This was the case, for example, for a generation of Americans who heard many conspiracy theories about the assassination of President John F. Kennedy or the attacks of September 11, 2001.

Why do we turn to myths so often to help us make sense of the world? Psychologists, anthropologists, and others who study child development in cultures the world over note that myth making is a common cognitive skill we develop when we are very young.[6] Some have argued that the human capacity to conjure up myths emerges even before we are able to grasp the basics of language. As we grow up, we learn about the stories and narratives

When Americans are asked about the nation's most significant presidents, almost all lists include Washington and Lincoln. Their answers have been supported over the years by stories that stress their honesty. The myths of Washington admitting to cutting down the cherry tree ("I cannot tell a lie") and Lincoln's honesty in his work as a shop clerk have been part of the elementary school curriculum since the nineteenth century.

of our families and friends, and soon we develop a repertoire of myths we rely on to help us make greater sense of the world in general. It is little wonder that we initially turn to myths when faced with new or baffling situations.

Perhaps no society in history best exemplified the role played by myths in everyday life (social, economic, and political) than the city-states of ancient Greece, and in fact the term *myth* itself is derived from the Greek concept of *mythos*.[7] For the ancient Greeks, *mythos* was composed of the stories about their heroes and gods, and it helped them make sense of everything from daily routines to the tragedies and disasters that befell them.[8]

As much as they relied on *mythos*, the Greeks also understood that there were problems if they relied on myths alone for making sense of their surroundings. For one thing, although mythology (the composite of stories about heroes and gods) helped them deal with their psychological need for answers in the short run, over time the myth-based narrative proved insufficient or too simplistic. Furthermore, because many (if not most) myths were based on fictions or partial truths, they all too often failed to provide credible predictions or guidance for actions. This flaw led many Greek thinkers to depend more on alternative approaches to making sense of the world.

Those alternative approaches to reality general fell under the idea of *logos*—that is, the application of reasoned thinking and practical wisdom to

When faced with events such as presidential assassinations or terrorist attacks, many people turn to conspiracy theories. As a form of myth, we use these narratives to make sense of unfathomable realities. Unfortunately, almost all provide a distorted view of the facts and make it difficult to understand what really took place.

understanding the world. Although most ancient Greeks did not abandon their reliance on myths, they did supplement it with the philosophical, ethical, and practical cognitive tools developed under the rubric of *logos*, or what we would call "reasoning."

In a similar way, when it comes to making sense of our complex political world, we often start with the stories and narratives of myths, but just as often we turn to other ways for comprehending and making sense of political realities. But we never quite completely abandon those myths. It is that tendency to initially rely on myths and eventually turn to other means for understanding the complexities of American government and politics that informs and shapes the following chapters.

Consider the widely held belief about presidents seeking reelection discussed at the outset of this chapter. As the 2012 election approached, the story often told by media analysts was that President Obama could not be reelected if the unemployment rate in the country were higher than 7.2 percent by Election Day. Where did this story come from? It developed from the fact that no president since Franklin Roosevelt had been reelected during difficult economic times. The 7.2 percent figure was derived from facts: first, that Ronald Regan had been reelected in 1984 when the unemployment rate stood as 7.2 percent and, second, that George H. W. Bush lost his bid to be reelected in 1992 when the rate was at 7.4 percent. Of course, there were all sorts of other "facts" that prognosticators should have taken into consideration, but in the months leading up to the 2012 election, the mythical 7.2+ narrative had taken hold not only in the media but also in the campaigns themselves. It was a narrative that the Obama campaign took seriously as early as June 2011, when they developed their strategy for his reelection bid.[9] Moreover, it was a storyline that bolstered the confidence of Republicans, who believed they had a considerable advantage going into the election, as the unemployment rate hovered around 8 percent in the summer and early fall of 2012.

At the same time, while acknowledging that the storied link between economic conditions and reelection seemed plausible, political scientists Robert Erikson and Christopher Wiezien were not quite ready to accept the myth, and—relying on data and models focused on economic conditions prior to the election—they correctly predicted an Obama victory.[10] The myth, in this case, carried considerable weight and actually influenced the conduct of the presidential campaigns. In the end, however, a more reasoned and empirical analysis like that provided by Erikson and Wiezien would probably have proven more useful.

There are many tools that can help us make better sense of U.S. government and politics, and not all require specialized knowledge or sophisticated statistical models. In fact, you are probably already using many of them. Throughout this book you will encounter views of the realities of American government and politics based on credible but admittedly imperfect sense-making tools. In the final sections of this chapter we consider some of those tools, but before doing so we need to address some basic questions and important concepts that will make our journey to understanding much easier.

The Nature and Role of Government and Politics

> **How do we define government and politics? What has been the role of government in American history?**

We begin by addressing three fundamental questions:

1. What is government, and how does it carry out its varied responsibilities?

2. What is politics, and how does it relate to the work of government?

3. How important has government been in our lives and in those of past Americans?

What Is Government?

What is government, and how does it carry out its varied responsibilities? In brief, **government** consists of those institutions and officials whose purpose it is to write and enact laws and to execute and enforce public policy. In broader perspective, we can regard government as the major mechanisms through which we determine, articulate, adopt, and carry out collective actions to deal with problems that cannot be addressed individually. Some of those problems are of a very general nature, and some are quite specific. Thus, Americans generally rely on government (1) to maintain order through the rule of law, (2) to provide goods and services that benefit the lives of all citizens, and (3) to promote equality among members of society. On a more specific level, we turn to government to make certain the water we drink is safe, the roads we drive on are clear on a snowy morning, and the food on our tables is plentiful. Of course, there are other mechanisms (such as the marketplace) we can rely on to achieve these objectives, but it is government we often depend on. (See Policy Connection 1, which follows this chapter.)

The activities directed at solving those problems and achieving those goals are conducted by legislators, presidents or other chief executive officers (such as governors and mayors), judges, bureaucrats, and other elected and appointed officials who work in the institutions that make up the executive, legislative, and judicial branches of federal, state, and local governmental systems. Ultimately, these officials carry out their responsibilities through their authority to enact and enforce laws and public policies that are crucial to the functioning of government.

Government Those institutions and officials whose purpose it is to write and enact laws and to execute and enforce public policy.

What Is Politics?

In its most general sense, **politics** refers to activities aimed at influencing or controlling government for the purpose of formulating or guiding public policy. In the chapters that follow we discuss the politics of running for or being appointed to office; choosing policy alternatives; and bargaining, negotiating, and compromising to get policies enacted and executed. The politics of federal student loan programs, for example, involves presidents and legislators (who are influenced by students, parents, bankers, and college administrators), who negotiate the issue of who receives loan benefits and who pays the bills.

Politics Those activities aimed at influencing or controlling government for the purpose of formulating or guiding public policy.

The Role of Government in American History

Has government always been important in the lives of most Americans? Despite some popular feelings to the contrary, the answer is probably yes. Here we come across one of the most important myths about American politics—and the realities behind it. Historian Arthur M. Schlesinger Jr. has pointed to a "cherished national myth" ascribing the economic development of the nation "to the operations of unfettered individual enterprise."[11] In fact, history shows that American government has always affected economic and social life. As early as colonial times, citizens expected government to perform such traditional functions as ensuring law and order and resisting foreign aggression. But even then, government often did more.

From the time the first European settlers established communities in America, colonial governments, under the general authority of the British government, played a major role in developing and regulating local economies. Colonial (and later state) governments helped finance new enterprises, build ports, and construct turnpikes and canals; they sometimes even controlled wages and prices in local markets.

Shortly after the United States gained its independence, Congress wrote a series of laws collectively called the Northwest Ordinance, which established rules for selling land and organizing local governments in the large territory stretching from the Ohio River to the Mississippi River and north to the Great Lakes. Land was even reserved to support public schools. One of the earliest examples of the national government's role as an active promoter of

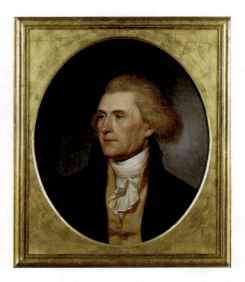

Thomas Jefferson took advantage of an opportunity to purchase the Louisiana Territory from France in 1803. As this 1805 map indicates, Americans did not have a clear idea of what they acquired. Jefferson would send Meriwether Lewis and William Clark on a three-year expedition to explore the new territory.

the economy was its 1803 purchase of the Louisiana Territory. That vast region was vital to the prosperity of the farmers who worked the lands along the entire length of the Mississippi. Historians have also found other examples of early government efforts to plan, manage, and promote the new country's resources.[12]

The role of government continued to expand during the 1800s and early 1900s. Attempts to solve the economic and social problems that arose during the Great Depression of the 1930s—an economic downturn that left millions of Americans jobless and homeless—led to an explosion of new programs that are associated with Franklin D. Roosevelt's "New Deal" presidency. Soon an army of bureaucrats was managing the economy, promoting stable economic growth by helping to find jobs for the unemployed, and enforcing price controls designed to hold down the prices of goods and services.

As the United States became a more complex society, Americans demanded that the national government pay more attention to problems that had once been solved by families and communities: problems of the poor, the handicapped, and the elderly, among others. Ever since the New Deal, all Americans have been touched directly or indirectly by programs in such areas as early childhood nutrition, health care, unemployment benefits, food stamps, and Social Security.[13]

Moreover, the government has not limited its interest to economic and social welfare programs. As destruction threatened the vast American forests and pollution tainted air and water, Americans turned to government for environmental management, in the form of interventions ranging from conservation programs to regulations affecting many polluting industries. In support of such goals as preventing environmental damage and ensuring a steady supply of energy, government has lowered speed limits on highways, pushed for the development of nuclear energy, and implemented a variety of other policies.[14]

In recent years, a growing number of Americans have concluded that perhaps we have been depending too much on government to solve our problems. In his 1981 inaugural address, Ronald Reagan famously noted that "government is not the solution to our problem; government is the problem"; by 1996 the Clinton White House too was admitting that it was time for a change. "The era of big government is over," declared President Bill Clinton in his State of the Union address.

But the arguments against "big" government failed to undermine the public's demand for government action when crises struck. Demands for more government action followed the events of September 11, 2001, the natural disasters that struck New Orleans in the wake of Hurricane Katrina in 2005 and Hurricane Sandy in 2012, and the financial crisis of 2007–2008 that nearly brought the United States and global economies to a standstill. Each event generated calls for more government action, and a growing number of Americans indicated that "government should do more to solve problems and help meet the needs of people."[15] Instead of focusing on shrinking the size of government, policymakers have turned their attention toward reorganizing and enhancing government

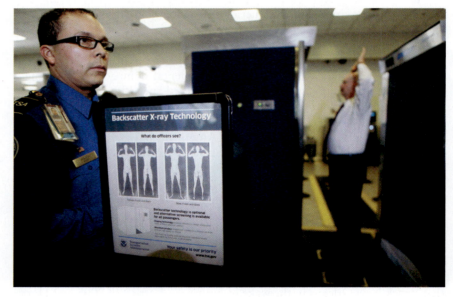

Soldiers patrolling New York's Penn Station and air passenger screening at Los Angeles International Airport are just two signs of how the role of government has changed in the post-September 11 world.

agencies at all levels to deal with the threats posed by terrorists, natural disasters, and economic vulnerabilities. Thus, government has played, and continues to play, an important role in the development of the modern American social and economic system.

What Are the Fundamental Issues of Government and Politics?

> **How does the U.S. political system deal with the issues of who should govern and where authority should be vested?**

The fact that government has always played an important role in the lives of Americans does not mean that its activities have not been controversial. Two basic questions about government and politics have consistently emerged: "Who should govern?" and "Where should governmental authority be located?"

Who Should Govern?

Because the government plays such a critical and pervasive role in everyone's life, it is natural that questions arise about who should control the use of this important social institution. In other words, *who* should govern? Answers to that general question have taken two forms: one focused on governmental authority and one on the wielding of governmental power.

Authority. For many students of government, the question "Who should govern?" refers to who should be officially authorized to control governmental institutions. In other words, who should exercise formal authority in government? **Authority** can be defined as the capacity to make and enforce public policies that is possessed by individuals who occupy formal governmental roles.[16]

Authority The capacity to make and enforce public policies that is possessed by individuals who occupy formal governmental roles.

As was already noted, government is composed of the institutions and officials who make and enforce public policies. The roles that those officials play in conducting the business of government are derived from a variety of sources. Some are defined in constitutions and other legal documents (see the discussion of constitutional foundations in Chapter 2), whereas others may be the result of long-standing traditions. In either case, when we are concerned with who should occupy those official roles, we are dealing with the issue of authority.

Among the first to try to answer the question of who should govern through the exercise of authority was the ancient Greek philosopher Aristotle (382–322 B.C.E.). He classified governments into three types: government by one, government by the few, and government by the many. Each type, he believed, has a good, or "right," form and a bad, or "wrong," form. A right form of government by the one—a monarchy—serves the common interests of the community, whereas a wrong form—tyranny—serves the personal interests of the ruler. In the same way, the good form of rule by the few—aristocracy—stood in contrast to a bad form—known as oligarchy—in which those few would govern in a manner that would serve their own interests.

When it came to rule by the many, or democracy, Aristotle believed that the best form of government would be that in which the population was capable of ruling in the interests of all, but he was realistic enough to know that this was unlikely. In any community, he argued, it is the poor who would dominate such a government, and they would not be capable by themselves of putting aside their own needs on behalf of the common interests of society. Aristotle's solution was to call for a modified form of democratic governance—which he termed a *polity*—in which the many would rule in conjunction with an aristocratic few. In his well-known work *Politics*,[17] Aristotle offers an elaborate description of all the ways that democracies can deteriorate into tyrannical, oligarchical, or even mob rule, but in the end he regards the mixed-rule polity to be the best alternative.

The notion of **democracy** held by most Americans can best be summed up as a belief in government in which authority is based on the consent and will of the majority. If asked the question "Who should govern?" a vast majority of Americans would respond that the people should govern.

Nevertheless, the American concept of democracy does not mean a commitment to direct rule by the majority. As we will see (in Chapter 2), the Framers of the Constitution did not believe that governmental authority should be directly in the hands of the people. They envisioned the United States as a **republic**, or **representative democracy**, in which the people *govern indirectly by electing certain individuals*—the president, members of Congress, governors, mayors, state legislators, and others—*to make decisions on their behalf*. Thus, the people do not vote on or directly make specific policy decisions; they do so indirectly, through those they elect to represent their interests.

Despite this general acceptance of representative democracy, controversies still arise over the need for greater or lesser citizen participation in government decision making. Some observers argue that much more should be done to increase public input into policy decisions through electoral procedures (see the discussion of initiative and referendum in Chapter 8). Others have called for greater public involvement in the deliberative processes that lead to policy decisions that impact their lives, especially at the local government level (see Chapter 3 on federalism and intergovernmental relations). In contrast, others believe—as Aristotle did—that too much democracy can produce bad outcomes. For them, institutional authority has to be designed to offset the misuse and abuse of the power that comes along with authority.

Power. We can also approach the question "Who should govern?" from the perspective of political power. As defined previously, politics involves activities intended to influence or control what goes on in government. Those who have the ability to wield such influence are said to possess power. From this perspective, the question about who governs should really be "Who should wield power over the operations of government?"

What does it take to possess power?[18] Reduced to its basics, **power** is a relationship between two parties, A and B. Let's say that A (we'll call her Alice) has power relative to B (we'll call him Ted) if Alice can influence Ted's choices or decisions. To do that, Alice should probably possess something that Ted finds desirable or irresistible. That something, called a *resource*, can be some special knowledge or expertise, a dynamic and winning personality, the promise of financial reward, or even an outright threat to do Ted harm if he does not cooperate. Just as important, Ted must find Alice's knowledge, reward, or threat credible. If

Democracy To Americans, a government in which authority is based on the consent and will of the majority.

Republic A system in which people govern indirectly by electing certain individuals to make decisions on their behalf.

Representative democracy See Republic.

Power The capacity and ability to influence the behavior and choices of others through the use of politically relevant resources.

Ted, for instance, does not believe that Alice is an expert, then Alice will not have that form of influence over him.

From the perspective of power, the answer to the question "Who should govern?" rests on how dispersed the resources for wielding power are in a society. Those who believe in democracy want to see such resources distributed as widely as possible. For them, the ideal situation would be that each and every citizen is able to exercise the same degree of influence over governmental actions. Under such conditions, government would do what the majority of citizens want done. This is called the **majoritarian view of power**.

However, most students of government agree that politically influential resources are unequally distributed in society; consequently, some members of society will be able to influence governmental actions more than others. Thus, the question really becomes whether it is more desirable to have those resources concentrated in the hands of a few (*elitism*) or dispersed as widely as possible (*pluralism*).

Those who advocate the **elitist view of power** argue that the general public is best served when a basic consensus regarding fundamental issues exists among a country's top leaders. Although these leaders may disagree on minor issues, or may even compete against one another for positions of authority in government, the fact that they share a common view on issues that might otherwise split the nation is regarded as an important foundation for governing.

In contrast, although they do not deny that power-relevant resources are unequally distributed in society, those who support the **pluralist view of power** advocate a political system in which many elites, not just one, influence government. For pluralists, it is not important that members of some small elite agree on fundamental issues. Rather, it is crucial that membership in the elite be open to all in society; members need only agree to abide by the rules of the game in government and politics. From the pluralist perspective, members of this open elite serve the public good by competing among themselves for the attention of government, as well as for control of public offices.

Whether it is focused on authority or on power, the issue of who should govern is an important one. It helped to shape the American political system, and as we will see in our discussions of public opinion, political parties, and campaigns and elections in Chapters 6 through 8, it remains a critical question in today's hotly contested political environment.

Where Should Governmental Authority Be Vested?

Should governmental authority be vested in local communities, in governments close to the people? Should it be vested in the political center of the nation, Washington, D.C.? Or should it be vested in the fifty state capitals—in Harrisburg, Springfield, Austin, Sacramento, Columbus, Tallahassee, and all the others? Because of the broad range of governmental activities, these questions do not have simple answers.

To illustrate, would it make sense for the national government to run your town's fire department? Who should be responsible for collecting your town's garbage, running your town's parks, and hiring your school district's schoolteachers?

Majoritarian view of power The view that political power should be distributed as equally as possible in a political system to facilitate meaningful majority rule.

Elitist view of power The view that political power should be in the hands of a relatively small part of the general population that shares a common understanding about the fundamental issues facing society and government.

Pluralist view of power The view that political power should be dispersed among many elites who share a common acceptance of the rules of the game.

Many people trust local government to deal with these important issues because towns and cities or even states are regarded as better able to do so. At the same time, it is generally agreed that local governments cannot deal effectively with foreign policy, national defense, regional unemployment, and other major economic and social issues that challenge the nation as a whole. Therefore, many Americans believe that it is the national government's job, with its vast economic resources and national perspective, to tackle these issues. Many also argue that national policies can better reflect the general will and values of the American people and are less likely to discriminate against racial, religious, and political minorities than local policies are.

However, views about which level of government is best suited to carry out the functions of government will vary depending on the level of trust reflected in public attitudes. The Pew Center for the People and the Press has been tracking the public's views toward different levels of government since 1997, and, although federal government has been viewed favorably in the past (especially immediately following the attacks of September 11, 2001), the trend since 2005 has been steadily downward for the national government and relatively positive for both state and local governments during that same period.

Most complex societies have found that to ensure effective governance, they need intermediate levels of government as well. Different nations have solved this problem in different ways. The United States has developed a unique solution that allows national, state, and local governments to share power. But even this solution is incomplete, and the debate continues over the role of each level of government in delivering services to the American public. We will discuss the struggles over the vesting of power in greater detail in Chapter 3, when we examine federalism and intergovernmental relations.

Understanding American Government and Politics

> **How do we understand and make sense of our political system and government? What are the roles of myths, reason, beliefs, and ideologies in that effort?**

With some of those basic definitions and concepts in mind, we can now return to the major question addressed in this book: How do we understand the world around us? This is a question that has intrigued philosophers for centuries and is still being studied daily by a range of scholars from psychologists and neuroscientists to sociologists and literature professors. The answers provided by all these students of human understanding are as varied as their approaches to the subject. But one thing they seem to have in common is the assumption that the world around us is much too complex for anyone to easily make sense of, and therefore each of us uses some form of mental tool or intellectual shortcut to make sense of our surroundings.

Political Myths

We have already discussed the tendency for most of us to rely on myths (i.e., stories and narratives) to make sense of the political world. As each of the following chapters demonstrates, myths can play and have played an influential role in shaping how we view the U.S. political system. For example, in Chapter 2, which discusses constitutional foundations, we consider how the *myth of the "living Constitution"* has helped determine the way the public and the courts have interpreted what the various provisions of the 227-year-old document means today, as well as how an alternative *myth of the "enduring Constitution"* is finding expression among some of today's Supreme Court justices.

In the realm of American foreign and defense policy, the *myth of American vulnerability* has played a role in the public's understanding of how our political system operates (see Policy Connection 4). That particular myth has its roots in the earliest years of the Republic, when Americans still felt vulnerable to threats from England and other European powers that surrounded the newly independent nation. The fact that the British had attacked Washington, D.C., during the War of 1812 and burned down the capitol and White House reinforced that myth, and it was still influential during the Cold War period, when Americans felt vulnerable to nuclear attack from the Soviet Union. And, although the feeling of vulnerability seemed to recede after the end of the Cold War, the myth reemerged on September 11, 2001, after terrorists attacked the World Trade Center and the Pentagon.

As noted earlier, myths come in a variety of forms. In some cases the myths we'll encounter take the form of *stories* (fictional as well as historical) about national heroes. As noted earlier, generations of school-age children have often been told stories about the young ("I cannot tell a lie") George Washington and about "Honest Abe" Lincoln, as well as tales about the military genius of Andrew Jackson at the Battle of New Orleans and the bravery of Theodore Roosevelt as he led the cavalry charge up San Juan Hill in the Spanish-American War.

The media have played a major role in developing and sustaining many of the most popular myths. In the nineteenth century, widely read rags-to-riches novels by Horatio Alger Jr. promoted the sense that anyone can succeed in America by commitment and hard work. During the 1950s and 1960s, prime time TV featured the heroic, justice-seeking exploits of characters such as the Lone Ranger and Marshall Matt Dillon on *Gunsmoke*. For more than two decades, the series *Law & Order* (along with its various spinoffs) created a popular narrative about the interaction between police investigations and criminal prosecution. Equally powerful stories abound in the popular press about our nation's leaders—about the lives and accomplishments of political families like the Roosevelts, Kennedys, Bushs, and Clintons; about individual presidents like Richard Nixon and Barack Obama; and about key institutions like the U.S. Senate and the Pentagon.

Such stories are powerful forces in shaping the public's views about government, as are stories about the actions of bureaucratic agencies and historical figures. A story about a government agency spending tens of thousands of taxpayer dollars on Las Vegas "training" conferences confirms

In 1802, John James Barralet issued this print, which depicts George Washington being raised from his tomb by Father Time and the Angel of Immortality. Such myth-creating imagery would eventually adorn everything from household china to the dome of the U.S. Capitol Building.

for many people the widely held belief that government bureaucracy is inefficient and wasteful.[19] On a different level, the story of John Hancock signing the Declaration of Independence supports the popular images of the American Revolution, what it stood for, and the risks and sacrifices made by those who chose to break with England in 1776. In each case, the story-turned-myth helps to shape our understanding of and attitudes toward our system of government.

But not all myths involve stories in the form of straightforward narratives. Instead, some of today's most important myths take the form of *stereotypes* (such as "All Democrats are big-spending liberals" and "The Republican party represents big business"), *proverbial sayings* (such as "You can't fight city hall"), and *pervasive attitudes* (such as "All politicians are crooks") that have an impact on the way we think about government and the American political system. Although not full-blown narratives in the standard sense, myths in these forms imply an underlying storyline that has gained wide and unquestioned acceptance.

Although there is no denying the pervasive presence of myths in our lives, the fact that many are based at least in part on falsehoods and distortions raises the question of why we would even consider maintaining our reliance on them. Why not acknowledge their shortcomings as reflections of reality and just toss them? The answer lies in the important functions that myths perform—functions that have helped provide us with a relatively stable political system for more than two very tumultuous centuries. Among other things, we depend on myths because we need them to do the following:[20]

- Simplify our complex world

- Define our place in the world and provide us with a shared identity

- Guide and rationalize our behavior

- Make sense of the behavior of others

- Orient our views of the past, present, and future

First, like the ancients, we sometimes use myths to *help us simplify the complex world in which we live.* Myths help us "to live in a world in which the causes" of our problems "are simple and neat and the remedies are apparent."[21] During the economic downturn of the early 1990s, for example, many Americans blamed the Japanese for the United States' economic woes. Stories about unfair pricing strategies used by Japanese firms as well as widely publicized remarks by Japanese officials regarding poor American work habits helped to fuel a myth about an "economic war" with Japan.[22] The popularity of both Japan bashing and "buy American" campaigns reflected a tendency on the part of too many Americans to seek scapegoats. In the meantime, these same Americans ignored the more complex national and international economic transitions that were responsible for the problems.[23]

Second, myths often *help us define our place in the world and provide us with a common social and political identity.*[24] Many of us perceive the United States in mythical terms: "as a community of free and equal self-governing citizens pursuing their individual ends in a spirit of tolerance for their religious and other forms of diversity."[25] This and other myths held by Americans are supported by stories—for example, of the first Thanksgiving, Washington's cutting down the cherry tree, and the noble deeds of young Abe Lincoln—that reinforce our national "belief in innocence, in honesty, in freedom, in the use of the wilderness, in adaptability, in the right of the individual to act freely without restraint. . . . Like all myths, their function is to say this is the way it was with Americans, this is the way it is, and this is the way it ought to be."[26] Without such myths, the political system might crumble, as those of the former Soviet Union and other parts of Eastern Europe did in the late 1980s and early 1990s.[27]

Third, we frequently depend on myths to *help guide and rationalize our behavior.* The myth of good citizenship tells us that we ought to vote because that is the only effective way to influence the behavior of government officials.[28] As already noted, myths also have an impact on how we conduct our foreign policy.[29] In addition to the myth of vulnerability, many critics of American foreign policy feel that our national behavior in international affairs is shaped by a national myth of progress—a vision of "America as the wave of the future."[30] "Americans see history as a straight line," comments essayist Frances FitzGerald, "and themselves standing at the cutting edge of it as representatives for all mankind."[31]

Fourth, myths often *help us make sense of the behavior of others.* In foreign affairs, and especially during wartime or periods of great tension, we often rely on images and stories of our enemies and allies that help guide our behavior. The negative images of our German and Japanese enemies found in movies and posters during both world wars helped to keep the war efforts going, as did the stereotypical pictures of the Soviets during the Cold War. President Ronald Reagan, for example, labeled the Soviet Union an "evil empire" during his terms in office, and after September 11, President George W. Bush spoke of the "evildoers" and the "axis of evil" when referring to those countries that he claimed supported terrorism. In contrast, positive images and stories of our allies took on mythical tones during the same periods.[32]

A fifth and final function of myths is that many of the most significant ones *reflect views of the past or the future, as well as the present.* Many of the myths surrounding our most important governmental institutions—the U.S. Constitution, the presidency, Congress, and the Supreme Court—reflect the judgments of history on those bodies and the people who served in them. For example, although Abraham Lincoln is regarded today as one of the nation's great presidents, he was highly criticized by other politicians and the media while he occupied the White House. His status as a great president—much of it reflected in stories and myths—is well established in our eyes, despite the low regard in which he was held by many of his contemporaries.

In today's American mythology, Abraham Lincoln is venerated and rarely ridiculed. While he was president, however, he was often the subject of critical attacks questioning his wisdom and motives.

We also adopt many future-oriented myths that often shape our expectations of what government officials can or will do. For example, among military professionals, the failure of America's military venture in Vietnam during the 1960s and early 1970s was often blamed on the civilian authorities' lack of commitment to the military's efforts. What emerged from that experience can be called the *Vietnam War myth*, a widely held belief among our nation's top military leaders that American military forces will not be successful in the future unless enough forces are sent to do the job and military commanders are allowed to act without interference from the politicians back in Washington. This myth had a significant influence on President George H. W. Bush's decisions concerning the use of military force against Iraq in 1991: He committed more than 500,000 U.S. troops and gave military commanders considerable freedom to determine how to deal with the forces of Saddam Hussein that had invaded Kuwait.[32] Given the relative success of that mission, some would argue that the myth was proved correct. However, for our purposes, what is important is that the Vietnam War myth had a significant impact on the attitudes and decisions of key policymakers as well as those of the American public.

And, of course, many of our myths focus on the present to help us deal with what is taking place in Washington, Topeka, or Sacramento, for example, right at this moment. Many people believe in the myth of special-interest government, which, correctly or incorrectly, helps many of us understand why Congress or a state legislature passes a law providing a new tax break for some major or local industry, even though this will ultimately increase the general taxpayer's burden. According to this myth, such laws are passed because special interests are able to hire high-priced lobbyists in Washington or a state capital who are effective in influencing legislators, whereas the general public has no one representing its interests (see Chapter 9 on interest groups).

From these examples, it should be obvious that myths focus on a wide range of subjects—from the nature of American society and our national Constitution to everyday political and governmental activities and our perception of world affairs. Individually, many of us have adopted myths about whether American society is racist or sexist, about the efficiency and effectiveness of local firefighters and law enforcement personnel, and about how important our participation in the political system is or can be. The wide range of topics covered by myths will become increasingly evident as you read through this textbook.

The Power of Reason

As noted earlier in our discussion of how the ancient Greeks used both *mythos* and *logos* to make sense of the world, the fact that myths shape our view of political reality does not mean we have to rely on stories and narratives alone. Rather, we can apply a variety of other cognitive tools to make sense of political complexities, and each can provide us with important and useful perspectives on what is really taking place. Another way of thinking about these tools is that they offer us a way of enhancing and/or modifying our myth-based understanding of political life by suggesting a number of different realities to compare it with.

Just as the ancient Greeks turned to *logos* as an alternative to myth-based thinking, today we regard reasoned analysis as the ideal means for making sense of our political world. We typically hope that the reasonable citizen has a basic knowledge about the political system and its government institutions and is capable of making sense of what he or she reads or hears in news reports. A knowledgeable and well-informed citizen who has access to relevant facts and evidence is able to understand by applying his or her analytic skills in a reasoned way.

Although some Americans can live up to that ideal, the complex nature of the U.S. political system often proves too difficult and time-consuming for many people to comprehend (recall the perplexing examples at the beginning of the chapter). In addition, some would argue that, as our private lives become more hectic and complicated, we have less and less time to deal with our public or civic lives.

The results are evident in recent surveys that tested the "civic literacy" of Americans. In 2008, the Intercollegiate Studies Institute (ISI) funded a survey in which a random sample of 2,508 American adults were asked to complete a thirty-three-question "quiz" involving basic civic knowledge drawn from a variety of sources. Of those who participated, more than 70 percent had failing grades (scored below 60 percent correct) on those thirty-three questions (see Figure 1.1; see also Asked & Answered, page 23).

Political scientists who study the American electorate express a wide range of opinions on the low number of citizens who rely on reason and evidence to make sense of their political lives and choices. To some, the American voter is so ignorant or irrational about politics that elections are really meaningless expressions of the public will. To others, the electorate is not ignorant but rather ill informed, and votes and elections are meaningful to the extent that they reflect decisions

America's Report Card		
In spring 2008, a random sample of Americans took a straightforward test designed to assess each respondent's "knowledge of America's founding principles and texts, core history, and enduring institutions"—ISI's definition of civic literacy. As detailed below, more than 70% of Americans failed this basic test of the kind of knowledge required for informed and responsible citizenship.		
Grade	Number Surveyed	Percent Surveyed
A (90 to 100%)	21	0.8
B (80 to 89.9%)	66	2.6
C (70 to 79.9%)	185	7.4
D (60 to 69.9%)	445	17.8
F (59.9% and below)	1,791	71.4
Total	2,508	100.0

FIGURE 1.1 Civic Illiteracy?

Source: Intercollegiate Studies Institute American Civic Literacy Program, "Our Fading Heritage: Americans Fail a Basic Test on Their History and Institutions."

made on the basis of less-than-adequate knowledge. Samuel Popkin, an advocate of that last view, argues that Americans use "heuristic shortcuts" in making sense of the choices they face in an election, and although such voters do not live up to the ideal model of a reasonable citizen, they do represent something more than an ignorant or indifferent voter.[34]

The use of reasoned analysis in American political life, however, is not always tied to the image of the ideal citizen or voter. Some would argue that many of the institutions of American government operate in a way that applies the power of reason to resolve disputes and solve public problems. One of the major characteristics of the American judicial system (see Chapter 14, on the judiciary) is the use of legal and constitutional reasoning in dealing with the many and varied issues that come before the courts.[35] Others would point to the increasing use of policy-analysis techniques by government agencies (see Chapter 13 on the bureaucracy) as another example of the growing power of reason in how we make sense of government. In fact, many of the efforts made to reform American government and politics over the past century can be regarded as attempts to enhance the use of reasoned analysis in the U.S. political system.

Beliefs and Ideologies

A third set of tools we use to make sense of our complex political world comes from those beliefs and ideologies that we adopt during our lifetime. **Beliefs** differ from reasoned analysis because they do not rely on empirical evidence or logic but instead are based on assumptions and attitudes we grow up with or develop over time. And although myths may play a role in generating and reinforcing beliefs, we can still regard them as a distinct sense-making tool. Many of our beliefs are implicit in the way we think about the world around us and are often reflected in the actions we take based on what we regard as common sense and stereotypes. Thus, if we are brought up to believe that all bureaucrats are incompetent or

Beliefs Those strongly held assumptions and attitudes about politics and government we grow up with or develop over time. In contrast to reasoned analysis or myths, beliefs do not rely on empirical evidence or narratives.

ASKED & ANSWERED

ASKED: How knowledgeable are U.S. students about their government?

ANSWERED: How much do American college students know about their government, its history, its values, or the U.S. economy? Do they score any higher on the civic literacy quiz than the general public (see Figure 1.1)? The answer is yes, but not by much. In the ISI study, those who held a bachelor's degree had an average score of 57 percent correct on the quiz, a full 13 percentage points higher than those with high school degrees. Nevertheless, a majority still failed the test. Giving the same quiz to college freshmen and seniors in 2005 and 2006, the ISI found not only that most students failed but that the three years of college education made little difference in the scores—and that students in elite schools often did worse on the test. In a follow-up survey focused on whether college education led to greater levels of civic engagement, ISI concluded that "a college degree appears to have the same negligible participatory impact as frequently listening to music, watching prime-time television, utilizing social networking sites, and emailing."

Are American students less civically literate than students in other countries? Do American students know less about political life and their political systems than students of the same age in Europe, Asia, or Latin America?

To find answers to those questions, we turn to the multinational 1999 Civic Education Study conducted by the International Association for the Evaluation of Educational Achievement (IEA). The study involved nearly 90,000 fourteen-year-olds in twenty-eight countries, asking a range of questions that would provide an assessment of how much these adolescents knew about politics, their views on civic engagement (what citizens are expected to do), and their attitudes on certain key issues. According to the IEA study's findings, America's fourteen-year-old cohort (mostly ninth graders) scored well in the categories of civic knowledge and understanding of civic engagement. Among the twenty-eight countries included in the study, the U.S. students ranked sixth overall, scoring 106 on a scale in which 100 was the average for all edge, the U.S. ninth graders scored 102 (100 = sample average) and ranked tenth among the twenty-eight-country sample, but in questions related to an understanding of the civic skills of citizens, the United States topped the list, with a score of 114 (100 = sample average).

Based on this survey data, when compared to students in other countries, American students tend to be above average in their understanding of both civic knowledge and civic skills. What makes these findings even more interesting is that the group of ninth graders tested in 1999 were of the same demographic cohort as the college seniors who scored so poorly in the 2005–2006 civic literacy tests.

Sources: For ISI, all material is found at http://www.americancivicliteracy .org/index.html. The findings for the 1999 IEA study are found at http://www.iea.nl/cived.html. A follow-up study was conducted in 2009, but the United States did not participate.

unresponsive (see Chapter 13, on the bureaucracy), we are likely to distrust all government officials, even in the face of evidence that they are people of integrity who are doing the best job they can under demanding circumstances and conditions of uncertainty.

Beliefs also differ from myths because they have an influence over us that is independent of stories and narratives about political and social life. Rather, our political beliefs emerge from an ongoing process we call *political socialization* (see Chapter 6 on public opinion and political participation). Thus, the widely shared belief among many Americans that all Democrats are liberals and all Republicans are conservative may have its roots in the attitudes expressed by our parents, schoolmates, or friends. Such basic beliefs will play a role in the political myths we adopt, and they might even shape the reasoned analysis we engage in when deciding which candidate to vote for in an election. But at their core, these attitudes probably come from fundamental beliefs we develop early in life and tend to retain over time.

The relationship between beliefs and myths can be a complicated one. We all face situations in which our beliefs are challenged by the evidence before us or are in direct conflict with the strongly held beliefs of others. Social psychologists call this situation *cognitive dissonance*, and they find that people who face such challenges will often filter out or ignore information that does not fit their beliefs. There are times, however, when those who hold strong beliefs will open themselves to alternative views and conflicting evidence—and this can have political consequences.

Consider what happens when a widely held belief that all Republicans are politically conservative is challenged by the candidacy of a liberal politician who is running as a Republican. This was the case in Rhode Island in both the 2000 and 2006 elections, when Lincoln Chaffee, the son of a popular Republican U.S. senator, ran to fill his father's seat. Rhode Island is regarded as a Democratic Party stronghold and one of the most "liberal" states in the country, and in preceding decades, Republicans had not done well in statewide elections. In 2000, however, many liberal Democrats voted for the younger Chaffee, giving him a 57 to 41 percent victory over his rival. But, although many liberal Democrats were willing to suspend their beliefs about Republicans in the 2000 election, Chaffee was not as lucky in 2006. Despite having established himself as one of the most liberal members of the U.S. Senate during his six years in office, not enough Rhode Island liberal Democrats were willing to give up their negative views and beliefs about Republicans to reelect the otherwise popular Chaffee. He lost the election by a 53 to 46 percent decision—and a year later quietly announced that he was no longer a Republican.

When our beliefs become more explicit and coherent, they take the form of ideologies. In politics, **ideologies** are the *conceptually coherent beliefs we use to think about whether government is doing what it ought to be doing.* They offer us general priorities and principles about what government could or should do and suggest the means for doing it.[36] Whereas myths help us to understand and deal with the world, ideologies tend to reflect our beliefs about the way we think the political world does or should operate. For example, those who adhere to a Marxist ideology view politics and the political system as the means by which the capitalist class maintains its power over the working class. For Marx and others, government should—and eventually will—be in the hands of the workers. At the other extreme, the American author and philosopher Ayn Rand used her writings to promote an ideology called objectivism that stressed the values of individualism and called for minimal government intervention in the economy.

But not all ideologies reflect extreme positions on issues. Consider, for example, the question of what the scope of governmental activity should be. When addressed explicitly as ideologies, this question's answers vary from society to society and

POLITICS & POPULAR CULTURE: Visit the book's companion website at **www.oup.com/us/gitelson** to read the special feature *Mirrors and Shapers of Images.*

Ideologies Conceptually coherent beliefs used to help us think about whether government is doing what it should be doing.

When conservative Orrin Hatch (R-Utah) ran for the U.S. Senate in 1976, he explicitly promised to work against the "liberal" agenda of the late Senator Ted Kennedy (D-MA). Over the years, however, Hatch and Kennedy (who died in 2009) developed a close relationship, resulting in the passage of major health and social legislation.

from era to era. Although some governments have attempted to establish an official ideology, in most democratic nations there is competition among two or more dominant ideologies. Until the middle 1980s, the leaders of the Soviet Union endorsed and enforced a Marxist-Leninist ideology that made opposition to the government a crime.[37] More common, however, is the situation in many Western European democracies, where competition among followers of different ideologies is at the heart of the representative system. In France, Italy, Belgium, Denmark, and even Great Britain, differences in ideology are often reflected in differences among the political parties.[38]

Although no "official" or dominant political ideology exists in the United States, most of us would probably support one of four major types of popular ideologies based on how we would respond to two central questions regarding how much government should do:

1. To what extent should government intervene in economic affairs?

2. To what extent should government interfere in the private affairs of Americans?

As for the first question, some Americans believe that government should not interfere in the marketplace unless absolutely necessary, whereas others believe that government regulation and management of the economy are crucial for the nation's health. In response to the second question, at one extreme are those who believe that government has no right to intrude in their personal choices and that the areas of personal freedom must be extended as much as possible. At the other end of the spectrum are those who believe that government sometimes has a moral obligation to intercede in the private lives of people who might otherwise

Liberalism A set of ideological beliefs that usually favor government intervention in the economy but oppose government interference in the private lives of individuals.

Conservatism A set of ideological beliefs that tend to resist government interference in economic matters but favor government action to regulate private affairs for moral purposes.

Populism A set of ideological beliefs that favor government intervention in both economic and personal affairs.

Libertarianism The ideological belief that government should do no more than what is minimally necessary in the areas of both economic affairs and personal freedom.

make unwise decisions. From that perspective, governments should be permitted to make and enforce laws related to smoking, abortion rights, same-sex marriage, and so on.

Taken together, the intersection of American beliefs on these two issues has generated four ideologies that seem to represent four general answers to the question of the extent to which the government should intervene in the economic life of the country and the activities of private citizens (see Figure 1.2).[39] **Liberalism** is the label typically applied to the position of those who favor increased government intervention in the economy but oppose increased limits on personal freedom. **Conservatism** is the label usually given to the position of those who favor increased regulation of private lives for moral purposes but oppose government interference in the economy.

Traditionally, liberalism and conservatism have constituted the mainstream ideological positions of most Americans. But in recent years many Americans have found that their views do not fit neatly into either perspective: They are liberal on certain issues and conservative on others. As a result, two other popular ideological perspectives have emerged: Modern-day **populists** are inclined to favor government intervention in both economic and personal matters, whereas **libertarians** take a strong stand against intervention in both.

The growing popularity of the populist and libertarian ideologies reflects some fundamental problems and potential shifts in the American ideological landscape. Initially the changes were subtle. During the 1990s some observers of American government and politics suggested that our dominant ideological perspectives—liberalism and conservatism—seem increasingly inconsequential to Americans. Some argued that there is a growing gap between the dominant ideologies and the realities of American political life. "The categories that have dominated our thinking for so long are irrelevant to the new world we face," contends E. J. Dionne Jr.[40] Others remarked on the widening "discrepancy" and tension between our dominant ideologies and the myths of American government that help define our expectations of how our political system should operate.[41]

By 2010, the ideological landscape of American politics had radically changed. Political divisions began to erupt in the form of what the popular press

FIGURE 1.2 Issues and Ideologies

The four major ideologies of American politics have been shaped by debates over government's role in economic and personal matters.

Source: Adapted from Maddox, William S. and Stuart A. Lilie. Beyond Liberal and Conservative: Reassessing the Political Spectrum. *Washington DC: CATO Institute, 1984. Reprinted by permission.*

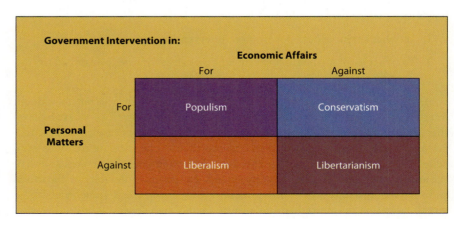

characterized as "culture wars." Antigovernment movements such as the Tea Party movement emerged to challenge elected officials they regarded as too moderate, and a significant change in the tone of political debate led many to worry about the "civility" of American political discourse.[42] Political scientists such as Morris P. Fiorina argue that these recent changes are limited and reflect a sharpening ideological divide only at the extremes of partisan politics. To him and his colleagues, the majority of Americans remain uncommitted to any strong ideological position.[43] Others, like Alan I. Abramowitz, think that there is something more significant taking place, and that ideologies are playing an increasing role in shaping the views and behavior of the general citizenry. His view is that the increasing prominence of ideologies in American political life is a reflection of growing demographic, geographic, cultural, and socioeconomic divisions.[44] In either case, ideological orientations and responses to questions about what government does or ought to do are important factors in making sense of American government (see the discussion of public opinion in Chapter 6).

Conclusion

We live in an increasingly complex and rapidly changing world, and many of us are barely able to keep up with the uncertainties and ambiguities of everyday life. Coming to terms with these turbulent conditions requires that we try to make sense of our everyday lives. We engage in sense making all the time. When you made the transition to college, for example, it probably took a while for you to make sense of where you were physically and what was expected of you socially and academically. When you change your residence or start a new job or make your first visit abroad, you engage in sense making as you get oriented to the new places and people that surround you. The same is true as you start to engage in the civic and political life of your community, state, or country. The first steps involve making sense of things.

Our approach and goal in this textbook is to get you started on the road to making sense of American government and politics. As we have highlighted in this chapter, the major ways to do this are with reasoning, beliefs, and myths. Although you may not realize it, unless you have been completely isolated from the outside world, you have already begun to make sense of our political and constitutional system, mostly through the adoption of the myths you learned in school or through the media. You may also hold some very strong beliefs about political life that you have picked up along the way. And it is likely that you have engaged in political reasoning at some point when discussing current issues and events with friends and family.

In the chapters that follow, we hope to raise your awareness of how you and other Americans make sense of our complicated political system. In the process, we highlight a few myths and strongly held beliefs related to specific topics—and explore some of the evidence and reasoning behind the "reality" of our subject matter. The main purpose of this book is to enhance your knowledge of American government and politics, but it is just as important that you increase your capacity to make better sense of it all.

Key Terms

Authority p. 13
Beliefs p. 22
Conservatism p. 26
Democracy p. 14
Elitist view of power p. 15
Government p. 9
Ideologies p. 24

Liberalism p. 26
Libertarianism p. 26
Majoritarian view
   of power p. 15
Myths p. 4
Pluralist view
   of power p. 15

Politics p. 9
Populism p. 26
Power p. 14
Public goods p. 33
Public policy p. 32
Representative democracy p. 14
Republic p. 14

Focus Questions Review

1. How do we define government and politics? What has been the role of government in American history? > > >

Government consists of those institutions and officials whose purpose it is to write and enact laws and to execute and enforce public policies that are expected to (1) maintain order through the rule of law, (2) provide goods and services that benefit the lives of all citizens, and (3) promote equality among members of society.

   Politics refers to the activities aimed at influencing or controlling government for the purpose of formulating or guiding public policy.

   Governments at the national, state, and local levels have played active roles in the nation's development from colonial times to the present.

- Traditionally, government has been active in economic and social policy areas, and the national government has been especially active since the days of the New Deal in the 1930s.
- Government has been increasingly involved in efforts to deal with environmental issues and the country's growing energy dependence.
- In recent years there has been greater concern about the size of government and the need to consider changing public priorities.

2. How does the U.S. political system deal with the issues of who should govern and where authority should be vested? > > >

From the perspective of governmental institutions, Americans are committed to the values of democracy, but the form of government is closer to that of a republic or representative democracy.

   From the perspective of politics and the wielding of power, the U.S. political system reflects a mixture of three major approaches:

1. A *majoritarian model*, in which power is distributed as equally as possible in a political system to facilitate meaningful majority rule
2. An *elitist model* based on the idea that, at times, the general public is best served when a basic consensus exists among a country's top leaders regarding fundamental issues
3. A *pluralist model* that accepts the role of power elites as long as membership in the elite is open to all in society and the members of this open elite serve the public good by competing among themselves for the attention of government, as well as for control of public offices.

Americans operate under a system that distributes authority over public policies among different levels of government—a system termed *federalism*.

How do we understand and make sense of our political system and government? What are the roles of myths, reason, beliefs, and ideologies in that effort? > > >

We make sense of our political system through three means:

   Political myths, which help us understand the political world around us through historical narratives, proverbial sayings, and other popular storylines that allow us to make sense of the complex settings and problems we face. These myths and stories, in short, help us by giving us a framework within which we can comprehend and navigate

complicated governmental structures and procedures, as well as many of the baffling issues that
challenge our political system. They do this by
1. Simplifying our complex world
2. Defining our place in the world and providing
   us with a shared identity
3. Guiding and rationalizing our behavior
4. Making sense of the behavior of others
5. Orienting our views of the past, present,
   and future.

Reasoned analysis, which relies on a citizen's basic
knowledge about the political systems and the
issues that confront it. Those citizens using this
approach would develop and apply their knowledge and analytic skills when faced with a choice
of candidates or when engaged in discussions
about policy issues.

Beliefs and ideologies, which we adopt and develop
over time, and which provide us with our basic
assumptions about the operations and role of
government, the political system, and the various
actors involved in both.
1. Beliefs are typically derived from our socialization into the political system and help
shape the content and role of reason and
myths in our political lives.
2. Ideologies reflect basic beliefs and attitudes
   toward government and its role in society. In
   the United States, four major ideological views
   tend to dominate:
   a. Liberalism, which takes a positive
      view of the government's efforts to deal
      with economic issues but a more cautious
      view of the government's incursions into
      the private lives of Americans
   b. Conservatism, which believes govern-
      ment involvement in the economy is not
      desirable but is willing to see government
      take action to restrict private behavior
      that is deemed socially questionable
   c. Progressivism, which is open to govern-
      ment involvement in both the economic
      and social lives of Americans for the
      greater good
   d. Libertarianism, which takes a dim
      view of government involvement in either
      sphere if it restricts individual freedom
      and choice

Review Questions

1. What are the three major goals of American government?
2. In what ways do myths help us make sense of politics and government?

For more information and access to study materials, visit the
book's companion website at
www.oup.com/us/gitelson.

Policy Connection

How do we make sense of public policies and programs?

The Policy Challenge

In Chapter 1, we learned about the different ways by which we make sense of the complex and often confusing nature of American government and politics. We use many of the same tools—myths, reason, beliefs, and ideologies—to make sense of what government does (or does not do) in response to public problems. The challenge we face in this and the thirteen other Policy Connections in this text is to show how we can use those sense-making tools to better understand and appreciate the role that public policies have in our lives.

The Legal Label

It is among the most common and mundane experiences facing all Americans as they grow up. At some point in our lives we decide to read that bothersome tag that is attached to the mattresses and pillows we sleep on, the upholstered chairs and couches we sit on, and even to the throw rugs and door mats we step on daily. Although the main purpose of the tag is to inform us of the material used in the product (e.g., "Minimum 75% Down," "Colored Urethane Foam," "10% Synthetic Fibers"), the phrase that stands out for most of us is printed at the very top in bold font: "Under Penalty of Law This Tag Not to Be Removed Except by the Consumer."

Initial reactions to reading the strong message printed on the "law label" vary from surprise to curiosity. Is this seemingly trivial bit of information from the product's manufacturer really the subject of a law? The simple answer is yes, and in fact it is the subject of a federal law (15 U.S. Code § 70C—Removal of Stamp, Tag, Label, or Other Identification) and more

detailed laws in thirty-one states. If you want to know the reason for the existence of the law label, a bit of research on the Internet will give the answer.

Early in the twentieth century, the states and federal government passed laws regulating the materials used as textile stuffing with the intent of stopping some manufacturers from using such things as horse hairs, corn husks, and old rags in their product. Over the decades, the rationale for the labeling law grew as the public became more aware of allergies and other hazards associated with various materials used for stuffing. The policy against removing the tag was designed to prevent the wholesalers and retailers who actually sold the item from tearing off the label. The labels themselves come in a range of sizes and shapes, although almost all seem to fit a standard familiar to most Americans. Manufacturers accept the labeling as just a part of doing business, and some have taken advantage of the tags by including basic warranty information on them. Consumer response to the tags, however, has been interesting.

Although the wording explicitly allows consumers to remove the tag, many leave the label on and accept it as just another part of the product's design. There may be a good reason for doing so (e.g., keeping the warranty information), but a popular explanation for consumer reluctance to removal of the law label is the belief that you might be subject to penalties for doing so. Over the years, the mythical fear of being arrested by the "mattress police" has provided comedians, cartoon satirists, and TV sitcoms with one-liners and plot lines guaranteed to get a laugh, but underlying the punch lines are some insights into the role that public policies play in our lives—and how we make sense of them.

THE ANATOMY OF A LAW LABEL

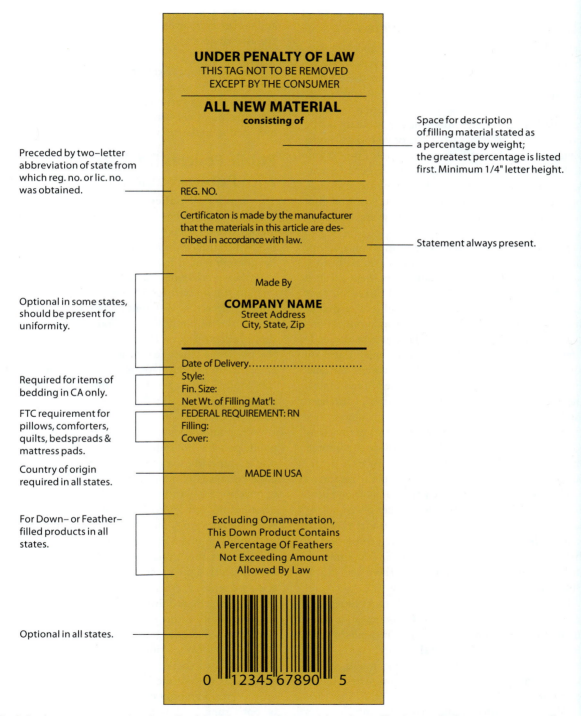

UNDER PENALTY OF LAW
THIS TAG NOT TO BE REMOVED
EXCEPT BY THE CONSUMER

ALL NEW MATERIAL
consisting of

REG. NO.

Certificaton is made by the manufacturer
that the materials in this article are described in accordance with law.

Made By

COMPANY NAME
Street Address
City, State, Zip

Date of Delivery.................................
Style:
Fin. Size:
Net Wt. of Filling Mat'l:
FEDERAL REQUIREMENT: RN
Filling:
Cover:

MADE IN USA

Excluding Ornamentation,
This Down Product Contains
A Percentage Of Feathers
Not Exceeding Amount
Allowed By Law

0 12345 67890 5

Space for description
of filling material stated as
a percentage by weight;
the greatest percentage is listed
first. Minimum 1/4" letter height.

Statement always present.

Preceded by two–letter
abbreviation of state from
which reg. no. or lic. no.
was obtained.

Optional in some states,
should be present for
uniformity.

Required for items of
bedding in CA only.

FTC requirement for
pillows, comforters,
quilts, bedspreads &
mattress pads.

Country of origin
required in all states.

For Down– or Feather–
filled products in all
states.

Optional in all states.

The federal government requires that a "law label" describing the material used as stuffing be attached to every mattress, pillow, couch cushion, and similar product sold in the United States. Over time, the label has been used for other purposes as well-such as an official product warranty-but its primary purpose reflects an effort to protect and inform consumers about the product they are purchasing.

The Pervasiveness of Policies

Law labels are just part of a more important fact about public policies. Unless you live a very sheltered existence, probably every aspect of your daily life is somehow connected to the work of government. If you believe that claim is an exaggeration, take up this challenge: from the moment you wake up in the morning and throughout the rest of your day, keep a detailed diary of your activities and note (as best you can) how those actions connect with government. Assuming you lead a reasonably normal life of attending school and/or going to work, you will find that by midday you have already filled several pages of your diary.

As you begin this exercise, consider some advice for how to start your diary. Many of you will begin with an entry noting that your alarm went off at a specific time and you got out of bed to launch your day. On careful examination you will realize that at that very moment you have had several connections to government. First consider the mattress and bedding you slept on. In addition to the label, there are government standards as to what material can and cannot be used in bedding sold in the United States. There are even standards for the material in those pajamas you slept in.

If, as is likely, your alarm clock (or its many component parts) was manufactured outside the United States, the price you paid for it was in part determined by a government tariff levied on imported goods. As significant, the very time of day you chose to awaken is influenced by government decisions regarding time zones, whether you are under standard or daylight savings time, and the determination of the exact setting of time by the U.S. government's official atomic clock, located at the U.S. Naval Observatory (see http://www.time.gov/).

If you awoke to an alarm sound, most likely it is patent protected under law; if it was music or news emanating from a broadcast station, it came through airwaves regulated by a federal agency; and if it was music from your private playlist, the music, lyrics, and performance itself are likely protected under government copyright laws.

Walk to bathroom, and you are using facilities built to code under local construction codes, using appliances (yes, even that electric toothbrush) that are also subject to a range of government standards and protections.

And you haven't even started your day!

It would be an understatement to point out the obvious: that government decisions are a pervasive factor in our lives—and thus another challenge to our need to make sense of the political world.

Public Policies Dealing with Public Problems

The term **public policy** covers a wide range of government actions that directly and indirectly impact on our lives. Public policies are broadly defined as the composite of decisions made and actions taken by government officials in response to problems identified and issues raised through the political system. As we will see in the chapters that follow, policies often take different names, typically associated with the institution or branch of government that produces them. Thus, Congress makes "laws," the president issues "executive orders," the bureaucracy enforces "regulations," and the courts issue "decisions." What ties these different activities together is that they all reflect the decisions and action of public officials.

We should develop our capacity to make sense of public policies, not only because they play a pervasive role in our daily lives but also because such knowledge enhances our understanding and appreciation of government—and vice versa. Developing that understanding and appreciation of public policies can prove challenging, however, because the choices policymakers make are often difficult.

Consider the "guns-or-butter" problem that has been central to the most important policy debates of the past century. At its simplest level, the guns-or-butter problem requires that policymakers decide what portion of the governmental budget will be devoted to defending the nation against external threats and what portion will go to dealing with the economic and social problems we face within our borders. If we assume the budget is finite—that is, only a certain amount of money is available to spend on both guns and butter—the policy choices involve a zero-sum decision in which an additional dollar

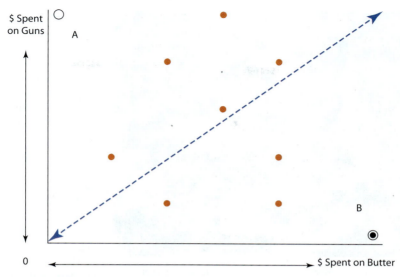

FIGURE 1PC.1 Possible Choices That Policymakers Face
Some policymakers will want all the money to be spent on guns, whereas others will
prefer it all to be spent on butter. However, an almost infinite number of alternative
positions are available.

spent on one means a dollar less for the other. Figure 1PC.1 illustrates the possible choices that policymakers face. There might be some, like policymaker A, who want all the money spent on guns, whereas B prefers it all be spent on butter. Of course, an almost infinite number of alternative positions are available within the parameters of the budget, and we can argue that an ideal policy choice might be one that lands somewhere along the dashed line.

Of course, the guns-or-butter problem is never quite so simple in reality, as all sorts of other factors come into play. How dire is an external threat? How severe is the economic recession? How serious are the social conditions (e.g., crime, poverty) that cry out for attention? Are the policymakers willing (and will the public support) borrowing money to fund additional guns or butter? How strong is the opposition against increasing the national debt in order to fund more of either or both?

If the guns-or-butter problem seems difficult, consider the problem of providing **public goods**. Also known as *collective goods*, these are products or services that cannot be provided through normal marketplaces.

The classic example is that of a lighthouse built along a dangerous coastline. If you owned a fleet of cargo ships and suffered losses from vessels that sank because they came too close to some rocky shore, you would give serious thought to constructing a lighthouse on the shoreline that would prevent further shipwrecks. But once your lighthouse is functional, its warning beam of light can be used by anyone—including your competitors! Economists call this the "nonexcludability" feature of public goods, because once it is provided, no one can be excluded from making us of it. If someone could be excluded, you would be in a position to charge the person a fee for its use, thereby enabling you to recover your costs—and perhaps earn some profit. But even if you could come up with some technological solution that allowed you to charge for use of the lighthouse service, what would you set as the price? After all, because the marginal cost of operating the lighthouse does not increase with any additional use—a property economists call "nonrivalrous consumption"—anything you charge might be regarded as unwarranted and unfair.

Lighthouses are regarded as public goods that have characteristics that make it difficult (if not impossible) to treat them as marketable commodities. It is assumed that such public goods ought to be provided by government.

Of course, the benefits to you and your shipping enterprise may be so considerable that you are willing to provide the lighthouse service without protest; but more often than not, the provision of a public good is put in the hands of government. The question facing policymakers is whether to take on the task of providing the public good and, if so, how to produce it and pay for it.

There are times when the service or product in question is clearly public in nature because it meets the criteria of nonexcludability and nonrivalrous consumption, as is the case with national defense. Thus, it comes as no surprise that national security is provided to all and funded out of general tax dollars.

There are other instances, however, when some good or service does not meet the technical criteria but is treated as a public good nonetheless. Public education (usually defined as kindergarten through twelfth grade, or K–12) is regarded as a collective good even though it meets neither standard: Individuals can be excluded from consuming it, and those who receive the schooling can be charged for the costs of the service. The decision to provide public education as a public good is left up to policymakers, and with few exceptions a general consensus has

supported this view for at least a century, if not longer. The power of that consensus becomes evident each time there is discussion about altering the way public education is provided or funded (see Policy Connection 3).

The U.S. space program is another interesting example. In the late 1950s and throughout most of the 1960s, the space program was regarded as a national priority, closely tied to our national defense interests during the Cold War. Starting in the early 1970s, however, policymakers began to question whether the costs of the program (run primarily by the National Aeronautics and Space Administration, or NASA) were warranted, especially in light of the growing demands of domestic problems. At first this issue was regarded as a classic guns-or-butter problem, as decisions focused on which parts of the space program were to be cut and which would be retained in light of demands for more social spending. Eventually, however, attitudes have shifted about the public goods nature of the space program. The shift began when the U.S. government decided to turn over control of communication satellites to private companies (e.g., COMSAT), and today private enterprises provide many of the services that were once operated as strictly public goods.

Conclusion
How do we make sense of public policies and programs?

The provision of public goods and the issue of guns or butter are just two examples of the many kinds of challenges facing public policymakers. For our purposes, they represent cases in which our tools to make sense of public policies can easily come into play.

Our understanding of the guns-or-butter dilemma, for example, is shaped by those myths and beliefs we have about America's vulnerability to foreign attacks or our reactions to stories about bureaucratic waste and welfare fraud in social programs. It is also subject to reasoned analysis and debate as we examine the trade-offs for each proposal to build a new weapon system or to increase funding for disaster relief. The same approach is true for the public goods issues, especially as we analyze the costs and benefits of public versus private provision of services such as health care, national parks, highway maintenance, and so forth. But even if a rational analysis demonstrates that we are better off providing some service through government, our ideological commitment to the free market might alter our perspective and understanding. The goal of this Policy Connection and all those that follow is to help us make sense of these policies and the choices they represent and to understand how they pervade our daily lives.

QUESTIONS FOR DISCUSSION

1. Our lives are increasingly tied to social media and the world of smartphones, tablets, and desktop and laptop computers. Each and every day we hear about problems and issues related to our life on the net, from cyberbullying to efforts by major media companies to control access to the web. What role should government play in addressing these issues? What kinds of public policies are needed to make certain the Internet is operated in the public interest?

2. In many countries, health care is regarded as a public good to be provided through government at little or no cost to all and paid for out of taxes. In the United States, health care is still provided through the private marketplace, although government now requires that affordable health care insurance be available to all. Should the United States change its approach and treat health care as a public good?

CHAPTER 2

MYTHS & REALITIES

Is the Constitution a living document?

Constitutional Foundations

The Constitutional Trade-Off

During the 1970s and early 1980s, New York City was regarded as a terrifying place to live, work, or even visit. In 1980 there were 1,814 homicides (compared to 417 in 2012), and serious crime increased each year, as did reports of street gang warfare, widespread drug use, and prostitution.[1]

By the early 1990s, New York was starting to transform itself into one the most desirable places to live if you wanted to achieve fortune and fame in the United States. During the past two decades, the change has been even more dramatic. New York City's crime statistics[2] indicated that the city was a much safer place. Between 1993 and the end of 2012, murder, burglary, and robbery rates had declined by more than 75 percent; rape and felonious assaults were down by more than 50 percent for the same period.

There is no shortage of theories about what caused the turnaround in New York, but a good deal of credit is given to the enhancement of police and law enforcement authority. Under Mayors Rudolph Giuliani and Michael Bloomberg, the police developed strategies that stressed maintaining social order and that focused on crime prevention. However, one of the more controversial practices was "stop and frisk," an approach that allowed NYPD officers to stop, question, and bodily search pedestrians for weapons or other indications of possible criminal activity.

Stop and frisk raises a number of issues regarding civil liberties and civil rights (as discussed in Chapters 4 and 5). One source estimates that there have been nearly 4 million stops under this policy since it was instituted in

2002, and that in nine of ten cases there was no violation of the law detected. Moreover, a disproportionate number of those stopped were from the African American and Latino communities. Despite protests from members of those communities, the program continued with the full support of the mayors and others. What supporters of stop-and-frisk have highlighted is just how "effective" the policy has been in reducing crime and improving the lives of those who live and work in New York City.

In August 2013, however, a federal court judge ordered a halt to the stop-and-frisk program until the NYPD could demonstrate that it had policies and procedures in place that would meet "constitutional" standards. For the judge, it did not matter whether the program worked or did not work. "This Court's mandate," wrote Judge Shira A. Scheindlin, "is solely to judge the constitutionality of police behavior, not its effectiveness as a law enforcement tool. Many police practices may be useful for fighting crime—preventive detention or coerced confessions, for example— but because they are unconstitutional they cannot be used, no matter how effective."[3]

That statement made no sense to those who favored the stop-and-frisk approach, and city officials appealed the ruling. After all, they argued, don't we as a public expect government to keep us safe by maintaining law and order, even if it means some minimal inconvenience? Few of us would raise questions about the procedures we go through whenever we travel by air (removing our belts and taking off our shoes), for we understand the trade-offs—we tolerate a bit of inconvenience in exchange for a greater sense of security. So why not accept the seemingly random stop-and-frisk efforts of the NYPD—especially because the numbers indicate that the program has been effective?

On appeal, a higher court stayed Scheindlin's order that the program cease until constitutional problems were addressed. For New York, however, the issue was resolved politically when the voters elected an opponent of the policy, Bill de Blasio, as the next mayor. Within a few weeks of taking office in January 2014, he announced an end to stop and frisk.

The goal of this chapter is to show that perhaps the judge's decision makes sense if we understand the status and role of our Constitution in our political system. Yes, we want a government that is effective, that can adapt to the need to reduce crime or prevent terrorism or deal with the aftermath of natural disasters or severe economic distress. And yet we also want that government to act in accordance with fundamental and enduring constitutional principles, and especially the rule of law—we want a government that is as effective in protecting us from the arbitrary exercise of government power as it is effective in establishing law and order while delivering the public goods and services we require to sustain the quality of life in our communities.

To help us strike the necessary balance of effective and constitutional governance, we have increasingly relied on the *myth of the living Constitution*—a narrative that tells us it is possible to have a government based on enduring principles set forth in the late eighteenth century that can adapt to the demands of our complex and ever-changing world. As we shall see, as comforting as that myth has been for those seeking to make sense of our constitutional system, it has not been unchallenged.

An Imperfect Document

> **What were the circumstances surrounding the framing of the Constitution?**

In 1987, along with thousands of other Americans, political historian Sanford Levinson visited an exhibit at Philadelphia's Independence Park that celebrated the two hundredth anniversary of the Constitution. At the end of the exhibit was a display of the final draft of the Constitution presented to the delegates for their acceptance or rejection on September 17, 1787. At that point, Levinson was confronted with a sign that asked visitors: "Will You Sign This Constitution?" Levinson hesitated. The author of several books on American constitutional history, he knew that many of the delegates to the 1787 convention that drafted the document also hesitated before putting their signatures to the very document that we now venerate, and at least three of those present on that day refused to add their names to what they regarded as a fundamentally flawed document. The Framers of the Constitution, it seems, had their own doubts about this imperfect document and its possible rejection by the states. And, even if it were ratified, several Framers openly wondered whether it would last.[4]

In what ways was the proposed Constitution flawed? The answer depended, of course, on who you were and your expectations of government. If you wanted a democracy in which the voice of the people would be directly and clearly represented in the laws of the land, then you would have found the proposed arrangements difficult to accept. You would have also been disappointed if you believed that every American should have an equal voice in the national legislature. As drafted, in our constitutional system, the voices and influence of some people are intentionally given more weight than others.

For example, at the time of the founding, the state of Virginia had ten times the population of Delaware—yet each state would have the same number of votes in the proposed U.S. Senate. Despite changes in how senators are selected (see the Seventeenth Amendment), the Constitution still guarantees each state two seats in the Senate. This means that the 12 percent of the U.S. population that live in California have the same representation—the same voice in the Senate —as the 0.2 percent that reside in Wyoming.

If you favored the abolition of slavery or were opposed to the continuation of the slave trade, you probably would have regarded the proposed Constitution as morally flawed in how it responded to those issues. Those who came from states whose economies depended on the continuation of slavery were not pleased with provisions that ended the slave trade in twenty years and would not allow slaves to be counted as whole persons when determining representation in the U.S. House of Representatives. In contrast, those who identified with the growing antislavery sentiments of the time found those very same provisions reprehensible, although they did set a definite end to the importation of more slaves and allowed Congress to impose taxes based on the number of slaves held in each state.

In the eyes of those who wanted a stronger national government to deal with the economic problems of the former colonies, the proposed Constitution did not go far enough in clearly establishing the authority of a central government. For those who feared too much power in the newly formed national government, the proposed Constitution seemed to take too much authority away from the states and failed to protect the rights of the people.

Given all these shortcomings, it is little wonder that Levinson—and many of the Framers—was hesitant to endorse that draft. How did such a flawed document get the support of enough delegates attending the convention to be sent forward to the states for ratification? And how did such a controversial and imperfect arrangement eventually get ratified by enough states to become the supreme law of the land? More importantly, how has such a flawed constitutional system remained an effective foundation for governing the United States for more than 225 years?

The Setting for Constitutional Change

Part of the answer is that the so-called flaws and imperfections we see in the Constitution are actually the result of the necessary bargains and compromises made by a group of individuals who understood that they were engaged in a major act of politics that would leave no one completely satisfied with the result. In that sense, we can make sense of the Constitution as a reasonable product generated by reasonable individuals engaged in a very challenging political process.

Why the Framers of the U.S. Constitution undertook the task of constitution writing is not clearly or simply answered. When they met in Philadelphia in May 1787, a constitution was already in place. The **Articles of Confederation** were written in 1777 by the same Continental Congress that had issued the Declaration of Independence one year earlier. It was ratified in 1781—in the midst of rebellion against Britain—as America's first national constitution, as each colonial legislature debated the pros and cons of joining together to form a government where none had existed before. The result was a loose union of states built around a relatively weak national congress.

The national congress under the Articles consisted of a single body in which each state had one vote. That body could exercise significant powers if it could muster the nine-thirteenths majority that was needed to pass any major legislation. For instance, under the Articles, the congress was empowered to make war and peace, send and receive foreign ambassadors, borrow money and establish a

Articles of Confederation
The first constitution of the United States, ratified in 1781. They established a loose union of states and a congress with limited powers.

monetary system, build a navy and develop an army in cooperation with the states, fix uniform standards of weights and measures, and even settle disputes among the states. However, it was powerless to levy and collect taxes or duties, and it could not regulate foreign or interstate commerce. No executive was appointed to enforce acts of the congress, and no national court system existed to hear disputes that might arise under the Articles. As for amending the Articles themselves, it would take a unanimous vote of all thirteen member states to make such fundamental changes in the national government.

The 1787 meeting at Philadelphia was convened because many of the country's political leaders believed that the national government under the Articles lacked the strength to cope with the young republic's problems. For example, by 1787 it was clear to many officials that the national government under the Articles could not conduct an effective foreign policy. Despite the colonists' victory in the American Revolution, the British had not relinquished, as they had promised, the Northwest Territories along the Great Lakes. Furthermore, the Spanish remained a hostile presence in Florida and what was then the Southwest. Encouraged by both Britain and Spain, Native American tribes harassed settlers all along the new nation's frontier.

Even worse was the Articles' inability to deal with the nation's financial problems. Lacking the power to tax, the national congress had to rely on funds provided by the states. However, its requests for funds from the states were increasingly ignored. The country had accumulated a large public debt during and immediately after the Revolutionary War, and much of it remained unpaid. Because they were not prohibited from doing so under the Articles, some states began to print worthless paper money to pay off their debts, and as a result, spiraling inflation hit the economy.

Economic conditions under the Articles were not good. Within the states, many small farmers faced bankruptcy and the loss of their farms. In western Massachusetts, where the situation was particularly bad, a group of farmers, led by a former Revolutionary War officer, Daniel Shays, disrupted court foreclosure proceedings in September 1786 and several months later tried unsuccessfully to seize a national government arsenal. That incident, known as *Shays' Rebellion*, convinced some of the country's most politically influential leaders that changes had to be made in America's system of government.[5] Several of those leaders were no doubt motivated by a genuine concern for the future of the young republic. Others, however, were stirred to action by fear and anxiety about their own economic future.

The Framers

We can better understand the Constitution if we know more about the individuals who wrote it and their motivations.[6]

What we know for certain is that the fifty-five people who came to Philadelphia in 1787 were all white males. Women and African Americans, as well as other racial minorities, were excluded. Among the "Founding Fathers" were merchants, physicians, bankers, planters, and soldiers. More than half of them were trained in law, and more than two-thirds had served in the Continental

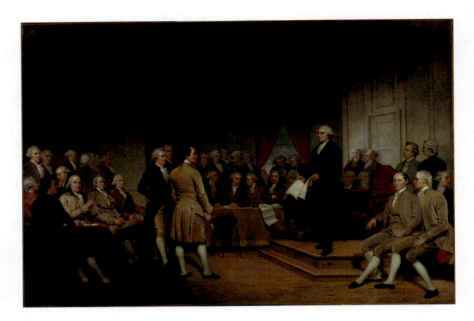

The Constitution was shaped by several compromises reached through the debates at the 1787 convention.

POLITICS & POPULAR CULTURE: Visit the book's companion website at **www.oup.com/us/gitelson** to read the special feature *HBO's Favorite Founding Father.*

Congress, which had governed the new nation during the Revolutionary War. That summer they took part in a rare moment of "decisive political creation": They applied their knowledge and experience of government to the design of a new constitution.[7]

At least two individuals who played important roles in the American Revolution and the writing of the Declaration of Independence were not in attendance. Both Thomas Jefferson and John Adams were in Europe at the time, where they were serving as the American ambassadors to France and England, respectively. One individual who played a central role in the convention's work was James Madison. Madison not only engaged in the debates and political bargains that shaped the Constitution but also lead the fight for its approval. He played such a significant role that today he is often called the "Father of the Constitution."

The delegates included at least two men of international reputation at the time: George Washington and Benjamin Franklin. Washington, a popular and imposing figure,[8] was unanimously elected to chair the meeting. Franklin[9] was well regarded by the other delegates, and many constantly sought his opinions. At eighty-one years of age, however, his physical powers were failing him. He was so ill at times that prisoners from the city jail were assigned the task of carrying him from his home to the nearby sessions. Nevertheless, he was influential in the eventual adoption of the document. During the final days of the convention, he expressed his support by noting that whenever a group of men are gathered to write a constitution, "you inevitably assemble with those men all their prejudices, their passions, their errors of opinion, their local interests, and their selfish views." One can hardly expect, he argued, that any such gathering would produce a "perfect" government. "It therefore astonishes me," he continued, "to find this system approaching so near to perfection as it does. . . . Thus I consent . . . to this Constitution, because I expect no better, and because I am not sure that it is not the best."[10]

The Roots of the Constitution

> What were the important traditions underlying the Constitution?

The Framers of the Constitution were hardly as diverse in their "prejudices" and "passions" as Franklin thought. Despite many disagreements and debates over specifics, the Framers shared a common legal and intellectual heritage. In that sense, the roots of the Constitution run deep. To understand the unique circumstances that led to its creation, we must explore the traditions that guided its authors.[11]

The Colonial Heritage

Most British colonies[12] were established under royal charters that allowed settlers to govern themselves in many matters. In several colonies, the settlers modified or supplemented these agreements. For example, the **Mayflower Compact**, which the Pilgrims wrote, set forth several major principles for the Plymouth Colony's government. That agreement and similar ones existing throughout the colonies became part of the colonial heritage that helped shape the Constitution.

Mayflower Compact A document, composed by the Pilgrims, that set forth major principles for the Plymouth Colony's government.

When we think about colonial rule, we often picture an oppressed people who are dominated by foreign rulers. We rarely think of colonial government as a breeding ground for self-government and openness. Yet, from the 1630s until the American Revolution, England let its North American colonies govern themselves, making no major effort to establish a central administration for its growing empire.[13]

Each of the colonies remained primarily a self-governing entity, and by the early 1700s most of them had developed similar governmental structures. A typical colony had three branches of government: (1) a governor appointed by the king, (2) a legislature, and (3) a relatively independent judiciary. Local government consisted of self-governing townships and counties. The future leaders of the American Revolution gained political experience and an understanding of how governments operate through participation in these colonial institutions.[14]

The Intellectual Background

The intellectual atmosphere of the time also influenced the Framers of the Constitution.[15] Raised in a society that took its religion seriously, they grew up with such concepts as equality before God and the integrity of each human life—concepts rooted in their *Judeo-Christian religious traditions*. The idea of a covenant, or contract, among members of society developed from those traditions, as did the distrust of the monarchy and the perception of a need for a system of laws to protect individual rights.[16]

Enlightenment The period from the 1600s through the 1700s in European intellectual history. It was dominated by the idea that human reason, not religious tradition, was the primary source of knowledge and wisdom.

The Framers were also children of the **Enlightenment**.[17] Usually dated from the 1600s through the 1700s, that period in European intellectual history was dominated by the idea that human reason, not religious tradition, was the primary source of knowledge and wisdom. On issues related to government and politics, a number of writers set the tone for the discussions among the Framers and their peers in the colonies.

Among the most controversial of Enlightenment writers was Thomas Hobbes. In his most famous work, *Leviathan* (1651), Hobbes contended that governments were formed by an agreement among rational individuals who, living without government in a brutish state of nature, realized that it was in their self-interest to subject themselves to an all-powerful ruler. Thus, Hobbes argued that government depended on the consent of the governed. Although he was no advocate of democracy (he wrote in defense of the British monarchy), his views proved helpful in establishing the rational basis of government.[18]

Another British political philosopher, John Locke, was perhaps the most influential of the Enlightenment authors among the colonists. He offered an explanation of political life that carried Hobbes's argument further by asserting that people possess an inherent right to revolution. In *Two Treatises on Government* (1690), Locke argued that individuals form governments as a matter of convenience to deal with the depraved behavior of some individuals. Thus, a government can continue to exist as long as it proves convenient to its citizens and does not interfere with their pursuit of life, liberty, and property. But, if the government violates this arrangement, the citizens have a right to emigrate or resist. Ultimately, this view sanctions the right of citizens to replace a government that does such things to them.[19]

The work of French aristocrat Charles de Montesquieu clearly influenced the writers of the Constitution. The Framers relied especially on his book *The Spirit of the Laws*, which was first published in Paris in 1748. In that work, Montesquieu argued that the best government is one that is designed in such a way that no person or group can oppress others. This end is best achieved, Montesquieu wrote, by separating the legislative, executive, and judicial functions into three distinct branches of government.[20]

Finally, just as the seeds of the American Revolution were being planted in the 1750s and 1760s, Swiss-born philosopher Jean-Jacques Rousseau published several works arguing for a more extreme version of **popular sovereignty** than that offered by Locke. According to Rousseau, the best form of government is one that reflects the general will of the people, or popular sovereignty, which is the sum total of the interests that all citizens have in common. He was read widely and had many followers in the American colonies. Among them was Thomas Paine, a British-born American revolutionary whose pamphlets had enormous influence during the American Revolution. His best-known work, *Common Sense* (1776), is among the most often cited of the writings that came out of the American Revolution.

The Onset of Revolution

In the 1760s, British policies toward the North American colonies changed. After nearly 150 years of relative freedom from direct interference from England, some of the colonists found themselves under increasing pressure from London. Britain needed men and resources to fight the French and so began to impose demands and commercial restrictions on the American colonies.

Popular sovereignty The concept, first described by Jean-Jacques Rousseau around the time of the American Revolution, that the best form of government is one that reflects the general will of the people, which is the sum total of those interests that all citizens have in common.

In 1765, the British passed the *Stamp Act*—the first tax levied directly on the colonists by Parliament. Relying on their view of the rights granted to all British subjects under English law, various colonial leaders protested against this "taxation without representation." The British Parliament repealed the Stamp Act within a few months, but other controversies soon arose. For instance, the British granted and enforced a monopoly on the sale of tea to a British firm, thus interfering with the interests of the colonial merchants who had developed lucrative business trading in that important commodity. In 1773, a group of Boston citizens responded by raiding a ship loaded with tea and dumping its contents overboard. That incident, now known as the *Boston Tea Party*, caused the British to close Boston Harbor and tighten control over the colonial government in Massachusetts. The events leading to rebellion soon escalated, and by 1774 even some of the previously moderate voices in colonial politics were calling for change.

Representatives from the colonies gathered as the First Continental Congress in Philadelphia in September 1774. After passing resolutions protesting the recent British actions, the delegates set a date for reconvening the next year and adjourned. By the time they met again, as the Second Continental Congress in May 1775, rebellious colonists and British troops had exchanged gunfire at Concord and Lexington.

The Second Continental Congress took a number of steps that officially launched the American Revolution. It organized itself as a provisional government, and in June 1775 it created a continental army, to be headed by George Washington. In May 1776, the congress voted to take the final step of drawing up a statement declaring the colonies free and independent states. Realizing the need to make their case for independence as strong as possible to potential supporters at home and abroad, on July 2, 1776, it adopted the **Declaration of Independence** drafted by a committee composed of Thomas Jefferson, John Adams, and Benjamin Franklin. Two days later, the congress formally declared independence.

Declaration of Independence A document declaring the colonies to be free and independent states, and also articulating the fundamental principles under which the new nation would be governed, which was adopted by the Second Continental Congress in July 1776.

The Declaration of Independence achieved several objectives. In the short term, it denounced the British for abusing the rights given the colonists under the British constitution and for disrupting the long-standing traditions of self-government. It also proclaimed the intention of the colonial revolutionaries to sever their ties with England and explained the reasons for such drastic action. More important, in the long term, it articulated two fundamental principles under which the newly formed nation should be governed, and these have become central to what is known as the "American creed."

1. The Declaration held that governments have one primary purpose: to secure the "unalienable rights" of their citizens, among which are "life, liberty, and the pursuit of happiness."

2. It stated that governments derive their powers and authority from the "consent of the governed." The signers of the Declaration asserted that when any government violates the rights it was established to secure, "it is the Right of the People to alter or to abolish it" and to create a new government in its place.[21]

What the Framers Did

> **> What do the various provisions of the Constitution accomplish?**

As noted earlier, the new government created in the immediate aftermath of the American Revolution—the Articles of Confederation—had developed some significant flaws by 1787, leading to the Philadelphia meeting. Although originally charged with just recommending changes to the Articles, the delegates soon assumed the broader task of constructing an entirely new set of institutions and rules.

To shape a viable national government, the Framers needed to establish its legitimacy and work out its basic structures. Through the Constitution, they created the three branches of government and defined and limited their powers. They also devised formal procedures by which the Constitution itself could be amended.

Establishing Legitimacy

A government cannot be effective unless it possesses power—that is, unless it has the ability to carry out its policies and enforce its laws. Even more important, its citizens must believe that the government has the ability to exercise authority and power (see the discussion in Chapter 1).

The power and authority of any government are enhanced by the willingness of its citizens to obey governmental officials. A government is most effective when its citizens believe that those officials have a right to pass and enforce laws. That is why the establishment of government **legitimacy** is so important. It provides government with the effective authority that it needs if it is to govern.

Legitimacy The belief of citizens in a government's right to pass and enforce laws.

The legitimacy of the U.S. government is rooted in the Preamble to the Constitution. In the beginning of the Preamble, the Framers make clear the source of authority for the republic: "We the People." The choice of words is of extreme importance. The government created under the Articles of Confederation in 1777 was called a "firm league of friendship" among the states. Ultimately, all authority was retained by the states. The Constitution, in contrast, leaves no doubt that the national government's right to exercise authority—its legitimacy—comes directly from the people and not from the states (see Table 2.1).[22]

Structuring Authority

In deciding how to structure the authority of the new government, the Framers of the Constitution faced these two challenges:

1. They had to create a stronger national government while at the same time allowing the states to retain their authority.

2. They had to deal with the issue of how to allocate authority within the national government itself.

Confederation An arrangement in which ultimate governmental authority is vested in the states that make up the union, with whatever power the national government has being derived from the states' willingness to give up some of their authority to a central government.

Balancing National and State Authority. Under the Articles, ultimate governmental authority rested with the states. Whatever power the national government had was the result of the states' willingness to give up some of their authority to a central government. Such an arrangement is called a **confederation**—hence the title of the Articles.

TABLE 2.1 **Comparing America's Two Constitutions**

	Articles of Confederation	**Constitution of the United States**
Establishing legitimacy	Through a "firm league of friendship" among the states	Through "We the People"—all citizens of the nation
Structuring authority	Through a confederacy, with ultimate authority residing in the states Within the national government, in a single body—the congress	Through a federal arrangement, with national and state governments dividing and sharing authority In three distinct branches of government: legislative, executive, and judicial
Describing and distributing powers	A number of foreign and domestic powers listed in Article IX, many limited so as not to interfere with state authority	Delegated and implied powers for national government in Article I Concurrent and reserved powers for states
Limiting powers	Many limitations on national powers, with deference to states	Provision in Article I Bill of Rights
Allowing for change	An amendment process requiring unanimous vote of states No national courts to interpret the meaning of the Articles	An elaborate amendment process requiring significant majorities rather than unanimity Judicial review implied

In considering alternatives, the Framers could have proposed a constitution based on a **unitary system** of government. In a unitary government, the ultimate authority rests with the national government, and whatever powers state or local governments have are given to them by the central government. The Framers would not have had to look far for examples, as each of the thirteen states was in fact a unitary government. Although each state contained towns, counties, and boroughs, those local governments exercised only such powers as were granted to them by a charter issued by the state government.

Although they sought to move toward a stronger national government, the Framers realized that their new constitution would not be ratified if it called for a unitary form of government. In the end, they created a hybrid: a mixture of confederation and unitary system that is now called a **federation**. In a federation, the authority of government is shared by both the national and the state governments. In its ideal form, a federal constitution gives the national government exclusive authority over some governmental tasks, while giving the states exclusive authority over other governmental matters.[23] In some areas, the two levels of government share authority. We discuss which areas of government were given to the national government and which to the states later in this chapter.

Structuring Authority Within the National Government. Having established a national government with authority, the Framers also had to develop structures of authority within the national government so it could exercise its powers. Under the Articles of Confederation, whatever powers the national government possessed

Unitary system A form of government in which the ultimate authority rests with the national government, with whatever powers state or local governments have being given to them by the central government.

Federation (federal system) A system in which the authority of government is shared by both national and state governments. In its ideal form, a federal constitution gives the national government exclusive authority over some governmental tasks, while giving the states exclusive authority over other governmental matters; in some areas the two levels of government share authority.

were exercised by a single body: the congress. In contrast, the Framers created three branches of government: Congress, the presidency, and the courts.

The basic structure of American government was the result of a series of compromises reached among the delegates to the Constitutional Convention. The delegation from Virginia offered a series of resolutions for the meeting to consider. Under the *Virginia Plan*, a **bicameral** (two-house) congress would be established, in which each state's representation would be based on its population relative to that of other states. Under the Articles of Confederation, a state could send several representatives to the congress, but each state had only a single vote. The Articles of Confederation also did not provide for a separate executive or judicial branch of government at the national level; the Virginia Plan called for both.

Delegates from states with larger populations welcomed the provisions of the Virginia Plan. However, some delegates from the smaller states put forward a counterproposal. Known as the *New Jersey Plan*, it called for strengthening the existing Articles by adding executive and judicial offices. It also increased the powers of the Articles' **unicameral** (one-house) congress, especially its ability to force reluctant states to cooperate with the national government.

The delegates voted to reject the New Jersey Plan. However, the discussions about it drew attention to the many delegates who remained uncomfortable with key provisions of the Virginia Plan, especially the question of representation. To avoid a stalemate, the delegates adopted what has become known as the **Great Compromise**. That proposal, offered by the Connecticut delegation (and therefore sometimes called the Connecticut Compromise), led to the structure of the American national government as we know it today. It called for the establishment of a bicameral congress consisting of a house of representatives, in which states would be represented according to their population size, and a senate, in which each state would have an equal voice. Furthermore, the Great Compromise also contained provisions for executive and judicial branches of government. The Great Compromise was just one of many agreements among the Framers to resolve the complex issues that they faced (see Table 2.2). Out of such compromises came major provisions of the Constitution.

The Case of the Electoral College. Of all the compromises developed by the Framers, perhaps none has proved more troublesome—for them as well as for many generations of Americans—than the decision to establish the **Electoral College** as the means for selecting the president and vice president of the United States.

Unlike most of the other issues faced by the Framers, the presidential selection issue did not have two clear sides pitted against each other. It was not a matter of deciding between direct election and indirect election of the president and vice president. Instead, it was a question of how to design a selection system that would fit into the complex arrangements for balancing national and state interests that had already been agreed on, while at the same time making certain that the presidency would not be beholden to either chamber of Congress. The Framers established the special Committee of Eleven to deal with several "postponed matters," including how to select the president. Out of the committee came the basics of the Electoral College proposal. Its flaws became evident in the

Bicameral Refers to a legislature that is divided into two separate houses, such as the U.S. Congress.

Unicameral Refers to a legislature that has only one house.

Great Compromise The proposal offered by the Connecticut delegation to the Constitutional Convention in 1787. It called for the establishment of a bicameral congress, consisting of a house, in which states were represented according to their population size, and a senate, in which each state had an equal voice.

Electoral College The constitutional body designed to select the president. This system is described in Article II of the Constitution.

TABLE 2.2 The Major Compromises

Demands	Compromises	Demands
GREAT COMPROMISE		
States to have equal representation in Congress (New Jersey Plan)	A bicameral Congress with equal representation in the Senate and population-based representation in the House	States to be represented in Congress on the basis of population (Virginia Plan)
THREE-FIFTHS COMPROMISE		
Slaves to be counted for representation purposes, but not for taxation purposes	All slaves to be counted as three-fifths of a person for both representation and taxation purposes	Slaves not to be counted for representation purposes, but to be counted for taxation purposes
COMMERCE/SLAVE TRADE COMPROMISE		
National government not to regulate slave trade or exports	Congress given the power to regulate interstate and foreign commerce but not to impose a tax on exports from any state; Congress not to act on slave trade until 1808	National government to have authority over all interstate and foreign trade
FEDERALISM		
States to retain their legitimate authority in the governmental system	Division of legitimate authority between the states and national government	An effective national government to be established

elections of 1796 and 1800,[24] when it was put through its first real tests and was found wanting. Despite efforts over the decades to change the system, nothing was done to modify its basic structure. Then came the presidential election of 2000, and again the Electoral College compromise of 1787 became a critical issue that drew the attention of Americans for six frantic weeks.[25]

Distributing and Describing Governmental Powers

Having established a two-level structure of authority in the federal system, and having created the three branches within the national government, the Framers next faced the task of dividing up the powers among the various institutions.

Powers in the Federal System. The history and present-day operations of the federal system are discussed in greater detail in Chapter 3. It is important at this juncture to understand how the Framers allocated governmental authority between the national government and the states. The powers given to Congress in Article I are central to the operation of the national government. The article includes a detailed list of these powers, such as the authority to tax, borrow money, regulate interstate commerce, coin money, declare war, and raise and support an army and navy. These and other powers identified in Section 8 of Article I constitute the **delegated powers** of the American national government

Delegated powers The powers the Constitution gives to Congress that are specifically listed in the first seventeen clauses in Section 8 of Article I; they are sometimes referred to as "enumerated powers."

(see Figure 2.1). Many of these powers—such as the power to coin money and make treaties—are granted exclusively to the national government; that is, they are denied to the states. Other delegated powers, however, are granted to the national government but not denied to the states—for example, the power to

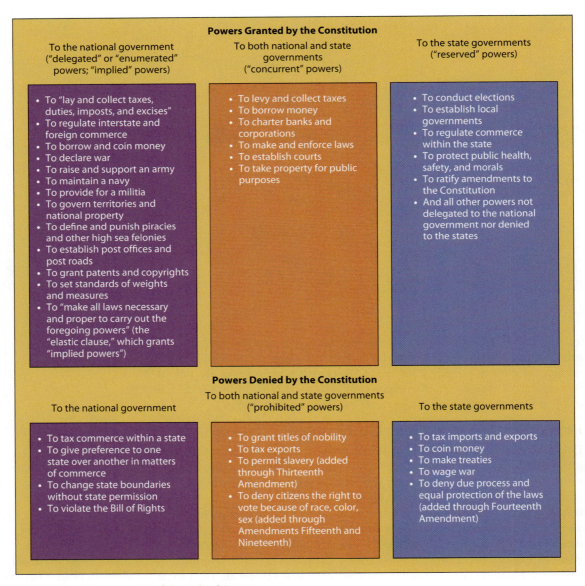

Powers Granted by the Constitution

To the national government ("delegated" or "enumerated" powers; "implied" powers)	To both national and state governments ("concurrent" powers)	To the state governments ("reserved" powers)
• To "lay and collect taxes, duties, imposts, and excises" • To regulate interstate and foreign commerce • To borrow and coin money • To declare war • To raise and support an army • To maintain a navy • To provide for a militia • To govern territories and national property • To define and punish piracies and other high sea felonies • To establish post offices and post roads • To grant patents and copyrights • To set standards of weights and measures • To "make all laws necessary and proper to carry out the foregoing powers" (the "elastic clause," which grants "implied powers")	• To levy and collect taxes • To borrow money • To charter banks and corporations • To make and enforce laws • To establish courts • To take property for public purposes	• To conduct elections • To establish local governments • To regulate commerce within the state • To protect public health, safety, and morals • To ratify amendments to the Constitution • And all other powers not delegated to the national government nor denied to the states

Powers Denied by the Constitution

To the national government	To both national and state governments ("prohibited" powers)	To the state governments
• To tax commerce within a state • To give preference to one state over another in matters of commerce • To change state boundaries without state permission • To violate the Bill of Rights	• To grant titles of nobility • To tax exports • To permit slavery (added through Thirteenth Amendment) • To deny citizens the right to vote because of race, color, sex (added through Amendments Fifteenth and Nineteenth)	• To tax imports and exports • To coin money • To make treaties • To wage war • To deny due process and equal protection of the laws (added through Fourteenth Amendment)

FIGURE 2.1 Constitutional Basis of the Federal System
The top-middle box lists powers shared by the two levels of government; the bottom-middle box shows powers denied to both. Powers on the upper left belong to the national government exclusively; those on the upper right belong to the states.

assess and collect taxes and the power to define criminal behavior and set punishments. These are called **concurrent powers.**

Article I, Section 8, of the Constitution also provides Congress with the authority "to make all Laws which shall be necessary and proper for carrying into Execution the foregoing Powers, and all other Powers vested by this Constitution in the Government of the United States." This **necessary and proper clause**, found in paragraph 18 of Section 8, establishes **implied powers** for Congress that go beyond those powers listed elsewhere in the Constitution. In *McCulloch v. Maryland* (1819), the U.S. Supreme Court resolved the issue of the constitutionality of implied powers.

In that case, the Court considered whether Congress had the right to charter a bank of the United States. The national bank was a controversial institution from the moment it was created by the first Congress, especially in the South and along the young nation's western frontier, where bank policies were blamed for the nation's economic woes. Several states decided to challenge the constitutionality of the bank by imposing a tax on its local branches. When Maryland officials assessed a tax of $15,000 on the bank's Baltimore branch, the head cashier took state officials to court, charging that they did not have the authority to tax an agency of the national government. Maryland countered that the Bank of the United States was not a legally constituted agency of the federal government, because no provision in the Constitution explicitly gives Congress the power to establish a national bank. The bank's lawyers, however, insisted that the power to charter a bank was implied in the constitutional authority to collect taxes, borrow money, and regulate commerce.

The Supreme Court unanimously sided with the national government. "Let the end be legitimate," stated Chief Justice John Marshall, "let it be within the scope of the Constitution, and all means which are appropriate, which are plainly adapted to that end, which are not prohibited, but consistent with the letter and spirit of the Constitution, are constitutional."[26] In that decision Marshall was agreeing with the national government that by giving Congress the explicit power to regulate commerce, the Framers of the Constitution implicitly granted Congress the right to charter a bank. This broad interpretation of the necessary and proper clause (also called the "elastic clause") altered the position of the states by greatly expanding the potential powers of the national government. The Bank of the United States survived until the 1830s, when President Andrew Jackson's opposition to it caused it to close. In 1913, Congress once again set up an agency for managing the banking system. That agency, the Federal Reserve System, still regulates the nation's major banks.[27] The right of Congress to establish such an agency is implied in the necessary and proper clause.

The Constitution does not provide a specific list of the powers left to the states. The Framers felt that there was no need for this, because the only powers given to the newly formed national government were those "enumerated" in the body of the Constitution. This approach left to the states the power over "all other objects."[28] This position was made explicit in the Tenth Amendment, which was added to the Constitution in 1791 (see the discussion of the Tenth Amendment and the current controversies surrounding it in Chapter 3). That amendment declares that "powers not delegated to

Concurrent powers Those powers that the Constitution grants to the national government but does not deny to the states—for example, the power to lay and collect taxes.

Necessary and proper clause The eighteenth clause of Article I, Section 8, of the Constitution, which establishes "implied powers" for Congress that go beyond those powers listed elsewhere in the Constitution.

Implied powers Those powers given to Congress by Article I, Section 8, clause 18, of the Constitution that are not specifically named but are provided for by the necessary and proper clause.

Reserved powers The powers that the Constitution provides for the states, although it does not list them specifically; they are sometimes called "residual powers." As stated in the Tenth Amendment, these include all powers not expressly given to the national government or denied to the states.

Writ of habeas corpus A court order that protects people against arbitrary arrest and detention by requiring officials to bring the "body" (i.e., the person) before the court.

Bill of attainder A legislative act declaring a person guilty of a crime and setting punishment without the benefit of a formal trial.

Ex post facto law A law declaring an action criminal even if it was performed before the law making it illegal was passed.

Bill of Rights In the United States, the first ten amendments to the Constitution, which collectively guarantee the fundamental liberties of citizens against abuse by the national government.

the United States by the Constitution, nor prohibited by it to the States, are reserved to the States respectively or to the people." Historically, these **reserved powers** have included such responsibilities as providing for public education, building local roads and highways, and regulating trade within a state's borders.

Powers Within the National Government. The Framers gave each of the three branches of the national government a distinct part of the functions that any government must perform: (1) pass laws (legislate), (2) enforce those laws (execute), and (3) settle disputes or controversies that arise from application of the laws (adjudicate).

In Article I of the Constitution, the Framers established Congress as the legislative branch. It is notable and important that they also chose Article I as the place to locate the delegated powers of the national government. That placement reflects the Framers' desire to make certain that the representative parts of the national government—the House of Representatives and the Senate—would be the primary fount of authority at the national level.

In contrast, the description of executive power in Article II takes the form of noting what roles the president will play and what duties he will carry out. Chapter 12 describes in greater detail how those roles and duties have expanded since the Constitution was written.

Article III says little more than that the "judicial power of the United States shall be vested in one Supreme Court" and in whatever lower courts Congress establishes. As we discuss in more detail in Chapter 14 the meaning of *judicial power* was articulated in the landmark case of *Marbury v. Madison* in 1803.

Limiting Governmental Powers. The Constitution also sets limits on the powers of both the national and the state governments. For example, Section 9 of Article I forbids Congress to suspend the privilege of a **writ of habeas corpus** except in times of rebellion or invasion. A writ of habeas corpus is a court order that individuals can seek to protect themselves against arbitrary arrest and detention. By issuing such a writ, a court can order public officials to bring a suspect or detainee before a judge to determine whether he or she is being held on legal grounds. But the fact that the Constitution permits its suspension in time of war ("rebellion or invasion") has made it the focus of debate since the events of September 11, 2001.[29]

Another provision prohibits the national government from passing a bill of attainder or an ex post facto law. A **bill of attainder** is a legislative act that declares a person guilty of a crime and sets punishment without the benefit of a formal trial. An **ex post facto law** makes an action criminal even though it was legal when it was performed.

Perhaps the best-known limits on the powers of the national government are provided in the **Bill of Rights**, a term usually applied to the first ten amendments to the Constitution, which were added in 1791 (see Table 2.3). Most of these amendments guarantee the fundamental liberties of citizens. They were appended to the Constitution to satisfy the demands of critics who complained during the ratification process that the original document did not adequately protect individual rights.[30]

After 9/11, hundreds of suspected terrorists and "enemy combatants" were held at the U.S. naval base at Guantanamo Bay, Cuba, without any right of habeas corpus. In June 2008, however, the U.S. Supreme Court noted that the remaining detainees had a right to seek a writ of habeas corpus in federal courts. The first detainee petitions were heard on November 6, 2008, and more than half of those filed were granted in the first year after the ruling. After July 2010, all but one of the petitions filed for the remaining detainees were rejected.

The Constitution also places limits on the powers and actions of the states. Section 10 of Article I, for instance, contains a list of powers denied to the states. Other sections set limits on the power of the states in relation to one another and to the national government. Article IV requires that each state give **full faith and credit** to the "Acts, Records, and judicial Proceedings of every other state." Thus, a divorce granted in Nevada must be honored in New York, and vice versa. There are exceptions, of course. In 1996, as several states began to consider revising their

Full faith and credit The requirement, found in Article IV of the Constitution, that each state respect in all ways the acts, records, and judicial proceedings of the other states.

TABLE 2.3 The Bill of Rights Adopted in 1791

Rights Addressed	Amendment
Freedom of expression Personal security	**1.** Freedom of religion, speech, press, assembly, and petition **2.** Right to bear arms **3.** No quartering of troops without consent **4.** Protection against unreasonable searches and seizures
Fair treatment under the law	**5.** Right to presentation of indictment; guarantee against double jeopardy and self-incrimination; guarantee of the due process of law and just compensation **6.** Right to a speedy and public trial **7.** Right to a jury trial in civil cases **8.** Guarantees against excessive bail, fines, and punishments
Reserved rights and powers	**9.** Powers reserved to the people **10.** Powers reserved to the states

marriage laws to permit same-sex unions, Congress passed the Defense of Marriage Act, which allowed each state to make its own laws related to that subject, but also allowed other states to avoid honoring such legal unions. In 1999, Vermont passed a law to allow civil unions, and in 2004 Massachusetts decided to allow same-sex marriages for its citizens (see Asked & Answered, page 56). In both cases, the 1996 act precluded the recognition of those legal unions and marriages under the full faith and credit provision of the Constitution.

The Constitution also mandates that the "Citizens of each State shall be entitled to all Privileges and Immunities of Citizens in the Several States." For example, before 1984, when the federal government passed legislation that required all states to limit the sale and public possession of alcohol to individuals age twenty-one and older, state laws differed on the minimum age for purchasing and consuming alcohol. Under this **privileges and immunities** guarantee, an eighteen-year-old resident of New Jersey, who could not purchase alcohol under that state's laws, could cross over to New York and buy alcoholic beverages without fear of violating the law. New York State could not apply the law differently just because that person was a resident of New Jersey. We take these provisions of the Constitution for granted today, but they were the source of considerable debate and compromise at the convention, as the Framers sought to create a strong national government while maintaining state autonomy.

Another problem the Framers faced was how to ensure that the laws of the national government would take priority over the laws of the states. In the end, the delegates settled for a statement found in Article VI. It declares that the Constitution and all laws and treaties "made in Pursuance thereof" would be considered "the supreme Law of the Land." Commonly referred to as the **supremacy clause**, this provision was to be enforced through both national and state courts.

Allowing for Change

If constitutions are to endure, they need to include means and mechanisms that allow them to change. Students of constitutions focus on at least four ways in which constitutions can be changed: revolution, formal amendment, interpretation, and construction.

Revolution. *Change through revolutionary action* would involve tossing out the current system and replacing it with an entirely new one. Such a revolution does not necessarily have to involve violence, as demonstrated by the Framers when they met in Philadelphia in 1787. They were sent as delegates to a meeting that was to consider changes in the Articles of Confederation, but instead they took the revolutionary initiative of starting with a clean slate.

Amendments. The Framers included an elaborate *formal amendment process*, but they did not make it easy for those who wanted to change the Constitution. The procedures require action at both the state and the national levels (see Figure 2.2 and Asked & Answered feature, page 56).

Many proposed amendments are introduced in Congress but never come to a vote in either body. Some come to a vote in Congress but fail to get the required two-thirds majority in each chamber. Other proposals are not adopted because

Privileges and immunities
A provision in Article IV of the Constitution requiring that the citizens of one state not be treated unreasonably by officials of another state.

Supremacy clause A provision in Article VI declaring the Constitution to be the supreme law of the land, taking precedence over state laws.

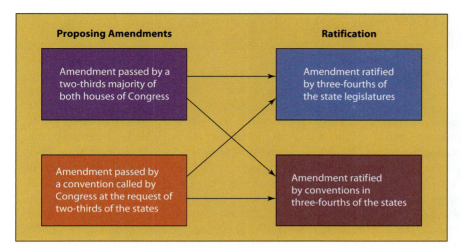

Proposing Amendments

Amendment passed by a two-thirds majority of both houses of Congress

Amendment passed by a convention called by Congress at the request of two-thirds of the states

Ratification

Amendment ratified by three-fourths of the state legislatures

Amendment ratified by conventions in three-fourths of the states

FIGURE 2.2 How the **Constitution Can Be Amended** The framers created four methods for amending the Constitution. With the exception of the Twenty-First Amendment, all amendments so far have used the Congress/ state legislature route (at top).

they fail to get the required number of states to ratify them (see Asked & Answered, page 56). The Constitution has been successfully amended seventeen times since the Bill of Rights (see Table 2.4).[31]

Interpretations and Constructions. Although they made the formal amendment process difficult, the Framers left the door open to changes that might occur by other means.[32] As a document built through many compromises, the Constitution leaves a great deal of room for elaboration.[33] One of the Framers, Alexander Hamilton, stated that a constitution "cannot possibly calculate" the effects of changing conditions and must therefore "consist only of general provisions."[34] Giving meaning to those general provisions can be accomplished through constitutional interpretation and constitutional construction.[35]

Constitutional interpretation involves attempts to discover the meaning of the words used in the different provisions. Consider the phrase *necessary and proper*, found in Article I, Section 8. The meaning of that phrase was subject to controversy even among the Framers once they took office. George Washington's secretary of the treasury, Alexander Hamilton, interpreted those words broadly (as an "elastic clause") and pushed for the establishment of the national bank that became so controversial during the early history of the United States. Clearly the words can be read differently—for example, they can be read as stating that the national government could do only what was absolutely necessary and proper to carry out its functions and no more. As it turned out, in the case of *McCulloch v. Maryland*, discussed earlier in this chapter, the Supreme Court upheld Hamilton's more liberal interpretation.

Or consider the various interpretations we might give to the term *commerce*, which is also found in Article I, Section 8: "The Congress shall have the power . . . to regulate commerce with foreign nations, and among the several states, and with the Indian tribes." Early in our constitutional history, the term *commerce* was strictly defined to mean real goods and services crossing real borders. That narrow

Constitutional interpretation A process of constitutional change that involves attempts to discover the meaning of the words used in the different provisions of the Constitution as they might apply to specific situations.

ASKED & ANSWERED

ASKED: So you want to change the Constitution?

ANSWERED: In November 2003, the Supreme Judicial Court of Massachusetts declared that, under that state's constitution, Massachusetts officials are required to offer marriage licenses for same-sex unions. On February 24, 2004, President Bush announced that he supported a constitutional amendment that would define marriage in the United States as a union only between a man and a woman. What would have to happen for such an amendment to become part of the U.S. Constitution?

Formally amending the U.S. Constitution is no easy task, as many advocates of such changes have learned over the years. In one form or another, literally thousands of amendments have been proposed in Congress, but only thirty-three have made it through the congressional part of the process, and thus far only twenty-seven have actually been ratified and have become part of the Constitution. Of that number, twelve were sent out to the states by the first Congress in 1789, and ten of those made it into the Constitution as the Bill of Rights. In short, the odds against changing the Constitution through the amendment process are considerable.

What is that process? Amendments can be formally proposed in two ways: either by members of Congress who submit resolutions to be considered in their respective chambers or by two-thirds of the state legislatures who request that a constitutional convention be convened to consider their proposals (this process has never been used). In the case of a proposal made in Congress, a two-thirds vote of both houses of Congress is required for the proposed amendment to be sent to the states for ratification. Congress decides how the amendment will be ratified: by three-fourths of the legislatures or by ratifying conventions in three-fourths of the states (a method used for only one of the Constitution's twenty-seven amendments—the single exception was the Twenty-First Amendment, which repealed the Eighteenth; see Figure 2.2 on p. 55).

Congress can also set a time limit for the amendment's ratification by the states, typically seven to ten years. For example, the proposed Equal Rights Amendment (ERA) stated that "equality of rights under the law shall not be denied or abridged by the United States or by any State on account of sex." Beginning in 1923, the ERA was introduced in Congress at almost every session, but it remained tied up in the legislative process until 1972, when it finally received the approval of both the House and the Senate. As proposed, the ERA needed to be ratified by thirty-eight states by June 30, 1982,* to become an amendment to the Constitution. Thirty-five states had given their approval of the ERA by 1978, but supporters could not muster enough votes in three other state legislatures to pass the proposed amendment. Despite that defeat, the ERA has been reintroduced into Congress at each session since 1983.

But in some cases no time limit is set. In the case of the Twenty-Seventh Amendment, it took 203 years for it to receive the ratification of enough states to become part of the Constitution. Originally proposed as part of the Bill of Rights in 1789, that amendment set limits on the power of sitting members of Congress to increase their own compensation. Unlike the ERA, the original proposal sent to the states had no set deadline for ratification. By the end of 1791, only six of the ten states needed for adoption at that time had voted to ratify the proposal. The proposal languished until the effort to pass the amendment was revived in the 1980s, when it became the pet project of a political science graduate student at the University of Texas who had stumbled on the proposal. On May 7, 1992, the Michigan legislature formally ratified the amendment, giving it the support of the thirty-eight states required for adoption.

As for the role of the White House in all this, despite President Bush's announced support for the definition-of-marriage amendment, he actually would have had no formal role in the process. Although some presidents in the past have added their signature to the thirty-three congressional resolutions proposing amendments for ratification, such an action was legally meaningless.

As it turned out, the effort to pass a definition-of-marriage amendment through Congress failed, and in 2013 the Supreme Court decided that federal legislation that attempted to define marriage (the 1996 Defense of Marriage Act) for legal purposes was an unconstitutional infringement on the rights of states to regulate who can or cannot be regarded as married.

The deadline, originally set for 1979, was later extended for thirty-nine months by congressional action.

TABLE 2.4 Amendments Eleven to Twenty-Seven to the Constitution

Amendment	Year Proposed by Congress	Year Adopted	What It Does
11	1794	1798	Gives states immunity from certain legal actions
12	1803	1804	Changes the selection of the president and vice president through the Electoral College
13	1865	1865	Abolishes slavery
14	1866	1868	Defines citizenship and citizens' rights; provides due process and equal protection of the laws
15	1869	1870	Extends the right to vote to African American males
16	1909	1913	Gives Congress the power to impose an income tax
17	1912	1913	Provides for direct election of U.S. senators
18	1917	1919	Outlaws alcoholic beverages
19	1919	1920	Extends the right to vote to women
20	1932	1933	Changes the dates for the start of congressional and presidential terms
21	1933	1933	Repeals the Eighteenth Amendment
22	1947	1951	Limits presidential tenure in office
23	1960	1961	Extends the right to vote in presidential elections to residents of the District of Columbia
24	1962	1964	Prohibits the use of tax payment (poll tax) as a basis for the eligibility to vote
25	1965	1967	Establishes procedures for presidential succession, for determining presidential disability, and for filling a vacancy in the vice presidency
26	1971	1971	Lowers the voting age to eighteen
27	1789	1992	Limits Congress's ability to change its own compensation

view limited the authority of Congress to pass laws regulating such things as the manufacture or quality of goods and services produced within states. Thus, even though there was growing public support during the late 1800s and early 1900s for federal laws regarding child labor or the quality of agricultural production, Congress could do nothing. However, as the courts began to define commerce more broadly, the arena for national governmental actions broadened considerably. This was most clearly demonstrated by passage of the 1964 Civil Rights Act, which included provisions that prohibited racial discrimination in all "public accommodations," such as restaurants and hotels. What made that landmark legislation possible was a broad interpretation of the term *commerce* so that it applied to any product or activity that was involved in the flow of commerce across state lines. Thus, the fact that a Heinz Ketchup bottle manufactured in Pennsylvania sat on the table of an Alabama diner meant that the owners of that diner could not refuse to serve anyone on the basis of race—a blow to the segregationist behavior that was prevalent in the South in those days (see the discussion of civil liberties and civil rights in Chapters 4 and 5).

Constitutional construction

A form of constitutional change that occurs as public officials fill in the institutional "blank spaces" left by the Constitution.

Constitutional construction involves actions taken by public officials to fill in the institutional "blank spaces" left by the Constitution. For example, the term *executive privilege* is applied to a president's assumed right to refuse to provide Congress with information that the White House claims the legislators have no right to see. The privilege was first asserted by George Washington in a disagreement with the House of Representatives over details involving the negotiation of a controversial treaty. President Obama asserted it when Attorney General Eric Holder refused to honor a subpoena from a committee for documents related to a failed policy initiative.

Many other constructions play an important role in our constitutional system, from judicial review and the creation of congressional committees to the creation of the U.S. Postal Service and the opening prayer at each daily session of the U.S. House of Representatives. Some of these emerge from custom and practice over time, whereas others are the result of congressional action or executive orders.

Adaptability and Endurance

There is little controversy over the assertion that the Framers fulfilled their obligations as constitution makers. They provided a foundation for the American constitutional system through the establishment of "We the People" as a source of constitutional legitimacy, and they put into place the basic structures necessary to make, enforce, and adjudicate laws. Just as important, they established an elaborate system of power that distributed the functions of governing among different branches and levels of government, while addressing the need to limit those powers or their abusive exercise. Moreover, they allowed for both formal and nonformal (e.g., through constitutional interpretation and construction) means of bringing about constitutional changes that gave the system a chance of surviving over the long haul.

Whether the Framers succeeded in establishing a constitutional system that would survive over time is an important question. Initially, this question took the form of asking whether the Framers had built governmental machinery that would operate effectively in the relatively homogeneous and stable environment that characterized pre–Civil War America. Eventually, the question became whether the Framers' handiwork would prove to be adaptable to the tumult and demands that characterized the industrialized and urbanized America that emerged in the late 1800s. As noted earlier, the myth of the living constitution was part of the response to that concern.

Those who adhere to the myth of the living constitution credit the Framers with creating more than just the machinery of government. In their view, the Framers also created a constitutional system that is endowed with the capacity to withstand all kinds of adverse conditions and challenges, including changing technologies, public values, and mores.

Some scholars and jurists argue that the myth of the living Constitution is not a good thing, and that today's constitutional system has become too adaptable. They argue that we have paid too great a price for the changes brought about through the living-constitution approach. For them, the value of the Framers' Constitution lies not in its capacity to adapt but in its ability to provide a firm foundation on which problems can be solved and controversies resolved. "The Constitution that I interpret and apply is not living but dead," states Supreme Court Justice Antonin Scalia, "or—as I prefer to call it—enduring." The Constitution "means today not what current society and much less the Court thinks it ought to mean, but what it meant when it was adopted."[36] We can consider this the *myth of the timeless and perfect Constitution*, and it forms an alternative position from which to make sense of the Constitution.

Still others assume a third and more critical approach, arguing that the so-called living Constitution has not really adapted well to the demands of modern times and the changing values of the American people. For them, the Framers' Constitution reflects the antidemocratic biases and fears of its authors, and it was established to limit change rather than promote adaptation to changing conditions.[37] From this perspective, the Constitution is a political document that has been used to promote the interests of those in power, and it is only through major political movements that relevant constitutional changes can be made.[38]

The Five Principles

> **What are the major principles of American constitutionalism?**

If there is a point of agreement among those alternative views of the Constitution, it is that, over the years, the Framers' work has been associated with several basic principles that are central to any understanding of the American constitutional system: rule of law, republicanism, separation of powers, checks and balances, and national supremacy.

Principle 1: The Rule of Law

Although the words ***rule of law*** are never used in the Constitution, this idea is one of the most important legacies of the Framers. As a general concept, the rule of law has its roots deep in Western civilization, but it emerged in its modern form in Europe during the 1600s. According to the rule-of-law concept, there exists "a body of rules and procedures governing human and governmental

Rule of law The principle that a standard of impartiality, fairness, and equality against which all governmental actions can be evaluated exists. More narrowly, this includes the concept that no individual stands above the law and that rulers, like those they rule, are answerable to the law.

behavior that have an autonomy and logic of their own." Under such rules and procedures, government and public officials are bound by standards of fairness, impartiality, and equality before the law.[39]

The rule-of-law principle, found in a number of constitutional provisions, implies that those provisions limit the powers of both national and state governments. The Bill of Rights added strength to the rule-of-law principle through the Fifth Amendment by requiring "due process of law" and "just compensation" whenever government initiates adverse actions against a citizen. The "equal protection of the laws" clause in the Fourteenth Amendment is still further evidence of how important this principle has been throughout our history.[40]

Another way of thinking about the rule-of-law principle is that in American government, the rulers, like those they rule, are answerable to the law. No individual stands above the law, regardless of that person's background or the office that he or she holds. Just as there are laws that address the behavior of general citizens, so there are laws that focus on the behavior of public officials. Those laws generally set limits on the powers of these officials or prescribe the procedures they must use in carrying out their duties. Under the rule-of-law principle, those limits and prescriptions must be adhered to if the American constitutional system is to function properly.

No one is exempt from the rule-of-law principle. In August 1974, for example, President Richard M. Nixon resigned in the face of charges that he took part in a criminal cover-up of White House involvement in a break-in at the Democratic Party's national headquarters at the Watergate office complex in Washington, D.C. Although Nixon and many of his supporters perceived the Watergate cover-up as a relatively minor offense, the president's attempt to circumvent the law resulted in enough political pressure to bring about the first presidential resignation in American history. Nixon and others learned that no public official, not even the president, stands above the law.

Principle 2: Republicanism

Republicanism A doctrine of government in which decisions are made by elected or appointed officials who are answerable to the people, not directly by the people themselves.

Despite the phrase *We the People*, the Framers questioned the ability of the American people to rule themselves directly. In turning to **republicanism**, the Framers created a government in which decisions are made by elected or appointed officials who are ultimately answerable to the people. The Framers opposed establishing a direct democracy because they distrusted human nature and the capacity of ordinary citizens to govern themselves.

The Federalist Papers A series of editorials written by James Madison, Alexander Hamilton, and John Jay in 1788 to support the ratification of the Constitution in New York State. This collection is now regarded as a major source of information on what the Framers were thinking when they wrote the Constitution.

We know something about the Framers' views on democracy thanks to documents such as *The Federalist Papers*, a series of editorials that James Madison, Alexander Hamilton, and John Jay wrote in 1788 in support of ratification of the Constitution. In "Federalist No. 10," Madison argued that democracies "have ever been spectacles of turbulence and contention; have ever been found incompatible with personal security, or the rights of property; and have ever been as short in their lives, as they have been violent in their deaths."[41]

What did the Framers see in republicanism that they did not see in direct democracy? Again we turn to "Federalist No. 10," in which Madison argued that the problems of government could be traced to the "mischiefs of faction." He defined a faction as a group that puts its shared interests ahead of the rights of others or the interests of the community as a whole. These self-serving factions can be small or large; they can even include a majority of the people. According to Madison, all factions pose a threat to the general well-being of society. Because the causes of faction are basic to human nature, eliminating them is impossible. Thus, if any government is to serve the general interest of the people, it must be designed so that the potentially destructive power of factions can be eliminated or controlled.[42]

Madison and the Framers favored a republican form of government in which the people had some voice, but that voice was filtered through their representatives. The community was to be governed "by persons holding their offices . . . for a limited time or during good behavior."[43] And although all officials would be answerable to the people, some would be more insulated from public pressure than others. Members of the House of Representatives were to have the most exposure: They alone would be elected directly by the American voters, and they would have comparatively brief terms: two years. Senators and the president were assigned longer terms, and, under the original provisions of the Constitution, the people did not elect them directly. Instead, state legislators selected senators, and the Electoral College, with members selected by the states, chose the president. These methods were later changed by constitutional amendments and by the action of state legislatures, which effectively left the selection of the electors up to voters (see Chapter 8). Supreme Court judges received additional protection from the whims of constantly changing public opinion: They were given lifetime appointments and could be removed only through the lengthy and difficult process called impeachment (see the discussion later in this chapter).

Although the Framers felt impelled to take these precautions, they never lost sight of the basic principle of republicanism: that the ultimate responsibility of government officials is to the American public.

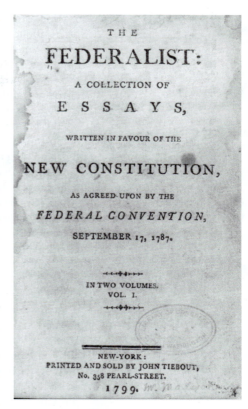

Little is known of what the Framers were thinking as they developed the various provisions of the Constitution. Their ideas became clearer during the ratification debate, when advocates wrote pamphlets and editorials supporting passage. *The Federalist Papers*, among the most often cited of those writings, were authored under the pen name of Publius by James Madison, John Jay, and Alexander Hamilton in their efforts to get New York to ratify.

Principle 3: Separation of Powers

The principle of the **separation of powers** is also linked to the effort to control factions. By splitting governmental authority among several branches of government and giving each an area of primary responsibility, the Framers sought to minimize the possibility that one faction could gain control. "The accumulation of all powers, legislative, executive, and judiciary, in the same hands," states Madison in "Federalist No. 51," "may justly be pronounced the very definition of tyranny."[44] Thus, to help avoid tyranny, the power to make, to execute, and to judge the law was divided among the three branches: Congress, the presidency, and the courts.

Separation of powers The division of the powers to make, execute, and judge the law among the three branches of American government: Congress, the presidency, and the courts. This principle was adopted by the Framers to prevent tyranny and factionalism in the government.

This principle was an important one for the Framers, who debated for many hours about the design of the national government. The idea was to distribute powers among the three branches, not in order to increase the efficiency of the government but to prevent efficiency, which they regarded as potentially dangerous.[45] Each branch was to be independent of the others when exercising its governmental authority. In this way, the American public would be protected against the tyranny that Madison and others so feared.

The Framers reinforced this principle in several ways beyond just giving each institution a distinct role in government. The Constitution makes certain that those holding a position in one branch will not serve in either of the others at the same time. Over the years, this prohibition has been both tightened and loosened in practice. During the 1960s, for example, Supreme Court Associate Justice Abe Fortas withdrew from his nomination to be chief justice after it was revealed that he had provided advice to his old friend Lyndon Johnson and that he had sat in on political meetings at the Johnson White House.[46] Then again, members of Congress have been allowed to serve as reserve officers in the U.S. military—a situation that places them under the command of the president while they are in uniform.[47]

The separation of powers was also reinforced by the Framers through the different constituencies and term lengths assigned to the various branches of the national government. The eligible voters of the respective districts, for example, directly elect members of the House of Representatives every two years. U.S. senators, on the other hand, were originally selected by the legislatures of their states for six-year terms, implying strongly that they represented the interests of the state governments that sent them to Washington. The design of the Electoral College, which was to select the president (see the discussion earlier in this chapter and that in Chapter 8), was intended to guarantee that the winner would regard the entire nation as his constituency during a four-year term in office. Along with the lifetime appointment, the elaborate process set up for naming federal court judges—nomination by the president and confirmation by the Senate—was intended to guarantee that those positions were filled by people who were more accountable to the law than to shifting political moods.

Principle 4: Checks and Balances

Although separation of powers provides independent roles for Congress, the presidency, and the courts, the principle of **checks and balances** forces them to work together. By giving each institution the capability of counterbalancing the authority of the other branches, the Constitution makes these institutions interdependent.

The key element in the system of checks and balances is the distribution of shared powers among the three branches of government. Each branch depends on the others to accomplish its objectives, but each also acts as a counterweight to the others (see Figure 2.3). The president's power to **veto**, or reject, legislation checks the legislative actions of Congress. The veto, in turn, can be overridden by a two-thirds vote of both chambers of Congress.

Checks and balances The principle that lets the executive, legislative, and judicial branches share some responsibilities and gives each branch some control over the others' activities. The major support for checks and balances comes from the Constitution's distribution of shared powers.

Veto The president's power to reject legislation passed by Congress. Vetoes can be overruled by a two-thirds vote of both chambers of Congress.

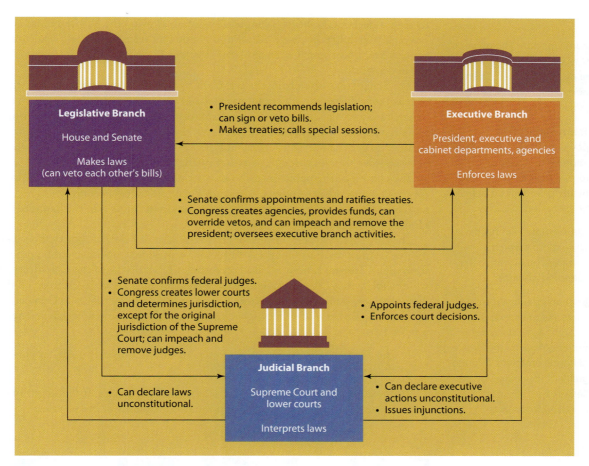

FIGURE 2.3 Separation of Powers and Checks and Balances
Under separation of powers, governmental authority is divided among the three branches: Congress exercises the power to make laws; the president exercises the power to execute laws; and the courts have the power to judge disputes that arise under the laws. A system of checks and balances provides each branch with a means to counterbalance the authority of the other two, thus making the three branches interdependent.

Although the veto can be a powerful presidential tool, some critics have complained that it is of limited value because it leaves the president with no alternative but either to sign or to veto an entire bill. The president has had no option for dealing with a specific provision of a bill that he finds troublesome. Many state constitutions give their governors *line-item veto* power, which permits them to strike out a particular clause of a bill that comes before them. In 1995, Congress passed a limited version of a presidential line-item veto, but in June 1998 the U.S. Supreme Court declared the act unconstitutional.

Congress can restrict presidential power in a variety of other ways. Beyond the powers granted to the president in the Constitution, presidents must have **congressional authorization** to undertake any official course of action.

Congressional authorization The power of Congress to provide the president with the right to carry out legislated policies.

Confirmation The power of the U.S. Senate to approve or disapprove a presidential nominee for an executive or judicial post.

Treaty ratification The power of the U.S. Senate to approve or disapprove formal treaties negotiated by the president on behalf of the nation.

Appropriation of funds The actions taken by Congress to authorize the spending of funds.

Impeachment A formal charge of misconduct brought against a federal public official by the House of Representatives. If found guilty of the charge by the Senate, the official is removed from office.

In recent decades, however, Congress has often allowed the White House considerable flexibility in many areas, and presidents have used their "executive" control over government agencies (see Chapters 12 and 13) to counter congressional constraints.

The Senate may also check the president's power by using its right to confirm or reject presidential nominees for judicial and executive positions. Although the Senate rarely says no during these **confirmation** procedures, many such nominations have been withdrawn (or have never been submitted) because they were unlikely to get the necessary votes. The Senate also has the authority to approve or disapprove treaties through its **treaty ratification** powers.

The control of the public sector's purse strings by Congress is another powerful check on presidential power. Although the president can recommend a budget for Congress to consider, the actual **appropriation of funds** is in the hands of the House and the Senate.

The ultimate restraint on presidential (and also judicial) authority, however, resides in the power of Congress to remove a president or other public official from office. **Impeachment** is based on Article II, Section 4, of the Constitution, which holds that "the President, Vice President and all civil Officers of the United States, shall be removed from Office on Impeachment for, and Conviction of, Treason, Bribery, or other high Crimes and Misdemeanors." Such removals involve two steps:

1. The House of Representatives votes articles of impeachment, or formal charges, against the official.

2. Once impeached, the official is tried by the U.S. Senate. If found guilty by a vote of the Senate, the official is removed from his or her position.

With Chief Justice Rehnquist presiding, the U.S. Senate conducted an impeachment trial of President Clinton in 1999.

The most significant check that the courts have is found in their power of **judicial review**, by which they can declare acts of Congress to be in conflict with the Constitution. Although not explicitly provided for in the Constitution, the power of judicial review was established in the case of *Marbury v. Madison* (1803). (See the discussion of this concept in Chapter 14.) The power of Congress over the courts derives in part from its constitutional authority to create or abolish any court other than the Supreme Court. Congress can also impeach and remove judges.

The principle of checks and balances is strengthened by the different methods of selecting officials, which the Framers believed would ensure that the different branches represented different public perspectives. Variations in terms of office were intended to add a further check. For example, senators, responding from the perspective of their six-year terms in office, were expected to act in a more measured and conservative way than their peers in the House, who have only two-year terms.

In setting up the elaborate system of checks and balances, the Framers pitted the three branches of government against one another. This has resulted in a slow and ponderous system that often frustrates officials who are trying to deal quickly with critical issues. Too rapid decision making, however, was exactly what the Framers feared. More often than many of us like, the system works the way they planned it to: deliberately and with care.

Principle 5: National Supremacy

Earlier we pointed out that the U.S. Constitution provides for a federal system in which national and state governments divide the authority of American government. Such a complex arrangement can work only if there is some principle that helps government officials settle fundamental disagreements among the different levels of government. If such a principle did not exist, then "the authority of the whole society" would be "everywhere subordinate to the authority of the parts." That, argued Madison, would have created a "monster" in which the head was under the control of its member parts.[48]

In the American constitutional system, that principle is **national supremacy**. As noted earlier in this chapter, the supremacy clause of Article VI of the Constitution makes the Constitution and those laws and treaties passed under it the "supreme Law of the Land." As you will see in Chapter 3, which discusses federalism and intergovernmental relations, that principle has been a central factor in the evolution of the American federal system. It is impossible to understand the operations of American government today without grasping the meaning of federalism and the role of the national supremacy principle in American government.

Applying the Five Principles

The role that these basic principles play in the American constitutional system is subject to much debate. For those who rely on the myth of the living constitution, each of these principles is viewed as a means or mechanism through which government is able to deal with ever-changing challenges.

Judicial review The power assumed by the courts in *Marbury v. Madison* to declare acts of Congress to be in conflict with the Constitution. This power makes the courts part of the system of checks and balances.

National supremacy The principle—stated in Article VI, the "supremacy clause"—that makes the Constitution and those laws and treaties passed under it the "supreme Law of the Land."

Originalism An approach to interpreting the Constitution that seeks to rely on the original understanding of its provisions by the Framers.

Textualism An approach to interpreting the Constitution that relies on a literal, "plain words" reading of the document.

Alternatively, those opposed to the living-constitution perspective can also rely on these constitutional principles. Those who regard the Constitution as enduring would see these principles as ends rather than means. For this group, constitutionalism involves acting according to the meaning of these principles as they were developed by the Framers, treating them as fundamental precepts to be applied to today's problems. Among lawyers, adherents to this view are said to follow one of two legal philosophies. The first is usually labeled **originalism**, to reflect reliance on the original understanding of the Framers when they wrote the Constitution.

Alternatively, other jurists associated with the enduring-Constitution view adhere to a position labeled **textualism**. According to this approach, the meaning of the Constitution should be derived literally from a "plain reading" of the words used in the document. The third perspective, which regards the Constitution as a political document, views the principles as if they were a set of fundamental "rules" under which government operates.

Conclusion

Americans have developed a complex relationship with the Constitution in their efforts to make sense of the gap between their urge for democracy and the undemocratic provisions of that document. In public opinion polls and in other forums, Americans continue to express a reverential pride in our constitutional system, and few advocate radical changes in the structure of government established by the Constitution. For most, in fact, the document represents the American people as a nation.[49]

In an important sense, what many (perhaps most) Americans have developed over the years is what Sanford Levinson has called "constitutional faith"—that is, a "wholehearted attachment to the Constitution as the center of one's (and ultimately the nation's) political life."[50] As an act of faith, this attachment does not need to be justified with clear reasons linked to some benefits gained from it, nor can it be easily undermined by the expressed dissatisfactions with the inequalities and injustices that sometimes result from the constitutional exercise of authority. That is why sense-making myths play such a significant role in how we relate to the American constitutional system. Believing in a living constitution not only helps us understand how a document written more than two centuries ago is able to operate as well as it does today but also allows us to have some faith in the system's ability to deal with the uncertainties of the future.

But it would also be a mistake to give in to blind faith; this is one reason why there are powerful and credible alternatives to the myth of the living constitution. Those who see the fundamental principles of the Framers as an enduring anchor believe in a Constitution that provides for sound and time-tested guidance in an era of constant turmoil and change. Their constitutional faith is not weaker; it is just based on a different myth. The same can be said of those whose constitutional faith is based on the hope that through open political deliberation, the system's rules can be used to make American government more democratic and more just in the future.

Key Terms

Agenda setting p. 70
Appropriation of funds p. 64
Articles of Confederation p. 40
Bicameral p. 48
Bill of attainder p. 52
Bill of Rights p. 52
Checks and balances p. 62
Concurrent powers p. 51
Confederation p. 46
Confirmation p. 64
Congressional authorization p. 63
Constitutional construction p. 58
Constitutional interpretation p. 55
Declaration of Independence p. 45
Delegated powers p. 49
Democratic model of
    policymaking p. 74
Electoral College p. 48
Elite model of policymaking p. 74
Enlightenment p. 43

Ex post facto law p. 52
The Federalist Papers p. 60
Federation p. 47
Full faith and credit p. 53
Great Compromise p. 48
Impeachment p. 64
Implied powers p. 51
Incremental model of decision
    making p. 73
Issue identification p. 70
Judicial review p. 65
Legitimacy p. 46
Mayflower Compact p. 43
National supremacy p. 65
Necessary and proper clause p. 51
Originalism p. 66
Pluralist model of policymaking
    p. 74
Policy adoption p. 71
Policy evaluation p. 72

Policy formulation p. 71
Policy implementation p. 72
Popular sovereignty p. 44
Privileges and immunities p. 54
Rational model of decision
    making p. 73
Republicanism p. 60
Reserved powers p. 52
Rule of law p. 59
Separation of powers p. 61
Supremacy clause p. 54
Textualism p. 66
Treaty ratification p. 64
Unicameral p. 48
Unitary system p. 47
Veto p. 62
Writ of habeas corpus p. 52

Focus Questions Review

1. **What were the circumstances surrounding the framing of the Constitution? > > >**
   The Framers of the Constitution came together to solve fundamental problems that had arisen under the Articles of Confederation.

2. **What were the important traditions underlying the Constitution? > > >**
   The roots of the Constitution can be found in the British legal tradition, including the principles that government officials, as well as ordinary citizens, must obey the law and that there exists a higher (constitutional) standard against which laws made by legislatures can be measured. The colonial experience of self-government and the political philosophy of the Enlightenment espoused by such writers as Hobbes and Locke also helped guide the Constitution's Framers.

3. **What do the various provisions of the Constitution accomplish? > > >**
   The Constitution's Framers accomplished a number of purposes, including the following:
   - Establishing the legitimacy of the government of the United States as coming directly from the people
   - Dividing authority within the new national government among the legislative, executive, and judicial branches of government
   - Describing the delegated and implied powers of the national government
   - At the same time, setting limits on both national and state power
   - Specifying the rules for amending the Constitution

4. **What are the major principles of American constitutionalism?** > > >

The Framers established in the Constitution the fundamental principles of American government: the rule of law, republicanism, the separation of powers, the system of checks and balances, and national supremacy.

From the perspective of the myth of the living constitution, those principles have been the primary means by which the Framers' handiwork has been adapted to deal with the challenges of today's world.

Alternatively, those principles can be regarded as enduring precepts of the Framers that should be used to guide government officials in turbulent times, or as the basic rules through which the constitutional system can be made to serve the political urge for greater fairness and justice and enhanced democratic participation.

Review Questions

1. "Many of today's politicians believe 'compromise' is a dirty word. What they fail to realize is that our constitutional system was founded on the willingness of the Framers to compromise." Explain this statement in light of what you've learned about the foundations of the American Constitution. Do you agree or disagree with the opinion? Why or why not?

2. "The U.S. Constitution was a reflection of its times, but times change and so should our Constitution." Many Americans would agree with this statement. There can be little doubt that our constitutional system has changed over time through a process of amendment and adaptation. But has it changed enough? Is our constitutional system appropriate to deal with the demands of the twenty-first century? Do we need to consider calling a new constitutional convention to "reconstitute" our constitutional system?

 For more information and access to study materials, visit the book's companion website at www.oup.com/us/gitelson.

Policy Connection

How can we use models to make sense of American policymaking?

The Policy Challenge

The story behind the work of the Constitution's Framers outlined in Chapter 2 is one of bargains and compromises among a group of individuals who wanted to deal with the fundamental issues that divided them as they gathered in Philadelphia. Although they were obviously aware that any government framework they put forward would have to issue laws and carry out public programs, they were not preoccupied with designing an efficient or rational policymaking machine. In fact, the complex system of separated powers and checks and balances seems to have been intentionally created to be ponderous and filled with all sorts of barriers and hurdles for those trying to come up with rational solutions to public problems.

Nevertheless, over the many decades of governing under the Framers' complicated constitutional arrangements, those charged with making and implementing public policies have managed to do so with relative success. At times, policymaking has proved critical to the nation's survival. Although the question of slavery and demands for abolition would ultimately be settled on the bloody battlefields of the Civil War, policy compromises delayed that inevitable clash for more than four decades. And, although the Great Depression of the 1930s and the Great Recession of recent years posed major threats to the nation's economic stability, both short- and long-term policy responses have put the economy back on track. As significant has been the everyday successes of policies that play a central role in shaping our daily lives.

In this Policy Connection we examine some concepts and models that can help make sense of how public policymaking emerges from within our complicated constitutional system. Most of these sense-making models do not do justice to the political drama of conflict and compromise of the policymaking process, but they do help us better understand what might otherwise seem baffling.

Making Sausage

Were you to attend a meeting of modern historians and ask those attending to name the top ten individuals who have helped shape government over the past two hundred years, one name likely to show up on their lists is Otto von Bismarck, the nineteenth-century Prussian aristocrat who served as German chancellor during the 1870s through the 1880s. Most would agree he was the master politician of his age, credited with creating the modern industrial Germany from a hodgepodge of principalities as well as dominating European diplomacy during his years in office.

For Bismarck, politics was the "art of the possible," and historians agree that this was reflected in his other great achievement: the creation of the modern welfare state. Ideologically a conservative, in the 1880s he nevertheless helped establish the first major social security pension system, national unemployment insurance, and universal health care coverage in Europe, a significant accomplishment considering that he faced opposition from both ends of the political spectrum. "The less the people know about how sausages and laws are made," Bismarck is believed to have said, "the better they sleep in the night."

In short, Bismarck knew that making public policy involved trade-offs and compromises. Although he understood what it took to make public policy, he also knew that to the outside world it looked like a messy affair—similar to what sausage making must look like to someone peering over the butcher's shoulder.[1]

The Process Models

As we look over the policymaker's shoulder, we can capture what we see by understanding a number of perspectives and models. Among the most widely used models are those that focus on the overall process by which the government tackles issues. The most common of these are the lawmaking model, the policymaking stages model, and the multiple stream model.

The Lawmaking Model. Perhaps the most obvious model is the one laid out in the U.S. Constitution—that is, the process by which a bill (i.e., a proposed policy) becomes a law (i.e., an enforceable policy). As Figure 2.3 illustrates (p. 63), after being introduced in the U.S. House and/or Senate, the successful bill goes through a legislative process involving committees, rules for debate, and consideration on the floor of each chamber (see Chapter 11, on Congress). Implied in this process is the existence of some idea or problem

that generates interest such that members of Congress are encouraged to propose the bill. Assuming that the two chambers agree on the legislation, the bill moves to the White House for the presidential signature, or a veto that will send the bill back to Congress for consideration of an override. Although this policymaking sequence seems logical on the surface, a simple presentation of it can only hint at its complexity.

The Policymaking Stages Model. Another model focuses on different stages of the policymaking process, without reference to which specific constitutional body or policymaker is involved (see Figure 2PC.1). In the initial **issue identification** stage, some event, person, or group calls attention to a problem needing governmental action. During the early 1980s, for example, the increasing number of deaths attributed to acquired immune deficiency syndrome (AIDS) brought demands for money to fund research into the cause of the deadly disease. Health care professionals, the surgeon general of the United States, and groups representing homosexual men (who were at high risk for the disease) used every possible opportunity to get the attention of policymakers at all levels of American government.[2]

In the second stage, **agenda setting**, the policymaking institution seriously considers the issue. Not all problems identified in the first stage of the process get this far, and for those that do, it often takes many years to draw serious attention from policymakers. The problem of obesity, for example, was perceived as a social problem from the early 1900s, and the rise of the multi-billion-dollar diet industry offers testimony to the fact that it was certainly identified as an issue for the general public. Little was heard from the medical community until the 1950s, however, when the American Heart Association highlighted obesity as a major health problem

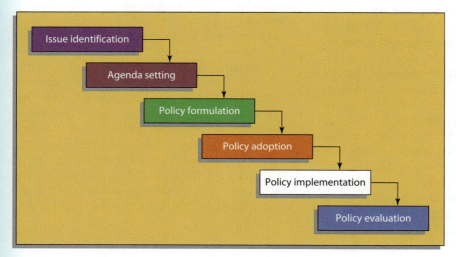

FIGURE 2PC.1 The Six Stages of Policymaking

related to the growing number of deaths from heart disease. By 1974, *The Lancet*—one of the most respected medical journals in the world—had declared that it was a significant *public* health problem. That year, the United States National Institutes of Health became the first federal agency to actively address obesity, and in 1977 it issued a report that was the subject of widely publicized congressional hearings. By 1980, several other agencies (e.g., the Department of Agriculture and the Department of Health and Human Services) were engaged in promulgating dietary and nutritional standards specifically aimed at obesity, a clear indication that it had finally made it onto the wider policymaker agenda.[3]

That an issue on the government's agenda gets serious attention does not necessarily mean that a policy will immediately emerge. Someone must develop a proposal or program addressing the issue. This third stage of the policymaking process, **policy formulation**, may take years, as policymakers and their staffs deliberate the pros and cons of different courses of action. Policies may be formulated within government agencies, in Congress, or by groups outside the national government, working separately or together. Proposals that would ultimately lead to a major congressional overhaul of America's welfare programs in 1996 first emerged at meetings of the National Governors Association more than ten years earlier.[4] Similarly, the 2010 Dodd-Frank Wall Street Reform and Consumer Protection Act is often treated as a single piece of legislation, but it was actually a composite of various proposals made by individuals and interest groups who worked with the congressional staff to meet the challenge of reforming the banking industry after the 2008 collapse of the financial markets.[5]

The next step, **policy adoption**, includes efforts to obtain enough support for a proposal so that the proposal can become the government's stated policy. At this point, most policy proposals—particularly

congressional legislation—begin a process of bargaining and compromise and emerge significantly changed. When Congress considers tax reform proposals, for instance, what begins as an attempt to close large tax loopholes may wind up creating more or different loopholes.[6] As we will see in Chapters 11 and 12, when members of Congress propose amendments to bills, they can radically change the intent of a bill or give it added meaning through the process of adding *riders* or *earmarks* to the legislation. In 1988, a bill intended to create a new cabinet post—the Department of Veterans Affairs— became the vehicle for passing a law giving veterans the right to sue the government.[7]

Policy adoption is no less complex in the executive branch. Executive orders, vetoes of legislation, and other presidential actions are not made arbitrarily, for the White House cannot operate in a legal or political vacuum.[8] Any executive order must be based on some authority granted by Congress, and vetoes are always subject to congressional override (see Chapter 12, on the presidency).

In 2014, President Obama proposed that Congress increase the federal minimum wage from $7.25 per hour to $10.10 per hour. The request was unlikely to pass Congress, but under the statutory authority given to the White House to oversee the provisions of federal government contracts, Obama was able to issue an executive order requiring future contractors to pay a minimum wage of $10.10. Although it had a limited impact on wages, the order established a policy designed to reflect how strongly Obama felt about the issue.

Decisions of the Supreme Court are a special type of public policy, often rooted in legal doctrines. Nevertheless, even policy adoption in the Supreme Court involves some political give and take among the Court's members, which has an impact on the resulting policies (see Chapter 14, on courts, judges, and the law). In recent years, we have learned much more about what happens when the Supreme Court justices decide an important case. Conferences involving all the Court's members are held regularly, and the discussions in those closed meetings supposedly sometimes focus on the political, as well as the legal, implications of a case.[9]

The policy adoption stage can continue for a long time. The first national air pollution laws were passed in 1960, but these did little more than authorize the surgeon general to study the problem. Three years later, Congress set up a technical committee to monitor air pollution problems and to assist state and local governments that chose to develop and maintain antipollution programs. In 1965 and 1967, Congress required states and localities to develop antipollution programs and required federal agencies to set emission standards for new automobiles. In 1970, President Richard Nixon acknowledged the importance of environmental problems by creating the Environmental Protection Agency (EPA). A few weeks later, Congress gave the EPA significant powers to clean America's air. Additional amendments followed during the 1970s and 1980s, and policy adoption in this area continued with passage of the Clean Air Act amendments in 1990.

Critical to the policymaking process is the stage of **policy implementation**—carrying out policy mandates through public programs and actions. The national bureaucracy traditionally performs this task, although in recent years it has used contractors and other methods associated with proxy administration (see Chapter 13, on the bureaucracy). In addition, many policies require the cooperation of state and local officials and of individuals outside government. For example, when Congress passed an income tax law, it created the Internal Revenue Service (IRS) to implement it, but the government still relies on the American people to do most of the paperwork. Washington also depends on state and local officials to enforce a variety of environmental laws.

As noted in Chapter 3, on federalism and intergovernmental relations, most domestic policies require the cooperation of either private individuals or the intergovernmental relations system.

The final stage in public policymaking is **policy evaluation**—reviewing the government's actions and programs to see whether their goals have been achieved or to assess their effectiveness and efficiency. Changes in the policy or program may then be instituted quickly, slowly, or not at all. A major plane crash caused by poorly maintained equipment is likely to result in the immediate issuing of new directives by the Federal Aviation Administration. A report indicating that public schools are not giving students an appropriate education for the changing world economy will not result in quick changes, but it might generate plans for major long-term changes in high school curricula and instruction.

The Multiple Stream Model. The stages model can very useful in making sense of policymaking, but some critics say it oversimplifies the complicated reality of the process, making it seem too sequential and rational. Political scientist John Kingdon contends that, at any point in time, there are "streams" of public problems and possible policy solutions, but that policymaking takes place when relevant political actors seize on an opportunity—that is, some crisis or perceived issue demanding attention—to match problems with potential solutions.[10]

During the 1970s and 1980s, for example, the United States was suffering from what President Jimmy Carter termed a "crisis of confidence," reflected in a recession that hit many parts of the economy. Energy shortages, unemployment, inflation, stagnant growth, trade deficits—the problems were numerous and seemingly intractable. Many potential solutions (from price controls to manipulation of interest rates by the Federal Reserve) were tried. One that stood out was *deregulation*: having government reduce or eliminate the web of rules and costly regulations that seemed to be holding back the economy. Whenever the opportunity arose to deal with a specific sector of the economy, policymakers would focus on the need to deregulate. In the 1970s this approach led to deregulation of the airline industry and other forms of transportation that had been subject to government oversight and intrusion for decades. In the late 1980s and through the 1990s, deregulation was extended to the financial services sector (banks)—a development that some analysts link to the eventual financial crisis of 2007–2008 and the Great Recession.

The Decision Models

Although each of the process models focuses on various stages in the development of public policies, none explicitly addresses what occurs at each decision point. Here we discuss three relevant perspectives, each based on a distinct view of the policymaker.

Rational Choice. Those who believe decision makers can approach policy problems logically will look at the choices made at each stage of the policymaking process as rational—that is, reflecting their view of which choice will maximize what they prefer or value.

Consider members of Congress, who, we assume, put a high value on those options or choices that will enhance (if not assure) their reelection. To get reelected requires that they satisfy the preferences or priorities of likely voting constituents in their district or state. In its simplest formulation,[11] the **rational model of decision making** holds that, when faced with a decision regarding a policy choice, the representative (or senator) will carefully analyze options, assess which would satisfy enough of the likely voters, and decide accordingly.

The neat logic of this model makes it inviting for those trying to make sense of policymakers' choices, and some believe that making rational choices is the ideal or standard we should apply when judging a policymaker's actions. But critics believe the model to be unrealistic—that few individuals can be as rational as this model requires and that only under the rarest of circumstances can a decision maker meet this model's requirements.[12] Moreover, many students of decision making are convinced that policymaking systems operating under rational choice conditions are likely to result in policy gridlock and stalemate.

Incrementalism. Those who accept that few of the conditions required for rational decision making exist in the real world of public policy often rely on an alternative view that sees decision makers as pragmatic and willing to settle for working with the choices at their disposal. They assume that policymakers rarely have enough information to analyze all the alternatives, and even if they did, they would operate under time constraints that restrict their ability to carefully consider all possible options. Moreover, no matter how much information they have, there is always some uncertainty about the outcome of policy choices.

According to this **incremental model of decision making**,[13] public policymaking is a process by which, little by little, decisions add to or subtract from policies that already exist. Each year, for example, the national government reconsiders the amount of money it will spend on highways and education. However, the White House and Congress rarely start their annual deliberations with a clean slate. Instead, in most cases executive officials and members of Congress begin by assuming that most current highway and education programs will remain intact; usually, the major issues are whether to expand or reduce spending for these programs and, if so, by how much. Sometimes this approach leads to marginal changes in the policies. For instance, each time a major program such as Social Security comes up for congressional reauthorization, amendments are added to meet, for its recipients, new or special needs that have emerged since the law was last revised. As a result, public policies and programs develop and change from year to year through marginal adjustments.

Bargaining and Compromise. Another way of making sense of policymaking is to see it as a process involving bargaining among the different actors involved. According to this view, decision makers come to the policymaking situation with resources (e.g., their vote) that they are willing to exchange to get what they want. To that extent, the policymakers are rational actors, but rational actors who are willing to settle for what they can get through bargaining and compromise with other policy actors. In short, policymakers are politicians willing to strike deals to achieve some of what will serve their interests.

U.S. history is filled with examples of policies created through bargains and compromises. As noted in Chapter 2, the U.S. Constitution is the product of many important compromises. The decision to locate the nation's capital in the District of Columbia was also the result of a famous compromise.[14] Other notable bargains were the controversial Missouri Compromise (1820) and the Nebraska Act (1854), which put off (for a time at least) an inevitable civil war. More recent compromises have formed the foundation of early civil rights legislation as well as federal policies for funding highways, schools, and health care. At times the resulting policies are better because of the bargains and compromises struck during the policymaking process. At other times, the results can be unwieldy and confusing. The 2010 Affordable Care Act (ACA, or "Obamacare"), for example, included so many provisions—many of which were the result of numerous compromises—that the final bill filled thousands of pages by the time it went to the president's desk for his signature. Many unsolved problems were buried in that massive legislation—a problem that only became evident as the ACA was being implemented several years later.

The Who Factor

Focusing on the overall process and/or decision-making approaches certainly helps clarify the otherwise complex world of policymaking. However, some

analysts think that what really matters is not *how* policies come into existence and are carried out, but rather *who* makes them.

Given the high value Americans place on democracy, we often rely on **democratic models of policymaking** as an ideal against which to assess the way policymaking is really made. Thus, we often tend to approach policymaking with the sense that policies *ought to be* the product of public deliberation in which those whose lives are affected by a decision are given the opportunity to participate.[15]

In contrast, some models emphasize the role of ruling elites in shaping and directing public policy choices. Closely related to the concept of elite power discussed in Chapter 1, this perspective makes sense of public policymaking by determining the preferences and priorities of those holding powerful positions in society and the economy as well as in government. These **elite models of policymaking** often become the basis of conspiracy theories in which certain groups (e.g., the military-industrial complex or Wall Street) are regarded as the key to understanding what really takes place when policies are formulated and implemented.[16]

Another set of models focuses on the policymaking activities of interest groups and those who engage in political activities (e.g., lobbying) on behalf of the groups they represent (see Chapter 9, on interest groups). Political scientists often refer to this as the **pluralist (or plural elite) model of policymaking**, in which the most active members of these groups are elites within their respective communities, and public policy is the result of bargains and agreements among those interest group leaders.[17] Thus, as noted previously, to make sense of a complex policy such as Obamacare, you need to view it as a product of compromises, and the plural elite model focuses attention on who was involved in the give and take that ultimately produced the 2010 Affordable Care Act.

The Occupy Wall Street protests began in September 2011 as people gathered in New York City's Zuccotti Park. The slogan of the protest—"We Are the 99%"—reflected the view that American public policies were being determined by the banking and financial elite class who made up less than 1% of the population.

Conclusion

How can we use models to make sense of American policymaking?

Each model offered in this Policy Connection helps us make sense of how our complex constitutional system generates solutions to public problems. But each model succeeds only by portraying policymaking as less messy than it really is. Therefore, when we use these models, we need to remember that *public policies are, in fact, the result of a complex, dynamic process involving a variety of participants and a wide range of factors that change over time*.[18] Because there is likely no single sense-making model that we can apply to all policymaking situations, we must rely on these and other views of how the policy sausage is made. What we must avoid, however, is becoming so attached to one view that we ignore other possible factors in the complex business of policymaking.

QUESTIONS FOR DISCUSSION

1. The Framers succeeded in creating a policymaking system that would be slow and deliberate. Although such a system might have been suitable for eighteenth-century America, is it time for major changes in our constitutional system so that our government can respond more quickly and effectively to twenty-first-century issues? If so, what kinds of changes would you suggest?

2. Although most Americans proudly think of the United States as a democracy, those who study public policymaking would argue that most policy decisions are really made by the few—an elite who directly or indirectly determine how government responds to various problems. Pick an area of public policy that interests you (for example, education or the environment) and look into who was involved in passing a major piece of legislation in that area.

CHAPTER 3

Federalism and Intergovernmental Relations

MYTHS & REALITIES

Do the individual states retain constitutional sovereignty?

The Importance of Federalism

Among all the compromises and bargains struck at the Constitutional Convention in 1787, none remain more central to the design and future of American government than those that created federalism. Almost at the outset, the relationships between the states and the national government were controversial, just as they are today. What have changed are the issues at the center of those controversies.

We live in the Nuclear Age and have been for at least the past half century. Every so often, that fact makes front-page news as the spread of nuclear weapons threatens world peace or some meltdown at a nuclear power plant releases dangerous levels of radiation into the atmosphere.[1] As significant and worrisome as those headline events have been, a quiet crisis has been growing daily that rarely shows up in the news: the need to deal with radioactive waste disposal. There are many technical and logistical (i.e., handling and transport) issues related to nuclear waste disposal,[2] but as important are the legal and political issues related to American federalism.

According to the two government agencies most directly involved in these issues—the Nuclear Regulatory Commission (NRC) and the U.S. Environmental Protection Agency (EPA)—there are six types of nuclear waste. Three types—spent nuclear reactor fuel, high-level waste (designated as HLW) generated by the treatment ("reprocessing") of the spent fuel, and "transuranic" waste generated in the production of nuclear weapons—can pose direct threats to public health and are therefore treated as a national problem. The other three types—naturally occurring radioactive materials, mill tailings from the

The Evolution of American Federalism

> How has federalism changed over the past two centuries of American constitutional development?

The Actors of American Federalism

> Who are the major actors in the U.S. federal system, and what roles do they play in the federal system?

< Most of the news reports about government and politics we hear on a daily basis relate to what is taking place in Washington. But most of the important business of governing actually occurs at the state and local levels and through the institutions of federalism. Pictured is the Texas State Capitol, located in Austin.

mining and milling of uranium ore, and low-level waste (LLW) (which is the contaminated material generated by the daily and routine use of nuclear material in local power plants, industrial parks, medical and dental facilities, universities, and other institutional settings)—also pose dangers to public health. But the threat of these three is more containable and does not necessarily require a national (central site disposal) solution.

Most Americans go about their daily routines without giving a second thought to the problem of radioactive waste disposal. But that has not been the case for residents of Nevada and New York whose lives have been directly impacted by policies designed to deal with radioactive waste disposal.

For Nevadans, the issue was a decision by federal officials to locate a high-level radioactive waste disposal facility just 100 miles northwest of Las Vegas. In 1982, in attempting to come up with a solution to the disposal of high-level wastes, the U.S. Congress passed the Nuclear Waste Policy Act, which authorized the Department of Energy (DOE) to develop a single geologic repository for HLW that would replace the more than 120 sites scattered throughout the United States. Scientists and policymakers had been studying various options and locations for decades prior to the act, and in 1985 the search for a site was narrowed to three locations: Hanford, Washington; Deaf Smith County, Texas; and Yucca Mountain, Nevada.

There was little local enthusiasm or support for hosting the facility at any of those locales, and while the Department of Energy was in the midst of conducting final evaluations of the three sites, the political battles in Congress over the selection process turned fierce. In 1987, the congressional delegations of Washington and Texas won an amendment to the original act that ordered the DOE to limit its study to Yucca Mountain. Nevadans would term the amendment the "Screw Nevada Bill," and over the next twenty-five years they did everything they could to kill the Yucca Mountain site project.

Politically united against the Yucca site, both Republicans and Democrats in the state used every strategy they could to defeat the project. It made no sense to them that the national government could come into their state and operate a facility that most Nevadans regarded as a threat to their health as well as an environmental catastrophe in the making. Constitutionally and legally, however, they were unable to make any headway, for through legislation and long-standing judicial precedent, the U.S. Congress absolutely had the constitutional authority to locate the Yucca site project on federal lands in Nevada. When it comes to matters of nuclear power, the national government's power (mainly through the interstate commerce clause) trumped any state's authority in the area. Despite official and unofficial protests from Nevada, in 2002 President George W. Bush signed a congressional resolution designating Yucca Mountain as the official site and ordering the DOE to proceed with preparation, with the intent to open the site in 2017.

But Nevada's politicians understood that American federal-state relations were not merely constitutional—they were also political. Over the years, the state's congressional delegation stayed united, and its influence grew, culminating in the selection of Senator Harry Reid as majority leader of the U.S. Senate. At the same time, the state had become a key battleground state in close presidential elections, and in their campaigns both John Kerry (2004) and Barack Obama (2008) promised to halt the Yucca site's development if elected. It came as no surprise, therefore, that in March 2009, President Obama's energy secretary, Steven Chu, announced that Yucca Mountain was no longer being considered as a waste disposal site.[3]

After withdrawing from Yucca Mountain, the DOE began the extended process of searching for an alternative site, and by 2014 they were focusing on a location in New Mexico that was already being used to dispose of plutonium waste from defense projects conducted at the nearby Los Alamos National Laboratories. Although there was local support for the site, there were signs of opposition from other corners of the state similar to those the DOE faced in Nevada. The story is likely to take years to unfold.[4]

Residents of New York State faced a different issue. Unlike the high-level variety, low-level waste involves those things that have come into

Despite bipartisan opposition from Nevadans, the federal government attempted to locate the nation's only high-level radioactive waste dump at Yucca Mountain (near Las Vegas). It took several years of tough political maneuvering, but eventually the state was able to get the Obama administration to reverse that decision.

contact with or have been contaminated by radioactive material—items such as plastic bags, protective clothing, rags and mops used to clean contaminated areas, filters, medical syringes, and so on. The disposal of LLW is also a national problem, but federal law (the Low-Level Radioactive Waste Policy Act of 1980 and the amendments of 1985) leaves it up to individual states to determine how to handle it. In most cases, LLW remains stored at the site where it was generated, but eventually it has to be transported to a safe site for long-term storage or disposed of once the danger has passed. It was up to the states to make arrangements for disposal.

Interstate compacts
A formal agreement among two or more states allowed under Article I, Section 10, of the Constitution with the consent of Congress.

The 1980 act encouraged states to enter into **interstate compacts**—that is, formal agreements among two or more states allowed under federal law—and the 1985 amendments made some adjustments to facilitate such agreements for opening LLW sites at several locations. Most significantly, it allowed each site established through a compact to limit access to the site to the compact members. If a state did not join a compact, it was required to develop an LLW site that met federal standards within its own borders, thus providing those who generate the waste a location for disposal. If the state failed to establish such a site for LLW, it was required by the act to "take title" of (own) the waste and assume any and all responsibility for the LLW subject to federal rules and federal regulations. In short, the state would lose its ability to develop its own policies and regulations for LLW and instead carry out the policies and orders of federal government regulators.

During the 1980s and into the 1990s, New York State attempted to comply with the federal law. It negotiated with other states, but the amount of LLW generated by New Yorkers was so great that no other state would agree to a compact arrangement. Unlike the situation facing Nevada, New York did not have the political power to alter the law or the decisions being made at the EPA under the George H. W. Bush administration. Turning inward, New York attempted to find a suitable site within its borders—but in each instance local opposition and a general "not-in-my-backyard" (NIMBY) attitude defeated each option. Finally, facing the day that it would have to take title of all LLW, New York went to court, arguing that under the American system of federalism, a state cannot be legally coerced by the federal government to assume responsibility for LLW.

In this instance, it was the constitutional path that gave New York a way out of its dilemma. In *New York v. United States* (1992), the Court majority held that the provision of the act that required state to take title would effectively commandeer New York's government "into the service of federal regulatory purposes, and would for this reason be inconsistent with the Constitution's division of authority between federal and state governments."[5]

In their distinct efforts to counter federal policies related to radioactive waste disposal, policymakers in Nevada and New York had to engage both politically and legally with federalism as a key part of the American constitutional system. As we will see in the sections that follow, the history of federalism is filled with debates, including one that literally split the nation in two and led to the bloodiest war in U.S. history. Central to these controversies has been a powerful narrative about federalism, one relying on the *myth of state sovereignty*.

The myth of state sovereignty holds that a fundamental and enduring characteristic of the American constitutional system is a division between the national and state governments in which each is capable of exercising some authority over certain matters under its jurisdiction. Although seemingly a very abstract idea, **sovereignty** was an important legal concept for the Framers. Like the other myths discussed in this book, it is neither inherently true nor inherently false; rather, different interests have regarded it as more or less true over the decades. For those who work in government, the myth can help them make sense of many of the complex relationships that emerge under the federalism arrangement. For state and local officials, the myth stresses their responsibility in dealing with many governmental functions close to the people, and for national officials it highlights the importance of taking into consideration the priorities and needs of state and local governments. The resulting interactions have proved so important that many use the phrase *intergovernmental relations* (IGR) as a way of describing federalism in action.

But the myth of state sovereignty has a problematic side as well, as we see in our overview of the history of federalism that follows.

Sovereignty The ultimate source of authority in any political system.

The Evolution of American Federalism

> **How has federalism changed over the past two centuries of American constitutional development?**

As the product of constitutional compromise among the Framers, federalism had only a vague form when it was first implemented in 1789. As noted in Chapter 2, the proceedings of the convention were held behind closed doors, and the Framers had agreed that no one would discuss what took place that summer in Philadelphia—a promise that most of them kept for decades. During the debates over ratification, however, many expressed their opinions about the proposed arrangement, and some did so in response to comments and questions made by opponents of the new government. And so, without a clear idea of how the attempt to mix national and state sovereignties should be worked out, the nation's new rulers engaged in an ongoing debate from the outset.

Battles over Meaning (1790s–1860s)

At first, the debate focused on the question of which of the two levels of government should take precedence when the two were in conflict: Was the national government primary, or could states ignore the laws of Congress when they chose? Two competing answers emerged, one centered on the states and the other on the nation.[6]

State-centered federalism The view that the Constitution allowed the national government only limited powers and that the states could overrule national laws if they determined that those laws were in violation of the Constitution.

Supporters of **state-centered federalism** wanted to allow the national government only limited powers. Led by Thomas Jefferson and James Madison, they argued that states could overrule national laws if they believed that those laws violated provisions of the U.S. Constitution.[7]

Nation-centered federalism The view that the authority of the national government goes beyond the responsibilities listed in Article I, Section 8, of the Constitution; it is based on the necessary and proper clause and the principle of national supremacy.

Proponents of **nation-centered federalism** argued that the authority of the national government goes beyond the responsibilities listed in Article I, Section 8, of the Constitution. They contended that the necessary and proper clause and the principle of national supremacy give the national government additional powers to act. Alexander Hamilton and, later, Daniel Webster took this position, as did Chief Justice of the Supreme Court John Marshall in *McCulloch v. Maryland* (1819; see the discussion of that case in Chapter 2, on constitutional foundations). Five years later, in *Gibbons v. Ogden* (1824), the Supreme Court dealt another blow to the proponents of state power. It held that a New York law that established a steamboat monopoly between New York City and New Jersey was not constitutional. Only the national government, the Court ruled, could regulate "commercial intercourse"—that is, **interstate commerce**—between states.

Interstate commerce Trade across state lines , in contrast to intrastate (within state boundaries) trade and foreign trade.

The supporters of the state-centered approach did get some relief when, starting in the late 1830s, the Supreme Court made a number of rulings that established the existence of sovereign **police powers**, which a state could exercise as part of its duty "to advance the safety, happiness, and prosperity of its people."[8] The existence of these police powers was used to justify state jurisdiction over economic matters.

Police powers The powers of state governments over the regulation of behavior within their borders. These police powers were used to justify state jurisdiction over economic matters.

The debate between advocates of state-centered and nation-centered federalism was also conducted on the floor of Congress. Much of it focused on the issue of slavery, and at times the heated discussions turned bitter and even violent. In one particularly notable episode in the period leading up to the Civil War, a senator from Massachusetts was beaten unconscious with a cane on the Senate floor by an angry member of the House.[9] Ultimately, the conflict over slavery was settled on the battlefields of the Civil War. Out of that bloody confrontation between the North and the South, nation-centered federalism seemed to emerge victorious. The Civil War, it seemed, made it formally possible for the national government to claim a dominant position in the federal system. In reality, however, the story was quite different. As we will see, the myth of state sovereignty was not killed by the Civil War.

From Separation to Cooperation (1860s–1920s)

Instead of domination by the national government, what developed after the Civil War was a system of dual federalism, under which the national and state governments were regarded as equal partners—that is, as equally sovereign.

SOUTHERN CHIVALRY — ARGUMENT versus CLUB'S.

Prior to the Civil War, disputes over federalism and slavery were taken quite seriously. Senator Charles Sumner, an ardent abolitionist from Massachusetts, was nearly caned to death on the Senate floor by Preston Brooks, a member of the U.S. House of Representatives from South Carolina. Brooks had taken exception to remarks Sumner had made about some proslavery members of Congress.

Under **dual federalism**, each level of government is perceived as being responsible for distinct policy functions, and each is barred from interfering with the other's work. Thus, whereas earlier cases had established that the states could not interfere with the national government's regulation of interstate trade, post–Civil War decisions held that the national government could not interfere with the power of the states to regulate the sale or manufacture of products or services within their own borders. Starting immediately after the Civil War, the Supreme Court declared in a series of rulings that insurance, fishing, lumbering, mining, manufacturing, building, banking, and a variety of other economic activities were not subject to federal regulation but rather could be regulated under the police powers of individual states.

The most explicit statement of dual federalism was issued in 1871, when the Court held that within the borders of each state there are "two governments, restricted in their sphere of action, but independent of each other, and supreme within their respective spheres." Neither, the Court said, can intrude on or interfere with the other's actions.[10] Then, in *Hammer v. Dagenhart* (1918), the Court declared that those powers "not expressly delegated to the National Government are reserved" for the states.[11] The Court's use of the word *expressly* was important, for it is not a term found in the Constitution; in particular, it is not found in the Tenth Amendment. In fact, when the Tenth Amendment was debated in the U.S. Congress in 1789, the inclusion of this term was voted down.[12] But the myth of state sovereignty was an important feature of the way many people were viewing federalism at the time of the *Hammer* case. Thus, the decision was an expression of dual federalism at its height.

Despite the Court's reliance on dual federalism during this period, the formal separation between the two levels of government was breaking down in the world of practical politics. The first step in this process was **grant-in-aid programs**, through which state policies and programs were partially funded or

Dual federalism The perspective on federalism that emerged after the Civil War. It saw the national and state governments as equal but independent partners, with each responsible for distinct policy functions and each barred from interfering with the other's work.

Grant-in-aid programs Federal appropriations that are given to states and localities to fund state policies and programs. The Morrill Act (1862) was the first instance of such a program.

given other support. The Morrill Act (1862) gave federal land grants to states for the purpose of establishing agricultural colleges.[13] Later, cash grants helped states with agricultural experiment stations, textbook programs for the blind, marine schools, forestry programs, agricultural extension services, state soldiers' homes, vocational schools, road construction, and a variety of other projects. By 1927 these grant programs were bringing state governments $123 million in national funds annually.[14]

Toward Cooperation and Local Participation (1930s–1950s)

The Great Depression of the 1930s significantly altered the relationship between Washington and the states. Demand for public services grew. At the same time, state and local governments were in an extremely tight financial situation, because tax revenues had fallen as the economy declined. The national government was expected and willing to respond. There was an explosion of new and cooperative programs in which the national and state governments shared an increasing number of functions. A new kind of relationship had emerged that recognized the interdependence of Washington and state and local governments. Called **intergovernmental relations**, or IGRs, it is a system in which the various levels of government share functions, and each level is able to influence the others.

The emergence of intergovernmental relations was an important development in the history of American federalism. It meant that the formal and highly legalistic form of federalism that had previously existed was being replaced by a more flexible and informal approach to nation-state relations. Furthermore, once interactions among various levels of government were treated as IGRs rather than as federalism, the door was open for greater participation by many more actors on the federalism stage. Local and regional governments and even private and community groups could now find a role to play.

Under the new system, a variety of grant-in-aid programs were offered, which covered a wide range of policy concerns. The number and size of these programs grew dramatically during this period, increasing from $100 million in 1930 to $6.8 billion in 1960.[15] The emergence of intergovernmental relations was the foundation for this period of **cooperative federalism**. Conflict between Washington and the states diminished as public officials worried less about what level of government performed certain functions and more about their specific program responsibilities. State and national officials began to see each other as "allies, not as enemies."[16]

At the heart of the system of intergovernmental relations were a variety of grant-in-aid programs that financed highways, social and educational projects, and other programs. Many were **categorical, or conditional, grants-in-aid**, under which state governments received federal funding for specific purposes only if they met certain general requirements. For example, state highway departments were expected to operate in an efficient and businesslike fashion, free of corruption and undue political influence. Similar standards were applied to welfare programs. If states failed to meet those standards, federal support was withdrawn, or sometimes the program was taken over. Thus, during the Depression, Washington took charge of public assistance programs in six states where officials could not meet federal requirements. And they closely watched

Intergovernmental relations The style of federalism that recognizes the interdependence of Washington and state and local governments. The various levels of government share functions, and each level is able to influence the others.

Cooperative federalism A period of cooperation between state and national governments that began during the Great Depression. The national government began to take on new responsibilities, and state and local officials accepted it as an ally, not an enemy.

Categorical, or conditional, grants-in-aid Money given to the states and localities by Congress to be used for limited purposes under specific rules.

During the 1950s and 1960s, many cities built major airports with the help of large grants provided by the federal government. However, the controversial and expensive Denver International Airport, opened in 1995 after much delay, was the first major facility to be built since the early 1970s.

public welfare programs in other states to make sure that they were following federal rules.

Under other federal programs, states received **formula grants** based on population, the number of eligible persons, per capita income, or some other factor. One of the largest of these grants, the Hill-Burton program, used a formula that was heavily weighted to favor states with substantial low-income populations. By 1986, more than $3 billion of Hill-Burton funds had been used to construct and modernize health care facilities throughout the United States.

Project grants are awarded only after submission of a specific proposal for a project or plan of action. The Housing Act of 1937 was one of the earliest and largest of these programs. Under the provisions of that act, local governments could obtain funds to build public housing. By the 1960s, there were more than 4,000 such projects, with more than half a million dwelling units. In many instances, the national government required recipient governments to provide a certain percentage of the funds needed to implement the programs. Among these **matching grants** was a program that provided aid to dependent children under the Social Security Act of 1935 and one that gave states $9 for every dollar spent to build interstate highways.

Cities and other local governments also became participants in the federal system during this period. Before the 1930s, American cities were regarded as merely subdivisions of the states. Grants or other forms of support came from state capitals, not from Washington. In 1932, for instance, only the nation's capital received aid from the national government. By 1940, however, the situation had changed. That year, the national government handed out $278 million in direct grants-in-aid to local governments for a variety of public housing and public works programs. In the 1950s, the national government expanded the

Formula grants Grants given to states and localities on the basis of population, the number of eligible persons, per capita income, or other factors.

Project grants Grants awarded to states and localities for a specific program or plan of action.

Matching grants Programs in which the national government requires recipient governments to provide a certain percentage of the funds needed to implement the programs.

types of projects it would support to include slum clearance, urban renewal, and airport construction. By the start of the 1960s, local governments were receiving $592 million worth of direct grants.[17]

The Urban Focus (1960s–1970s)

The intergovernmental relations system continued to grow during the 1960s and 1970s, and by 1980 grant-in-aid programs to state and local governments had surpassed $85 billion. Starting in 1960, other notable changes also took place.[18] For example, grant systems expanded into new policy areas. The percentage of funds devoted to highways and public assistance declined, and funding for programs in the areas of education, health care, environmental protection, worker training, housing, and community development increased significantly.

In a shift in the flow of funds, a growing number of intergovernmental programs were targeted at local, rather than state, governments. President Lyndon B. Johnson's Great Society policies included dozens of new and innovative grant programs with an urban focus. For the first time, community-based programs for feeding the urban poor, training the unemployed, and educating the children of low-income families received support. One important initiative, the Model Cities Program, was designed to help cities develop projects addressing a variety of economic and social problems. In 1974, many of these and related programs were consolidated under community development grants. By 1985, the national government was disbursing nearly $5 billion directly to local governments through these programs.

Until the early 1960s, Washington used federal grants simply to help states and localities perform their traditional governmental functions. State and local governments might have been asked to modify their personnel policies or their methods of bidding for contracts, but they rarely had to take on new policy responsibilities as a requirement for receiving federal funds. In contrast, the grant programs of the 1960s and 1970s were increasingly designed to involve these governments in achieving national policy objectives. States or localities that initiated new or special programs promoting national goals received substantial grants. The Model Cities Program, for example, encouraged cities to institute programs for improving the quality of life for poor and low-income groups. In other instances, Washington threatened to reduce or cut off funding to governments that failed to change their old policies or to adopt new ones that complied with national standards. It was during this period, for example, that the national government used the threat of withholding highway funds from states that did not lower their maximum speed limits to fifty-five miles per hour.[19]

Reforming and Devolving (1970s–1990s)

Inevitably, the rapid spread of grant programs and their requirements led to problems. Local recipients criticized federal officials for administering programs without regard for the unique circumstances and dilemmas that they were facing. State officials complained that the national government ignored them in designing and implementing many new programs. Both state and local officials complained about the increasing number of strings attached to federal grants, especially policy mandates, which many recipient governments regarded as costly, irrelevant, and inappropriate. At the same time, members of Congress reacted impatiently to the poor coordination and cooperation in the massive intergovernmental relations system. As a result, there was almost constant pressure to reform the grant system.

Responding to pressures for an increased role for state and local officials, Washington took a number of steps designed to loosen its control over grant programs and to enhance state and local authority. During the early 1970s, for instance, the federal government provided funds to support the formation of local and regional **councils of governments**. These associations of local governments helped their member governments contend with such common problems as coordinating local applications for federal grants. In addition, President Johnson and his successor, Richard M. Nixon, reorganized the administration of the grant system, increasing the power of federal regional offices in order to ease the burdens on both state and local governments.

In two additional reform efforts, the national government introduced new funding systems designed to further reduce its control and make procedures more flexible. Most of the programs established before this time had been based on categorical, or conditional, grants, in which money given to the states and localities was to be used for limited purposes under specific rules. In the mid-1960s, however, Congress introduced block grants. **Block grants** were a way of consolidating categorical grants in a given area so that the recipients would have greater freedom in their use of funds and so that paperwork would be reduced. By 1974, seven major block grants were in existence that covered such areas as health, education, and other social services. These grants gave state and local officials more freedom in running their programs and freed them from some of the annoying mandates attached to categorical grants. Nevertheless, in financial terms, they represented only a small portion of the total amount of federal aid flowing to states and localities.

The other new form of federal aid was called **general revenue sharing**. This small but innovative grant-in-aid program had no significant conditions attached to it. State and local governments received funds according to a complex formula based on population and related factors. In the late 1970s, the program was modified considerably, and its funding was reduced. By 1988, it had disappeared from the intergovernmental system.

The late 1970s and early 1980s produced major changes in intergovernmental relations. Most obvious was the reduction in federal funding to states and localities through grants-in-aid. Grant money began to decline in 1979, but the most significant drops occurred during President Ronald Reagan's first years in office. It was nearly a decade before federal aid returned to its pre–Reagan administration levels.[20]

In addition to reducing federal funding, Reagan also attempted a major overhaul of the intergovernmental system. He formally proposed to Congress that many government functions be returned to the states. In exchange, the national government would assume most public welfare programs. When that strategy failed, Reagan administration officials tried to bring about changes by adjusting the way in which grant-in-aid programs were administered. These efforts had a major impact on the federal system.[21]

Councils of governments Local and regional bodies created in the early 1970s with federal funds to help solve problems such as coordinating applications for federal grants.

Block grants Money given to the states by Congress that can be used in broad areas and is not limited to specific purposes, as categorical grants are. They were introduced in the mid-1960s as a means of giving states greater freedom.

General revenue sharing A small but innovative grant-in-aid program, used in the 1970s and 1980s, that had no significant conditions attached to it. State and local governments received funds according to a formula based on population and related factors.

Putting the principles of federalism into practice often poses a challenge for even its most ardent supporters. Traditionally, the Republican Party has favored a more decentralized approach that favors state policies in lieu of national standards. Yet, reacting to auto industry opposition, the Bush administration rejected California's 2008 request that it be allowed to impose tougher auto emission standards on new vehicles. A year later, however, the Obama administration granted the necessary waiver.

At the same time, Congress was consolidating more categorical programs into broad block grant programs. During the first half of the 1980s, Congress converted dozens of categorical programs into about a dozen block grants. Despite these efforts, however, hundreds of categorical grant programs remained on the books. By 1988—the last year of the Reagan administration—the national government was spending an estimated $116 billion on grants-in-aid to states and localities.

There is little dispute, however, that the Reagan administration significantly changed the direction of intergovernmental relations, at least for the short term. Although the absolute amount of federal dollars going for grant-in-aid programs increased through most of the 1980s (from $91.3 billion in fiscal year [FY] 1980 to $121.9 billion in FY 1989), the total amount in constant-dollar terms (adjusted for inflation) declined during most of that period, actually dropping from $168.5 billion in FY 1980 to $148.1 billion in FY 1989 (in 1996 dollars). Only after Reagan left office did grant expenditures increase in both absolute and constant terms.[22]

More importantly, during this period states and localities were becoming less dependent on federal dollars for carrying out their work. For example, in 1978, 26.5 cents of every dollar spent by state and local governments came from the national government. By 1990, however, only 17.9 cents of every dollar spent by states and localities could be linked to a federal grant-in-aid. As one observer put it, the Reagan years represented the years of "fend-for-yourself" federalism.[23]

President George H. W. Bush launched no major initiatives in the area of intergovernmental relations. Nevertheless, two factors emerged that gave cause for concern. First, the combination of cutbacks in federal funding and an extended economic recession created fiscal crises in states and localities throughout the nation. Because many states and localities were required to have balanced budgets, the fiscal crises of the early 1990s had an immediate impact and could not be resolved through governmental borrowing. States from Connecticut to California were forced to take the unpopular steps of cutting budgets and/or raising taxes. However, the flow of federal grant-in-aid money to states and localities picked up once again, and by the time Bush left office, the amount had increased from $121 billion in FY 1989 to $193 billion in FY 1993.

A second factor shaping intergovernmental relations during the early 1990s was the growing number of policy pressures and federally mandated costs that states and localities had to shoulder. The policy pressures came primarily from the White House as President George H. W. Bush made education and the "War on Drugs" program two of his top priorities. Although Bush called for major reforms and initiatives in these specific areas, he made no request for additional federal funding for the states and localities that would have to carry out many of the policy changes he was suggesting. Thus, although he held conferences and made speeches on the need for local schools to engage in costly educational reforms, President George H. W. Bush did not support funding for any major new or special programs to accomplish those objectives. Similarly, his much-touted War on Drugs required nearly $500 million in federal funds, but most of the money was earmarked for federal law enforcement efforts and aid to foreign countries. State and local officials complained bitterly that they needed more money if they were to do their part. After all, they argued, it was the states and localities that had to deal with drug use and its consequences.

Congress was also a source of problems. Members offered and passed well-intentioned legislation requiring state and local action but failed to deal with the associated costs of the new programs. In addition to the previously passed requirements for environmental cleanup, Congress in 1990 passed the much-heralded Americans with Disabilities Act, which included provisions for greater public access to services, transportation facilities, and so forth that would require millions of dollars in additional state and local expenditures for years to come.

Known as **unfunded mandates**, these unfinanced or underfinanced burdens on states and localities became a major issue in national politics and policymaking. By 1994, federal lawmakers had developed greater sensitivity to these burdens. The debates on legislation, such as that dealing with clean water, increasingly included consideration of those responsibilities and who should pay for them. A bill addressing the issue of unfunded mandates—one part of the Republican Party's "Contract with America" agenda, which the Clinton administration supported—became the first substantive item passed by the 104th Congress in January 1995. The legislation required the Congressional Budget Office (CBO) (see Chapter 11, on Congress) to monitor proposals and highlight those that might generate unfunded mandates for state and local governments that exceeded a $50 million (in 1996 dollars) threshold amount. Since 1996, fewer than twelve laws met that criteria, but state officials are quick to point out that, over time, the costs of such laws were well over $130 billion.[24] Thus, despite efforts to deal with this problem, it remains a potentially significant issue.[25]

President Bill Clinton was also sensitive to the growing demands being made on states and localities when he came into office in 1993. As governor of Arkansas

Unfunded mandates
Required actions imposed on lower-level governments by federal (and state) governments that are not accompanied by money to pay for the activities being mandated.

for twelve years, he had developed a national reputation as an innovative leader who understood and appreciated the role of states in the federal system.[26] After less than two weeks in office, Clinton held a meeting with the nation's governors to hear their complaints and suggestions. Although his administration did not propose any major reforms of the intergovernmental system, Clinton did establish a policy that permitted federal officials to loosen program requirements in order to allow states and localities greater flexibility to innovate. This approach of giving states and localities more room to determine the policies they were to enforce became part of a more general movement toward devolution in the intergovernmental relations system. **Devolution** involved having the national government turn over more functions with greater responsibility to state and local governments. During the Clinton years, federal outlays for state and local grants continued to climb, even as welfare programs were reformed and other responsibilities were devolved. By FY 2001—the final budget of Clinton's term in office—the national government was spending $317.2 billion on grants—more than double what it had been sending to states and localities a decade earlier. As important, in constant-dollar terms (again based on 2005 dollars), the value of those grants had risen to $354.8 billion in FY 2001 from $210.4 billion in FY 1991.

Devolution A term indicating the effort to give more functions and responsibilities to states and localities in the intergovernmental system.

Twenty-First-Century Challenges (2001 and Beyond?)

The growth in federal grants to states and localities has continued under the George W. Bush and Obama administrations, with events such as the attacks of September 11, 2001, the financial market collapse of 2008, and the increasingly divisive nature of US politics playing critical roles in some of the increases.

The presidency of George W. Bush began with plans to continue the efforts at devolution,[27] but also to bring about at least two major changes in intergovernmental relations. One initiative was in the area of education, in which Bush received bipartisan support for passage of the No Child Left Behind initiative in 2002 that greatly expanded the federal government's influence in the operations of local schools (see Policy Connection 3 immediately following this chapter).

A second important initiative came early in his term, when Bush endorsed an effort to allow **faith-based organizations (FBOs)** to play a major role in the delivery of social and community services that were funded through the federal government. The idea was to remove the legal and administrative obstacles that stopped federal funding of church-related organizations, such as the Salvation Army and local African American congregations that were effectively providing social services in local communities. Bush created the high-profile White House Office of Faith-Based and Community Initiatives,[28] but the initiative immediately ran into opposition from those who feared that it would violate the separation of church and state (see the discussion of First Amendment rights in Chapter 4) and also from some religious leaders, who regarded it as a threat to church autonomy. Nevertheless, the Bush administration pushed ahead. By 2008, the White House enhanced that effort by requiring all federal intergovernmental grant programs to give consideration to faith-based initiatives and organizations. The effort was modified and extended to include secular neighborhood organizations by the incoming Obama administration in 2009 which maintains a White House office to oversee and promote FBO involvement in intergovernmental programs.[29]

Faith-based organizations (FBOs) Church-related social service organizations.

But perhaps the most significant developments in intergovernmental relationships during the Bush years were unplanned and came in response to the events of September 11, 2001. The first priority of the Bush administration's federalism agenda became strengthening **homeland security** in the fight against terrorism. The war on terrorism has had a major impact on the policies and programs of American government. Whereas initially most attention was given to military responses, by the spring of 2002 attention had turned to domestic security concerns. State and local authorities played a central role in dealing with homeland security issues, from providing security at airports to making plans to guard and protect water supplies and other major public facilities. A request for billions of dollars of federal assistance to first-response agencies—that is, state and local law enforcement, emergency management, and firefighting units—was high on the list of priorities, as were plans to help improve communications and cooperation among governments at all levels.[30]

In addition to White House initiatives, many changes in intergovernmental relations have resulted from innovative state programs and some important U.S. Supreme Court decisions. In areas in which some states believe the federal government is not doing enough, a number of states have taken the lead with innovative policies and programs. In 2006, a bipartisan effort led by California governor Arnold Schwarzenegger led to the passage of groundbreaking laws designed to cut the state's greenhouse gas emissions by 25 percent by 2020. That same year, a major reform of state health insurance laws in Massachusetts was being viewed by some as the model for other states—and eventually the national government. More controversially, in response to what was perceived as lax federal enforcement of national immigration laws, Arizona in 2010 passed legislation that made illegal immigration a state crime. The law immediately drew critical reactions from the Obama administration and was soon successfully challenged in the courts.[31]

In the Supreme Court, starting in the late 1980s, a slim majority of the justices began to lean in the direction of a more state-centered view of federalism that took the constitutional concept of state sovereignty seriously. The influence of that majority has become increasingly evident over the years, and in 1999 the Court issued several decisions that indicated that it would play a major role in shaping the federalism of the future. The trend has continued. Within the Court, at least, the myth of state sovereignty has been taken more seriously with each passing year. This was reflected in a 2002 decision that overturned an effort by a federal agency (in this instance, the Federal Maritime Commission) to hear a private citizen's complaint against a state agency (the Ports Authority of South Carolina). "Dual sovereignty is a defining feature of the Nation's constitutional blueprint," wrote Justice Clarence Thomas in the majority opinion. "States, upon ratification of the Constitution, did not consent to become mere appendages of the Federal Government. Rather, they entered the Union 'with their sovereignty intact.'"[32]

Economic and political conditions have also had major impacts on today's federalism. In response to the economic crisis created by the collapse of financial markets in the fall of 2008, Congress passed the American Recovery and Reinvestment Act of 2009 (ARRA), a large "stimulus package" that contained increases in funding for many state programs as well as state and local **capital expenditures** (for road and bridge repairs, school facilities, and other **infrastructure** projects).

Homeland security
Domestic programs intended to prevent and, when necessary, deal with the consequences of terrorist attacks on U.S. soil.

Capital expenditures In the public sector, that part of a government budget allocated to the construction or major repairs of large, fixed assets such as roads, buildings, dams, and so on.

Infrastructure In government, those basic physical and organizational structures that support the operations of a system or program. The term is typically applied to utilities such as water supply, waste disposal (sewers), electrical grids, information technology systems, and telecommunications, as well as bridges, tunnels, and other public assets.

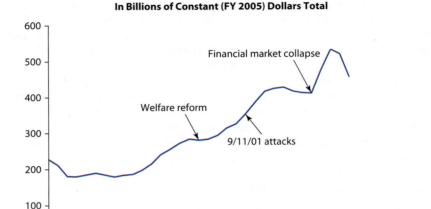

In Billions of Constant (FY 2005) Dollars Total

FIGURE 3.1 The Growth of Federal Grants to State and Local Governments (FY 2005 Dollars), 1980–2012

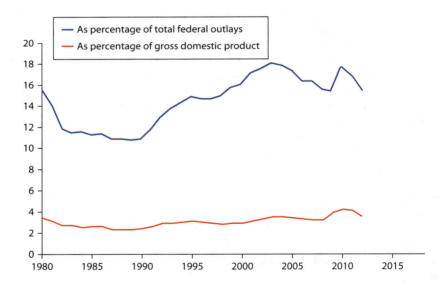

FIGURE 3.2 The Growth of Federal Grants to State and Local Governments, as Percentage of the Total Federal Outlays (blue) and as Percentage of the Gross Domestic Product (red), 1980–2012.

Source: U.S. Government Printing Office, Historical Tables, Budget of the United States Government, Fiscal Year 2015, Table 12.1 — Summary Comparison of Total Outlays for Grants to State and Local Governments.

After the 2010 election, however, most of the stimulus funding was reduced or not renewed due to political concerns over the growing deficit, leading to a downturn in federal aid (see Figures 3.1 and 3.2).[33]

Federalism was a key factor in the policy and political gridlock that emerged after the mid-term elections of 2010 as reaction to the passage of the Patient Protection and Affordable Care Act (also known as the Affordable Care Act or Obamacare). Opponents of the law not only assumed control of the U.S. House, but also several state legislatures and other state offices, and the situation did not change even after President Obama won reelection in 2012. In addition to Obamacare, many of the most controversial issues that led to political stalemates at the national level—for example, immigration, abortion, and climate change—were played out on the state level, where the Tea Party factions gained and solidified their majority positions in many state legislatures. Several states passed laws designed to toughen enforcement of U.S. immigration laws; others limited access to abortion by imposing new requirements for clinics and by prohibiting the procedure after twenty weeks. When states were given the option in a 2012 U.S. Supreme Court decision to opt out of sections of the nation's new health care program, many states did so despite strong political pressures and financial incentives not to do so. The divisions that emerged on the national political scene were clearly being played out on the federalism stage.[34]

The Actors of American Federalism

> ### Who are the major actors in the U.S. federal system, and what roles do they play in the federal system?

Although the issues surrounding federalism and intergovernmental relations have long histories, they have never been as complicated as they are today. This complexity is in part due to the very nature of modern life, but it is also a result of the number of people and institutions involved in the system. Today's federalism is an intergovernmental relations system involving a cast of hundreds of agencies, thousands of political and administrative personnel, and millions of citizens who depend on government for daily public services. In short, the underlying story is that the American federal system has grown wider and deeper as interactions among the different levels of American government have increased and become more complex. Here we briefly describe the many actors who occupy the modern stage of American intergovernmental relations.

National Government Actors

Formally, the American federal system has only one national government. In practice, however, dozens of national-level actors play out daily dramas on the intergovernmental relations stage.

The Supreme Court. In the two centuries of American federalism, no national institution has been more important than the U.S. Supreme Court. We have already seen how, in *McCulloch v. Maryland*, the Court helped establish the national government's dominant role and how the post–Civil War Court supported the notion of dual federalism.

As noted previously, until recently Supreme Court rulings seemed to be reducing the role of the states as effective policymakers.[35] In the late 1980s, however, some Supreme Court decisions indicated a growing willingness to give state and local governments more power to shape public policies on a wide range of issues, from abortion rights and the right to die to local campaign financing and the use of sobriety tests for drivers suspected of drunk driving. In other areas, such as civil rights, however, the Court seemed more reluctant to defer to states. Then, in a 1992 case we discussed earlier in this chapter (*New York v. United States*), the Supreme Court held that the national government could not "simply

The Supreme Court has heard a number of important cases involving states' rights in recent years, including those related to same-sex marriage. In March 2013, large crowds demonstrated in front of the U.S. Supreme Court as it held two days of oral arguments on that issue.

compel" a state to take policy actions. Four years later, in the case *Seminole Indian Tribe of Florida v. Florida* (1996), the Court declared unconstitutional a law that authorized individuals to sue state governments in federal court for violations of national laws.

Similar cases followed. In 1997, the Court overturned a law that required local law enforcement officials to implement provisions of a federal handgun control law (*Printz v. United States*). This was followed by a 1999 decision in which the state of Florida was held to be immune from lawsuits brought against it under the provisions of a federal law dealing with patent rights and false advertising. In another, the Court held that the state of Maine was not subject to federal fair labor standards legislation. In January 2000, the Court went even further, specifically exempting states from provisions of federal laws aimed at preventing age discrimination (*Kimel v. Florida Board of Regents*). With its decision in the Federal Maritime Commission case (discussed earlier), the Court has made it clear that it is once again a significant factor in shaping both the present and future of federalism.

This was clearly in evidence in two highly controversial cases decided in 2012 and 2013. A 2012 decision upholding the constitutionality of the Affordable Care Act (*National Federation of Independent Business v. Sebelius*) did declare one important exception—that the law's mandate that states expand their Medicaid programs was not valid (upholding the decision in *New York v. United States* that a state's legislative function cannot be "commandeered") and that the states could opt out of that part of the program. Then, in a widely anticipated 2013 decision (*United States v. Windsor*), the Court found that a federal statute (the Defense of Marriage Act, or DOMA) interfered with the states' right to define and regulate marriage and was therefore unconstitutional.

Congress. Although presidents often receive credit for major policy innovations, Congress has always played a central role in the evolution of the federal system. This has been especially true in the past forty years, during which Congress has increased its authorization of grant programs.

Some students of Congress point to strong incentives for members of the House and Senate to create and fund federal grant-in-aid programs for state and local governments. These programs give almost every state and local government an opportunity to obtain federal funding. Therefore, members of Congress can claim credit for passing and supporting their constituents' grant applications. As a result, even fiscally conservative members of Congress often found it difficult to avoid supporting requests for new and larger intergovernmental grant programs. "Philosophically, I have not been one to jump rapidly to new programs," commented one member of the House of Representatives from Virginia. "But if programs are adopted, my district is entitled to its fair share. And I do everything I can to help—if they decide to apply for aid."[36]

POLITICS & POPULAR CULTURE: Politics & Popular Culture: Visit the book's companion website at **www.oup.com/us/gitelson** to read the special feature *The Political "Image" of the South.*

The White House. American presidents have proposed new federal grant programs and worked to reform the intergovernmental system. Johnson's Great Society agenda, for example, emphasized the Model Cities Program and other new and innovative projects. As previously noted, the administrations of both Johnson and Nixon strove to improve the coordination of federal grant programs. In the late 1970s, President Jimmy Carter issued several executive orders aimed at simplifying grant application and reporting procedures, which by then had grown very complex.

Other White House initiatives have sought to expand the role of state and local governments in the federal system:

- Johnson called for the establishment of a "creative federalism" involving a partnership of all levels of government as well as community and private organizations.

- Nixon proposed a "new American revolution" that would give "power to the people" by turning many national domestic programs back to state and local governments.

- Reagan announced a "new federalism" that would have revamped the intergovernmental grant system over a ten-year period.

- Clinton ordered members of his administration to administer programs that allowed states to experiment with innovative ways of dealing with the nation's health and welfare problems.[37]

Some changes in the American federal system resulted from each of these presidential initiatives, but none led to radical alterations in intergovernmental relationships. Instead, it has been changes in specific programs that have had the greatest impact on the federal system.

For example, when he ran for the presidency in 1992, Bill Clinton promised that if he were elected, he would bring about "an end to welfare as we know it."[38] On August 22, 1996, he signed into law perhaps the most sweeping changes in welfare programs since the early 1960s. The Personal Responsibility and Work Opportunity Reconciliation Act of 1996 significantly altered the system of assistance to the needy, which had generated criticism from both sides of the political spectrum. The new law was aimed at ending the cycle of poverty and dependence that had caused concern among even the most ardent supporters of government assistance to the poor. But for those who administered the vast web of federal programs that had developed over several decades, the law represented even more important changes. For them, in many respects, the new welfare law meant an end to the intergovernmental relations system as they had known it for more than half a century.

Before the passage of the reform legislation in 1996, assistance to the poor was effectively a set of national programs administered by the states. Thus, despite the significant role played by the states, there was an unmistakable national flavor to the welfare system. As in many other policy areas—from education to environmental protection to highway construction and maintenance—states and localities had taken on significant financial and administrative burdens but were severely limited in deciding on such matters as who was eligible for the programs or how the funds would be spent. After the 1996 reforms supported by the Clinton administration, the role of the states in welfare policy was radically transformed, as they took on most of the responsibility for determining the kinds of assistance programs they would administer.

As noted previously, the George W. Bush administration's major initiative in changing intergovernmental relations was the push for the involvement of faith-based organizations in federal programs. In the longer term, however, it was the need to bring states and localities into homeland security programs that took top priority for the Bush White House.

The Obama administration's approach to intergovernmental relations has been described as one stressing "flexibility"—a "hybrid model of federal policy innovation and leadership, which mixes money, mandates, and flexibility in new and distinctive ways."[39] This was especially true in regard to education policy and the push to get economic stimulus funding to states and local governments during the Great Recession (see Policy Connection 3).

The Federal Bureaucracy. Perhaps the greatest increase in the number of national-level actors on the intergovernmental stage has taken place in the bureaucracy, especially in such agencies as the U.S. Departments of Housing and Urban Development, Health and Human Services, Agriculture, Interior, Transportation, and Education. Some bureaucrats in these agencies determine the eligibility of state and local grant applicants and the appropriateness of their proposals. Others monitor the use of grant-in-aid funds and constantly consult with other actors in the intergovernmental system about the need to modify specific grant programs.

The emergence of these intergovernmental bureaucracies has added a new dimension to U.S. government. On the one hand, the bureaucrats in these agencies are expected to disburse funds and assist state and local governmental officials in making effective use of those resources (see Figure 3.3). On the other hand, they are expected to ensure that state and local programs meet federal standards and live up to federal requirements. In other words, the growing federal bureaucracy

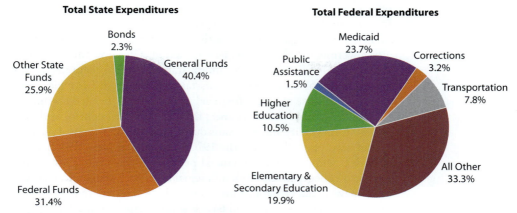

FIGURE 3.3 Total State and Federal Expenditures by Funding Source (FY 2012)

A little less than one-third of state budgets are funded through federal grants, with most of the funding allocated to Medicaid, education, and transportation.

Source: National Association of State Budget Officers (NASBO), State Expenditure Report, FY 2012 *(Washington, DC: NASBO, 2013), p. 4.*

assigned to intergovernmental programs is supposed to both facilitate the grant process and regulate state and local grant recipients. These bureaucrats are actors on the intergovernmental stage with dual, and often contradictory, roles (see Chapter 13, on the bureaucracy).

Two developments are likely to shape the role of the federal bureaucracy in the federal system in the future. First is the continued trend toward devolution and program reform, especially in welfare, health care, environmental protection, and education. Although the national government is unlikely to withdraw from these areas, its role will be increasingly linked to the work of state, local, nonprofit, and (sometimes) private sector agencies. Second, the emergence of homeland security as a high priority for the national government will continue to pose issues for Washington. If federal officials are to make any headway in this area, an enhancement of the intergovernmental system will necessarily be required, with a special emphasis placed on establishing a significant role for local public services, such as law enforcement and fire protection.

States in the Federal System

Even during periods when the national government has seemed to be playing the leading role in the federalism drama, the states have remained important and active participants in the intergovernmental arena. Through all the various changes that have taken place, they have been sustained by the myth of state sovereignty and have retained significant responsibilities in the areas of education, public health, criminal justice, and the regulation of gambling and liquor. They also play major roles in enforcing environmental, safety, and health regulations. For years they have been the chief regulators of public utilities and savings banks.

An important but often unappreciated legal fact about states is that they empower and determine the organization of local governments.[40] Legally, local governments are created by the actions of state legislatures. Thus, theoretically, state officials acting in their constitutionally sovereign role can legally terminate them. In practice, however, states rarely use this life-and-death power over the legal existence of local governments, although they have on occasion eliminated entire city governments through legislative action. City governments cannot impose their own sales or income taxes unless state laws grant them that authority. There are examples of state governments taking over or shifting local governmental functions because of severe financial problems or unbridled corruption and inefficiency. In Missouri, for instance, the state assumed control of the police forces in both Kansas City and St. Louis during the twentieth century because of widespread corruption.[41] And in the 1970s, the state of New York helped New York City deal with its critical financial problems by assuming responsibility for all four-year colleges in the city's municipal university system. In recent years, some states have taken control of inner-city school districts that were failing to perform up to state standards and have assumed responsibility for the governance of entire cities as financial crises forced some into bankruptcy.[42]

States have also made their mark through creative approaches to solving public problems. Wisconsin regulated railroads and democratized the political nomination process long before such policies were adopted nationally. California led the way in developing building-construction standards to help reduce energy costs, in establishing auto-emission standards to help reduce air pollution, and more recently in taking steps to reduce the state's contribution to greenhouse gas emissions by 25 percent by 2020. The Massachusetts approach to health care reform became the model for the federal Affordable Care Act of 2010. Such state-initiated innovations are common in almost every major area of domestic policy, from welfare to education and insurance reform.[43] One of the strongest arguments for giving more responsibility to the states has been their ability to come up with novel and effective programs, even in the face of budgetary cuts.

Most important today, however, is the states' pivotal role as liaison in the intergovernmental relations system. As noted earlier, the national government uses state agencies to administer its grants in a wide variety of policy areas. Furthermore, local governments rely on state officials for technical assistance, as well as for financial aid. In short, state governments may be the key link—and not necessarily the weak link—in the U.S. federal system.

The role of the states in the intergovernmental relations system is always changing. When their influence wanes, students of American government tend to pronounce their doom. According to one prominent observer in the 1930s, the American state was "finished." He said, "I do not predict that the states will go, but affirm that they have gone."[44] At other times, the states have been so important that some can hardly imagine how American government could operate without them, whereas others are extremely critical of their importance.[45]

What accounts for these gains and losses in power?

- *The states' authority changes dramatically as the Supreme Court shifts between strict and flexible interpretations of the Constitution.* As noted previously, the current Court majority has signaled its intent to decide in favor of a state-centered view of federalism when issues come before it.

- *The states' role depends on the actual political power they can mobilize.* During certain periods of American history, state officials have managed to exercise considerable influence in Washington through their representatives in the House and Senate. At other times, state governors and legislators have carried relatively little weight either at the White House or in the halls of Congress.

- *Public opinion plays a role in determining the extent of states' influence.* Although state governments have always been important policymakers, the American public has not always looked to the states for solutions to its collective problems. At times the public has depended on local governments, and more recently it has expected Washington to help. The question of public support for state government is complicated by citizens' attitudes toward their state governments, which tend to vary over time. Over the past several decades, public opinion regarding the capacity of states and localities has become more positive.[46]

- *The role of the states in the federal system depends on their administrative capabilities.* If states lack the administrative resources and managerial talent to deliver the goods and services demanded by the public, then they cannot play a major role for very long. Most observers believe that the administrative capabilities of the states have improved markedly since the 1960s. Ironically, much of that improvement has come about as a result of pressures imposed by Washington through the requirements attached to grant-in-aid programs.

Local Governments

When you think of local governments, you probably picture city halls and county courthouses occupied by small councils of elected officials and a few offices occupied by record-keeping clerks, who collect taxes and issue dog tags and automobile licenses. American local governments are much more than that, however, and their role in the intergovernmental relations system is a major one.

As noted earlier, all local governments are creations of the individual states. Under the formal provisions of the federal system established in the Constitution, governmental powers are divided between the national government and the states. Local governments, in other words, have no formal constitutional standing except as subdivisions of the states. Their very existence and legal authority are derived from charters granted to them under state laws. This does not mean that they are powerless or insignificant actors in the federal system, for states often give local government considerable authority. Just how powerful these local governments can be was made clear in 2005, when the Supreme Court issued a decision that upheld the authority of local governments to take private property for public purposes. In that particular case (*Kelo v. City of New London* [125 S. Ct. 2655]), the city of New London, Connecticut, used its power of eminent domain to force 115 private homeowners to sell their residences so that the city could give the land to a private developer who had offered to construct a hotel and conference center complex in that economically depressed city. The power of **eminent domain**—or the right of a sovereign government to take property for public purposes for just compensation, even if the owner of that property objects—is a power that most states give to local governments in their charters so

Eminent domain The right of a sovereign government to take property for public purposes for just compensation , even if the owner objects.

they can acquire real property needed for such public purposes as building roads and highways or constructing public facilities such as schools or a city hall. Local governments have also been given the authority to use eminent domain to clear areas of urban blight, or to replace slums with public housing. In recent years, a growing number of localities have used eminent domain to promote economic development, and it was for that purpose that New London sought to take possession of those 115 residences. The homeowners took the city to court, and in a controversial 5–4 decision, the U.S. Supreme Court sided with the city. Like it or not, the Court majority ruled, local governments do possess whatever power of eminent domain their state charters grant them, and they have wide discretion in determining what is or is not a valid public purpose. Any limits on that power have to come from the state, so the federal courts may not interfere.

Even though local governments formally depend on the state for their legal authority, in practice Americans have always treated local governments as if they had separate and legitimate standing in the federal system.[47] As of 2012, there were 90,056 local governments in the United States. This figure includes county (3,031), municipal (19,519), township (16,360), and other **general service governments** that provide a wide range of public services to those who live within their borders. It also includes 12,880 independent school districts and 38,266 other **special district governments** dealing with one or two distinctive governmental functions, such as fire protection, public transportation, or sewage treatment. Each of these local governments can participate in some way in the intergovernmental relations system—and a great many do.[48]

The problems of local governments are not all alike, because those governments reflect a variety of physical, social, cultural, political, and economic conditions. Between the extremes of small, rural, sparsely populated townships and huge, densely populated metropolitan areas are cities, towns, counties, and districts of every conceivable size and shape. To understand the distinctive role played by local governments in the intergovernmental system, we need to perceive their differences.

Of particular importance are the wide economic disparities among various local governments. These differences in wealth influence the way community leaders approach the intergovernmental system. For example, according to recent estimates, the per capita income in Laredo, Texas, is less than half the per capita income of Tulsa, Oklahoma, or Bremerton, Washington, and barely one-third the per capita income of residents of Naples, Florida. A city such as Laredo or Newark, New Jersey, would want more federal aid programs targeted at job training, public housing, public health, and similar needs of the urban poor. Naples's government, in contrast, would seek more federal funding for new highways, construction of new recreation facilities, and other such amenities.

Not only the economic status but also the age and ethnic background of the citizenry bear on local problems and needs. The interests and concerns of those living in Scottsdale, Arizona, where the median age is more than 45 years old, are different from those living in Loredo, Texas, where it is 27.9 years old. The people of Scottsdale would seek federal and state help in funding special programs for the elderly, whereas the citizens of Loredo would be more interested in state and federal aid for elementary and secondary school programs. Ethnic

General service governments Local governments, such as counties, municipalities, and townships, that provide a wide range of public services to those who live within their borders.

Special district governments Local governments that deal with one or two distinctive government functions, such as education, fire protection, public transportation, or sewage treatment.

concerns can also be a factor. The existence of a very large Hispanic community in El Paso, Texas, is relevant to what that city wants from Washington. The intergovernmental relations system, for instance, can offer El Paso's schools funding for bilingual education programs. Such funds might not be available if the schools had to depend on local resources.

These and other factors make it difficult to generalize about the roles played by local governmental actors on the intergovernmental relations stage. Nevertheless, local officials have undoubtedly become major participants in the federal system during the post–World War II period and will remain important. They exercise much of their influence through local members of Congress, who are responsive to the needs of their constituents back home. They also exert influence through membership in intergovernmental lobbying groups, which make up an increasingly important set of actors in the federal system.

Nongovernmental Actors

Those outside the formal governmental system also have issues that they act on. Within this category are the intergovernmental lobby and the largest group of potential participants—the citizens of the United States.

Intergovernmental Lobby. The **intergovernmental lobby** includes individuals and groups that have a special interest in the policies and programs implemented through the growing intergovernmental relations system (for more on interest groups, see Chapter 9). Some of these lobbyists represent private interests that hope to benefit from or expect to be harmed by some intergovernmental program. For example, environmental lobbyists push for effective state and local enforcement of national air-quality and water-quality standards. Other intergovernmental lobbyists support social regulations to strengthen automobile safety, consumer protection, or occupational health. Representatives of businesses seek to reduce these regulations and to weaken state and local enforcement.

Lobbyists for the poor and the disabled are also active on the federalism stage. In many instances, their goal is to ensure continued federal funding of social services, health care, and educational programs. At other times these groups seek better treatment by government agencies for groups who do not have the resources or capacity to protect themselves. The Southern Poverty Law Center, for example, has successfully filed legal actions on behalf of foreign guest workers in order to protect their right to "fair wages" under federal law. Disability rights organizations, in the meantime, have filed a number of class action lawsuits on behalf of individuals who have lost their benefits because of some change in state of federal policy, whereas still other nonprofit law firms have initiated court actions to end overcrowding in America's prisons and to promote improved treatment for mental illness within those facilities. In a 2011 landmark decision, for example, the U.S. Supreme Court declared that overcrowding in California's prisons constituted "cruel and unusual punishment" and ordered the release of 32,000 prisoners.[49]

In recent years, a new kind of intergovernmental lobby has emerged: **public-sector interest groups** that represent the interests of elected officials and other major governmental actors involved in the intergovernmental relations system.

Intergovernmental lobby
The many individuals and groups that have a special interest in the policies and programs implemented through the growing intergovernmental relations systems. These lobbyists represent private, consumer, and business groups.

Public-sector interest groups
A lobby that represents the interests of elected officials and other major governmental actors involved in the intergovernmental relations system. An example is the National Governors' Association.

For example, the National Governors' Association and the U.S. Conference of Mayors are two of the most active groups in Washington that lobby on domestic policy issues. The National Conference of State Legislatures (NCSL), based in Denver, is one of the best sources of information on what is taking place in the intergovernmental system, and that has made them an effective participant in policy debates surrounding IGRs. Still other groups—such as the National League of Cities, the National Association of Counties, and the Council of State Governments—lobby on behalf of their own governmental jurisdictions. The American Society for Public Administration and the International City and County Management Association are active representatives of the interests of public administrators and other nonelected public-sector workers.

Individual governments also hire lobbyists to represent their interests. In 1969, Mayor John V. Lindsay of New York City took the brash step of opening a Washington, D.C., office to lobby on behalf of the Big Apple. Two decades later, New York City had eight full-time lobbyists looking after its interests in Washington. Similar offices have been opened by just about every major government in the United States.

The increase in the number of public-sector interest groups, as well as their political influence, paralleled the growth of the intergovernmental system itself during the 1960s and 1970s. In recent years, however, the reduction in federal aid for states and localities has led several of these public-sector interest groups to reconsider their priorities and roles. Many have cut back their Washington-based staffs and focused more of their attention on lobbying state legislatures or on providing technical assistance to their members, who must adapt to Washington's reductions in grant-in-aid funding.[50]

Citizens. The largest group of potential participants in the intergovernmental system are the citizens of the United States—the intended beneficiaries of all the

The U.S. Conference of Mayors is a public-sector interest group that can wield considerable influence in Washington. Here, Attorney General Eric Holder addresses a session at the organization's 2013 winter conference asking the mayors to lobby Congress in support of pending gun control legislation.

policies and public services of American government. Hardly an area of American domestic policy remains untouched by the intergovernmental relations system, yet many Americans remain unaware of the role of intergovernmental relations. Every person who drives a car on the highways, attends public schools, uses city buses, or receives emergency care at a community hospital benefits from intergovernmental programs.

Of course, the American people are more than just the beneficiaries of the many goods and services provided through the intergovernmental system. As taxpayers, citizens also pay for those programs, often indirectly. Most intergovernmental programs are paid for with general tax revenues collected by the various levels of government. However, a portion of the money comes from special trust funds established for a particular program. For instance, each time you purchase a gallon of gasoline for your car, you pay a special federal tax. That tax is deposited in the Highway Trust Fund, which is used primarily to pay for the construction and maintenance of interstate highways and other roads (see Asked & Answered, page 104).

Most important, the American people generate the demand for intergovernmental programs. The pressures that the public can bring to bear on the system are most evident when popular grant programs are threatened with major cuts, or when a community faces a crisis that cannot be handled with local resources. Consider, for example, social service programs for the elderly or handicapped. When members of the Reagan administration suggested cutbacks in social security in 1982, the public reacted so negatively that President Reagan felt compelled to promise never to cut those benefits.

And when a crisis or tragedy strikes some community—when a tornado or flood devastates a small town, or when buried hazardous wastes contaminate a

When disaster strikes, significant political differences among intergovernmental leaders are put aside. When Hurricane Sandy devastated the New Jersey shore in 2012 in the midst of the presidential election, President Obama and New Jersey's Republican governor, Chris Christie, put aside their differences to deal with the disaster.

ASKED & ANSWERED

ASKED: Who is responsible for America's elaborate systems of roads and highways?

ANSWERED: Part of the answer to this question is found in the U.S. federal budget.

In early 2009, the U.S. Department of Transportation (USDOT) requested that the Federal Highway Administration (FHWA) budget for FY 2010 be set at just slightly more than $41 billion. Most of that money came from a special trust fund that motorists paid into through a tax imposed on every gallon of gas purchased at the pump and was used to pay for the construction, repair, and maintenance of the American highway system. In addition, a special appropriation of $26.6 billion was given to the FHWA under the American Recovery and Reinvestment Act (ARRA) of 2009—also known as the Stimulus Act—which was used to fund more than 12,000 highway-related projects not covered under the regular budget.*

But despite all the federal money that goes toward the construction and maintenance of roads and highways, it is more likely that, to get a pothole fixed, you would have to call your local road department or state highway agency. In fact, almost all those federal funds—as well as billions in additional state and local funding—is spent by the states and their subdivisions.

Consider these statistics: Of the 3.9 million miles of roads and highways in the United States, about 3.1 million—a full 77.5 percent—are controlled by local governments, including cities, towns, counties, local special districts, and so forth. Another 776,000 miles are designated as state roads, and a relatively small number of miles—a little more than 120,000— are under the jurisdiction of federal agencies that operate national forests, parks, military reservations, and other federal government lands.

The Constitution does give the national government a potentially powerful source of authority over roads and highways in Article I, Section 8, when it empowers it "to establish post offices and post roads." From the outset, however, the national government has avoided assuming too much responsibility for the actual building or maintenance of roads. Instead, with a few minor exceptions, it left that task up to states and localities and instead focused attention on designating certain state and local routes as national "post roads," and providing some advice and support for new forms of transportation, such as canals and railroads. In the twentieth century, the national government emerged as the primary source of funds for projects at all levels of government.

The result is that today the construction and maintenance of the country's major roads and highways are intergovernmental responsibilities shared by local, state, and national governments, as well as some private companies. Privately owned and operated roads were once commonplace in the United States. In the nineteenth century, many toll roads, mostly access roads and privately financed bridges that crossed private property, were privately owned and maintained. Although at one time these were all but eliminated by the modern government-financed highway systems, today privately owned highways are making a reappearance in many states. The fourteen-mile Dulles Greenway that stretches between Leesberg, Virginia, and Dulles International Airport is one such road, as is the twenty-two-mile Camino Colombia Toll Road in Texas. Other privately funded and operated roads are now found in Florida, Colorado, and California, and several more are under construction.

Even so, the role of private roads is likely to remain very minor, and to get any potholes filled, you will likely have to speak with your local government.

For detailed information on the ARRA, see the unique website launched by the Obama administration to track the various expenditures under the stimulus at www.recovery.gov.

community's soil and water supply—the call for action goes out to Washington as well as to the state capital and city hall. These are the kinds of actions that generate intergovernmental activity regardless of concerns over the constitutional niceties of federalism. The massive mobilization of public-sector resources from all levels of government in response to the tragic events of September 11, 2001, was a case in point, and that effort received generally favorable marks. But there are also examples of terrible failures of this system, the most notable in recent years being the response to Hurricane Katrina in August 2005.

Conclusion

Before embarking on a political career that eventually led him to the governorship of Maryland, Parris Glendening was a scholar who wrote books about federalism. What he observed as a scholar—and attempted to put into practice as an elected public official—is an approach that he calls "pragmatic federalism." From his perspective, intergovernmental relations "are constantly changing, fashioned to address current needs while emphasizing problem solving with minimal adherence to rigid doctrine."[51]

The type of federalism that Glendening and others practice on a day-to-day basis is indeed pragmatic and practical—a type of federalism quite different from the contentious interactions that marked the first years of this institution. The old form of federalism resulted in confrontation rather than cooperation. This new form of federalism took decades to evolve into a system of intergovernmental relations, and most of those engaged in it find debates over such things as state sovereignty quite unproductive and irrelevant.

This is not to say that there are no problems with the intergovernmental relationships that are at the heart of today's pragmatic federalism. Depending on the issue, you will always hear people in city hall or the state capitols complaining about too much interference from Washington; and in the federal bureaucracy, the administrators of various programs feel constantly challenged by local and state officials who they feel are unwilling or unable to meet the minimal requirements established for specific programs. Those outside the system have other issues as well. Some complain about the inequities and inefficiencies that result from having national programs implemented by local and regional governments, whereas others express frustration at the one-size-fits-all mentality reflected in some federal programs.

In the day-to-day world of intergovernmental relations, the myth of state sovereignty seems irrelevant and insignificant. Nevertheless, today's system of intergovernmental relations cannot ignore its roots in the federalism bargain. The legacy of the seemingly ancient debates over sovereignty and authority lingers in the form of the myth of state sovereignty, and it manifests itself in congressional debates over health care and during times of economic and environmental crises as well as in cases before the Supreme Court. If we are to truly make sense of and understand the institution of federalism, we need to take into account both the realities of daily government operation and the myths from the past.

Key Terms

Block grants p. 87
Capital expenditures p. 91
Categorical, or conditional,
   grants-in-aid p. 84
Cooperative federalism p. 84
Councils of governments p. 87
Devolution p. 90
Dual federalism p. 83
Eminent domain p. 99
Faith-based organizations
   (FBOs) p. 90
Federal Poverty Level p. 112

Food stamps p. 111
Formula grants p. 85
General revenue sharing p. 87
General service governments p. 100
Grant-in-aid programs p. 83
Homeland security p. 91
Infrastructure p. 91
Intergovernmental lobby p. 101
Intergovernmental relations p. 84
Interstate commerce p. 82
Interstate compacts p. 80
Matching grants p. 85

Medicaid p. 111
Nation-centered federalism p. 82
Police powers p. 82
Project grants p. 85
Public-sector interest groups
   p. 101
Sovereignty p. 81
Special district governments p. 100
State-centered federalism p. 82
Supplemental Security Income
   (SSI) p. 111
Unfunded mandates p. 89

Focus Questions Review

1. **How has federalism changed over the past two cen-turies of American constitutional development?>>>**
   - The evolution of the American federal system has been shaped by debates over the meaning of federalism, especially the issue of whether it was intended to be nation centered or state centered.
   - It has also been shaped by the distinctive challenges that have faced the United States during the past two centuries.
   - Out of that evolution has emerged a complex system of intergovernmental relations based on a variety of grant-in-aid programs. The intergovern-mental relations system has been characterized by periods and episodes of conflict and cooperation.

2. **Who are the major actors in the U.S. federal system, and what roles do they play in the federal system?>>>**
   - Many different actors engage in the federal system, and all of them contribute to the complexity of the system. In addition to the major branches of the national government (the Supreme Court, the White House, and Congress) are states, local governments, the intergovernmental lobby, and the citizens of the United States—each with a role and stake in the system.

Review Questions

1. In what ways do intergovernmental relations (IGRs) differ from federalism?
2. "Almost any issue you see on the front page of the nation's papers has something to do with federalism." Test this statement against some item in today's newspapers.

For more information and access to study materials, visit the book's companion website at www.oup.com/us/gitelson.

Policy Connection

How are education policies and aid to the poor affected by American federalism?

The Policy Challenge

The complicated policymaking process discussed in Policy Connection 2 is most evident in those areas where national, state, and local governments must work together to deal with some of the nation's most challenging issues. In this Policy Connection, we focus on aid to the poor and education—two areas in which the topics discussed in Chapter 3 (that is, federalism and intergovernmental relations) have provided a dynamic setting within which governments at all three levels attempt to engage with one another. In many respects, the story of how American government has addressed these issues reflects the evolving nature of the federal system.

The Constitutional Setting

Understanding that story begins by our recalling some of the most important provisions of the Constitution itself. As noted in Chapters 2 and 3, the first eighteen paragraphs of Article I, Section 8, of the Constitution establish the authority of Congress in a range of subjects, from the power to declare war and coin money to the power to fix weights and measures and establish post offices and post roads. The section ends with the *necessary and proper clause*, a provision that we can interpret in two ways. On one hand, we could regard it as a means for limiting the national government to *only* those activities that were absolutely necessary and proper to conduct its business. On the other hand, we might read it as a license to expand the jurisdiction of Congress, allowing it to do *whatever* is deemed

necessary and proper to fulfill its other obligations. Which view prevailed would have significant implications for the national government's role in many policy areas—including education and aid to the poor.[1]

The pivotal decision as to which view would prevail came relatively early in the nation's history—in the *McCulloch v. Maryland* decision (discussed in Chapters 2 and 3), which allowed for the more expansive view of Congress' powers. Although the reasoning in *McCulloch* would prove to be a watershed decision, it would take decades before Washington took major steps to expand its role, a role normally regarded as within the purview of states and localities.[2] The pull of localism has been a powerful factor in American politics, and it was reinforced by the Tenth Amendment to the Constitution, which made explicit what was left implicit but unstated in the original document—that those "powers not delegated" to Congress "nor prohibited" to the states were in fact "reserved to the States respectively, or to the people."

Education Policy

The Constitution does not mention education, and it is one of the areas in the American federal system in which states and localities still tend to dominate. Nevertheless, over the past two centuries, the national government has become a major player in this policy arena, particularly in response to four general issues: (1) access to education, (2) education funding, (3) educational content, and (4) the quality of education.[3]

Access to Education. The national government's involvement in issues of *access to education* actually predates the Constitution. In establishing a plan for the settlement of the northwestern territories (today's Ohio, Indiana, Illinois, Michigan, and Wisconsin), the congress under the Articles of Confederation passed the Northwest Ordinance (1787), requiring that "schools and the means of education shall forever be encouraged" by the governments formed in that region.[4] For the next two centuries, all legislation related to the governing of territories and the admission of states included similar provisions. In addition, the Morrill Act of 1862 granted federal land grants for the establishment of colleges devoted to "the agricultural and mechanical arts," and the act became the basis for many of today's state universities. In 1914, Congress passed the Smith-Lever Act, which promoted the educational missions of colleges and universities through off-campus cooperative extension programs. Access to higher education was a key component of the GI Bill of Rights (1944),

which provided benefits to veterans returning from World War II.

In the 1950s and 1960s, access to education was redefined to stress *equal access* for all Americans. In *Brown v. Board of Education* (1954; see Chapter 5), the Supreme Court struck down government policies supporting segregated access to public education, and in the civil rights and education policies that followed, specific provisions made discriminatory policies illegal at all levels of education.

Today, the mission of the Department of Education's Office of Civil Rights is to enforce the antidiscrimination policies in the following:

- Title VI of the Civil Rights Act of 1964 (prohibiting discrimination based on race, color, or national origin)

- Title IX of the Education Amendments of 1972 (prohibiting sex discrimination)

- Section 504 of the Rehabilitation Act of 1973 (prohibiting disability discrimination)

  - Age Discrimination Act of 1975 (prohibiting age discrimination)

  - Title II of the Americans with Disabilities Act of 1990 (prohibiting disability discrimination by public entities, whether or not they receive federal financial assistance)[5]

Funding of Education. The national government's ability to shape educational policies at the state and local level has long been tied to its ability to deal with *educational funding issues*. Initially, these programs emerged because the national government was intermittently faced with surplus funds and often used them for education-related purposes. Eventually, however, specific programmatic objectives led to the creation of small grant programs.

The major breakthrough, however, came with passage of the National

GI Bill benefits gave World War II veterans the opportunity to attend colleges and universities. Long lines to register for classes formed at campuses nationwide. In a matter of one or two years, schools such as the University of Houston (pictured here in 1946) were transformed from relatively small city colleges to large state universities.

Defense Education Act of 1958 (NDEA), which focused on higher-education programs, and the Elementary and Secondary Education Act of 1965 (ESEA). ESEA was the first major effort to provide a broad range of federal financial support for K–12 education; its provisions targeted districts serving large numbers of children from low-income families. In 1968, Congress extended ESEA's reach to programs for handicapped and other special needs students, as well as to rural areas and bilingual education. The next major revisions to ESEA came in the 1994 Improving America's Schools Act, which covered items ranging from school building repair to multicultural education programs. This effort continued under presidents Bill Clinton and George W. Bush. In 2002, Congress passed the No Child Left Behind Act, which tied funding to achieving national standards (see the subsequent discussion).

Educational Curriculum. Federal programs that deal with specific educational curricula are implied in most of the early access and funding policies. However, it was the Cold War–era fear that the Soviet Union was outdoing the United States in critical areas of science that initiated a major effort by the federal government to shape the curriculum of America's classrooms. The National Defense Education Act of 1958 declared that "an educational emergency exists and requires action by the federal government . . . to help develop as rapidly as possible those skills essential to the national defense." Although the language of the act emphasized that this was not an attempt to impose federal control of education, it had a major impact on education at all levels. It emphasized enhancing the teaching of foreign languages, science, math, and other areas deemed critical to the Cold War effort.[6]

The first comprehensive federal programs covering curriculum issues in K–12 programs were passed in the Goals 2000: Educate America Act of 1994, which promoted the adoption of programs in math, the sciences, literacy, and lifelong learning. Along with the Improving America's Schools Act of 2000, Goals 2000 became a content-relevant bridge between federal funding and quality education programs.

Perhaps because of sensitivity about state and local control, federal funding to promote curriculum change has remained indirect, with the U.S. Department of Education being supportive rather than explicitly involved. In 2009, the National Governors Association and Chief State School Officers (both public-sector interest groups; see Chapter 3) announced a joint initiative to have each state adopt the Common Core State Standards, with the expectation that each would develop statewide standards for school curricula leading to diplomas. By 2013, forty-five states as well as the District of Columbia had adopted the standards, but by August 2014 several states had withdrawn due to local opposition to federal involvement (see http://www.corestandards.org/ for updates on the program's status). As the initiative moved forward, the secretary of education made it clear that this was not a federal project. "With governors and state leaders making major progress on standards, we gave them all the support we could, within the bounds of what's appropriate for the limited federal role in education."[7]

Educational Quality and Accountability. Federal involvement in *educational quality and accountability* concerns is increasingly evident. George W. Bush's No Child Left Behind Act (NCLB) initiative was a key part of his run for the presidency. This 2002 act stressed the need for states to develop educational standards in specific subject areas and to implement testing programs for assessing how well the schools were helping students—including those with special needs—to meet those standards. The NCLB represented an effort to make schools more accountable, and it gave the national government a prominent role in education policy for the future.

The debate over federal education policy is a prime example of how Americans have increasingly relied on the national government to deal with problems that cannot be handled by state and local officials alone. Although most details of education policy have always been the responsibility of states and localities, federal policymakers have obviously not been reluctant to get involved if the public seems supportive.

We cannot assume, however, that federal involvement in education has always been welcome or successful. Opposition to school desegregation in the South during the 1950s and early 1960s was widespread and sometimes violent. Later efforts to integrate schools in cities outside the South, such as Boston and Kansas City, met with significant opposition, especially when they involved mandatory busing of students away from the neighborhood schools. There was also vocal opposition to the No Child Left Behind policies of the Bush and Obama administrations, especially from teachers who complained that the underlying approach of NCLB was ill conceived.[8]

Aid to the Poor

Social welfare policies have deep roots in American history. America's earliest social policies were based on England's poor laws—enacted in the early 1600s—which made local communities responsible for taking care of their own needy and sick. State governments became involved in aiding the needy during the 1800s. Many states abolished local debtors' prisons, instituted child labor laws, mandated public education, and supported the creation of institutions to care for those in physical and economic need. These state and local efforts continued to expand into the twentieth century.[9]

Except for a few small federal grant-in-aid programs to the states (described in Chapter 3), the national government was not actively involved in social welfare policy until the Great Depression. Beginning in the 1930s, however, national policies focused on promoting the general welfare through social programs for all Americans, regardless of income level.[10] Here we focus on those policies related to assistance for those in economic distress.

Old and New Welfare. Federal policies aimed explicitly at helping those in need went through a major overhaul in 1996. To appreciate the significance of those changes, we must understand the welfare system that the 1996 act replaced.

Under the previous system, three distinct forms of federal assistance programs were enacted:[11]

1. *General assistance* (such as emergency assistance) given in cash or in the form of food and other commodities or the means for buying them

2. *Work assistance* offering jobs or job-training programs

3. *Categorical assistance* targeting specific populations (for example, aid to families with dependent children and supplemental assistance to children with disabilities)

Almost all these programs were intergovernmental programs, involving state and local funding and participation. The resulting welfare system was a complex arrangement that drew criticism from all corners of the political arena. Among those criticisms, three specifically helped shape the 1996 reforms.

1. The system was *too centralized and inflexible.* Many of the federal programs were designed to guarantee that people who needed help had approximately equivalent access to minimal welfare benefits, whether they resided in New York City or Jackson, Mississippi. This goal required that the national government establish basic program standards and ensure the implementation of minimal eligibility requirements throughout the country. Although the level of benefits might vary from state to state, Washington enforced and set program standards and a minimal level of benefits.

2. The older system created *too much dependence* on government programs among the poor.[12] Existing welfare programs gave recipients little, if any, incentive to seek employment or job-related training, creating a "culture of poverty" that increased the dependence of welfare recipients on government programs.

3. The system was proving *too expensive* for a nation increasingly concerned about the climbing national debt. *Entitlement programs* in which all eligible individuals qualified for the program's benefits dominated the welfare approach and required open-ended funding.

These and related criticisms of the welfare system eventually led to the passage of the Personal Responsibility and Work Opportunity Reconciliation Act, which President Clinton signed into law in 1996. Another factor that spurred elected officials to action was the growing political popularity of reform, which created the incentive for policymakers to make the most significant changes in American welfare policies in more than three decades.

The 1996 legislation addressed the major criticisms of the previous system.[13] It empowered the states to control the funding it received through federal programs, focused on reducing dependence on welfare, and placed limits on government spending for welfare programs. It replaced many of the highly centralized and inflexible categorical programs of the past with a block grant that provided each state with resources to accomplish the legislation's four basic goals:

1. Assisting needy families so children could be cared for in their own homes or in the homes of relatives

2. Ending the dependence of needy parents on government benefits by promoting job preparation, work, and marriage

3. Reducing the incidence of out-of-wedlock pregnancies

4. Encouraging the formation and maintenance of two-parent families

Although the block grant gave the states considerably more power to shape their own welfare policies and programs, Congress did set some standards requiring the states to submit plans for approval by the federal government and to show how their policies and programs would achieve the primary objectives of the reforms while keeping costs in check.

Other Program Changes. Although the 1996 act changed the structure of several major entitlement programs, it did not make radical changes in some other parts of the welfare system. For example, **Supplemental Security Income (SSI)** was created in 1972 to provide direct monthly benefits from the federal government to the aged, those with visual handicaps, and those with mental or physical disabilities, regardless of their level of assistance from other programs. However, a major portion of the SSI that affected children with disabilities was modified to tighten eligibility requirements.

Another major entitlement program, **food stamps** (now called the Supplemental Nutrition Assistance Program, or SNAP), was also left mostly intact.

Begun in 1961 as an experiment, the program had become the primary source of food assistance for the poor. By 1994, more than 27 million people were receiving some level of food-stamp support, and the program was modernized to take advantage of newer technologies for delivering program benefits. Because it is an entitlement program, the economic downturn of 2008 resulted in an expansion of SNAP, and by 2013 there were roughly 48 million Americans receiving an average of $133 in benefits each month.[14]

Many other federally funded programs—including housing assistance, child nutrition, child care, and child support—were linked in some way to programs modified by the 1996 act, and each was affected in some way by the legislation. The long-term implications of welfare reform on these and other programs became clear as the new act was implemented. By 2006, state welfare programs had experienced major changes, caseloads had declined significantly, and participation in the workforce as well as income among welfare recipients had increased. But signs of success were tempered by other issues, especially the economic situation of families that had moved off welfare rolls into low-wage jobs. Overall, however, the 1996 reforms were regarded as a positive development.[15]

One aspect of assistance to the poor that was not directly part of the 1996 reforms was related to health care. **Medicaid**[16] has remained the primary health care program for aiding the poor. Established in 1965 as part of the Social Security system, it is financed jointly by the states and national governments, with states having some flexibility within broad federal guidelines in the design and operation of the program. The welfare reforms of 1996 did not directly affect Medicaid, although some provisions indirectly gave states the right to slightly modify eligibility standards. The bigger change came in 1997, with the passage of what is now known as the Children's Health Insurance Program (CHIP), through which the federal government provided matching funds for state programs that provided coverage to low-income families with children. By 2013 the combined Medicaid/CHIP programs covered 62 million Americans, half of them children.

The eligibility requirements, level of benefits, and operations of these programs has varied among the states. Eligibility for both Medicaid and the CHIP has to be tied to income, and specifically to an individual's (or family's) annual income above or below a threshold calculated each year by the U.S. Census Bureau. In response to President Lyndon Johnson's call for a "war on poverty," the bureau first established the threshold in 1964 based on how much income was required for a nonfarm family of four (two adults and two children) to sustain "an adequate nutritional level" over a one-year period. Modified a number of times to take into account regional and other factors, the threshold—now called the **Federal Poverty Level (FPL)**—went from just more than $3,000 in the mid-1960s for that family of four to $23,850 in 2014.

The variation among the states can be significant. For example, to have been eligible for the CHIP in North Dakota in 2012, your family income must have been under 160 percent of the FPL. In New York, however, your children were eligible if your family income was below 400 percent of the FPL. Most states had eligibility requirements at the 200–250 percent threshold during that year.

The 2010 Affordable Care Act (popularly called "Obamacare") originally contained provisions that required the states to enhance the coverage of their Medicaid program in order to include those whose incomes were above a state's eligibility criterion for Medicaid but below the level at which they would be eligible for subsidies for purchasing private health care under the act. Initially, that would have required all states to set their Medicaid eligibility up to 138 percent of the poverty line, as set by the U.S. government. To offset the increased costs to the states' Medicaid programs, the federal government would

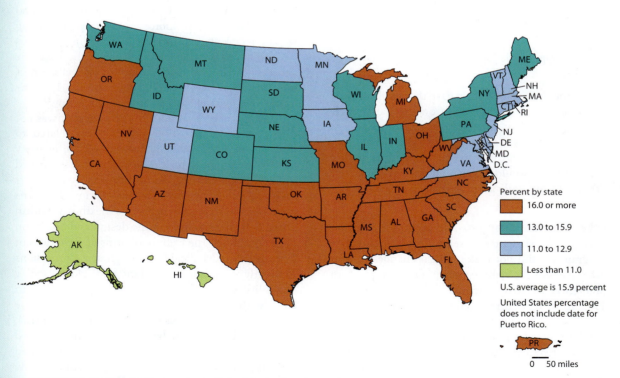

FIGURE 3PC.1 The Level of Poverty in the United States (2012)

Each year, the U.S. Census Bureau determines the federal poverty level income threshold for individuals and families and uses that measure to determine the level of poverty in the states.

Source: U.S. Census Bureau, 2012 American Community Survey; U.S Census Bureau, 2012 Puerto Rico Community Survey.

assume the costs of all increases through 2017, at which time the states would pick up 20 percent of the increased burden. Several states balked at this provision and sued; the result was a Supreme Court decision that allowed individual states to opt out of the Medicaid expansion program. As of February 2014, when the policy came into effect, only 25 states and the District of Columbia had decided to participate. Nevertheless, this modification of Medicaid is another of the long line of changes made in America's social welfare policies.

Conclusion

How are education policies and aid to the poor affected by American federalism?

Public policies are designed to solve public problems, but they are also designed to fit into the limits imposed by constitutional structures and constraints. Indeed, the nation's education and social welfare policies and program would look a lot different if it were not for federalism. There have been benefits as well as drawbacks to the complicated nature of America's domestic policy arenas. Adapting to the demands of federalism—and its blend of federal, state, and local authority—has led to many innovations and a flexible approach that may seem incoherent from the viewpoint of those who seek uniformity and consistency above all else. It does make sense, however, if we view it from the perspective of a highly diverse and constantly changing society.

QUESTIONS FOR DISCUSSION

1. The education you received throughout high school was shaped primarily by decisions made in your state and by your local school board. In other countries, education policies and standards are set at the national level. How different do you think your education would have been had the U.S. Constitution given the federal government power over education policies?

2. Why have the roles of national, state, and local jurisdiction changed as the government established new social welfare policies for the poor?

CHAPTER 4

Civil Liberties

Defining and Preserving Liberty

Writing to her husband in June 1775, Abigail Adams lamented her father's profound despondency over the recent burning of his beloved hometown of Charleston, Massachusetts. She provided her husband a long list of the horrors experienced by the citizens of Boston and other seaport towns. John, a delegate to the Continental Congress, responded to Abigail expressing his condolences and thanking her for the descriptions of the war casualties in New England. As for the suffering experienced by the residents of the seaport towns, John made clear that he too grieved their losses. He took the occasion of the letter to remind Abigail about the reason for the war and assured her that cities could be rebuilt and lost property could be replaced, but "a Constitution of Government once changed from Freedom, can never be restored. Liberty once lost is lost forever."[1]

John Adams's admonition is a warning to all of us. The future president of the United States understood that civil liberties are both vital and precarious. **Civil liberties**, most of which are spelled out in the first ten amendments to the Constitution (the Bill of Rights), were intended to protect individuals from excessive or arbitrary government interference. Civil liberties are distinguished from **civil rights**, which are guarantees of protection by the government against discrimination or unreasonable treatment by other individuals or groups.

Many Americans believe that the guarantee of civil liberties *should* mean that we can do whatever we want.

< The original Constitution lacked a full listing of individual rights and freedoms. To appease those who feared a loss of freedoms, in 1789 the First Congress proposed twelve amendments guaranteeing individual rights and reserving some powers for the states or the people. Ten of the proposed amendments were ratified by three-fourths of the states in 1791. These ten are known today as the Bill of Rights.

Civil liberties Freedoms, most of which are spelled out in the Bill of Rights, from excessive or arbitrary government interference.

Civil rights Guarantees of protection by the government against discrimination or unreasonable treatment by other individuals or groups.

As we will see in this chapter, that belief is a myth—the *myth of absolute or complete liberty*. Liberty is rarely absolute, and our Founders did not think it could be. Moreover, few Americans really believe in complete liberty when it comes to the government's treatment of unpopular groups or detested actions.

When asked general questions about First Amendment liberties, Americans almost universally support them. But support for these liberties drops significantly in regard, for example, to members of the Westboro Baptist Church conducting antigay protests at military funerals and others who express unpopular views. The exercise of liberties may also conflict with other goals and values in society. In that case, we often favor curtailing liberty in the name of national security or domestic peace. As you read this chapter, notice how our understanding of liberty has changed. It is not a static concept enshrined in the Bill of Rights and other constitutional provisions. Instead, our liberties are often balanced against these competing values.

In this chapter, we explore the expansion and contraction of our civil liberties as the courts have interpreted and reinterpreted the Bill of Rights.

Pictured here are members of the Topeka, Kansas, Westboro Baptist Church picketing the funeral of Marine Lance Corporal Kevin A. Lucas at the Arlington National Cemetery. The church's congregation became notorious for traveling the country picketing funerals, most notably the funerals of American soldiers killed in war. Rather than grieving the dead soldiers, the Westboro demonstrators celebrated each death as proof that God hates Americans for their acceptance of homosexuality. Even though most Americans find the demonstrators repulsive, they still have First Amendment rights.

Applying the Bill of Rights to the States

> **How has the Bill of Rights been applied to the states?**

As we discussed in Chapter 2, the original U.S. Constitution, unlike several state constitutions, made no mention of a bill of rights. Most historians argue that the Framers simply felt that a listing of rights and liberties was unnecessary. The national government was to have only the powers granted to it, and the Constitution did not give the national government any power to infringe on people's liberties. Therefore, many delegates reasoned, there would be no problem. No doubt they also assumed that the separation of powers and the system of checks and balances would thwart any effort to diminish individual liberties.

The failure to include a bill of rights in the Constitution caused clashes at state-ratifying conventions. State after state ratified the Constitution only on the understanding that the new Congress would strengthen the document with a guarantee of certain personal liberties. Consequently, the First Congress, which met in September 1789, proposed twelve amendments to the Constitution, and within two years the states ratified ten of them. These ten amendments, collectively referred to as the Bill of Rights, constitute a list of specific limits on the power of the national government.

Originally, the provisions of the Bill of Rights were understood to limit only the actions of the national government. States were restricted only by the provisions of their individual constitutions. The Supreme Court decision in *Barron v. Baltimore* (1833) clarified that view.[2] Baltimore city officials had redirected several streams that fed into the city's harbor. As a consequence, large deposits of sand built up around John Barron's wharf and made it inaccessible to ships. Because the city had destroyed his business, Barron claimed, the city was required by the Fifth Amendment to provide just compensation.

After reviewing the precise wording of the Bill of Rights and the historical justification for adopting it, Chief Justice John Marshall, writing for a unanimous Court, ruled against Barron. According to Marshall, the Bill of Rights applied only to the national government. That is why, Marshall argued, the first word of the First Amendment is *Congress*. That position remained unchallenged until the ratification of the Fourteenth Amendment in 1868.

Drafted chiefly to provide equality before the law to the recently emancipated slaves, the Fourteenth Amendment contains much broader language. Its very first paragraph includes the statement "nor shall any State deprive any person of life, liberty, or property, without due process of law." This statement is critically important for understanding the role of the Bill of Rights in modern society. To some, this "due process" clause clearly indicates that the framers of the Fourteenth Amendment intended to reverse the *Barron v. Baltimore* decision. For instance, Supreme Court Justice Hugo Black (1937–1981) steadfastly maintained that the Fourteenth Amendment *incorporated* (that is, made applicable to the states) the entire Bill of Rights.[3]

Although a majority of the Supreme Court has never fully accepted Black's sweeping interpretation of the Fourteenth Amendment, most provisions of the Bill of Rights have since been applied to the states. Beginning in 1925, the

The first test of the Bill of Rights came in 1833, when John Barron, the owner of a wharf in the Baltimore harbor, unsuccessfully sued the state of Maryland for a violation of his Fifth Amendment rights to just compensation.

Selective incorporation
The Supreme Court's practice of making applicable to the states only those portions of the Bill of Rights that a majority of justices felt to be fundamental to a democratic society.

Supreme Court slowly increased the number of provisions applicable to the states through **selective incorporation**—the application to the states of only those portions of the Bill of Rights that a majority of justices believed to be fundamental to a democratic society. The 1937 case of *Palko v. Connecticut* illustrates that approach.[4]

Frank Palko was found guilty of second-degree murder and sentenced to life in prison. The prosecutor, desiring a conviction for first-degree murder, successfully appealed the trial court's decision and retried Palko. This time, Palko was found guilty of first-degree murder and sentenced to death. He then appealed his case to the Supreme Court, claiming that the second trial was unconstitutional because the Constitution protected an individual from double jeopardy, or being tried twice for the same crime. Writing for the Court, Justice Benjamin Cardozo acknowledged that the Bill of Rights contains guarantees that are so fundamental to liberty that they must be protected from state as well as national infringement. He did not, however, include among these guarantees the protection against double jeopardy. Cardozo granted that this protection was valuable and important, but he concluded that it was not "the essence of a scheme of ordered liberty." Consequently, Frank Palko was executed.

Ultimately, the *Palko* decision was overturned in 1969, and by the early 1970s the Supreme Court had incorporated almost all the provisions of the Bill of Rights. The last right to be incorporated was the Second Amendment, which became applicable to the states in 2010. As Table 4.1 shows, however, some provisions of the Bill of Rights have yet to be incorporated.

TABLE 4.1 Selective Incorporation of the Bill of Rights

Specific Right(s)	Amendment	Year of Incorporation	Court Case(s)
RIGHTS INCORPORATED			
Public use and just compensation in the taking of private property	Fifth Amendment	1896 and 1897	*Missouri Pacific Railway Co. v. Nebraska* *Chicago, Burlington & Quincy Railway Co. v. Chicago*
Freedom of speech	First Amendment	1927	*Fiske v. Kansas*
Freedom of the press	First Amendment	1931	*Near v. Minnesota*
The right to a fair trial and to counsel in capital cases	Sixth Amendment	1932	*Powell v. Alabama*
Freedom of religion	First Amendment	1934	*Hamilton v. Regents of the University of California* (dictum only)
Freedom of assembly and association	First Amendment	1937	*DeJonge v. Oregon*
Free exercise of religion	First Amendment	1940	*Cantwell v. Connecticut*
Separation of church and state; protection against the establishment of a religion	First Amendment	1947	*Everson v. Board of Education*
Right to a public trial	Sixth Amendment	1948	*In re Oliver*
Protection against unreasonable searches and seizures	Fourth Amendment	1949	*Wolf v. Colorado*
Application of the exclusionary rule in regard to unreasonable searches and seizures	Fourth Amendment	1961	*Mapp v. Ohio*
Protection against cruel and unusual punishment	Eighth Amendment	1962	*Robinson v. California*
Right to counsel in felony cases	Sixth Amendment	1963	*Gideon v. Wainwright*
Protection against self-incrimination	Fifth Amendment	1964	*Malloy v. Hogan*
Right to confront witnesses	Sixth Amendment	1965	*Pointer v. Texas*
Right to privacy	Deduced from the penumbra of several provisions in the Bill of Rights	1965	*Griswold v. Connecticut*
Right to an impartial jury	Sixth Amendment	1966	*Parker v. Gladden*

(Continued)

TABLE 4.1 **Continued**

Specific Right(s)	Amendment	Year of Incorporation	Court Case(s)
Right to a speedy trial	Sixth Amendment	1967	*Klopfer v. North Carolina*
Right to a compulsory process for obtaining witnesses	Sixth Amendment	1967	*Washington v. Texas*
Right to a jury trial in cases of a serious crime	Sixth Amendment	1968	*Duncan v. Louisiana*
Protection against double jeopardy	Fifth Amendment	1969	*Benton v. Maryland*
Right to counsel in all cases entailing a jail term	Sixth Amendment	1972	*Argersinger v. Hamlin*
Right to bear arms	Second Amendment	2010	*McDonald v. City of Chicago*
RIGHTS NOT INCORPORATED			
Protection against the requirement to quarter soldiers	Third Amendment	---	---
Requirement of indictment by grand jury	Fifth Amendment	---	---
Right to a trial by jury in all civil cases in which the value in controversy exceeds $20.	Seventh Amendment	---	---
Protection against excessive bail and excessive fines	Eighth Amendment	---	---

Source: Adapted from Craig Ducat, *Constitutional Interpretation-Cases-Essays-Materials*, 10th ed. (Boston: Wadsworth/Cengage, 2013).

Incorporating the Bill of Rights is one thing, but defining the scope of its provisions is another.

The First Amendment Freedoms

> **What balances has the Court established in applying the First Amendment?**

Because the First Amendment is written in absolute terms ("Congress shall make no law . . ."), it is more likely to be subject to the myth of absolute liberty than the other amendments. But the exercise of First Amendment freedoms often conflicts with other highly desirable goals of society. Most justices have realized that it is impossible to protect First Amendment liberties without qualification. Therefore, the issue has been one of balance. Sometimes the Court has interpreted the safeguards of the First Amendment strictly, giving maximum protection to individual liberties. At other times, it has allowed the government great latitude in pursuing its interests. Drawing the lines has never been easy, but it has always been necessary.

Freedom of Speech

Freedom of speech is essential for a democracy. As Justice Black observed, "Freedom to speak and write about public questions is as important to the life of our government as is the heart to the body."[5] The First Amendment states that "Congress shall make no law . . . abridging the freedom of speech or of the press." Nevertheless, the freedom to speak has often been the target of government regulation. No matter how highly we value free speech, each of us is likely at some time to see its exercise as dangerous. This is simply a recognition that ideas have consequences—consequences that we may disapprove of or even fear.

Changing Standards. Although the phrasing of the First Amendment seems to prohibit any limitations on speech, the Supreme Court has never viewed freedom of speech as immune from all government restriction. Justice Oliver Wendell Holmes once noted that freedom of speech does not protect someone who is "falsely shouting 'fire' in a crowded theater." The Court has tried to define the circumstances under which the government may limit speech. To that end, it has employed a series of tests designed to strike a balance between the constitutional protection and the need for public order or security.

The first of these tests was developed by Justice Holmes in *Schenck v. United States* (1919).[6] Charles T. Schenck had been convicted under the Espionage Act of 1917 for distributing leaflets urging young men to resist the World War I draft. Writing for a unanimous Court, Justice Holmes rejected the proposition that speech was always protected from government restriction and instead expounded the **clear and present danger test**. The question, Holmes said, was whether speech would cause evils that the government had a right to prevent. If the speech could be shown to present a grave and immediate danger to the government's interests, the government had a right to punish it. In ordinary times, the justice admitted, the defendant would have been within his constitutional rights, but these were not ordinary times. Urging young men to resist the draft during a war was, Holmes said, a serious threat to the nation's safety.

Soon after the *Schenck* decision, the majority of the Court began to substitute for clear and present danger the **bad tendency test**, which allowed the government to punish speech that might cause people to engage in illegal action. Announced in *Gitlow v. New York* (1925),[7] the bad tendency test removed the need to prove a close connection between speech and the prohibited evil. To justify a restriction of speech, the government needed to demonstrate only that the speech might, even at some distant time, present a danger to society. Thus, Benjamin Gitlow, a member of the Socialist Party, could be convicted under a criminal anarchy law that prohibited anyone from advocating the overthrow of the government, even though there was no evidence showing that his efforts had had any effect.

During the 1960s, questions of free speech became numerous, as the civil rights movement and anti–Vietnam War activists generated a succession of mass

Clear and present danger test The proposition, proclaimed by the Supreme Court in *Schenck v. United States* (1919), that the government has the right to punish speech if it can be shown to present a grave and immediate danger to the country's interests.

Bad tendency test The principle that the Supreme Court began to prefer, in First Amendment cases, over the clear and present danger test. It allowed the government to punish speech that might cause people to behave illegally.

Preferred freedoms test
The principle that some freedoms—such as free speech—are so fundamental to a democracy that they merit special protection. The test was instituted by the Warren Court of the 1960s.

protests. Sit-in demonstrations, protest marches, and draft-card burnings raised new issues of free speech. The Supreme Court of that era, led by Chief Justice Earl Warren, rejected the bad tendency test of the earlier period. It substituted the **preferred freedoms test**, which proposed that some freedoms—free speech among them—are so fundamental to a democracy that they merit special protection. The government can restrict these freedoms only if some particular exercise of them presents a grave and immediate danger to the larger society. Theoretically, government may limit speech, but, designing a law that passes the test is very difficult.

Symbolic Speech. Not all speech is verbal. A person may engage in what is called *symbolic speech* without uttering a word: gestures or even the wearing of a certain type of clothing may convey an opinion. Because symbolic speech is a form of communication, the Supreme Court has often accorded it the protection of the First Amendment. In 1989, for instance, the Court upheld the right of protesters to burn the American flag. In *Texas v. Johnson*, the majority argued that laws that prohibit the burning of the flag infringe on a form of constitutionally protected speech,[8] and the opinion was greeted by a storm of outrage.

Saying that "flag burning is wrong, dead wrong,"[9] President George H. W. Bush called for a constitutional amendment to overturn the decision. Although Bush's proposed constitutional amendment failed in the Senate, Congress did pass the Flag Protection Act of 1989, which provided criminal punishments for anyone who knowingly "mutilates, defaces, physically defiles, burns, maintains on the floor or the ground, or tramples upon any flag of the United States." In 1990, however, with Justice Brennan again writing the majority opinion, the Court, in *United States v. Eichman*, ruled that the new law also violated the Constitution's guarantee of freedom of speech.[10] Since 1990, several constitutional amendments outlawing flag desecration have been introduced in Congress, but none has received the necessary two-thirds vote in both houses.

Not all symbolic acts have gained protection from the Court, however. In 1994, for instance, the Court upheld a lower court's order prohibiting protesters from blocking the entrance to an abortion clinic. Writing for the Court in *Madsen v. Women's Health Center*,[11] Chief Justice William Rehnquist argued that the state's interest in protecting the well-being of the clinic's patients justified the restraint on free speech. This ruling was further extended in 2000, when, in *Hill v. Colorado*, the Court upheld a Colorado law that prohibited approaching within eight feet of anyone within one hundred yards of a health care facility.[12] But in the 2014 case of *McCullen v. Coakley* a unanimous court declared that a Massachusetts law banning demonstrations within thirty-five feet of an abortion clinic was an unconstitutional restriction of speech. Although the Court did not specifically overturn *Hill*, many observers believe the decision effectively did.

Another example can be seen in *Morse v. Frederick* (2007). Mr. Frederick was suspended from school for ten days after unfurling a banner that read, "Bong Hits 4 Jesus." Writing for the majority, Chief Justice John Roberts admitted that the banner may have been gibberish, but he concluded that the principal had every right to believe that it promoted, or at least glorified, illegal drug use, a viewpoint he said schools do not have to tolerate. In a concurring opinion, Justice Thomas went further, arguing that the Constitution does not give students any free speech rights in public schools—students, Justice Thomas argued, "have a right to speak in schools except when they don't."

Whether or not students have free speech rights was tested again recently; this time the issue was whether schools can prohibit students from promoting breast cancer awareness by wearing bracelets emblazoned with the slogan "I [heart] boobies." School officials in Easton, Pennsylvania, banned the bracelets because they believed the phrase was the kind of sexual double-entendre that the school dress code policy prohibited. At trial, a U.S. district court ruled that the school violated the First Amendment rights of its students by banning the bracelets. Similarly, the Third U.S. Circuit Court upheld the trial court decision, saying that when it comes to social or political commentary, speech may not be banned by schools unless it is "plainly lewd." Believing that the lower courts had misinterpreted precedent, the school district appealed to the U.S. Supreme Court. But in 2014, the Court refused to hear the case, leaving the Circuit Court decision standing as the final word on the case.

The First Amendment's guarantee of free speech, including symbolic speech, also covers the freedom *not* to engage in symbolic action, such as saluting the flag. This freedom not to speak, in words or symbols, was first articulated by the Court in *West Virginia State Board of Education v. Barnette* (1943). In that case, Walter Barnette, a parent of school-aged children, challenged a West Virginia statute that required all teachers and schoolchildren to recite the Pledge of Allegiance while maintaining a stiff arm salute. Barnette, a Jehovah's Witness, claimed that the

In 2010, the school district in Easton, Pennsylvania, banned middle school students from wearing bracelets that read "I [heart] boobies! (Keep a breast)." The school district contended that the bracelets, which were meant to indicate breast cancer awareness, violated the school dress code. Two students who were suspended from school for wearing the bracelets sued the district, contending that their First Amendment rights had been violated. The case has yet to be decided.

action violated a religious commandment against worshiping graven images. Speaking for the majority, Justice Robert Jackson held that the state could not compel any student to salute the flag. To those who argued that a compulsory flag salute was necessary to foster national unity, Jackson answered, "If there is any fixed star in our constitutional constellation, it is that no official, high or petty, can prescribe what shall be orthodox in politics, nationalism, religion, or other matters of opinion, or force citizens to confess by word or act their faith therein."[13]

Technology and Free Speech. Sites like Twitter, Facebook, Google+, LinkedIn, MySpace, and tumblr aid in the construction of social networks among people with common interests or experiences, but at the same time they breed numerous challenges to our understanding of free speech.

Whether we are dealing with cyberbullying, cyberstalking, harassment, or trolling, the world of social networks presents serious challenges to our understanding of the freedom of speech. Several states, as well as the federal government, have criminalized bullying, stalking, and harassment, yet a great deal of uncertainty accompanies these laws. In most states, as well as for the national government, electronic communications that threaten, torment, stalk, or cause distress to a reasonable person are illegal. What the courts call "true threats" are not protected speech. But the line between, for instance, rudeness and true threats is far from clear. This is especially true in regard to trolling. Are the troller's relentless attempts to cause distress and wreak havoc among members of an online community merely rude behavior protected by the First Amendment or do they rise to the level of criminal actions?

Recently, some social networks have begun to respond to harassing content. In 2013, a well-known female historian in the United Kingdom received multiple rape

In September 2010, an eighteen-year-old Rutgers freshman, Tyler Clementi, jumped to his death off the George Washington Bridge. Clementi's roommate, Dharun Ravi, and Molly Wei, a resident of the dorm, used Ravi's webcam to secretly record and then transmit to Wei's computer images of Clementi kissing another man. Clementi's death heightened the awareness and consequences of cyberbullying.

threats because she tweeted her wish to see Jane Austin on the ten-pound note. After feminists called for a boycott of Twitter, the company offered an apology and made it easier for users to report abusive messages.[14]

Another issue is sexting, the transmission of sexually explicit messages or photos, usually by cell phone. Sexting became part of the political world when U.S. Representative Anthony Weiner of New York resigned after he admitted to sending a series of explicit tweets to about six women over a three-year period. This is also an issue for schools, albeit not a new one. School policies vary dramatically, as some make it clear that students have no expectation of privacy, and searches of the content of phones are common. (The argument from schools with more aggressive policies is that because students have no expectation of privacy in their lockers or backpacks, they should not expect searches of their phones to be exempt.) Other school districts have less aggressive policies and tend to leave the matter to police departments. In many cases of sexting, it is not clear what crime has been committed; however, when the sexting involves children, police departments in most jurisdictions have treated it as the distribution of pornography.

Participation in social networks also raises serious work-related issues. Many companies and governmental agencies have created policies regulating the content of employees' online postings. Are such policies legitimate, or are they illegal infringements of employees' protected speech rights? In a series of rulings, the National Labor Relations Board (NLRB) has taken the lead in answering workplace questions of this nature. The agency has generally ruled that employers may not discipline employees for their comments on social networks so long as the comments represent "concerted activity" designed to promote "mutual aid." Thus, if a group of employees post online comments in an effort to improve wages or working conditions, they are exercising their First Amendment rights. Put another way, employees have a right to talk about working conditions around the water cooler or on Facebook—in both cases the speech is protected. If, on the other hand, a single employee uses the postings simply to rant, making no effort to engage colleagues in "concerted effort," that employee is not protected by the First Amendment and thus may be disciplined.

Several federal courts have also accepted the argument that posts on social networks are protected speech. In one recent example, the U.S. Court of Appeals for the Fourth Circuit in Richmond, Virginia, ruled that "liking" something on Facebook was the "Internet equivalent of displaying a political sign in one's front yard," an action long regarded as free speech. Thus the free speech claims of six employees of a sheriff's office fired for "liking" the web page of the sheriff's electoral opponent were vindicated.[15]

As has often been the case, our laws trail behind technology. These and other emerging issues serve as a reminder that our understanding of free speech (or, for that matter, any of our liberties) is not static.

Freedom of the Press

Given the close link between free speech and freedom of the press in the language of the First Amendment, it isn't surprising that many of the lines of reasoning that apply in free speech cases also fit those of freedom of the press. As with free

Prior restraint The government's blocking of a publication before it can be made available to the public. The Supreme Court has repeatedly struck down laws that imposed prior restraint on publications.

Libel The use of print or pictures to harm someone's reputation; it is punishable by criminal law and subject to civil suits for damages.

Slander Injury by spoken word. Like libel, it is outside First Amendment protection and punishable by criminal law and civil suits.

speech, the majority of Supreme Court justices have rejected the proposition that freedom of the press is an absolute.

Prior Restraint. Even though the Supreme Court has never accepted complete freedom of the press, it has repeatedly struck down laws that impose prior restraint. **Prior restraint** means blocking a publication from reaching the public. The First Amendment has stood as a strong check against would-be censors. The first significant prior restraint case, *Near v. Minnesota* (1931), illustrates this stance.[16]

At issue in *Near* was a state statute that provided for the banning of "malicious, scandalous and defamatory" newspapers or periodicals. After he had printed a series of articles criticizing the local police department, Jay Near, the publisher of the Minneapolis-based *Saturday Press*, was ordered to cease publication of the weekly scandal sheet. In addition to his attacks on city officials, every issue had an anti-Semitic, pro–Ku Klux Klan tone.

Clearly, the *Saturday Press* was malicious, scandalous, and defamatory. Yet the Supreme Court lifted the ban on publication, with Chief Justice Charles E. Hughes observing that prior restraint could be applied only in "exceptional cases." Hughes admitted that under some circumstances the government might prohibit the publishing of truly harmful information—for example, information about troop movements in wartime. But in ordinary circumstances, the presumption should be in favor of publication.

A more serious challenge to freedom of the press arose in *New York Times v. United States* (1971), also known as the Pentagon Papers case.[17] Both the *New York Times* and the *Washington Post* published portions of a classified report on the history of American involvement in Vietnam. Citing a breach of national security, the government sought an order preventing further publication of the material by the two newspapers. A divided Court (six to three) ruled that the newspapers could continue publishing the report because the government had not justified the need for prior restraint. Only Justices Black and William Douglas took the position that the government could never restrain publication, however. The four others in the majority assumed that, in extreme cases, national security could justify an injunction, thus raising the possibility of a constitutional exercise of prior restraint.

The great leeway that the Court has granted the press in the area of prior restraint does not mean that the press is free to do as it pleases without regard to consequences. The press can be punished *after* publication. Two forms of expression, libel and obscenity, are particularly open to punishment.

Libel. **Libel** is the use of print or pictures to harm someone's reputation, whereas **slander** is injury by spoken word. Traditionally, these actions have not received First Amendment protection; therefore, they have been punishable under criminal law and subject to civil prosecution for damages.

Until 1964, a plaintiff could win a libel suit simply by proving that the statements in question were substantially false. In 1964, however, the Court expanded protection of the press by requiring public officials who claimed to have been libeled to prove that the statements were made with "actual malice."[18] To recover damages, a public official must prove not only that the accusation is false but also that the publisher acted "with knowledge that it was false or with reckless disregard of whether it was false or not." This actual malice standard was later extended to cover public figures—private citizens who, because of their station in life or their activities, are newsworthy. Actual malice is virtually impossible to prove; therefore, the Court's decisions immunized the press against libel suits by public officials and public figures.

Obscenity. Obscenity has never been considered deserving of First Amendment protection. Any work that is judged obscene may be banned. But what is obscene? Again and again the Court has confronted that question, and each time the justices have struggled to give meaning to the elusive concept.

In the first of the modern obscenity cases, *Roth v. United States* (1957),[19] Justice Brennan observed that sex and obscenity are not synonymous. Consequently, Brennan tried to formulate a legal test for obscenity that would protect the right to deal with sexual matters and yet reserve to the government the power to prohibit what was truly obscene. The test he proposed was "whether to the average person, applying contemporary community standards, the dominant theme of the material taken as a whole appeals to prurient interest." Later cases attempted to clarify this test by (1) describing the community standards as national standards, not local ones, and (2) requiring proof that the work was "utterly without redeeming social value."[20] This latter aspect of the test made it virtually impossible for prosecutors to obtain pornography convictions.

In the 1970s, believing that previous decisions had gone too far in protecting offensive materials, the Court, led by Chief Justice Warren Burger, reworked the standards in an effort to limit the spread of sexually explicit materials. Beginning with *Miller v. California* (1973), the Court has held that prosecutors do not need to demonstrate that the work is "utterly without redeeming social value."[21] Instead, prosecutors have to prove only that the work "lacks serious literary, artistic, political, or scientific value."

In the *Miller* decision, the Court also rejected the previous rulings that community standards mean national standards. Arguing that it is unrealistic to require the same standard in Maine or Mississippi as in Las Vegas or New York, Chief Justice Burger expressed faith in the ability of jurors to draw on the standards of their local community. Nevertheless, the question of what constitutes obscenity remains a perplexing judicial and social issue, with the Court's decisions allowing considerable variability among communities.

None of these standards, however, is directly applicable to materials that depict children. Over the years the Court has consistently held that the government's interest in protecting children from abuse allows for greater latitude in regulating the production and distribution of materials. Works that depict children may be obscene without appealing to the prurient interest of the average person or portraying sexual conduct that is patently offensive.

POLITICS & POPULAR CULTURE: Visit the book's companion website at **www.oup.com/us/gitelson** to read the special feature *What Does a Wardrobe Malfunction Cost?*

Freedom of Religion

The freedom to worship was one of the dominant motives behind the founding of the American colonies. Yet, surprisingly, the original Constitution makes only one mention of religion: Article VI states, in part, "No religious test shall ever be required as a qualification to any office or public trust under the United States." Not until the First Amendment do we find guarantees of religious freedom. The amendment begins, "Congress shall make no law respecting an establishment of religion, or prohibiting the free exercise thereof."

As we have seen, the myth of absolute liberty has seldom been upheld, because First Amendment rights have often conflicted with other rights and important social values. The problem is particularly acute in the case of religious freedom. The guarantee of the free exercise of religion clearly means that the state must avoid coercion with regard to religious beliefs. But what should be done when social policies offend particular religious beliefs? Does the state have the right to require school attendance and vaccination of public school students whose religious beliefs forbid such practices? Of course, the easy answer is to make an exception, but exceptions run the risk of violating another First Amendment provision—the establishment clause—by showing favoritism to one religion.[22]

Accommodationist interpretation A reading of the establishment clause that bars only the establishment by Congress of an official public church. Accommodationists agree with state support of religion as long as all religions are treated equally.

Wall of separation An interpretation of the establishment clause that requires a complete separation of government and religion.

Establishment of Religion. What does the establishment clause mean? One view, known as the **accommodationist interpretation**, holds that the clause was meant to be interpreted narrowly, merely barring Congress from establishing an official, publicly supported church. Proponents of this view contend that nothing in the establishment clause forbids state support of religion as long as all religions are treated equally.

Others see the establishment clause as a broad-based prohibition against any governmental support of religion. They read the First Amendment as banning governmental involvement in all religious affairs, even when such involvement is conducted in a completely even-handed way. Advocates of this view claim that the First Amendment requires a complete separation of the government and religion, or, as Thomas Jefferson put it, a "**wall of separation**" between church and state.

The Supreme Court has consistently espoused the wall of separation view. Yet in many cases the Court's decisions appear contradictory. They indicate that the justices have not completely rejected the idea of governmental aid to religious institutions so long as the government does not favor one religion over others. The debate over the establishment clause usually focuses on two issues: aid to religious schools and prayer in public schools. The question of governmental aid to church-supported educational institutions has long been a problem for the Court. In 1947, the Court allowed to stand a New Jersey plan that provided free bus transportation for children attending parochial schools.[23] Justice Black, writing for the Court, reasoned that the plan was designed to aid the children and their families, not the religious institutions. Using this so-called child-benefit theory, the Court has sustained state programs providing parochial schools with textbooks on secular subjects, school lunches, and public health services that are normally available in public schools.

Currently, the Court seems divided over establishment clause questions. Some members seek an accommodation of secular and religious practices, whereas others are intent on maintaining a high wall between church and state. A third group on the Court seeks to present a middle position. As a result, the Court has had difficulty drawing a clear line between permissible and impermissible aid programs.

Until 2002, this difficulty in assembling a coherent majority on the Court left open the question of the validity of **school vouchers**—programs that provide state funds to parents who want to send their child to a school other than the assigned public school. In 2002, however, the Supreme Court seemingly settled this issue. Writing for a sharply divided Court, Chief Justice Rehnquist upheld Ohio's Pilot Project Scholarship Program. Under this program, parents of Cleveland schoolchildren can receive up to $2,250 for tuition at any public or participating private school in the city. Any private school in the city, including religious schools, is eligible to participate as long as it meets state standards and pledges not to discriminate on the basis of race, religion, or ethnicity. The effect of the program, at least in the short term, is to provide, through the parents, state funds to religious schools. In the first year of the program, 3,700 Cleveland students participated, and 96 percent of the vouchers went to religious schools. Nevertheless, the majority ruled that the program was "entirely neutral with respect to religion" and therefore was constitutional. Because the program allowed parents a true choice between public and private—whether secular or religious—education, it did not violate the establishment clause.[24]

With regard to the second question, the Court's decisions on prayer in public schools have created intense controversy. In 1962, public protests followed a ruling that a nondenominational prayer of twenty-two words composed by the

School vouchers Programs that provide state funds to parents who want to send their child to a private school rather than the assigned public school.

Prayer in public schools is not, the Supreme Court has told us, constitutional if it is government sponsored. Athletic teams, like the East Brunswick High School football team, pictured here, often gather together for prayer prior to the start of a game. Whether or not these activities are constitutional depends on whether the Supreme Court believes the prayer to be government sponsored or a matter of individual choice.

New York State Board of Regents for daily recitation by New York schoolchildren violated the establishment clause.[25] One year later, the Court added to the controversy by declaring unconstitutional a Pennsylvania law requiring public schools to begin each day with a short reading from the Bible.[26]

Despite the fierce opposition of many religious and political leaders, the Court has maintained its stance that government-sponsored prayers in the classroom violate the First Amendment. In fact, the Court has never prohibited prayer in public schools; rather, it has forbidden governmental encouragement of or involvement in prayer. However, none of the frequent efforts to institute voluntary prayer in schools has met with the Court's approval. Indeed, the 2000 case of *Santa Fe Independent School District v. Doe* carried these decisions a step further when the Court struck down a Texas school district's practice of permitting a student, elected by the student body, to deliver an invocation before all home football games. According to Justice John Paul Stevens, "The religious liberty protected by the Constitution is abridged when the state affirmatively sponsors the particular religious practice of prayer."[27]

We must understand, though, that the Court has not opposed all exercise of religion in public life. For example, the Court has sustained the practice of opening sessions of Congress and state legislatures with a prayer.[28]

Tests like these may be relegated to history, however, if the Court's 2010 decision in *Salazar v. Buono*[29] becomes the norm. The Salazar case involved a small Latin cross honoring World War I veterans in the Mojave National Forest. Critics claimed that placing the cross on public land amounted to a governmental endorsement of religion—specifically Christianity. Writing for the five-member majority, Justice Kennedy argued that the First Amendment calls for "a policy of accommodation toward religious displays on public land, not strict separation of church and state." Besides, the Latin cross was more than a religious statement; in the context of a war memorial "it evokes thousands of small crosses in foreign fields marking the graves of Americans who fell in battles, battles whose tragedies are compounded if the fallen are forgotten." Only time will tell, but Justice Kennedy's language in the Salazar case suggests that the accommodationists may have finally found the majority that they have been lacking.

Free Exercise of Religion. The First Amendment also guarantees that Congress shall not prohibit the free exercise of religion. Thus, we are free to adopt any set of beliefs and to call anything a religion.

Freedom to believe, however, is not the same as freedom to act. You can believe in a religion that demands human sacrifice, but the state has a right to make such sacrifices a crime. Following this reasoning, the Court has upheld a law that made it a crime to have more than one husband or wife at the same time, despite objections from some religious sects.[30] It has also sustained Sunday-closing laws that have caused problems for Orthodox Jews[31] and laws that require children to be vaccinated despite their parents' religious objections.[32] In each of these cases, the Court argued that the guarantee of free exercise cannot be absolute. The justices did, however, recognize that laws that apply to the general population but unduly burden the free exercise of religion violate the First Amendment, unless the state demonstrates an especially important and compelling interest in the regulations. Illustrative of this approach was the Court's 1972 decision in *Wisconsin v. Yoder*, which exempted Amish children from compulsory school attendance laws.[33] The Court concluded that Wisconsin's general interest in an educated population did not justify restricting the free exercise of Amish religious beliefs.

Radically departing from this precedent, in *Employment Division v. Smith* (1990), the Court ruled that state drug laws need not make exceptions for the sacramental use of drugs by religious sects.[34] Specifically, the Court concluded that the state of Oregon did not have to provide unemployment benefits to a worker who was fired for violating state drug laws because he had ingested peyote as part of a ceremony of the Native American Church. Although the Oregon Supreme Court reasoned that the use of the hallucinogenic plant was protected by the free exercise clause, the U.S. Supreme Court disagreed. Such restrictions on the exercise of religion were, according to Justice Antonin Scalia, permissible, as they were "merely the incidental effect of a generally applicable and otherwise valid provision." In other words, so long as the restrictions applied to all persons and were not intended to deny the free exercise of religious belief, the states needed to offer no compelling justification for the restraints. Under this reasoning, the states were given far more latitude in regulating religious institutions.

Following the *Employment Division v. Smith* decision, Catholic teaching hospitals in Maryland lost their accreditation for refusing to perform abortions. Distressed by the ramifications of the decision, a nearly unanimous Congress passed the Religious Freedom Restoration Act of 1993 (RFRA). Under the terms of the act, government may not "substantially burden" a person's religious practices, even if the burden results from a generally applicable law, unless the government can demonstrate that the law (1) is in furtherance of a compelling governmental interest (e.g., health or safety) and (2) is the least restrictive means of furthering that compelling interest. With this act, Congress directly overturned the *Smith* case.

Congress did not have the last word on the subject, however. In the 1997 case of *City of Boerne v. Flores*, the Court considered the constitutionality of the RFRA.[35] In *Boerne*, a Roman Catholic church in Boerne, Texas, sought to overturn a local zoning ordinance that prevented it from expanding its original building. Claiming that the ordinance substantially burdened the free exercise of religion, the church argued that the RFRA exempted it from the zoning ordinance.

Justice Anthony Kennedy delivered a stinging rebuke to Congress, declaring that the lawmakers had seized power that was not granted to the legislature. Congress had justified the passage of the RFRA under Section 5 of the Fourteenth Amendment (which empowers Congress to enforce the provisions of the Fourteenth Amendment by legislation). However, Justice Kennedy argued, Congress had not attempted to enforce a right guaranteed by the Fourteenth Amendment. Instead, he charged, it had attempted to create a right by changing the meaning of the free exercise clause. In passing the RFRA, Justice Kennedy declared, Congress had attempted to determine "what constitutes a constitutional violation." In other words, Congress had sought to overturn a Supreme Court interpretation of the Constitution by simple statute. This action, he argued, is not within its powers.

Seventeen years after the *Boerne* decision, the Court resurrected the RFRA in granting religious liberties to some companies. In the 2014 case of *Burwell v. Hobby Lobby*, a divided court ruled that closely held (family owned) companies could assert religious rights under the RFRA. The owners of Hobby Lobby contended that Affordable Care Act provisions that required them to provide female employees no-cost birth control coverage violated their religious beliefs. Justice Alito, writing for the majority, argued that closely held for-profit corporations could assert religious rights under the RFRA. Moreover, Alito asserted that requiring the owners of the company to provide contraceptive coverage constituted a substantial burden on their religious views.

The Second Amendment and the Right to Keep and Bear Arms

> **To what extent is gun ownership protected by the Second Amendment?**

The Second Amendment to the Constitution specifies that "a well-regulated Militia, being necessary to the security of a free State, the right of the people to keep and bear Arms, shall not be infringed." Prior to 2008, the U.S. Supreme Court had handed down only four decisions that interpreted the Second Amendment; all had consistently ruled that the right is qualified by the clause stating that it is "necessary for the security of a free State." To the Court, this meant that the amendment protects a collective right, preventing the national government from abolishing state militias, not an individual right of gun ownership. In 1939, for instance, the Supreme Court ruled that a federal law prohibiting the transportation of sawed-off shotguns was not in violation of the Second Amendment. Justice McReynolds made this clear when he wrote, "In the absence of any evidence tending to show that possession or use of a 'shotgun having a barrel of less than eighteen inches in length' at this time has some reasonable relationship to the preservation or efficiency of a well regulated militia, we cannot say that the Second Amendment guarantees the right to keep and bear such an instrument."[36]

In the 2008 case *Heller v. District of Columbia*, however, the Supreme Court rejected that view. Writing for the majority, Justice Scalia stressed the amendment's use of the phrase "the right of the people" as demonstrating that this was indeed an individual, not a collective, right—the individual right here being the right to own a gun for self-defense. Although Justice Scalia's decision pointed out that the Second Amendment right to own guns is not unlimited, the decision rejected as unconstitutional the District of Columbia's absolute ban on the possession of handguns. Because the District of Columbia is not a state, the question of incorporation was not an issue. That issue came before the high Court almost two years to the day after *Heller*. The Court, in *McDonald v. City of Chicago*, ruled that the right protected by the Second Amendment was applicable to the states

Left: In September 2013, Howard Schultz, CEO of Starbucks, wrote a public letter respectfully requesting that people not bring firearms into the chain's stores. Until that letter, Starbucks had been described as a friendly place for gun owners. In many regions, gun owners had held meetings at their local Starbucks.

Right: The U.S. Supreme Court has ruled that the Second Amendment grants individuals the right to own guns, but it has also said that the states could enact some reasonable restrictions. Just what constitutes reasonable restrictions remains bitterly debated in the country. Pictured here are people supporting what they believe to be reasonable restrictions following the tragedy at Sandy Hook, Connecticut, in which twenty students and six adults were killed by a gunman who then killed himself.

because that right was fundamental to our system of ordered liberty. Notably, Justice Alito's decision reaffirmed the *previous ruling* that states could enact some restrictions on firearms. Acceptable restrictions, Alito reasoned, included those meant to "prohibit . . . the possession of firearms by felons or mentally ill." Furthermore, states could prohibit the "carrying of firearms in sensitive places such as schools and government buildings." They could also impose "conditions and qualifications on the commercial sale of arms."

In the wake of a series of high-profile rampages, gun control advocates stepped up their push for stronger laws on gun ownership. They have had some success: Both Delaware and Illinois, for example, passed laws requiring background checks for private sales of guns. California limited the right to purchase semiautomatic rifles with detachable magazines, and Connecticut added more than one hundred more firearms to its banned list. Similarly, both New York and Colorado toughened their gun laws. Gun-rights activists, however, have had many more victories. Illinois, for instance, became the last state to allow concealed-carry permits. Moreover, as a reaction to the stricter controls passed in Colorado, two prominent state legislators lost recall elections, elections in which gun control law was the only issue.[37] In New York, several upstate sheriffs have sworn to disregard the new laws. The two sides will continue to promote their positions, and the Supreme Court will be challenged to define when government can limit gun rights.

Due Process and Crime

> **What are the constitutional rights of those accused of crimes?**

Like the liberties discussed earlier, the rights of persons accused of crimes are rooted in the Bill of Rights, especially the Fifth Amendment's guarantee of "due process of law." These rights are meant to protect the individual from the arbitrary use of police power. When it comes to criminal suspects, however, there is little public support for the myth of absolute liberty. The Court has tried to balance the majority's demand for protection from criminals against the individual's need to be protected from excessive governmental power.

Right to Counsel

The Sixth Amendment to the Constitution guarantees an accused person the right to representation by a lawyer. For most of our history, however, the states were not required to provide attorneys to poor defendants, even though most prosecutions occur in state courts. In 1932, the Supreme Court did declare, in *Powell v. Alabama*, that in capital offenses—those carrying the death penalty—the state was obligated to provide a lawyer to those unable to afford one.[38] The occasion for the ruling was a famous trial known as the Scottsboro case. In that trial, which lasted only one day, Ozie Powell and seven other young black men were charged with and convicted of raping two young white women. Before the trial, the local magistrate had appointed all members of the local bar as counsel for the defendants. None of these lawyers stepped forward to mount an actual defense, and the eight were sentenced to death without ever having had adequate time to secure effective counsel.

Not until 1963 did the Supreme Court, in *Gideon v. Wainwright*, extend the state's obligation to provide a lawyer to everyone charged with a felony.[39] Nine years later, the Court broadened the guarantee to cover any penniless defendant being tried for an offense for which the penalty is a jail term.[40] Considerably more controversial were the Court's decisions providing for the right to counsel before trial. The Warren Court expanded the right to counsel to include the investigative stages preceding the trial. Justice Arthur Goldberg, speaking for the Court in *Escobedo v. Illinois* (1964), announced that the right to counsel applied whenever the investigation turned from a general inquiry to a focus "on a particular suspect."[41]

Two years later, the Court bolstered the *Escobedo* decision by requiring that police officers inform suspects of their constitutional rights. In overturning the rape-kidnapping conviction of Ernesto Miranda, the Court, in *Miranda v.*

Pictured here with Sam Leibowitz, an out-of-state lawyer provided by a labor organization, are the Scottsboro defendants. The young men underwent four trials, and the last of the group remained in jail until 1950. In 2013, eighty-two years after their convictions, the Scottsboro boys were granted a posthumous pardon.

Arizona (1966), created specific guidelines for police interrogations.[42] All suspects must be informed that

- They have the right to remain silent

- Anything they say may be used against them in a court of law

- They have the right to the presence of an attorney, and if they cannot afford an attorney, one can be appointed prior to any questioning

These warnings do not have to be given in this exact form, however. Police officers need only provide their equivalent.[43]

Miranda rights have become a basic part of police practices, but subsequent Supreme Court decisions have allowed several exceptions to the rule. For instance, the Court let stand the rape conviction of Benjamin Quarles in 1984. Before the *Miranda* warnings were read to him, Quarles, at the request of the police, implicated himself in the crime by pointing to the place where they could find the weapon he had used in the attack. In upholding Quarles's conviction, the Court argued that considerations of public safety may outweigh the need to strictly adhere to the *Miranda* decision.[44] Carving out an even more important exception, the Rehnquist Court ruled that the admission at a trial of an illegally co-erced confession does not require overturning the conviction if, given all the other evidence, the impact of the confession was harmless.[45] The admission of an illegally acquired confession may be considered simply a harmless error if other evidence, gathered independently of the confession, substantiates a guilty verdict.

Moreover, according to the 2010 decision in *Berghuis v. Thompkins*, suspects who have been given the Miranda warnings must explicitly invoke their rights. Silence alone does not constitute an assertion of the right to be silent. In this case, Thompkins remained silent for almost three hours of interrogation. Eventually, an interrogator asked him, "Do you pray to God to forgive you for shooting that boy down?" Thompkins said simply, "Yes." That one-word answer was used at the trial in which Thompkins was convicted. On appeal, the U.S. Court of Appeals ruled that the answer could not be used at trial because Thompkins's long silence was clear evidence to the interrogators that he wished to invoke his constitutional right to remain silent. The Supreme Court disagreed, however. Writing for the five-justice majority, Justice Kennedy noted that silence alone does not invoke the constitutional right to silence. Instead, that right can be asserted only by an unambiguous statement that the suspect does not wish to talk.

Searches and Seizures

The Fourth Amendment states that "the right of the people to be secure in their persons, houses, papers, and effects, against unreasonable searches and seizures, shall not be violated." Notice that only "unreasonable" searches are prohibited. Unfortunately, the amendment does not tell us what is considered reasonable, making an absolute application of the amendment impossible.

As a general rule, a search may be conducted after a neutral magistrate issues a **search warrant**, which grants written permission. The authorities must fill out an application describing what they expect to find and where they expect to find it.

Search warrant A written grant of permission to conduct a search issued by a neutral magistrate to police authorities. Police must describe what they expect to find and must show probable cause.

In addition, the officers must set out facts that enable the magistrate to conclude that there is "probable cause" to justify issuing the warrant. Over the years, however, the Court has recognized certain exceptions to the warrant rule:

- If a suspect consents, a warrantless search is legal, even if the suspect was unaware of his or her right to refuse.[46]

- Recognizing that cars are mobile and relatively public places, the Court has allowed them to be searched without a warrant if the officer has probable cause.

- In 1991, the Court significantly expanded that exception by ruling that police officers may conduct warrantless searches of closed containers found in automobiles if they have probable cause to believe that those containers conceal contraband or evidence.

- Instances of "hot" pursuit also constitute an exception to the warrant requirement. Thus, police officers who are chasing a suspect need not turn back and acquire a warrant.

- In 1989, the Court created an additional exception by allowing drug agents, without warrants or probable cause, to use "drug courier" profiles to stop and search people who look like possible drug dealers.

- Police officers need not ignore evidence that they accidentally discover; the officers may seize anything that is in plain sight.

Since 1968, the Supreme Court has accepted a practice known as "stop and frisk," a tactic that allows police officers to briefly detain an individual for questioning while also doing a pat-down search. In *United States v. Terry* (1968), the justices referred to the importance of crime prevention. In order to prevent crime, the Court said, police officers needed flexibility. Rather than requiring probable cause, the Court allowed that, in the case of a stop (an act short of an arrest), police needed only to demonstrate reasonable suspicion. Nor was the Fourth Amendment violated if, in the cause of personal safety, the officer performed a frisk, checking for guns or other weapons. Over the years, the Supreme Court became increasingly lenient in defining what constitutes reasonable suspicion.

Given the leeway provided by the Supreme Court, police in New York City originated a program called Operation Clean Halls, based on an aggressive practice of stopping and frisking thousands of New York pedestrians each year. In August 2013, U.S. district court judge Shira Scheindlin ruled that the stop-and-frisk practice violated the Fourth Amendment (see Chapter 2). Judge Scheindlin noted that tens of thousands of New Yorkers each year were subject to stop and frisk and that 90 percent of them were cleared and sent on their way. The judge also noted that the practice was applied disproportionally to African Americans and Hispanic Americans. Although former mayor Michael Bloomberg vowed to appeal any decision limiting the city's stop-and-frisk policies, his successor, Mayor Bill de Blasio, entered into a settlement agreeing to implement the reforms ordered by the court.

Before 1961, few effective checks on police searches existed. An individual who was subjected to an illegal search could sue the police for civil damages, but juries rarely sympathized with criminal suspects. Evidence found through a search was admissible in state trials even if it had been gathered illegally. Thus, in 1957, police officers in Cleveland, Ohio, broke into the home of Dollree Mapp and seized pornographic materials while looking for a fugitive. Mapp was convicted of possession of the pornographic materials seized in the warrantless search. On appeal, the Supreme Court in *Mapp v. Ohio* (1961) overturned Mapp's conviction, ruling that evidence that was gathered illegally was inadmissible in state trials.[47] This **exclusionary rule** means that evidence, no matter how incriminating, cannot be used to convict someone if it is gathered illegally. (See Asked & Answered, p. 138, for more on the legality of police entering a private home.)

> **Exclusionary rule** The principle that evidence, no matter how incriminating, cannot be used to convict someone if it is gathered illegally. This concept was established by the Supreme Court in *Mapp v. Ohio* (1961).

Perhaps no other criminal law ruling has stirred up as much controversy as the exclusionary rule. The exclusionary rule provoked such a furor because it dramatizes the conflict between the due process rights of individuals and society's interests in controlling crime. Despite this, the Court has continued to enforce the exclusionary rule, although the justices have limited its reach by creating some broad exceptions. In 1984, for instance, the Court adopted what is called an "inevitable discovery exception." It permits the introduction of evidence that was collected illegally when such evidence would have been discovered anyway.[48] More important, that same year the Court allowed what is called the "good faith exception." If the police conduct a search using a warrant that later turns out to be invalid, the evidence discovered during the search is admissible at trial.[49]

Cruel and Unusual Punishment

In the 1962 case *Robinson v. California*, the Supreme Court made the Eighth Amendment's protection against the imposition of "cruel and unusual punishments" applicable to the states.[50] But beyond noting that the punishment must fit the crime, the justices did little to explain what the terms *cruel* and *unusual* meant. Lawrence Robinson had been convicted under a statute that made it a misdemeanor to be addicted to narcotics. Robinson was not under the influence of narcotics at the time of his arrest, nor were any narcotics found on him. The police officer made the arrest after observing needle marks on Robinson's arms. Likening this situation to being punished for having an illness, the Court argued that even one day in jail would be excessive.

Court decisions that followed, however, have cast doubt on whether the punishment must fit the crime. In 1991, for instance, a majority of the Court upheld a Michigan law that mandated a prison term of life without the possibility of parole for a defendant found guilty of possessing 650 grams of cocaine.[51] Writing for Chief Justice Rehnquist and himself, Justice Scalia argued that nothing in the text or the history of the Eighth Amendment supported the belief that the harshness of the penalty must be proportional to the severity of the crime. According to Justice Scalia, the Court's Eighth Amendment analysis should be limited to death penalty cases. Justices Sandra Day O'Connor, Anthony Kennedy, and David Souter agreed that the Eighth Amendment did not require proportionality, but they did conclude that it prohibited extreme sentences that are "grossly disproportionate" to the crime. It is unclear what constitutes a grossly disproportionate sentence, but the Court will certainly revisit that issue as litigants begin to appeal the state and federal laws requiring mandatory life sentences for repeat offenders—the so-called three-strikes-you're-out statutes.

ASKED & ANSWERED

ASKED: Do police officers who are conducting a search have to knock and announce their presence before entering your home?

ANSWERED: Under English common law, "a man's home is his castle." This age-old maxim, known as the Castle Doctrine, provides that a homeowner may use all manner of force, including deadly force, to protect his or her house and its occupants. In the 1995 case *Wilson v. Arkansas*, the Supreme Court, relying on this doctrine, ruled that the police may not enter a home without first knocking and announcing their presence.

But the Court has acknowledged exceptions. Under certain exigencies, officers may acquire so-called no-knock search warrants, whereby police officers may forcibly enter a home without warning. It has been generally acknowledged, for instance, that officials may obtain a no-knock warrant from a judge if they reasonably believe that announcing their presence will endanger the lives of police officers or others in the home. No-knock warrants may also be issued if police have reason to believe that evidence may be destroyed if advance notice of the search is given. Additionally, courts have commonly accepted the evidence garnered from no-knock searches conducted without a specific no-knock warrant, if police can demonstrate that unanticipated exigencies existed at the scene of the search that demanded quick entry into the home.

Still, the Supreme Court has continued to rule that no-knock searches should be the exception and not the rule. In *Richards v. Wisconsin* (1977), the Court invalidated a conviction based on evidence (drugs) seized as the result of a no-knock search, because the state had legislated a blanket exception to the need to knock and announce in all felony drug cases.

Writing for the majority, Justice John Paul Stevens made it clear that the validity of a no-knock search would have to be established on a case-by-case basis and not by legislating the use of such searches for whole categories of crimes.

Conversely, in 2003 the Supreme Court ruled that federal agents executing a search warrant were constitutionally justified in waiting only fifteen or twenty seconds after knocking and announcing before forcibly entering a home. Writing for a unanimous Court in *United States v. Banks*, Justice David Souter argued that it was not how long it could reasonably take for someone to answer the door that mattered but rather how long it might take the occupants to dispose of any evidence that dictated how long the police have to wait before entering.

In principle, this fifteen- to twenty-second standard still applies, but the Court's 2006 decision in *Hudson v. Michigan* suggests a greatly diminished importance for the standard. The *Hudson* case involved a search by Detroit police in which they knocked and announced their presence but waited no more than five seconds before entering the property. A search of Mr. Hudson's home produced substantial quantities of cocaine. He was subsequently convicted. Because the lower courts in Michigan ruled that the police had conducted an illegal no-knock search, the Supreme Court did not reexamine the question of how long police officers had to wait before entering the house. Nevertheless, the Supreme Court upheld Mr. Hudson's conviction, ruling that the evidence gathered from an illegal no-knock search is not subject to the exclusionary rule and thus can be admitted at trial. Even though police officers executing a search warrant still need to wait at least fifteen seconds after knocking and announcing their presence, failure to do so does not invalidate any evidence they may seize.

In 1972 the Court addressed the most controversial of punishments: the death penalty. In *Furman v. Georgia*, a divided Court concluded that capital punishment was, in that particular case, a violation of the Eighth Amendment.[52] The Court did not reject the death penalty itself as unconstitutional; instead, the Court focused on what one justice referred to as the "wanton and freakish" pattern of the penalty's imposition (see Figure 4.1). Thus, although the Court declared

In recent years the number of U.S. prisoners executed has declined. Nevertheless, executions are still carried out in this country. Americans are divided on the question of executions. Many believe that the possibility of execution deters some from committing capital crimes, whereas others reject the idea that the death penalty provides deterrence.

Executions by Year Since 1976

FIGURE 4.1 Number of Executions in the United States by Year Since 1976

Source: Death Penalty Information Center, http://www.deathpenaltyinfo.org/executions-year.

Georgia's death penalty unconstitutional, it also encouraged states to draft more precise laws that would guide judges and juries.

In the past few years, the Court has imposed additional limits. In 2002, the Court ruled that executing the mentally retarded violated the ban on cruel and unusual punishment. That same year, the Court ruled that the death penalty may be imposed only by a jury or a judge acting on the recommendation of a jury. Judges may not independently impose capital punishment.[53] In 2005, the Court, in *Roper v. Simmons*, concluded that the Constitution prohibits execution for crimes committed before the age of eighteen. In the 2008 case *Kennedy v. Louisiana*, the Court ruled that applying the death penalty as punishment for child rape violates the Eighth Amendment. Justice Kennedy argued that applying the death penalty to such cases actually provides victims with less protection, as the rapist, facing the death penalty, would have greater incentive to kill the victim, removing, in most cases, the only witness to the crime.

With the focus still on sentencing juveniles, the Court overturned the life-without-parole sentence that a Florida court had given Terrance Graham. As a sixteen-year-old, Mr. Graham had been convicted of armed robbery, following his participation in a series of violent home invasions. In writing the opinion, Justice Kennedy returned to the idea of a national consensus that sentencing a juvenile to life without parole is cruel and unusual punishment, especially if the crime was not murder. The state does not have to guarantee that the juvenile will be released at some point, but it does have to offer some realistic opportunity for release.

Privacy

> ### Does the Constitution provide a right to privacy?

In the 1890s, Charles Warren and Louis Brandeis first articulated the notion of a right to privacy.[54] They hoped to establish the "right to be let alone," but the concept did not easily find a place in American law. In fact, the Supreme Court did not recognize or create such a right until its 1965 decision in *Griswold v. Connecticut*.[55] Dr. Estelle Griswold had been convicted under a Connecticut law that made it illegal to provide birth control devices or even give instruction on their use. When the case was appealed to the Supreme Court, the majority argued that the law unduly interfered with married couples' right to privacy. Because the Constitution does not specifically mention a right of privacy, it took great pains to demonstrate that, taken together, several provisions of the Bill of Rights created such a right.

Abortion

In one of the most controversial decisions it ever delivered—*Roe v. Wade* (1973)—the Supreme Court extended the right of privacy to cover abortions.[56] The Court ruled that in the first trimester of a pregnancy, the decision about abortion rested with the woman. In the second trimester, the state could, to protect the health of the woman, dictate general rules governing the procedure, such as requiring that it be performed in a hospital. Only in the third trimester could the state prohibit abortion altogether.

For sixteen years the Court continued to apply the trimester approach developed in *Roe*. In 1989, however, the Court signaled a clear change in direction. In *Webster v. Reproductive Health Services*, the majority let stand state regulations that significantly limited a woman's right to an abortion.[57] The Missouri law that was at issue in *Webster* required doctors to conduct tests of viability—tests to determine whether the fetus could survive outside the womb—whenever there was reason to believe that the woman was twenty or more weeks pregnant. Because twenty weeks is within the second trimester, the Court, by upholding the law, placed the trimester structure developed in *Roe* in grave doubt. Another provision that the Court let stand banned the use of public facilities for abortions and prohibited state employees from performing abortions. Although the decision stopped short of overturning *Roe*, the case demonstrated that the majority was willing to uphold a wide array of restrictions.

The *Webster* decision led many to assume that a constitutionally protected right to abortion could not survive further Court scrutiny. Expecting a definitive overturning of *Roe*, both supporters and opponents of abortion rights anxiously awaited the Court's 1992 decision in *Planned Parenthood of Southeastern Pennsylvania v. Casey*.[58] The Court disappointed both sides. The 5–4 decision in *Casey* upheld several restrictions on abortions, including a requirement that a woman first be counseled on the risks of and alternatives to abortion and then wait at least twenty-four hours after the counseling to have the abortion. The narrow majority also upheld the state's ban on abortion after twenty-four weeks of pregnancy unless it was necessary to save the woman's life. More important, the Court rejected the trimester framework developed in *Roe*. Nevertheless, the Court fell short of overturning *Roe*, declaring that a woman's right to terminate her pregnancy "is a rule of law and a component of liberty we cannot renounce." In place of the trimester formulation of *Roe*, the Court substituted the "undue burden" test. An undue burden is any law that "has the purpose or effect of placing a substantial obstacle in the path of a woman seeking an abortion of a nonviable fetus." Nevertheless, in the 2007 case *Gonzales v. Carhart*, the Court upheld the federal Partial-Birth Abortion Act.[59] The *Gonzales* decision encouraged states to pass more laws testing the Court's commitment to precedent, guaranteeing that the issue of abortion is bound to appear before the Court yet again.

Doctor-Assisted Suicide

The controversial question of doctor-assisted suicide is an intensely divisive moral issue. The Supreme Court has denied that there is a constitutional right to doctor-assisted suicide. In 1997, the Court unanimously rejected a lower court decision that the right to die with dignity was an aspect of liberty protected by the Fourteenth Amendment. The state, Chief Justice Rehnquist argued, has "an unqualified interest in the preservation of human life." The state also has an interest in protecting vulnerable groups (the poor, the disabled, and the elderly) from the risk of "subtle coercion and undue influence in end-of-life situations."[60] These interests, Rehnquist argued, outweigh whatever interests individuals may have in assisted suicide.

In a second case decided in 1997, the Court rejected a lower court's ruling that banning doctor-assisted suicide constituted a denial of equal protection of the laws. The lower court had reasoned that because the terminally ill have a right to discontinue life-support systems and therefore end their lives, it is a denial of equal protection to prohibit terminally ill patients who are not on life-support systems from choosing immediate death. Again speaking for a unanimous Court, the chief justice wrote, "Unlike the court of appeals, we think the distinction between assisting suicide and withdrawing life-sustaining treatment, a distinction widely recognized and endorsed in the medical profession and in our legal traditions, is both important and logical."[61] Nevertheless, five justices clouded this distinction by conceding that patients are entitled to pain relief, even if the doses needed to relieve the pain might result in the death of the patient.

Far from resolving the issue, these cases are only the beginning of the debate. The Court has ruled that states may prohibit doctor-assisted suicide, but nothing in its decisions requires states to make the practice illegal.

Conclusion

Americans are of two minds when it comes to making sense of civil liberties. On the one hand, many of us adhere to the desirability of absolute liberty—that is, a life in which we can live with minimal or no government interference. On the other hand, we are well aware of the fact that we cannot operate in a world of absolute liberties, and we therefore accept the fact that somebody needs to deal with the conflicts that result when our desire for complete freedom is challenged by other, widely held values. As we have discussed throughout this chapter, the Supreme Court—the federal institution that is most directly responsible for reconciling conflicting values—has never accepted the myth of absolute freedom. Nevertheless, for many citizens, the myth lives on, especially with regard to First and Second Amendment freedoms.

The Court's role in dealing with these conflicts is particularly important when it comes to the liberties guaranteed to those suspected of criminal activity. There tends to be little public support for the myth of absolute freedom when it comes to the liberties of criminal suspects. The Court has tried to balance the majority's demand for protection from crime against appropriate constitutional protections for suspects. A society that disregards the rights of defendants risks creating a police state that ignores all individual rights. Yet all societies must be able to prevent lawless behavior.

Key Terms

Accommodationist interpretation
  p. 128
Bad tendency test p. 121
Civil liberties p. 115
Civil rights p. 115
Clear and present danger
  test p. 121

Exclusionary rule p. 137
Homeland security p. 147
Libel p. 126
National security
  policies p. 146
Preferred freedoms
  test p. 122

Prior restraint p. 126
School vouchers p. 129
Search warrant p. 135
Selective incorporation
  p. 118
Slander p. 126
Wall of separation p. 128

Focus Questions Review

1. How has the Bill of Rights been applied to the states? > > >
- Originally, the Bill of Rights did not restrict the actions of state governments. Through a process known as selective incorporation, however, the Supreme Court has made most of its provisions applicable to the states as well as to the national government.

2. What balances has the Court established in applying the First Amendment? > > >
- Rejecting the position that all forms of speech are protected, the Court has attempted to balance conflicting interests, using a series of tests that consider the impact of the speech. Sometimes the Court has favored comparatively few restrictions on free speech, but at other times it has permitted more restrictions.
- As with freedom of speech, the Court has rejected the argument that freedom of the press is an absolute; however, the justices have been unwilling to permit prior restraint—that is, blocking a publication from reaching the public. After publication, the press can be punished for libel or obscenity.
- The First Amendment prohibits the government from establishing a religion, and it also guarantees the free exercise of religion. The Supreme Court's interpretation of these provisions has

generated considerable controversy in American society.

3. To what extent is gun ownership protected by the Second Amendment? > > >
- The Supreme Court has ruled that the Second Amendment's reference to the right to keep and bear arms does grant an individual right. These rights are not unlimited, however. The Court has acknowledged that some regulation of firearms may pass constitutional muster.

4. What are the constitutional rights of those accused of crimes? > > >
- Although it has made some exceptions recently, the Court continues to require that a person suspected of a crime be allowed representation by counsel and be informed of that right, as well as of the right to remain silent. Evidence seized illegally cannot normally be used to convict, although the Supreme Court has recently made broad exceptions to that rule.

5. Does the Constitution provide a right to privacy? > > >
- Although neither the Constitution nor any of the amendments specifically mentions a right to privacy, the Supreme Court has decided that, taken together, several provisions of the Bill of Rights created such a right.

Review Questions

1. Write an essay in which you discuss how the ratification of the Fourteenth Amendment changed the understanding of the application of the Bill of Rights.
2. Write an essay in which you discuss the various constitutional protections that the Supreme Court has provided to criminal suspects.

For more information and access to study materials, visit the book's companion website at www.oup.com/us/gitelson.

How can the government maintain its commitment to civil liberties while minimizing the nation's vulnerability to attack?

The Policy Challenge

In the years following the attacks of September 11, 2001, Americans were confronted with a major policy challenge. As important as it is for the government to generate and maintain the support of the American people during a national security crisis, the social controls and intrusions into their private lives that might have to take place—actions that they would find unacceptable during peacetime—may require a reconsideration of those basic constitutional liberties we Americans hold so dear.

In this Policy Connection we consider the various policy approaches that the government has applied under conditions related to our national security or other national emergencies, especially those that seem to threaten our civil liberties, as we have discussed in Chapter 4.

President George W. Bush is informed of the attacks of September 11, 2001, by Andrew Card, his chief of staff.

"We Are Going to War"

Bob Woodward, one of America's best-known journalists, wrote of the moment that President George W. Bush learned of the attacks of September 11, 2001:

> A photo of that moment is etched for history. The president's hands are folded formally in his lap, his head turned to hear [Andrew] Card's words. His face has a distant sober look, almost frozen, edging on bewilderment. Bush remembers exactly what he was thinking: "They had declared war on us, and I made up my mind at that moment that we are going to war."[1]

The decision to commit the United States to any war effort has obvious policy implications, and the War on Terror initiated in response to 9/11 was no different. Not only do armies and navies have to be mobilized on behalf of the war effort, but so too do the nonmilitary human and economic resources necessary to conduct the war, including the hearts and minds of the American people.[2]

The Myth of Vulnerability

National security policies are those actions taken by government to safeguard the physical, economic, and social institutions that are deemed critical to our survival as a country. Implied in this definition is the idea that there exists a threat to that survival that must be responded to, and that the threat is aimed at not merely our physical territory but also our way of life.

In making sense of national security, we often rely on a myth that has deep roots in our history: *the myth of America's vulnerability*. According to the myth of vulnerability, from the time of its founding, the United States has always been under threat militarily, politically, and economically from a variety of external forces. With this in mind, Americans feel they must constantly guard against challenges to their territorial, political, and economic integrity. "We are and have always been a nation preoccupied with security," argue James Chace and Caleb Carr.[3] For at least the decades of the Cold War (generally dated from the end of World War II in 1945 to the collapse of the Soviet Union in 1991), this preoccupation led to an urge to achieve "absolute security" in the face of immediate and potential challenges, both real and perceived.

Many observers believed that after the fall of the Soviet Union, with America the one remaining superpower in the post–Cold War era, Americans would feel less vulnerable and more secure. But that has not been the case. From the Persian Gulf War of 1991 to the war on terrorism initiated after the attacks on the World Trade Center and the Pentagon in 2001, Americans have retained their sense that the United States will never escape from the many threats emanating from a hostile world.

In its contemporary version, the myth of vulnerability has been accompanied by a belief that America cannot address its exposure to these threats by withdrawing behind a wall of isolation, as it did before World War II. Rather, there is a strong commitment to the idea that the country's vulnerability would increase if it ever decided to disengage from world affairs. Between the two world wars, most Americans supported this nation's withdrawal from world affairs. The United States involved itself in only those events and crises that seemed to be in its narrowly defined national interest.

A vocal minority, however, has taken an opposite stand, expressing the position of putting "America first" and calling for the United States to assume a perspective that would minimize its involvement and entanglements in world affairs. During the 1990s, led by national figures such as former third-party presidential candidates Patrick Buchanan[4] and Ross Perot, this group advocated a return to an earlier era when the myth of vulnerability was complemented by a strong belief in America's "virtuous isolation" from world affairs.[5] The American public's reaction to September 11, however, demonstrated that the once strong pull of isolationism has been replaced with a worldview that accepts the inevitability of U.S. involvement in world affairs.

There are indications, however, that this view has changed in recent years. Perhaps as a result of America's post–9/11 commitments of tens of thousands of troops and billions of dollars to wars in Iraq and Afghanistan, public opinion polls began to reflect a growing sense of war wariness. More than 75 percent of the Americans surveyed in one major poll conducted in 2013 agreed or strongly agreed with the proposition that the United States needs to reduce its role as the world's policeman, and more than 80 percent felt that, at a time of economic and social stress, we should spend less on foreign assistance to other nations and devote more resources to solving problems at home. Nevertheless, that same poll indicated clear support for maintaining a strong military—an indication that Americans still view the world as threatening and the nation as vulnerable.[6]

Responses to Vulnerability

The Garrison-State Approach. How Americans view the country's vulnerability to national security threats gives us some interesting insights into public policies related to our civil liberties.[7] To the extent that we Americans have perceived the external enemies as a major and immediate threat, we have responded by creating what political scientist Harold Lasswell called the *garrison-state approach*.[8] During World War I, in order to deal with the threat of espionage and sabotage, Congress passed a number of acts limiting the freedom of speech and the press, and giving President Woodrow

Wilson the power to deport aliens and prosecute citizens for disloyalty or "seditious" acts that undermined the war effort. In World War II, Franklin Roosevelt issued an executive order that led to the forcible relocation of 110,000 residents of Japanese descent—two-thirds of them being either American born or naturalized citizens—from the West Coast to inland relocation camps.[9]

The Temporary-State-of-War Approach. In contrast to the garrison state approach, there have been times in our history when we adhered to what can be termed the *temporary-state-of-war approach*. This perspective reflected the belief that some measures taken during wartime or under emergency conditions are necessary but short term. Such actions do not rely on acts of Congress or major executive orders such as the one that led to the internment of the Japanese; rather, they are based on short-term declarations of emer-

At the start of World War II, a garrison-state mindset took hold in the United States. It led to a presidential executive order resulting in the internment of more than 110,000 individuals of Japanese ancestry, most of them U.S. citizens. More than four decades later, the U.S. Congress passed the Civil Liberties Act of 1988, which required government payment and a formal apology to survivors.

gency or martial law (military rule) that can involve the temporary suspension of everyday liberties. The public often accepts these edicts because they deem them necessary to bring an end to chaotic conditions. Underlying this approach is the belief that the sooner the immediate danger or threat passes, the sooner life—and liberties—can return to normal. During the Civil War, for example, Abraham Lincoln suspended the constitutional guarantee for a writ of habeas corpus (see Chapter 2) in certain parts of the country, and he also curbed freedom of speech and assembly in those areas placed under martial law.

Today, presidents and governors can and do declare state-of-emergency conditions after some major natural catastrophe. At times, those declarations suspend the normal operations of government and make demands on citizens to evacuate an area subject to flooding or to limit travel during a major snowstorm—demands that many citizens regard as temporary intrusions on their civil liberties. After September 11,

2001, however, the domestic capacities to deal with natural disasters through a short-term declaration of emergency became closely tied into the national security network designed to prevent more attacks on American soil, thus creating programs that come under the umbrella of **homeland security**. The result has been a change in state-of-emergency procedures in which the system, once triggered by an event such as the Boston Marathon bombings of 2013, defaults to procedures that immediately impose constraints on civil liberties.[10]

The Glass-Firewall Approach. Still another approach creates a *glass firewall* between those areas that are deemed important to national security and those that are not. This includes policies that limit civil liberties in matters classified as top secret or sensitive enough to warrant special treatment. Under this approach, freedoms associated with access to information or the distribution of information can be severely restricted.

The logic behind these policies is that keeping an "open society" requires that some information be kept confidential—what was described in a government manual as "secrecy in the public interest."

The amount of information behind the firewall expanded greatly during the Cold War, and what emerged was, according to one government study, a "culture of secrecy" that was threatening basic civil liberties. In 1997, Senator Daniel Patrick Moynihan headed a commission that concluded that the government must completely revamp its policies, giving as much consideration to the rights of individuals as to the need for confidentiality.[11]

A number of changes took place in response to the Moynihan Commission report, including a program of declassification throughout government and enhancement of the federal government's Freedom of Information Act policies. However, the 9/11 attacks and the War on Terror resulted in the passage of the USA Patriot Act of 2001. This act contained many provisions restricting or affecting civil liberties and permitting the application of new technologies that enhanced the glass firewall.

The act included the following provisions:

- It established a policy allowing preventative detention.

- It loosened the requirements for surveillance.

- It expanded government access to public and private records previously regarded as protected from such scrutiny.

- It imposed requirements on commercial transactions among individuals.

- It gave considerable power to immigration and customs personnel in their treatment of individuals at U.S. borders.

- It gave more discretion to law enforcement officials in their investigations of terrorist threats and acts.[12]

The implementation of the Patriot Act and related policies has drawn considerable criticism and reaction in recent years, and the unauthorized release of classified information regarding the activities of the U.S. government under post–9/11 national security policies has embarrassed American officials here and abroad.[13] Although the U.S. government has pursued prosecution of those who leaked documents related to U.S. intelligence, there has been a growing call for change from both the public and some members of Congress.

The Enemy-Within Approach. Perhaps the most controversial national security policies related to civil liberties have been those based on an *enemy-within approach*. This view emphasizes that the threat to our security emanates from within our borders, and that, as good Americans, we should ferret out disloyal and subversive individuals. We can find this perspective throughout U.S. history, starting with passage of the Alien and Sedition Acts of 1797, which dealt with the perceived threat to government posed by those

Post-9/11 fears of the enemy within led to policies that allowed the National Security Agency and other intelligence agencies to monitor the communications of millions of individuals around the world. Former CIA employee and NSA contractor Edward Snowden downloaded classified documents about NSA surveillance and in 2013 began releasing them to the press. Regarded as a hero and patriotic whistleblower by some, he was viewed as a traitor by others.

supposedly inspired by the French Revolution. After the end of World War I, many of the programs developed to stop spying and sabotage were used as part of the Red Scare, which focused on dealing with those Americans suspected of communist or socialist sympathies. Similarly, during the initial phases of the Cold War, fear of the enemy within fueled antiespionage investigations by federal agencies and congressional committees. And, despite official denials and explicit declarations against targeting Muslims, dating back to the 2001 Patriot Act, it is widely believed that several law enforcement agencies have been carrying out surveillance and investigations of U.S. mosques and their attendees.[14]

Conclusion

How can the government maintain its commitment to civil liberties while minimizing the nation's vulnerability to attack?

As we discussed in Chapter 4, most Americans think about civil liberties in absolutist terms, but in reality the courts have had to limit and define our most fundamental freedoms for a wide range of reasons. As this Policy Connection makes clear, civil liberties have also been the focus of policies developed in response to national and homeland security concerns. Thus, although we Americans aspire to greater freedom under the protections guaranteed by our constitutional liberties, we find ourselves having to make compromises in the face of threats and fears about our vulnerability.

QUESTIONS FOR DISCUSSION

1. The War on Terror is unlike past conflicts in that the enemy is not another nation-state but rather loosely knit groups that operate in cells located throughout the world. Is the United States capable of fighting against this type of enemy, given its emphasis on civil liberties and reliance on traditional military approaches? If not, what needs to be changed to win this new type of warfare?

2. In what ways, if any, have you personally been affected by recent national security policies, such that your civil liberties have been limited or even taken away?

Civil Rights

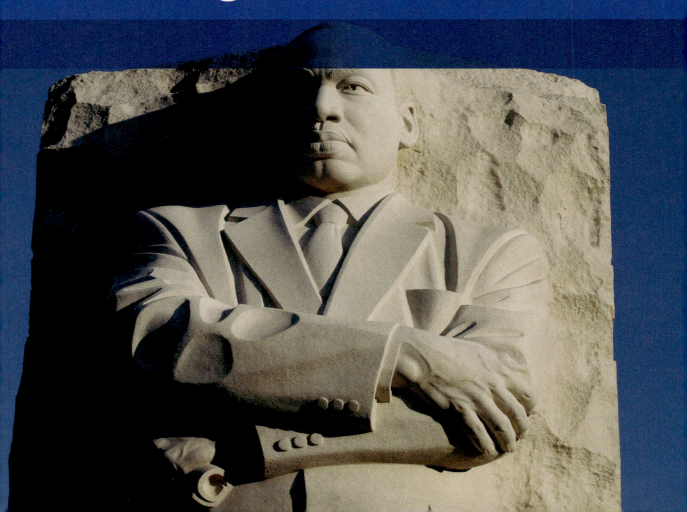

The Crime of "Driving or Shopping While Black"

On August 17, 1988, a New Jersey state trooper pulled over, for speeding, a Porsche driven by an African American male. Although the trooper did not use a radar gun to clock the speed of the vehicle, she observed that the late-model sports car was traveling "faster than the flow of traffic." As the trooper approached the vehicle, the driver made "furtive movements" toward the passenger side of the car—movements that she considered suspicious. The trooper later admitted that the driver was cooperative and polite and had complied with all requests. Nevertheless, she asked him to exit the car; she conducted a pat-down, and in a subsequent search of the vehicle she found a fully loaded handgun on the passenger side rear floor. She asked the driver if he had a gun permit as required by New Jersey state law. He did not, and the trooper placed him under arrest, charging him with possessing an unregistered dangerous weapon. One month later, a judge dismissed the charge on grounds that there was insufficient cause for the trooper's search of the vehicle.

Nearly twenty-five years later, a young African American went into Barneys, a high-end department store on New York's Madison Avenue, where he purchased a $350 designer belt. The clerk asked for some form of identification when he presented his personal debit card to pay for the item. With the sale completed and item in hand, he left the store. In the meantime, the sales clerk alerted the police because she suspected that the identification used for the purchase was a fake and the debit card must have been stolen. A block away from Barneys, the customer was approached by a New York City police officer, who asked to see the item and proof of purchase. He produced

< Forty-eight years after Dr. Martin Luther King Jr. led the March on Washington for Jobs and Freedom, his likeness was carved in granite. Dr. King's inspirational leadership in the cause of equality and dignity for all has long since made him a worldwide symbol for civil rights.

CHAPTER OUTLINE AND FOCUS QUESTIONS

The Continuing Struggle Against Racism

> What have been the breakthroughs in the movement toward racial justice in America?

Sex Discrimination

> How have the rights of women evolved?

Sexual Orientation

> How has the legal status of gays, lesbians, and transgender people changed?

Equality and Citizenship Status

> What constitutional rights do noncitizens have?

the receipt, the debit card, and an ID. Questioning "how a young black man such as himself could afford to purchase such an expensive belt," the officer handcuffed and took him to the nearest precinct. Several hours later, after his identity and the debit card were eventually verified, the nineteen-year-old student was released.

On the surface, both cases seem to involve instances in which an individual's civil liberties were violated (see Chapter 4).[1] In the New Jersey traffic stop, the court determined that the search of the car was unwarranted, a violation of the Fourth Amendment protection against unreasonable searches and seizures. In the Barneys incident, the issue is false arrest.

Ask members of the African American community, however, and they will tell you that what was involved in both instances has more to do with civil rights—that is, protection against discrimination and unequal treatment under the law—than civil liberties. The 1988 case made news across the country because the driver of the Porsche was Charles Barkley, at the time a well-known professional basketball player with the Philadelphia 76ers. Although not brought up in court at the time, questions were raised as to whether the traffic stop was really an example of **racial profiling**—a practice in which decisions about whether to enforce a law are based on the race or ethnicity of an individual rather than on any suspicious or illegal act. A secret internal study conducted by the state police a few years later indicated that the practice of racial profiling was pervasive among the troopers who patrolled the New Jersey Turnpike. Finally, in 1999 the state attorney general issued a public report that noted that African Americans were "routinely targeted" for traffic stops. The practice was so common that African Americans claimed that the only reason they were stopped was for the crime of "driving while black."

The 2013 Barneys case made headlines when the New York media picked up the story behind the lawsuit filed by the shopper, Trayon Christian. Again, for African Americans there was nothing shocking about what happened outside Barneys, and many spoke of the suspicious and discriminatory treatment they regularly encounter in many stores as part of "shopping while black."[2] In a rare comment related to race, President Barack Obama had taken note of the situation a few months earlier:

> There are very few African-American men in this country who haven't had the experience of being followed when they were shopping in a department store. That includes me. And there are very few African-American men who haven't had the experience of walking across the street and hearing the locks click on the doors of cars. That happens to me, at least before I was a senator. There are very few

Racial profiling A practice in which decisions about whether to enforce a law are based on the race or ethnicity of an individual rather than on any suspicious or illegal act.

African-Americans who haven't had the experience of getting on an elevator and a woman clutching her purse nervously and holding her breath until she had a chance to get off. That happens often.[3]

Unfortunately, the experiences of African Americans like President Obama are not unique. Latino Americans as well as other ethnic and racial groups have been subjected to various forms of discrimination by both government officials and private individuals. The same holds true for women, the elderly, the disabled, and Americans of different sexual orientations. Few Americans would deny the existence of discrimination and unequal treatment, but almost all would agree that such behavior poses a direct threat and challenge to our common belief in the basic principles of our political system.

We regard ourselves as a nation committed to protecting **civil rights**— guarantees of protection by the government against discrimination or unreasonable treatment by other individuals or groups—reflecting the widely held *myth of guaranteed political and social equality*. According to the myth, participation in our political, economic, and social systems is *and ought to be* open to all. We understand that discrimination has been and still is a feature of American society and that the rights of minorities have often been ignored in favor of the interests of the majority. But the myth of guaranteed political and social equality throws a negative light on acts of discrimination and unequal treatment. It helps us make sense of the actions government takes in order to move our political and social reality closer to our aspirations.

Our understanding of the meanings of civil rights, like our understanding of civil liberties, is constantly changing. In this chapter, we consider how choices are made regarding the way in which civil rights have been and are protected. What forms of discrimination are constitutionally impermissible? What is meant by invidious discrimination? These are some of the issues we discuss in an effort to understand and assess the effects of laws and, most importantly, the Fourteenth Amendment.

Civil rights Guarantees of protection by the government against discrimination or unreasonable treatment of certain individuals or groups.

The Continuing Struggle Against Racism

> **What have been the breakthroughs in the movement toward racial justice in America?**

A central element of post–Civil War Reconstruction was the adoption of three key constitutional amendments: the Thirteenth, Fourteenth, and Fifteenth:

- The Thirteenth Amendment abolished slavery and involuntary servitude.

- The Fourteenth Amendment addressed several aspects of individual freedom, but its key provision on civil rights is the clause declaring that no state shall "deny to any person within its jurisdiction the equal protection of the laws."

• The Fifteenth Amendment states that the right to vote cannot be denied on "account of race, color, or previous condition of servitude."

These three amendments, plus the congressional acts passed under their authority, promised the recently freed slaves a future of political and civil equality. Indeed, as C. Vann Woodward pointed out in his classic study *The Strange Career of Jim Crow*, the period immediately following the Civil War was a time of great progress in assimilating the former slaves.[4] But the gains did not last. During Reconstruction, the recently freed slaves enjoyed the protection of Northern soldiers. In 1877, however, the troops were withdrawn, and white Southerners quickly reestablished their hold on power, rendering the freedmen second-class citizens. When all is said and done, most political historians agree with Eric Foner, who wrote, "What remains certain is that Reconstruction failed, and that for blacks its failure was a disaster whose magnitude cannot be obscured by the genuine accomplishments that did endure"[5] (see Asked & Answered, page 7).

One of those accomplishments was the Civil Rights Act of 1875 (also called the Enforcement Act). Antedating President Lyndon Johnson's 1964 Civil Rights Act, the 1875 version forbade the separation of the races in places of public accommodation—transportation, hotels, and theaters. The 1875 act also banned states from excluding blacks from jury duty. Congress had assumed that the equal protection clause of the Fourteenth Amendment and the Thirteenth Amendment's prohibition against slavery authorized the act. Unfortunately, the 1875 act never did provide much protection. Once the troops left the South, there was little chance that the laws would be enforced. Thus, when in 1883 the Supreme Court, in a set of five separate cases known simply as the Civil Rights Cases, ruled the act unconstitutional, it was anticlimactic. Nevertheless, the Court's reasons for the ruling constituted a major setback for equality. The Fourteenth Amendment, the majority said, applied only to state-imposed segregation, not to discrimination practiced by private individuals. This interpretation implied that Congress could act if a state affirmatively discriminated, but not if the state simply allowed segregation to exist. As for the Thirteenth Amendment, the Court argued that it does apply to private individuals but it prohibits only the ownership of people and does not prescribe equal treatment of people.[6]

Thirteen years later, the Court dealt another blow to those seeking an end to racial distinction when it ruled, in *Plessy v. Ferguson*, that the Fourteenth Amendment did not even prohibit state-sanctioned segregation.[7] On the contrary, the Court argued, separation of the races is permitted as long as they receive equal treatment. This is the infamous separate-but-equal doctrine.

The Court's narrow ruling on the Fourteenth Amendment, along with presidential lack of interest in racial equality, gave rise to Jim Crow laws. Community after community decreed the separation of the races, and almost no aspect of life was too trivial to escape the reach of these laws. Not only did states require separate drinking fountains and public bathrooms for blacks and whites, but some went so far as to require different courtroom Bibles.[8] The stress was on separation.

POLITICS & POPULAR CULTURE: Visit the book's companion website at **www.oup.com/us/gitelson** to read the special feature *Writing History with Lighting*

ASKED & ANSWERED

ASKED: What do we mean by *Jim Crow*?

ANSWERED: Between 1877 and 1965, many state and local governments, particularly those of the former Confederacy, sought to enshrine racial segregation in their communities by constructing often elaborate legal codes that prohibited consorting among the races. These laws and the social norms surrounding this era came to be called "Jim Crow," the stage name of Thomas Dartmouth Rice, a white minstrel performer (1808–1860). With his blackened face and grotesque manner, Rice became famous for his extravagant and demeaning caricatures of slaves. Although it is not certain how the minstrel character came to symbolize a regime of apartheid, they both demeaned African Americans and furthered the separation the races.

Jim Crow is best known for the laws requiring segregated schools, drinking fountains, restrooms, restaurants, and transportation services. But these were only the tip of the iceberg. Few activities were beyond the purview of the Jim Crow laws. In Alabama, for instance, it was illegal for African Americans and whites to play pool or billiards together. Birmingham, Alabama, took it one step further and barred the races from playing checkers or dominoes together. Nor could any white nurse in Alabama be required to work in a hospital room where African American men were placed. Louisiana required that all circuses expecting the attendance of more than one race establish separate ticket offices not less than twenty-five feet apart. In Mississippi, it was illegal to advocate social equality. North Carolina, after requiring separate schools, then required that no textbooks could be interchangeable between the segregated schools. All textbooks were to be reused by the first race that used them. One couldn't escape Jim Crow even in death. Georgia, for instance, required separate burial ground for the races. Few business or social activities were spared legal controls.

Of course, the most common Jim Crow law was the absolute prohibition of intermarriages. But miscegenation laws were not limited to former confederate states. States as far flung as California, Connecticut, Indiana, Montana, and North Dakota had at some point, during this period, prohibited interracial marriages. Likewise, laws requiring segregation in public schools were not limited to the South. After all, the schools in the nation's capital were segregated by race. Even Wyoming specified that schools should be segregated anytime there were fifteen or more African American children in the district.

Legal codes, however, were only one part of the Jim Crow era. Jim Crow was also about attitudes and unwritten codes of behavior. As the author and folklorist Stetson Kennedy noted, African Americans were expected to show deference to whites at all times. No African American could ever imply that a white person was lying or dishonest. Nor could an African American man comment on the appearance of a white woman or demonstrate superior knowledge or intelligence. Generally, such infractions were dealt with by personal rebukes or, in more serious cases, mob violence, not law. Indeed, mob violence played a crucial role in enforcing Jim Crow. Sometimes, mobs would attack individuals believed to have violated some norm, but often the mobs, angered by some alleged violation of Jim Crow norms, would raid whole neighborhoods, destroying property and killing or injuring African Americans, simply because they lived in the community. More prominent were the public lynchings. Numbers are not easy to verify, but the Tuskegee Institute has documented the lynching of 3,446 African Americans between 1882 and 1968. In many of these cases, local police departments were actively involved. That lynching was a public act demonstrated the intention to further terrorize African Americans into accepting second-class treatment. Lynching was a means of suppressing any thoughts of social equality.

ASKED & ANSWERED *continued*

Want to learn more about Jim Crow? Visit the New Jim Crow Museum at www.youtube.com/user/jimcrowmuseum.

Sources: The examples of Jim Crow laws were taken from a much longer list compiled by the Martin Luther King Jr. National Historic

Site Interpretive Staff. The fuller list can be found at http://www.nps .gov/malu/documents/jim crowlaws.htm. To learn more about the norms associated with Jim Crow, see Stetson Kennedy, Jim Crow Guide to the USA: The Laws and Customs and Etiquette Governing the Conduct of Nonwhites and Other Minorities as Second-Class Citizens *(Tuscaloosa: University of Alabama Press, 1990).*

Even the Supreme Court paid little heed to equality. Three years after *Plessy*, the Court let stand as a local matter a Georgia school board's decision to close the black high school while leaving open the all-white high school.[9] "Separate but equal," then, simply meant "separate."

Public Education

Despite such setbacks, the struggle to end segregation in American society continued. The National Association for the Advancement of Colored People (NAACP), formed in 1909, became the driving force in these efforts. At first, the NAACP tried to persuade Congress to pass federal legislation forbidding segregation. Failing in the legislative arena, the organization created a separate unit, the Legal Defense Fund, directed by Thurgood Marshall (who later became a justice of the Supreme Court). The primary tactic of the Legal Defense Fund was to attack segregation in the courts.

In the late 1930s, the Legal Defense Fund began a series of court battles that challenged segregation in all areas of American life. It was, however, most successful in the realm of education. As a result of the fund's efforts, the Court struck down a Missouri law that reimbursed African American law students for out-of-state tuition rather than admitting them to the University of Missouri.[10] Then, in 1950, the Court ruled that a separate University of Texas law school for blacks was not equal to the University of Texas law school attended by whites, because the former lacked certain intangible factors such as prestige and reputation.[11] Although the Court failed to overturn the separate-but-equal doctrine in its Texas decision, it came close to doing so.

Finally, on May 7, 1954, the Supreme Court startled the nation by issuing a unanimous decision, in *Brown v. Board of Education of Topeka*, that the Fourteenth Amendment prohibits a state from compelling children to attend racially segregated public schools. In a brief opinion that specifically overturned *Plessy v. Ferguson*, the Court simply declared that "in the field of public education the doctrine of 'separate but equal' has no place." No other conclusion was possible, the justices argued, because "separate educational facilities are inherently unequal."[12]

Pronouncing segregation unconstitutional was one thing; compelling desegregation was another. Recognizing that fact, in the following term the Court set the case for reargument to consider remedies, and *Brown II* (1955) required desegregation of

In 1963 the growing civil rights movement found its voice in Alabama, where Governor George Wallace, standing on the steps of the state capitol declared, "Segregation now, segregation tomorrow, segregation forever." Birmingham, Alabama, became the focal point for demonstrations. In turn, the state authorities turned dogs and fire hoses on demonstrators. Pictured here are Birmingham police officers and their attack dogs patrolling the city.

public schools to proceed with "all deliberate speed."[13] "All deliberate speed," however, was interpreted by many school districts and lower courts to mean "all deliberate delay."

In the decade following the *Brown* decisions, little changed in the public schools of the South. For those ten years, the percentage of African American children attending integrated schools never exceeded 2 percent. Across the South, efforts to resist desegregation swelled as state and local governments passed laws and regulations designed to counter court decisions. Using a tactic known as massive resistance, state and local governments fought all efforts to desegregate their schools. **Massive resistance** hinged on a belief or a hope by segregationists that, if they could hold off long enough, the rest of America would come to believe that desegregation would not work and would give up on the idea. As part of this movement, local governments routinely ignored court orders or complied so slightly that they had to be dragged through each step. When mere resistance failed, local governments took more extreme actions. Prince Edward County, Virginia, for instance, closed the entire school system from 1958 to 1964. White children went to the Prince Edward Academy, a private, segregated school established to evade desegregation. African American children went without a school until 1963, when the Ford Foundation funded a private school for them. Opposition by local officials and school boards was compounded by the fact that many lower court judges were also opposed to the *Brown* decision. In several instances it was the lower court judges who resisted the decision.

What progress was made came at a high cost. For instance, in 1957 President Dwight D. Eisenhower used a thousand members of the 101st Airborn Division to protect black students enrolled in a Little Rock, Arkansas, high school. The admission of the University of Mississippi's first black student sparked riots that resulted in two deaths.

Massive resistance A practice in which some state and local governments routinely either ignored court - ordered desegregation or complied so slightly that they had to be dragged through each step. Many public officials believed that if they held off long enough, the rest of America would come to believe that desegregation would not work and would give up on the idea.

Responding to this resistance, the Court proclaimed in 1969 that "'allowing all deliberate speed' is no longer constitutionally permissible." Every school district was "to terminate dual school systems at once."[14] Ironically, by this time real progress toward desegregation was clearly taking place in the South. The motivation for acting after a decade of resistance came from the vigorous enforcement of the Civil Rights Act of 1964. Under the 1964 act, officials could withhold federal education funds from school districts that refused to desegregate. Fearing the loss of funds, many school districts found the will to desegregate that had been missing in the ten previous years.

Implementing the *Brown II* decision in southern schools was hard enough, but in the 1970s the Court began to confront the seemingly more difficult problems of segregation in the North. Southern schools had been segregated by state law. (Segregation mandated by law is known as *de jure*.) By the 1970s, urban school systems in the North were considerably more segregated than their counterparts in the South, but this segregation was the result of housing patterns rather than state laws. This *de facto* segregation—segregation not officially established by law—proved to be much more difficult to erase or even minimize. Having ruled that courts could order remedial action, such as busing, only to correct instances of de jure segregation,[15] the Supreme Court had made it extremely difficult to remedy segregation triggered by the movement of white families from the cities to the suburbs. Even limited efforts to desegregate by busing children out of their neighborhood proved extraordinarily unpopular and led to violent confrontations in some northern cities. In 2007, further limitations to remedies compounded the problem when, in *Meredith v. Jefferson County Board of Education*, the Court invalidated school programs in Seattle and Louisville that considered race as a criterion in assigning children to schools. Without the ability to use race as a criterion in assigning children to various schools, the courts were left with very few tools to confront de facto segregation.

Public Accommodations

The *Brown* decision had little bearing on the widespread practice of private discrimination in public accommodations. As court efforts to eliminate discrimination against blacks continued, public protest against discrimination began to mount. In December 1955, Rosa Parks, a seamstress in Montgomery, Alabama, was arrested for refusing to give up her seat on a bus to a white man. Her arrest sparked a yearlong boycott of the Montgomery bus system—a boycott led by Dr. Martin Luther King Jr. Eventually the system was integrated, but not before Dr. King's home was bombed and he and several others were arrested for "conspiracy to hinder the operations of business."

The Montgomery bus boycott was only the beginning, however. In the early 1960s, unrest grew among the opponents of segregation: Blacks and white sympathizers increasingly turned to public protest. Marches and sit-in demonstrations received wide publicity as police reacted to the protests with increasing force. In 1963, President John F. Kennedy proposed legislation to desegregate public accommodations, which Congress finally passed at the urging of Kennedy's successor, President Lyndon B. Johnson.

The Civil Rights Act of 1964 made it a crime to discriminate in providing public accommodations. It barred racial discrimination in hotels, restaurants, and gas stations; at sporting events; and in all places of entertainment. The act also included provisions against discrimination in employment. Although the ground it covered was similar to that of the Civil Rights Act of 1875, the 1964 statute invoked congressional power over interstate commerce rather than the Fourteenth Amendment. To justify an attack on discrimination on the grounds that it interfered with the flow of interstate commerce may seem strange and even dehumanizing to us today; however, it was an effective way of getting around the reading of the Fourteenth Amendment given by the Supreme Court in the Civil Rights Cases of 1883.

Although the Civil Rights Act of 1964 did much to open up a wide array of public accommodations to African Americans and other minorities, one glaring issue was not covered. The 1964 act did not repeal **anti-miscegenation laws**— anti-miscegenation laws criminalized interracial marriages. This matter was finally resolved by the Supreme Court when, in a 1967 case known as *Loving v. Virginia*, it declared these laws in violation of the equal protection clause of the Fourteenth Amendment and therefore unconstitutional.

Anti-miscegenation laws
State laws that made interracial marriage a criminal offence.

Voting Rights

As we noted earlier in this chapter, the Fifteenth Amendment states that the right to vote cannot be denied on account of race. Nevertheless, after 1877— the year the federal government stopped supervising elections in the South— southern states excluded the vast majority of blacks from the voter registration rolls. They did so through diverse and inventive means that commonly involved the use of some type of highly subjective test. Potential voters might, for instance, be given portions of the Constitution to read and explain. Because the examiners had complete freedom in selecting questions and answers, rejecting applicants was an easy matter. Even African American lawyers sometimes failed the Constitution test. So effective were these efforts that in 1961 less than 10 percent of the African American population was registered to vote in the 129 southern counties surveyed.

To address this inequality, Congress passed the Voting Rights Act of 1965. Expanding on the mandate of the Fifteenth Amendment, the act states that "no voting qualification or prerequisite to voting, or standard, practice, or procedure shall be imposed or applied by any State or political subdivision to deny or abridge the right of any citizen of the United States to vote on account of race or color."

Furthermore, Section 4(b) of the act identified some states and local jurisdictions, mostly but not exclusively in the South, as having a history of discriminatory voting practices. In these states and subdivisions, all tests and devices were banned, and the U.S. attorney general was empowered to assign federal registrars to enroll all applicants meeting state requirements. Those states and subdivisions identified as having a history of discriminatory voting practices were also subjected to continued scrutiny. Under Section 5 of the act, these states and local jurisdictions were required to seek preclearance from the U.S. attorney general or the U.S. District Court for the District of Columbia prior to implementing any changes linked to voting.

Extensions of the act in 1970 and 1975 banned literacy tests nationwide and broadened coverage to areas where large numbers of citizens spoke languages other than English—both languages spoken by immigrants, such as Spanish and Asian languages, and those spoken by Native Americans and the Inuit.[16] After a protracted struggle between Congress and the White House, in 1982 the major portions of the act were extended—this time for twenty-five years. Thus, in 2006 Congress took up once again the renewal of the Voting Rights Act, and again the move was contentious. Indeed, the 2006 debates about the act were more divisive than any previous debates over the act. Southern states objected to continuing the preclearance requirement of Section 5. It was, they argued, unwarranted and outdated, because discriminatory voting practices were a thing of the past. Other states objected to an amendment requiring states with large Spanish-speaking populations to provide bilingual ballots. Nevertheless, the act—now named the Fannie Lou Hamer, Rosa Parks, and Coretta Scott King Voting Rights Act Reauthorization—passed, thereby extending all the major provisions for another twenty-five years.

Seven years after reauthorization of the act, the Supreme Court significantly altered the Voting Rights Act. In the 2013 case of *Shelby County v. Holder*, Chief Justice John Roberts proclaimed that a five-member majority of the Court had found that the congressional formula determining which states presented evidence of discriminatory voting practices was unconstitutional. Echoing the act's congressional opponents in the 2006 debate, the Court majority ruled that the formula was outdated. What opponents of the act could not achieve in Congress they won in the Court.

The *Shelby County* decision did not invalidate the preclearance required in Section 5 of the act; it just rejected the idea that, under the current formula, any states or local jurisdictions were subject to preclearance, at least until such time as Congress satisfactorily replaces the coverage formula. In the meantime, the Department of Justice is free to bring suits against states and subdivisions it believes are engaged in voter discrimination based on race or color. Such cases will be very difficult to win, however. The Department of Justice will have to prove that the laws in question were intended to discriminate on the basis of race or color—it will not be enough to prove that the laws adversely affect racial minorities. Obviously, proving intention is far more difficult than proving effect.

Immediately after the *Shelby County* decision was announced, several states previously covered by the Voting Rights Act altered their voting laws. Texas revealed yet another redistricting plan and a new voting-identification law. Additionally, Alabama, North Carolina, Mississippi, Virginia, and South Carolina passed new voter-identification laws. Although the states defended the new voter-identification laws as necessary to prevent voter fraud, many observers noted that the weight of these new laws would fall disproportionally on minority groups. To critics, these laws looked like voter suppression.

Sex Discrimination

> ### How have the rights of women evolved?

White women have always held citizenship in the United States, but for a long time it was citizenship without political rights. Women could not vote, and married women were recognized by law as subservient to their husbands. They could not own property, contract debts, or even keep any money they themselves earned. In return for a woman's giving up her separate existence, the law guaranteed that her husband would provide for her necessities. He was not responsible, however, for anything beyond what he decided were the necessities of life.

The first generation of feminists, led by Lucy Stone, Elizabeth Cady Stanton, Susan B. Anthony, and others, were dedicated to working for women's rights and the abolitionist cause. In the organized opposition to slavery, these feminist leaders developed political skills that laid the foundation for the first women's movement.

Crucial to the movement was the first women's rights conference, held in 1848 in Seneca Falls, New York. However, suffrage—the most dramatic of the many reforms proposed by the Seneca Conference—was submerged in the Civil War effort and then in the struggle over the post–Civil War amendments. Although some feminists wanted to add sex to the Fifteenth Amendment's list of attributes that could not be used to deny the right to vote, others opposed such an effort. Many supporters of the Fifteenth Amendment maintained that the issues of race and sex had to be treated separately if they were to be successfully resolved. Despite being shunned by many of the abolitionists and deprived of the support the early leaders had hoped for, those in the movement continued to press for women's rights, particularly the right to vote. Susan B. Anthony, for instance, was arrested for voting in the 1872 election. She was tried in a federal court by a judge who ordered the jury to return a guilty verdict. Not surprisingly, she was found guilty and fined $100. She never paid the fine, but she used the publicity around the trial to expand her audience. Unfortunately, because she died in 1906, she did not live to see women granted suffrage. That task was left to another generation of feminists.[17]

Among the many groups that continued to press for suffrage, none was more dedicated than the Congressional Union. Using techniques that would become more common in the 1960s, its members held marches, picketed the White House, and staged hunger strikes. Several members were jailed and beaten for their protests. Finally, in 1920, the Nineteenth Amendment was ratified. After years of struggle, the Constitution now contained the guarantee that "the right of the citizens of the United States to vote shall not be denied or abridged by the United States or by any State on account of sex."

After the adoption of the Nineteenth Amendment, the women's movement lost steam. The movement had always been broader than the issue of suffrage, but the long and difficult battle for the vote had displaced most other issues. Not until the early 1960s did the women's movement revive. This "second wave" has been seeking the eradication of sexism in all areas of life, and their efforts continue today.

Paternalism and Discrimination

The ratification of the Nineteenth Amendment did not eliminate sex discrimination from American society, in part because sex discrimination, even more than race discrimination, stems from a strong tradition of paternalism. Discrimination against women has been routinely defended as a means of protecting them, even when the goal is exploitation.

For many years the Supreme Court rather uncritically accepted distinctions based on sex if they appeared to benefit women. The Court's 1948 decision in *Goesaert v. Cleary* illustrates that approach.[18] The Court upheld a Michigan law that prohibited a woman from working as a bartender unless she was the wife or daughter of the bar's owner. Women could, however, work as waitresses. The Court accepted the argument that the statute protected women from the unwholesome elements encountered by bartenders. The exception for wives and daughters was reasonable because the woman's husband or father would protect her. What the Court overlooked was that the statute maintained male domination of the better-paying jobs, while women were relegated to the less lucrative role of servers.

In the past thirty years or so, the Court has been less tolerant of statutes that supposedly benefit women. Thus, the Court struck down an Oklahoma law that set a lower drinking age for women than for men.[19] Nevertheless, the Court continues to accept some classifications that treat men and women differently. For instance, the Court accepted as constitutional Florida's tax exemption for widows but not widowers. Noting the economic inequality that existed between men and women, the Court argued that the law was designed to compensate for past discrimination.[20]

Despite the Court's willingness to include sex discrimination under the equal protection clause of the Fourteenth Amendment, it has traditionally not received the same strict scrutiny as racial and ethnic discrimination. This approach may be changing, however.

Indications of a change in the Court's approach appeared in its 1996 decision on the status of the Virginia Military Institute (VMI) as an all-male school. VMI is a state-supported, four-year institution of higher education providing a unique experience. Students at VMI are subjected to an environment emphasizing "physical rigor, mental stress, absolute equality of treatment, absence of privacy, minute regulation of behavior, and indoctrination in desirable values." In order to stave off a constitutional challenge to the all-male admissions policy, the state of Virginia proposed the creation of a parallel military leadership program at nearby Mary Baldwin College. This Virginia Women's Institute for Leadership (VWIL) would not offer the same rigor that characterized VMI, but it would, the state argued, provide women with an education as citizen soldiers.

When this matter was appealed to the Supreme Court, Justice Ruth Bader Ginsburg, writing for the seven-member majority in *United States v. Virginia*, ruled that the all-male policy violated the equal protection clause of the Fourteenth Amendment.[21] Furthermore, Justice Ginsburg argued, the establishment of the VWIL fell far short of the necessary remedial action required. Virginia could comply with the equal protection clause only by opening VMI to women.

More important than the immediate case was Justice Ginsburg's apparent elevation of the level of review employed by the Court. Although the justice denied that classifications based on sex were to be treated like classifications based on race or national origin, she went on to announce a very high standard of review. Accordingly, Ginsburg noted that when reviewing classifications based on sex, "the reviewing court must determine whether the proffered justification is 'exceedingly persuasive.'" To most observers, "exceedingly persuasive" seems to be another way of saying "strictly scrutinized." Whether such scrutiny is taking place will have to be determined by future cases. It may be that, in the future, questions of sex discrimination will receive the same scrutiny as those involving race and national origin.

Women in the Workforce

One of the most dramatic changes in society has been the growing importance of women in the workforce. In 1987, for instance, the Census Bureau reported that, for the first time in American history, more than half of all women with children under the age of one were either working or actively seeking employment. Indeed, by 2013 women constituted 40 percent of primary breadwinners in American families.

Although Title VII of the Civil Rights Act of 1964 prohibits discrimination in employment on the basis of "race, color, religion, sex, or national origin," the application of this provision to women has been slow in coming. Initially, the national government was reluctant to apply the act to cases of sex discrimination. In fact, Herman Edelsberg, a former executive director of the Equal Employment Opportunity Commission, portrayed the ban on sex discrimination in the workplace as a "fluke . . . conceived out of wedlock."[22] The federal courts often tolerated discrimination based on sex plus some other characteristic. For example, the Court used the "sex-plus" distinction to justify company policies that provided for compensation for all non-job-related disabilities except pregnancy. Such policies, the Court argued, do not constitute sex discrimination because they are based not on sex alone but rather on sex plus the characteristic of

In the last few decades, women have become a large and vital part of the American workforce, even entering into jobs and careers once thought to be the sole domain of men. Still, the number of women in top jobs remains small, and few break through the so-called glass ceiling. Pictured here is Mary Barra, the CEO of General Motors. She is the first woman to head an American automobile manufacturing company.

Glass ceiling A phrase used to denote the subtle barriers preventing women and minorities from attaining the upper-level jobs in organizations.

pregnancy.[23] Congress overturned that decision, however, by passing the Pregnancy Discrimination Act of 1978.

Title VII has unmistakably opened up employment opportunities for women. There have even been cracks in the **glass ceiling**—subtle barriers preventing women or minorities from attaining the upper-level jobs in organizations. Yet women's wages still lag behind those of men. Currently women employed full-time are paid 77 cents for every dollar earned by a man working full-time. Moreover, as of 2013, the size of the disparity had not changed in 10 years. Economists disagree over how much of the wage gap is the result of wage discrimination and how much is the result of other factors. Men and women, for example, tend to cluster in different occupations, and those jobs most populated by men pay better. Whether such clustering is the product of individual preferences or occurs because choices are often constrained by discrimination is certainly debatable.

Plainly, there are multiple explanations for the pay gap, but it cannot be denied that one of those is simple wage discrimination by employers' failure to abide by the Equal Pay Act of 1963, which requires "equal pay for equal work." Illustrative of the problem is the case of Lilly Ledbetter, a production supervisor at a Goodyear tire plant. As she was nearing retirement, Ms. Ledbetter discovered that she had, for some time, been paid considerably less than male colleagues performing the same tasks. Failing to secure any redress from her employer, Ledbetter filed an equal pay lawsuit under Title VII of the Civil Rights Act of 1964. At the trial, a jury found in her favor and awarded Ledbetter back pay and more than $3 million in compensation and punitive damages. On appeal, however, the U.S. Supreme Court in *Ledbetter v. Goodyear Tire and Rubber Company* (2007) threw out the jury's verdict, ruling that, under the law, Ledbetter was required to file her complaint within 180 days of the date that the company first discriminated against her. (Of course, she did not learn of the discrimination until years after it first happened.) Disappointed by the majority decision, Justice Ruth Bader Ginsburg took the unusual step of reading her dissent from the bench. Scornfully referring to the decision as a "parsimonious reading of Title VII," she urged Congress to overturn the decision.

Lilly Ledbetter's case became an important issue in the 2008 presidential election. Barack Obama campaigned on a promise of correcting the Supreme Court decision. Indeed, Ledbetter made an appearance on behalf of Candidate Obama at the Democratic National Convention in Denver. Thus, it may be fitting that the first law signed by President Obama was the Lilly Ledbetter Fair Pay Act of 2009. Under the law, the 180-day clock for filing suit is reset with each discriminatory paycheck. Unfortunately, the act is applicable only as far back as 2007. Ms. Ledbetter will never receive compensation. As she said at the signing ceremony: "Goodyear will never have to pay me what it cheated me out of." But, she went on to say, "with the President's signature today, I have an even richer reward."[24]

The Ledbetter bill may not be the final word, however. Congress now has before it another bill known as the Paycheck Fairness Act. This bill would amend and strengthen the fifty-year-old Equal Pay Act. Although this new act has the support of the White House and several outside groups, it also has its opponents. What will happen is unknown, but what is unmistakable is that women are now a vital part of the workforce and that expectations of equality of the sexes in the workplace will not subside.

President Obama is pictured here signing his first piece of legislation. The act before him was the Lilly Ledbetter Fair Pay Act, named after Lilly Ledbetter (second from the left in the front row). The act extended the time women have to sue for back pay when they have illegally suffered payroll discrimination.

Women and Educational Achievement

A major reason that women have come to play a sizeable role in the workforce is that they have become increasingly better educated. The post–World War II period has witnessed an extraordinary growth in the number and percentage of women seeking higher education. In 1947, only 29 percent of the students enrolled in a degree-granting institution were women. Gradually, the percentage of women enrolled increased. Indeed, in 1980, for the first time in American history, women composed the majority of students enrolled in degree-granting institutions. By 2010, women made up 57 percent of all students registered in degree-granting institutions. Likewise, the graduation rates of women now exceed those of men; in 2010 the difference was 8 percent.[25]

Central to expanding the educational opportunities for women was Title IX of the Education Amendments of 1972. That act provides that "no person in the United States shall, on the basis of sex, be excluded from participation in, be denied the benefits of, or be subjected to discrimination under any education program or activity receiving Federal financial assistance." Broadly written, the act was intended to root out all forms of gender discrimination in education. Colleges and universities that limited female admissions suddenly were on notice that such actions were not acceptable. Neither were school policies that expelled pregnant women or limited young women to certain classes.

These days, Title IX is best known for its dramatic changes in the domain of sports, at both college and high school levels. Across the board, schools of all types are required to provide equal opportunities to participate in organized sports. Without a doubt, the results have been dramatic. Opportunities for women have increased considerably. The year Title IX was passed, 7.4 percent of high school athletes were young women; 40 years later, that percentage was 41.4.

Title IX of the Higher Education Act opened up athletic opportunities to women throughout the educational system. Although some inequalities continue to exist, a few women's sports have gained national attention. Shown here, the University of Connecticut's women's basketball team raises the 2014 championship trophy. The game was nationally televised and played before more than 17,000 fans.

Similarly, there has been enormous progress on equal opportunities for women at the collegiate level. Forty years ago, only about 30,000 women played on a National Collegiate Athletic Association (NCAA) varsity team. By 2012, over 191, 000 women participated in NCAA varsity sports. Despite this progress, truly equal opportunities remain elusive. Men's sports still receive the bulk of athletic department budgets, and the proportion of scholarship athletes is higher for men than women. Enforcement of Title IX has also created some backlash, as some blame the law for the elimination of so-called minor sports.

Sexual Harassment

Sexual harassment
Unwelcome sexual advances, requests for sexual favors, or other verbal or physical conduct of a sexual nature by an employer or coworker.

Title VII of the Civil Rights Act of 1964 eventually became the vehicle used to attack sexual harassment in the workplace, as the Court came to view **sexual harassment** as a form of sexual discrimination. (*Sexual harassment* is generally defined as unwelcome sexual advances, requests for sexual favors, or other verbal or physical conduct of a sexual nature by an employer or coworker.) But judicial acceptance of harassment as discrimination was slow in developing. Initially, courts ruled that harassment was a private matter that was not covered by Title VII. Slowly, however, courts began to accept that at least some types of sexual harassment constituted sex discrimination. In the 1976 case of *Williams v. Saxbe*, the district court for the District of Columbia became the first court to rule that sexual harassment could violate Title VII.[26] Diane Williams brought suit against the U.S. Department of Justice, alleging that she was fired less than two weeks after refusing her supervisor's sexual advances. In finding in Williams's favor, the district court ruled that the type of sexual harassment known as *quid pro quo* constituted sex discrimination. (Quid pro quo harassment occurs when a supervisor demands sexual favors from an employee in exchange for some employment advantage.)

Although several lower courts followed the *Williams* decision and permitted Title VII suits for sexual harassment, the U.S. Supreme Court did not rule on the issue until 1986. Writing for the majority in *Meritor Savings Bank v. Vinson*, Chief Justice Rehnquist argued that sexual harassment need not involve questions of promotion or job loss to be prohibited.[27] The creation of an offensive or hostile working environment, Rehnquist said, is sufficient to satisfy the definition of sex discrimination. Not every instance of offensive or annoying behavior in the workplace constitutes harassment, but the Court argued that a pattern of behavior that includes such things as requests for sexual favors, sexual innuendoes, or sexual insults creates a condition of employment disparity that Title VII prohibits. The Court's 1993 decision in *Harris v. Forklift* broadened this ruling. The Court decided that a woman claiming sexual harassment need not prove that she was psychologically injured in order to receive a damage award. She need only prove that the work environment was such that a reasonable person would find it hostile or abusive.[28]

Over the years, the courts and the U.S. Equal Employment Opportunity Commission have broadened the understanding of sexual harassment so that "both the victim and the harasser can be either a woman or a man, and the victim and harasser can be the same sex."[29] Of course, not everyone is protected by Title VII. As we discussed earlier, the Civil Rights Act of 1964 was based on congressional control over interstate commerce. For Title VII purposes, the law defines business establishments with 15 or more employees as engaged in interstate commerce. Thus, Title VII does not protect employees working for small businesses. Similarly, unpaid interns may not claim protection under Title VII, because their voluntary work does not, the courts have said, constitute employment.

Sexual Orientation

> ### How has the legal status of gays, lesbians, and transgender people changed?

Among the groups that have sought or are seeking coverage under the equal protection clause of the Fourteenth Amendment, none has been more controversial than gay, lesbian, and transgender people. For more than two decades, gay rights organizations and social conservatives have waged an ideological battle over the constitutional rights of homosexuals.

Equal Protection and Sexual Orientation

Initially, the Supreme Court was reluctant to extend judicial protection to homosexual acts. In the 1986 case of *Bowers v. Hardwick*, the Court ruled that state laws prohibiting homosexual sodomy, even between consenting adults, did not violate the constitutional right to privacy.[30] Writing for the five-member majority, Justice Byron White argued that whatever residual rights to the privacy of the bedroom existed were clearly outweighed by the majority's belief that homosexual sodomy is "immoral and unacceptable." Although the *Bowers* case, based as it was on the right to privacy, did not involve an equal protection claim, the decision did not suggest that the Court would be open to the advocates of gay rights. After all, if the majority's belief in the immorality of homosexuality outweighs the right to privacy, it stands to reason that it may also constitute grounds for discrimination.

Thus, the Court surprised both sides on this issue when, in the 1996 case of *Romer v. Evans*, it struck down an amendment to the Colorado constitution that prohibited any law protecting homosexuals from discrimination.[31] The amendment (known as Amendment 2) was the voters' response to ordinances in three Colorado cities that made it illegal to discriminate against homosexuals, as well as women and racial minorities, in housing, education, employment, and health and welfare services. Ignoring the *Bowers* decision, Justice Anthony Kennedy argued that Amendment 2 violated the Fourteenth Amendment by depriving homosexuals of the right to seek legal protection against any form of discrimination except by the extraordinary method of a constitutional amendment. In overruling Amendment 2, Justice Kennedy very carefully avoided defining homosexuals as a constitutionally protected class that was entitled to strict judicial scrutiny. Discrimination against homosexuals could, Kennedy argued, be justified as long as it served a legitimate governmental interest. But the justice went on to argue that the majority's "animus" toward a group does not constitute a legitimate governmental interest. No group, Kennedy argued, could be put at an electoral disadvantage simply because a majority disapproved of it. Therefore, as Justice Antonin Scalia pointed out in a biting dissent, the juxtaposition of *Bowers* and *Romer* means that a practicing homosexual may be jailed but not put at an electoral disadvantage. This apparent anomaly was eliminated in 2003, however, when the Supreme Court overruled *Bowers* and declared the existing sodomy laws in twelve states unconstitutional.[32]

Same-Sex Marriage

Only a few years ago, the goal of uniting same-sex couples in marriage seemed highly implausible. After all, in 1996, Congress, fearing that Hawaii might legalize same-sex marriage, rushed through and President Clinton signed the Defense of Marriage Act (DOMA). The act defined marriage for the purposes of receiving federal benefits (e.g., Social Security) as "the legal union between one man and one woman as husband and wife." Furthermore, the act relieved the states of the legal responsibility—under the full faith and credit clause of the Constitution (Article IV, Section 1)—to recognize same-sex marriages performed in any other state.

Flash forward from 1996 to 2004, when the high court of Massachusetts granted legal status to same-sex marriages. That ruling created a firestorm in the middle of a presidential election. Both candidates George W. Bush and John Kerry rejected the idea. (Kerry did accept civil unions.) Additionally, twelve states used ballot measures to make same-sex marriages impossible in their states. (The measures passed in all twelve states.)

Now flash forward again, this time to 2013. By a vote of 5 to 4, the U.S. Supreme Court in *United States v. Windsor* ruled that the provision of DOMA prohibiting couples legally married in any state from receiving federal benefits violated the Fifth Amendment to the U.S. Constitution. (Ironically, 2013 was also the year that Hawaii finally legalized same-sex marriages.) Writing for the majority, Justice Anthony Kennedy said that DOMA was driven only by the desire to injure gay and lesbian couples. Moreover, Kennedy wrote, "DOMA writes inequality into the entire United States Code."[33]

On the same day that they announced the *Windsor* ruling, the Court also handed down *Hollingsworth v. Perry*. In 2008, the California Supreme Court had insisted that the state's constitution required that the term *marriage* include same-sex couples. Later that year, however, California voters passed Proposition 8, a constitutional amendment that limited marriage to a man and a woman. Two couples, one gay and one lesbian, sued, arguing that Proposition 8 denied them of their Fourteenth Amendment right to equal protection of the law. At the trial, state officials informed the court that they would not defend Proposition 8. Nevertheless, the trial in *Hollinsworth* proceeded, with a group of Proposition 8 proponents replacing state authorities. On the completion of the trial, the court ruled that Proposition 8 violated the constitution, a decision affirmed by the U.S. Court of Appeals for the Ninth Circuit. Supporters of Proposition 8 then appealed to the U.S. Supreme Court. Rather than deciding the case on its merits, the Court dismissed it, contending that the parties bringing the appeal lacked standing—that is, they were not the right parties to bring suit. Chief Justice John Roberts, who wrote the opinion, noted that "we have never before upheld the standing of a private party to defend the constitutionality of a state statute when state officials have chosen not to." Then Roberts added, "We decline to do so here."[34] Dismissing the case meant that the trial court decision stands. With Proposition 8 declared unconstitutional at the trial court level, California was cleared to begin offering same-sex marriage licenses.

Neither of these decisions means that same-sex marriages are the law of the land. In neither case did the Supreme Court validate a fundamental right for gay people to marry. That decision rests with the states. At this time, same-sex marriages are still prohibited in a clear majority of the states. The Court's decisions mean that the struggle will continue on a state-by-state basis.

In 2011, New York state governor Andrew Cuomo signed into law the Marriage Equality Act and thus legalized same-sex marriages. Pictured here are Brenda Sue Fulton (left) and Penelope Gnesin (right) exchanging vows in the chapel at the West Point Military Academy.

Changing Views

As dramatic as Supreme Court decisions can seem, we should remember that changes have occurred outside the courts. Obviously the most important change has been in public attitudes. Over the years, pollsters have shown a consistent increase in public support for same-sex marriage. Gallup, for instance, notes that 27 percent of Americans supported same-sex marriage in 1996—the year DOMA was passed. But just months before the Supreme Court's 2013 decision regarding *Windsor*, 53 percent approved. By the time the Supreme Court addressed the issue, almost all polls showed a solid majority supporting gay marriage.[35]

As public attitudes have changed, so has policy. In 1992, presidential candidate Bill Clinton promised that, if elected, he would lift the decades-old ban on homosexuals in the uniformed services. To the surprise of many, President Clinton turned to this issue very quickly after the election. Confronted by opposition on several fronts, the president compromised by supporting a policy that allowed homosexuals to remain in the military so long as they did not talk about their sexual orientation or engage in sexual activity. In exchange, officers were not allowed to question service members about their sexual orientation. Attacked by both sides in the debate, this policy—called "don't ask, don't tell"—did allow gays and lesbians to serve in the military.

"Don't ask, don't tell" never did work, however. Indeed, in the years after the implementation of the policy, thousands of servicemen and servicewomen were discharged from the service for being homosexuals. Many were forced out by a culture that promoted tireless investigations designed to purge the military of gays and lesbians. In 2010 Congress repealed the act. By then a substantial majority of the public favored allowing gays and lesbians to serve openly in the military.[36]

Changing public attitudes again altered policy. Gays, lesbians, and transgendered people nevertheless confront many obstacles to the full enjoyment of their rights. Notably, none of the federal laws overseeing employment practices covers discriminatory acts against gays, lesbians, or transgendered people. As far as federal law is concerned, employers may refuse to hire based solely on sexual orientation or identity. Likewise, employers may fire those who announce their orientation. A bill presently pending in Congress, the Employment Non-Discrimination Act (ENDA), if signed into law, will bar workplace discrimination based on sexual orientation or gender identity. The bill passed the Senate but languished in the House. Convinced early in 2014 that the House would not pass the bill, President Obama, in the summer of 2014, signed an executive order providing workplace protections to those that work for federal contractors, no matter their sexual preferences or gender identity.

Equality and Citizenship Status

> **What constitutional rights do noncitizens have?**

Although it may seem ironic in a nation of immigrants, immigration policy and the legal status of immigrants have often been hotly debated in American politics. In recent years, the debate over the rights of both legal and undocumented immigrants has gained new urgency. The state of California, a major destination for both legal and undocumented aliens, has spearheaded this reexamination of the legal status of immigrants. On November 8, 1994, California voters opened a nationwide debate over the rights of undocumented aliens by adopting Proposition 187. Among its many provisions, Proposition 187 required police officers, health care professionals, social service workers, and teachers in public schools to verify the immigration status of persons with whom they came into contact and to report to state and federal officials any individuals who lacked proper documentation. The proposition also denied health care, education, and social services to those who were undocumented.

This broad denial of benefits and services to undocumented aliens raised legal issues that had never before been fully addressed. In 1982 the U.S. Supreme Court, in *Plyler v. Doe*, had ruled unconstitutional a Texas law that allowed local school districts to deny educational services to children who were in the country illegally.[37] In denying public services, Proposition 187 went well beyond the law that led to the *Plyler* decision. In 1998, a federal district court declared virtually all the provisions of Proposition 187 unconstitutional.

Many of the goals embodied in Proposition 187 were given federal expression by the Welfare Reform Act of 1996. Hailed as "the end of welfare as we know it," the act, among other things, terminated Supplementary Security Income and Medicaid benefits to all immigrants, no matter what their legal status. One year later, Congress restored these benefits for most legal immigrants who were in the country when the legislation went into effect.

Immigration policy remains controversial. Indeed, since 2007, efforts to produce a new national immigration policy have been the source of bitter dispute. Recent proposals have provided, among other things, "a path to citizenship" for those undocumented people currently living in the United States. But even the mention of eventual citizenship generates passionate responses from those who believe that such a path rewards those who have taken up residence without the proper

Even as our government seeks to develop workable immigration policies, government authorities continue to deport undocumented aliens by the thousands. In 2013, the United States deported 368,644 people. Pictured here are demonstrators in front of the U.S. Capitol Building protesting the deportations, especially those that separate parents from their children.

documentation. The argument, simply put, is that providing a path to citizenship for undocumented residents rewards those who jumped the line at the expense of others who obeyed the law. Most of those who object to providing a path to citizenship also reject any significant reform until our borders have been sealed. Reform, they argue, can come about only after the borders have been closed.

In his first term, President Obama's administration deported more immigrants than any administration under any other president since 1950.[38] Moreover, President Obama created a program (Secure Communities) that encouraged local police departments to cooperate with the Department of Homeland Security in deporting the undocumented. Yet President Obama has consistently urged Congress to pass comprehensive immigration reform—reform that includes a path to citizenship.

With Congress unable to move an immigration bill, the president used (critics say abused) his executive powers to revise current policy. In June 2012, the president announced that, on his order, the Department of Homeland Security would cease deporting some undocumented people who came to the United States before age sixteen. To be eligible for this exception, the immigrants in question cannot be older than thirty and must have lived in the United States for five years, be in school or have graduated from high school, or have served in the U.S. military. Finally, they cannot have a criminal record. Individuals who fit this profile may apply for a two-year (renewable) deferment on deportation, and during that time they may seek work permits. The executive order does not provide amnesty, nor does it provide a path to citizenship. It is, however, highly controversial and subject to congressional countermand.

Because Congress was unable to agree on a comprehensive immigration policy, the states have become a hotbed of legislative action. Since 2007, forty-eight states have passed one or more laws on the subject. The result of all this legislation is a multiplicity of solutions, producing a confusing and contradictory array of

Opponents of migration across our southern border have long advocated the creation of a wall separating the United States and Mexico. Pictured here is one part of the wall, separating Nogales, Arizona, and Nogales, Mexico.

policy options. Some states, Arizona and Texas in particular, have adopted aggressive law enforcement and deportation as the key policy—the so-called attrition through enforcement approach. Other states have adopted more accommodating policies. Twelve states, for example, have promised in-state tuition at state universities to undocumented residents of the state. In 2013, California became the tenth state to allow the undocumented to obtain a driver's license. Obviously, so long as the national government is unable to take a lead, the states will continue to develop their own policy responses.

Affirmative Action

Affirmative action is a set of procedures that attempts to correct the effects of past discrimination against members of racial minorities and women. In its least controversial form, affirmative action seeks only to ensure that members of minority groups are fairly considered for educational and employment opportunities. Much more subject to dispute are affirmative action plans that establish specific goals and quotas for hiring minority applicants. Attacked by opponents as reverse discrimination, such plans have increasingly provoked criticism.

In its first full review of the affirmative action issue, *Regents of the University of California v. Bakke* (1978), the Court sent mixed signals as to the constitutionality of affirmative action measures. In 1973 and 1974, Alan Bakke had sought admission to the medical school at the University of California at Davis. Both times he was denied admission, even though the school accepted others with lower test scores under its special admissions program for disadvantaged students. Bakke finally sued the school, claiming that he was a victim of reverse discrimination.

A majority of the justices agreed with Bakke and ordered the school to admit him. They argued that because the medical school did not have a history of racial discrimination, it could not establish numerical quotas for minority students. It could not, as had been done on the Davis campus, set aside seats for minority candidates. The Court held, however, that the school could take minority status into account when deciding on admissions; to ensure a diverse student body, the university could treat the applicant's status as a member of a minority group as a plus.[39]

Even though in the *Bakke* case the Court seemed to conclude that affirmative action was constitutional, the confusion surrounding the decision encouraged opponents to continue challenging affirmative action programs. In 2003, the Supreme Court reentered the fray over affirmative action in education by deciding a pair of cases from the University of Michigan, one involving its law school and the other its undergraduate admissions policies. Writing for the Court in *Grutter v. Bollinger*, Justice Sandra Day O'Connor upheld the law school's program of using race as a factor in admissions. Justice O'Connor noted that the law school had no quota for minority students and that each applicant was considered individually. Furthermore, the justice noted that the law school frequently accepts nonminority students with lower grades and test scores than minority applicants who are rejected. The justice did point out, however, that the Court expects that within twenty-five years' time, the use of racial preferences would no longer be necessary. On the other hand, the Court rejected the university's affirmative action program for undergraduate admissions. Students

Affirmative action A set of procedures that attempts to correct the effects of past discrimination against minority groups. It can include specific goals and quotas for hiring minority applicants.

applying to the College of Literature, Science, and Arts were rated on a 150-point scale; they needed at least 100 points to guarantee admission. Minority applicants were automatically awarded 20 points, and the Court found this discriminatory. This mechanistic approach of automatically awarding some students 20 points amounted, the Court majority concluded, to a quota system, a practice banned as far back as *Bakke*[40] The future of affirmative action programs was thrown into further doubt in 2007, when the Court invalidated public school assignment plans in Seattle and Louisville that took race, along with other characteristics, into account. According to Chief Justice Roberts, the way to eliminate racial discrimination was to eliminate racial discrimination. Indeed, in the 2014 case *Schuette v. Coalition to Defend Affirmative Action,* the Court ruled that states may prohibit any use of race in university admissions decisions.

Affirmative action plans associated with employment practices have also come under Supreme Court scrutiny. In 2009 the Court ruled that white firefighters in New Haven, Connecticut, were the victims of racial discrimination when the city tossed out their promotional exam results. No African American applicant scored high enough on the exams to be considered for promotion. Fearing that the city would be sued for racial discrimination, New Haven officials discarded the exam results and restarted the promotion process. The nineteen applicants, seventeen of whom are white and two of whom are Hispanic, sued the city, claiming that they were the victims of racial discrimination. Justice Kennedy, speaking for the five-justice majority, ruled that the fear of litigation could not justify ignoring the exam results. Ignoring the results of legitimate promotional exams out of fear that not enough minorities would be promoted would, Justice Kennedy argued, "amount to a de facto quota system." Only when there is "a strong basis in evidence" that the employer would lose a discrimination suit may the results of a previously administered exam be discarded.

Conclusion

Using the equal protection clause of the Fourteenth Amendment, the Supreme Court has done much to ensure civil rights for African Americans, but so too has Congress. Unfortunately, full equality is yet to be achieved. Even in the case of African Americans, the record has been one of progress and regress. Other groups that feel the burden of discrimination perhaps have not gained as much in the battle for equal rights, but, like African Americans, their struggle has produced improvements. Obviously, as is evident in the cases of Charles Barkley and Trayon Christian, highlighted at the opening of this chapter, the myth of guaranteed equality does not describe reality. The myth remains an aspiration. Without the aspiration, without the hope that the myth creates, it is unlikely that any progress would be possible.

Key Terms

Affirmative action p. 173
Anti-miscegenation laws p. 159
Civil rights p. 153
Cold War p. 177
Containment p. 177
Glass ceiling p. 164

Focus Questions Review

1. **What have been the breakthroughs in the movement toward racial justice in America?** > > >
   We regard ourselves as a nation committed to protecting minorities against discrimination and unreasonable treatment by others, but discrimination was and still is a feature of American society. Our understanding of civil rights is constantly undergoing change, leading us to continually question what forms of discrimination are impermissible. The Supreme Court has ruled that invidious discrimination—discrimination based on characteristics that are not fundamentally related to the situation—is not permissible.

   Racism has from the nation's founding burdened many in American society. The struggle for equality has led to the end of the separate-but-equal doctrine and some decreases in discrimination, particularly in education, public accommodations, and voting. But African Americans are still subject to discrimination.

2. **How have the rights of women evolved?** > > >
   Women first organized for equal rights as part of the antislavery movement, but it took until the second decade of the twentieth century to get the right to vote. In the 1960s the second generation of the women's movement made progress toward equality in the courts and Congress. Nevertheless, several issues remain unsolved

3. **How has the legal status of gays, lesbians, and transgender people changed?** > > >
   The twenty-first century has seen the growth of the gay rights movement and its increasing success in changing policies and attitudes. Rapid changes in public opinion have opened up new opportunities for gays, lesbians, and transgender people, but they have yet to achieve full equality.

4. **What constitutional rights do noncitizens have?** > > >
   Questions regarding the undocumented remain a highly controversial subject in American politics. Because Congress has been unable to agree on a comprehensive immigration policy, the states have become active in setting policy.

Review Questions

1. Write an essay in which you discuss how the level of scrutiny applied in cases involving racial discrimination differs from the level used in cases concerning discrimination based on gender.
2. Write an essay in which you discuss the progress that gays and lesbians have made in advancing their claims for equality.

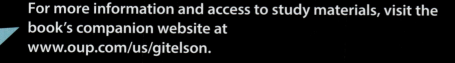

For more information and access to study materials, visit the book's companion website at www.oup.com/us/gitelson.

Policy Connection

What is the relationship between American domestic policies and U.S. foreign policy?

The Policy Challenge

Among the major challenges facing those who shape and direct American foreign policy is how to reconcile what they do on the international stage with the realities of how the United States handles many of its toughest domestic issues. Similarly, those who work on domestic policy problems can hardly ignore that, in a sense, the whole world is watching how America deals with important issues, especially those related to the treatment of minority populations.

The image of students being escorted to and from Little Rock Central High School in 1957 was the cause of considerable embarrassment for U.S. foreign-policy makers and diplomats.

In this Policy Connection we consider those policy dilemmas, highlighting the post–World War II struggles to advance civil rights that we discussed in Chapter 5.

The Whole World Was Watching

In September 1957, President Dwight D. Eisenhower sent a thousand members of the 101st Airborne Division to protect nine black children who were attempting to enter the Little Rock, Arkansas, Central High School. In doing so, he was enforcing a federal court order that required the school district to end its policy of forced segregation. Eisenhower's actions marked the culmination of several months of negotiation and heated debate between federal and state officials over the desegregation orders and how they would be carried out.

Media coverage of the events grew as the crisis unfolded. At first there were stories in the local press, followed by coverage by major African American press outlets that sent reporters to Little Rock. Eventually the mainstream media (see Chapter 10), including the major TV networks, began sending reporters and camera crews to the scene as confrontations between local and federal officials escalated. By the time the troops arrived, the efforts to integrate Central High had turned violent—and the riots in the streets of Little Rock became an international news story.

From the perspective of American foreign-policy makers, the picture of U.S. race relations painted by those news stories was not helping America's efforts to win the Cold War that was being waged abroad. For America's diplomats abroad, the Little Rock confrontations were just the latest in long line of stories that were having a negative impact on American foreign policy. President Truman's secretary of state, Dean Acheson, wrote to the head of one government agency that:

[D]iscrimination against minority groups in this country has an adverse effect upon our relations with other countries. We are reminded over and over again by some foreign newspapers and spokesmen that our treatment of various minorities leaves much to be desired. . . . Frequently we find it impossible to [respond] to our critics in other countries.[1]

Chester Bowles, the U.S. ambassador to India, told an audience in 1952 that:

A year, a month, or even a week in Asia is enough to convince any perceptive American that the colored peoples of Asia and Africa . . . seldom think about the United States without considering the limitations under which our 13 million Negroes are living.[2]

The **Cold War** is a period dating from just after the end of World War II until the collapse of the Soviet Union in 1991, and it was characterized in part by American efforts (as the leading nation of the West) to win over the hearts and minds of those nations in Africa, Asia, and Latin America emerging from colonialism or from under the yoke of dictatorships. In very general terms, U.S. policy during the Cold War was based primarily on **containment**—a commitment to diplomatically, economically, and militarily counter the expansionist tendencies of the Soviet Union and its allies in Eastern Europe and Asia. The approach was a middle ground between doing nothing in the face of growing Soviet influence and directly confronting the USSR and its allies on the battlefield.

News stories like those coming out of Little Rock were not helpful on the diplomatic front, where the United States wanted to project the most positive image of its political system, especially to those in Asia, Africa, and Latin America who might be attracted to the influence and appeal of Soviet-style communism. The millions of dollars invested in foreign aid and the creation of cultural exchanges were quickly offset by events in Arkansas. Moreover, the Soviet Union took full advantage of the ongoing crises in Little Rock and elsewhere by making certain the news reached every corner of the globe.

Within this context, it was not surprising that advancing civil rights policies became a critical concern and high priority for the decision makers involved in making and implementing U.S. foreign affairs. Whatever the policymaking establishment might have thought about the plight of African Americans before the Cold War, it gave it a great deal of attention as the media expanded its news coverage from Little Rock and other parts of the American South. Some prominent historians of the period have concluded that the support of the foreign policy establishment was a central factor in the advancement of civil rights policies during that period.

The Little Rock crisis highlights a major issue that has puzzled political observers for decades: What is the relationship between American domestic policies and its foreign policies? Were the major advances in civil rights policies that took place in the 1950s and 1960s the result of America's policymakers realizing that winning the Cold War required such changes? Or was the opposite the case—that is, did the emerging civil rights movement and other progressive economic and social policies of the post–World War II era shape American foreign policies, especially those in support of **Third World nations**, that is, those newly independent and nonaligned nations that regarded the United States as a model to emulate?

Students of American foreign policy have developed four distinct responses to questions about the relationship between domestic and foreign policies. Some believe that domestic policies are indeed subject to the influence of foreign-policy priorities. Historian Mary L. Dudziak writes:

From the immediate postwar years until the mid-1960s, race in America was thought to have a critical impact on U.S. prestige abroad.

Civil rights crises became foreign affairs crises. Domestic difficulties were managed by U.S. presidents with an eye toward how their actions would play overseas. In this context, secretaries of state promoted civil rights reform, and progress on civil rights was counted as a foreign affairs achievement.[3]

Advocates of this view also see the impact of foreign-policy pressures in other areas of domestic policy. The oil embargo imposed by the Organization of Arab Petroleum Exporting Countries (OAPEC) in response to U.S. support for Israel in the Yom Kippur War of 1973, for example, generated a number of changes in domestic policies designed to enhance energy-conservation efforts. In fact, decades later, the drive for energy independence from foreign oil remains a key factor in shaping policies from highway speed limits and regulations regarding the sale of light bulbs to state and local building codes. And, as noted in Policy Connection 4, the effort to combat terrorism has altered many aspects of our lives. There is also support for the argument that globalization and the emergence of a new international economic order based in East Asia and elsewhere have led to shifts in our domestic economic policies, especially toward deregulation and away from protectionist barriers to free trade. The North American Free Trade Agreement (NAFTA) involving the United States, Canada, and Mexico, for example, was a hotly contested treaty that passed the U.S. Senate in 1994 primarily because of the way it altered many parts of the American economy.

Other observers assume a quite different view, emphasizing that domestic factors shape and direct much of U.S. foreign policy. They point to the significant role that Martin Luther King Jr. and other prominent leaders of the civil rights movement played in the anti–Vietnam War movement, which has had a lasting impact of the conduct of American foreign policy. In terms of energy policy, they stress the impact that the years of domestic policies promoting overconsumption and waste of carbon-based fuel resources has had on creating our dependency on foreign oil, thus exposing us to the kind of crisis that took place in the 1970s. As for our foreign economic policies, these critics point to the decisions to deregulate the U.S. banking sector and lax enforcement of regulations of other domestic industries as major reasons for the collapse of global financial markets in 2008 and the subsequent changes in the U.S. role in the international political economy.

In contrast to both those views is a perspective holding that there is little or no significant relationship between the two policy spheres. Known as *political realists*, analysts taking this view regard the international arena of nation-state relationships to be distinct and completely different from the domestic arena. They argue that the influence of civil rights, economic and social policy disputes, and other "internal matters" is—and ought to be—minimized when it comes to the pursuit of America's national interest on the world stage. Political

On December 23, 1973, cars formed a double line at a gas station in New York City. The Arab oil embargo caused gas shortages nationwide and has shaped U.S. foreign policy to this day.

scientist Hans J. Morgenthau (1904–1980) was an advocate of this perspective, and his view of the history of American foreign policy was that although policymakers often spoke to domestic audiences as if their decisions reflected the unique values and preferences of American society, the reality was that the United States had always acted like every other country in pursuing power and its national interest in foreign relationships.[4]

Finally, there are those who see the two policy arenas as closely intertwined. One cannot understand American foreign policy unless one appreciates its domestic politics and the policies it generated—and vice versa. Former secretary of state Henry Kissinger understood this quite well. Although as a scholar writing in the 1950s and 1960s he expressed admiration for some practitioners of the political realism approach (known as *Realpolitik*),[5] as a key foreign-policy decision maker under President Richard Nixon, he knew that, in practice, no foreign policy could or should ignore the political divisions and controversies that characterized U.S. politics during the 1970s. Similarly, as President Jimmy Carter learned a few years later when he faced an ongoing energy crisis as well as the taking of hostages in Iran, domestic problems and issues are difficult to address when the country is preoccupied with international crises.

Any serious analyst of U.S. foreign policy should appreciate that each of those four perspectives has some merit. But knowing the historical details of those "theories" is of little use if you are the average American trying to make sense of what is taking place in U.S. foreign policy today. That is why many of us tend to rely on two myths that help us understand why our policies are as they are.

Vulnerability and Exceptionalism

The *myth of American vulnerability*, introduced in Policy Connection 4, has deep roots in our country's approach to foreign affairs. We can see it in George Washington's advice that the United States avoid "entangling alliances" that can make the nation vulnerable to the influence of foreign powers. "Observe good faith and justice towards all Nations," he advised in his farewell address; "cultivate peace and harmony with all. . . . It will be worthy of a free, enlightened, and, at no distant period, a great Nation, to give to mankind the magnanimous and too novel example of a people always guided by an exalted justice and benevolence."[6]

Implied in Washington's comments, however, is another myth—one stressing America's unique standing among the world's nations. The *myth of American exceptionalism* reflects the idea that the nation's role on the global stage ought to be tied to a vision of a world order in which America can stand as a "magnanimous and too novel example." According to Walter Russell Mead,[7] U.S. foreign policy has been linked historically to four such visions of that exceptionalism:

1. *The Wilsonian vision:* In one such vision, the mission or purpose of American foreign policy is a moral one in which the United States seeks to play a major role in establishing and defending a benign international legal order in which democracy and free markets can thrive in peace. Associated with President Woodrow Wilson's efforts to create the League of Nations after World War I, it is a vision that links American security to the support and success of organizations like the United Nations.

2. *The Hamiltonian vision:* A second vision for American foreign policy would have it foster a world order that best serves the economic interests of the United States. This view is closely associated with the views of Alexander Hamilton, the first secretary of the treasury, who was committed to doing whatever was necessary to give the new nation a stable economic standing in the world economic order of the day.

3. *The Jeffersonian vision:* A third vision for American foreign policy stresses the need for the United States to shape its foreign and defense policies to protect and sustain our country's democratic institutions. Linked historically to the views of Thomas Jefferson, this vision regards the United States as an exceptional political

system and society that require its leaders to be on guard against risky entanglements that might put the nation's unique political qualities at risk. The mission of the United States in world affairs is to stand out as an example for others to emulate, but to avoid getting involved in alliances or international arrangements that might sacrifice America's special "democratic experiment."

4. *The Jacksonian vision:* Finally, a fourth, more nationalistic, vision of American foreign policy gives weight to national honor and the wisdom and judgment of the American public and its leaders at any particular time. This view is associated with the domestic populism of President Andrew Jackson, and in many respects shares the Jeffersonian vision of the United States as an exceptional country that should avoid foreign entanglements. But, whereas the Jeffersonians are skeptical and weary about international affairs, the Jacksonians are explicitly hostile to the idea of engaging in global politics on terms set by other nations. For Jacksonians, the special status of American democracy extends to how the United States conducts itself once it is drawn into world affairs. Jackson had little tolerance or respect for the niceties of diplomacy or international rules, and he believed the United States should follow its own code of behavior in its relations with other nations.

It is easy to see how each of these four visions of America's mission in the world would have a significant impact on the conduct of U.S. foreign policies as well as the average American's understanding of them. Mead argues that these visions of the American role in world affairs (Wilsonian, Hamiltonian, Jeffersonian, and Jacksonian) have, in various forms and mixtures at various times in U.S. history, provided the logic for the country's foreign policies. Indeed, when tied to the diverse feelings of national vulnerability over time, they offer us a means for understanding how these policies emerged and how they have changed over the years.

For the Wilsonians, Americans will only be safe in a democratic world, and U.S. foreign-policy makers should be guided by a sense of moral obligation to promote a world order reflecting those democratic values so central to our view of government. For the Hamiltonians, because the greatest threats come from a world order that undermines the economic interests of the United States, American policymakers must see foreign affairs in terms of serving our national economic self-interest. Jeffersonians, by contrast, regard the United States as an exemplar of modern democratic governance—a model to be nurtured and protected as much as possible from the corruption of international entanglements and intrigues. Finally, for Jacksonians, it is the integrity and honor of the United States that is most exceptional as well as vulnerable, and the country's foreign-policy makers must be prepared to do whatever is necessary to defeat those who might threaten either.

Conclusion

What is the relationship between American domestic policies and U.S. foreign policy?

Of course, there is much more to American foreign policies than actions to make us less vulnerable and to help us pursue some vision of America's role in the world. There are the strategies and instruments through which we conduct foreign policy, and these are the subject of Policy Connection 12. The focus of this discussion was to highlight different views on the complex relationship between domestic and foreign policies. In the case of civil rights, what seemed like a completely internal matter that was of interest and concern to Americans turned out to be a significant issue on the world stage, as the United States engaged in the Cold War for more than four decades. At the same time, in conducting our foreign affairs, policymakers find it difficult to ignore the American public's attitudes toward the pain and suffering around the world that they view in daily news reports.

But there are instances when policymakers have to confront the realities of political events. When a bomb exploded at the 16th Street Baptist

Church in Montgomery in September 1963 and killed four young African American girls, the stain on America's reputation was obvious worldwide.[8] The U.S. foreign-policy establishment that had pushed so hard to advance the cause of civil rights could do little more than mourn along with the rest of the world.

That same feeling of frustration and helplessness emerged more than three decades later when U.S. policymakers could do little or nothing to prevent the outbreak of genocidal conflict in the African nation of Rwanda in May 1994. "When I wake up every morning and look at the headlines and the stories and the images on television of these conflicts," stated Anthony Lake, President Bill Clinton's national security advisor,

President Jimmy Carter's appointment of civil rights leader Andrew Young as ambassador to the United Nations was intended in part to send a sign to the world that the United States was overcoming its past problems with race relations.

> I want to work to end every conflict. I want to work to save every child out there. And I know the president does, and I know the American people do. But neither we nor the international community have the resources nor the mandate to do so. So we have to make distinctions. We have to ask the hard questions about where and when we can intervene. And the reality is that we cannot often solve other people's problems; we can never build their nations for them.[9]

It seems like the primary conclusion we can draw about the relationship between domestic and foreign policies is that "it's complicated." But for those of us trying to make sense of American public policy, perhaps there is some comfort in appreciating just how complicated that relationship gets.

QUESTIONS FOR DISCUSSION

1. **During the Cold War era, the United States was very concerned about how the world viewed how America responded to its domestic problems such as civil rights. Are we any less concerned today about how the rest of the world sees us? Can you think of any issue or policy that might cause us embarrassment on the global stage? And what, if anything, should we do about it?**

2. **We now live in a globalized and interconnected world. How have globalization and the revolution in telecommunications impacted our domestic policy agenda?**

CHAPTER 6

Public Opinion and Political Participation

Witches, Ghosts, and Public Opinion

When Halloween arrives every October, the proverbial questions always seem to be raised about what people find scary. Do you believe in witches? Do you believe in ghosts or extraterrestrial beings? These are strange questions, no doubt, for an American government textbook. But they are questions that reputable polling organizations have asked, and that Americans have opinions on. (You may find it interesting that 21 percent of Americans believe in witches, 31 percent believe in ghosts, and 24 percent believe that extraterrestrial beings have visited the earth.)[1] Although attitudes about witches and ghosts have little to do with American government and politics, public opinion and polls do play a central role in the shaping of politics and policy in the United States.

The role that public opinion plays in public policy decisions often presents a complex problem for elected officials. In general, policymakers feel compelled to pay close attention to public opinion on an issue, whether that opinion is held by a majority of the public (more than 50 percent) or simply by a plurality (the largest percentage among those polled, but not a majority). Yet public opinion is often difficult to assess, and in many cases no definitive opinion carries the day. Consider poll findings during one of the most heated periods of debate over the Affordable Care Act (also known as Obamacare) during the fall of 2013. One reputable polling center found that 53 percent disapproved of the act, whereas 42 percent approved. Of those who disapproved of the act, approximately half thought that elected officials who oppose the

CHAPTER OUTLINE AND FOCUS QUESTIONS

What Is Public Opinion?
> How do we define political public opinion?

How We Develop Our Beliefs and Opinions
> What agents of political socialization help to shape and influence our opinions about government and politics?

How Polls Work
> What factors contribute to a well-designed and effective poll? What factors contribute to a poorly designed poll?

The Paradox of Public Opinion
> Do the findings from public opinion polls suggest that Americans question the principles of democracy and representative government?

Group Opinion: Diversity and Uniformity
> How does public opinion vary between women and men and within and among different ethnic, religious, racial, and age groups?

Avenues of Political Participation
> What are the different ways in which Americans participate in the political system?

< One of the most polarizing issues in recent years has been immigration reform and whether illegal immigrants to the United Sates should be able to gain legal status and be provided with a path to citizenship. Here, a person dressed in a skeleton costume makes his or her anti–immigration reform feelings very clear.

law should make it work as well as possible, whereas the other half thought they should make it fail. At the same time, only 25 percent of the respondents said that they had a very good understanding of how the law would impact them. Forty-four percent of the public were unsure whether the act remained a law, including 13 percent who thought it had been either overturned by the Supreme Court or repealed by Congress.[2] Public opinion was polarized and confused on this issue, and although many people were uncertain about the act's content and status and how it would affect them personally, they still expressed an opinion about it.

How does a member of Congress sort out the conflicting information supplied by polls on any policy issue? Although the ideology and the party identification of many legislators often play an important role in shaping their policy positions, public opinion frequently makes any attempt by policymakers to write laws and establish policies highly controversial and open to considerable debate. If the members of Congress try to please a portion of the public by supporting legislation regarding a specific policy, they could very well end up offending another portion of the public with those same policies.

Consider the controversial subject of abortion rights. Figure 6.1 reflects the results of more than a decade (1996–2013) of polling by the Gallup organization focused on whether respondents perceived themselves as *pro-choice* (favoring abortion rights) or *pro-life* (opposing abortion rights). Starting in the late 1990s, public attitudes toward abortion—both pro-choice and pro-life—have hovered around 50 percent. In light of the emotions associated with opinions on this issue, one can see why the politics of abortion rights has been so heated.

FIGURE 6.1 Public Opinion About the Abortion Issue, 1996–2013
With respect to the abortion issue, would you consider yourself to be pro-choice or pro-life? This chart shows the trends from polls in which respondents were asked whether they were pro-life or pro-choice after a question on the legality of abortion.
Source: Gallup Poll, 2013.

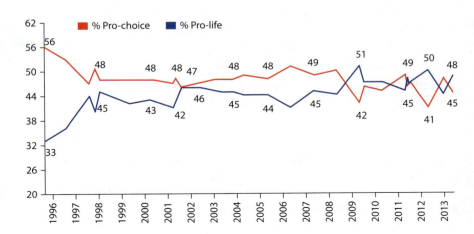

Behind these examples, however, is the question raised by the polls themselves. Are the people who respond to these polls representative of the American public? Can a sampling of public opinion be a credible measure of how the American people really feel about these issues? Moreover, are the issues as black and white as the polling questions infer? That is, can the public be divided between those for and those against every aspect of the Affordable Care Act? Or do Americans have a more nuanced view, being willing to support parts but not all of the mandates of the program? Or can Americans support a more liberal policy on abortions in the case of incest or rape but be against it during the second trimester of a pregnancy?

As flawed or ambiguous as some may be, public opinion polls play a central role in the shaping of politics and policy in the United States, and they can often help both ordinary citizens and politicians make sense of public policy preferences. This is the case not only for predicting election outcomes but also for providing a tool that politicians, scholars, and the media use to measure and assess the public's opinions on everything political, from its favorite presidential candidate to its attitudes toward specific issues and laws.

In making sense of the role that public opinion and opinion polls play in our political system, we focus specifically on the *myth of majority opinion*. According to that myth, many Americans and officeholders frequently believe that on important issues there is a prevailing majority view held by most people. Either side of an issue can selectively interpret polling data as supporting its position and therefore believe its position is the right one. In reality, although citizens share majority feelings on some issues and values—for example, as early as 2013, a significant majority believed and continues to believe that we should get our troops out of Afghanistan as soon as possible—the public often cannot be viewed as having a monolithic, majority viewpoint on numerous important issues. Public officials must balance a diverse set of opinions voiced by a variety of groups, resulting in consensus through compromise. By understanding the facts behind the myth of majority opinion, we can gain a sense of how the public influences government decisions and how we can better make sense of the political system.

The importance of public opinion in our political system reflects the general view that, in a democracy such as ours, the more the voice of the people is heard, the better. In this chapter we also examine different forms of participation in the political system, for it is often the strength and intensity of public opinion that leads to political participation on the part of citizens.

What Is Public Opinion?

> **How do we define political public opinion?**

Political public opinion
The collective preferences expressed by people on political issues, policies, institutions, and individuals.

V. O. Key Jr., a respected scholar of public opinion, said that "to speak with precision of public opinion is a task not unlike coming to grips with the Holy Ghost."[3] And yet no democratic government can afford to ignore public opinion, for it is public opinion that links the values, demands, and expectations of the citizens to the actions of their government. What, then, is this elusive concept? Stated formally, **political public opinion** is the collective preferences expressed by people concerning political issues, policies, institutions, and individuals. In using the term *collective*, we are arguing that public opinion is not always majority opinion but, more precisely, is a collection of opinions that generally reflect a variety of beliefs on a given issue or problem.

Opinion intensity The strength of one's opinion about an issue.

To better make sense of what public opinion is, we must understand the four different components of public opinion. Public opinion varies in **intensity, saliency, stability**, and **direction**. Not every issue evokes intense feelings, and not every issue is equally salient or stable. In addition, public opinion varies in terms of direction—that is, whether it is in favor of or against a particular issue. Much of the time, there are various levels of support for an issue, with no clear and precise direction of public opinion.

Opinion saliency One's perception of the relevancy of an issue.

For example, many Americans are concerned about the treatment of laboratory animals, but few feel intensely about this issue. Even when they do, it may not be the most salient issue for them, either because it does not appear to directly affect their lives or because they believe there are more important issues to worry about. In contrast, most people feel strongly, or intensely, about the state of the economy and high unemployment rates. These issues are salient, or important, to them because they affect them directly. On issues such as abortion, however, the wide disparity among the intensities of opinion about it makes the policy direction supported by the majority of the public unclear.

Opinion stability The degree to which public opinion on an issue changes over time.

Public opinion also varies in stability. For example, a 2004 poll dealing with the economy found that 21 percent of those surveyed said that that issue was the most important in determining their vote in a presidential election. A survey taken five years later, however, found that the number of individuals who considered the economy the most important issue had grown to 50 percent of those surveyed. By 2014, only 20 percent of Americans thought that the economy was the most important problem facing the country.[4] The stability of public opinion over longer periods of time also fluctuates. In 1968, 42 percent of Americans favored the death penalty for individuals convicted of murder. By 1995, that percentage had grown to 80 percent. Today, that percentage has declined to 63 percent.[5] Thus, far from being stable, public opinion on many issues may be vulnerable to the expectations and demands of the people.

Opinion direction One's position in favor of or against a particular issue. Much of the time there are various shades of support for an issue, with no clear and precise direction of public opinion.

Many public officials use measures of intensity, saliency, stability, and direction as a guide to the public's political preferences. If a majority, or even an active minority, of the public seems indifferent, or if opinions are unstable and shifting, officials may discount the public's views or not act at all. In contrast, salient issues that arouse intense feelings and popular passions are likely to generate action.

How We Develop Our Beliefs and Opinions

> **What agents of political socialization help to shape and influence our opinions about government and politics?**

What factors influence our political opinions? Using reasoned analysis based on data and facts is very important. By being better informed about issues and candidates, we can make sense of the political events and issues that affect our lives. Our underlying beliefs and ideologies also help shape our opinions about government and the political world we live in. As we noted in Chapter 1, whether we are liberal or conservative or libertarians or populists, the ideology we maintain often shapes how we view the political world and evaluate the facts and data others present to us. The myths we believe in also play an important role in shaping our political opinions and helping us make sense of the governmental process. Among other things, myths help us simplify the complex world in which we live, provide us with a political identity, guide our behavior, and help us make sense out of the behavior of others.

How do long-term political values and beliefs develop? How do we acquire our ideological commitments and our view of the world through the myths we adopt? According to social scientists, they are based on the different experiences that people undergo throughout their lives. Single historical events like that of September 11, 2001, the Great Recession that followed the banking crises of 2007–2008, the devastation of a natural disaster, or military combat experiences can have a lasting impact on citizens' values and beliefs. Everyday experiences and events can also have subtle, long-term impacts on our political beliefs and attitudes. Living in Boston, Houston, or San Diego is very different from living in rural Vermont, Mississippi, or North Carolina. These differences translate into regional (and even local) variations in what people believe in and value; further differences in opinion derive from gender, race, religion, class, and other factors.

Many Americans share a common, or core, **political culture**—that is, a set of shared values, beliefs, and traditions with regard to politics and government. These shared values (sometimes called the "American creed") include a general faith in democracy, representative government, the free-market system, freedom of speech, and the rights of individuals. The process by which people acquire these important values and gain knowledge about politics is known as **political socialization**. It is strongly influenced by the persons with whom an individual comes into contact from early childhood through adulthood.

Agents of Political Socialization

Children are influenced by many variables as they grow up and are exposed to the political world around them. They learn from songs, the celebration of holidays, the honoring of heroes, and a variety of patriotic rituals that we as Americans practice. Some institutions play a particularly strong role in our acquisition of political values and knowledge.

Political culture A set of values, beliefs, and traditions about politics and government that are shared by most members of society. Political culture in the United States includes faith in democracy, representative government, freedom of speech, and individual rights.

Political socialization The process by which individuals acquire political values and knowledge about politics. It is strongly influenced by the people with whom an individual has come into contact with from early childhood through adulthood.

Political efficacy The perception of one's ability to have an impact on the political system.

Party identification The tendency of citizens to think of themselves as Democrats, Republicans, or independents.

Family and Friends. Family members, especially parents, transmit to their children basic attitudes, beliefs, and values that mold the children's views of the political world. These general values include perceptions of right and wrong and attitudes toward authority figures—parents, teachers, police officers, judges, and political officeholders. They also include perceptions of our **political efficacy**—that is, our ability to have an impact on the political system. Family and friends also have an impact on our attitudes about the political system, including how trusting or cynical we may be toward government and politicians, how alienated from government we may feel, and how well we can make sense of the political system.

One specific belief often passed from parent to child that is particularly important in understanding political opinions and behavior is **party identification**, or whether people think of themselves as Democrats or Republicans, identify with another political party, or consider themselves independents. Peer groups and friends have relatively little influence on a person's party identification or voting behavior at the age of eighteen. Later in life, there are occasions when friends and peers with political opinions that conflict with those we hold can influence and alter our beliefs and attitudes about politics and government. As we get older, however, our peers tend to reinforce our already-established beliefs, because we tend to associate with friends and colleagues who share similar values and attitudes.

School. Another institution that potentially has a great impact on political socialization is school. At any given time, about a quarter of the population is enrolled, full or part time, in degree-granting educational programs, including primary and secondary schools, four- and two-year private and public postsecondary programs, and technical training schools. Schools teach such political virtues as patriotism, compliance with the laws, the importance of voting, and the desirability of a peaceful changeover of presidential administrations. By repeating many of the lessons about government that we learn at home, school reinforces many of the values we already hold about politics and government.

At their best, schools also help us develop our skills in analyzing government and the political process, as well as making us better informed and better able to make sense of the political world around us. They no doubt also contribute to some of the myths we hold about the political system, including the often-taught lesson that anyone can grow up to be president of the United States, a belief that, although it is an exaggeration (in more than two hundred years, we've had only forty-four presidents), reminds us that our nation believes in equality and opportunity for all.

The amount of schooling a person receives greatly influences that person's opinions on and views of the political world. Better-educated and less-well-educated individuals differ significantly in their attitudes and behaviors. Better-educated people generally know more about politics. Those who have been to college are more likely than others to hold liberal views on civil liberties and rights, foreign policy, and social questions. Education also brings confidence that one can affect political and governmental policy—what we earlier called political efficacy—which leads to a relatively high level of participation in politics.[6]

Like schoolchildren all over America, these second-grade students in Austin, Texas, begin their day by reciting the Pledge of Allegiance. Schools are an important influence in learning about politics, often reinforcing such political virtues as patriotism and support of our government systems.

The Media. The media, particularly television, are also important socializing agencies. Ninety-eight percent of households in the United States have at least one television. Because the average person spends close to five hours a day watching television, its potential effect as an agent of political socialization is enormous.[7] But what is its actual influence?

Although television teaches and reinforces general beliefs and attitudes, it has limited political impact, chiefly because such a small proportion of programming has direct political content. For example, in 1952, television network coverage of the Republican and Democratic presidential conventions averaged about sixty hours. During the 2012 conventions, the average evening coverage by the three major television networks— ABC, NBC, and CBS—was less than one hour a night, although ABC, CBS, NBC, Fox News Channel, PBS, and C-SPAN provided live streaming online from start to finish of both the Democratic and Republican conventions. Social media (Twitter, Facebook, and YouTube) also were used by the traditional media outlets to enhance their coverage of the conventions.[8]

The media in all their forms, including broadcast and print, play an important role in the socialization of Americans. But a careful examination of that role suggests that its impact is varied and is dependent on our viewing and reading habits. Although the time committed to local news broadcasts has increased over the past ten years, only 3 percent of the newscasts cover politics and government, whereas 40 percent of the time is allocated to covering the weather, traffic, and sports. Another 13 percent of local airtime is devoted to accidents, disasters, and unusual events.[9] (See Chapter 10 for more about the impact of the media.)

Religion. Religion can often serve, both directly and indirectly, as an important agent of political socialization. Indirectly, religion teaches morality and values that can apply to the way we think about government and politics. We may view

The development of the Internet and social media sites such as blogs, YouTube, and Twitter has played a growing role in the public's exposure to elections, politics, and the government. Here we see a man reading Barack Obama's tweet on November 7, 2012 after his re-election.

POLITICS & POPULAR CULTURE: Visit the book's companion website at **www.oup.com/us/gitelson** to read the special feature *The Biographical Film and Political Advertising.*

the acts of politicians through the value lenses afforded us by attending a church, synagogue, or mosque. Religious institutions also take overt positions on political issues that may affect our political beliefs.

Political Culture. Although Americans share a common political culture, a variety of political subcultures flourish.[10] Individuals who grow up and live in one region have different religious, ethnic, and racial backgrounds and customs and undergo different economic and social experiences from those living in other parts of the country. A carpenter who grew up and still lives in the rural poverty of West Virginia is far less likely to view the political system as responsive than a lawyer who grew up and prospered in Florida, a state that experienced great economic growth until the recent Great Recession. Such influences help shape the way we view the political world. They can generate or reinforce our beliefs and ideologies as well as the myths we adopt to better make sense of the political system. Variations in life experience inevitably result in differing political, social, and economic views.

Adult Socialization

Not surprisingly, political socialization is not just a childhood experience. As parents' influence declines, coworkers, neighbors, and friends reinforce—and sometimes shape—adults' opinions. Television, of course, affects adults' political views more than children's, because adults rely on it for the news more than children do. And a variety of additional media—newspapers, magazines, the Internet, blogs, and radio—provide wider exposure to political information.

In addition, adults bring their own established beliefs, facts, ideologies, and myths to their assessment of new situations. They are also likely to be influenced by the current conditions of their life. For example, parents may see more merit in a tax increase to support local schools than do childless adults. Events such as the crisis of failing financial institutions in 2008, as well as the wars in Iraq and Afghanistan, continue to shape the values and opinions of millions of adult Americans who view our social and economic welfare and our national security as major public policy issues. Thus, the development of public opinion is clearly a process that continues throughout one's entire life.

How Polls Work

> **What factors contribute to a well-designed and effective poll?**
> **What factors contribute to a poorly designed poll?**

Informal public opinion surveys in the United States date as far back as 1824, when a reporter from the *Harrisburg Pennsylvanian*, standing on a street corner in Wilmington, Delaware, asked 532 men whom they planned to vote for in the presidential race that year. But it was not until the 1930s that George Gallup and Elmo Roper began to experiment with scientific measures of public opinion. Gallup and Roper were able to measure opinion on many issues with a high degree of accuracy by taking into account differences in age, gender, ethnic background, race, religion, social class, and region.

Pollsters choose their interviewees by the method of **random probability sampling**, in which every person in the population theoretically has an equal chance of being selected. That system of sampling is not perfect, for in any population some individuals have little or no chance of being selected for an interview. Nevertheless, pollsters have developed elaborate and sometimes complicated procedures to deal with potential sampling errors. For example, after decades of relying on landline phone numbers, in recent years they have had to consider how to ensure that cell phone users will be included in their telephone surveys. The basic idea—that the opinions of individuals selected by chance will be representative of the opinions of the population at large—is highly effective and reliable. Since 1936, the Gallup Poll has correctly predicted the winner in all but two presidential elections and has been within a few percentage points of the actual results each time.[11]

In contrast, **straw polls** rely on an unsystematic method of selection. People are questioned in shopping centers or on street corners, with little or no effort being made to ensure that respondents are representative of the population at large. The results are often inaccurate and unreliable. For instance, in 1936, the *Literary Digest*, using a straw poll of 2.5 million people, predicted that Republican Alfred Landon would defeat Democrat Franklin D. Roosevelt in the presidential election; Roosevelt won overwhelmingly. The *Digest* poll failed because it selected its respondents from telephone directories and automobile registration lists. Conducted in the midst of the Great Depression, that *Digest* sample had too many middle- and high-income individuals and excluded voters who could not afford telephones or cars.

Currently, polls are essential to high-visibility campaigns, including presidential, congressional, and gubernatorial races, and are increasingly important to

Random probability sampling A method by which pollsters choose interviewees, based on the idea that the opinions of individuals selected by chance will be representative of the opinions of the population at large.

Straw polls Polls that rely on an unsystematic selection of respondents. The respondents in straw polls frequently are not representative of the public at large.

many lower-profile state and local campaigns. Candidates who can afford the high cost typically survey prospective voters to learn their concerns.

Major television stations and newspapers also survey the public on issues and candidates. When elections are under way, poll results are frequently the bread and butter of the evening news and the daily newspaper. In the months before major elections—and on election night—these reports often have a horse-race quality; that is, they focus on who is ahead or behind in a contest. The media spends significant amounts of time and money tracking voter preferences. Many elected officials use polls to assess the public's views on a variety of issues and use the results to help increase support for their positions or to fine-tune or eventually abandon policies.

The fact that public officials use polls, however, should not imply that presidential or congressional decision making is based solely on evaluation of public opinion. Although polls are an important source of feedback in making policy decisions, representatives also rely on their own values and on both their own and others' knowledge. In effect, polls provide one glimpse of the public's attitudes at the time that the poll is taken. Events, both personal and public, may have a significant impact on those opinions one day, week, month, or year later; thus opinions are susceptible to change.

What makes a good poll? As the failure of the *Literary Digest* poll demonstrates, the sample must be chosen with care. In addition, questions must be worded in such a way that their form or content does not influence the response. The way a question is asked may make a difference in the response that is

The U.S. Census dates back to the nineteenth century, when census workers not only collected demographic data on our growing population but also provided citizens with the opportunity to express their opinions and beliefs on a variety of topics.

solicited. This is known as the **framing effect**. For example, starting a question on a farm issue with the phrase "Most people believe that farms should be family owned" will increase the likelihood that a respondent will agree with what "most people" believe. This type of question is not designed to solicit an individual's true opinion on a matter but rather is used by political campaigns and interest groups, who employ such polling-like techniques (called "push polls") as campaign tools designed to persuade an individual to give the answer the pollster wants. A more neutral, unbiased opening phrase, such as "People have different beliefs regarding support for family-owned farms," avoids the suggestion on the part of the pollster that there is a right and a wrong answer to the question.

Good questions are another important ingredient. Many surveys ask numerous questions and allow for only brief answers, often a simple yes or no. The pro-choice/pro-life survey conducted by Gallup discussed earlier (see Figure 6.1) is an example. Although such questions may improve the efficiency of the survey, they do so at the expense of more thorough information. Consequently, such questions may distort the intensity, saliency, stability, and direction of opinion and may obscure complex shades of opinion, giving support to the myth of majority opinion when, in fact, there is no such view.

Finally, pollsters ought to measure what people know about an issue, as well as what their opinions are, in order to distinguish between informed and uninformed responses. Many Americans recognize the difficulties of keeping up with the issues and also often find government baffling and mysterious. In one poll, 60 percent of the public indicated that government was "so complicated that a person like me can't understand what's going on."[12] Still, lack of knowledge and failure to understand do not keep people from answering questions. As implementation of the Affordable Care Act national health insurance exchange program approached in the fall of 2013, 49 percent of Americans expressed disapproval of the program, whereas 41 percent approved, with 11 percent having no opinion. However, despite media campaigns by both sides of the issue to increase awareness of the health care law, only15 percent of Americans said they were "very familiar" with the law (53 percent said they were "somewhat familiar," 18 percent "not too familiar," and 12 percent "not at all familiar"). In a poll taken at the beginning of President George H. W. Bush's administration, 83 percent of those interviewed rated the president's cabinet appointments as excellent, good, fair, or poor. Yet when asked to name a cabinet member, four out of five could not name a single appointee.[13] Even when the public has limited knowledge about an issue, it is hardly shy about expressing an opinion.

Poorly designed and poorly administered polls are likely to provide inaccurate and misleading findings. The level of confidence we have in a survey may depend on who conducted the poll, and polls commissioned and released to the public by a candidate's campaign committee are generally more suspect than those conducted and reported by a reputable media outlet. But when carefully done, professional polls can help to link citizens with the officials who represent them, amplifying, not distorting, the public's voice.

Framing effect The effect that the wording of a question or the way the question is asked may have on the response by an individual in a survey. That wording may influence the response of the person being interviewed.

The Paradox of Public Opinion

> **Do the findings from public opinion polls suggest that Americans question the principles of democracy and representative government?**

In the 1950s and early 1960s, Americans viewed government optimistically. Seventy-eight percent of Americans felt that the national government tended to improve conditions in the nation.[14] The nation had triumphed in World War II, the economy was flourishing, and no domestic or foreign policy problem seemed too difficult to solve.

Starting in the early 1970s and continuing into the twenty-first century, however, Americans gradually lost confidence in government. The Watergate scandal and resignation of President Nixon, the impeachment and trial of President Clinton, and the public's disapproval of President Bush's handling of Hurricane Katrina as well as the Iraq and Afghanistan wars all served to fuel confusion and cynicism concerning government and politics. A 2013 Pew research poll indicated that only 26 percent of Americans trusted government "always or most of the time."[15] Although some reports indicated that public trust and confidence in the government had increased shortly after the terrorist attacks on September 11, 2001, analyses by a number of prominent political scientists contended that fundamental levels of public trust had not increased and that "there was no sudden affection for big government."[16]

The decline in confidence and trust in government has been matched by a rise in cynicism among many Americans regarding the ethics of elected officials. In 2013, during the partial shutdown of the federal government because of a congressional-presidential dispute over the budget, only 18 percent of the public rated the federal government favorably; 60 percent said that they would vote to replace every member of Congress.[17] Fifty-four percent of citizens believed that the federal government has too much power, whereas 53 percent believed that the federal government poses an immediate threat to the rights and freedoms of ordinary citizens.[18] The cumulative impact of a number of government missteps and scandals at the local, state, and national levels seems to have taken its toll (see Table 6.1). Trust in the national government has declined over the past forty years. In one poll taken in 2014, only seven percent of Americans expressed confidence in Congress; 29 percent in the presidency; and 30 percent in the U.S. Supreme Court.[19] Trust in state government has remained relatively stable over this same time period, while trust in local government has increased.

The question asked is straightforward: How much trust and confidence do you have in our national, state, and local governments when it comes to handling national, state, and local problems, respectively—a great deal, a fair amount, not very much, or none at all? Do these findings suggest that the public no longer believes in democracy and representative government? The answer is no. Most citizens are proud to be Americans. A recent poll found that 85 percent of respondents said they were proud or extremely proud to be Americans.[20] Although one poll found that Americans are unsatisfied with many aspects of how government works, a majority praised the federal government's work on natural disasters, national parks and open spaces, homeland security, transportation programs,

TABLE 6.1 How Much Do You Trust the Government?

Over the past four decades, Americans' trust and confidence in their national government's abilities have decreased, while state and local governments have fared better in the minds of the public. How much trust and confidence do you have in our national, state, and local governments when it comes to handling national, state, and local problems, respectively—a great deal, a fair amount, not very much, or none at all?

	% Great Deal/Fair Amount				% Not Very Much/None at All			
	National (Domestic Issues)	**National (International Issues)**	**State**	**Local**	**National (Domestic Issues)**	**National (International Issues)**	**State**	**Local**
1972	70	75	63	63	29	22	33	33
2012	51	66	65	74	47	33	34	24

Source: Gallup Poll, September 2012.

and military and national defense.[21] Despite major disagreements over a wide range of policies, Americans believe that no other country or government provides the opportunities found in the United States. A majority of Americans believe that government will be an important force in the future in terms of improving the lives of the American people.[22]

Group Opinion: Diversity and Uniformity

> How does public opinion vary between women and men and within and among different ethnic, religious, racial, and age groups?

You should not infer from the preceding discussion that divisions among the American public are trivial or that we should ignore them. The differences both among and within groups in our society do produce a notable fragmentation of public opinion. Political views may differ between men and women, African Americans and whites, young and old, and southerners and northerners. Of course, not all members of a group are necessarily unified in their views. Nevertheless, some generalizations are possible.

Gender

Compared with men, women express greater support regarding certain social issues including gay marriage and the problems of the poor, children, and the elderly. Women are more likely to favor an active role for government than are men, particularly regarding stronger regulation of food production and packaging, workplace safety and health, and environmental protection.[23] Historically, men are more concerned about the budget deficit, the cost of living, and the trade deficit. Men are more likely than women to support the death penalty for persons convicted of murder.[24] A larger percentage of women than of men consider themselves Democrats, although approximately an equal proportion of men and of women support the Republican Party.

TABLE 6.2 **The Gender Gap Between the Democratic and Republican Presidential Candidates, 1980–2012**

Year	Presidential Candidates	% of Female Votes Received	% of Male Votes Received	Gender Gap (Percentage Points) for Winning Candidate
2012	Barack Obama–D	55	45	0
	Mitt Romney–R	44	52	
2008	Barack Obama–D	56	49	7
	John McCain–R	43	48	
2004	George W. Bush–R	48	55	7
	John Kerry–D	51	41	
2000	George W. Bush–R	43	53	10
	Al Gore–D	54	42	
	Ralph Nader–Green	2	3	
1996	Bill Clinton–D	54	43	11
	Bob Dole–R	38	44	
	Ross Perot–Reform	7	10	
1992	Bill Clinton–D	45	41	4
	George H. W. Bush–R	37	38	
	Ross Perot–Reform	17	21	
1988	George H. W. Bush–R	50	57	7
	Michael Dukakis–D	49	41	
1984	Ronald Reagan–R	56	62	6
	Walter Mondale–D	44	37	
1980	Ronald Reagan–R	46	54	8
	Jimmy Carter–D	45	37	
	John Anderson–I	7	7	

Source: Center for the American Women and Politics (CAWP), Eagleton Institute of Politics, Rutgers University, December 2012, www.cawp.rutgers.edu.

There are no strong gender differences regarding the right to choose abortion, with a majority of men as well as of women believing that abortion should be legal in all or most cases. Both men and women have concerns that government does too much for the wealthy. In the 2012 presidential elections, Democrat Barack Obama received an overall advantage over Republican Mitt Romney of 10 percentage points from female voters (see Table 6.2).

Age Groups: College Students and Twentysomethings

Despite popular images of youthful extremism, most college students and people in their twenties hold middle-of-the-road political views (see Table 6.3).[25] Their interest in political affairs is relatively weak, however. A 2012 survey of freshman college students found that only about 30 percent discussed politics frequently during their senior year in high school (although this number is the highest it has been since the mid-1960s), and only 9 percent worked on a local, state, or national political campaign.[26]

Table 6.4 shows that the opinions of college students, like those of the rest of the population, are diverse. (See Asked & Answered, page 197, for more about college students and youth participation.)

Race and Ethnicity

Diversity and divergence also hold true when people are grouped by race and ethnicity, although whites, African Americans, Hispanics, Asian Americans, and others manifest some group consciousness on important issues. Recent polls indicate that more than 85 percent of African Americans feel "very satisfied" or "somewhat satisfied" with their lives, comparing favorably with an 89 percent satisfaction rate for whites.[27] Compared with whites, African Americans favor greater government participation in resolving economic and social issues.[28]

TABLE 6.3 **The Political Orientation of College Freshmen: The Class of 2016**

	% Average	% Male	% Female
Far left	2.8	---	---
Liberal	26.8	---	---
TOTAL (LEFT):		26.4	32.5
Middle of the road	47.5	48.0	47.0
Conservative	21.8	---	---
Far right	1.8	---	---
TOTAL (RIGHT):		25.6	20.7

Source: Data from John H. Pryor, Kevin Eagan, Laura Palucki Blake, Sylvia Hurtado, Jennifer Berdan, and Matthew H. Case, *The American Freshman: National Norms Fall 2012* (Los Ángeles: The Cooperative Institutional Research Program at the Higher Education Research Institute at UCLA, December 2012), pp. 7, 37.

TABLE 6.4 What Do College Freshman (Class of 2016) Think?

	% Support for Statement
The death penalty should be abolished.	35.5
Abortion should be legal.	61.1
Racial discrimination is no longer a major problem in America.	23.0
Realistically, an individual can do little to bring about changes in our society.	28.2
Wealthy people should pay a larger share of taxes than they do now.	64.6
Same-sex couples should have the right to legal marital status.	75.0
A national health care plan is needed to cover everybody's medical costs.	62.7
Dissent is a critical component of the political process.	61.0
Students from disadvantaged social backgrounds should be given preferential treatment in college admissions.	41.9

Source: Data from John H. Pryor, Kevin Eagan, Laura Palucki Blake, Sylvia Hurtado, Jennifer Berdan, and Matthew H. Case, *The American Freshman: National Norms Fall 2012* (Los Angeles: The Cooperative Institutional Research Program at the Higher Education Research Institute at UCLA, December 2012), pp. 8, 37.

Although a significant majority of blacks—80 percent—have a positive attitude toward President Obama, only 37 percent of whites share that opinion.[29]

For African Americans, federal programs, including affirmative action programs, remain a key strategy in dealing with civil rights, voting rights, and other pressing problems. African Americans are more likely than whites to indicate that the economy in general is the most critical issue facing the nation, with unemployment as the most important problem.[30] When Hurricane Katrina devastated the city of New Orleans in 2005, whites and nonwhites strongly disagreed with each other over the role of race in the government's response to the tragedy. Sixty-five percent of nonwhites felt that race accounted for the slow response to those trapped in New Orleans, whereas 64 percent of whites said that race played no role.[31] Public opinion polls found that, after George Zimmerman was acquitted in 2013 of the killing of Trayvon Martin, an unarmed black teenager in Florida (based on a stand-your-ground law), racial divide was heightened between blacks and whites. One poll found that "78 percent of black respondents thought the case 'raised important issues about race that need to be discussed.' But only 28 percent of white respondents agreed with that statement, with 60 percent saying race was 'getting too much attention.'"[32]

There is agreement across race on some issues. For example, a majority of African Americans and whites agree that government is often wasteful and inefficient. Both groups are concerned about the concentration of corporate power in

ASKED & ANSWERED

ASKED: *Are young people in the United States and in other nations inattentive and inactive in the political process?*

ANSWERED: For many years, the most common answer to this question was yes; eighteen- to twenty-nine-year-olds did not participate in significant numbers in the political process. The general belief was that many were too preoccupied with their studies, busy with jobs or attending institutes of higher education, and generally caught up in planning for their futures.

Historically, research has supported the finding of low levels of voting among the eighteen- to twenty-nine-year-old cohort in many nations. No other age group, including those seventy-five years old and older, has a lower percentage of eligible citizens turning out on Election Day.

Current elections have revealed a mixed picture in regard to trends toward voter turnout among eighteen- to twenty-nine-year-olds, with their voter turnout still lagging behind all other age groups. In the United States, although voter registration rates and presidential Election Day turnouts among this age group have been at their highest in recent years, the 2012 elections found a decline (45 percent) from 2008 (51 percent) among eighteen- to twenty-nine-year-olds. As with all other age cohorts, youth participation in off-year elections is lower than in presidential-year elections. Turnout among eighteen- to twenty-nine-year-olds in some other parts of the world has been relatively high—and considerably higher than turnout among young people in the United States. For example, in the 2004 European Union (EU) parliamentary elections, the average eighteen- to twenty-nine-year-old turnout in fifteen of the most established Western member states was more than 55 percent. Of this age group's eligible voters, turnout was 81 percent in Italy and 77 percent in France.

Do young people do more than just vote? One recent survey conveyed a picture of limited engagement by eighteen- to twenty-nine-year-olds: 30 percent always voted; 18 percent had contacted a government official in the past two years; seven percent served as a campaign volunteer in the past two years; and 35 percent discussed politics nearly every day or a few times a week.

If this evidence doesn't suggest a strong emergent participation by youth in the political process, UCLA's highly regarded annual survey of entering undergraduates for the class of 2016 finds that students are motivated regarding community activity as well as staying abreast of political affairs. Approximately 31 percent of first-year college students believe that it is very important to participate in community action programs, and more than 37 percent feel it is very important to become a community leader. More than 35 percent believe it is very important to keep up to date with political affairs.

Although some evidence indicates a growing level of interest and participation by youth in the political process in the United States and Europe, we must arrive cautiously at any conclusions. The eighteen- to twenty-nine-year-old age cohort still lags behind the voting and participation rates of every age group thirty years or older. In turn, the data that are cited represent incremental changes over time. Indeed, only time will tell whether young people will, in fact, steadily increase their level of participation in the political system. Would you predict a growing participation by youth in the political and governmental process?

Sources: Harvard University Institute of Politics, Survey of Student Attitudes: Toward Politics and Public Service, *23rd ed., April 30, 2013, www.iop.harvard.edu/; Center for Information and Research on Civic Learning and Engagement (CIRCLE),* **2012 Election Fact Sheet**, *www.civicyouth.org; John H. Pryor, Kevin Eagan, Laura Palucki, Sylvia Hurtado, Jennifer Berdan, and Matthew H. Case,* **The American Freshman: National Norms for Fall 2012** *(Los Angeles: Cooperative Institutional Research Program, Higher Education Research Institute at UCLA, 2013), pp. 32, 43; Pew Research Center for the People & the Press, "Youth Engagement Falls: Registration Also Declines," September 28, 2012; Pew Research Center for the People & the Press, June 12, 2014, Tables 3.9 and 5.1; www.people-press .org/2014/06/12/poltical-polarization-in-the-american-public/.*

the United States.[33] Among whites, Republicans hold an edge over Democrats, whereas African Americans have been more heavily Democratic since the 1940s. Approximately 30 percent of African Americans describe themselves as independents, whereas 38 percent of whites consider themselves independents.[34] In the 2012 presidential election, 93 percent of African Americans voted for Democrat Barack Obama.[35]

Hispanic opinion is difficult to characterize, because the label serves as an umbrella term for Mexican Americans, Puerto Ricans, Cuban Americans, Central Americans, and others who trace their origins to the diverse cultures of Central and South America and the Caribbean. Except for Cuban Americans (a majority of whom identify with the Republican Party), Hispanics tend to be Democratic in their politics. In the 2012 presidential election, Democrat Barack Obama received 71 percent of the Hispanic vote, a 4 percent increase over the 2008 election.[36]

Mexican Americans, Puerto Ricans, Central Americans, and Cuban Americans have played a growing role in local and state politics. In fact, according to *ThinkProgress*, "collectively, Hispanics, African-Americans, Native Americans, and Asian-Americans are currently a majority of the population in California, Hawaii, New Mexico, Texas, and the District of Columbia."[37] Nevada, Maryland, Georgia, and Florida are projected to achieve minority-majority status by 2020, with Arizona, New Jersey, Delaware, and New York to follow suit.[38] Minorities will certainly gain political strength in many regions of the nation as we move through the twenty-first century.

Religion

Although religion does not necessarily shape political beliefs, members of a particular religious group often share similar opinions. Given their liberal to moderate bent, Jews lean toward the Democratic Party, whereas non-Hispanic Catholics are increasingly supporting the Republican Party, although a plurality (39 percent) identify as independents (as recently as 2008, Democrats held a slight edge among white Catholics).[39] White Protestants tend to identify as Republicans. Individuals who are regular attendees of church are more likely to support the Republican Party.

Within each religious group, however, there are differences on many important issues. Catholics are divided on abortion, public support of birth control programs, and the public funding of parochial schools. Both Jews and Muslims are divided over the Arab-Israeli conflict and U.S. policy toward the Middle East. A significant number of Protestant evangelical groups oppose a broad spectrum of liberal government policies, but other Protestant evangelicals decry these traditional stands on social welfare and environmental issues as too conservative.[40] Once again, majority opinion can be difficult to define within groups.

In recent years, some observers have argued that economic and social class influences are more important than religious influences.[41] In addition, more than 75 percent of Americans believe that religion is "losing its influence on American life."[42] Nevertheless, the issue of religion was at the forefront in the 2012 elections. Republican presidential candidate Mitt Romney, a devout Mormon, faced some voter bias because of his religious beliefs. Religion continues to have a direct and indirect effect on political life, influencing tolerance toward political candidates, protection of disadvantaged groups, moral and ethical opinions regarding political behavior, and conformity with the rules of the system.[43]

Avenues of Political Participation

> ### What are the different ways in which Americans participate in the political system?

The development of public opinion is a long and complex process, and having opinions is just the beginning. We must also consider whether Americans act on their opinions by participating in the political system. **Political participation** encompasses a broad range of activities, from voting and learning about politics to engaging in efforts that directly affect "the structure of government, the selection of government authorities, or the policies of government."[44]

As we discussed in Chapter 1, **political ideologies** shape our attitudes and opinions about specific political issues and institutions. As political scientist Max Skidmore suggests, ideology also provides "a form of thought that presents a pattern of complex political ideas simply and in a manner that *inspires action to achieve certain goals*."[45] It is also true that the more information we have about an issue, the more likely it is that we will participate in the political system.

Most Americans participate in limited ways—for example, by discussing politics with family and friends and by following campaigns, elections, and other political events on television and in the newspapers. Others are more active; they write letters and e-mail governmental officials, attend community meetings and legislative hearings, and join in interest-group activities. In 2014 approximately 41 percent of the eligible electorate voted in the congressional elections. Those who are deeply involved in politics contribute money to campaigns, attend political rallies and speeches, take part in campaigns, and run for political office. A smaller but growing number of people bypass traditional avenues of action and engage in **civil disobedience**, the willful, and at times violent, breach of laws that these people regard as unjust.

One highly regarded study found "a populace in the United States [that] is highly participatory in most forms of political activity and even more so in nonpolitical public affairs (from a vast variety of organizational memberships to charitable giving and volunteer action)."[46] Nevertheless, as Table 6.5 makes clear, participation varies depending on the particular activity. Relatively few individuals attend organized protests or political meetings. Many more citizens are likely to sign a petition or contact a government official about an issue.[47] Nearly two-thirds of all Americans have participated in some form of political activity, as measured in Table 6.5. In the age of the Internet, 66 percent of Internet users have gone online for one or more of the reasons discussed in Table 6.6.[48] Research tends to support the idea of a growing level of participation by the American people.

Political participation
Taking part in any of a broad range of activities, from involvement in learning about politics to engagement in efforts that directly affect the structure of government, the selection of government authorities, or the policies of government.

Political ideology
A pattern of complex political ideas presented in an understandable structure that inspires people to act to achieve certain goals.

For further updates visit the companion website at **www.oup.com/us/gitelson**.

Civil disobedience A refusal to obey civil laws that are regarded as unjust. This may involve methods of passive resistance such as sit-ins and boycotts.

TABLE 6.5 **Political Participation in America**

The Proportion of Adults Who Did Each of the Following in the Last 12 Months	%
Sign a petition	32
Contact a national, state, or local government official about an issue	30
Work with fellow citizens to solve a problem in your community	28
Attend a political meeting on local, town, or school affairs	24
Contribute money to a political candidate or party or any other organization or cause	18
Function as an active member of a group that tries to influence public policy or government	15
Attend a political rally or speech	12
Send a letter to the editor of a newspaper or magazine	10
Work or volunteer for a political party or candidate	8
Make a speech about a community or local issue	7
Attend an organized protest	4
Any of these	**63**

Source: Pew Internet & American Life Project August 2008 Survey. The margin of error is $+/-$ 2 percent based on all adults ($n = 2,251$).

For some individuals, however, political inactivity does not necessarily indicate a lack of interest. Here are some of their reasons for not participating:

- Threats of violence have kept some groups out of politics; in particular, African Americans in the South were kept out of politics until the 1960s.

- Work and family responsibilities leave little time for political involvement.

- For people between the ages of eighteen and twenty-six, adjusting to new academic challenges or to being independent, self-supporting adults contributes to political inactivity.

- Some people believe that their participation will have no impact on government or are satisfied with how things are and therefore feel they have no reason to get involved.

Acting on Opinions

Those who do act on their opinions fall into six general categories, according to political scientists Sidney Verba and Norman Nie:[49]

1. Inactives participate by occasionally casting a vote.

TABLE 6.6 **Political Engagement on Social Networking Sites (SNSs)**

Sixty percent of American adults use social networking sites such as Facebook and Twitter; these are some of the civic behaviors they have taken part in on these sites.

	% of SNS Users Who Have Done the Following	% of All Adults Who Have Done the Following
"Like" or promote material related to political/social issues that others have posted	38	23
Encourage other people to vote	35	21
Post your own thoughts/comments on political or social issues	34	20
Repost content related to political/social issues	33	19
Encourage others to take action on political/social issues that are important to you	31	19
Post links to political stories or articles for others to read	28	17
Belong to a group that is involved in political/social issues, or that is working to advance a cause	21	12
Follow elected officials, candidates for office, or other public figures	20	12
Total % of respondents who said yes to any of the activities listed above	**66**	**39**

Source: Pew Internet & American Life Project, "Civic Engagement in the Digital Age," April 25, 2013.

2. Voting specialists vote regularly in presidential, state, and local elections but seldom join in other political activities.

3. Parochial activists vote and contact public officials only when their self-interest is involved.

4. Community activists work to solve problems in their localities and vote regularly but do not otherwise participate in party activities or elections.

5. Campaigners—the mirror image of the community activists—immerse themselves in partisan politics and campaigns rather than in community organizations.

6. Complete activists engage in activities ranging from community affairs to voting, campaigning, and running for political office.

Verba and Nie's categories represent traditional forms of political participation. What other tactics have evolved over the years as forms of political participation? In the early 1960s, African Americans in the South organized sit-ins at segregated lunch counters, boycotted segregated buses, and engaged in other acts of civil disobedience. Antiwar protests were a common occurrence during the Vietnam War in the 1960s and 1970s. Since that time, protest has become an increasingly common form of participation among those who find traditional avenues of action ineffective or closed.

We should not overlook the impact of even limited participation. In the 2012 presidential election, 67 percent of the electorate watched programs about the campaigns on television, 27 percent of voters read about the presidential campaign in a newspaper, and 67 percent of the electorate followed campaign news on the Internet. These forms of political activity may be less direct than voting or running for office, but they represent an important form of participation in the political process.[50]

Despite this evidence, there is certainly room for skepticism about, as well as improvement of, Americans' activism. Relatively few people work for parties or candidates. Even though the 2008 presidential election saw the highest turnout since 1960, turnout for presidential elections has been relatively low over the past thirty years, averaging around 50 percent of the eligible voters. In comparison with other democracies, the United States has ranked sixteen or seventeen globally in voter turnout (depending on whether it is a presidential-year or off-year election).[51] The 2012 presidential election saw a 58.2 percent turnout.[52] In the 2014 off-year elections, turnout was 41 percent of eligible voters. We cannot ignore the reality that active political participation in the United States is lower than many political observers believe it should be.

Yet this apparent apathy is balanced by activity. When election time rolls around, many political meetings are jammed with people, campaign buttons and bumper stickers decorate lapels and automobiles, and money pours into campaign headquarters. Political parties, particularly at the national level, thrive on millions of small contributions—most under $50; increasingly, many of these contributions are being made to candidates via the Internet. Tens of thousands of people participate in social and political movements aimed at affecting policy on issues that range from government involvement in Afghanistan and the Middle East to abortion rights. In addition, volunteerism in the United States is alive and well. Americans feel that volunteering time to community service is an essential or very important obligation of citizens. A recent poll found that more than 87 percent of college freshmen stated that they had participated in some form of volunteer work, ranging from helping the homeless to teaching, religious service, social work, and environmental and health care.[53] Historically, Americans have engaged in at least as much campaign and community activity as citizens of many other nations. In terms of volunteering and giving money to nonpolitical public affairs programs, Americans significantly outdistanced many other nations in the amount of time and financial support contributed.

What Influences Participation?

Why do people participate in politics? After all, an individual act of participation rarely has much impact. One answer is that people participate if the action does not take much effort. Sending a check or watching the nightly news is easy.

For further updates visit the companion website at **www.oup.com/us/gitelson**.

People also participate if they care a lot about the outcome. Both African American and white college students who took part in sit-ins at lunch counters and marched in demonstrations in the 1960s had a big stake in the success of the civil rights movement. Likewise, during the 1970s and 1980s, many women (and men) participated in demonstrations and marches for equal rights and opportunities for women. Finally, participation depends on life circumstances. Recent increases in political participation in the South can be attributed to rising educational and socioeconomic levels, as well as to enforcement of voting rights laws; in the past, poll taxes, literacy tests, and other barriers to registration prevented African Americans from voting.

Participation leads to more participation. For example, people who work in community and fraternal organizations are more likely than the average citizen to participate in politics. A strong sense of party identity also seems to encourage activism. Even such passive participation as having an interest in politics or holding strong opinions on issues and candidates can serve as a catalyst for political action.

Political activism also depends on age. Those between the ages of eighteen and twenty-four are less likely to vote or engage in other forms of political participation—for example, discussing politics, working for a political party, or running for political office—than those in any other age group through the age of seventy-five. A higher percentage of people ages forty-five and older than those younger than forty-five register and vote in national elections. As we indicated earlier in this chapter, these statistics often reflect the unsettled lives of young people who are working, starting families, attending school, or adjusting to their status as independent, self-supporting adults. To some extent, too, political activism is a function of the responsibilities of age. As taxpayers, parents, and homeowners, older people have more immediate reasons to get involved in politics.

A Closer Look at Women, African Americans, Hispanics, and Asian Americans

Participation has varied in recent years for women, African Americans, Hispanics, and Asian Americans.

Women. Women have a long history of activism in local and community work. Nineteenth-century feminists fought for equal rights, economic opportunity, and the right to vote. Yet women's roles in the partisan political arenas of the time were very limited. In recent years, barriers against women in national and state politics have diminished. Currently, as party leaders, candidates, voters, and community organizers, women are entering politics in greater numbers. The percentage of female voters has exceeded the percentage of male voters in every presidential election since 1980.[54] Their activity at the state and national level has increased significantly.

Since 1975, the number of women holding a local or state office has risen dramatically. In 2012, a record 231 women (145 Democrats and 86 Republicans) ran in U.S. House primaries.[55] In 2014, as of election night, 81 women were elected to the House of Representatives; 20 were elected to the Senate.

For further updates visit the companion website at **www.oup.com/us/gitelson**.

Although women are still underrepresented in politics, proportional to their numbers in the general population, their participation in government has increased significantly over the past thirty-five years. Here, female members of the House of Representatives pose for a group photo on the stairs of the Capitol Building in Washington, D.C.

Of the delegates to the 2012 Democratic National Convention, 50 percent were women. Female delegates to the 2012 Republican National Convention totaled 32 percent.

The 2008 presidential election was marked by the first serious challenge from a woman, Senator Hillary Clinton, for the nomination of a major political party for the office of the presidency. Although Clinton lost the Democratic nomination to Barack Obama, her candidacy demonstrated the growing role of women in our political system and the strong likelihood that the future will see women successfully competing for the office of the presidency of the United States (Clinton is regarded as a strong potential candidate for the Democratic presidential nomination in 2016).

African Americans. Discrimination, along with alienation from and lack of faith in the electoral process, has historically contributed to African Americans' low rates of political participation. African American voter turnout has increased greatly during the past three decades—in good part because of voting rights laws, key Supreme Court decisions, registration drives, and a rise in educational achievement and economic well-being. In 2012, approximately two out of every three eligible blacks (66.2 percent) voted in the presidential election; this percentage was higher than the total non-Hispanic white turnout (64.1 percent).[56]

Since the 1970s, increasing numbers of African American candidates have won political office. History was made in 2008, when the first African American, Barack Obama, was elected president of the United States; he was then reelected in 2012. In 2012, 8.4 percent of elected officials serving in the state legislatures were black.[57] Prominent black officials include Governor Deval Patrick of Massachusetts, Democratic Representative John Lewis of Georgia, and Republican Senator Tim Scott of South Carolina. African Americans have also increasingly won mayoral races in cities such as Atlanta, Chicago, Dallas, Los Angeles, and Newark.

Hispanics. Hispanic Americans have also faced major barriers to participation, including language problems, low levels of education and income, literacy tests, and residency requirements. Recently, registration drives in Florida, Texas, and California, where many Cuban Americans and Mexican Americans live, have produced increases in voter turnout. In the 2012 presidential election, 59 percent of eligible Latino voters were registered to vote in the United States.

Although Hispanic participation is still limited in the United States, candidates for office in many parts of the nation recognize the growing size and importance of the Hispanic vote. The twenty-first century will very likely see dramatic increases in Hispanic activism, particularly in states such as California, Arizona, New Mexico, Texas, Colorado, New York, Florida, and New Jersey, which are experiencing significant increases in the number of Hispanic voters.

Asian Americans. Although only limited data are available regarding the political participation patterns of different Asian American groups, we can draw some tentative conclusions. Historically, most Asian Americans, including Japanese,

In recent years, more and more Hispanic Americans have entered the political arena, running for local, state, and federal offices. Senator Robert Menendez (D-NJ) has served in the U.S. Senate since 2006, having earlier participated in politics and government as a member of a local school board; the mayor of Union City, New Jersey; a state legislator; and a member of the New Jersey House of Representatives.

Korean, Vietnamese, and Filipino Americans, are less likely than either whites or African Americans to participate in the political system. Chinese Americans, however, are as likely to vote as white Americans. In the 2012 presidential elections, members of Asian American ethnic groups supported Democrat Barack Obama with 73 percent of their vote. Republican Mitt Romney received 26 percent of the Asian American vote.[58] A recent study argued that factors that contribute to the relatively low voter turnout of many Asian American groups include limited English proficiency among older generations of voters and real and perceived biases against Asian Americans by poll workers.[59]

As members of various ethnic groups from Asia and the Pacific settle in the United States and assimilate into the political system, it is likely that there will be increases in their political participation. Asian Americans represent the fastest-growing collective ethnic group in the United States.

Conclusion

In this chapter we have looked at the myth of majority opinion. What is the reality behind this myth? Is there a majority opinion? The answer is yes—and no. Many Americans do share certain beliefs about the political system, including the importance of democracy and representative government, majority rule, and concern for minority rights. An overwhelming majority—in most polls, much more than 90 percent of the respondents—support a democratic form of government. And public officials pay attention to public opinion when it has strength and direction on a given issue.

The myth, however, obscures an important attribute of public opinion, one that is often difficult to clearly define. As obvious and unambiguous as it is that a large majority of Americans share a belief in a democratic form of government, it is equally clear that public opinion, on many specific issues, is often fuzzy and unstable; it is also frequently uninformed and sometimes does not exist at all. It rarely comes packaged in neat, easy-to-understand categories. In this vast and varied nation, differences in gender, age, race and ethnicity, religious background, region of residence, education, and class produce a broad spectrum of views about the political world. We tend to believe that public opinion is aligned with our own personal feelings, attitudes, and beliefs—beliefs that are often shared with our friends and family members. As a result, we may fail to take into account the full scope and breadth of beliefs held by other Americans on a multitude of issues and mistake public opinion for our opinions. To complicate matters further, even when people have similar backgrounds, they often do not share the same views.

Thus, in defining majority opinion on any issue, policymakers must tread carefully. Often the answers to a single survey question or even a series of such questions do not capture the diversity or ambiguity of public opinion. For many issues, the generalization that there is a majority opinion in the United States is a myth—comprising both truths and falsehoods.

We also discussed political participation in the United States. Americans are frequently criticized for their lack of participation in the political process. That criticism often focuses on the relatively low voter turnout in the United States, particularly when compared with higher turnout figures in other nations. If activism is defined by voting, the American public does seem apathetic. But if we broaden the definition to include other activities, including such forms of participation as political discussions, we see a reality of a more politically and socially concerned citizen, a citizen who is more active in the political system than was previously thought.

Key Terms

Civil disobedience p. 201
Framing effect p. 193
Opinion direction p. 186
Opinion intensity p. 186
Opinion saliency p. 186

Opinion stability p. 186
Party identification p. 188
Political culture p. 187
Political efficacy p. 188
Political ideology p. 201

Political participation p. 201
Political public opinion p. 186
Political socialization p. 187
Random probability sampling p. 191
Straw polls p. 191

Focus Questions Review

1. **How do we define political public opinion?** > > >
   - Public opinion is defined as the shared evaluations expressed by people on political issues, policies, and individuals. The four important characteristics of public opinion are as follows:
     Intensity: The strength of one's opinion about an issue
     Saliency: One's perception of the relevancy of an issue
     Stability: The degree to which public opinion on an issue changes over time
     Direction: One's position in favor of or against a particular issue
   - Often, support for an issue has many degrees, with no clear and precise direction of public opinion.
   - Although a majority opinion may exist, as well as well-defined, stable, and easily understood issues, public opinion is often difficult to define clearly and can be fuzzy and unstable, often uninformed, and sometimes completely absent on a given issue.

2. **What agents of political socialization help to shape and influence our opinions about government and politics?** > > >
   - Political socialization is the process by which people acquire political values and opinions about the political world.

   - The socialization process is strongly influenced by people and events from early childhood through adulthood. The five important factors that mold our political beliefs and opinions are as follows:
     Family and friends
     School
     The media
     Religion
     Political culture

3. **What factors contribute to a well-designed and effective poll? What factors contribute to a poorly designed poll?** > > >
   - Polls are a major instrument for measuring public opinion. Poorly designed and badly administered public opinion polls can provide inaccurate and misleading findings. When carefully designed and administered, however, professional polls offer sound and meaningful information about public opinion. Nevertheless, on many issues, a clear and unambiguous majority opinion is often difficult to assess from polls.
   - Factors that contribute to a well-designed poll include the following:
     1. Random probability sampling, by which pollsters choose interviewees based on the idea that the opinion of individuals selected by

chance will be representative of the opinions of the population at large

2. Questions whose form and content do not sway the respondent one way or another but encourage a person to answer a polling question in terms of how she or he thinks or would act

3. Both short-answer questions—also called closed-ended questions, in which the respondent is given a limited number of answer options—and open-ended questions that give the respondent the opportunity to provide more detailed answers to a question

4. Questions that distinguish between informed and uninformed responses

- Poorly designed polls do not fulfill these minimal requirements. Some factors that contribute to poorly designed polls include the following:

   1. Polling methods, like those used in straw polls, that rely on unsystematic methods of selection or are generally biased in terms of who is selected to be interviewed.

   2. Poorly worded questions that push a respondent to answer a question the way the pollster wants it to be answered. For example, starting a question on a farm issue with the phrase "Most people believe that farms should be family owned" will increase the likelihood that a respondent will agree with what "most people" believe. This type of question is used by disreputable pollsters who write questions that push an individual to answer a question the way the pollster wants it answered. Thus, it is called a "push poll."

4. Do the findings from public opinion polls suggest that Americans question the principles of democracy and representative government? > > >
Although Americans show a lack of confidence and trust in government and politics, they still have an overwhelming faith in the political system in general and in the principles of democracy and representative government.

5. How does public opinion vary between women and men and within and among different ethnic, religious, racial, and age groups? > > >

- The opinions of Americans are often influenced by age and gender and by ethnic, racial, religious, regional, socioeconomic, and educational backgrounds, although opinions can and do vary widely within any group. For example, many Hispanics favor the moderate to liberal positions of the Democratic Party, but this is not true of all individuals in this group. Cuban Americans, for example, tend to favor the more moderate to conservative positions of the Republican Party.

- Differences also exist among ethnic, religious, racial, and age groups. For example, Jews tend to be more liberal and moderate than white Protestants. In turn, African Americans identify with the Democratic Party in larger percentages than Caucasian Americans.

6. What are the different ways in which Americans participate in the political system? > > >

- Political participation can range from activities that involve taking part in the learning process about politics to activities that directly influence the structure of government, the selection of government authorities, or the policies of government.

- Participation in politics in the United States is more extensive if we include not only voting but also all forms of political participation, including discussing politics with friends and family, working on a campaign or making a donation to a candidate, running for political office, participating in a political protest, reading about political events, and watching political debates on television.

Review Questions

1. Define the terms *political culture* and *political socialization*, and explain how they relate to each other.
2. Discuss the factors that contribute to a good poll.

For more information and access to study materials, visit the book's companion website at www.oup.com/us/gitelson.

Policy Connection

How do public opinion and public attitudes affect environmental policies?

The Policy Challenge

In this Policy Connection we examine the relationship between public opinion and public attitudes in one major policy area—environmental protection. Government initiatives regarding the environment often rely on the work of scientists and other experts who attempt to approach problems objectively and empirically—that is, governmental policymakers would prefer to rely on evidence and avoid engaging in political debates over either defining problems or developing solutions. Nevertheless, when it comes to environmental issues, they often find themselves drawn into heated discussions about what government can or ought to do. In many cases, these discussions mean having to deal with public opinions and attitudes.

The Public and Climate Change

In 2007, a prestigious panel of climate scientists from thirty nations convened by the United Nations issued a report that called the problem of global warming "unequivocal" and identified human activity as the major cause. The Intergovernmental Panel on Climate Change (IPCC) issued a call to action that included getting all nations to adopt the UN Framework Convention on Climate Change and to take steps to reduce greenhouse emissions as much and as quickly as possible.[1] As significant as the substance of the report was the degree of consensus in the scientific community regarding its findings, which has been put at 97 percent or higher. And they supported their arguments with analyses showing that almost all the available scientific literature points to the same conclusion about both global warming and the human contribution to the problem.

We might expect the opinion of the scientific community to carry significant weight and influence in shaping U.S. policies related to climate change, but there has been considerable political opposition to such policies. Those who have raised doubts about the IPCC report and its findings—usually called climate skeptics or "deniers"—have succeeded in mobilizing a sufficient countermovement that has gained a foothold in American public opinion. Responding to a reporter's question about the success of the climate skeptics movement, one of its leaders was clear about their reliance on shaping public attitudes toward claims of global warming: "There are holdouts among the urban bicoastal elite, but I think we've won the debate with the American people in the heartland, the people who get their hands dirty, people who dig up stuff, grow stuff and make stuff for a living, people who have a closer relationship to tangible reality, to stuff."[2]

Anyone attempting to bring about changes in American public policy has to be concerned with public attitudes and opinion regarding the issue he or she is addressing. As we noted in Chapter 6, the myth of majority opinion plays a significant role in the way many Americans make sense of our political system and its claims to be a democracy. When it comes to public policy, there is a different but related myth at work: the *myth of effective public opinion*—that is, the belief that public opinion can be and often is reflected in public policies and other actions of our government.

For some observers who have examined the relationship between public opinion and government policies, the myth is a necessary partial truth we tell ourselves in order to sustain our support for the political system. Political scientist V. O. Key summarized that position as follows: "If a democracy is to exist, the belief must be widespread that public opinion, at least in the long run, affects the course of public action. In a technical sense that belief may be a myth, an article of faith, yet its maintenance requires that it possess a degree of validity."[3] Other students of American public policy have conducted research that does support the validity of the myth—at least to some degree.[4]

Linking Opinions to the Environment

The dates are a bit fuzzy, but in the two weeks preceding Thanksgiving Day in 1953, about two hundred New Yorkers died of illnesses attributable to exceptionally high levels of air pollution.

The pollution-related deaths did not make headlines at the time; in fact, they were only "discovered" nine years later, when studies of public health records indicated that there was a statistically significant increase in the number of deaths for the period of November 15–24.[5] In total, there were around two hundred more deaths during that period than during the same period in the years before and after 1953.

When investigators looked deeper, they determined that weather conditions had created an "air inversion" that settled into the area from November 12 to 21. New Yorkers were accustomed to "bad air" days, but these were typically twenty-four-hour episodes that moved on almost routinely as winds carried the pollutant-laden air out to the Atlantic. In this case, however, the soot, haze, and smoke lingered in the New York region for days.

The situation did draw some attention. Area astronomers focusing on a celestial event that would not occur again until 2012 expressed dismay about the heavy overcast conditions. There was a notable reduction of visibility for those driving on the New Jersey Turnpike, and the "cheerless atmosphere" created by air conditions was reported in coverage of weekend football games. The weather conditions were even enough to draw a comment in the editorial pages of the *New York Times*, which took note of the "headaches, nausea, and burning eyes, even the 'sluggish and distressed' pigeons in the parks." Nevertheless, although detailed records were kept about daily mortality rates and the levels of air pollution in New York City, at the time no one paid attention to the deaths resulting from this extended polluted air episode.[6]

The fact that no attention was paid to those deaths or their causes meant, of course, that the government took no action at the time. But even if those monitoring the air pollution levels in the region or the government workers recording reported deaths had made the connection, no policies or programs existed to deal with the situation. As implied in our previous discussions defining public policies (see Policy Connection 1) and the policymaking process (Policy Connection 2), government can take action only when it is aware of and attentive to the problems that require a response. By the early 1960s, the awareness of significant health problems associated with air and water pollution had resulted in a proliferation of local and state policies, especially in those regions like Los Angeles and Denver where smog made the toxic situation visible. The 1962 publication of Rachel Carson's *Silent Spring*[7] brought increased attention to pollution as a national problem, and by 1970 awareness and attention had generated a popular movement that mobilized support for federal policies to deal with air and water pollution as well as other problems associated with environmental conditions and the human impact on the ecology.

Today, environmental policy covers a wide range of issues, from the public health problems related to ambient air quality to those of climate change, from concerns regarding the pesticides we use in agriculture to the earth's limited capacity to sustain a growing and ever-more-demanding human population. In a little more than half a century, environmental policy has transformed from a local concern to become national and global in scope. And, all along the way, the "public"—its attitudes, opinions, and participation—has played a key role in shaping what has taken place.

Policy Developments

Prior to the emergence of environmental policy as a major concern of the national government in the 1960s, the federal government was involved in two closely associated efforts: federal land management and preservation.[8] In 1871, following the recommendation of explorers and surveyors in the region, Congress set aside vast tracts of federally owned land in what is now Yellowstone National Park so they might be used for the "pleasuring" of the public.[9] About twenty years later, John Muir and other naturalists engaged in a political struggle to save the Yosemite Valley in California as well as the Sierra from commercial exploitation.[10] During the same time period, conservationists dedicated to a more sustainable approach to forestry pressed the government to establish national forests in which the harvesting of trees could be better managed.[11] Although the objectives of the three movements differed—that is, the creation of parks for public enjoyment, preservation of natural wilderness areas, and the development of a more sustainable approach to

John Muir, a leading naturalist and advocate for wilderness preservation, used his writings and political connections to advance his cause with the American public. Here, at Yosemite National Park, he is pictured with a powerful ally, Theodore Roosevelt.

forests—each effort faced strong opposition from local and commercial interests, and each succeeded by mobilizing public support at the national level.

During the 1930s and 1940s, while continuing to promote and expand established programs related to the conservation and preservation of resources, the Roosevelt administration developed policies aimed at improving farming practices, especially soil and water conservation programs. Most of these efforts were focused on actions to enhance agricultural productivity rather than protection or preservation of the environment. In fact, many of these policies would produce the very conditions that were subject to environmental regulation in the 1970s and 1980s.

The first steps toward today's environmental protection policies took the form of legislation authorizing the U.S. surgeon general to assist (mainly through technical advice and information) states and local government in their efforts to deal with public health issues related to water (Federal Water Pollution Control Act of 1948) and air (National Air Pollution Control Act of 1955) pollution. These and related programs (e.g., grants for constructing water treatment plants) were driven primarily by the work of a small group of environmental lobbyists in Washington as well as pressure for funding assistance from state and local governments. As far as public attention was concerned, these policies and programs surfaced under the radar of mass public opinion.

The environmental picture began to change in the mid-1960s. There was increased media coverage of air pollution in southern California and other cities as well as reports about the dumping of toxic waste into already polluted rivers and streams. It was also a time of convergence of popular concerns about the overuse of pesticides in the United States, the use of chemical weapons (especially Agent Orange) in the Vietnam War, and the implications of unchecked population growth. As a result, what was relative public indifference and inattention in the early 1960s transformed into a mass social movement by 1970, culminating in the first Earth Day demonstration on April 22, 1970. Triggered by the reaction to a major oil spill on the California coast, the call for a major teach-in about the environment came from within the U.S. Congress itself. Led by Senator Gaylord Nelson of Wisconsin and Representative Pete McCloskey of California, the effort tapped into the energy and tactics of the antiwar movement as well as the organizational power of existing environmental groups to mobilize activities throughout the country—and in the process to generate broad public support for environmental protection.

By 1970, Congress had already approved several important pieces of legislation. It passed the Clean Air Act (CAA) in 1963, expanding the national government's involvement in dealing with air pollution. Following the lead of California, which had already imposed emission control standards for new vehicles sold in the state, Congress then passed the Motor Vehicle Air Pollution Control Act, which amended and strengthened the CAA. Additional amendments soon followed. In 1967, Congress authorized the setting of interstate air quality standards and put in place the means for federal monitoring and enforcement. A major extension of the CAA occurred in 1970, when Congress required the development of federal and state regulations of major industrial and mobile sources of air pollution. Those regulations were tied to national ambient air quality standards (NAAQSs, pronounced "knacks"), which would play a major role in the work of the newly formed Environmental Protection Agency (EPA).[12] For several years thereafter, the focus was on making sure badly polluted regions of the country could meet the NAAQSs. Another major strengthening of the CAA took place in 1977, when Congress gave the EPA the task of preventing the deterioration of NAAQSs in regions that had already achieved them.

On a more general level, the National Environmental Policy Act of 1969 (NEPA) committed the federal government to improvement and enhancement of the environment. In addition to establishing the Council of Environmental Quality in the White House, it also required that all federal agencies (as well as state and local agencies receiving federal funding) conduct assessments of and prepare environmental impact statements on the effect of their new and existing programs on their surroundings. For many, the NEPA was—and remains—the Magna Carta of environmental protection, effectively making environmental policy part of every federal government action.

Simultaneous developments occurred in regard to clean water policies. The Federal Water Pollution Control Act (FWPCA) was completely rewritten in 1972, considerably expanding the regulatory authority of the federal government in this area. This was followed by the Safe Drinking Water Act of 1974 and further amendments to the FWPCA in 1977. Similarly, during this period Congress enacted legislation addressing threats to U.S. fisheries (Marine Protection, Research, and Sanctuaries Act of 1972) and endangered species (Endangered Species Act of 1973). The use and the disposal of pesticides, hazardous waste, and toxic substances were also addressed in congressional actions between 1972 and 1977, establishing these concerns as among the most significant in the development of America's environmental policy regime.

Ironically, public support and enthusiasm for environmental policies seemed to decline and level off as congressional actions increased. Although environmental concerns reached significant highs in public opinion polls in 1970, the importance of these issues fell and leveled off by 1974, as concerns about the economy and the nation's energy resources became increasingly important. The sense that environmental regulation had gone too far crept into the political debate of the time, and when Ronald Reagan took office, he seemed to have a mandate to cut back on government intrusions. The Reagan agenda led to fewer environmental policy initiatives; however, his administration's efforts to reduce and even undermine enforcement of environmental rules drew negative media coverage and ultimately led to a public backlash that resulted in the resignation of the secretary of the interior and the head of the EPA. By the late 1980s and early 1990s, favorable public attitudes toward federal government involvement in environmental protection were once again showing up in opinion polls. Especially important during this period was a growing concern about climate change due to human activity.

The focus on climate change elevated the issue of environmental protection to a global level, and most of the efforts to raise awareness about global warming came from the scientific community. Public debate was stirred up once again when former vice president Al Gore presented the case for policies to deal with the threats of climate change in a widely seen 2006 documentary, *An Inconvenient Truth*. The impact of

Severe weather conditions, often seen as an indication of climate change, have captured the attention of the American public in recent years. Here, in February 2014, crews clean up a mudslide near Glendora, California. The neighborhood is adjacent to the area burned by the massive Colby Fire in the Angeles National Forest in January 2014. A lack of vegetation on the mountains led to the mudslide.

Gore's award-winning presentation was once again to place environmental concerns high on the policy agenda, but opposition to the conclusions of climate change science was well organized, and the economic problems of the Great Recession drew attention away from the issue. Climate change and related policy concerns also fell victim to the political polarization that characterized the Obama administration. Nevertheless, although not among the public's list of top policy issues, environmental concerns and the need for government action retain the support of a significant portion of the American public.

Reflecting on what was taking place in the area of environmental policy during the 1960s and early 1970s, policy analyst Anthony Downs offered a five-stage issue-attention cycle model for making sense of how environmental and other issues (e.g., poverty, health care, auto safety) are handled over time. Writing in 1972, he characterized the period up to the mid-1960s as the "pre-problem stage," in which there is acknowledgement that the problem exists but the public pays little attention to it. This is

followed by a stage of "alarmed discovery and euphoric enthusiasm"—in the case of environmental protection, this is the period from about 1967 to Earth Day and the policy actions that followed in its wake. Public awareness spreads quickly during this phase, and policymakers face demands for significant action to deal with the problem. It does not take long before the next (third) stage takes hold, as the public begins to become aware of the costs associated with making significant progress toward resolving the issue. Downs predicted that we then enter a fourth stage—the intensity and degree of interest in environmental concerns will decline as other issues emerge to take its place near the top of the policy agenda of the public. Finally, we enter the "post-problem stage" as the public devotes less attention to the problems of the environment, with "spasmodic recurrences of interest."[13]

Conclusion

How do public opinion and public attitudes affect environmental policies?

In retrospect, Downs's model seems to fit the general pattern we see in the relationship between public opinion and U.S. environmental policy. To an extent, the model supports the myth of effective public opinion, and public support of government actions to deal with the environment did produce policies, programs, and institutions that have continued to address the major issues long after the attention to environmental problems declined. At the same time, the model may understate the degree to which environmental issues have been transformed over the long term. Many analysts would argue that—given lack of water in the western U.S. states, huge lakes drying up around the world, ice melting in glaciers, and so on—the current focus on climate change is substantially different from the issues of air and water pollution that were central to the mass movement that reached its peak in 1970. Perhaps, they argue, we are just emerging from a new pre-problem stage, and the "alarmed discovery and euphoric enthusiasm" that will radically alter our approach to environmental problems is just over the horizon.

Only time will tell.

QUESTIONS FOR DISCUSSION

1. Downs's issue-attention cycle theory predicts that issues surrounding climate change will eventually enter the post-problem stage and fade into the background. Given the nature of climate change, do you think that will be the case, or will advocates for relevant policies be able to sustain public support for their efforts in the long term?

2. Environmental policies related to clean air, clean water, recycling, and so on have had a considerable impact on the daily lives of Americans since the early 1970s, but we are often unaware of just how much that is the case. To comprehend just how pervasive those policies are, monitor your daily routine and take note of those points in your day that are influenced by environmental policies. For example, does the campus bus operate using natural gas? What about the quality standards applied to the tap water you drink each morning, or the catalytic converter in you car?

CHAPTER 7

MYTHS & REALITIES

How much do the Democratic and Republican parties differ from each other?

Political Parties

Sorting Out the Puzzle of Political Parties

When we teach about political parties in our American government courses, we often start off by asking our students what single word comes to mind when they think about political parties. Although the initial response is frequently just "Republican" or "Democrat," the words that next come to mind are pretty consistent: "unnecessary," "corrupt," "one-sided," "bad," "untrustworthy," and "confusing." These words often suggest a negative image of political parties and politics in the United States as well as the proposition that they are irrelevant and unnecessary. Indeed, as we point out in Chapter 6, 64 percent of adults, when asked in a recent poll, "If you had a child, would you like to see [him or her] go into politics as a life's work," emphatically answered "no."[1] What do you think of political parties? Do you think they are irrelevant in our political and governmental system?

Our goal in this chapter is to make sense of parties and their roles in our political and governmental system. By informing ourselves of essential facts about the reality of political parties, by examining a central myth associated with parties—the *myth of party irrelevance*—and by understanding the basic assumptions, attitudes, beliefs, and ideologies associated with parties, we can better understand this important institution, reducing or even eliminating the confusion regarding myths often associated with the party system in the United States.

Like many Americans today, the nation's founders were also distrustful and suspicious of political parties. In a 1796 farewell letter addressed "to the People of the United States," George Washington warned about the "baneful effects of the spirit of party." In summary, he suggested that

< The symbol of the Republican Party—the elephant—and the symbol of the Democratic Party—the donkey—head-butting each other reminds us of the strong partisan differences between the two major political parties in the United States.

It [the political party], serves always to distract the public councils and enfeeble the public administration. It agitates the community with ill founded jealousies and false alarms, kindles the animosity of one part against another, foments occasionally riot and insurrection. It opens the door to foreign influence and corruption, which find a facilitated access to the government itself through the channels of party passions.[2]

Years earlier, John Adams wrote a colleague that "there is nothing I dread so much as the division of the republic into two great parties, each under its own leader." Even Thomas Jefferson, who is often given credit for helping establish America's earliest parties, had mixed feelings about them: "If I could not go to heaven but with a party," he wrote in 1789, "I would not go there at all."[3]

Given this general attitude among the most prominent of the founders, it is not surprising that political parties are not mentioned at all in the Constitution. Yet, as individuals who devoted their lives to politics, each of those notable figures understood what all other observers of American political life have known for more than 225 years—that political parties are an inevitable consequence of governing in a democracy and a fact of political life in America that no one can ignore.

Nevertheless, in the words of one observer of political parties, "The public is highly skeptical of the parties and their activities."[4] How can we make sense of this deep-seated and widespread public skepticism about parties? We argue that public criticism of the Democrats and Republicans reflects the myth of party irrelevance—a myth that allows us to believe that parties are unnecessary and perhaps even worthless, while at the same time knowing that they are central, even critical, to the day-to-day operations of our representative democracy. In this chapter we focus on the reality, and you will learn that parties still matter in the country's politics, even though fewer people now strongly identify with them.

@

POLITICS & POPULAR CULTURE: Visit the book's companion website at **www.oup.com/us/gitelson** to read the special feature *The Politics of Hollywood.*

What Parties Are and What They Do

> **What are the three parts of a party that political scientists often refer to, collectively, as the "three-headed political giant"?**

Political parties differ from country to country. In most Western European democracies, for example, parties tend to be highly centralized, stable, and tightly knit coalitions of men and women with commonly held opinions and beliefs. In these countries, parties take clear-cut, sometimes extreme, ideological positions. In a number of the European nations, where you often have a multiparty system with more than two parties successfully competing in elections, socialist or liberal parties on the left of the political spectrum face ideologically conservative parties on the right of the political spectrum.

Parties in the United States

In the United States, some minor parties are strongly ideological—for example, the Libertarian Party, the Conservative Party, and the Socialist Workers Party. Recently, the Tea Party movement (not a single party but a loose coalition of political organizations), which has supported economic and social conservative issues, has attracted both local and national attention. However, historically, the two major parties, the Democrats and the Republicans, have not based their positions strictly on ideology; rather, they have followed a set of guiding principles, most of which focus on the role that government should play in supporting and enhancing our democratic system. Each party's positions reflect a wide range of beliefs about what government should do in particular areas, and each party seeks to attract a broad spectrum of supporters. Because some of their beliefs overlap, the Democratic and Republican parties may, at times, seem alike, especially because they share a strong democratic, capitalist tradition. But they differ on many economic and social issues; in recent years the Democrats and Republicans have been highly polarized on economic and social issues at both the national and state levels of government. And they draw differing proportions of liberals, moderates, and conservatives into their political folds.

In the United States, **political parties** are coalitions of people organized formally to recruit, nominate, and elect candidates for public office. In addition to organizing elections, political parties are instrumental in the following activities:

- Running the government

- Creating and implementing shared political goals through the election of officials to the executive and legislative branches of government

- Bringing stability to the political system

As strange as it may seem to many people who are cynical about political parties, the parties do serve as a major link between the public and governmental officials.

Political party In the United States, a coalition of people organized formally to recruit, nominate, and elect individuals to office and to use elected office to achieve shared political goals.

One of the most important tasks of a political party is to get out the vote on election day. Here, both Republicans and Democrats vie for the attention of prospective party loyalists with lawn signs.

Decentralization A term that contends that many different individuals within the party share the decision-making power, with power dispersed. No single individual or organization controls the entire system. In effect, party organizations in the United States are fragmented and multilayered, often operating independently of each other.

Party-as-organization An entity with few members, primarily consisting of state and county chairpersons and local ward and precinct captains, who work for the party throughout the year, recruiting candidates and participating in fundraising activities.

Party-in-the-electorate The coalition of everyone who identifies with a particular party and tends to vote for that party's candidates; these people may also contribute to and work on campaigns.

Party-in-government The individuals who have been elected or appointed to a governmental office under a party label. They play a major role in organizing government and in setting policy.

The Republicans and the Democrats, the two major parties, are decentralized organizations, regulated at the state level.[5] The concept of decentralization is not as confusing as it may seem. In this context, **decentralization** means that many different individuals within the party share the decision-making power. No single individual or organization controls the entire system (as compared, for example, with Great Britain, Germany, and Italy, which have highly centralized party organizations controlled by relatively few individuals or central committees). In effect, parties in the United States are fragmented and multilayered. The comments of one local party leader perhaps best describe that structure: "No state leader, not even the president of the United States, is going to dictate to us whom we slate for local office. They can't even tell us what issues are important." All state party organizations and most local party organizations operate more or less independently of one another, although the authority of one party organization may overlap that of another. Compared with other nations, the United States has one of the most loosely integrated party systems in the world.[6] The Constitution makes no mention of parties, and Congress has passed relatively few laws regulating party activities. By and large, individual states are free to set the rules for their own state parties' operation, although recent Supreme Court decisions have enhanced the power of the national parties to regulate some aspects of state party activity—for example, the primary and caucus systems for nominating the party's presidential candidates (see Chapter 8).

The Three-Headed Political Giant

In describing political parties, we might best characterize them as *three-headed political giants*.[7] Like our own relationships with brothers, sisters, or friends, sometimes these three alliances cooperate, and sometimes they pull in different directions. The three heads represent three different alliances of members: the party-as-organization, the party-in-the-electorate, and the party-in-government.

The **party-as-organization** is small and relatively informal. American party organizations consist primarily of state and county chairpersons and local ward and precinct captains (who are sometimes paid employees but more often volunteers) who work for the party throughout the year, recruiting candidates and participating in fundraising activities. The **party-in-the-electorate** includes all those who identify with the particular party and tend to vote for that party's candidates; some of these may also contribute to and work on campaigns. Anyone of voting age can choose to be a member of the party-in-the-electorate. American parties depend on such public support for their electoral strength. The **party-in-government** consists of the individuals who have been elected or appointed to a governmental office under a party label. Contrary to the myth of party irrelevance, parties play a major role in organizing government and in setting policy. For example, in the U.S. House of Representatives and the U.S. Senate, the Republican Party supports policies different from those supported by Democrats.

If a party is going to be successful, it must attract people like you and me to its fold. Parties need paid and volunteer workers to ring doorbells, distribute campaign literature, register voters, and staff party headquarters. They need voters who will support the party's candidates, donate money to campaigns, and volunteer their services around election time. Finally, parties need candidates who can successfully run for office and, once elected, work to attain the party's policy goals.

Who Belongs to Major Parties and Why?

> **What are some of the key differences between the Republican and Democratic parties?**

Given the high level of skepticism about parties in the United States that we've discussed thus far, it may seem strange for us to ask you the question, "Do you belong to either the Democratic or the Republican party?" Interestingly, for many college students, even those who are cynical about the role of parties, the answer is often yes, although the attachment may be weak. Despite the widespread belief that the two major parties are alike, more than 55 percent of the voting-age population identifies with one or the other.[8]

As you can see in Figure 7.1, attachment to the Democratic Party is historically stronger than attachment to the Republican Party, although it is noteworthy that a plurality of voters regard themselves as independents.

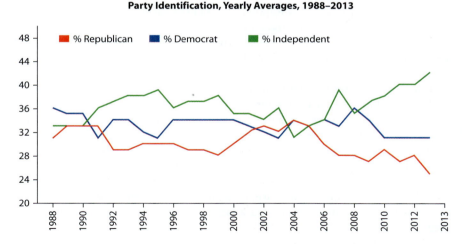

Party Identification, Yearly Averages, 1988–2013

■ % Republican   ■ % Democrat   ■ % Independent

FIGURE 7.1 A Record-High 42 Percent of Americans Identify as Independents Forty-two percent of Americans, on average, identified as political independents in 2013, the highest percentage Gallup has measured since it began conducting interviews by telephone twenty-five years ago. Meanwhile, Republican identification fell to 25 percent, the lowest over that time span. At 31 percent, Democratic identification is unchanged from the last four years but down from 36 percent in 2008.

Source: The results are based on more than 18,000 interviews with Americans from thirteen separate Gallup multiple-day polls conducted in 2013.

What difference does party identification make? Clearly, it often determines citizens' political choices. In a typical election, for example, a voter may face a ballot listing candidates for ten, twenty, thirty, or more offices. Because few people can thoroughly study every issue and every office seeker's record, many voters select candidates on the basis of party affiliation. Not surprisingly, one of the reasons individuals who identify with a political party are more likely to vote in an election is that the party label often serves as a shortcut or cue as to how to vote, allowing individuals to vote for a candidate they may know little or nothing about. These voters rely on a candidate's party label to help guide their choice. Self-declared independents are less likely to vote, because they don't have a party label cue to rely on when they know little or nothing about a candidate other than her or his party identification.

Sometimes voters find, to their disappointment, that a candidate does not represent their views, but the party label often indicates a candidate's political philosophy and positions on issues with reasonable accuracy. As one party loyalist in Michigan recently put it, "If you are a Democratic candidate in this state and don't support labor, you won't be a Democratic candidate for very long."

In the Driver's Seat: Democrats and Republicans

Who are the Democrats and the Republicans? These parties tend to attract different groups of supporters. Democrats maintain their greatest strength among African Americans and Hispanics, Jews, women, and individuals between the ages of eighteen and twenty-nine and those over the age of fifty. White southerners were once a critical part of the Democratic coalition, but a majority of them have voted as Republicans over the past three decades, although Democrats still maintain a foothold in the South through the support of African Americans. Republicans are scattered across the country. They tend to be white, Protestant, and middle to upper class, and their views are comparatively conservative.

Immediately after the September 11, 2001, terrorist attacks in the United States, Republicans and Democrats, both partisan supporters and officeholders, came together to present a united front against our enemies. In a time of crisis, this is not surprising. This cooperation has historically been the case in wartime and during national emergencies. But partisanship has strong roots in our nation, and within months after September 11, many traditional partisan divisions were evident in Congress and state legislatures.[9] The issue that most sharply divides Democrats and Republicans is the role of government. Since the 1930s, Democrats have favored a large governmental role in such policy areas as social welfare and business regulation. Republicans, on the other hand, are more likely to favor reducing taxes and, as a result, governmental services, including aid to minorities and social welfare programs. They also prefer that government have less of a role in regulating business. The polarization of the two parties over issues including economic recovery, job programs, immigration policy, and national health care legislation has been especially apparent over the past seven years, as Democrat and Republican members of Congress

TABLE 7.1 Comparisons Among Democrats, Republicans, and Independents on Important Issues

	% Democrat	% Republican	% Independent	% Partisan Gap
Creating more jobs	90	84	85	6
Helping the economy grow	88	84	86	4
Making government work more efficiently	80	84	81	4
Improving education	89	76	78	13
Reforming Social Security and Medicare	74	77	79	3
Reducing health care costs	78	59	70	19
Reducing the deficit	61	84	65	23
Improving access to health care	83	47	70	36
Reducing poverty and inequality	75	52	66	23
Reforming the tax code	57	64	57	7
Reducing gun violence	73	40	50	33
Reforming immigration	44	55	53	11

Source: Gallup Daily Tracking, May 4–5, 2013.

strongly opposed each other on these and other issues. When it comes to the question of which issues are the most important, Republicans and Democrats hold both similar and different views (see Table 7.1).[10] How do your values and issue concerns match up with the party lines suggested by these poll findings in Table 7.1?

Independents: Taking a Back Seat in Politics?

Independents—individuals who do not identify with any party—often claim that their voting patterns are influenced by issues and leadership qualities, not by party labels. The increase in the number of independents during the 1960s and 1970s, particularly among young voters between the ages of eighteen and twenty-nine, and the leveling off of this trend in the 1980s and 1990s parallel the belief in the myth of party irrelevance—that is, the tendency of many Americans to question the ability of parties and government to solve the nation's major problems. The United States has faced a series of major crises in the past three decades, from Watergate to economic recessions. Many people, including college students, believe that these events have contributed to a general feeling that the political system is ineffective and to a corresponding increase in indifference toward both parties. Forty-seven percent of Americans think that neither political party represents the American people.[11]

This indifference is reflected, in part, in the growth over the past thirty years of self-declared independents. Independents make up an important part of the voting population, especially in presidential elections. Less evidence exists, however, that they maintain an independent position in state and local elections.[12] In these contests, voters often lack information on candidates' policy positions or leadership qualities. In an average election, voters may be faced with dozens of candidates seeking dozens of offices at all levels of government. It is not easy to learn about and understand all of the issues involved and all of the candidates' positions. Therefore, there are not many voters who are pure independents and totally avoid using party labels to identify the candidates for whom they will vote. Thus, party label remains one of the best predictors of voter choice in many elections, even for self-declared independents.

A majority of Americans appear to accept the Democratic and Republican parties as relevant symbols, particularly when it comes to voting. In fact, when independents who lean toward one or the other of the two major parties are included, between 80 and 85 percent of the electorate identify to some extent with either the Democratic or the Republican party.[13]

If Parties Are So Important, What Do They Do?

To no one's surprise, a basic task of political parties is to win elections. Once parties have successfully run candidates for political office, they offer a way to organize the political world and provide elected officials with a means to organize the government. Had they not developed as a link between the public and the institutions of government, parties would have had to be invented.[14] Let us look more closely at some of the functions of parties.

Simplifying Voting. Many citizens, who often vote in dozens of elections at the local, state, and national levels, cannot adequately research all of the candidates and issues. Thus, as just mentioned, most of these individuals rely on a candidate's party identification to identify his or her positions on general issues and to serve as a shortcut or cue for voting decisions. In a complex world of issues and problems, this shortcut method is probably not a surprising tool for many voters, including college students. This use of party identification also explains why partisans often vote more frequently, across the ballot and in both state and local offices, than self-declared independents do. Independents have fewer useful cues or shortcuts to help them make their electoral choices.

Electoral coalitions Groups of loyal supporters who agree with the party's stand on most issues and vote for its candidates for office.

Building Electoral Coalitions. Parties exist to organize people into **electoral coalitions**: groups of loyal supporters who agree with the party's stand on most issues and vote for its candidates for office. Although individual ties to political parties have weakened over the past fifty years, party labels remain an important electoral symbol in the United States, and for many Americans no other institution or organization embraces as broad a range of issues and goals on the national, state, and local levels as the Democratic and Republican parties.

Developing Public Policy. Parties also play a role in developing positions on what government should do about various problems and in translating those positions into legislation. Research on presidential and state platforms indicates that opposing candidates usually have distinctly different positions on certain issues. Both the candidates and the parties take **platforms**—statements of party goals and specific policy agendas—very seriously, although they are not binding on either candidates or elected officials.[15] Political scientists Gerald Pomper and Susan Lederman argue as follows: "The parties do not copy each other's pledges, but make divergent appeals, thereby pointing to the differences in their basic composition. [The platform] is important because it summarizes, crystallizes, and presents to the voters the character of the party coalition. We should take platforms seriously because politicians seem to take them seriously."[16] Although party platforms do serve as a form of propaganda—an attempt to put a positive light on the party's programs and goals—they also represent a serious declaration of policy. The Democrats' positions are relatively liberal, with strong support for social spending, and the Republicans' positions are relatively conservative, with emphasis on individual enterprise.

Platforms Statements of party goals and specific policy agendas that are taken seriously by the party's candidates but are not binding.

Winning Elections. A party's ability to recruit the best possible candidates and to win elections determines its success. Party organizations do not monopolize that process; many candidates seek nomination on their own. In recent years, however, parties have offered their candidates a growing list of services. Party organizations,

Campaign victories are always a time for celebration by the winners. Here, Pat McCrory is introduced on January 5, 2013, as the newly elected Republican governor of North Carolina.

drawn to the major party coalitions at election time, and those parties try hard to maintain middle-of-the-road positions that will attract voters.[23] The result has been two broad-based party coalitions, such as the Republicans and the Democrats of today.

A Division of Interests. A second explanation, advanced by political scientists V. O. Key Jr. and Louis Hartz, points to a natural division of interests in our nation as the source of the two-party system.[24] From the time of the country's founding until recently, divisions have existed: between eastern manufacturers and western frontier interests, between slaveholders and abolitionists, between urban and rural interests, and among various regional interests. These divisions have stemmed from tensions over the power of the national government and over questions of economic and social policy. That situation, according to Key and Hartz, has fostered the two-party competitive system, which is really a response to the national duality of interests.

A Similarity of Goals. Still another view focuses on the overriding consensus in the United States regarding our political, social, economic, and governmental systems. For example, most Americans believe in capitalism, virtually no Americans want to institute a monarchy, and most Americans believe in some form of free enterprise in the United States. By contrast, in many European countries, the people support a variety of radically different social and economic alternatives, ranging from socialism to anarchy, and differences in social class and religion have given rise to a broad range of parties.

Divisions do exist in the United States, of course—for example, between the poor and the wealthy. But a basic acceptance of the political and governmental system by most Americans makes compromise possible. As a result, according to this view, the two major parties can adequately serve us all, and we do not need a complex multiparty system.

State Laws. Because the U.S. Constitution does not mention political parties, the definition of what a *party* is and the laws that regulate parties have been left, for the most part, to the individual states. Because the two major parties, the Republicans and the Democrats, have dominated the state legislatures, with the exception of that of Nebraska, state laws, in general, have historically made it difficult for third parties to get on the ballot. These restrictive state laws have helped to perpetuate the two-party system in the United States (although recent court challenges have eliminated some of those restrictions in various states).

The Hidden Actors: Third Parties in the United States

Despite the strength of the two-party system, minor parties have always existed in the United States. There have been more than nine hundred of these "third" parties, and occasionally they even do well in national elections, although only one of them—the Republicans in 1860—has developed into a permanent national party. In 1992, independent candidate Ross Perot mounted a highly visible campaign for the presidency and received 19 percent of the popular vote. In 1996, however, running as the Reform Party presidential candidate, he received only about 8 percent of the vote. In 2012, no third party presidential candidate attracted as much as 1 percent of the national vote, a number far short of that in recent presidential elections.

Sometimes a minor party forms around a single issue, such as prohibition, or an ideology, such as socialism. Other minor parties are splinter groups that leave a major party because they feel that their interests are not well represented.

Most of the third parties' electoral successes have come at the state and local levels. But even at those levels, they must overcome many barriers. Dominated by the two major parties, state legislatures have created complicated electoral rules—often requiring petitions, nominating conventions, minimum levels of registered voters, organizational requirements, or a combination of all of these provisions—that can make it hard for the minor parties to place their candidates on the ballot.

Federal election laws also work against the minor parties. For example, the major parties automatically receive funding for presidential campaigns. A third party cannot obtain such funding until its candidate has demonstrated the ability to garner a certain amount (at least 5 percent) of the national popular vote.

Third parties have been a part of the political landscape in the United States for more than two hundred years. Here, Libertarian Party chair Geoff Neale speaks before an audience of loyal supporters.

Despite these obstacles, third parties endure, attracting devoted members and serving as a force for change in American politics (see Table 7.2). These parties put new issues on the political agenda—issues that the major parties may overlook in their search for the broad middle ground, where most voters are perceived to be. For example, social security, unemployment insurance, the five-day workweek, workers' compensation, national health insurance, and governmental aid to farmers were first introduced by the Socialist Party in its 1932 party platform and only later recognized as important programs by both the Republicans and the Democrats.

Future elections will no doubt provide voters with a number of third-party candidates for the presidency, as well as for Congress and state and local offices. In 2014, dozens of minor parties ran candidates in Senate, House, and gubernatorial races and in many local elections. (See the Asked & Answered feature on page 235.)

TABLE 7.2 A Sampling of the More Than Nine Hundred National and Regional Parties That Have Spotted Our Political Landscape Since the Early 1800s

	Number of States in Which Party Is Present	Date Founded
Federalist Party*	---	1789
Anti-Masonic Party*	---	1826
Democratic Party	50 (plus Washington, D.C.)	1828
Free Soil Party*	---	1848
Republican Party	50 (plus Washington, D.C.)	1854
Socialist Labor Party of America*	---	1876
National Women's Party*	---	1913
Vegetarian Party*	---	1948
American Nazi Party*	---	1959
Independent Citizens Movement**	1 (U.S. Virgin Islands)	1968
Libertarian Party	50 (plus Washington, D.C.)	1971
Alaskan Independence Party**	1 (Alaska)	1973
Green Party	37 (plus Washington, D.C.)	1991
Constitutional Party	37	1992
Boston Tea Party**	1 (Massachusetts)	2006
Blue Enigma Party**	1 (Delaware)	2006
Rent Is Too Damn High Party**	1 (New York)	2005
Ecology Democracy Party**	1 (Minnesota)	2010
Sovereign Union Movement**	1 (Puerto Rico)	2010

*Historical party, no longer functioning.

**Party based only in one state.

ASKED & ANSWERED

ASKED: *Shouldn't we have more than just two party options on the ballot?**

ANSWERED: During every election year cycle, this lament is often heard among voters: "Shouldn't we have more than two party options on the ballot?" Countless election pundits follow that question by observing that many other nations have multiparty systems. But perhaps this is yet another case of "the grass is always greener on the other side"? What are some of the disadvantages associated with the multiparty parliamentary systems so often found in other countries around the globe?

- **Unstable government coalitions.** With proportional representation in government, it is often the case that no single party controls a majority of the legislative seats. As such, larger parties are often forced to form coalitions, drawing on the support of other, smaller parties to create a majority alignment in the legislative body. Depending on how fragile the alignments are, even the exodus of a small, weak party from the coalition may wind up upsetting the entire governmental apple cart. Israel and Italy have had to call for early elections in many instances during past decades due to coalition breakdowns—and, often, the entrance of one party into an alliance has meant the exit of another.

- **Party-based campaigns.** When people vote for a member of Congress in the United States, they often have a reasonably good idea of whom they are putting into office. But elections that are centered on the party rather than on the candidates, as is often the case in parliamentary systems, can produce representatives whom the public knows little about—which likely would not sit very well with most American voters.

- **Radical ideologies in government discourse.** France's National Front Party would be hard-pressed to gain political representation in a two-party system; its ultranationalistic views (which in the past have included a proposal to expel all French residents not of European descent) would relegate it to the sidelines in national debate, just as extreme candidates in the United States fail to survive the electoral process. But the electoral parliamentary system of France, based on proportional representation, encourages extreme, fascist parties like the National Front to run candidates for office and frequently allows them to succeed, as they have in recent years. Although some political pundits argue that the inclusion of extreme candidates on the right and the left siphon off attention from the more "serious" candidates, proponents of parliamentary systems often claim that more political voices equal an increase in voter participation.

No doubt the issue of a two-party system versus a multiparty system in the United States will continue to occupy the attention of many American voters in the future, especially as we gain new insights into politics at the global level. No doubt, too, the question, "Shouldn't we have more than just two realistic options on the ballot?" will continue to be asked by us as we debate our choices of which individuals and political parties will represent us in the White House, Congress, governor's mansions, city halls, state legislatures, and the thousands of other governmental offices across the nation.

---

*Kevin Fullam contributed to this feature.

Precinct The bottom of the typical local party structure—a voting district, generally covering an area of several blocks.

Ward A city council district; in the party organization, this is the level below the citywide level.

Patronage The provision of jobs for party loyalists in return for their political support at election time.

Preferments The provision of services or contracts in return for political support. Party committee members use patronage and preferments to court voters and obtain campaign contributions.

Party Structure from the Bottom Up

> **What are the different roles of parties at the local, state, and national levels?**

Decentralization is the key word to remember when you think about the structure of parties. Just as in our governmental system, power in the parties is fragmented among local, state, and national organizations. The two national parties are loose confederations of state parties, and state political parties are loose confederations of city and county political organizations.

Local Parties

You may be most familiar with the structure of political parties at the local level. At the bottom of the typical local party structure is the **precinct**, a voting district that generally covers an area of several blocks. An elected or appointed precinct captain may oversee electoral activities in the precinct, including voter registration, distribution of leaflets, and get-out-the-vote efforts. Above the precinct level, several different organizations exist. **Wards**, or city council districts, are important in big cities such as Chicago. Elsewhere, party organizations exist at the city, county, congressional district, state legislative district, or even judicial level. Members of these committees may be elected or appointed. Their responsibilities include registering voters, raising money, recruiting candidates, conducting campaigns, getting out the vote, and handling **patronage**—that is, jobs for party loyalists—and **preferments**—services or contracts provided to individuals and companies in return for campaign support.

In many places around the country, local parties scarcely exist at all. Nonpartisan elections are the rule—a result of antiparty reforms during the early 1900s—and politics is relatively informal. Indeed, two-thirds of cities with populations of more than 50,000 use the nonpartisan form of election. In many of these communities, formal or informal *political clubs* raise money and run campaigns. These clubs actively compete with each other in elections and may identify with either major party.[25]

Even in communities where partisan elections are the rule, party organization and strength vary tremendously. If one party dominates, the weaker party may find it impossible to recruit workers and candidates and to raise money for elections. Until its recent resurgence, the Republican Party had to cope with this kind of handicap throughout a Democrat-dominated South. In communities that show little interest in politics, neither party may be able to put together a strong local organization.

Nevertheless, it is at the grassroots local community level that party organization often finds its greatest strength, and it is at that level that we have seen growth in party

Political machines dominated many party organizations in the nineteenth century. One of the most infamous party bosses, Boss Tweed, a powerful leader of New York City's Tammany Hall Democratic Party organization, was often satirized by cartoonist Thomas Nast in the 1870s.

organizations in recent years. Indeed, recent research suggests that local party organizations are becoming increasingly active in various aspects of the campaign process in communities.[26]

State Parties

The influence and power of state party organizations vary from state to state. The Democratic state party organizations in Alabama, Georgia, and New Jersey and the Republican state party organizations in Alaska, Iowa, Minnesota, and Nevada have been described as "dysfunctional."[27] In contrast, parties in states such as Connecticut, Indiana, and Michigan wield considerable power. Often a good deal of that power is in the hands of the state chairperson. It is not unusual for the governor of a state to control the state's party organization, although, as we shall see in Chapter 8, which discusses elections and campaigns, governors are often motivated to establish their own candidate-centered organization devoted to their campaign for reelection. Party organization varies from state to state, however, and depends on the preferences of officeholders and other influential party members and on state laws and party rules and regulations.

In recent years, state party organizations have assumed an important role on the political scene.[28] State parties have increasingly begun to offer state and local candidates fundraising, polling, and research services as well as technical help in establishing candidate websites. They may also provide computer analyses of voting behavior. In addition, most state party organizations help orchestrate the state presidential campaigns.

National Parties

The national party organizations come into their own every four years when they organize the national conventions and support candidates for major office. Although the national parties are less visible the rest of the time, their staffs, directed by the national chairpersons and the national committees, which include representatives from all the states, are hard at work. They raise money for national and state elections, run workshops on campaigning and fundraising techniques for congressional candidates, and maintain the loose, decentralized structure that is the national party. The Democrats and the Republicans, by devoting greater resources to their national party organizations, have undergone a national resurgence during the past twenty-five years. The electoral role of the national party organizations has been challenged in recent years by interest groups and their **political action committees (PACs)**. Because federal laws, as well as many state laws, prohibit various interest groups from donating money to political campaigns, such groups have set up affiliated PAC organizations for the purpose of contributing money to the campaigns of candidates who sympathize with their aims. (See Chapter 9, on interest groups, for a more detailed discussion of the role of PACs.) The involvement of professional consultants and the media in the campaign process has also challenged the role of the national organizations. (See Chapter 8, on elections, for more on this topic.)

Despite these challenges, the national organizations have refused to accept a secondary role in national politics and during the past twenty-five years have

Political action committee (PAC) An independent organization that can be established by interest groups, officeholders, and political candidates for the sole purpose of contributing money to the campaigns of candidates who sympathize with its aims. PACs are the result of federal laws that prohibit most interest groups from donating money to federal political campaigns.

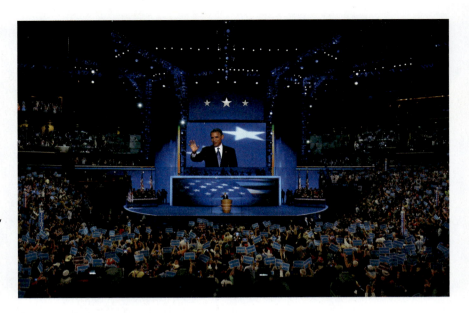

National party conventions, although serious events that confirm the selection of a party's candidate for the presidency of the United States, are filled with celebration and hoopla. Here, President Barack Obama celebrates with his supporters at the 2012 Democratic National Convention.

worked to revitalize themselves.[29] Both the Republican and Democratic parties have strengthened their fundraising and candidate support systems. They now provide sophisticated technical campaign expertise to state and local parties in addition to providing financial support for campaigns. The Democrats have also redefined the rules governing the selection of presidential convention delegates

National conventions are an opportunity for the party's presidential nominee to rally his supporters. Here, Republican vice-presidential candidate Paul Ryan addresses delegates to the 2012 Republican National Convention.

to make the party's decision-making structure more democratic and to increase grassroots participation in the party.

Conclusion

What does the future hold for the Democratic and Republican parties? Some scholars insist that both parties are in a period of decline and see them as weak, inconsistent in their policies, lacking accountability for their actions, disorganized in pursuing their goals, and less effective in organizing government than in the past.[30] In recent presidential campaigns, we have seen both the Democratic and the Republican parties faced with contentious battles over which faction of the party—moderate, liberal, or conservative—will control the nomination of candidates and the writing of the party platform. We seem to have moved from **party-centered campaigns** to **candidate-centered campaigns**, reflecting the shift in control over the candidate recruitment and campaign process from the political parties to candidate-controlled campaign organizations. Given the decrease in party identification and the weakening of party control over some aspects of the campaign and election process, it is not surprising that many people believe in the myth of party irrelevance.

Are the parties identical? It often seems that way because in some areas their policies can be difficult to distinguish. On certain broad issues, such as concerns over terrorism and the need for energy independence, their general positions are often the same. To confuse matters further, groups of legislators from both parties occasionally join forces to support or oppose legislation. However, over the past ten years, Congress and many state legislatures have accurately been described as highly polarized, with Democratic and Republican legislators divided on many policy issues.

The evidence suggests that the parties are not irrelevant. The fact that they attract different coalitions of voters and office seekers and that Democrats and Republicans in the electorate and in government tend to view many issues differently attests to their relevancy in the political system.

The significant number of independents, along with the increase in ticket splitting, suggests that parties may be less relevant than they have been in the past, as does the takeover of some traditional party roles by interest groups, political action committees, the media, and professional political consultants. We will discuss these issues further in Chapters 8, 9, and 10. However, the parties have changed in response to such challenges. Furthermore, although parties attract fewer strong supporters, particularly among college students, a significant majority of voters still feel some attachment to either the Democrats or the Republicans and believe that one party can do a better job than the other in tackling the nation's most serious problems.

If parties are still viable, what kind of change is taking place? How can we explain, for example, the growing independence of political candidates and legislators from their parties? Some scholars have suggested that a transformation is taking place in the roles and functions of parties in our society.[31]

Although parties are now sharing many traditional functions with other groups, they have also taken on new tasks, as our discussion in this chapter has

Party-centered campaign A campaign in which the party coordinates activities, raises money, and develops strategies.

Candidate-centered campaign A campaign in which paid consultants or volunteers coordinate campaign activities, develop strategies, and raise funds. Parties play a secondary role.

shown. Both national and state organizations have enhanced their roles in the campaign process, and parties continue to play an important role at the local level. In fact, most of the elections held in our nation during the four years between presidential races—and they number more than 500,000—are not touched by any other organized group. Party influence in the Senate and House remains strong, and on many partisan issues the members vote along party lines more often than not. This pattern is also typical of state legislators.

Thus, despite the myth of party irrelevance, and our inability, at times, to make sense of their role in our political system, parties remain a key institution in American politics and are still one of the most important cues for voters making electoral decisions. They also play a dominant role in organizing and coordinating public policy on literally thousands of issues. Finally, parties represent many individuals and groups that are not adequately served by other organizations. All of them have benefited from strong party platforms and legislative action. Challenged by the entry of new and competing institutions into the electoral process, parties have increasingly adapted to these challenges and have maintained their unique role in our political system.

If you are confused about the role that political parties play in your life, think about the potential confusion you would confront in determining, without the party label as a cue, how you will vote in the thousands of elections you will be asked to participate in over your lifetime. Also give some thought to how government, and particularly our large legislative bodies—including the 435 members of the House of Representatives—would organize and coordinate public policy on literally thousands of issues without the help of party organizations. Making sense of the political system would surely be even more difficult, complex, and confusing without the party system.

Key Terms

Balance of trade p. 247
Candidate-centered campaign p. 239
Decentralization p. 222
Economic development policies p. 247
Electoral coalitions p. 226
Fiscal policy p. 246
Free trade p. 247
Globalization p. 247
Industrial policy p. 248
Keynesians p. 246

Monetarists p. 246
Monetary policy p. 244
Party-as-organization p. 222
Party-centered campaign p. 239
Party dealignment p. 230
Party-in-government p. 222
Party-in-the-electorate p. 222
Party realignment p. 230
Patronage p. 236
Platforms p. 227
Political action committee (PAC) p. 237

Political party p. 221
Precinct p. 236
Preferments p. 236
Primary p. 228
Proportional representation p. 231
Single-member district, winner-take-all electoral system p. 231
Supply-side economics p. 248
Tariffs p. 247
Tax incentives p. 248
Ward p. 236

Focus Questions Review

1. **What are the three parts of a party that political scientists often refer to, collectively, as the "three-headed political giant"?**
   - Parties represent three different alliances of members—what we sometimes refer to as the "three-headed political giant":
     1. *The party-as-organization*: an entity with few members, primarily consisting of state and county chairpersons and local ward and precinct captains, who work for the party throughout the year, recruiting candidates and participating in fundraising and campaign activities.
     2. *The party-in-the-electorate*: the coalition of everyone who identifies with a particular party and tends to vote for that party's candidates; these people may also contribute money to and work on campaigns.
     3. *The party-in-government*: the individuals who have been elected or appointed to a governmental office under a party label. They play a major role in organizing government and in setting policy.

2. **What are some of the key differences between the Republican and Democratic parties?**
   - Ideologically, Republicans tend to be more conservative; Democrats, more liberal.
   - The two parties attract different supporters: Democrat support comes more from African Americans and Hispanics, Catholics and Jews, women, and citizens over the age of fifty. Republican supporters tend to be white, Protestant, and middle to upper class, and now include white southerners. Democrats and Republicans have differences of opinion on key issues, including economic problems, health care, immigration policy, and terrorism.

3. **Why does the United States have a two-party system?**
   - Parties developed slowly in the United States, but by the 1860s the Republicans and the Democrats had laid the foundation for the two-party system. Four major party realignments, or major shifts in party coalitions, have occurred in U.S. history. Currently, scholars are debating whether we are in a period of realignment or dealignment.
   - Explanations for the existence of the two-party system include single-member district, winner-take-all electoral rules; a division of social and economic interests; a basic consensus on political goals; and restrictive state laws regarding third parties.
   - Despite the strength of the major parties, minor parties thrive and present program alternatives that are often adopted by the Democratic and Republican parties. More than nine hundred minor parties have existed in the history of the United States.
   - Although many Americans' identification with the Republican or Democratic party seems to be weak, the parties continue to be relevant symbols, particularly when it comes to voting.

4. **What are the different roles of parties at the local, state, and national levels?**
   - The key roles that political parties play in our political system include the following:
     1. Organizing and coordinating public policy on literally thousands of issues
     2. Providing the American electorate with different ideological orientations
     3. Serving as a cue for voters who don't know very much about the candidates or the issues they stand for
   - In addition, political parties act as an organizational structure for our legislative bodies and represent hundreds of millions of Americans, including many individuals and groups that are not adequately served by other organizations.
   - The party organizations at all levels play a number of roles, including encouraging voter registration and getting out the vote on Election Day.
   - Local party organizations raise money, recruit candidates, and conduct campaigns.
   - State party organizations also raise money, recruit candidates, and conduct campaigns and increasingly offer state and local candidates polling and research services. They provide technical assistance

and help maintain candidate websites. In addition, they provide support for the national party organizations for presidential campaigns.

- The national party organizations, in addition to supporting all of the types of services provided by local and state party organizations, every four years organize and support the national convention, the place where the party's presidential and vice-presidential candidates are confirmed, and where the national party platform is written.

- Both local and state political parties have grown in importance in recent years. Although the national party organizations have been challenged by competing groups, they have responded to the challenge and, in changing, have revitalized themselves.

Review Questions

1. What are the different functions of political parties?
2. What explanations have been given for why we have a two-party system and not a multiparty system?

 For more information and access to study materials, visit the book's companion website at www.oup.com/us/gitelson.

Policy Connection

Do the two major parties really offer different approaches to managing the American economic system?

The Policy Challenge

Chapter 7, focusing on the realities that lie behind the popular myth of party irrelevance, highlighted the important function parties play in the operations of our electoral system. It also noted the role they play in articulating policy options for voters to consider when they go to the polls. In this Policy Connection, we will see how, throughout our history, the parties have reflected different approaches to economic policies. The policy challenge for both parties is to reinforce the impression that voting for one or the other really matters when it comes to shaping the national government's role in dealing with economic issues.

Images and Realities

For America's political parties, images matter.

Most of us are familiar with the parties' political symbols—the donkey for the Democrats and the elephant for the Republicans—not only because the parties make use of them on almost all their campaign material but also because political cartoonists and editorial writers have used them for more than 150 years to represent the existence of differences between the parties on issues of the day. Over time, those specific partisan differences began to reinforce one another as each party attempted to take consistent stands that reflected the voters who had supported them on past issues. Soon it became clear that each party represented distinct choices that had been reframed and reduced to their simplest form.[1] The differences are particularly true in one area that has special importance to Americans: the role of government in managing the economy.[2]

After the Civil War, the platforms of the two parties began to take different approaches from each other regarding economic issues. By the 1896 presidential campaign, it was evident that the Republican Party (led by William McKinley) favored policies in support of the growing urban, industrial sector, whereas the Democrats (led by William Jennings Bryan) took positions more favorable to agrarian interests, mainly in the western United States. Throughout the Progressive Era and the 1920s, party positions on economic matters evolved as the GOP became increasingly identified as pro-business, while the Democrats aligned increasingly with the economic interests of the "common man," especially those of labor. The Great Depression solidified these identities in the public mind, and the positions became associated with probusiness, small-government views on the Republican side and antibusiness, big-government views on the side of the Democrats.

By the 1960s, two associated myths had emerged that mirrored the partisan differences and helped average Americans to make sense of where the parties stood on economic policy matters. On the one hand, the *myth of too little government* became a powerful narrative in the minds of those who were prone to favor Democratic candidates in elections. This myth held that economic matters can be most effectively handled by government policies and programs, and that there is a need for even more government involvement to assure economic growth in the future. On the other hand, the *myth of too much government* held sway among voters who took the GOP perspective. In this narrative, although government involvement may be required, it has become too

243

intrusive and needs to be rolled back, with fewer programs and a lower budget (including fewer taxes) as well as reductions in costly regulations.

In this Policy Connection, we provide an overview of the policies resulting from this partisan divide on a key issue.

The Role of Government in the Economy

Behind the partisan divide reflected in the myths is the fact that the national government has been engaged in economic policymaking for most of American history. We can trace government intervention in the marketplace to colonial times.[3] Colonial governments offered payments to businesses that made large investments in the manufacture of certain products or increased the exportation of locally produced goods. Many of these activities continued long after the Revolution, as states and local governments actively promoted their economies.

Alexander Hamilton, the first secretary of the treasury, and others tried to give the national government a major role in the economy during the presidencies of George Washington and John Adams. Hamilton felt that the young nation's future depended on its having a strong economy, and he believed that the national government should play a major role in shaping that economy. In contrast, Thomas Jefferson and his successors (especially Andrew Jackson) strongly opposed any form of central control. They believed that economic policy should be left to local and state governments. This opposition, however, did not stop some national policymakers. Between 1816 and the early 1830s, members of Congress from the northeastern states won passage of banking and tariff legislation that was favorable to their small but growing manufacturing and trade businesses. During the 1830s, the power in Congress shifted toward agricultural interests in the South and West. With that shift came lower tariffs and other economic policies favoring farmers and plantation owners. Because railroads were important to agrarian America, between 1850 and 1857 Congress turned over more than 25 million acres of public land to railroad companies.

After the Civil War, Congress became much more involved in the nation's economy, by promoting westward expansion and the growth of business and by establishing regulatory agencies to control and monitor certain industries. In spite of these efforts, throughout the late nineteenth and twentieth centuries, the economy remained subject to boom-and-bust cycles, culminating in the Great Depression of the 1930s.

The Great Depression became a watershed era, as President Franklin D. Roosevelt's administration responded with a series of popular programs, known as the New Deal, to help promote recovery and stabilize the economy. Out of those efforts came a collection of policy tools designed to deal with economic issues. As we will see, all of those tools once again came into play during the period after the collapse of financial markets in the fall of 2008—and the "Great Recession" that followed.

Macroeconomic Policy Tools

To understand the steps taken by both the Bush and Obama administrations in response to the financial market crisis of 2008, we need to become familiar with two major economic policy tools—monetary and fiscal policies—that focus on dealing with the varying conditions of the general economy, or what economists term "macroeconomic" issues.

Most discussions of policies in the news and basic economics textbooks focus on monetary and fiscal policies. When focusing on **monetary policies**, economists talk of tight and loose money supplies. A *tight money supply* exists when the amount of money circulating in the economy is low relative to the demand for money by consumers and investors. Basic economics teaches that when the money supply is tight, interest rates (the cost of using someone else's money) tend to be high and the cost of most goods and services is likely to fall. A *loose money supply* exists when the amount of money circulating is high relative to the demand for money. During these periods, interest rates decline and the prices of goods and services increase. Thus economists attribute a variety of related economic conditions to the supply of money circulating in the economy.

Monetary policies involve the manipulation of the money supply to control the economy, and historically they have been favored by Republican policymakers. The principal mechanisms for carrying out monetary policy in the United States are in the hands of the Federal Reserve System, also known as the "Fed" (see Figure 7PC.1). The Federal Reserve System, established in 1913, consists of twelve regional banks and the Federal Reserve Board, which is empowered to regulate the circulation of currency in the U.S. economy. When the economy is sluggish—when not enough money is being invested to maintain economic growth or when unemployment is high—policymakers at the Fed

FEDERAL RESERVE BANKS

Twelve banks representing the nation's twelve Federal Reserve districts. The twelve manage the day-to-day needs of the banking system by maintaining a stable flow of money.

The banks, by districts:
1 Boston	7 Chicago
2 New York	8 St. Louis
3 Philadelphia	9 Minneapolis
4 Cleveland	10 Kansas City
5 Richmond	11 Dallas
6 Atlanta	12 San Francisco

What They Do

- Act as lender of last resort to banks, savings associations, and credit unions in trouble
- Keep reserves deposited by depository institutions
- Supply currency and coins to banks
- Destroy worn-out bills, coins
- Operate clearinghouses for checks
- Serve as fiscal agent for the U.S. Treasury
- Conduct domestic and foreign monetary operations through the New York Federal Reserve Bank as agent for the Federal Open Market Committee

BOARD OF GOVERNORS

Seven members appointed by the president and confirmed by the Senate. Terms are 14 years. The president names one member as chairman for a four-year term. The board is based in Washington, D.C.

What It Does

- Helps carry out policy for regulating the supply of money and credit by:
  –Setting reserve requirements for the depository institutions
  –Setting the discount rate on the Fed's loans to banks
- Makes margin rules for purchases of securities on credit
- Oversees major banks by regulating the nation's bank holding companies
- Inspects and regulates state-chartered banks that are members of the reserve system
- Monitors the economy
- Deals with international monetary problems
- Enforces consumer-credit laws
- Supervises Federal Reserve banks

FEDERAL OPEN MARKET COMMITTEE

Twelve members: The seven Federal Reserve governors and the president of the New York Federal Reserve Bank plus four of the presidents of the other eleven Federal Reserve banks on a rotating basis.

All twelve bank presidents attend the FOMC meetings, held every five to eight weeks.

What It Does

- Sets overall policy for regulating the supply of money and credit in the country
- Helps carry out that policy by directing the "trading desk" of the Federal Reserve Bank of New York to buy and sell government securities in the open market

FIGURE 7PC.1 The Long Reach of the Federal Reserve

Source: U.S. News & World Report.

often stimulate economic activity by increasing the supply of money. With more money in circulation, people should be more likely to make purchases or investments, which, in turn, should generate business activity and jobs. If policymakers think that the economy is overheated and is generating too much inflation, they can reduce the supply of money in an attempt to slow down economic activity.

Fiscal policy came to prominence as a policy tool during the Great Depression, when policymakers realized that changes in how much the government spent and how much it collected in taxes could influence overall economic performance. The use of fiscal policy, which tends to be favored by Democratic policymakers, became another way to manage the general performance of the economy. According to this policy theory, the federal government can stimulate economic activity during sluggish periods through its purchases of goods and services. By reducing taxes, it can put money in the hands of consumers, who can further stimulate economic activity through their own increased purchases and investments. If, on the other hand, the economy is overheating, the government can cut spending and raise taxes; this procedure takes money away from consumers and investors and thus reduces demand. The advocates of governmental activism tended to favor fiscal policy alternatives and were often called **Keynesians**, because of their reliance on the theories of the British economist John Maynard Keynes (1883–1946).

In contrast, the **monetarists**, a group of prominent economists led by University of Chicago economist Milton Friedman (1912–2006), tended to favor monetarist policies and rejected the argument that constant government intervention in the economy can bring either constant prosperity or stability. Not only is government intervention in the economy not a solution, they argue, but in fact it has prevented even stronger economic growth. Government intervention should be limited to maintaining a consistent growth in the nation's money supply in order to control inflation.

Although regarded as opposing approaches to ensuring overall economic growth, both monetary and fiscal policies have played a major role in U.S.

economic policy throughout the post–World War II period. At the heart of the debate between the monetarists and those favoring fiscal policies was the extent to which the federal government should be actively engaged in managing the overall direction of the economy. The sustained period of relative prosperity from the late 1940s until the late 1960s led many economic analysts to assume that such government intervention had made the threat of economic stagnation, let alone major recessions, a thing of the past.[4] During the 1970s and early 1980s, when the U.S. economy went through a period of both high inflation and rising unemployment, the country's economic policymakers gave greater attention to the monetarists' argument that government was doing too much through fiscal policies.[5]

By the late 1990s, however, many analysts had come to the conclusion that neither the Keynesians nor the monetarists had the definitive answer to how the economy should be managed. Some have argued that a "new economy" emerged in the last decade of the twentieth century, and that a new approach to managing the economy must be developed to deal with the changed conditions brought about by technological innovations and globalization (see the subsequent discussion).[6]

But, when faced with the economic downturn generated by the 2008 financial market collapse—a downturn labeled by many as the Great Recession—the government relied on both monetary and fiscal policy responses.[7] On the monetary side, the Fed reduced interest rates to historically low levels and took other steps designed to inject more money into the economy in order to counter recessionary pressures that might otherwise have taken hold. On the fiscal side, the Obama administration asked Congress for both tax cuts and a massive "stimulus package" that would boost government spending. The tax cuts were designed to put more money in the hands of consumers as well as to reward businesses for creating new jobs, whereas the stimulus spending was aimed at getting shovel-ready projects (mostly public works projects like roads and bridges) under way as well as injecting more money into areas of the economy that would lead to future growth.

By the summer of 2010, however, there was a growing concern that these policies might have long-term negative consequences for the American economy. At the heart of the growing debate was the question of the growing national debt—an issue that often emerges whenever government economic policies seem to be too aggressive. As we will see in Policy Connection 11—on deficits, surpluses, and the national debt—economic policies remain closely tied to the long-standing partisan divide between the two major political parties.

Economic Development Policies

In addition to using monetary and fiscal policies to manage the economy and help stabilize it, policymakers have used **economic development policies** to help the economy grow. These policies have involved a range of approaches, from trade policies to industrial strategies. The Democratic Party favors some; the Republican party, others—but neither has been adamant about adopting any particular approach.

Trade Policies and Globalization

For much of our history, our national economic development policies were closely associated with our **tariff** policies. In the 1800s, both political parties supported tariffs, but for different reasons. Generally, the Democrats supported them because they were a major source of government revenue in the era before the income tax. Nevertheless, they favored keeping tariffs low. In contrast, the Republicans tended to see tariffs as a policy tool—one that could protect and thereby foster the growth of domestic industries. Their policies tended toward keeping tariffs high.

From 1900 through the 1920s, there was a shift toward a more bipartisan stand on tariffs. But in reaction to the economic crisis that developed in 1929, Republicans enacted the Hawley-Smoot Tariff of 1930, which substantially raised tariff rates and actually exacerbated the deteriorating global economic situation.

By 1934 there was a general agreement that trade liberation was the preferred policy option. Consequently, the two parties have been less vocal on trade protection, and Congress has been reluctant to pass protective tariff legislation for more than three-quarters of a century. Most policymakers believed that **free trade** (the abolition of tariffs and other trade barriers) was the best policy to follow. Although there was opposition to lowering barriers to trade on specific imports, the general reliance on tariffs was no longer a significant partisan issue as the United States entered the post–World War II era.[8] During those years, the U.S. **balance of trade**—the net difference between the value of what Americans bought and what they sold overseas—ran a surplus, as Americans exported more goods and services than they imported. In 1975, for example, the United States exported $18 billion more in merchandise than it imported.

In contrast, by 1985 the United States had become a debtor economy: The value of foreign investment in America exceeded U.S. overseas investment by more than $110 billion. Responding to these conditions, some members of Congress advocated raising tariffs or taking other policy measures to protect U.S. industries and jobs from foreign competition. The administrations of Ronald Reagan, George H. W. Bush, and Bill Clinton, as well as other advocates of free trade, opposed such proposals, insisting that free and open international markets are the answer to trade deficits. The problem, they contended, was rooted in the barriers to free trade imposed by other countries, especially Japan. They preferred diplomatic and other kinds of political pressures to persuade those nations to lower their barriers to the importation of U.S. goods and services.

By 2012, however, Americans imported more than $436 billion more in goods and services than they exported. The issues raised by free trade policies in recent years are associated with a worldwide debate about **globalization**. The term actually implies several related trends. Politically and economically, it implies the need to pay greater attention to international issues and to come to terms with the fact that national borders are less relevant to our daily lives than they were in the past. It also involves the emergence of a global culture and what many people see as the eventual disappearance of cultural and national distinctions. Finally, some perceive globalization as a process of modernization and

Westernization, in which democracy and capitalism become the global standards.[9]

The debate centers on whether or not these trends are desirable. If they are, the United States should vigorously pursue free trade policies, as in free trade agreements with other nations; if they are not, we should develop policies to counter these powerful trends, especially those that would help protect American jobs and keep U.S. capital in the country. There is bipartisan agreement for globalization among many of the top leaders of both parties, but the issues it raises have also been accompanied by divisions within each party. These have been evident in the pro–free trade positions taken by Presidents Clinton and Obama—positions that have been criticized by major segments of the rank-and-file Democrats, especially those affiliated with organized labor. On the GOP side, although the moderate parts of the party are aligned with pro–free trade and globalization positions, there is considerable sentiment for protectionism among the conservative right.[10]

Tax Incentives

The government has also used **tax incentives** to promote growth.[11] Tax breaks can promote economic activity in certain industries. For example, the home-building industry has benefited greatly over the past several decades from a provision of the tax law that allows Americans to deduct their home mortgage interest costs from their personal income taxes. Another well-known but less popular tax break was an oil depletion allowance introduced during the 1920s. The tax break promoted oil and gas exploration, but many critics thought that its benefits were excessive and much too costly. It took more than fifty years, however, to get that specific tax break eliminated. Nevertheless, many tax breaks and incentives remain, not only for the oil and gas industry but also for just about every conceivable form of business, from agriculture to high technology. We will discuss these in greater detail in Policy Connection 11.

Industrial and Supply-Side Policies

During the 1980s, economic policy discussions often centered on a debate between two strategies. Some analysts argued that policymakers must develop a comprehensive economic development strategy for restructuring the economy. Under this approach, known at the time as **industrial policy**, the United States would abandon certain industries in which labor costs were too high for successful competition with other nations.[12] At the same time, it would rescue other industries and make them competitive in the world market.

By contrast, advocates of **supply-side economics** believed in putting more emphasis on policies that would promote increased production of goods by giving incentives to private producers.[13] Thus, supply-siders supported cutting taxes to help stimulate investment, lifting regulations in the marketplace, and eliminating other government restraints on private business initiatives. According to supply-side advocates, only through policies that increase suppliers' incentives can jobs be created and the economy grow.

The debate between advocates of both approaches was highly partisan during the 1980s, with Democrats advocating industrial policy positions and Republicans closely identified with supply-side economics. As economic times improved in the 1990s, the debate cooled off, only to return in a somewhat different form after the financial crisis of 2008. The government used bailouts and tax breaks aimed at saving and sustaining banks and other sectors of the economy to confront the immediate impact of the crisis. The Bush administration's initiative to support a failing banking industry that was deemed "too big to fail" played out in a way that let some firms fail while shoring up others. The Obama administration used the same scenario in its attempt to save the auto industry during the worst parts of the downturn.[14]

But there was a quick reaction to these bailouts and stimulus package programs (advocated primarily by Democrats). In what became known as the austerity approach, those formerly associated with supply-side policies backed policies aimed at reducing the size of government and reducing—if not eliminating—taxes in order to provide greater incentives for private investment. The debate continued through 2014, as the economy continued its slow but steady recovery from the Great Recession.

Conclusion

Do the two major parties really offer different approaches to managing the American economic system?

In this brief survey of the major tools used in designing economic policies, we have seen that certain approaches are favored by the Republican Party and others by Democrats. But being inclined toward using certain policy tools has not stopped policymakers from taking a pragmatic approach when faced with real-world economic crises, as was the case during the global financial market collapse of 2008. Given the gravity of the immediate situation, the Republican administration considered all options, including those that ran fundamentally counter to the beliefs of some of the major policymakers. Going well beyond just fiscal and monetary policy, the government engaged in bailouts and literally took ownership in some major corporations. Democrats found themselves supporting huge financial concessions to banks while Republicans backed major spending programs to stimulate the economy. Policymakers at the Fed, previously committed to policies that would prevent inflation, found themselves pumping money into the economy at unprecedented levels. Partisan differences on economic policy seemed to disappear overnight.

But these emergency measures were not without controversy, and it did not take long before the partisan divide reasserted itself and the powerful myths of too much and too little government returned. The differences between Democratic and Republican views of economic policy run so deep that it is likely that they will continue well into the future.

QUESTIONS FOR DISCUSSION

1. **Many observers argue that the revolution in information technology (IT) has completely transformed the American economy, and that the traditional policies advocated by both political parties are irrelevant to the new economic realities of the computer age. What difference, if any, has the IT revolution made in the economy? And have party positions become irrelevant?**

2. **At the core of political debates over economic policy are different views of the appropriate role of government in managing the economy. Some call for greater involvement, whereas others would like to see government remove itself from this arena. What is your view of the role of government in economic matters? Should it be involved? If so, what should be the limits of government policy?**

CHAPTER 8

Campaigns and Elections

Campaigns and the American Public

In 2012, President Obama became the first candidate to raise and spend more than $1 billion on a single campaign. If we take into consideration expenditures by all candidates and supporting political action committees in the primary and general election, Republican Senator Mitch McConnell's 2014 reelection bid in Kentucky resulted in the first Senate contest to top the $100 million spending mark.[1] Not all campaigns are costly to run. With more than 500,000 elections held every four-year cycle (between presidential races) in the United States, most of these races do not involve vast sums of money. But most high-visibility races, including the presidency and competitive Senate, House, gubernatorial, and mayoral races, are expensive. It is estimated that more than $4 billion was spent on the 2014 midterm congressional elections.

The public clearly disapproves of the significant amounts of money spent on election campaigns. Such views are reinforced when the public learns how much it may cost for a candidate to lose an election for public office. For example, in the 2008 presidential party nomination races, Rudy Giuliani, an unsuccessful candidate for the Republican nomination, spent more than $60 million on his campaign before he withdrew from the nomination race. How many delegates did Giuliani win for his $60 million? None. No wonder many voters sit back and contend that the nomination process makes no sense. It simply is too costly.

The American public has some misgivings about other aspects of the election process. The public is often suspicious of candidate promises and platforms and, more often than not, is confused by the complexities of the

< In many polling districts, long lines of citizens waiting to cast their ballots for favored candidates are a familiar occurrence every Election Day.

For further updates visit the companion website at **www.oup.com/us/gitelson**.

campaign process. Opposing candidates exchange harsh criticisms, including accusations that an opponent distorted the candidate's records or lied about the policy positions and intentions of his or her opposition.

Poll findings also suggest that many Americans do not believe that our elected representatives respond to their demands and expectations. For example, about two-thirds of Americans "don't think public officials care much about what people like [them] think." Almost 80 percent feel that they can trust government in Washington only some of the time or never.[2]

Why have so many Americans come to doubt the usefulness of elections? Why do so many stay home on Election Day? And why are so many Americans both confused and distrustful of the campaign and election process, suggesting that it makes little or no sense? One study found that nearly three in five eighteen- to twenty-nine-year olds "agree strongly or somewhat that 'elected officials' seem to be motivated by selfish reasons."[3] This widely held view reflects the story that many voters tell themselves when they try to understand elections and campaigns. According to this narrative, politicians make all sorts of promises and commitments to get themselves elected, but once they are in office, they are more likely to serve their own interests than those of the voters who elected them. Not surprisingly, it's a story that creates skeptics out of voters, for they feel the present electoral system will inevitably disappoint. "If the people can choose only from among rascals," quipped political scientist V. O. Key, "they are certain to choose a rascal."[4] That view of American elections and campaigns is embodied in the popular *myth of broken promises*, which holds that elections do not affect government policies—that candidates, once they are elected, fail to keep the promises they made during their campaigns.

Every campaign has included advertising posters, cartoons, and campaign literature. When William McKinley ran for president in 1896, his campaign literature emphasized his link to prosperity, prestige, and economic well-being.

The reality of the election process, however, differs from that myth. We will see in this chapter that most politicians seek to achieve not only their own career goals but also the social and political goals put forth in their campaigns. In addition, we show that, although money is very important in campaigns because it pays for television time, polls, consultants, and the like, a variety of other factors also have a significant impact on who is elected. This chapter helps us to make sense of the elections and campaigns in the United States, drawing on reasoned analysis and a realistic look at the myth of broken promises.

Nominations: The Selection Process

> **What roles do party caucuses, primaries, and conventions play in the nomination process?**

Every year thousands of individuals decide to run for political office. In many cases, before they can get on the ballot, a political party must select, or nominate, them, often after a costly, time-consuming, and exhausting primary campaign. What motivates these individuals?

Why Do People Run for Office?

"The stakes are too high for government to be a spectator sport," the late member of Congress Barbara Jordan from Texas told a commencement audience. Few of those who run for office would disagree. What motivates people to enter the proverbial election rings?[5]

- Public service

- Personal ambition

- Policy goals

These factors often drive politicians to climb what Joseph Schlesinger refers to as the **opportunity structure**: the political ladder of local, state, and national offices that brings one greater prestige and power as one moves toward—at the very top—the presidency.[6]

Opportunity structure The political ladder of local, state, and national offices that results in greater prestige and power as one moves toward the presidency.

The Caucus: Old-Fashioned Politics

Anyone who wants to run for political office in most partisan elections, including the presidency, must first secure a party nomination. One of the oldest methods of nomination is the **caucus** (the word means "meeting").

Until the Progressive Era, a period of political reform starting around the end of the nineteenth century, most party nominations were decided by caucuses or conventions. These meetings were closed to the public, and party leaders usually chose the nominees. Most contemporary caucuses are local meetings that are open to all who live in the precinct. These citizens "caucus"—that is, meet and discuss—and then vote for delegates to district and state conventions. These delegates then nominate candidates for congressional and statewide offices. In about 20 percent of the states, delegates to the national presidential conventions are chosen by the caucus/convention method. Many of these delegates are committed in advance to a particular presidential candidate. Some, however, choose to run as uncommitted delegates, awaiting the national convention to declare their candidate preference.

The most celebrated of modern presidential caucuses takes place every four years in Iowa, where candidates compete for the Democratic and Republican presidential nominations. Traditionally, the Iowa caucus is the first of the

Caucus A forum for choosing candidates that was closed to the public until the Progressive Era; contemporary caucuses are local party meetings, open to all who live in the precinct, in which citizens discuss and then vote for delegates to district and state conventions.

Primary An election in which party members (in some states, nonparty members and independents may participate) select candidates to run for office under the party banner.

Open primary A primary election in which any qualified voter may participate, regardless of party affiliation. The voter chooses one party ballot at the polling place.

Closed primary A primary election in which a voter is allowed to obtain only a ballot of the party in which he or she is registered.

Partisan primary A primary in which candidates run for their own party's nomination.

Nonpartisan primary A primary in which candidates are listed on a ballot with no party identification.

Runoff primary An electoral contest between the top two vote getters in the primary that determines the party's candidate in a general election. Such primaries are held in the ten southern states in which a majority of the vote is needed to win the primary.

Front-loading The scheduling of primaries very early in the campaign season by states eager to have an early influence on the Republican and Democratic nomination process.

presidential campaign cycle, and candidates are anxious to do well in order to demonstrate their appeal both to the voters and to potential campaign contributors who want to support a winner.

Primaries: The New Kid on the Block

Except in presidential contests and when minor political parties select their candidates, caucuses are relatively uncommon in contemporary politics. Most Democratic and Republican nominees, whether at the national, state, or local level, are chosen in a **primary**: an election in which—for the most part—party members (in some states, nonparty members and independents may participate) select candidates to run for office under the party banner. In 2012, presidential primaries were held in thirty-eight states.[7]

Because the rules that govern how a primary is conducted differ from state to state, let's make some sense of the process. In an **open primary**, any qualified, registered voter may participate, regardless of party affiliation. On entering the polling place, voters select a Democratic, Republican, or other party ballot and choose among the names on the ballot to select that party's candidates for the various offices. In a **closed primary**, used in a majority of the states and in Washington, D.C., voters are allowed to obtain only a ballot for the party in which they are registered.

In a **partisan primary**, candidates run for their own party's nomination. In a **nonpartisan primary**, candidates are listed on a ballot with no party identification. All presidential primaries are partisan, but many local primaries and the Nebraska state primary are nonpartisan.

In most states, the winning candidate in local and statewide office primaries is the one who receives the most votes. In ten southern states, however, a candidate must receive a majority (more than 50 percent) of the vote in order to win; if no candidate receives a clear majority, a **runoff primary** between the top two vote getters determines the party's candidate in the general election.

In presidential contests, the first presidential primary is always held in New Hampshire. Although the state is small and its population is not representative of the nation's population as a whole, this primary plays a significant symbolic role in the nomination process. Like victory in the first caucus, held in Iowa, victory in the New Hampshire primary brings the winning candidate a great deal of media coverage, which helps in attracting campaign donations. From New Hampshire's point of view, having the first primary is a benefit because it draws the candidates, their entourage, and the media into the state. This means not only prestige and honor but also additional revenue for various businesses, local governments, and the state, all of whom profit from the primary campaign.

Historically, presidential primaries were spread out over the first six months of the calendar year in which the presidential election took place, beginning with the New Hampshire primary in February and culminating with several state primaries in June. In the 2000, 2004, and 2008 presidential primary races, however, many states, eager to have an early influence on the Republican and Democratic nominating process, moved their primaries ahead. Such scheduling of primaries very early in the campaign season is called **front-loading**. Although fewer primaries were front-loaded in 2012, the early scheduling of a state primary is still popular among many states.

Why is front-loading important? It tends to give the candidates who are the front runners at the beginning of the primary season an advantage: With a shorter primary season, underdogs have only a brief window of opportunity to overtake the front runner. Candidates must demonstrate that they have public support very early in the primaries (indeed, well before the primaries begin) if they are going to have any chance of getting their party's nomination. In addition, with the primaries clustered so close together, campaign money must be raised early and in large amounts if a candidate is to compete successfully. In 2012, fourteen Republican presidential aspirants collectively spent more than $1.3 billion on their nomination campaigns.[8] The incumbent, President Barack Obama, faced no major primary challengers.

The Changing Role of Nominating Conventions

The rise of the presidential primary has meant that the national party conventions no longer select the candidates but rather ratify the choices that have already taken place in statewide primaries and caucuses.[9] Conventions still serve a number of traditional functions, however. They give the party faithful a place to transact business, which includes changing rules and writing the party platform. When a convention runs smoothly, it serves as an important media event, publicizing the party's candidates and issues to a nationwide audience.

This cartoon spoofs the often complicated path to the race for the presidency.

Superdelegates Individuals who automatically are designated delegates to the national party conventions because they are members of Congress or hold statewide offices or are prominent party leaders.

Until the rule reforms of the late 1960s and early 1970s, state and local party leaders appointed most convention delegates. The delegates were largely well-educated, white, male professionals. One survey in the 1940s found that nearly 40 percent of them were lawyers.[10] In 2012, a majority of the delegates to the Democratic and Republican conventions were elected through primaries; the remainder were selected by state caucuses or were made up of **superdelegates**, individuals who automatically were designated delegates to the national conventions because they were members of Congress, held statewide offices, or were prominent party leaders. Delegates still tend to come from elite groups, however: They tend to be well educated and predominantly white, with relatively high family incomes. The Democrats attract more African Americans, young people, union members, and women to their conventions, whereas Republican delegates tend to be older, white, and predominantly Protestant. Loyal supporters of one of the major candidates, most delegates stand for election in a primary or caucus in that candidate's name.

Although for both parties the nomination process is critical to the success of any presidential aspirant, it apparently matters less to most voters. In most primaries, fewer than 30 percent of the eligible voters turn out to vote; often the percentage is less than 20 percent.

Who Gets Nominated?

In the past, almost all the Democratic and Republican presidential nominees have been white, male, wealthy, and Protestant. The barrier against Catholics fell with the Democratic nomination of Al Smith in 1928 and the nomination and election of John F. Kennedy in 1960. In 2012, Mitt Romney, the Republican presidential candidate, was the first Mormon nominated by a major political party. Furthermore, with the exception of General Dwight D. Eisenhower, a World War II hero who was elected in 1952, all successful presidential candidates for the past hundred years have previously held some high elective office—the vice presidency, a seat in the U.S. Senate, or the governorship of a state. These elected positions give candidates the visibility and prestige necessary to attract campaign financing and to mount a national campaign.

Social barriers to the nomination of women and of African Americans and Jews seem to be weakening. In 1984, Congresswoman Geraldine Ferraro was the Democratic vice-presidential nominee. In 2000, the Democratic Party nominated the first Jewish vice-presidential candidate on a major party ticket, Senator Joseph I. Lieberman. In 2008, for the first time in the history of either of the two major political parties, the Democrats nominated an African American, Barack Obama, to run for the presidency. What made this nomination even more historically significant was that his major competitor for the Democratic nomination was the first serious female candidate for the office of the presidency, Hillary Clinton. At the Republican National Convention, Governor Sarah Palin of Alaska was nominated as the vice-presidential candidate for the party, an historical first for the Republicans. Although barriers still exist in the political system based on religion, gender, race, age, and ethnicity, few people would question that many of those roadblocks are gradually coming down.

January 2007 marked a new era in congressional politics when Congresswoman Nancy Pelosi (D-CA) became the first woman to serve as Speaker of the U.S. House of Representatives. She served as Speaker for the next four years until, in 2011, the Republicans won control of the House.

The Race for Office

> **What impact does money have on political campaigns? What recent changes have occurred in federal election campaign finance laws?**

In recent years, few issues revolving around elections have afforded more controversy than the raising and spending of money on political campaigns. Recent changes in federal election campaign laws along with important U.S. Supreme Court decisions have had an impact on the election and campaign landscape.

Financing Campaigns: The Buying and Selling of Offices?

Much of the public regards the way many, if not most, campaigns are financed as suspect. The feeling prevails that campaigns consume far too much money.

Candidates can be offered large campaign contributions in return for favors. No doubt, some candidates accept such offers; others do not. One would-be contributor to Edmund Muskie's 1972 presidential campaign offered $200,000 with the following stipulation: "You understand . . . I want to be an American ambassador. Not a big country, you understand, not France or England. I couldn't afford those anyway. But can you give me a little one, Switzerland or Belgium?"[11] Muskie summarily declined the offer.

Financing campaigns is an expensive proposition. In 2012, all presidential and congressional candidates (including unsuccessful candidates for the presidency),

TABLE 8.1 **Summary of Campaign Spending for the 2011–2012 Election Cycle**

	Disbursements
Presidential candidates*	$1,359,800,000
Congressional candidates	$1,847,200,000
Party committees	$1,599,300,000
Political action committees (PACs)	$2,198,400,000
TOTAL:	**$7,135,700,000**

Source: Federal Election Commission, news release, April 19, 2013.

Includes fourteen candidates seeking their party's nomination.

For further updates visit the companion website at www.oup.com/us/gitelson.

as well as party committees and political action committees (PACs), spent more than $7 billion on the primaries, general election campaigns, and national conventions (see Table 8.1).[12] In 2014, a nonpresidential election year, congressional candidates, parties, and PACs spent more than $4 billion on the campaigns.

Act I: The Federal Election Campaign Act. In 1971, and again in 1974 and later, Congress stepped in to limit the amount of money presidential candidates could receive and spend. The problem that Congress was trying to solve was not the overall size of campaign expenditures but rather the imbalances created when some individuals and groups could afford to contribute far more than others.

The Federal Election Campaign Act (FECA) of 1971, as amended in 1974 and later, created a system to monitor the flow of funds and set limits on contributions made by individuals. It also provided for public financing of presidential campaigns and restricted total spending by those candidates who accept federal funding. The spending limits, however, applied only to presidential campaigns. Congress has never restricted its own election expenditures.

The act, along with its amendments, had four key features:

1. It set up the Federal Election Commission, a bipartisan, six-member commission, to administer and enforce federal regulations regarding the contribution and expenditure of campaign funds.

2. It limited individual contributions to primary, runoff, and general elections, as well as contributions to any PAC or national party committee (see Table 8.2).

3. It provided for public funding of the major parties' presidential election costs, including the costs of the Democratic and Republican national conventions.

4. It placed important controls on the amount of money that could be spent in presidential primaries and general elections.

TABLE 8.2 Limits to Contributions for Federal Elections by Individuals and Groups to Candidates, Committees, and Political Action Committees (PACs) in 2013–2014

Group	Contribution Limit ($)				
	To Each Candidate or Candidate Committee per Election	**To the National Party Committee per Calendar Year**	**To State, District, and Local Party Committees per Calendar Year**	**To Any Other Political Committee per Calendar Year[a]**	**Special Limits**
Individuals	2,600*	32,400*	10,000 (combined limit)	5,000	123,200* overall biennial limit: • 48,600* to all candidates • 74,600* to all PACs and parties[b]
National party committees	5,000	No limit	No limit	5,000	45,400* to Senate candidate per campaign[c]
State, district, and local party committees	5,000 (combined limit)	No limit	No limit	5,000 (combined limit)	No limit
PACs (multicandidate)[d]	5,000	15,000	5,000 (combined limit)	5,000	No limit
PACs (not multicandidate)	2,600*	32,400*	10,000 (combined limit)	5,000	No limit
Authorized campaign committees	2,000[e]	No limit	No limit	5,000	No limit

Source: Federal Election Commission, www.fec.gov.

* These contribution limits are increased for inflation in odd-numbered years.

[a] A contribution earmarked for a candidate through a political committee counts against the original contributor's limit for that candidate. In certain circumstances, the contribution may also count against the contributor's limit to the PAC. See public laws 11 CFR 110.6 and 11 CFR 110.1(h).

[b] No more than $48,600 of this amount may be contributed to state and local party committees and PACs.

[c] This limit is shared by the national committee and the Senate campaign committee.

[d] A multicandidate committee is a political committee with more than fifty contributors that has been registered for at least six months and, with the exception of state party committees, has made contributions to five or more candidates for federal office (11 CFR 100.5[e][3]).

[e] A federal candidate's authorized committee(s) may contribute no more than $2,000 per election to another federal candidate's authorized committee(s) (2 U.S.C. 432[e][3][B]).

In 2008, Republican presidential candidate John McCain chose to accept $84.1 million in federal funding for the general election. By accepting this funding, a candidate agrees not to spend any additional funds on the campaign, although, as we shall shortly see, other organizations and individuals can spend money supporting or opposing a presidential candidate. Democratic presidential candidate Barack Obama chose not to accept public funding. He raised funds by appealing for contributions from his supporters, thus avoiding any spending limits on his campaign. In 2012, most of the serious candidates seeking the Democratic or Republican presidential nomination turned down the federal matching grants in the primaries and raised their own campaign funds. Thus, they were free of any restrictions on the amount of money they spent in the primaries. Many political observers believe that future presidential candidates for the Republican and Democratic parties will choose to reject public funding for their campaigns, thus leaving few, if any, constraints on fundraising and campaign spending.

In implementing the Federal Election Campaign Act, Congress did not intend to reduce the importance of money in the election process, however. Expenses covered by campaign funds included the rental and furnishing of campaign headquarters, communication and transportation, polls, television and newspaper advertisements, political consultants, and, of course, accountants to keep track of how the money was collected and spent. In presidential races, the bulk of the money goes to media advertising (e.g., more than $650 billion was spent on media in the 2012 presidential race),[13] although travel, staff payrolls, polls, and consultants all contribute to the overall costs of a campaign.

Although these campaign expenditure figures are, indeed, substantial, keep in mind that the advertising budgets for many corporations are much higher. In past years, the advertising budget for Proctor and Gamble has approached $3 billion a year; Comcast, General Motors, and AT&T have each spent more than $1.5 billion a year to advertise their products. Television advertising costs aren't cheap. The charge for a thirty-second advertisement during the 2014 Super Bowl was $4 million. A thirty-second advertisement during *Sunday Night Football* costs more than $550,000, and advertising during the popular program *American Idol* costs about $350,000. All advertising spending just on television exceeded $139 billion in 2012.[14]

These examples do not suggest that political campaigns are cheap by comparison. In 2012, for example, more than $50 million was spent by Connecticut Republican senatorial candidate Linda McMahon (co-owner of the World Wide Wrestling Association), in her losing race against Democrat Chris Murphy, who spent $10.5 million on his campaign. Where does the money come from? Some wealthy candidates finance their own campaigns or lend themselves the needed funds. This move can give them a significant advantage over their opponents. In the 2010 California gubernatorial campaign, Republican Meg Whitman spent more than $142 million of her own money in both the primary and the general election races. Most candidates, however, must solicit gifts and loans from interested individuals, their party, or other groups, including PACs.

One major consequence of the Federal Election Campaign Act has been the rise of PACs. They were set up to bypass a provision of the act that prohibits unions, corporations, and other groups from contributing directly to candidates for national office. PACs distribute voluntary contributions from such groups to candidates. During the 2014 election cycle, PACs contributed approximately $1 billion to congressional candidates, thus continuing their significant impact on the financial resources available in federal elections.

For further updates visit the companion website at **www.oup.com/us/gitelson**.

PACs (and individuals) can legally spend any amount of money on a candidate as long as they do not coordinate their spending efforts or otherwise cooperate with the candidate's campaign. Thus, their participation can circumvent the spending and contribution limits of the campaign act. As important as PACs have become, however, they are still overshadowed by individual contributors, who supply the bulk of candidate election funds. (See Chapter 9 for further discussion of PACs).

Act II: The Bipartisan Campaign Finance Reform Act. Although money may not be the only important factor in a successful campaign, many people believe that even the appearance of impropriety on the part of candidates in raising campaign funds is reason enough for reforming the system. The millions of dollars in **soft money** contributed to political parties by individuals, corporations, and unions have also made voters uneasy about the role of money in campaigns. Soft money is unrestricted contributions by individuals, corporations, and unions that can, under Federal Election Commission (FEC) regulations, be spent on party-building activities such as voter registration drives and get-out-the-vote efforts or on campaign issue advertising, but not in support of a specific candidate. For many Americans, the campaign funding system is broken and needs to be replaced.

Critics have suggested many reforms. These have ranged from spending limits for candidates and the elimination of soft money to restrictions on PAC contributions, an increase in the size and enforcement powers of the FEC, and the public financing of elections. (For other strategies, see Asked & Answered on page 263.)

Under growing pressure from the public and the media, Congress enacted and President Bush signed into law the Bipartisan Campaign Finance Act of 2002 to further reform federal campaign financing. This act focuses on weaknesses in the existing laws that were targeted for change by Senators John McCain (R-AZ) and Russell Feingold (D-WI) and Representatives Christopher Shays (R-CT) and Martin Meehan (D-MA).

The act, which took effect after the November 2002 elections, had four key features that modify some of the provisions of the Federal Election Act:

1. It banned soft money contributions to the national political parties.

2. It increased the limits on hard money contributions by individuals to individual candidates and the total overall contributions to all candidates and political parties.

3. It allowed multicandidate PACs to contribute up to $5,000 per candidate per election, $5,000 to other PACs per year, $15,000 per national political party committee per year, and $5,000 per state or local party committee per year. There was no ceiling on the total contributions that a PAC can make.[15]

4. The act initially prohibited corporate, union, or trade associations from sponsoring candidate-targeted ads just before elections and primaries. In 2010, the U.S. Supreme Court decision *Citizens United v. Federal Election Commission* ruled that corporations and unions could spend unlimited sums calling for the election or defeat of individual candidates so long as these efforts were not coordinated with a candidate's campaign.

Soft money Unrestricted contributions to political parties by individuals, corporations, and unions that can be spent on party-building activities such as voter registration drives and get-out-the-vote efforts. The problem is that loopholes in the law allow soft money also to be spent in support of party candidates so long as key words such as *elect*, *vote for*, or *vote against* do not appear in the ads.

A number of problems remain concerning campaign finance reform at the federal level. The FEC, which was given the responsibility for implementing "the new law's candidate and party soft money provisions[,] . . . has opened loopholes that could allow elements of the current state party soft money system to continue."[16] These provisions would allow contributors to continue to make indirect soft money contributions to federal campaigns by contributing money to state party organizations, who then funnel that money to federal campaigns. As one political observer has noted, "the States have been the backdoor to American politics for years," and they may very likely continue in this role.[17] Proponents of campaign finance reform argue that actions taken by the FEC may distort and undermine the spirit of the act.

A second major concern regards the growth of **527 committees** and **super PACs**. A 527 committee isn't regulated by the FEC. These committees are tax-exempt groups "organized under section 527 of the Internal Revenue Code to raise money for political activities including voter mobilization efforts, issue advocacy, and the like."[18] Unless a 527 committee is also a political party or PAC specifically engaged in advocating the election or defeat of a federal candidate, it is not required to file disclosure reports with the FEC. In effect, 527 committees can raise unlimited soft money to mobilize targeted voters for the election and to support certain types of issue advocacy, so long as there is no expressed support for or against a specific candidate.

Super PACs may raise unlimited contributions from corporations, unions, professional and business associations, and individuals for the purpose of making unlimited expenditures in favor of or against a candidate running for the presidency or for Congress. Like traditional PACs, a super PAC must report the names of all its donors to the FEC. Unlike traditional PACs, super PACs are barred from making direct contributions to the campaign of any political candidate.

The use of 527 committees and super PACs to spend millions of dollars in the 2012 presidential election and the 2014 congressional elections illustrates that candidates in federal elections can circumvent federal laws designed to reform the campaign finance process. (Super PACs are discussed in greater detail in Chapter 9).

A third major concern has been the establishment of 501(c)(3) and 501(c)(4) organizations involved in promoting and supporting public policies often associated with election campaigns and candidates. These organizations are not regulated by the FEC. Traditionally, the Internal Revenue Service (IRS) reserves designation as a 501(c)(3) organization for not-for-profit groups that are involved in public charities work, foundation work, education work, or religious functions with no political orientations or connections. Public charities designated as 501(c)(3)s may, however, lobby to influence legislation if that activity does not constitute a substantial part of its activities and is not partisan in nature. A 501(c)(4) organization is generally a civic organization focusing on social welfare issues. Unlike contributions to a 501(c)(3), which are tax deductible, a contribution to a 501(c)(4) is not tax deductible (except under certain circumstances regarding the dues paid to be a member of the organization). However, unlike a 501(c)(3) organization, a 501(c)(4), although

527 committees Tax-exempt groups that can raise unlimited soft money to be used to mobilize targeted voters and for issue advocacy if there is no expressed support for or against a specific candidate. These 527 committees are not regulated by the Federal Election Commission.

Super PACs Officially known as "independent-expenditure only committees," super PACs may raise unlimited contributions from corporations, unions, professional and business associations, and individuals for the purpose of making unlimited expenditures in favor of or against a candidate running for federal office. Like traditional PACs, a super PAC must report the names of all its donors to the Federal Election Commission. Unlike traditional PACs, super PACs are barred from making direct contributions to the campaigns of any political candidate.

ASKED & ANSWERED

ASKED: Why can't we reduce the role of money in elections as other nations do?*

ANSWERED: American politicians have quarreled over various proposals for campaign and election reform since the founding of the United States, but no aspect of reform has drawn more attention than that of campaign finance. Some observers believe campaign-spending limits could positively reform the system, whereas others argue that these limits would restrict freedom of speech and would serve to increase, rather than diminish, the power of incumbency (because, whatever the limits, incumbents tend to receive a larger share of campaign contributions than challengers). These opposing stances on the issue can and do cause confusion for many Americans regarding the role of money in elections. Will there ever be a campaign finance solution that satisfies all parties? Might other democracies employ strategies that could be successful in America? For an alternate perspective, let's take a look across the Atlantic to see how countries in Western Europe are dealing with similar issues.

- **Length of political campaigns.** It's harder to burn through huge sums of money when you don't have much time to spend it. Whereas American presidential candidates often start establishing bases in New Hampshire and Iowa at least a full year before the general election (often shortly after the previous presidential election), by comparison, British campaigns last about four weeks from beginning to end. That's just one month's worth of print advertisements, television commercials, and massive voter outreach efforts to pay for.
- **Size of the voting population.** There's simply no way to get around the fact that the United States is a huge country, and campaigning with 317 million citizens who are spread out over fifty states is much more difficult than reaching, for example, 60 million French citizens residing in a

smaller, much more densely populated area. Even at the U.S. congressional level, the number of House seats has remained constant since 1911, which means that each representative is responsible for reaching an increasing number of constituents with each passing year. In 2014, the average congressional district numbered about 710,000 citizens.

- **Party-centered versus candidate-centered campaigns.** Many American political campaigns are centered on the individual, with messages tailored to detail specific points on why a candidate is the most qualified to represent her or his particular district or state. In Western European parliamentary elections, campaigns are focused on the parties, and it is much more efficient for a party to coordinate a single, national message than it is to run one hundred variations on the same theme. This arrangement, of course, leads to the question of whether our country would actually have to modify its style of government in order to overhaul the way that campaigns are financed.
- **Television ad time.** As already discussed, the United States is a much larger country than any of its Western European counterparts. Even running a statewide race can be prohibitively expensive, given the need to buy commercial airtime. However, many parties in Western European countries are given free television time, drastically reducing the obligation to raise huge sums of money. Some American critics have called for television networks to assume more responsibility for the public's civic education by granting free access time to candidates. However, others view this practice as yet another example of government overstepping its bounds and potentially limiting the free flow of ideas.

For all the talk of upwardly spiraling campaign spending in the United States, some political scientists believe that this isn't a pressing concern for our

ASKED & ANSWERED *continued*

democratic institution, pointing out that the advertising budgets of some Fortune 500 companies greatly dwarf what is spent on politics each year (see p. 260 for some examples). Sorting out the answers to the complex question of how much money and resources should be devoted to all elections in the United States is not an easy task. Still, as the costs of campaigns spiral up, we may well want to look to our global neighbors for answers to the complex issue of campaign finance reform. Otherwise, we may never be able to reduce the increasingly high costs of running campaigns in the United States.

* Kevin Fullam contributed to this feature.

primarily a social welfare organization, can educate and attempt to influence the public regarding legislation germane to its programs. It may also participate in campaigns and elections as long as their primary function and focus is on social welfare issues. What constitutes a "social welfare function" can be and often is highly debatable.

Another advantage of a political group organizing as a 501(c)(4) is that it does not have to make public the names of the individuals who contribute to the organization. For this last reason alone, the use of the 501(c)(4) designation by politically oriented organizations has come under increased public scrutiny and criticism as a misuse of this not-for-profit status. Many contributors to politically organized 501(c)(4) organizations do so in order to assure the anonymity of their contributions to assist a Republican or Democratic campaign. As with 527 committees, by using 501(c)(3) and 501(c)(4) committees, federal candidates and PACs are able to skirt federal laws meant to reform the campaign finance process.

Act III: *Citizens United v. Federal Election Commission.* As noted previously, in a 2010 case, *Citizens United v. Federal Election Commission*, the U.S. Supreme Court ruled "that corporations [and unions] may spend freely to support or oppose candidates for president and Congress."[19] The 5–4 decision by the Court strikes down part of the Bipartisan Campaign Finance Act of 2002, which banned unions and corporations from paying for political ads. The decision allows unions and corporations to make expenditures on campaigns as long as they don't coordinate their spending with candidates' campaigns. The decision also opened up the opportunity for individuals to form PACs to make unlimited expenditures on campaign ads and other political tools in support of candidates and their policies.

In another significant case, decided on April 2, 2014, *McCutcheon v. Federal Election Commission*, the Supreme Court, in a 5–4 decision, struck down a contribution cap that previously limited the overall contributions that individuals can make to federal candidates, national parties, and political committees. The majority decision, based on the First Amendment's freedom of speech clause,

TABLE 8.3 Impact of *McCutcheon v. Federal Election Commission* on Individual Campaign Contributions

To Candidates	To National Parties and Other Political Groups	Combined
$2,600 to each candidate per election. NO LIMIT on the total amount contributed directly to candidates	$32,000 to each national party committee; $10,000 to a party's state, district, and local committees; and $5,000 to any other political committee per year. NO LIMIT on the total amount contributed to parties and other political groups.	NO LIMIT on the total amount contributed to candidates, parties, and political committees in an election.

Source: "Before and After the Supreme Court's Ruling," *The New York Times*, April 2, 2014.

while continuing limited caps on contributions to individual candidates per election, ruled that no limitations could be placed on total contributions to federal candidates, parties, and other groups (see Table 8.3). As with *Citizens United v. Federal Election Commission*, the long-term impact of this decision will have to await future analysis of individual campaign contribution patterns.

Despite the actions of Congress, decisions by the courts, and the public's ongoing distaste of campaign financing, the future of campaign finance reform remains uncertain; what is clear is that the issue will not disappear. Only time will tell whether pressures from the public for reform and the actions of Congress and the federal courts will continue to have an impact on elected officials at both the state and national levels of government.

Does Money Buy Victory? Since 1976, the federal government has funded presidential campaigns, giving the Democratic and Republican candidates equal support. As a result, the major party candidates have entered the race for president, at least initially, on a more or less equal financial footing. As we discussed previously, Barack Obama chose not to accept public funds in the 2008 general election. In 2012, both Barack Obama (D) and Mitt Romney (R) chose not to accept public funds but depended on contributions from their supporters to finance their campaigns. The clear advantage of not accepting public funding for Obama and Romney in 2012 was their ability to spend as much money as they could raise. Obviously, the Bipartisan Campaign Finance Reform Act of 2002 does not resolve all the issues and problems regarding campaign financing in presidential campaigns. The public remains justifiably skeptical of laws that supposedly limit the influence money has on campaigns.

Money also plays a large part in congressional campaigns, which are not funded by the federal government, and it affects more than just the election outcome, in at least three ways:

1. Both incumbents and challengers must spend a considerable amount of time raising funds for a congressional election, time that takes them away from campaigning and, for incumbents, from governing and policymaking. A competitive, high-visibility Senate race costing in excess of $10 million

requires a senator who is running for reelection to raise more than $32,000 every week of her or his six-year term.

2. The need to raise large sums of money to campaign for Congress (as well as for many other offices) prevents many citizens from even contemplating a run for political office.

3. The large sums of money spent on campaigns often give the public the impression that contributors can buy the favor of elected officials.

However, it is important to recognize that money is not the only factor determining the outcome of congressional elections. Who wins also depends on the circumstances of the race, particularly whether one of the candidates is an **incumbent**—that is, in office at the time of the election. Incumbents are hard to beat, because they are usually well known to voters and because they have already served the state or district. The retention rate of incumbent members of the House of Representatives who were running for reelection in 2014 was more than 95 percent.

Furthermore, incumbents often find it relatively easy to raise funds. A strong, competitive challenger may have a chance against an incumbent,[20] although the race may be lost before it begins unless the challenger can raise enough money to create name recognition. Spending has the greatest impact on an election in which there is no incumbent in the race—known as an **open race**—and the outcome is uncertain. Thus, the reality is that money is a necessary but not sufficient factor in a successful bid for many political offices.

Incumbent A candidate who holds a contested office at the time of an election.

Open race An election in which there is no incumbent in the race.

Organizing Campaigns: The Old and the New

Even though most state and local campaigns are unorganized or underorganized and lurch from one improvisation to another as the year unfolds, the most visible campaigns—including those for the presidency, the Senate, and many House seats and governorships—are highly organized.

Campaign Organization. John F. Kennedy's 1960 presidential campaign was the first to make significant use of an organization recruited from outside the party structure. Kennedy relied heavily on a personally selected team of advisers and staff, including his brother Robert, to take on the major burdens of running the campaign. That model has been followed in most presidential campaigns since the 1960s, and in many state and local races as well.

Candidates assemble personal staffs because the parties historically were slow to develop polling and media-consulting programs and other support systems. The existence of such staffs also reflects the growing sophistication of campaigns. Staff members write speeches, schedule appearances, plan strategy, and recruit additional talent as needed. Major state and local candidates now receive sophisticated training and support from the parties. Nevertheless, presidential candidates and many congressional and statewide candidates still seek the guidance of their own professional consultants as well as that of their personal advisers.

Campaign Strategy. A critical part of the campaign process is the development of themes (reasons why the public should support the candidate) and campaign strategies. The plausibility of these themes is critically important to a candidate's success. If voters do not believe that a candidate will fulfill his or her campaign promises—if the candidate's words evoke the myth of broken promises—the election is lost.

In most presidential, House, and Senate races, campaign strategy depends on whether the candidate is an incumbent or a challenger. Congressional incumbents generally have the advantage of name recognition, a record of accomplishments, and a loyal constituency. Not surprisingly, then, most incumbents in the House—between 80 and 99 percent since World War II—have succeeded in their quest for reelection.

Incumbency is also important in presidential elections. No other officeholder in the United States has as much visibility, name recognition, or prestige, or as many opportunities to speak to voters on the issues, and incumbent candidates take full advantage of these assets. Incumbency does not guarantee a second term, however. Since the end of World War II, six out of eleven incumbent presidents have not served second terms (including John F. Kennedy, who was assassinated).

Differences among election outcomes reflect something more than incumbency, however. Winners and losers alike are profoundly affected by the political environment: the partisan leanings of the electorate and the candidates' experience, personality, personal values, leadership skills, and positions on policy issues. Many candidates try to ensure that none of these factors polarizes the electorate and drives away potential supporters. In 2014, however, many Republican and Democratic candidates took competing, polarized positions on a variety of issues ranging from health care and the national debt to immigration reform and foreign policy.

The New Campaign Style. The tools, and consequently the style, of campaigns have changed over the years. One major innovation has been the use of polls, an expensive campaign tool that can dramatize or establish proof of a candidate's viability for major office.[21] In Chapter 6, which discusses public opinion, we looked at the way candidates use polls to evaluate their strengths and weaknesses, assess the relevance of specific issues, and determine the campaign's impact on the voters.

Professional pollsters have established strong reputations for the accuracy of their estimates of candidates' standings and the voters' views on the issues. Pollsters' services are now almost universally used by candidates in presidential races and are used in many congressional and statewide races as well. Costs depend on the size of the state and the kind of polling. The cost of a statewide poll can run from $5,000 to $50,000 or more.

Another "miracle" of modern campaigning is the use of technology, including computers, iPads, and smartphones. Most congressional and statewide candidates seeking political office in 2014, as well as many local office seekers, created an electronic version of their campaign brochure on a website, posting everything from their personal leadership qualities and their policy positions to baby pictures

POLITICS & POPULAR CULTURE: Visit the book's companion website at **www.oup.com/us/gitelson** to read the special feature *Twitter Campaigning in the Digital Age.*

Political consultant An individual, often trained in public relations, media, or polling techniques, who advises candidates on organizing their campaigns.

and favorite Bible passages. In addition, many candidates have engaged in online fundraising. Millions of dollars for the 2014 congressional and statewide races were raised through the Internet. Two very popular modes of promoting contemporary campaigns and raising funds at all levels of government are the use of Facebook and Twitter. These social networks can serve as important organizational tools for political office seekers, as they allow candidates and supporters to interact with one another and to rally around issue positions for the purpose of aiding candidates. These new campaign tools have already had a growing impact on presidential, congressional, state, and local races.

Technological changes over the past three decades have been accompanied by the rise of **political consultants**. These individuals, often trained in public relations, media, or polling techniques, have replaced traditional campaign managers in the most visible elections. Some consultants organize all aspects of the race, from the physical appearance of the candidate to the strategies that he or she adopts in presenting his or her positions on issues. Most consultants specialize in certain aspects of the campaign, such as polling, fundraising, or the media,[22] and most generally work for either Democratic or Republican candidates exclusively.

The Media and Campaigns: Are We Brainwashed?

> **What is the impact of the media on political campaigns?**

Use of the media, particularly television, has become almost a way of life in recent presidential, congressional, and gubernatorial races, and many mayoral contests as well. A campaign is often organized around media coverage. Candidates make decisions about trips, rallies, and press conferences with an eye to attracting the press and meeting its schedules. Because advertising costs so much, campaign managers work hard to maximize free coverage by television news as well as radio and newspapers to promote their candidates. Consequently, they often schedule a candidate's speeches and rallies before large crowds so that these can appear on the evening local and network news programs.

The media also manipulate the coverage of important campaigns in order to maximize the attention of their audience. Often this tactic entails highlighting and even promoting conflict. Candidates are encouraged to attack one another's policies, and television debates, especially among presidential candidates, have become contests, with "winners" and "losers." The Kennedy-Nixon debates in 1960 marked the beginning of face-to-face discussion between presidential candidates. In the 2012 presidential campaign, three presidential debates were held, as well as one debate between the vice-presidential candidates. Many political pundits believe that a presidential candidate's success is clearly tied to his or her performance in the debates. However, there is relatively little evidence to support this belief. As one analyst argued after reviewing the evidence, "when it comes to shifting enough votes to decide the outcome of the election, presidential debates have rarely, if ever, mattered."[23]

Of course, candidates do not rely on free coverage alone. Advertising is also a crucial part of campaigns. The high cost of network television advertising has been tempered somewhat in recent years by the significant growth in cable television. Many cable outlets provide candidates with relatively inexpensive access to the public. Although broadcast television gets the greatest share of political ad dollars, in 2012 cable television earned close to $1 billion in total political advertising revenue, a 100 percent increase over 2008.[24] Instead of paying for a political advertisement that may reach hundreds of thousands of viewers outside their election district, local candidates can use cable television to limit their campaign advertising to their prospective constituents. Such access can be cost-effective when cable television advertising rates are relatively low.

The evidence regarding the impact of the media on campaigns and elections is still very sketchy. Clearly, the use of television has increased the costs of running presidential, congressional, and gubernatorial campaigns, as well as campaigns for other highly visible public offices. But do the media brainwash us into voting for specific candidates?

- Media advertising is probably more effective in motivating and encouraging a candidate's supporters to go to the polls than in changing the minds of already committed opponents of a candidate. With marginal

President Obama's Facebook page is an example of one important way in which an incumbent president publicizes the achievements of his administration.

voters, both media news coverage and advertisements are effective. Because such voters lack strong or even moderate commitment to a candidate, they are more open than partisan voters to the opinions and influence of a news anchorperson or reporter or to the appeals of a paid political advertisement.

- The media also provide a relatively unknown political candidate with increased name recognition. This can be vital to the success of a candidate who is challenging a well-known and highly visible incumbent.

- Finally, the media help to shape the issues that candidates focus on in an election, thus serving as an agenda-setting force in a campaign. This can have a dramatic effect by determining the quality of debate throughout the race. (See Chapter 10 for a more far-reaching discussion on the role of the media in politics.)

Campaigns and Political Parties

> **What have been the consequences of the shift from party-centered campaigns to candidate-centered campaigns?**

By using the media, as well as independent campaign consultants, online advertising, fundraising, data analysis and budgeting, and polls, many high-visibility office seekers have been able to bypass the political parties, which traditionally played a major role in the campaign process. Presidential, congressional, gubernatorial, and mayoral candidates are now no longer dependent on party volunteers or party campaign-funding events to jump-start their campaigns. That change has shifted the focus from **party-centered campaigns** (in which the party coordinates activities, raises money, and develops strategy) to **candidate-centered campaigns** (in which paid consultants or volunteers perform those tasks).

However, as we discussed in Chapter 7, the role of parties in the campaign process is still evident at most levels of government. In recent years, parties have learned to adapt to the changing campaign strategies, providing candidates at the national, state, and local levels with consultants, advisers, and workshops on campaign funding and strategy, and, as political brokers, with access to PACs and to individual contributors who seek out the party's advice on their campaign contributions. That last function is critical for candidates who rely on the party to direct individual and PAC contributions to their campaigns.

Political parties are unlikely to return to the center stage of many political campaigns, but evidence suggests that the parties have adapted to the new campaign style, including the participation of political consultants, who play a central role in the shaping of that style, and PACs, who play a growing role in the financing of high-visibility campaigns.

Party-centered campaign A campaign in which the party coordinates activities, raises money, and develops strategies.

Candidate-centered campaign A campaign in which paid consultants or volunteers coordinate campaign activities, develop strategies, and raise funds. Parties play a secondary role.

Voting and Elections

> **What factors influence the way people vote in an election?**

Voting rules and regulations have changed considerably in the past two hundred years. Until 1920, women could not vote in most states. African Americans and women faced voting restrictions for much of the country's history. Although the vote has now been extended to most adult citizens (one exception is in the forty-eight states in which felons serving time in prison lose their voting rights), not everyone chooses to exercise that prerogative. Therefore, it is important that we look at who votes and why.

Who Is Allowed to Vote?

The Constitution originally left the decision on voting qualifications to the individual states. Article I, Section 4, specifies that Congress may regulate by law only the time, place, and manner of federal elections. Any extension of voting rights by the federal government must come in the form of a constitutional amendment or a federal law.

State leaders in the 1780s had little sympathy for the idea of universal voting rights. All of the original thirteen states restricted voting rights to white males, and only three of these states—New Hampshire, Pennsylvania, and Georgia—admitted adult males into the electorate without a property requirement. Even in those states, however, a voter without property had to be a taxpayer. As a result, in 1789, only some 10 percent of the population could cast ballots.[25]

Over the past two centuries, voting rights have been extended to those who do not own property and to African Americans, Native Americans, and women, and in 1971, passage of the Twenty-Sixth Amendment lowered the voting age in national, state, and local elections from twenty-one to eighteen.

During the 1960s, the Supreme Court struck down property ownership requirements and shortened residency requirements. Today, a citizen needs only to have resided in a state for thirty days in order to vote in national elections and in most state elections.

Who Votes?

Americans are proud of their electoral system. Indeed, many citizens would argue that the freedom to select political leaders is one of the most important differences between a democracy and a dictatorship or a communist government. Yet, as we saw in Chapter 6, on public opinion and political participation, a limited number of Americans vote. On average, since 1964, about 50 percent of Americans take part in presidential elections. Although approximately 58 percent of eligible voters participated in the 2012 presidential elections, it is not clear whether that level of participation will be sustained in the future. In 2014, the turnout for the off-year election was estimated at 41 percent of eligible voters.

For further updates visit the companion website at **www.oup.com/us/gitelson**.

Other nations show higher rates of voter turnout. For example, 95 percent of Australians regularly go to the polls, and the turnout in other democracies in recent elections has ranged from 65 percent in Great Britain to 70 percent in Spain and 90 percent in Belgium. These comparisons are not entirely fair, however, because voting is often easier and simpler in other nations, and in twenty-two countries voting is mandatory (although not often enforced). Americans face much longer ballots and relatively brief and inconvenient polling schedules, although many states have laws that now provide for early voting opportunities. In many European countries, voting takes place on weekends. Many European nations also have automatic universal registration, which is not widespread in the United States. As a final incentive to ensure voting, some European countries, regarding voting as the civic responsibility of their citizens, levy fines on those who stay at home.

Demographics and Voter Turnout. In Chapter 6, we also learned about the social and economic factors that influence political participation patterns, particularly voter turnout. Individuals who vote regularly are likely to have higher levels of education, higher incomes, and better jobs than nonvoters. Education seems to be a key to voter turnout.[26] As political scientists Raymond Wolfinger and Steven Rosenstone point out, education "imparts information about politics . . . and about a variety of skills, some of which facilitate political learning. . . . Educated people are more likely to be well informed about politics and to follow the campaign in the mass media."[27] In addition, for non-English-speaking citizens, education provides fluency in English, a necessary tool for efficiently following the campaign process. The Voting Rights Act of 1965, renewed most recently in 2006, provides for bilingual ballots to be printed in electoral jurisdictions where there are substantial populations who don't speak or read English proficiently.

Older Americans (except those who are handicapped and therefore have difficulty getting to the polling booths) are more likely to vote than younger ones. The reasons for that pattern are complex:

- Young people are frequently preoccupied with the demands of school, military service, or new careers.

- Young people also tend to believe that they have little impact or influence on the political system.

- In states that provide for early voting opportunities, older citizens who may be infirm or physically handicapped can vote, at their convenience and leisure, in advance of Election Day.

In the past, turnout for women trailed that for men. Today, however, the percentage of women voting is slightly higher than that for men.

The Disappointed Electorate. There are many reasons that citizens choose not to vote, as evidenced by the data in Table 8.4, which lists the reasons for nonvoting in the most recent presidential and general elections. However, other reasons, too, have an impact on nonvoting in the United States. Barriers such as preregistration requirements and long ballots reduce the numbers of citizens who vote. But another obstacle is the myth of broken promises. Many Americans do not take part in elections because they do not believe that government in general and elected officials in particular can solve the country's problems. Voting, for many, simply doesn't make sense.

TABLE 8.4 Reasons for Nonvoting in the 2012 Elections (in Thousands)

		Reason for not voting (percent distribution)											
	Total Number of Nonvoters*	Illness or Disability	Out of Town	Forgot to Vote	Not Interested	Too Busy	Transportation Problem	Dislikes Candidate or Issues	Registration Problems	Bad Weather	Inconvenient Polling Location	Other Reasons	Don't Know or Refused
Total population	19,141	14.0	8.6	3.9	15.7	18.9	3.3	12.7	5.5	0.8	2.7	11.1	3.0
18- to 24-year-olds	3,073	3.1	14.8	5.0	14.0	20.8	4.9	9.9	9.4	0.7	2.1	11.5	4.0

Source: U.S. Census Bureau, Current Population Survey, November 2012.

* The total figure is the number of registered citizens who reported not voting. If a respondent answered "Don't Know" or "Refused" to either the voting or the registration question, he or she was not included in this table.

Some Americans also question the honesty and integrity of many political leaders. The Watergate scandal in the early 1970s and the subsequent resignation of President Richard Nixon undermined confidence in government. In 1999, President Bill Clinton was impeached by the House of Representatives and became only the second president in our history to be tried for misconduct by the Senate. Although he was acquitted of all charges brought against him, the events surrounding the impeachment and the Senate trial were seen as bringing discredit not only on President Clinton but also on the political and governmental system in general. In 2000, the highly controversial election of President George W. Bush, who received a majority of the Electoral College vote but lost in the popular vote to Democratic candidate Al Gore by more than 500,000 votes, also weakened many Americans' confidence in the political process, as have the protracted wars in Iraq and Afghanistan, financial failures, and high unemployment rates as a result of the 2007–2009 Great Recession.

In this atmosphere of cynicism, many potential voters doubt that their vote matters and simply stay home on Election Day. Several studies have documented the reasons for failure to vote.

- Many people believe that government cannot solve the nation's problems.

- As we pointed out in Chapter 7, people are less likely than in previous years to strongly identify with one political party, an identification that once got out the vote.

- Some people have even questioned whether it makes any difference who wins elections.

Should we be concerned about the disappointed voter? Some observers say yes, arguing that low turnout undermines representative government, which, they argue, depends on full electoral participation. Others disagree, suggesting that people who are ill informed may make poor choices when they vote. Some have even argued that low levels of voter turnout are a sign of a healthy system—that is, they show that people are satisfied with their government.

Why Do People Vote the Way They Do?

What draws voters to the polls? What influences their choices of candidates? How did voters make their choices for president and Congress in 2012 and Congress in 2014? Obviously, the supporters of the various candidates thought that their man or woman was the better candidate, and that he or she would better serve their interests. But a number of factors influence voter choice.

Issues. Political observers often accuse American voters of focusing on frivolous aspects of campaigns. In fact, many American voters do pay attention to issues and take them into account when making their choices. Of course, no one can review all the positions of every candidate who is running for office. Given that hundreds of issues arise at the local, state, and national levels each year, no one could possibly follow them all, or even have an interest in most of them.

In presidential elections, however, there seems to be some relationship between the issues that citizens support and the candidates whom they vote for.[28] In the

2014 congressional elections, voters viewed the policy positions of the Democratic and Republican contestants differently. The state of the economy, unemployment, the Affordable Care Act (Obamacare), and immigration reform were among the most important issues to voters.

Candidate Image. The candidate's personal qualities, particularly her or his experience and leadership, also count. Furthermore, voters ask themselves how well the candidate represents their own interests and whether the candidate is honest, trustworthy, and approachable by the electorate. One observer labels this process "politics by psychoanalysis."

Party Identification. As we saw in Chapter 7, party identification gives voters a general sense of how candidates are likely to approach various issues and policies. This identification can be misleading, as opinions within the parties are diverse. Nevertheless, in a world in which voters may know little or nothing about many of the candidates, the party label serves as an indication of their policy positions.

Retrospective Voting. When individuals base their votes on the candidates' or parties' past performance, they are engaging in **retrospective voting**.[29] Incumbents are judged on their records in office; challengers may be judged on what they did in the offices they previously held. In effect, voters are looking at the past to help them evaluate the future—one rational way to make judgments. Is retrospective voting common? Evidence suggests that it is and that it can have an important impact on voting behavior. In the 2014 congressional elections, voters scrutinized past issue positions and voting records of Democratic and Republican candidates alike.

> **Retrospective voting** When individuals base their votes on the candidates' or parties' past record of performance.

Group Influences. People of different genders, races, age groups, and educational and political backgrounds vote in predictable and yet divergent ways for political candidates. In the 2012 election, for example, Mitt Romney drew support from conservatives, who are traditionally allied with the Republican Party, whereas, not surprisingly, Democrat President Barack Obama drew deep support from liberals. Republican Mitt Romney received strong support from white voters sixty years or older, Protestants, regular churchgoers, and voters living in rural communities and small towns. President Obama received his strongest support from first-time voters between the ages of eighteen and twenty-nine, Latinos, Jews, and African Americans.

The Other Elections: Referenda and Initiatives

Despite the general acceptance of elections in a representative democracy, controversies still arise over the need for greater or lesser citizen participation in government decision making. Some argue that more should be done to increase public input through a procedure called **initiative and referendum**. Both initiatives and referenda involve placing questions of public policy on the ballot for voters to consider directly; however, the initiative process allows members of the general public to place such questions on the ballot, whereas it is the state or local legislative body that places a referendum on the ballot. (For specific information on referenda and initiatives, see the Policy Connection feature on p. 284.)

Others believe that too much public input through direct participation can be damaging. It is argued by some that the initiative process poses dangers to

> **Initiative and referendum** A method of democratic decision making that places questions of public policy on the ballot for voters to consider directly. Initiatives are placed on the ballot by citizen petition, whereas a referendum is generated by the legislature.

our constitutional system of checks and balances and that initiatives can be subject to manipulation by special interests. Others have noted that state and local requirements that proposed tax increases and increases in school budgets, which were put before voters in a referendum, have created budgetary crises in recent years because voters have turned down requests to increase revenues. The argument against the use of the referendum and initiative system is the danger of public policy being made by small groups of individuals with a vested interest in an issue or by an uninformed public voting on detailed policy issues.

The 2014 Elections

> **A changing political landscape?**

Tip O'Neal, the late Speaker of the U.S. House of Representatives, argued that "all politics are local." The 2014 midyear elections proved that while the impact of local issues is important, national politics can have a significant impact on congressional and state races. The low popularity ratings of the president and Congress, along with a polarized environment in Washington D.C., provided the pretext for major changes in the political landscape.

The president's party (the Democrats in 2014) traditionally loses congressional seats in an off-year election. True to form, the Republican Party was the major benefactor of the high level of discontent with Washington politics in 2014. The elections saw the Republicans capturing control of the Senate while maintaining control of the House of Representatives. The Republican Party also fared well at the state level, picking up two additional gubernatorial seats and winning control of both houses of the legislature in twenty-three states.

A significant change in the political landscape as a consequence of the Republican victories is an even more divided government with a Republican-controlled Congress and a Democratic president. Given the history of presidential–congressional relations over the past ten years, some have argued that Washington will continue to experience political polarization. A major question is whether the 114th Congress (2015–2017) will be as ineffective as the previous Congress, which generated fewer statutes than any modern Congress in over one hundred years. Certainly some of the major issues facing the president and Congress will include the economy and jobs, immigration policy, tax reform, climate control, terrorism, and the Middle East, relations with Iran, and the weak economy in Europe. According to many political analysts, the uncertainty created by the 2014 elections may continue to endure as we approach the 2016 presidential elections.

The Electoral College

> **How does the Electoral College function? What alternatives have been suggested as a replacement for the Electoral College?**

The constitutional environment in which presidential campaigns take place is the Electoral College. Although the founders believed in representative government, they hesitated to place the selection of the president directly in the hands of the

Joni Ernst, Iowa Republican 2014 candidate for the U.S. Senate, casts her ballot—accompanied by a half-dozen reporters. A few hours later she would be a surprise Senator-elect.

people. The system that they devised provides for the election by the people of each state of a number of electors equal to the number of senators and representatives representing that state in Congress. For example, the congressional delegation of Georgia includes two U.S. senators and fourteen members of the House. Thus, in presidential elections, that state's voters elect sixteen electors to the Electoral College. (See also Chapter 2 for a discussion of the Electoral College.)

Until the drama of the 2000 presidential election, when George W. Bush had a minority of the popular vote but was elected to the presidency with a slight majority of the Electoral College vote, most Americans understood little about the Electoral College but assumed that when they cast their ballots, they were voting directly for the presidential candidate of their choice. Instead, they are really voting for a slate of electors (equal to the size of the state's congressional delegation) who have committed their support to that presidential candidate. State law determines how a person becomes an elector. In Pennsylvania, the presidential candidates select their electors. In thirty-eight states, the electors are nominated at state party conventions. In most of the remaining states, electors are selected in primaries or by state party committees.

There is nothing in the Constitution about how a state is to select it electors. In most states, the presidential candidate who wins a plurality of the vote in the state receives all its Electoral College votes. Two states, Maine and Nebraska, use what is called a "district plan." In Maine, for instance, each of the two congressional districts chooses an elector, and the two remaining electoral votes are awarded to the ticket that receives the plurality of statewide votes. Thus, a ticket may receive four electoral votes, or one ticket may pick up three electoral votes, while the other ticket is awarded one elector. The Nebraska plan is the same, except that the state has three congressional districts.

The members of the Electoral College chosen in the November general election in each state meet in December and vote for the president. The votes from each state are forwarded to Congress, where an official count takes place on the first day of the congressional session in January. Only after completion of that vote count is the official winner of the presidential election declared. A total of 538 Electoral College votes are cast in the fifty states and the District of Columbia; the presidential candidate receiving the majority of these votes wins the election. The vice president is selected in the same manner. (If no candidate receives a majority of the Electoral College vote, the House of Representatives selects the president, and the Senate selects the vice president in special sessions.)

Critics have noted at least two problems with this system. First, in twenty-four states, the electors whose party candidate wins a plurality of the state's popular vote are required to vote for that candidate. In the remaining twenty-six states, however, an elector is not required by law to support the candidate who has won the popular vote in the state.

A second problem is that a president can be elected by a majority of the Electoral College without having a majority of the national popular vote. A number of reforms have been proposed to deal with this problem, including the selection of the president by direct popular vote (see Table 8.5). Yet no consensus for a constitutional amendment has emerged, and thus the indirect election of presidents through the Electoral College has remained intact.

When they are campaigning for the presidency, candidates are well aware that gaining a majority of the popular vote is not enough. A candidate must be successful in garnering pluralities in a sufficient number of states to ensure that he or she receives a majority of the Electoral College vote (see Figure 8.1 for an example).

TABLE 8.5 Six Modern Presidential Election Outcomes Under Alternative Plans

Election	Electoral College[a]	Direct Election[b]	Proportional Plan[c]	District Plan[d]	Bonus Plan[e]
2012	Obama wins Obama 332 Romney 206	Obama wins Obama 51.1% Romney 47.2%	Obama wins Obama 267.2 Romney 253.4 Others < 4%	Romney wins Obama 262.0 Romney 273.0	Obama wins Obama 434 Romney 206
2008	Obama wins Obama 365 McCain 173	Obama wins Obama 53.0% McCain 46.0% Others < 1.0%	Obama wins Obama 291.0 McCain 247.0 Others < 1.0%	Obama wins Obama 298.0 McCain 240.0	Obama wins Obama 467 McCain 173
2004	Bush* wins Bush 286 Kerry 252	Bush wins Bush 51.0% Kerry 48.1% Others 0.9%	Bush wins Bush 274.0 Kerry 257.8 Others 6.2	Bush wins Bush 320.5 Kerry 217.5	Bush wins Bush 388 Kerry 252
2000	Bush* wins Bush 271 Gore 266 One blank vote	Gore wins Gore 48.4% Bush 47.9% Others 3.7%	No one wins a majority Bush 259.4 Gore 258.4 Others 20.3	Bush wins Bush 271.0 Gore 266.0 One blank vote	Gore wins Gore 368 Bush 271 One blank vote

Election	Electoral College[a]	Direct Election[b]	Proportional Plan[c]	District Plan[d]	Bonus Plan[e]
1996	Clinton wins Clinton 379 Dole 159 Perot 0	Clinton wins Clinton 49.2% Dole 40.7% Perot 8.4%	No one wins a majority Clinton 262.1 Dole 222.0 Perot 45.2	Clinton wins Clinton 345.0 Dole 193.0 Perot 0.0	Clinton wins Clinton 481 Dole 159 Perot 0
1992	Clinton wins Clinton 370 Bush** 168 Perot 0	Clinton wins Clinton 43.0% Bush 37.4% Perot 13.9%	No one wins a majority Clinton 231.1 Bush 202.2 Perot 101.8	Clinton wins Clinton 324.0 Bush 214.0 Perot 0.0	Clinton wins Clinton 472 Bush 168 Perot 0

[a] *Electoral College plan*: The existing system of selecting a president—the candidate winning a majority of the Electoral College vote (at least 270 votes) wins the election.

[b] *Direct election plan*: The candidate receiving a majority of the popular vote wins the election.

[c] *Proportional plan*: The Electoral College vote is kept, but candidates receive a proportion of each state's Electoral College vote based on the percentage of the popular vote they win in each state. (Results are divided to the nearest tenth.)

[d] *District plan*: The Electoral College vote is retained in each state, but it is apportioned according to the plurality popular-vote winner in each congressional district, plus two votes for winning the state (the plan presently used by Maine and Nebraska).

[e] *Bonus plan*: This plan keeps the Electoral College system but awards 102 extra votes to the candidate who wins the national popular vote (originally proposed by the Century Fund).

* George W. Bush.

** George H. W. Bush

Source: Sections of this table appear in Robert L. Dudley and Alan R. Gitelson, *American Elections: The Rules Matter* (New York: Longman, 2002), pp. 150–151. The table is an updated version of a table constructed by Nelson W. Polsby and Aaron Widavsky, *Presidential Elections: Strategies and Structures of American Politics* (New York: Chatham House, 2000), p. 251.

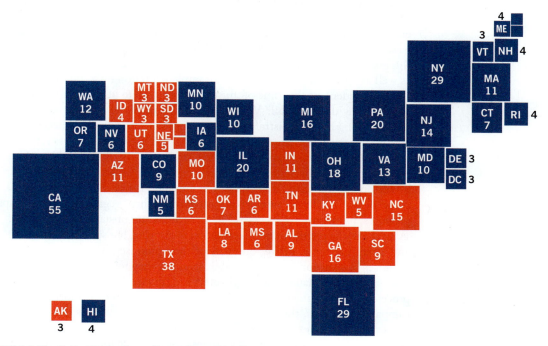

FIGURE 8.1 The United States According to Electoral College Votes

This distorted map will give you a sense of the electoral power of the most populous states, such as California, New York, Texas, Pennsylvania, Florida, Ohio, Illinois, and Michigan.

Source: U.S. National Archives and Records Administration, Washington, D.C.

Not surprisingly, most candidates focus much of their attention on the larger competitive states, such as New York, Pennsylvania, Illinois, Ohio, Florida, and Michigan—states that have significant numbers of Electoral College votes.[30]

Promises, Promises: The Link Between Campaigns and Public Policy

> **Do candidates, when elected to office, try to keep their campaign promises?**

As we have discussed, poll results show that the public doubts whether the promises a candidate makes in a campaign have any bearing on the policies that candidate promotes once in office. We believe that this perception of broken promises is a myth—a simplification of the facts. How do we make sense of this assumption?

Of course, candidates do not fulfill all the promises they make. How could they? The wish list of most candidates, let alone that of Americans collectively, is dauntingly long. But candidates try hard to keep many of their promises.[31] Party platforms are, in effect, their agreements with the electorate. It is as if they were saying, "This is what I think. This is what I will try to do. If you agree with what I think, at least on many of the issues, then vote for me."

Recent presidents have been reasonably successful at fulfilling the promises in their party platform and persuading Congress to act on those promises.[32] For example, during the Obama administration, the president pledged to create and pass legislation dealing with national health care insurance. He accomplished this goal (although the Affordable Care Act has been plagued by technical problems as well as strong ongoing resistance to implementation by Republicans).

All presidents make some promises that they fail to keep—but not for want of trying. Why did they fail? Why was Obama unable to get gun control reform passed during his administration? A president's programs can fail because they are poorly conceived or ineffective. They can also fail because Congress refuses to cooperate. Obama faced opposition from Congress, including members of his own party, regarding gun control reform. Sometimes one or both houses are controlled by the opposition party. Sometimes the president is not able to persuade his own party or the public to support his programs. Thus, regarding their campaign promises, presidents are successful in some areas and unsuccessful in others.

In short, the politics of implementation is complex, but successful candidates try and often manage to deliver on many of their promises. They do not make these promises in a vacuum, and more often than not they represent the genuine intentions of the candidates. Although voters are frequently disappointed by the slow processes of government and the incomplete realization of platform agendas and campaign promises, they also often "win" when they place their wishes, desires, and expectations in the hands of our elected officials. For the voters, elections do more than just select their representatives. They provide for citizen empowerment. At their best, elections also help make sense of policy needs and the expectations of the public.

Conclusion

Americans are ambivalent about, and sometimes confused by, elections. Although they acknowledge the importance of elections in the democratic process, they take part in them in relatively low numbers, compared with many Western European democracies. To understand better and make more sense of the election process, we examined in this chapter the facts behind the myth that candidates break their campaign promises. Although that myth contains some truth, it is by and large inaccurate and misleading.

What is the reality? Although some campaign promises are not fulfilled, many are. Furthermore, although candidates run for office for personal reasons—power is a strong motivator—they also run in order to implement their promised policies. And they are often successful in achieving that goal.

We also examined the relationship of a number of variables to election campaigning and voting behavior, particularly the influence of money. Money is a very important—indeed, a necessary—part of most campaigns, but it is not the only important factor in most elections. Other elements, such as incumbency, issues, personalities, skills, national trends, and partisanship, strongly influence election outcomes. The voters' characteristics—religion, ethnic identity, race, age, and so forth—also appear to affect how they view the political world and for whom they cast their ballots. Although the campaign and election processes seem confusing, if we can gain a better understanding of how the system works by examining the myths, facts, and beliefs surrounding the process, we can make sense of the political system.

Key Terms

Candidate-centered campaign p. 270
Caucus p. 253
Closed primary p. 254
527 committees p. 262
Front-loading p. 254
Incumbent p. 266
Initiative and referendum p. 275

Nonpartisan primary p. 254
Open primary p. 254
Open race p. 266
Opportunity structure p. 253
Partisan primary p. 254
Party-centered campaign p. 270
Political consultant p. 268
Primary p. 254

Recall p. 286
Retrospective voting p. 275
Runoff primary p. 254
Soft money p. 261
Superdelegates p. 256
Super PACs p. 262

Focus Questions Review

1. **What roles do party caucuses, primaries, and conventions play in the nomination process? > > >**
   - Candidates are nominated in open meetings (caucuses) or, most commonly, in primary elections that select candidates to run for office under the party banner. A closed primary election is one in which only registered party members participate.

   In an open primary, any qualified voter may participate, regardless of party affiliation or as an independent. The voter chooses one party ballot at the polling place.
   - Although some states and minor political parties still use conventions to nominate candidates, the most prominent conventions are at the national level, held

every four years by the Republicans and Democrats to nominate their presidential candidates.
- Presidential nominations take place at national conventions, which today generally ratify the outcome of primary and caucus campaigns in which delegates to the national conventions are selected.

2. **What impact does money have on political campaigns? What recent changes have occurred in federal election campaign finance laws? > > >**
- Although money is not the only important variable affecting the outcome of an election, it is often critical in the success of many campaigns.
- The escalation of campaign costs led Congress to pass the 1971 Federal Election Campaign Act, which set limits on contributions and expenditures in federal elections. The law gave rise to a new source of funds: political action committees (PACs).
- Congress enacted and President Bush signed into law the Bipartisan Campaign Finance Act of 2002 to further reform federal campaign financing. This act focuses on weaknesses in the existing law, although it does not eliminate all of the loopholes that allow campaigns to legally circumvent the intent of the law through the establishment, for example, of 527 committees and super PACs. Recent Supreme Court cases have overturned congressional reforms aimed at limiting the impact of campaign contributions.

3. **What is the impact of the media on political campaigns? > > >**
- The media can have an impact on political campaigns because it can serve as an important and effective tool in motivating and encouraging a candidate's supporters to go to the polls on Election Day, in influencing a voter who is undecided, and in helping shape the issues that candidates focus on in an election. Thus, the media can have an impact on the quality of the debate throughout a race.
- More often than not, the media focus on the horse-race nature of a campaign, spotlighting which candidate is ahead or behind in the polls as well as conflict between the candidates. The media spend less time following the issues of a campaign.

4. **What have been the consequences of the shift from party-centered campaigns to candidate-centered campaigns? > > >**

- The shift from party-centered campaigns to candidate-centered campaigns has weakened the role of political parties and placed more control over many campaigns in the hands of candidates and their political consultants. Nevertheless, the role of parties in the campaign process is still evident at most levels of government.

5. **What factors influence the way people vote in an election? > > >**
- Factors that influence the way people vote include the following:
  1. Issue preferences
  2. The personal qualities and past records of the candidates
  3. Party identification and social identities

6. **A changing political landscape? > > >**
- The 2014 midyear elections proved that while the impact of local issues is important, national politics can have a significant impact on congressional and state races.
- The low popularity ratings of the president and Congress, along with a polarized environment in Washington D.C., provided the pretext for major changes in the political landscape.
- A significant change in the political landscape as a consequence of the Republican victories is an even more divided government with a Republican-controlled Congress and a Democratic president.
- Certainly some of the major issues facing the president and Congress will include the economy and jobs, immigration policy, tax reform, climate control, terrorism, and the Middle East, relations with Iran, and the weak economy in Europe. According to many political analysts, the uncertainty created by the 2014 elections may continue to endure as we approach the 2016 presidential elections.

7. **How does the Electoral College function? What alternatives have been suggested as a replacement for the Electoral College? > > >**
- Although the founders believed in representative government, they hesitated to place the selection of the president directly in the hands of the people. The system they devised, the Electoral College, provides for the election by the people of each state of

a number of electors equal to the number of senators and representatives representing that state in Congress. With the exception of Maine and Nebraska, in most states, the presidential candidate who wins the popular vote also wins the state's Electoral College votes. The Electoral College vote determines the winner of the presidential election.

- Alternative methods of selecting the president include the following:
    1. Direct election
    2. The proportional plan
    3. The district plan
    4. The bonus plan

8. **Do candidates, when elected to office, try to keep their campaign promises? > > >**
    - The candidates' positions are not idle promises. Once elected, candidates try to fulfill many of their campaign pledges.

Review Questions

1. What dynamics impact the way people vote in an election?
2. What are the differences between primaries and caucuses in the selection of candidates to run for political office?

For more information and access to study materials, visit the book's companion website at www.oup.com/us/gitelson.

Policy Connection

Are elections an effective way to make public policies?

The Policy Challenge

Every election is important, for the outcomes help shape the agenda and tone of government for the next two or four years. In that sense, the results broadcast on the evening of November 6, 2012, were not exceptional. A president was reelected, his party held on to the U.S. Senate, and—although the Republicans retained a comfortable majority in the U.S. House—the Democrats had made some gains. The stage was set for the political drama that would unfold over the next two years.

But some other significant results did not go unnoticed by the national media, even though they involved election results that would have an impact only at the state or local levels. These results concerned elections held at the state and local levels that made public policy decisions, and in this Policy Connection we consider what such direct legislation entails.

Electing a Public Policy

In the 2012 election, two state *ballot measures* received almost as much attention from the media as did elections for Senate and House seats. Although differing in details, the Colorado and Washington state measures effectively legalized the regulated sale of marijuana—a controlled substance that remains illegal under federal drug laws. Two other results also made some headlines, as voters in Maine and Maryland backed legislation to allow same-sex marriages in those states. Given the heated political debate surrounding the legalization of both pot and same-sex marriage, all four votes were regarded as worthy of national news coverage.

That year, many other policy issues appeared on ballots in other states—and most did not grab national headlines.[1] Californians had decided not to do away with the death penalty, and Oklahoma voters passed a measure that effectively

In 2012 the voters of Colorado passed ballot question 64, which led to the legalization of recreational sales of marijuana starting in 2014. A similar ballot initiative passed in Washington State the same day.

undermined the use of affirmative action in state programs, including admission to state universities. In Montana, voters resoundingly voted to deny state services to undocumented immigrants, whereas in Maryland they approved allowing undocumented immigrants to pay in-state tuition at the state's schools. Physician-assisted suicide, which had been approved through popular vote in Oregon (1994) and Washington (2008), was defeated by a close vote in Massachusetts. And voters in other states supported fifteen of sixteen state funding measures that were on the ballot in 2012.

These decisions are the results of campaigns and elections that allow the citizens of a state (and, more frequently, local governments) to play a direct role in the making of

In 2004, the voters of Arlington, Texas, held a referendum imposing a local sales tax increase devoted to helping fund construction of a local stadium to house the NFL's Dallas Cowboys. The tax would provide $325 million of the $1.3 billion needed for the project. The stadium opened in 2009.

public policies. Although the procedures for holding such policy-focused elections vary from state to state, the practice of allowing *referenda* and *initiatives* is actually widespread. One estimate declares that some form of policymaking through direct elections can occur in several thousand local jurisdictions as well as all fifty states. And the implications of such elections for national policy can be significant.

Touted as the closest we come to direct democracy, initiative and referendum procedures have drawn increasing attention in recent years. In a true direct democracy, of course, all those eligible to participate in the making of a decision would assemble at a designated location at a given time, discuss the issues they face as a community, consider and debate proposals to deal with the issues, and cast votes establishing policies that can then be carried out by individuals appointed to do so. Such mechanisms do exist in smaller communities, with the primary example often being the New England town meeting.[2]

A **referendum** is an alternative means for engaging citizens in direct policymaking by using elections as the way in which voters express their

positions—yea or nay—on a policy appearing in the form of a ballot proposition. For those who favor a "pure" democracy approach to policymaking, the referendum process leaves much to be desired. The proposal on the ballot is not the result of deliberation among the voters but rather comes directly from some legislative body or indirectly through a process that allows a group of citizens to put legislative actions on the ballot for the electorate to reconsider. All fifty states allow their legislatures to put a measure on the ballot—often called a "referred measure" or "legislative proposition." Only twenty-four states, however, allow for a "popular referendum," whereby citizens can petition to have an act of the legislature put before the voters for reconsideration. In either case, how the item gets on the ballot depends on the state or local laws governing the process. Whatever the prescribed path,[3] the process results in a proposal to be "referred" to the citizenry, usually at the next scheduled election.

An **initiative** process also leads to a ballot question, but without dependence on any action by the legislature. Although the exact requirements vary from jurisdiction to jurisdiction, the initiative process permits any citizen or group of citizens to collect a sufficient number of valid signatures on petitions in support of a proposition to be placed on the ballot. Three states—Florida, Illinois, and Mississippi—limit the initiative process to proposals to amend the state constitution; Alaska, Idaho, Utah, Washington, and Wyoming allow citizens to seek votes on proposed laws but not on the constitution. Another fifteen states allow initiatives of both types.

A related mechanism is a **recall**, which involves petitioning to have an elected official leave office before her or his formal term is over. Some recalls have been related to issues about the competence or integrity of the official, but others have been tied to policy disagreements. In 2013, for example, two members of the Colorado legislature were recalled because of their positions on limiting gun rights. Technically, however, recalls are not votes on policies per se.

A Brief History of Referenda and Initiatives

Although policies involving the legalization of pot and same-sex marriage have drawn considerable attention, few referenda or initiatives make front-page news in national newspapers. For that reason, most Americans tend to regard them and other forms of direct public involvement in policymaking as rare or uncommon political events. In reality, they have played a significant role in making both major and relatively minor policy decisions throughout American history. As noted in Chapter 2, on America's constitutional foundations, the Framers were no fans of mass democracy. Nevertheless, there were times when those same political leaders would go to the voters to seek the approval of some change in a state constitution or local charters. The voters of Massachusetts, for example, rejected a proposed state constitution in 1778, primarily because of the way it was drafted by the state legislature.[4] Today, forty-nine of the fifty states require that changes to their constitutions be put before the voters.[5]

It was not until the 1890s, however, that calls for widespread adoption of state and local initiative and referendum procedures took hold.[6] Reformers associated with the Progressive Movement realized that their efforts to end political corruption and establish more efficient and open government would go nowhere if they had to rely on those entrenched office holders who felt threatened by the proposed reforms. The initiative and referendum process would give them a means for advancing their agenda, so they often made it their top priority. They recorded their first success in 1893, when California approved initiatives for local governments, and in 1898, when the initiative process became part of the new South Dakota constitution. These successes were followed by adoption of the procedures in a number of western states. By the 1930s the use of referenda and initiatives had become widely adopted; however, with a few exceptions, their popularity on the state level declined significantly through the 1970s. In the meantime, ballot measures became increasingly commonplace at the local level.

California's experience with the initiative process is especially noteworthy for two reasons. First, since 1912 there has been at least one initiative on the state's ballot every two years—as well as in some special elections in odd-numbered years. In fact, in some years there have been as many as seventeen or eighteen ballot questions!

Given California's growth and prominence among the states, some of its more recent initiatives established popular policy trends that quickly spread across the country. In 1978, for example, Californians launched a nationwide taxpayer's revolt with the passage of Proposition 13. Many—if not most—public services (especially public schools) at the local and state level are funded through property tax assessments. As housing prices and values increased during the 1970s (primarily due to inflation), many homeowners reacted to higher property tax bills. Prop 13, as it came to be known, reduced property taxes by 30 percent, placed a cap of 1 percent on the value to be assessed, and required a two-thirds majority vote in the state legislature for any tax rate or revenue-collection increases. Within the next five years, nearly half the states imposed some limit on the taxing powers of their legislatures or local governments, and many of those were passed through the referenda and initiative process. Many political analysts see the election of Ronald Reagan in 1980 and a major federal income cut in 1981 as other consequences of the Prop 13 initiative movement.[7]

Use of initiative and referendum policymaking has also been associated with environmental and social issues. In 1972, for example, the voters of Colorado voted by an overwhelming margin to end the state's support for the 1976 Winter Olympics, which had been awarded to the Denver region two years earlier. The result was partly a taxpayer revolt, but growing public concern for the impact of the Olympics on the environment (see Policy Connection 6) played a major role as well. In 1976, the voters of Boulder, Colorado, passed a law putting a cap on housing construction in order to slow the city's growth; nine years earlier, they had voted to increase the local sales tax in order to purchase land for the development of a "greenbelt." Voters have also used the initiative and referendum process for environmentally inspired antigrowth laws and greenbelt development in many other cities over the years.

The effort to put social issues on the ballot has a long history, tracing back at least to the campaigns conducted by the Anti-Saloon League and other alcohol prohibitionists, who attempted (often unsuccessfully) to use direct legislation to impose restrictions on liquor sales and consumption. Today, the major social issues making it to the ballot involve abortion rights and laws related to the use of marijuana, same-sex marriage, and (most recently) minimum or "living" wage.

On abortion rights, those attempting to significantly limit access to abortion have taken various approaches. Since 2008, "personhood" ballot initiatives essentially giving human embryos the same civil rights as people have been pursued in several states. Such initiatives were defeated by wide margins when they first appeared on ballots in Mississippi and Colorado. Nevertheless, antiabortion forces have continued to put similar laws or constitutional amendments before the voters in elections through 2014. Voters in both Colorado and North Dakota soundly rejected personhood initiatives that were on the November 2014 ballots. In fact, antiabortion

initiatives have generally not fared well in any major jurisdictions, and pro-life interests have discovered that it is much less difficult to win victories in state legislatures than on straight yes-no ballot measures; thus, they have turned their attention to support of legislative candidates who would support their agenda in state houses.[8]

The legalization of marijuana use and sales got its major start with the passage of California Proposition 215 in 1996, which authorized the dispensing of cannabis for medicinal use. As of 2013, twenty states and the District of Columbia have passed medicinal use laws, some through the initiative and referendum process. The 2012 Colorado and Washington state initiatives mentioned previously allow for nonmedicinal sale of pot, and more states are considering doing the same. And, although the possession and sale of cannabis remains a federal crime, several states and localities have either decriminalized possession or given it a very low priority when enforcing drug laws. Although some of these steps were taken by legislative bodies or through administrative decisions, the most significant developments (e.g., those of California and Massachusetts) have been achieved through ballot measures.

As public attitudes toward civil unions and same-sex marriages have shifted over the past decade, so has the willingness of advocates to put the issue on state ballots. The major developments took place in California. In 2000, Californians passed an initiative, Proposition 22, outlawing same-sex marriages. When that law was declared unconstitutional by the state's highest court in 2004, opponents of gay marriage put a constitutional amendment (Proposition 8) on the 2008 ballot that would effectively overrule the earlier court decision. Emboldened by the changing public view of gay marriage, advocates took the state of California to federal district court and had the Proposition 8 vote thrown out. In 2013, the U.S. Supreme Court essentially upheld the lower court decision by holding that those who brought the appeal lacked "legal standing" to sue (see Chapter 14, on the judiciary).

As economic inequality emerged as an issue after the Great Recession, initiatives related to raising the minimum wage began to find their way to the ballot

Crowds gather outside the U.S. Supreme Court as justices decide the fate of Proposition 8, a California initiative that banned same-sex marriage in the state. The Court's ruling effectively overturned the Proposition 8 vote, and the same-sex marriage ban was lifted.

box. In 2013, despite the opposition of its popular governor, Chris Christie, New Jerseyans passed a $1 raise in the state's minimum wage. On the same day, voters in a Seattle suburb (SeaTac) that included the city's airport and hotel facilities passed an initiative to raise the minimum wage for jobs within their jurisdiction to $15 per hour. Although winning by only a slight margin and covering only jobs in SeaTac, the vote made national headlines as an indication that voters might support a "living wage" initiative that is nearly double that of the federal minimum. Other states and localities included minimum wage and related initiatives on their ballots in 2014.

Conclusion

Are elections an effective way to make public policies?

Are election ballots an effective—and appropriate—way to make public policy? The fact that almost every Western democratic country has constitutional provisions for—or has made use of—some form of national initiative or referendum might be the best answer we can provide to that question. In fact, the United States is the only major democracy that does not have the means for holding a nationwide plebiscite on policy issues. All of our states and thousands of localities have filled the gap in that regard, but the form and practice of the initiative and referendum process vary widely. What is true is that substantively direct legislation does play an important role in some of the more contested issues of the day.

As with most other topics related to public policymaking, the referendum and initiative processes have their advocates and opponents. Those voters in favor of them not only highlight the attention ballot measures give to critical issues facing the country but also note that even issues that do not generate widespread attention are important to the local and regional populations they influence. Where else, they argue, does the public really have a voice in shaping the laws and programs under which they live? They can also point to widespread public support for using the referendum and initiative processes at the national level. When asked by the Gallup Poll if they would be for or against a law that would require "a nationwide popular vote on any issue if enough voters signed a petition to request a vote to do so," 68 percent of those surveyed said they would.[9]

Opponents are quick to point out that relying on voters to make important policy decisions assumes a degree of reasonableness and knowledge that runs counter to all we know about the American electorate. Moreover, looking at the requirements for getting measures on the ballot, critics have noted the role played by special interests, who are able to invest the resources needed to manipulate the process. Initially designed as a means for reforming corrupt government, the initiative and referendum process has sometimes become a tool in the hands of those capable of fostering even worse forms of corruption.[10]

Whether we are for or against the process, there is little doubt that direct legislation is here to stay. Social media and related technologies are already altering the landscape, often making it easier to mobilize the support needed to get a measure on the ballot. In addition, there exists a consulting industry of specialists ready and willing to assist any group that seeks to develop campaigns either promoting or opposing a ballot question. As students of American government, our task is to approach each measure in a way that makes sense of it meaning and implications.

QUESTIONS FOR DISCUSSION

1. **Whereas advocates for initiative and referendum procedures believe they are the most democratic means for getting the public involved in policymaking, critics argue that today's public problems are too complex to be handled through oversimplified ballot questions. Given U.S. experience with these policymaking elections, which side of the debate would you support?**

2. **Do you believe there should be a constitutional amendment adding a national initiative and referendum process for federal legislation?**

CHAPTER 9

MYTHS & REALITIES
Are all interest groups corrupt
and self-serving?

Interest Groups

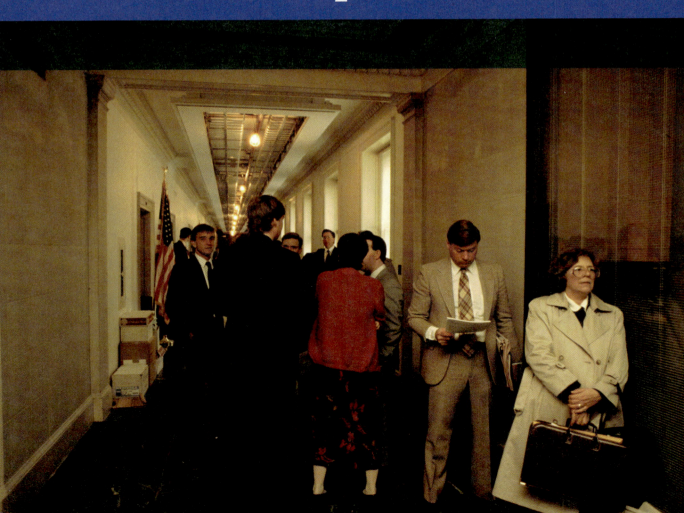

Interest Groups, Lobbying, and Congress

The newspaper and broadcast headlines didn't mince words: "Immigration Debate Attracts Wide Swath of Lobbyists," or "Lobbying Dollars Fly in Immigration Reform Debate." The references were to one of the hottest issues debated by Congress and the American people over the past ten years: immigration reform.[1] The Sunlight Foundation reported that between 2008 and 2012, companies, unions, trade associations, and other political groups had spent millions of dollars on lobbyists in an attempt to influence congressional consideration of hundreds of pieces of legislation that addressed immigration issues directly or indirectly.[2] In 2013, registered lobbyists reported that they were hired by 622 clients—among them the U.S. Chamber of Commerce, Microsoft, the American Federation of Labor and Congress of Industrial Organizations, Wal-Mart, Major League Baseball, the National Roofing Contractors Association, the Florida Fruit and Vegetable Association, the Catholic Church, and the National Association of Evangelicals—to address immigration issues. Political action committees (PACs) have contributed hundreds of thousands of dollars to the campaigns of members of Congress.[3] Even other nations, including South Korea, Ireland, Poland, Tibet, Hong Kong, and Canada, hire Washington, D.C., lobbyists to represent their interests and concerns regarding immigration policy, including visa quotas and allotments.[4] Clearly, comprehensive immigration reform was one of the biggest games in town.

Indeed, big money is always at stake when the president, members of Congress, and the public are debating

< Whenever Congress is in session, you will find lobbyists seeking access to our elected officials in order to try to influence their decisions. Here, interest-group representatives gather outside a congressional hearing room, awaiting the results of their lobbying efforts.

an important and controversial bill, and many institutions hire lobbyists to represent their interests and to seek benefits. These interest groups range from large corporations and labor unions to universities and colleges like the one you attend.

In 2013, nearly 12,000 registered lobbyists presented the interests of various groups and individuals before the members of Congress and their staffs and before executive branch officials. Together they accounted for $2.38 billion in spending for lobbying in 2013—a decline from 2010, when the tab for influencing Washington's policymakers was calculated to be $3.5 billion.[5] Although some groups that engage in lobbying—for example, universities, sports teams, and the American Red Cross—are seen as being as American as apple pie, many Americans consider most interest groups and the lobbyists that represent them in a different and harsher light. They see lobbyists as wheeler-dealers and government as being influenced by a relatively few big interests. They suspect interest groups of being driven by self-interest, dishonest, and prone to corrupting the political process by attempting to unduly influence government decision makers. They are convinced that these special interests are constantly attempting to "buy" members of Congress and other elected officials through campaign contributions.

Public opinion polls often reflect such skepticism. One recent poll found that 71 percent of the public believe that lobbyists have "too much" power, whereas 62 percent of the public rate the honesty and ethical standards of lobbyists as "very low or low."[6] These public sentiments are not new. Although he spoke of them in terms of "factions," James Madison (in "Federalist Paper No. 10") is often cited to show that there have been concerns about interest groups ever since our constitutional government was formed. But Madison understood that factions are a natural part of politics, and he and the other Framers attempted to design a system that would welcome the participation of many interests while curbing potential abuses through elaborate forms of institutional and political checks and balances. Although the Madisonian approach to dealing with factions and interests has endured for more than two centuries, many Americans continue to question the roles of special-interest groups and lobbyists in government activities.

Apparently many (if not most) Americans believe in the *myth that interest groups are a corrupting influence in politics*. Although there is no doubt that many interest groups attempt to exercise some influence over the policymaking process—that is, after all, a major reason for their having representation in Washington—the question of whether they exercise a corrupt influence requires a reality check. Before we can evaluate the myth and reality of interest groups, however, we must look at the role they play in American politics and at the resources and techniques that they use to influence politics. Only then can we make more sense of the role of interest groups in the political system.

Movers and Shakers: Interest and Other Advocacy Groups

> **What are the differences between interest groups and political action committees (PACs)?**

Our first task is to define three key terms: *interest groups*, *lobbyists*, and *PACs*.

Interest Groups

A political **interest group** is any organized group of individuals who share common goals and who seek to influence government decision making.[7] Such diverse groups as the National Rifle Association, the Sierra Club, the U.S. Chamber of Commerce, and the League of Women Voters all fit this definition. Universities frequently lobby for policies and programs that advance higher education (see Table 9.1 and the Asked & Answered feature on p. 294). Even college students are represented by interest groups—for instance, the United States Student Association and the American Student Association of Community Colleges.

Interest group Any organized group of individuals who share common goals and who seek to influence government decision making.

TABLE 9.1 **Federal Grant Funding, Lobbying Expenditures, and Campaign Contributions: The Top Ten Universities**

University	2011 Federal Grant Funding	2012 Lobbying Expenditures	2012 Campaign Contributions
Johns Hopkins University	$1,880,000,000	$800,000	$502,291
University of Washington	$949,000,000	$650,000	$674,959
University of Michigan	$820,000,000	$335,000	$651,142
University of Pennsylvania	$707,000,000	$913,358	$693,455
University of Pittsburgh	$662,000,000	$670,000	$243,612
Stanford University	$656,000,000	$470,000	$2,369,449
Columbia University	$645,000,000	$104,145	$1,116,537
University of California	$637,000,000	$1,000,000	$3,144,466
University of Wisconsin	$594,000,000	$400,000	$495,984
Duke University	$585,000,000	$585,000	$441,051

Source: OpenSecrets Blog, www.opensecrets.org, June 5, 2013.

ASKED & ANSWERED

ASKED: *Are college students represented by interest groups?*

ANSWERED: With nearly 12,000 lobbyists registered in Washington, D.C. (many more are not registered, because the rules are unclear and the penalties for not registering are small), you'd assume that college students would have interest-group representation in the nation's capital. After all, billions of dollars are spent every year by the federal government on higher education, and many laws enacted by Congress have a direct (or often an indirect) impact on college students. More than $90 million was spent on federal education lobbying in 2012 by colleges, universities, and higher-learning-related associations and industries.*

Indeed, groups in Washington represent college students on campuses across the country. As Philip Sharp, former director of Harvard University's Institute of Politics, suggested, college students are "rising activists and rising players in the political system."† With activism often comes organization, and with organization can come formal interest-group representation.

Two specific groups that represent college students are the United States Student Association (USSA) and the American Student Association of Community Colleges (ASACC). The USSA is, in its own words, "the country's oldest and largest national student organization, representing millions of students."‡ Founded in 1947, USSA regards itself as the major voice of college and university students from around the nation, representing more than 4.5 million students at more than four hundred campuses. The tools used by the USSA are similar to those employed by many other interest groups. As part of its mission, "The organization tracks and lobbies federal legislation and policy, and organizes students from across the country to participate in the political process, through testifying in official Congressional hearings, letter-writing

campaigns, and face-to-face lobby visits between students and their elected officials."§ In addition, employing the traditional tactics and tools of lobbyists, the USSA trains and organizes students on campuses, focusing on issues including school fee hikes, recruitment and retention of underrepresented students, and lobbying to improve campus safety. On March 26, 2010, two days before Congress passed the historic Health Care and Educational Reconciliation Act, which overhauled the federal student aid system, USSA cosponsored a major rally in Washington, D.C., in support of the bill.

The USSA is not the only interest group whose lobbying has had an impact on college students. The ASACC is an advocacy group for more than 12 million students attending community and junior colleges across the nation. An active voice in Washington, D.C., on many of the issues that the USSA also supports, the ASACC's work in recent years has included lobbying for increases in student Pell Grants, reauthorizing the Higher Education Act, and increasing other federal sources of student aid. The ASACC works with other groups in ensuring that the interests of community college students are represented in Congress and the executive branch.

All of these efforts are geared toward helping college students make sense of government's role in higher education. Indeed, these efforts make the answer to our original question crystal clear. Are college students represented by interest groups? They are, most definitely.

Source: United States Student Association homepage, www.usstudents.org, and American Student Association of Community Colleges homepage, www.asacc.org.

* *Center for Responsive Politics, opensecrets.org, 2013.*

†*National Press Club news conference, Washington, DC, April 19, 2005.*

‡*www.usstudents.org/about/history*

§*www.usstudents.org/about/history*

Students call for increased higher education funding during a rally sponsored by the U.S. Student Association.

Interest groups differ from political parties.[8] Chapter 7, on political parties, emphasized that parties are broad-based coalitions, with policies on a wide range of issues. A party's ultimate goal is to contest and win elections in order to control and operate government. In contrast, interest groups put forth a limited set of demands.* Although they sometimes try to affect the outcome of certain elections, they do not run candidates for office or attempt to control or operate government. Their primary concern is to influence policy in their own area of interest.

Interest groups differ in size and makeup and pursue varying objectives. They also serve as an important link between their members and elected and appointed government officials. What justifies the existence of interest groups in a democratic, representative form of government is their role in making members of the executive, legislative, and judicial branches of government more aware of the needs and concerns of various groups in America. Many people join interest groups to promote their own economic well-being or to effect political and social change. They believe that their goals are best served by acting together with other citizens. Indeed, although we regard ourselves as a very individualistic society, we also join groups fairly frequently. We are far more likely to join organizations and groups than are the English, the French, Italians, and Germans, for example.

Some interest groups, such as Common Cause and the Christian Coalition, have positions on a wide range of issues. Even these two groups, however, usually focus on a few key issues and direct their resources toward them.

Economic Interest Groups. Among interest groups, business, labor, professional, and agricultural groups are the most enduring and powerful types. That fact is hardly surprising, given the intensity of most people's preoccupation with their own economic welfare.

Thousands of individual corporations and businesses employ lobbyists, or spokespersons for the corporation or business, in Washington.[9] The concerns of these organizations depend on the business in question and on the political climate. Tax laws, government subsidies, antitrust laws, tariffs on imported goods, and consumer product and environmental regulations may all affect the cost of doing business. In recent years, issues such as the financial credit crisis, failing home mortgages, unemployment, changes to immigration policy, and the establishment of a national health insurance program have led to increased lobbying efforts on the part of the business community.

Business and trade associations are another type of economic interest group. Under the umbrella of business associations are the large and influential U.S. Chamber of Commerce; the Business Roundtable, made up of more than 160 chief executive officers of the largest industrial, commercial, and financial businesses in the nation; and many other groups. These associations represent some of the most powerful interests of corporate America.

Trade associations, which represent entire industries, also have widely divergent interests, ranging from government regulation of food and drugs to regulation of the import of beef from Argentina. These groups are interested in government regulations that may affect the way their members do business. The National Cable Television Association, for example, closely monitors government regulations covering the cable industry—regulations that may have an impact on how much you and I have to pay for cable television service. Even lobbyists have a trade association, the American League of Lobbyists.

Another important type of economic interest group is labor organizations. The American Federation of Labor and Congress of Industrial Organizations (AFL-CIO) is an umbrella organization of fifty-seven labor unions with 12 million members. Overall, the number of union members in the United States is approximately 15 million, although this figure represents a decline in membership over the past four decades. The AFL-CIO, along with large unions such as the American Federation of State, County and Municipal Employees (AFSCME); the United Auto Workers; and the Teamsters, has for many years represented the interests of labor in the state capitals, municipalities, and counties as well as in Washington. Smaller individual labor unions also lobby independently. For example, the Independent Federation of Flight Attendants keeps on top of airline industry issues, and representatives of the International Brotherhood of Boilermakers, Iron Ship Builders, Blacksmiths, Forgers & Helpers focus their attention on legislation related to their interests, including shipbuilding, tool making, and construction of nuclear and fossil-fuel plants.

Professional associations also bring the economic interests of their particular membership to the government's attention. Two of the most powerful, the American Bankers Association and the Association of Trial Lawyers of America, have large lobbying budgets and maintain full-time staffs in Washington and in many state capitals. Smaller, less powerful associations, such as the Clowns of

America, have fewer resources but also try to protect their members' interests with regard to workers' compensation, tax laws, and other legislation affecting their professions.

Farmers, as an economic interest group, are a relatively strong economic force in contemporary American politics, as upward of 20 percent of the workforce is directly or indirectly employed in agribusiness. One of the major goals of agricultural interest groups is protection from fluctuating prices for meat, grain, fruit, and other agricultural products, which affect the income of the groups' members.

Citizen Activist Interest Groups. Not all interests are purely economic. In the past three decades, there has been an increase in the number of citizen activist groups. These groups often represent what they deem to be the interests of the public and so are referred to as **public interest groups**.[10] Other organizations focus on specific causes or serve as advocates for those who are not able to represent themselves.[11]

Public interest groups such as Common Cause (a liberal grassroots organization supported by member dues), Public Citizen, Inc. (a loose affiliation of consumer groups supported by foundation grants), and the Christian Coalition (a conservative group seeking to protect the values of some Christians) were part of an explosion of citizen lobbies beginning in the 1960s. Public interest groups have tried to represent what they see as the public's interests on such issues as civil rights, consumer protection, campaign reform, environmental regulation, and family values.

An activist group with an extremely narrow focus is known as a **single-issue group**. For example, the major goal of the Bass Anglers' Sportsman Society is to further the interests of bass fishing. The National Rifle Association (NRA) and the Gun Owners of America work to preserve the right of Americans to own handguns and rifles. NARAL Pro-Choice America fights for legislation and court decisions that protect the right of women to have abortions.

Some citizen activist groups serve as advocates for people who may be unable to represent their own interests individually.[12] For instance, the National Association for the Advancement of Colored People, the Child Welfare League of America, and the American Cancer Society assist their target populations by lobbying on legislation relevant to their cause, providing the public with information, and taking cases to court.

Public-Sector Interest Groups. As we discussed in Chapter 3, on federalism and intergovernmental relations, not only do governments receive pressure from lobbyists, they also lobby other governments. San Francisco, Baltimore, Chicago, Chattanooga, and Newark are only a few of the cities that have lobbyists representing their interests in Washington on such matters as grants-in-aid, budget and appropriation legislation, Medicare, housing, and transportation. Indeed, the offices of hundreds of cities and states are listed in the *Washington Representatives Directory*. The efforts of these cities are directed toward ensuring that they receive their share of federal funding—funding that can ease the burden of local taxes. Cities also heavily lobby their state capitals for financial aid, as well as in support of or against legislation that affects them. With many programs and policies being jointly implemented or funded by local and state governments as

Public interest groups Citizen activist groups that try to represent what they deem to be the interests of the public at large.

Single-issue group An activist group that seeks to lobby Congress on a single issue or a narrow range of issues.

Left: Environmental issues have stirred controversy throughout the past four decades. Here, Sierra Club supporters demonstrate in favor of environmental protection reform.
Right: Supporters gather to demonstrate in favor of the Keystone Pipeline, a controversial construction project intended to tap energy sources in North America.

well as by the federal government, many government lobbying groups find that they have to lobby all three levels of government on policy issues ranging from environmental pollution to workplace safety.

In addition to lobbying by governments, many associations of governments and government officials—including the following—represent the collective interests of their members

- The U.S. Conference of Mayors
- The International City Management Association
- The National League of Cities
- The National Association of Counties
- The Council of State Governments
- The National Governors' Association

Local and state governments have come to depend on Washington for funds to pay for everything from public roads to new airports and schools. Public-sector interest groups (collectively made up of mayors, governors, state legislators, or other associations of elected or appointed government officials) often lobby for those funds.

Foreign Nation Interest Groups. As the introduction to this chapter indicated, even foreign nations have lobbyists looking after their interests. Nations such as Turkey, Saudi Arabia, Columbia, China, and Canada have lobbyists in the United States who represent their interests before Congress and the executive branch. Those interests can range from military and economic assistance programs to technical advice on how to build an electric power plant. This globalization of interest-group activity extends to the private sector, too. Groups like Amnesty International, a worldwide watchdog organization, lobby against any government's repression and torture of its citizens. Amnesty International has offices in the United States and Great Britain and throughout the rest of the world.

Lobbyists

Who does the work for an interest group? A **lobbyist** is an individual who works for a specific interest group or who serves as the spokesperson for a specific set of interests. Lobbyists engage in the act of lobbying—that is, they try to affect government decision making by influencing legislators and members of the executive branch to support or reject certain policies or legislation.

Lobbyist An individual who works for a specific interest group or who serves as the spokesperson for a specific set of interests.

Although some interest groups maintain their own staffs of full-time lobbyists, other groups hire a lobbying firm to represent them in Washington or in various state capitals. Increasingly, lobbying has become a professional, full-time occupation. Many lobbyists are lawyers, former members of the executive branch or of Congress, or former employees of one of the hundreds of federal and state agencies. Government experience and contacts, along with accumulated expertise, are valuable assets in the lobbying game.

As we shall see later in this chapter, when we discuss the tactics of interest groups, the effectiveness of the lobbyist as a spokesperson for an interest group is generally central to that interest group's success in achieving its goals.

PACs and Super PACs

If the myth of corruption has tainted interest-group politics in recent years, a major source of that concern has been **political action committees (PACs)**. As we discussed in Chapter 8, on campaigns and elections, these independent organizations are set up to collect campaign contributions from individuals who support their goals and to pass those contributions on to candidates. Many PACs also fund independent efforts at electing favored candidates to office or publicizing support for or against specific legislation.

Political action committee (PAC) An independent organization that can be established by interest groups, officeholders, and political candidates for the sole purpose of contributing money to the campaigns of candidates who sympathize with its aims. PACs are the result of federal laws that prohibit most interest groups from donating money to federal political campaigns.

PACs resulted from a change in campaign finance laws designed to limit interest groups' financial involvement in elections.[13] This change came about in the 1970s, when Congress passed the Federal Election Campaign Act. The act provides for a rigid reporting system covering money raised and spent for campaigns, and it restricts campaign contributions and prohibits corporations and labor unions from directly raising funds for or making contributions to political campaigns. However, Congress permitted unions and corporations to set up and administer independent organizations designed to collect and disburse campaign contributions (see the section on electioneering and policymaking later in this chapter).

Unions invented PACs, but as Figure 9.1 indicates, PACs sponsored by corporations rapidly surpassed union-sponsored PACs in number. Now almost every kind of group uses PACs. Trade and professional groups (e.g., the American Institute of Certified Public Accountants), unions (such as the American Federation of Teachers Committee on Political Education), corporations and businesses (e.g., the American Dental Political Action Committee), and cooperative groups (such as the Committee for Thorough Agricultural Political Education of Associated

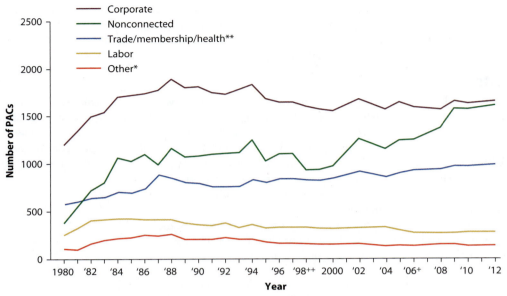

*"Other" category consists of PACs formed by corporations without capital stock and incorporated cooperatives.

**To better reflect statement of organization reporting, trade and membership organizations are now separate categories. Health organizations are no longer an organization type but are included in either the trade or membership categories. This category change occurred in July 2011.

+During the second six months of 2005, 189 PACs were administratively terminated because of inactivity.

++During the first six months of 1997, 227 PACs were administratively terminated because of inactivity.

FIGURE 9.1 An Explosion of PACs, 1974–2013

Unions invented PACs, but corporations forged ahead with them when they were in their infancy. Corporate, union, and trade PACs have tended to support candidates, whereas nonaffiliated PACs have worked on negative campaigns.

Source: Federal Election Commission press releases.

Milk Producers, Inc.) have PACs that solicit and contribute money to political campaigns. More than 12,000 PACs are registered in Washington, D.C.[14]

The outcome of two Supreme Court cases in 2010 prompted the formation of **super PACs**.[15] As discussed in Chapter 8, super PACs are barred from making direct contributions to the campaigns of any political candidate. However, unlike traditional PACs, super PACs may raise unlimited contributions from corporations, unions, professional and business associations, and individuals for the purpose of making unlimited independent expenditures in favor of or against a candidate running for the presidency or for Congress. Super PACs, as the name implies, are regarded by many critics of campaign financing as a significant force in distorting the campaign finance process and in providing unchecked influence on elections by wealthy individuals as well as corporations, unions, and professional and business organizations. Only time will tell whether this apprehension is justified.

What Makes an Interest Group Powerful?

> ## > What factors determine the power of an interest group?

What accounts for the success of interest groups? What problems do they experience or create? In this section, we focus on six factors that strengthen or weaken interest-group activity: size, unity, leadership, information and expertise, money, and countervailing forces.

Size

Size is a major factor affecting an interest group's power. Large organizations, such as the AFL-CIO or the U.S. Chamber of Commerce, have the potential to mobilize vast amounts of money, information, time, and energy in the service of an issue. The success of unions' support of the minimum hourly wage is a measure of the importance of size as a component of political power. The success in the mid-1990s of the U.S. Chamber of Commerce's efforts in support of the North American Free Trade Agreement with Mexico and Canada is an indication of the political impact of the chamber's membership and size.

The importance of the size of a group's membership varies among interest groups. Corporate interest groups that are not membership organizations and trade associations, which generally have relatively few members, obviously need not pay much attention to membership size. On the other hand, unions and citizens' groups, which traditionally claim large memberships and mass representation, do place a high value on membership size.[16]

In evaluating the impact of size, the key word is *potential*. Many large interest groups have little or no influence over the political opinions and participation of their membership. Indeed, a large membership is often difficult both to manage and to influence.[17] But, if the leaders of large interest groups such as the AFL-CIO or the U.S. Chamber of Commerce can convince elected officials, administrators, and congressional staff that they can mobilize their membership behind a policy, size becomes very important. Elected officials are often impressed and influenced by interest groups that have a large membership, including their constituents.

Unity

A group's power is also strongly affected by the unity of its members. In recent legislative battles to reform the Social Security and Medicare systems, the American Association of Retired People (AARP) was sure that its large membership was united. Such unity on the issues of Medicare and Social Security expressed by its membership gave the AARP enormous strength in overcoming changes it did not support. Congress, the president, and the bureaucracy cannot ignore the preferences of millions of organized individuals who are united by a common goal.

When an interest group lacks unity on an issue, its influence on the policymaking process drops considerably, even if the group is large. Internal disagreements

Super PACs Officially known as "independent-expenditure only committees," super PACs may raise unlimited contributions from corporations, unions, professional and business associations, and individuals for the purpose of making unlimited expenditures in favor of or against a candidate running for federal office. Like traditional PACs, a super PAC must report the names of all its donors to the Federal Election Commission. Unlike traditional PACs, super PACs are barred from making direct contributions to the campaigns of any political candidate.

often work against a group's interests. For example, agreement is rare across all of the petroleum industry, in which companies differ in size from giants such as Exxon Mobil to the smaller, independent "wildcat" companies. One lobbyist for the American Petroleum Institute, a trade association representing oil interests, suggested that consensus on some issues was a "long time coming." When such consensus is lacking, the institute often takes "no stand" at all, even if the issues affect its membership across the board.[18]

Leadership

Size and group unity do not necessarily ensure success, however. Interest groups must also have leaders who command respect and who can articulate and represent the issues and demands of the organization. Without such leadership, the interest group is headless and, more often than not, is ineffective in pushing its goals.

One example of effective leadership is provided by Marian Wright Edelman, head of the Washington-based Children's Defense Fund, which lobbies on health and social service issues on behalf of children. Highly respected by many members of Congress, she and her organization have been very successful in supporting programs that have a beneficial impact on the lives of children.

Information and Expertise

What lobbyists know—their ability to collect information, evaluate its importance, and pass it on to appropriate government officials—is critical to their success. Faced with the need to make decisions on a variety of issues, public officials need credible and trustworthy information. Thus, an interest group that can present its

Many interest groups representing less powerful constituencies must fight for the attention of elected officials. Shown here is Marian Wright Edelman, leader of the Children's Defense Fund and a leading advocate for the rights of children.

expertise cogently and convincingly has a distinct advantage over less informed and less articulate organizations. Patrick Healy, who was powerful and successful as chief lobbyist for the National Milk Producers' Federation, argues that facts are the major resource of lobbying and that being able to provide accurate information to members of Congress and their staffs is the key to a lobbyist's success. Few of his colleagues would disagree with him.

The effectiveness of a group's expertise and the delivery of its information also depend on the perception of the group's motives. The health insurance industry's position on smoking is presumed to be in the public interest and hence is heeded by Congress and the public. But its stand against the public option funding of national health insurance is often viewed with some skepticism, as it may have stemmed from the insurance company's economic self-interest.

Money

Lobbying, collecting information, and other such activities cost money. In addition to the lobbyists' salaries, there are expenses for office space, support staff, telephones, office equipment, and travel. Some groups hire professional lobbying firms, and the costs of these services can be significant. A large budget may not be an interest group's most critical resource, but adequate funding is essential.

Fundraising tactics differ from group to group. Many citizen activist groups, such as the Sierra Club and the American Automobile Association (AAA), rely on an annual membership fees. For these groups, finding enough members to maintain the organization can be a problem. A hiker or camper need not join the Sierra Club in order to benefit from its achievements in improving environmental conditions and preserving national parks. In turn, you don't have to be a member of the AAA in order to benefit from their lobbying efforts to increase federal and state spending on highways. To get around this problem of **free riders**—those who benefit from the actions of interest groups without spending time or money to aid them—groups may seek funding from foundations that favor an interest group's goals. Groups may also offer special services and resources to help recruit members.[19] They may provide members with free publications, technical journals, informative newsletters, reduced insurance rates, and even the opportunity to combine business with pleasure at annual meetings held in vacation resorts. For example, the AARP provides its members with low-cost health insurance policies and a money market fund as well as all sorts of travel and entertainment discounts.[20] The members of the National Rifle Association can buy ammunition, handguns, and rifles at discount prices.

Economic groups often have easier access to funds. Groups such as the U.S. Chamber of Commerce and the National Association of Manufacturers receive dues from their corporate and individual members. Many companies use corporate funds to cover the cost of maintaining a staff lobbyist or hiring a lobbying firm. Organizations that people must join in order to keep their jobs can certainly count on financial support from their members. This is typical of many trade and industrial jobs and even some professions. Carpenters and plumbers must join their unions, and physicians, lawyers, and other professionals find themselves under pressure to join professional associations.

Free riders Those who benefit from the actions of interest groups without spending time or money to aid those groups.

Countervailing Forces

Whether an interest group is challenged effectively by one or more other interest groups can have a significant impact on the influence and power of that interest group. In effect, the larger and more powerful the countervailing forces are, the less power an opposing interest group will have. Few or no countervailing forces can provide an interest group with a monopoly in influencing the policies and programs linked with that interest group. The American Boilermakers Association can often monopolize policy regarding its industry (construction of commercial boilers), for example, because of the absence or near-absence of any rival forces to oppose them. In turn, the American Automobile Association, a strong advocate for the funding of highways, often finds itself competing with trade associations like the Association of American Railroads and Airlines for America for scarce federal and state funding of transportation projects.

Interest-Group Tactics: "You Don't Lobby with Hundred-Dollar Bills and Wild Parties"

> **What tools do interest groups use in attempting to influence the policymaking process?**

Interest groups are as powerful as their size, unity, leadership, expertise, and funds enable them to be. A group need not have all of these resources, but the more of them that it has, the better. Of course, no single resource will make or break a group. More often than not, success comes from effectively combining organizational resources and the tactics used to influence policymaking.

"You don't lobby with hundred-dollar bills and wild parties. You lobby with facts," says former lobbyist Patrick Healy. As you will see, however, money counts, although it is only one of many tools used by interest groups to influence government.

Lobbying

Lobbying The act of trying to influence government decision makers; it is named after the public rooms in which it first took place.

As you learned earlier in this chapter, **lobbying** is the act of trying to influence government decision makers. Named after the public rooms, lobbies, in which it first took place, lobbying now goes on in hearing rooms, offices, golf courses, and restaurants—any spot where a lobbyist can gain a hearing and effectively present a case.

Lobbyists' stock in trade is their relationships with government officials and their staffs and, for the most part, their ability to provide accurate and timely information (see Table 9.2). There are, indeed, some unscrupulous lobbyists who use bribes to curry favors and support from dishonest and corrupt government officials. But most lobbyists, the more than 520,000 elected U.S. officials, and the administrators in the more than 89,000 units of government in the nation maintain relationships not with bribes and favors, as the myth of corruption implies, but with data—the technical information that members of Congress and

TABLE 9.2 What Lobbyists Do

Despite the myth of corrupting influence, lobbyists do not spend all of their time "endorsing candidates" or contributing to political campaigns. As these data demonstrate, building relationships and seeking and disseminating information are their main activities.

Type of Activity	Percentage of Lobbyist's Time Involved in Activity
Building relationships	23
Providing and seeking information	18
Research and analysis	17
Preparing and testifying before Congress	10
Working with congressional staff	6
Building legislative coalitions	5
Mobilizing public opinion	4
Lobbying legislators	3

Source: Rogan Kersh, "The Well-Informed Lobbyist: Information and Interest Group Lobbying," in *Interest Group Politics*, ed. Allan J. Cigler and Burdett A. Loomis (Washington, D.C.: Congressional Quarterly Press, 2007), p. 393.

bureaucrats need in order to carry out their committee and administrative assignments. Because their work demands a level of expertise on a wide range of topics that few can muster, they come to depend on lobbyists' information and recommendations regarding the thousands of issues on which they must decide. Lobbyists even draft legislation, write speeches, and help plan legislative strategy. For most lobbyists, however, building relationships and presenting research results or technical information to public officials are the most important and time-consuming parts of their jobs.[21]

Once an interest group proves itself as a source of dependable information, it has easier access to officials. Lobbyists also share that expertise at congressional hearings, presenting research or technical information or discussing the impact of a bill on national, state, or local interests. Knowing how important constituents' concerns are to legislators, lobbyists are quick to point to the impact of a bill on a representative's home district or state. Whenever they can, interest groups mobilize the folks at home to write and call members of Congress to stress the importance of particular issues.

As was mentioned previously, unethical lobbyists do exist, and they support the myth of corruption. In the early years of the republic, presenting gifts to or bribing willing legislators was a not uncommon way of influencing the passage of a specific bill. Indeed, in 1833, as prominent a senator as Daniel Webster was on retainer to the Bank of the United States, which was fighting for its survival. Webster wrote to the bank president: "My retainer has not been renewed or refreshed as usual. If it is wished that my relation to the Bank should be continued, it may be well to send me the usual retainer."[22]

An important way in which lobbyists can influence public policy is to have contact with members of Congress or their staff or to testify at congressional hearings on policies that they support or oppose. Here, representatives from Wall Street testify before the House Finance Committee.

Despite their reputation for bribery and corruption, however, most interest groups today function within the law. Nevertheless, Congress has found it necessary from time to time to pass laws regulating these groups and their representatives. It was in 1887 that Congress first required lobbyists to register with the House of Representatives. Additional laws since that time have mandated that lobbyists file reports listing their clients, describing their activities, and recording the amount of money spent. Recent legislation, including the 1995 Lobbying Restrictions Act and the Honest Leadership and Open Government Act of 2007, has sought to regulate lobbying in Washington, although there are still many loopholes in the law that prevent effective overall control over lobbying activities.[23]

In their relations with government officials, lobbyists' actions are governed by one major rule: *A lobbyist should never lie.* This may seem to you to be strange or untrue, but it is the way most lobbyists work. As one member of Congress put it, "It doesn't take very long to figure which lobbyists are straightforward, and which ones are trying to snow you. The good ones will give you the weak points as well as the strong points of their case. If anyone ever gives me false or misleading information, that's it—I'll never see him again."[24] When 175 lobbyists were asked what resources were most important to their success, an overwhelming majority singled out the reputation for being credible and trustworthy.[25]

Electioneering and Policymaking

Electioneering
Participating in the election process by providing services or raising campaign contributions.

Participating in the election process—**electioneering**—is an important tactic of many interest groups. As part of that tactic, both interest groups and political action committees have become very important to candidates.

During the 2012 election cycle, PACs raised approximately $1.48 billion, of which approximately $453.3 million was contributions to federal candidates and other costs related to Senate and House races. Few congressional candidates, incumbent or not, refuse PAC funding of their expensive campaigns. (See Table 9.3 for a list of major PAC contributors.)

PACs' patterns of giving reflect their partisan persuasions. In 2012, for example, labor-sponsored PACs, which are traditionally strong supporters of the Democratic Party, channeled their contributions primarily to Democratic candidates. Although corporate-sponsored PACs generally target a majority of their contributions to Republican candidates, who controls the presidency and the two houses of Congress can influence the business community's patterns of contribution.

Do PAC contributions influence politicians' decisions? Do the recipients of campaign funds support the donors' programs? Interest groups apparently think they do. In one study, 58 percent of interest-group representatives said that they used campaign contributions as a means of influencing the policymaking process.[26] Despite that belief, there is limited evidence that campaign contributions guarantee support of a lobbyist's position or votes on a bill. In general, what a gift may do is ensure that representatives of an interest group will have easier access to elected officials or their staffs. This is important in itself, for such access allows

POLITICS & POPULAR CULTURE: Visit the book's companion website at **www.oup.com/us/gitelson** to read the special feature *What's in a Name? The Case of Hidden Lobbies.*

TABLE 9.3 Top Twenty PAC Contributors to Candidates During the 2011–2012 Election Cycle

PAC Name	Total Amount	% to Democrats	% to Republicans
National Association of Realtors	$3,960,282	44	55
National Beer Wholesalers Association	$3,388,500	41	59
Honeywell International	$3,193,024	41	59
Operating Engineers Union	$3,186,387	84	15
National Auto Dealers Association	$3,074,000	28	72
International Brotherhood of Electrical Workers	$2,853,000	97	2
American Bankers Association	$2,736,150	20	80
AT&T Inc.	$2,543,000	35	65
American Association for Justice	$2,512,500	96	3
Credit Union National Association	$2,487,600	47	52
Blue Cross/Blue Shield	$2,401,398	35	65

Source: http://www.opensecrets.org/pacs/toppacs.php?Type=C&cycle=2012

lobbyists to present and argue their positions and to influence the agenda of Congress. However, although the list of the top twenty PAC contributors in Table 9.3 is impressive, we shouldn't be misled. A majority of the more than 5,570 registered PACs in Washington donate little or nothing to political campaigns but instead keep a safe arm's-length distance from the financing of the campaign process.

Although some studies claim that campaign contributions by PACs influence the policymaking process, other studies assert that there is no clear link between money and policymaking. Many legislators argue that PAC funds are not intended to buy congressional votes; rather, their purpose is to support legislators who are already committed to the PAC's positions. As former Representative Jack Fields said in responding to allegations of PAC influence through financial contributions, "I haven't changed my philosophy in the fifteen years I've been in Congress. My philosophy has always been free enterprise and to support whatever creates jobs, and those who want to contribute to me are free to do so."[27] Nevertheless, the 2014 congressional elections saw both record PAC contributions and a growing skepticism on the part of citizens about the role that money plays in the campaign and policymaking process.

According to the Federal Election Campaign Act (left unchanged by the Bipartisan Campaign Finance Reform Act of 2002), PACs can donate no more than $5,000 per candidate per election (primaries and general elections count as separate elections), a restriction motivated by a history of interest-group contributions that sometimes reached tens of thousands of dollars for a single candidate. Because candidates must now seek out more contributors to their campaigns to ensure sufficient funding, a single group may have less influence on a candidate than it expects. However, the $5,000-per-candidate restriction makes it possible for PACs to support more candidates, for the number of campaigns to which a PAC may contribute is unlimited. This outcome is disturbing to many reformers, who had hoped to restrict, not increase, the involvement of interest groups in campaigns.

Interest-group activity in campaigns has given rise to other concerns as well. As we discussed in Chapter 8, a recent U.S. Supreme Court decision declared unconstitutional a number of restrictions placed on campaign spending by corporations and unions. The decision expands the opportunity for well-funded corporations and unions to influence the election process.[28] The role of PACs in funding federal elections through contributions at the state level also continues to provide PACs with a very powerful campaign financing tool. Clearly, interest groups and their respective PACs will continue to have a significant impact on the election process.

Interest groups support campaigns in other ways besides PAC contributions. Labor, trade, and professional associations supply candidates with volunteers and offer public endorsements. The AFL-CIO, Americans for Democratic Action, and the American Conservative Union are just three of the many interest groups and PACs that provide their members and the public with voting scorecards on candidates they support or target for defeat. By listing key votes, the cards can praise or damn the candidate. The National Congressional Club PAC specializes in so-called negative campaigns, or putting down the opposition. This group has spent large sums in the past, particularly on television advertisements, in an effort to defeat liberal candidates. In turn, the AFL-CIO has financed expensive television advertising campaigns that have both directly and indirectly supported Democratic candidates for Congress as well as financing campaigns against candidates who have not been prolabor.

Interest groups do not limit their activities to congressional races. Besides pressuring the major parties to include the interest group's goals in the presidential party platforms, a group may turn out in force for important conventions—for example, its members may serve as delegates at the national conventions. Not surprisingly, with many union members in attendance at the 2012 Democratic National Convention, the party took strong platform positions on labor concerns. In 2012, the probusiness, antiregulation platform of the Republican Party was no doubt influenced, in part, by the strong representation of the self-declared conservatives who attended the Republican National Convention.

Building Coalitions

An interest-group tactic that has gained increasing importance is **coalition building**—the bringing together of diverse interest groups in a common lobbying effort. Various groups have formed coalitions to support or prevent the passage of congressional, state, or local legislation. One example of a diverse coalition that supports immigration reform includes groups from high-tech executives and conservative evangelical pastors to union officials, agricultural interests, law enforcement officials, and liberals and libertarians. Increasing the forces in favor of or against legislation can add legitimacy to the lobbying effort and can attract the attention of elected officials. Most signs point to increasing use of coalition building by interest groups and PACs in an effort to influence the policymaking process.

Coalition building
The bringing together of diverse interest groups in a common lobbying effort.

Grassroots Pressure: Power to the People

The word *grassroots* is a people-centered term. In interest-group politics, **grassroots pressure** refers to lobbying by rank-and-file members of an interest group—often just ordinary citizens—who use such tactics as letter writing and public protests to influence government.

When the National Beer Wholesalers Association wanted to be exempted from antitrust legislation, it mobilized grassroots support for a massive letter, telephone, and telegram campaign. Truly a "bottoms-up" effort to stimulate pressure from the grassroots level, the campaign was supported by political contributions from the association's political action committee—which, as you have no doubt guessed, is often called SIXPAC.

Grassroots activity includes face-to-face meetings between members of Congress and selected constituents, as well as demonstrations and protests. When interest groups mobilize grassroots mail and telephone campaigns, they tend to focus on narrow issues and to direct their efforts toward specific members of Congress. On any given issue, "lobbyists understand intuitively what political scientists have demonstrated empirically: members of Congress are more influenced by their constituents than by Washington lobbies."[29] For that reason, many interest groups stress grassroots efforts.

Grassroots pressure
Lobbying by rank-and-file members of an interest group who use such tactics as letter writing and public protests to influence government.

Indeed, grassroots mobilization has evolved into a highly professional undertaking. In an article appearing in *Campaigns & Elections* magazine, the author argues that "the planned orchestrated demonstration of public support through the mobilization of constituent action is . . . one of the hottest trends in politics today. . . . Interest groups that don't play the game risk becoming political eunuchs."[30] Today, professional grassroots lobbying is a billion-dollar industry. An interest-group representative may call members of the public and solicit their opinion on a topic; if their opinion coincides with the position of the interest group, the individuals are offered an immediate and direct telephone hookup with their representatives in Congress. In this way, interest groups try to ensure that grassroots opinions favorable to them reach the appropriate legislators. As *Washington Post* correspondents Haynes Johnson and David Broder point out, "there's nothing spontaneous about this kind of operation." It has been called "astroturfing"—a reference to the synthetic grass used on many football, soccer, and baseball fields.[31] Unlike spontaneous grassroots activity generated by citizens who are concerned about an issue, astroturfing is "public opinion" that is systematically organized and generated by an interest group.

Litigation

Many pressure groups, particularly public interest and advocacy groups, also use the courts to influence policy.[32] They bring direct suits, challenge existing laws, or file briefs as "friends of the court" to support one side in cases that are already before the court.

Although it is expensive and time-consuming, litigation can bring about remarkable political change. Perhaps the outstanding example is the use of the courts by the National Association for the Advancement of Colored People (NAACP). In a series of cases, culminating in the *Brown v. Board of Education* decision in 1954, NAACP lawyers argued and the Supreme Court affirmed that school segregation was illegal in the United States. Women's groups, consumer groups, environmental groups, religious groups, and others have followed the lead of the civil rights movement in taking their causes to the courts. Corporations and trade associations have also engaged in litigation. However, the high cost restrains many groups. One interest group, the Women's Equity League, was unable to appeal a court ruling against it in an important case because it could not afford the $40,000 necessary to pay for copies of the trial transcript.[33]

Using another approach, groups try to influence the composition of the Supreme Court by opposing or supporting judicial nominees. In 2005, President George W. Bush's nominee to the Supreme Court, Harriet Miers, was strongly opposed by both conservative and liberal groups. Miers was President Bush's chief White House counsel and a longtime

In 2010, the Supreme Court extended the power of corporations and unions to contribute to federal election campaigns. Here, Citizens United president David Bossie, a key actor in the litigation, talks to reporters in front of the Supreme Court in Washington, D.C., about campaign finance.

ally, dating back to the time he was governor of Texas. Many prominent conservatives opposed the nomination, questioning her qualifications and her judicial philosophy, which they felt was not conservative enough. Liberal groups charged cronyism and also expressed the belief that Miers was not qualified to be on the Supreme Court. President Bush eventually withdrew the nomination as support in Congress faded and public opinion turned against the nomination.

Hard-Line Tactics

In recent years, a number of interest groups have used hard-line tactics, including civil disobedience and illegal action, to further their cause. Groups like ACT UP drew public attention to the plight of AIDS victims by disrupting public events, and organizations like Operation Rescue have received a great deal of attention because they advocate illegally blocking access to abortion clinics. Hard-line tactics appear to be a growing mechanism for presenting an interest group's cause. Recent demonstrations and protests by members of the Tea Party movement against a national health care bill, deficit spending, and immigration reform have focused on placing pressure on elected officials to respond to the group's causes.

Interest Groups and Democracy

> Do interest groups play a role in the representative process?

Interest groups pose a number of problems for a democratic society. In "Federalist No. 10," James Madison argued that the rise of factions is inevitable in a democracy. Although he believed that factions could destroy the policymaking process, he did not want to prohibit them, for that would undermine the basic tenets of a participatory republic. Instead, Madison hoped that the divisiveness of factions would be tempered both by built-in checks and balances and by a political system that would ensure the creation of competing factions.

Interest groups do distort the democratic process to some degree, mainly because their membership is clearly biased toward the upper half of the socioeconomic ladder. To the extent that business, labor, and professional groups have exceptional influence, policy is distorted.

However, many groups, including some of the public interest groups that we discussed earlier in this chapter, seek to help and represent less affluent and underserved citizens, including the homeless and the poor. Although the distribution of representation by interest groups in the United States remains distorted, with the advantaged being better represented than the disadvantaged, there is reason to believe that the public increasingly recognizes the need for broad representation in a society based on strong interest-group representation.

Conclusion

Unquestionably, interest groups have come to wield increasing political power, and Americans' fear of these groups as a corrupting influence in politics has some basis in reality. With large treasuries to disburse and an inside track with public officials, at any given time they are potentially a distorting influence on the functioning of the political system. Broad national interests can be lost in the clamor of pressure-group activity and narrow self-interests. Interest groups also work out of public view, thus encouraging the popular belief that the public cannot adequately scrutinize their activities.

Some observers believe that we do not give enough credit to the benefits of interest-group activity. They argue that not every group with a shared interest is *self*-interested. Like the proverbial concept of beauty, an interest group's "goodness" or "badness" is often in the eye of the beholder. To see only the biasing effects of interest groups, they maintain, is to perpetuate the myth of corrupting influence. Interest groups are also a healthy feature of and a positive force in the political process. They are organizations that sometimes give voice to the voiceless and represent the unrepresented or underrepresented. According to this view, advances for many minority groups, the poor, the young, the aged, and others who are disadvantaged, and for farmers, laborers, and owners of small businesses, can be attributed in part to the effective activities of interest groups. For example, if it were not for organizations like the NAACP and their Legal Defense Fund, the civil rights movement might have taken decades longer to develop into an influential force. And where would the fight for medical advances, cleaner air and water, safe workplaces, and so on, be if it were not for the efforts of interest groups? In addition, increasing numbers of interest groups often support and fight for programs that benefit and contribute to our democratic process. They serve to supplement our representative body of elected officials by giving citizens an additional voice in government.

Although not everyone is a member of a powerful association with high-paid lobbyists in Washington and the state capitols, there are likely few citizens who are not represented either directly or indirectly by one or more interest groups, whether those groups are concerned with economic, social, or environmental issues.

Madison appropriately warned of the pitfalls of interest groups. He also argued that they are inevitable in any democratic system. We argue that the groups link citizens and public officials through corporate, labor, trade, and professional associations and through citizen activist groups. Such linkages may be worth the price of the real (and imagined) distortions that inevitably occur when interest groups are active in the policymaking process. Certainly, the groups are too useful to simply dismiss by invoking the myth of corrupting influence.

Key Terms

Coalition building p. 309
Electioneering p. 306
Free riders p. 303
Grassroots pressure p. 309
Interest group p. 293
Lobbying p. 304

Lobbyist p. 299
Medicare p. 318
Medicaid p. 318
Political action committees (PACs) p. 299

Public interest groups p. 297
Single-issue group p. 297
Super PACs p. 301

Focus Questions Review

1. **What are the differences between interest groups and political action committees (PACs)? > > >**
   - Interest groups are organized groups of individuals who share one or more common goals and who seek to influence government decision making.
   - PACs, cousin organizations of interest groups, serve as affiliated or independent organizations with the prime function of collecting and disbursing campaign contributions.

2. **What factors determine the power of an interest group? > > >**
   - A number of factors determine the power of an interest group, including size, degree of unity, quality of leadership, information and expertise, money, and the degree to which the interest group monopolizes the policy area.
   - In general, however, given different issues and different political environments, no single resource determines the success of an interest group. A group's influence is usually strongest when it brings a combination of organizational resources to bear on the policymaking process.

3. **What tools do interest groups use in attempting to influence the policymaking process? > > >**
   - Tools used by interest groups in attempting to influence the policymaking process include the following:
     Grassroots pressure
     Lobbying
     Electioneering (which includes financing and supporting campaigns through affiliated PACs)
     Coalition building
     Litigating
     Hard-line tactics

4. **Do interest groups play a role in the representative process? > > >**
   - Interest groups can pose problems for a democratic society because they often represent narrow interests that are biased toward the higher economic groups. Interest groups are important to the political process because they can and do focus our attention on important issues.
   - Although interest groups can be a distorting influence on the political and governmental process, they are also a positive force, giving voice to the voiceless and representing the unrepresented. They serve to supplement the representative process by providing an additional voice in the policymaking process.

Review Questions

1. Discuss the factors that determine the power of an interest group.
2. How do interest groups attempt to influence the policymaking process?

For more information and access to study materials, visit the book's companion website at www.oup.com/us/gitelson.

Policy Connection

How have some interest groups been able to shape American public policies?

The Policy Challenge

Interest groups play a major role in the workings of American government—especially in the policy-making process. Typically (and perhaps ideally), whenever an issue comes before Congress or some other policymaking body, various interest groups spring to action, each seeking to influence the outcome of the process. Which groups get involved and the extent of their efforts to shape a policy often depend on what is at stake. For example, significant numbers of interest groups pay attention to proposals to overhaul the tax code, a policy that affects almost every sector of the U.S. economy. In other areas—such as when the Commodities Credit Corporation, an agency in the U.S. Department of Agriculture, sets annual "loan rates" for raw cane sugar farmers—the number of interests actively paying attention is small.[1]

There are certain policy arenas, however, in which one or two interest groups become so influential that they effectively determine what government does—or does not do—on some specific issue. For example, for many years, the American tobacco industry was able to mount considerable resistance to laws that would limit or restrict the sale or consumption of cigarette—despite evidence of associated health risks.[2] Over the past three decades, the power of the National Rifle Association has been evident in almost every effort to formulate or implement any policy involving gun control.[3] And, as highlighted in the following story of the century-long pursuit of a national health insurance policy, the American Medical Association has been perhaps the most significant obstacle to consideration of such a law.

The Hundred Years War

On March 23, 2010, President Barack Obama signed into law the Patient Protection and Affordable Care Act, commonly called the Affordable Care Act (ACA) or "Obamacare." It was the culmination of a process started during the 2008 presidential election and, as we now know, the start of a long-term battle over the constitutionality, funding, and implementation of a controversial policy. Many analysts believe that the story of the ACA will be the defining narrative of the Obama presidency, and that its success—or failure—will determine how his years in office will be remembered.

For students of American public policy, however, the story behind Obamacare has deeper roots and represents the climax of a century-long struggle initiated by social reformers and pursued by advocates of universal health care coverage through seventeen presidential administrations and numerous sessions of Congress. It is the story of many failed attempts to establish for all Americans the kind of access to health care enjoyed by many Europeans since at least the 1880s. It is also the story of how the opponents of such a policy succeeded in blocking all efforts to develop any kind of national health insurance for more than fifty years, and how they helped to shape the limited health care coverage policies that finally emerged in 1965 and thereafter. Most significant, it is the story of how one particular interest group—the American Medical Association (AMA)—shaped and led that powerful opposition through all those decades.

In 1846, the Medical Society of New York put out a call to other local and state medical societies to convene a national medical convention that would address issues of common concern, including the formation of an association "for the protection of their interests, for the maintenance of their honour [sic] and respectability, and for the advancement of their knowledge, and extension of their usefulness."[4] As with many national interest groups that emerged in the middle to late 1800s, the AMA was a federation of local and state chapters that sent delegates to annual or biannual conferences. The AMA eventually formed a national office with a staff that worked on national issues. The local medical societies, however, remained powerful in their own right, and that strength would prove important for our story.

Other groups that would be important actors in the history of health care policy were also emerging at this time. In addition to labor unions such as the American Federation of Labor and business and trade associations such as the Chamber of Commerce, several other groups were dedicated to bringing about social reform. Of particular importance were the National Conference of Charities and Correction (NCCC) and the American Association for Labor Legislation (AALL).[5] Both pushed for the adoption of social insurance legislations modeled after those in place in the major industrial countries of Europe, especially Germany and England. Whereas the NCCC actively sought to get politicians and political parties to endorse and support legislation to ban child labor, institute ten-hour workdays, encourage safer workplaces, provide unemployment insurance and workman's compensation insurance, and bring about related progressive reforms, the AALL worked on developing and promoting model laws to achieve those goals at all levels of government.

By 1913, the AALL had formed a special committee focused on what was initially called "sickness insurance policies"; this was, in fact, the first serious initiative in the push for a national health insurance (NHI) policy. Their efforts attracted the attention of the AMA,[6] which formed its own committee to work on the proposal, and in 1917 the AMA House of Delegates actually endorsed the need for such policies as part of its commitment to public health. Passage of that resolution was bitterly opposed by a strong minority of delegates from several state medical societies. By the next meeting (1919), they had sufficient votes to table a proposal for an outright endorsement of a national health insurance proposal. That defeat was the beginning of the decades-long AMA war on any kind of NHI policy.[7]

Even before the 1919 meeting, many state and local medical societies had actively joined in the fight against government health insurance by aligning themselves with other groups that opposed the policy. The American Federation of Labor, viewing the AALL's model law as a threat to its own efforts to offer its members health care benefits, attacked the proposals as "paternalistic." Also opposed were major farming and business groups, especially private insurers, who saw government intrusion into their small but lucrative markets. As the United States entered World War I, these groups used anti-German sentiment (because social insurance was closely identified with German government policies) to defeat proposals as they emerged. And, after the war, the nation went through the Red Scare, during which any idea that smacked of European socialism was doomed to defeat.

During the 1920s, several state legislatures considered health care insurance, and it even appeared on the referendum ballot in some states (see Policy Connection 8)—but each time it met with opposition, which was increasingly led by the AMA and its state and local affiliates. In the late 1920s, to offset growing public demand for affordable health insurance, medical societies endorsed the creation of private insurance associations such as Blue Cross (for hospitalization) and Blue Shield (for nonhospital medical service). In addition, as labor unions gained bargaining strength, they made sure to include health coverage as part of the contracted benefits package. By the mid-1950s, nearly 70 percent of Americans were covered under these nongovernmental plans.[8]

But there remained the problem of the uninsured millions. The Great Depression and the electoral victories of Franklin Roosevelt's New Deal Democrats provided another opportunity for the advocates of social insurance legislation to push through an NHI plan.[9] After dealing with the immediate economic emergencies of 1933, FDR turned his attention to what he called "economic security policies." Initially, these involved a national unemployment insurance plan, an old-age pension insurance system (which would become Social Security), and a national health insurance policy similar to European (and particularly British) programs that would provide coverage for all Americans. FDR convened a committee composed of representatives from a wide range of interest groups—including the AMA—to draw up the legislation that would be sent to Congress as a single package. As the group turned its attention to the specifics of the NHI components, the AMA launched what was at that point an unprecedented grassroots campaign. It sent thousands of telegrams to committee members over a single weekend and mobilized anti–health insurance editorials throughout the nation.

Because FDR and his congressional allies realized that such opposition would lead to the defeat of the entire package, they decided to focus on the unemployment and social security insurance provisions. When he finally offered the proposed economic security package to Congress, FDR noted the need to consider health insurance in the future. Thus, despite both the popularity of a health insurance plan (the public opinion polls at the time indicated support ranging up to 80 percent) and FDR's considerable political power, the NHI law was put on the back burner.

NHI advocates in Congress would propose legislation in the years that followed, but they could never convince Roosevelt that the time was ripe. Besides the constant opposition by the AMA and its affiliates and allies, other opponents included conservative (mainly southern) members of Congress holding key committee positions whom FDR needed to keep as allies to deal with other domestic or foreign policy problems. The AMA factor, however, was significant, a fact supported by FDR's comments to a prominent U.S. senator seeking his support for a NHI proposal in 1943: "We can't go up against the State Medical Societies," he said; "we just can't do it."[10]

The effort to pass a national health insurance program gained momentum again after World War II, and President Truman made its passage a major part of his Fair Deal agenda in 1946.[11] With the backing of the American Hospital Association (AHA) and no opposition from the AMA, Congress did pass the Hill-Burton Act of 1947, aimed at funding the construction of hospitals in rural, underserved areas, especially in the South. But when it came to legislation dealing with universal health care coverage, the AMA again led the opposition, this time through its open support of the work of the National Physician's Committee for the Extension of Medical Services (NPC), an organization with close ties to the AMA. Truman's plans were stalled and eventually defeated, but he used the issue as the basis for his successful 1948 presidential campaign. Despite his victory and although opinion polls continued to indicate strong public support for an NHI proposal, the legislation was delayed again in the congressional process and eventually failed. In 1949 the AMA took the unprecedented step of assessing a $25 fee on its members to pay for a $4 million public relations campaign against Truman's legislation. By that point, the AMA also had significant help from an alliance of more than 1,800 national organizations, including the AHA, the American Bar Association, and a wide range of powerful agricultural, labor, and trade associations.[12] The AMA had clearly established itself as an almost insurmountable obstacle to any form of NHI.

Given the success of the AMA in mobilizing local opposition to health insurance initiatives, the Republican Party decided to cultivate the organization's active support for the 1950 midterm elections. The AMA became fully engaged in the election. Physicians mailed letters to their patients and posted notices in the waiting rooms asking them to support candidates (almost all of whom were Republicans) who would vote against "socialized medicine." In addition to local radio spots, AMA-affiliated organizations conducted house-to-house campaigns and ran phone banks on Election Day. Although historians disagree as to whether the AMA actually made a difference in the election's outcome, the group was quick to claim credit for Republican gains.[13] The effort paid off, and Truman's proposal never had a chance after the 1950 election.

The influence the AMA now had in Congress would also affect the presidency of Dwight Eisenhower. Although Eisenhower was no advocate of the NHI idea, he was concerned about the gap in private coverage for those high-risk individuals being turned away by private health insurers. In 1954 he endorsed a "reinsurance plan" that would, in effect, protect private insurers from losses they might incur by offering standard coverage to high-risk patients. He sought $25 million from Congress to effectively insure the private insurers against catastrophic losses. Even though this plan involved relying exclusively on the private market to achieve something closer to universal coverage, the AMA adamantly, aggressively, and successfully opposed it. The modest proposal was not even considered in the House and died in a Senate vote, and the AMA was clearly a factor in the defeat. In frustration, the otherwise even-tempered Eisenhower called the AMA leadership "just plain stupid . . . a little group of reactionary men dead set against any change."[14]

On July 30, 1965, President Lyndon Johnson traveled to Missouri so that an aging Harry Truman could be at his side as he signed Medicare into law. Recalling Truman's failed efforts to pass national health insurance sixteen years earlier, LBJ called Truman "the real daddy" of Medicare.

Eisenhower's lament was both an indication of the AMA's extraordinary influence by the mid-1950s and a signal that it may have gone too far in its strategy of obstruction. Its success was not without unforeseen consequences, for the advocates of some form of NHI had begun to rethink their approach. In the last months of the Truman presidency, certain members of his administration drew up a proposal that would seek the more limited objective of universal coverage of hospitalization for the elderly—a plan they called "Medicare." Although Truman himself never endorsed it, the program was often discussed during the Eisenhower years, because it struck a chord in the American media, in which access to health care for the aged and the needy was emerging as a newsworthy issue. By 1960, realizing that it needed to address the growing pressure, the AMA supported passage of the Kerr-Mills Act, a precursor to Medicaid (see the following discussion) that established a federal grant program (see Chapter 3). This act provided states with matching funds for welfare programs offering health care to indigent

and needy populations, especially the elderly. However, only twenty-eight states joined the program, and less than 1 percent of the senior population received needed coverage. Rather than countering the argument for Medicare, Kerr-Mills made it seem even more inevitable.

In 1961, President Kennedy proposed a Medicare bill that would cover hospital and nursing home costs for Social Security recipients over sixty-five, with funding to come from a one-quarter of 1 percent increase in social security taxes.[15] Even though it intentionally avoided coverage of medical services from physicians, the Kennedy proposal was doomed to failure because of strong opposition from key members of Congress backed by the AMA. Again, in 1962 the Kennedy administration tried to pass Medicare, but it fell short of the support needed to bring the bill to the floor of the House.

With a significant infusion of pro-Medicare members of Congress after Johnson's landslide election in 1964, Medicare seemed destined for passage as Congress convened in 1965. Faced with this inevitability, the AMA altered its strategy and began to engage in the process of helping to formulate the specific legislation. The result was a complex bill passed as the Social Security Amendments Act of 1965. The act actually created three different programs for providing health care coverage. **Medicare** Part A provided mandatory insurance coverage for hospitalization and nursing care and reflected the original Truman administration proposals. Medicare Part B was the result of AMA involvement. Following a plan proposed by the AMA under the label "Eldercare," Part B was a *voluntary* program that covered physician and outpatient services. In addition, the 1965 legislation established **Medicaid**, a program modeled after the Kerr-Mills Act, but with broader coverage for those in need—including seniors, children, and the disabled.

The impact of the passage of Medicare on the AMA and its membership was significant. Despite its active engagement in the policymaking process, the AMA House of Delegates did consider calling for a boycott of the new law in 1965, but the matter never came to a vote. Within a few years, there was a noticeable shift in the attitude of AMA members toward Medicare, with many expressing growing satisfaction with the law's main provisions.[16] By 1971, there were also changes within the AMA itself, as younger and more progressive members challenged the more conservative leadership that had led the anti-Medicare effort. By 1991, the organization was transformed from the leading opponent of any form of government health care insurance into a leading advocate of universal coverage. That year it launched Health Access America, a program that included calls for specific government actions to "improve access to health care for Americans who are, for various reasons, without health insurance."[17]

Thus, it was no surprise when the AMA initially endorsed major parts of Bill Clinton's 1993 Health Security Act proposals, which would have provided universal coverage. The political backlash that followed from within the medical community led to some backtracking and helped defeat the measure. In addition, it caused an internal division in which the anti-insurance conservatives temporarily reasserted control of the AMA House of Delegates and

replaced many of the key staff members who had worked with the Clinton administration.[18]

The ongoing strife over control of the AMA continued through the next fifteen years. It was heightened when President Obama sought and received the organization's support for the Affordable Care Act. The endorsement came in March 2010, just as the controversial bill was heading for a crucial vote in the U.S. Senate. Given the AMA's past opposition, the endorsement was regarded as important to the law's passage. Several state medical societies, however, expressed opposition to the bill, reflecting some of the heated internal disagreement. In response, the AMA took note of certain provisions of the ACA that it opposed, and it has continued to work for changes in the ACA ever since the law's passage.[19]

Conclusion

How have some interest groups been able to shape American public policies?

Whatever our opinions about the AMA's opposition to national health insurance proposals over the years, we cannot doubt the group's standing as an effective player in the policymaking and political arena. Political scientists have offered different explanations for its success (and, ultimately, defeat). One view is that there was no effective opposing or countervailing interest to stand in its way. The history of NHI policymaking, however, indicates that there were indeed powerful advocates for the proposals. Another explanation is that the AMA was only as powerful as the alliances it formed with other major interest groups, and that it eventually failed when allies such as organized labor and moderates such as Eisenhower took exception to the AMA's adamant and unswerving stands. A related explanation focuses on the eventual price paid by an AMA leadership that took positions and used tactics that created divisions within the organization itself and ultimately led to its decline as a powerful force in Washington policymaking circles.

None of this, however, takes away from the fact that the history of health care policy in America has been and is closely tied to the history of a single interest group: the American Medical Association.

QUESTIONS FOR DISCUSSION

1. Given the history of the AMA's effective opposition to national health insurance and current controversies surrounding the National Rifle Association's influence over gun control policies, do you think the activities of interest groups ought to be more strictly regulated? If so, and keeping in mind First Amendment rights related to free speech and the right to petition government, how would you attempt to limit their power?

2. Today, only 15–18 percent of physicians are paid members of the AMA; this percentage has come down significantly from 75 percent in the 1950s. In a 2011 survey of American physicians, 77 percent said the AMA's policy position in support of Obamacare did not represent their views. In light of those figures, is it reasonable for that group to claim to represent the interests of the medical community?

CHAPTER 10

MYTHS & REALITIES
Do the media have the power
to influence public opinion?

Media and Politics

The Tangled Trail of the Day Radio Panicked the Nation

On October 30, 1938, the day before Halloween, a couple of million Americans tuned their radios to the Columbia Broadcasting System and its presentation of the Mercury Theater on the Air. The Mercury Theater on the Air routinely presented plays or dramatized short stories. On this particular evening, the show's announcer introduced the evening's broadcast by saying, "The Columbia Broadcasting System and its affiliated stations present Orson Welles and the Mercury Theater on the Air in the *War of the Worlds* by H. G. Wells." The fact that the presentation was based on a novel was made clear at the start.

In adapting the book to radio, however, Welles altered the narrative so that it would sound like a legitimate news broadcast of a Martian invasion. Following an opening monologue from Welles, the listeners are offered a fake weather report, and then the show shifts to a hotel ballroom in New York where an orchestra is playing dance music. A little more than three minutes into the show, a correspondent interrupts the music to describe strange explosions on Mars. The journalist describes "blue flames" headed toward Earth.

What follows is a series of back-and-forth switches between the music and reporters in the field. A little more than ten minutes into the program, a reporter breaks into the show to tell the listeners that a large flaming cylinder has crashed into a farm field in Grover's Mill, New Jersey. But again there is a switch back to the music. A few minutes later, another special report interrupts the broadcast; a reporter at Grover's Mill describes large creatures with glistening tentacles arising from the fallen object. Using some

< The ever increasing assortment of electronic platforms useful for displaying information and entertainment has forced traditional outlets, like newspapers, to expand their offerings beyond ink and paper. Pictured here is an issue of the venerable *Wall Street Journal*, displayed on an iPad. Readers can also access the paper via their mobile phone.

kind of "ray gun," these creatures from Mars proceed to destroy the countryside and to defeat the New Jersey state militia. Meanwhile, more of these beings are landing in Virginia, Chicago—all over the country. The plot continues to unfold with a series of eyewitness accounts, many of which are cut off mid-sentence to imply an individual's death. Eventually the Martians rout all resistance and kill everyone in their way, leaving only the narrator to explain what happened to America.

At the close of the program, Orson Welles came back on the air to assure the audience that his presentation of "the *War of the Worlds* has no further significance other than the holiday treat it was meant to be." In other words, it was just a Halloween trick.

But, in the end, the joke was on Welles. Although he did not know it at the time, the *War of the Worlds* was to become the most famous radio play in history. Without a doubt, the Mercury Theater on the Air did a first-rate job of showcasing a great nineteenth-century work of science fiction. But it was not the outstanding writing or its superb cast of actors that made it famous. It is the most famous radio play in history because of the outrage that followed its airing. From coast to coast, newspaper headlines screamed out messages of mass panic and hysteria. The *Boston Daily Globe* headlined their paper with, "Radio Play Terrifies a Nation," even though the program did not air in Boston. All across the nation, newspapers featured front-page stories of people panicking, fleeing their homes, suffering heart attacks, and attempting suicide in the face of the Martian invasion. Even today, the story of a public panicked by a radio program is widely believed. As late as 2013, a major documentary film talked of "upwards of a million people, convinced if only briefly, that the United States was being laid waste by alien invaders."[1]

The problem here is that there is no evidence of the mass hysteria. Although it is true that some people were frightened by the show, widespread panic, heart attacks, attempted suicides, and people fleeing into the streets are simply not documented. There is, at best, only a grain of truth in the newspaper stories.[2]

Why, then, do we continue to believe that a radio play could and did cause such terror? The story of panic and hysteria is more believable because it conforms to

Legend has it that the broadcast of the *War of the Worlds* led, as the *Daily News* headline proclaims, to mass panic. Yet many contemporary observers have spurned that claim. Even the radio editor for the *Daily News* later denied that New Yorkers were in terror of a Martian invasion.

a widely held view that the mass media are capable of dominating and shaping the public's thinking about the world, especially the world of politics. This is the *myth of media manipulation*, and it reflects the partial truth that the media do indeed have some degree of influence over what people know about politics and how they might think about their political surroundings. Of course, few of us believe that we as individuals are susceptible to such influence and manipulation; we believe ourselves capable of sorting out the hype and distortions and avoiding becoming a victim of media manipulation. We do, however, suspect that other people are generally ill informed and less capable of resisting the media's influence.[3] Their views differ from ours, we believe, because of the pervasive effect of powerful media.

The myth of media manipulation is not confined to any particular group in society; it is shared by Americans with widely varying political perspectives. Conservatives worry about the effects on the public of what they see as a liberal conspiracy by the mainstream media, whereas liberals often describe the same media and the numerous radio talk shows as a capitalist plot serving the interests of the wealthy. In their own defense, journalists say that they are simply reflecting the world as it is—serving as a mirror to society. They just cover the story. Thus, Roan Conrad, a former political editor for *NBC News*, argued more than two decades ago that "the news is what happens. . . . The news is not a reporter's perception or explanation of what happens; it is simply what happens."[4]

As you will see in this chapter, although the media's choice of stories does much to define public concerns, the relationship between the media and public opinion is not as straightforward as the myth, or as Conrad, suggests. The media cannot dictate the political beliefs of the country. At the same time, journalists are not simply passive instruments through which events, called news, are transmitted. Indeed, the standards by which journalists decide what is newsworthy often work to the advantage of officials and candidates who know how to use the media to achieve policy and electoral goals.

The Rise of the Media

> ## How have the media evolved over the past two hundred years?

Although newspaper sales have declined precipitously, Americans continue to buy millions of newspapers, and they can choose from among 10,000 or so weekly and monthly periodicals. They keep their television sets on for an average of more than four hours each day. And there are almost 9,000 radio stations in the country. Moreover, the growth of the Internet is opening up an uncountable number of media sources. Estimates suggest that, as of 2013, there were 649[5] million websites and more than 2 billion web[6] users in North America. Additionally, YouTube estimates that one hour of video is uploaded every second.[7] Obviously, the attentive media watcher faces an incessant flow of information on topics ranging from foreign affairs to domestic scandals. Yet it has not always been this way. Less than two hundred years ago, news from Washington or the state capital arrived days, weeks, or even months after the events occurred, if it arrived at all.

The Early Days

Before 1830, the American press consisted of specialized publications designed to reach elite audiences. Many papers were simply organs of political parties or individual candidates. Appearing once or twice a week, these partisan papers rallied the party faithful and denounced political opponents, often through vicious personal attacks. The only alternative sources of news were commercial papers, which were designed for merchants and traders. The commercial papers provided extensive accounts of business activities, such as shipping dates, commodity prices, and business transactions, but they were short on politics and made no attempt to reach a wide audience.

With the 1833 publication of the *Sun* in New York, American publishing entered the age of mass journalism. Capitalizing on technological advances that made printing relatively fast and cheap, the *Sun* was the first paper to appeal successfully to the public at large. It was sold on street corners for a penny a copy, and it and its many imitators—known together as the **penny press**—cultivated readerships in the thousands. A breezy style and an emphasis on local news, especially scandalous events, ensured the popularity of these papers. Each vied fiercely with the others to produce the most sensational stories. At one point, the staff of the *Sun* came up with a hoax about life on the moon.[8]

Toward the end of the nineteenth century, the emphasis on sensationalism became even more pronounced. Joseph Pulitzer, a crusading spirit who owned the *New York World*, and William Randolph Hearst, owner of the *New York Journal*, created **yellow journalism**—named for the Yellow Kid comic strip, which appeared first in the *World* and then in the *Journal*. Yellow journalism utilized large, bold headlines; illustrations; cartoons; and color features to promote its tales of scandal and corruption. Not content with reporting the news, both Pulitzer and Hearst often made news by committing the considerable resources of their papers to various political causes. For instance, Hearst is usually believed to have aroused in the American public the strong anti-Spanish feelings that led to the Spanish-American War. Just before the war, Hearst sent an artist to Cuba to cover the conflict between Spain and Cuba. When the artist wired that war did not seem likely, Hearst replied, "Please remain. You furnish the pictures. I will furnish the war."[9] Many people believe that he did just that.

While Hearst and Pulitzer inflamed public opinion with their sensational appeals, a new style of journalism was developing. A conservative paper, the *New York Times*, attacked the excesses of yellow journalism as indecent and stressed objectivity in its reporting. Newspapers, according to Adolph Ochs, owner of the

Penny press The term for the first generation of newspapers with mass popular appeal. The name comes from the New York *Sun*, which was sold for a penny a copy in the mid-1800s.

Yellow journalism A type of journalism that flourished in the late nineteenth century and whose popularity was based on sensationalized stories of scandal and corruption.

The modern mass media were born in America with the creation of the penny press. Sold on street corners by young boys and girls, like those pictured here, the penny press specialized in sensationalism.

Times, had the responsibility to "give news impartially, without fear or favor, regardless of any party, sect or interest involved."[10] Although its circulation was small compared with that of the yellow press, the *Times* became a standard by which journalism was judged, and objectivity became the goal of serious journalists. As any trip to today's supermarkets will show, however, yellow journalism did not die; it just became less mainstream.

The Broadcast Media

Even as newspapers were undergoing change, the technology of the broadcast media was being developed. The first regularly scheduled radio station, KDKA in Pittsburgh, began operation in 1920. Its owner, Westinghouse, the nation's leading manufacturer of home receivers, initially viewed it as a means of creating a market for its products. Most of the early radio stations were owned by nonprofit institutions, such as universities, and they were seen as public service entities designed to educate citizens for life in a democratic culture. In 1928, however, the newly created Federal Radio Commission (the predecessor to the Federal Communications Commission, see the following discussion) reallocated frequency assignments in a way that greatly favored commercial owners. The commission reasoned that nonprofit owners would not act in the public interest, because they were not motivated by profits. Nonprofit stations quickly disappeared, to be replaced by commercial broadcasters that linked advertising to immensely popular and profitable entertainment programs.

POLITICS & POPULAR CULTURE: Visit the book's companion website at **www.oup.com/us/gitelson** to read the special feature *Fake News*.

Although broadcasters stressed entertainment, government leaders were quick to grasp the political potential of radio. During the Great Depression, President Franklin D. Roosevelt employed the medium skillfully to deliver his famous fireside chats. Speaking in a warm and informal manner, Roosevelt sought to reassure his millions of listeners by making his broadcasts sound like friendly discussions. Roosevelt demonstrated the vast possibilities of radio, as well as its potential for overt manipulation. During the 1944 election campaign, for instance, Roosevelt learned that his opponent, Thomas Dewey, had purchased airtime immediately following his own. Although he was scheduled to speak for fifteen minutes, Roosevelt stopped after fourteen. Millions of puzzled listeners turned their dials away from the silence and missed Dewey's address.

Despite the interest shown by political leaders, most broadcasters resisted programming news shows until the fledgling CBS network entered the business. Its owner, William Paley, saw news as a cheap source of programming and as a means of competing with NBC, the more established radio network. His team of journalists, including Edward R. Murrow and Eric Sevareid, quickly established a reputation for superior news coverage. Murrow's broadcasts from London during World War II captured the imagination of the entire country and made Murrow a national celebrity.

Like radio, television was, from the beginning, a commercial venture that stressed entertainment and advertising. (Appropriately, Philo T. Farnsworth, the inventor of television, used a dollar sign as his first test pattern.) Throughout the 1950s, each of the three television networks—CBS, NBC, and ABC—provided one fifteen-minute news program five evenings a week. Even CBS, which had pioneered radio news, was reluctant to use valuable television airtime for news and public affairs, preferring the popular and extraordinarily profitable quiz shows.

This focus changed in 1960, however, when all three networks televised the debates between presidential candidates John F. Kennedy and Richard M. Nixon. Although there is still disagreement over which candidate won, the debates definitely demonstrated the commercial potential of news and public affairs programming by drawing an audience of 60 to 75 million viewers. News programs ceased to be viewed simply as a means of improving a network's public image. Instead, the networks began competing to produce the most highly rated news programs, using such advanced technology as small handheld cameras, wireless microphones, and satellite transmissions. As news coverage broadened, the audiences grew into the millions, and a majority of Americans came to depend on television as their prime source of news.

As the twentieth century came to a close, the development of information technology exploded. By the end of the twentieth century, the Internet, including the World Wide Web, had radically changed the shape and volume of information available. The result is a flood of information that moves around the world at the speed of light. Countless websites exist to aggregate news from the "old media," whereas others—including blogs and Twitter—create news stories, many of which become embedded in the traditional media. Supplementing all of these are the multitude of social media outlets that connect people across countries with little regard to national borders. Facebook and its competitors provide opportunities to build countless communities of people speaking directly to one another (see Figure 10.1).

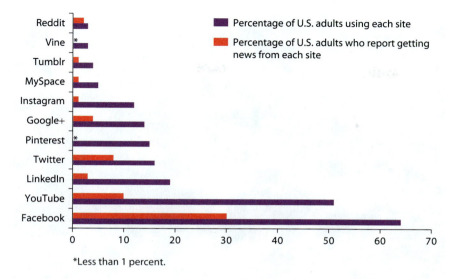

*Less than 1 percent.

FIGURE 10.1 Social Media as a Source of News

Source: PEW Research Center.

Unlike the established media that dominated most of the twentieth century, the new information tools were founded on the principles of transparency and openness. Most of the pioneers of the Internet world believed that they were creating the means for enhancing democracy and empowering the average citizen. Free use of the technology was not just assumed—it was inbred in the very conception of the web. Indeed, much of what has grown with the technology does promote social values of justice and equality. The role of social media in the revolts characterized as the Arab Spring (2010–2011) certainly lives up to the hopes and wishes of many. Nevertheless, the ability of the Internet to generate abundant revenue has not gone unnoticed. Social network sites like Facebook and Twitter are not popular on Wall Street because they promote democracy or social justice. To investors, these organizations have the potential to make millions, if not billions, in profits.

Diversity and Concentration

Although the media offer a staggering array of choices, merely reciting the number of outlets can be deceiving. The real issue, say media critics, is the increasing concentration of ownership in a few hands—a change that threatens to limit diversity of expression. About 80 percent of all daily newspapers published in the United States are owned by one of the large chains. The largest of all, Gannett, owns eighty-five newspapers, including *USA Today*. (Gannett also owns twenty-three television stations.) As chain ownership has grown, newspaper competition has decreased markedly. Less than 2 percent of American cities have more than one newspaper.[11]

Concentrated ownership and influence are even greater in the television markets. About 85 percent of the nation's commercial over-the-air television stations are affiliated with ABC, CBS, or NBC.[12] The three major networks, in turn, are owned by large conglomerates with multiple media interests that combine publishing, broadcasting, and Hollywood production studios.

Pictured here are Egyptians gathered in Cairo's Tahrir Square to celebrate their successful revolt against the dictator Hosni Mubarak. Many are using their mobile phones to record the festivity, but prior to the victory, mobile phones were used as tools to overthrow the old regime. Demonstrators stayed in touch with one another and coordinated their activities using their phones and Twitter.

All is not well for the networks, however. The growth of cable television alternatives has substantially eroded network dominance. Where once the three over-the-air network news programs—ABC, CBS, and NBC—were the major source of political information for almost all Americans, these days the audience is far more fragmented. Although as of 2012 the three traditional networks still commanded a combined audience of some 20 million viewers for the nightly news broadcasts, that was about 3 million fewer viewers than they had in the 1980s.[13] Many of those viewers have shifted to cable news programs, but the majority now use the vast options that cable and the Internet present to watch breaking news, entertainment shows, and sports.

The enormous growth of cable, direct satellite transmission, and a host of developing technologies that combine video and computer processing with microwave transmissions suggests a future of almost infinite choices. But who will control these outlets? Some observers believe that the technological revolution is destroying the centralized and concentrated media, as exemplified by the major networks, and is paving the way for a more democratic means of information production.[14] Still others expect the future to be much like the past, with major corporations becoming multimedia giants that will control the worldwide production, distribution, and technology of the new media.

During the past few years, the enormous growth of the Internet—and its availability not only on the computer but also on cell phones, tablets such as the iPad, and other devices—has indeed challenged the old alignment of media sources. Many Internet enthusiasts assume that the ability of users to produce high-quality programming at minimal cost will simply overwhelm the current media. Thus, John Perry Barlow (a political activist and former lyricist for the

Grateful Dead) dismisses the rise of huge entertainment conglomerates like Disney and Time Warner, arguing that they are "merely rearranging deck chairs on the *Titanic*."[15]

Certainly, the Internet is a revolutionary technology with unparalleled potential, but its potential has not been lost on media owners. Increasingly, a key component of media conglomerates is the ability to provide content for the World Wide Web. Disney already owns a substantial interest in the popular Infoseek search engine, and Rupert Murdoch, the owner of a vast media empire that includes the Fox Network, now owns Intermix Media Inc., which holds interests in popular social networking sites. Additionally, all of the major newspapers and also the television networks provide online versions of their products. Nor should we ignore the fact that some companies, rooted in the earlier days of the technological revolution (think, for instance, Google or Apple) have become formidable enterprises seeking to dominate or at least play a major role as an integrator of a wide range of products and services.

Even blogging, assumed by many to be a check against these mainstream conglomerates, has become increasingly mainstream. This medium catapulted onto the national scene in 2003, after bloggers circumvented traditional media channels to report on controversial, ostensibly prosegregation remarks made by Senate majority leader Trent Lott. When these reports, which were eventually picked up by the mainstream press, forced Senator Lott to give up his leadership position, bloggers were hailed as pioneers in democratizing the delivery of news to the American people. This single event marked the rise of bloggers. But, these days, the bloggers' world is increasingly populated by those with ties to the mainstream media—think tanks, interest groups, trade associations, mainstream reporters, and even politicians have their own online diaries. Moreover, it is no longer unusual for something posted by a blogger to become a mainstream media story, as reporters looking for new stories routinely follow bloggers.

Similarly, YouTube, Facebook, Twitter, and an increasing variety of other social network options have become common modes of communication and self-promotion for political leaders, business firms, and even governments. Indeed, tweeting has become a commodity in the marketplace, as those with sizeable followings may earn large payments for their tweets. In 2013, it was widely acknowledged that Kim Kardashian earned as much as $10,000 a tweet. Of course, Kim Kardashian is not alone; many celebrities profit handsomely from their tweets.

Whether the Internet and other technological creations will put an end to the current media structure or simply become arms of media conglomerates remains to be seen. What is clear, however, is that the Internet and the whole range of recent technological advances are a target of media owners, who are working to integrate them with their other holdings. Perhaps professor and lawyer Tim Wu, the former chair of the media reform group Free Press, is prescient when he warns, "History shows a typical progression of information technologies from somebody's hobby to somebody's industry, from jury-rigged contraption to slick production marvel; from freely accessible channel to one strictly controlled by a single corporation or cartel—from open to closed."[16]

About the only assurance that can be made about our information needs is that the ways in which we acquire knowledge will continue to change. The man pictured here is wearing Google glasses. Google is betting that its face computers will become the next essential knowledge platform.

Government Regulation

The American mass media are freer from government restrictions than the mass media in any other nation. Nevertheless, the government exercises some control, especially over radio and television. In the case of printed materials, regulation applies only to obscenity and libel (see Chapter 4, on civil liberties).

Government Licensing. Because of the limited number of frequencies over which radio and television signals can be transmitted, Congress created the **Federal Communications Commission (FCC)** in 1934 to monitor and regulate the use of the airwaves. Besides assigning frequencies so that stations' signals do not interfere with one another, the FCC issues licenses, which must be renewed every five years for television and every seven years for radio. According to statute, license renewals depend on "satisfactory performance" that "serve[s] the public interest, convenience, and necessity." The vagueness of that mandate gives the FCC tremendous discretion in awarding or denying license renewals, but as a matter of practice it has denied few applications and has exercised little control over the content of broadcasts. Illustrative of the FCC position is its refusal, in the face of heavy lobbying by advocacy groups, to require television broadcasters to present only family programming during the early evening hours; instead, it accepted a rating system created and managed by the networks.

Equal Time. The most significant FCC requirement is the **equal-time rule**. This provision stipulates that broadcasters who permit a candidate for political office to campaign on the station (including through paid advertisements) must allow all other candidates for the same office equal time at identical rates. Appearances on interview shows and news events are exempted from the requirement, but

Federal Communications Commission (FCC) The agency created in 1934 to monitor and regulate the use of the airwaves.

Equal-time rule A Federal Communications Commission rule that requires a broadcaster who permits one candidate to campaign on the station to provide all other candidates for the same office with equal time at identical rates.

entertainment shows are not. This exception presented a problem during the 2008 presidential campaign, when actor Fred Thompson announced his candidacy for the Republican Party nomination. Fearing that the other candidates would demand equal time, NBC pulled broadcast reruns of any *Law & Order* episodes in which Thompson had appeared.

Making News

> **What is news?**

Prominently displayed on the front page of the *New York Times* is the company motto: "All the News That's Fit to Print." Admirable as this sentiment may be, it is not, nor can it be, true. Indeed, a more accurate rephrasing of the motto provided by wags is "all the news that fits." The argument that the news is simply what happens is unrealistic. No form of mass media can carry every newsworthy event; all are constrained by costs and by the availability of space and time. For instance, the average daily newspaper fills approximately 62 percent of its space with advertising, leaving a mere 38 percent (called the news hole) to be shared by news accounts, human-interest stories, and pure entertainment features.

Network television news is even more limited. Each half-hour program contains only eighteen minutes of news and human-interest stories. Thus, the news is not simply what is happening out there; it must be selected from a multitude of events, only a few of which will be covered. What, then, is news? Perhaps the best explanation is that "news is what reporters, editors, and producers decide is news."[17]

Although the basis of news judgment often seems vague and unarticulated, it is possible to identify the criteria that newscasters most often use in selecting stories.[18]

- Newsworthy stories must be *timely* and *novel*. They must be what reporters call *breaking stories*. Routine matters are considered unworthy of coverage, even though they may have a significant impact on people's lives. As a former editor of the *Sun*, a nineteenth- and mid-twentieth-century New York paper, put it, "When a dog bites a man, that is not news, because it happens so often. But if a man bites a dog, that is news."[19]

- Newsworthiness is heightened by *the presence of violence, conflict, disaster, or scandal*. Violent crime, for example, was a staple of the penny press and continues to dominate contemporary news. Even nonviolent conflict makes news. Larry Speakes, deputy press secretary during the Reagan administration, once noted that no one pays attention when one hundred members of Congress come out of a White House meeting and say that the president's program is great. "But if one says it stinks, that's news."

- *Familiarity* is also an important element of newsworthiness. Events are more likely to be covered if they involve individuals whom the public already knows. Approximately 85 percent of the domestic news stories covered by television and news magazines involve well-known people—mostly those holding official positions.[20] Unknown people are most newsworthy when they are victims of crime or natural disasters.

- Newsworthiness is also heightened by the availability of *people to interview*. Reporters rely heavily on interviews rather than printed documents. This dependence on interviews results partly from the need to personalize the news. Interviews with adversaries also increase the sense of conflict, adding a dramatic element to the narrative while preserving the reporter's image of objectivity by presenting the story in the familiar point-counterpoint format. Whatever the cause, the result is a bias in favor of those who are willing and able to provide a pithy comment.

- For television, *video* footage is crucial. After all, television without film is simply radio.

These criteria mainly stress ways of keeping the audience interested. Because media outlets make their profits from selling their audience to advertisers, they must keep their ratings or circulation high. Indeed, cynics often claim that news is "that which is printed on the back of advertisements."[21] Ironically, the growth of cable and the Internet and the fierce competition produced by the proliferation of twenty-four-hour news programming have led to a relaxation of the standards for determining what constitutes news. To attract and keep an audience, media outlets increasingly rely on feature stories, or so-called soft news, as exhibited by stories highlighting the personal lives and peccadilloes of celebrities. A news cycle operating twenty-four hours a day, seven days a week also puts an emphasis on "gotcha" journalism—journalism based largely on interviews designed to trap the interviewees into saying things that can be used to attack their character or motives. Scandal still sells.

The doings of celebrities, like Kanye West, pictured here, saturate the media. No aspect of celebrity life is too trivial to be covered.

Moreover, the need to attract and hold an audience has blurred the line between newscasts and entertainment programming. Most of the programming for the all-news cable outlets is provided by talk shows and infotainment programs that stress opinion, not news. More importantly, in general, the opinions need to be sensational and extreme; remember: conflict sells. As you will see, this concern for audience appeal has an impact on the way politics is conducted in the United States.

The Effects of the Mass Media

> **How does media coverage affect people's attitudes?**

For many citizens, concern about media manipulation stems from a belief that the media have an extraordinary effect on public opinion. Critics of television have been particularly prone to view the media as dictating the attitudes of a largely passive audience. Indeed, the argument goes, if the media were not influential, why would companies spend so much money on advertisements? Social scientists who have examined the issue are far less certain of the media's impact. In fact, most research suggests that the media, by and large, fail to change people's settled political beliefs. In fact, individuals who already hold beliefs on particular issues or candidates are unlikely to change their minds as a result of what they are told by the media.

The media's power to change established political beliefs is limited, because people exercise selective exposure, absorbing only information that agrees with their existing beliefs.[22] They more easily incorporate such information than data that contradict preconceived ideas; they may dismiss or entirely ignore those data. Existing beliefs also influence the way people interpret what they see—a process known as selective perception. Thus, supporters may perceive a candidate's actions as demonstrating complete integrity, while opponents perceive the actions as demonstrating complete dishonesty.[23]

Nevertheless, the media are capable of swaying some individual beliefs. In matters in which a person has neither experience nor a firmly held opinion, the information and interpretation supplied by the media may shape that person's political attitude. Citizens who lack knowledge on a particular subject do often adopt the views expressed by media commentators.[24]

The irony is that the explosion of technology has created more choices, which in turn have lessened the media's role in influencing what people believe. Cable TV, for instance, has been a source of a large amount of partisan news programming (see Table 10.1). The cable networks have far lower operating costs than the over-the-air networks—an advantage that allows them to cater to fewer viewers and still make handsome profits. But how effective are these partisan news shows? The answer seems to be, not very. Viewers of partisan news gravitate to sources that express values they already hold. Those who watch partisan shows on FOX or MSNBC, for example, are what scholars call "news seekers." They are, compared to most Americans, more interested in politics and more knowledgeable about politics and therefore are less susceptible to influence. They already know what they believe.[25] Given that these shows have to appeal to and hold an audience, it may be that they program to please, not influence, their viewers.

TABLE 10.1   **The Most and Least Trusted Sources of Television News**

Most Trusted Networks		Least Trusted Networks	
Network	**% of Respondents***	**Network**	**% of Respondents****
Fox	35	Fox	33
PBS	14	MSNBC	19
ABC	11	Comedy Central	14
CNN	10	CNN	11
CBS	9	ABC	5
MSNBC	6	CBS	4
Comedy Central	6	NBC	2
NBC	3	PBS	2

Respondents were asked to select which network—out of those provided here—was most trustworthy.

**Respondents were asked to select which network—out of those provided here—was least trustworthy.*

Source: "Fox News Once Again Leads Most Trusted and Least Trusted List," *Public Policy Polling.*

A more serious consequence of the multiplicity of choices is that those people not interested in politics have a much greater array of entertainment options than ever before. Cable TV, for instance, provides dozens of alternatives any hour of the day and, of course, the Internet provides far more. All these options make it easy for people with less interest in politics to avoid news programming in favor of entertainment, furthering an information gap between the news seekers and the less informed.[26]

Setting the Agenda

Increasingly, the media influence the political agenda and the conduct of politicians. When deciding what to cover, journalists focus on some aspects of public life and ignore others. Because the media are often the public's only source of knowledge, what journalists do not report as news might as well not have happened. As political scientist Austin Ranney once suggested, the appropriate riddle for the media age may well be this: "If a tree falls in a forest but the event is not videotaped or broadcast on the nightly news, has it really happened?"[27]

When the public knows events and issues well, the media have less impact on its attitudes. For example, studies of individuals exposed to stories alleging that the nation's defenses were weak grew more concerned about national defense. Stories about inflation, however, had little effect on their opinions, undoubtedly because inflation affects everyone personally.[28] Thus, the media wield the most influence in shaping the public agenda when the events and issues are either outside an individual's experience or new to the society.

Of particular importance is the effect that the media's agenda setting has on the public's evaluation of candidates and public officials. Studies examining the effect of media have identified a process called **priming**, which "refers to the capacity of the media to isolate particular issues, events, or themes in the news as the criteria for evaluating politicians."[29] The more attention the media give to an issue or character trait, the greater that issue's weight in the formation of public evaluations of candidates and public officials. By highlighting some issues or attributes and ignoring others, the media influence the standards by which people judge governments, public officials, and candidates.

Priming The capacity of the media to isolate particular issues, events, or themes in the news as the criteria for evaluating politicians.

Conducting Politics in the Media: Old and New

Politicians are much more attuned to the media than the public is. The conduct of politics in the United States is changing, as candidates and public officials increasingly tailor their activities to meet journalists' needs. Thus, as mentioned previously, they plan and time speeches, rallies, and personal appearances to win maximum media coverage, especially on television. To further facilitate coverage, campaign staffers supply the media with daily schedules, advance copies of speeches, and access to telephones and fax machines. If they manage the campaign well, they will exploit the reporters' need for a story and influence the content of news coverage.

All these efforts are in vain, of course, if the campaign cannot get reporters to cover the candidate. Therefore, to attract reporters, campaigns routinely create **pseudo-events** —staged events that are intended to produce media coverage. Pseudo-events are often presented with the special needs of television in mind. Knowing that television producers dislike "talking heads" (footage of the candidate simply delivering a speech), campaign organizers work to provide interesting and symbolic visuals for the evening news. Whether candidates visit farms to indicate their concern for the family farmer or spend a little time serving food in a soup kitchen to prove that they care about the poor, the picture is the thing.

Pseudo-events Events, such as speeches, rallies, and personal appearances, that are staged by politicians simply to win maximum media coverage.

Even with all the planning, candidates have become increasingly frustrated with media coverage. Although the coverage is extensive, the established media give candidates little direct access to the public. As political scientist Thomas Patterson has pointed out, the candidates have become voiceless. For every minute that the candidates spoke on the three major networks' evening news shows in 2000, the reporters covering them talked for seven minutes.[30] Reports from the 2008 election further support this diminishment of candidate airtime. Stephen J. Farnsworth and S. Robert Lichter found that 68 percent of the time devoted to television coverage of the candidates was taken by the reporters and anchors. As they noted, "little of what the voters heard about the candidates actually was from the candidates."[31]

To reach the public directly, political candidates have adopted a variety of techniques designed to bypass the established media. One such technique, the video news release (VNR), is a newslike report or interview paid for by the candidate and delivered to local television stations. By renting time on a satellite transponder, the candidate can be interviewed by local television reporters all over the country without leaving a studio. The local stations get the chance to

Pictured here is President Obama answering questions put to him by Jorge Ramos and Maria Elena Salinas, co-anchors of a popular news program on Univision. Univision, a Spanish-language television network, has become a powerful force in the market and an increasingly important network for political candidates.

interview a national political figure at no cost to themselves, and the candidate covers several cities quickly. This technique also has the advantage that local anchors are seldom as hard on candidates as are the national reporters covering the campaign, and they are more likely to let the candidate talk directly to the audience.

Besides making extensive use of VNRs, the presidential candidates are turning to what have been called "the new media": radio call-in shows, early morning television programs, televised town meetings, and late-night entertainment productions. We can see the significance of these venues for candidates by looking at presidential candidates' frequent appearances on shows like the *Late Show with David Letterman*, where Senator John McCain first announced his intention to seek the presidency in 2008. Appearances on these shows give the candidates more time to talk directly to the public than they would get from a month of coverage by the network news programs.

Candidates are also increasingly using the Internet. In 2012, for instance, every major presidential candidate posted campaign videos on the popular Internet site YouTube, as well as maintaining expertly crafted campaign websites. The first presidential campaign websites occurred in the 2000 election—both Al Gore and George W. Bush set up a campaign website. Both sites were fairly bland operations, simply providing lots of details about the candidates' positions on the issues. By 2008, however, things had changed: For example, the Obama website was designed to be its own social network. Users could share content with their own groups and build their own platforms.[32] Moreover, candidates have discovered the power of the Internet as a source of campaign funding. During the 2008 presidential primaries, a candidate for the Republican nomination raised a record 6 million dollars in one day through appeals on his website.

Candidates now also make heavy use of Twitter in showering their followers with messages. Indeed, candidates are becoming increasingly skilled at tailoring their tweets to fit the interests of the recipients. In 2012, President Obama delivered a speech on student loans before a Chapel Hill, North Carolina, audience. In the speech, the president expressed his opposition to raising the interest rate on student loans. What made the speech unusual was that he urged the students to "tweet them,"(Congress) and he went on to say: "We've got a hashtag. Here's the hashtag for you to tweet them: #dontdoublemyrate."[33] Minutes later, thousands of posts using the president's hashtag appeared.

Of course, the use of Twitter is not limited to one political party. For campaigns, the advantage of Twitter is that it allows parties and candidates to test messages. The usual pattern is that the campaign managers release a tweet, and then a few hours later they check Facebook to see how it is playing out in the larger sphere. The next day, a Google search confirms how well the tweet performed.[34] If it works, the campaign may use the message in speeches and broadcast ads.

For the candidates, these new media offer irresistible opportunities to circumvent the press and speak directly to the American people. President Clinton, an early exploiter of the new media, described the advantages of the new media best in March 1993, when he told a group of radio and television correspondents, "You know why I can stiff you on press conferences? Because Larry King liberated me by giving me to the American people directly."[35] Since then, the information explosion has made it even easier to avoid the mainstream media.

Besides affecting the candidates' conduct, media-oriented politics also diverts attention from issues and draws it to campaign strategies. Because, as we have seen, journalists define news as involving conflict and personalities, they pay special heed to the horse-race characteristics of elections. Media attention focuses on who is winning and why. During the 2008 presidential election, 38 percent of the

President Obama talks about jobs at a town hall meeting hosted by the social network LinkedIn. Social networks like LinkedIn have become important ways of reaching potential voters.

televised news stories focused on candidates' changes in tactics, which candidates had the most money, and internal troubles in the candidates' campaign organizations. Domestic and foreign policy issues represented only 22 percent of the stories.[36] Even when issues were discussed, the question was often how the candidate's position on these issues helped or hurt the campaign.

For reporters, elections are simply games in which candidates devise tactics to defeat their opponents. Foremost among the tools for reporting campaign strategy is the public opinion poll. Even though polls are of little value to voters other than those making book on the election, the media saturate their audience with frequent and often hyped poll results. Illustrative of this tactic is coverage surrounding the Democratic Party's presidential nomination process in 2008. Following Senator Obama's victory in the Iowa caucuses, Senator Clinton was written off as a potential nominee—that is, until she won the New Hampshire primary. After that, the nation was barraged with poll results, all used to hype the closeness of the race and, in the process, keep the audience. Public opinion polls are the press's version of a pseudo-event; the press creates and pays for polls and then covers them as news.[37]

Of course, journalists defend this preoccupation with strategy by arguing that the audience prefers to hear about the campaign rather than about the issues. Whether or not they are correct about that, it is apparent that discussions of campaign strategies appeal to reporters, editors, and producers for several reasons. These stories are easier to do than more substantial reports, because reporting on campaign tactics requires little knowledge of complex political issues. Indeed, editors can easily reduce horse-race stories to the simple question of who is winning and who is losing. More importantly, reporting on strategy and mechanics provides the kind of dramatic themes that keep an audience interested.

Although no unanimity of opinion on the effects of horse-race coverage exists, many observers believe that the emphasis on elections as games has a detrimental effect on public opinion. By highlighting tactics and strategies, the media present a consistent image of candidates as political opportunists who are interested only in winning elections. According to many observers, the constant repetition of that vision simply increases the public's mistrust of candidates.

The Uneasy Alliance Between Government and the Media

> **How do government officials shape the news?**

Government officials and journalists are often portrayed as adversaries locked in combat, each trying to best the other. This is an accurate picture when their goals conflict—when, for instance, journalists, wanting the big scoop on governmental waste, fraud, or incompetence that will bring them instant fame, confront government officials, who want the press to present their actions in the most favorable light possible. At other times, however, the goals of journalists and officials overlap, and the two groups cooperate. Journalists court officials to obtain the information that is their livelihood, and government officials woo the media in order to build public support for their policies. As veteran newscaster Walter Cronkite once remarked, "Politics and media are inseparable. It is only the politicians and the media that are incompatible."[38]

Furthermore, government officials are avid consumers of journalism—more so than the general public—and this fact creates additional incentives for cooperation. The mass media provide an important communication link among officials, informing them of what others in and out of government are doing and saying. When, for instance, President George W. Bush wanted to send a rather undiplomatic warning to Iraqi prime minister Nouri al-Maliki, he did so in an off-the-record briefing to a few national reporters and the network anchors. As a result, his message that the administration's patience with the Iraqi government was running out was broadcast to the world without President Bush ever being identified as the source.

Given this mutual dependence, the media and government form an uneasy alliance. Journalists report the actions of government officials, particularly the president and the more prominent members of Congress, whereas government officials attempt to shape the content of the news.

Covering the President

Nowhere is the uneasy alliance between the media and government more apparent than in the coverage of the White House. Almost everything the president does becomes news. Even trivial events receive wide coverage. For presidents, this extensive coverage represents a valuable means of reaching the American public on a daily basis, but it is also a source of frustration. The frustration undoubtedly increases throughout a president's term. As political scientist Fred Smoller has demonstrated, television portrayals of a president become more negative as the president's term progresses.[39] John Kennedy undoubtedly spoke for all presidents when, in response to a question concerning some particularly critical accounts of his administration, he claimed to be "reading more and enjoying it less."[40]

Because the media provide the vital link between the president and the public, and because, from the president's perspective, journalists cannot be counted on to get their stories right, the White House goes to great lengths to put its view across to the media. Indeed, about one-third of the high-level White House staff are directly involved in media relations.[41]

Most of the responsibility for dealing with the media falls to the president's press secretary, who gives a daily briefing to the some seventy-five reporters and photographers who regularly cover the White House. Under constant pressure from their editors to file stories on the president, these reporters rely extensively on these briefings and on press releases provided by the press secretary. On occasion, the press secretary may also arrange interviews with the president or provide photo opportunities—a chance to take photographs of the president, although not to ask questions. Most White House reporters simply repeat the information given them by the press secretary. According to Bill Moyers, who was press secretary during Lyndon Johnson's administration, the White House press corps "is more stenographic than entrepreneurial in its approach to news gathering."[42] As a result, presidents are less subjects of news coverage than they are sources of news.

Press Conferences. Presidents communicate with the public through press conferences. Although press conferences often seem spontaneous, they are in fact highly structured events that allow the president a great deal of control. Typically, these thirty-minute affairs begin with a short statement. This enables the president to speak directly to the public. It also reduces the time available for questioning and focuses the audience's attention on a subject of the president's choosing.

Careful preparation and rehearsal further strengthen presidential control of press conferences. Days, or even weeks, before a press conference, the president's staff prepares a list of the questions that are most likely to be asked and then provides written answers so that the president can study and rehearse them. Ronald Reagan, for instance, held mock news conferences. Furthermore, presidents can and do frequently call on reporters who are known to be friendly to their administration. Such reporters are far more likely than others to ask easy questions, or even to ask questions furnished (planted) by the White House. At Reagan press conferences, reporters thought to be sympathetic to the administration, called the "known friendlies," were seated in front and to the president's right. If a line of questioning became uncomfortable, Reagan needed only to "go to the right."[43]

Although press conferences can be a valuable tool, they still pose risks. Even though they have a high level of control over what questions are asked and by whom, presidents cannot avoid embarrassing or politically charged queries. Few presidents are satisfied with press conferences as an institution, and most take part in them with some misgivings (see Figure 10.2).

Going Public. In addition to making use of a large staff dedicated to managing media relations in Washington, presidents increasingly try to shape press coverage by taking their policy proposals directly to the public. This strategy, known as "going public," has the president and often senior members of the administration fanning out across the country to give policy speeches. Most importantly, however,

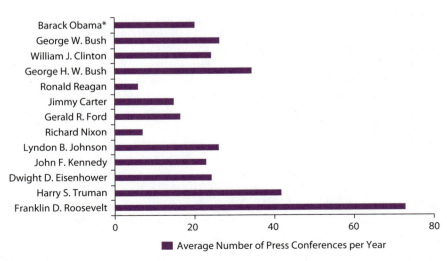

FIGURE 10.2 Presidential News Conferences

Source: Gerhard Peters, "Presidential News Conferences," in The American Presidency Project, ed. John T. Wooley and Gerhard Peters (Santa Barbara: University of California, 1999–2014).

■ Average Number of Press Conferences per Year

*From January 20, 2009 to January 20, 2014

ASKED & ANSWERED

ASKED: *What are leaks, and where do they come from?*

ANSWERED: We have all read or heard stories of a brewing White House scandal, an impending resignation from the administration, a policy proposal under consideration, or a disagreement among policymakers that get attributed to some unnamed source. Sometimes the source is described as "knowledgeable," "close to the decision makers," or even a "high White House official," and, whoever the source is, the information he or she provides is often described as a "leak." But what exactly is a leak, and why would someone use this method to convey information to the press?

Although there is no precise definition of a leak, Stephen Hess best defines the term as the "premature unauthorized partial disclosure" of information. To understand why individuals leak information requires an examination of motive. Some leaks (ego leaks) come from people who want to demonstrate how important they are, how much they are in the know in the political world. Other leaks (goodwill leaks) are an attempt to curry favor with a reporter in hopes that in the future the favor will be repaid. Alternatively, still others (animus leaks) may be part of an ongoing conflict between policymakers and, as such, are designed to embarrass an adversary. Finally, some leaks (whistle-blower leaks) may be the result of a person's frustration at his or her inability to use proper channels to correct what is perceived as a wrong being done by the government. Of course, there are many variations on these basic types, and often a leak serves more than one purpose.

Although presidents have long decried leaks, they, or people authorized by them, are often the sources of stories from unnamed officials. The information they provide is called a "plant," which Hess defines as a "premature authorized partial disclosure" of information. Presidents authorize the release of information this way for a variety of reasons. Often, presidents use reporters to send up "trial balloons." For example, a story about a proposal under consideration is planted with a reporter. If the public or Congress reacts negatively, the president can disclaim the story and drop the proposal, all the while denying that there was any basis to the story. This practice gives the president what is called "plausible deniability." Alternatively, a president, or someone authorized by the president, may plant a story in order to discredit a competing policy proposal or a political opponent. Plants, like leaks, have many justifications.

Washington is rife with both leaks and plants, which are not always a bad thing: Although leaks and plants always serve the purposes of those who release the information, they can also serve the democratic process by opening up matters of public concern for debate and discussion. But whatever the benefits or drawbacks, we can be certain that leaks and plants will continue to be part of American government; as the late journalist James Reston so famously said, "A government is the only known vessel that leaks from the top."

Source: Stephen Hess, The Government/Press Connection: Press Officers and Their Offices *(Washington, DC: The Brookings Institution, 1984).*

the strategy involves circumventing the national media by providing local reporters, who are often not used to covering national politics, with opportunities to report firsthand on national political figures. Not surprisingly, the local press tends to be far less critical of presidents than the national media. (For a discussion of "leaks" to the press, see the Asked & Answered feature, on page 341.)

Done well, going public can be a very effective strategy, garnering not only good press but also public support. In 2001, President George W. Bush, for instance, skillfully used this strategy to convince Congress that his proposed tax cuts were necessary. A president who calls for public response too often may, however, find a public that is losing interest. This may be what happened to President Bush in 2005, when he and several top administration officials crisscrossed the nation in the 60 Stops in 60 Days tour to promote his Social Security reform plan. Although his views were well covered by the local press, the tactic failed to move the plan in Congress.[44] Unfortunately for presidents, failure to move public opinion is the most likely outcome of the tactic of going public.[45]

Covering Congress

The media do not seem to pay as much attention to Congress as they do to the executive branch. To some extent, this apparent imbalance is due to the nature of the institution itself. Unlike the administration, Congress has no single leader who can be expected to speak authoritatively, although its members are generally more willing to talk and far less secretive than officials of the executive branch. Reporters cope with the multiple voices of Congress by concentrating their attention on party leaders, committee chairs, and others who hold key leadership positions or who are clearly identified as experts on a particular issue. As a result, many senators and representatives receive little or no national media attention. To political scientist Stephen Hess, such focus suggests that "where you sit determines how often you will be photographed."[46]

Illustrating the standard for defining news, coverage of Congress emphasizes partisan conflict and scandal. Policy accomplishments are generally ignored or trivialized. Debates over policy questions are most often described as power struggles, and compromise is characterized as unprincipled behavior motivated by electoral concerns.

Despite these constraints, individual members of Congress often receive favorable attention from parts of the media, especially their home-state media, which often depend heavily on their local senators and representatives to provide a regional perspective on national issues. Many members even become regular contributors to their local media, writing news columns and producing broadcast-quality radio and television tapes for distribution within their constituency. Additionally, members of Congress have adapted to the new technologies. They are, not surprisingly, avid users of the new media.

Covering the Courts

The branch of government that is least covered by the media is the courts. Although specific decisions of the U.S. Supreme Court may receive substantial media attention, most go unreported. When decisions are reported, the discussion is often superficial, concentrating, again, on who won and who lost.

The complex nature of judicial decisions and the specialized knowledge necessary to interpret them make judicial opinions particularly subject to misinterpretation by journalists, and justices often complain about such misinterpretation. Nevertheless, justices also remain indifferent to the needs of journalists. For instance, they do not hold press conferences or grant interviews to explain their decisions. Reporters are expected to read the decisions and draw their own conclusions. Most justices accept former justice William Brennan's observation that their opinions "must stand on their own merits without embellishment or comment from the judges who write or join them."[47]

Conclusion

We began this chapter by noting the general belief that the mass media have dramatically altered the conduct of American politics. But the increasingly sophisticated technology that made possible inexpensive newspapers and then the transmission of voice and images over the airwaves also changed the media. Slowly, newspapers began to emphasize objective reporting of public events. Similarly, radio and television turned into important sources of news, but only after it became apparent that there was an audience for such programming.

Along with the development of the mass media has come the fear, expressed as the myth of media manipulation, that Americans are in danger of being indoctrinated by their media. This myth exaggerates the power of the mass media to alter established political opinions. Citizens are not so susceptible to being told what to think as the myth suggests; they are not uncritical receptors of the media product. People with strong partisan views tend to gravitate toward sources that express the values that they already hold. Because they already know what they believe, they are less susceptible to influence. Nevertheless, the media do play an important role in framing the issues and setting the political agenda. Journalism may not change political attitudes, but it does have a significant effect on what people think is important and how they form political judgments. In many cases, the choices that journalists make define the political reality.

Furthermore, the mass media have greatly affected the conduct of political campaigns and government business. The media do not simply hold up a mirror to these processes; the reporters and cameras are not invisible observers. On the contrary, media coverage introduces distortions. However, there is little evidence that these distortions are journalistic attempts to manipulate the news. In fact, journalists often feel that they are the ones being manipulated when political candidates and public officials attempt to use them to get their stories across to the public.

Key Terms

Equal-time rule p. 330
Federal Communications
   Commission (FCC) p. 330

Penny press p. 324
Priming p. 335
Pseudo-events p. 335

Yellow journalism
   p. 324

Focus Questions Review

1. **How have the media evolved over the past two hundred years? > > >**
   - Early American newspapers were either organs of the political parties or commercial papers that reported business news to merchants. True mass media did not come into being until the 1830s, with the rise of the sensationalist penny press. Radio and then television developed initially as entertainment media. Only slowly did they come to be purveyors of news and public affairs programming.
   - Now the American mass media consist of numerous alternatives. Nevertheless, critics worry that the increasingly concentrated ownership of media outlets threatens the diversity of information. Few cities have more than one newspaper, and more than 85 percent of the local television stations are affiliated with one of the three major networks, which in turn are owned by huge conglomerates, comprising media outlets that combine publishing, broadcasting, and Hollywood studios.
   - Television and radio are subject to government regulation by the Federal Communications Commission (FCC), which has been reluctant to control the content of broadcasts. It does, however, require that stations that provide campaign airtime to a candidate for political office allow all other candidates for the same office equal time at identical rates.

2. **What is news? > > >**
   - News is what editors and reporters say it is. There are, however, several identifiable criteria for selecting stories. Events are more likely to be considered news if they contain conflict, involve people who are already well known, and are timely or novel. It also helps if there are people to interview, and, for today's media, if the event provides good visuals.

3. **How does media coverage affect people's attitudes? > > >**
   - What reporters and editors label as "news" is often the public's only source of information. By highlighting some events and ignoring others, the media have the capacity to influence what people think are the important issues.
   - The power of the media to change public opinion is limited, because many people accept only information that confirms the beliefs they already hold. The less familiar the issue, the more likely it is that the media will have an impact on people's attitudes.
   - Political candidates have become increasingly frustrated with media coverage that gives them very little direct access to the American public, while giving reporters and commentators a great deal more time on the air. To counter this, political candidates are turning to use of new media, including personal websites, blogs, and tweets.

4. **How do government officials shape the news? > > >**
   - Although government officials often view reporters as adversaries who must be controlled, they use the media to build public support for their programs. Press conferences, media interviews, going public, and planting information are some of the ways they convey information to the public.
   - The president is the prime focus of media coverage. Presidential administrations expend a great deal of time and effort on dealing with the media. Presidents commit substantial staff resources to media relations and plan their appearances before the public with the media in mind.
   - Congress is a more difficult institution for the national media to cover, but members of Congress receive a great deal of local media coverage.
   - The Supreme Court is the least covered institution in American government, in part because the justices are not particularly attentive to the needs of journalists.

Review Questions

1. Write an essay in which you discuss the criteria used to define what is news.
2. What does it mean to say that the press performs an "agenda-setting" function, and why does it matter?

For more information and access to study materials, visit the book's companion website at www.oup.com/us/gitelson.

Policy Connection

How do government policies shape the media landscape?

The Policy Challenge

In Chapter 10 we focused on the role of the mass media in our political lives and on issues related to the diversity and concentration of news and social media outlets. Issues related to media concentration take on even greater significance if we broaden our focus to include the nonnews fields of entertainment, sports, and publishing, which have considerable influence on what we know and how we feel about the world. From this perspective, the U.S. media market in 1983 was in the hands of fifty corporations, many of them operating in a particular part of the media landscape—for example, television, print journalism, movies, and book publishing. By 2013, through a combination of mergers, buyouts, reorganizations, and corporate failures, that number had been reduced to six major corporations, which are often described as "multimedia conglomerates": Comcast, 21st Century Fox (formerly News Corp), Disney, Viacom, CBS, and Time Warner.[1] Moreover, many analysts believed the consolidation of the media giants will continue into the future, and in February 2014 they were proven correct when Comcast announced its plans to buy Time Warner. The plans were immediately opposed by public interest groups who asked the Federal Communications Commission as well as the Antitrust Division of the Department of Justice to intervene.

It is clear that the consolidation and concentration that have taken place in the mass media market resulted in large measure from decisions made by the owners and managers of the various companies. But those decisions were not made in a vacuum. Government policies—especially those related to the regulation of the marketplace—were certainly a factor. In this Policy Connection we explore how certain public policies influenced the strategic decisions made by private corporations and how they affected the structure of the mass media marketplace.

By 2013, there was growing concern about the consolidation of America's media as they folded into six megacorporations. When, in February 2014, two of those companies—Comcast and Time Warner—announced plans to merge, there was an immediate reaction from groups who believed this move would not serve the public interest.

How Government Created Corporations

Our lives are touched daily by huge corporations, so it is often difficult to imagine that this form of business enterprise did not emerge as a major force in the American economy until the early twentieth century. In their classic work *The Modern Corporation and Private Property*, Adolph Berle and Gardiner Means noted that "the typical business unit of the 19th century was owned by individuals or small groups; was managed by them or their appointees; and was, in the main, limited in size by the personal wealth of the individuals in control."[2] They were also limited by the technology of the time, for whether you were a farmer or a blacksmith or a milliner, not having the capacity to extend the reach of your markets was significant.

Business conditions began to change in the mid-nineteenth century as new technologies such as the telegraph and railroad made it possible to expand the scope of your market, while new organizational forms allowed for the scaling up of production.[3] As a business owner, you could take advantage of these changed circumstances by challenging the competition in the next town or region and capturing the market all for yourself. Better yet, you could form a cooperative relationship with the potential competitor—join forces through a merger or some other arrangement that would serve both your interests.

The problem at the time was that the legal environment was not suitable for effective or long-term cooperation—that is, there were no legal provisions for one company to join with another company in an expanded venture that could take advantage of the new technologies. In addition, each state had it owns laws regarding the status of business enterprises, and these laws were often designed to prevent cooperative arrangements among different enterprises.[4] Thus, there was no direct or obvious way to merge or link the operations.

Starting in the 1850s[5] the legal picture changed, as privately owned railroad companies took advantage of state laws to form shareholder-owned corporations that combined the assets and operations of the smaller enterprises. As important, they formed regional alliances with other rail companies in order to take advantage of the economies of scale that came with cooperative arrangements on rates and operations. Businesses that increasingly relied on rail transport soon formed similar alliances and trade associations, in part to expand their markets and in part to counter the growing capacity of rail companies to demand higher prices. But such alliances were unstable (any member company could drop out of the alliance at any point), and their efforts to manipulate the market were increasingly subject to regulation under new state laws and successful court challenges.

In 1882, however, ten oil companies, led by John D. Rockefeller's Standard Oil of Ohio, entered into a "business trust" agreement in which the participating companies signed an "irrevocable deed of trust" that allowed a designated board of trustees to make all decisions for the combined enterprise.[6] The Standard Oil Trust eventually encompassed forty companies that effectively controlled most of petroleum production, refineries, and distribution in the United States. Over the next three decades, similar trusts emerged in all sectors of the growing U.S. economy, from steel, sugar, and whiskey to tobacco and stationary trusts.

The expansion of trusts was not welcome by all, and a strong populist movement among farmers and small business owners in the Midwest had begun to organize in the 1860s and 1870s against the growing economic power and monopolistic practices of railroads and grain elevator operators. As trusts emerged, these populist groups began to campaign for state and federal policies that would reign them in. Thus, by the late 1880s, there was not only a growing public demand for laws to deal with the anticompetitive nature of trusts but also a growing need among the trusts themselves for some other legal basis for forming and maintaining their giant enterprises.

In response, two major policy changes took place, one in the state of New Jersey and the other at the federal level. In 1888 and 1889, New Jersey liberalized its corporate laws to allow companies chartered in the state to legally merge and to own stock in other chartered companies, including companies chartered outside the state. Almost immediately, many of the largest trusts sought to be incorporated in New Jersey and moved their legal homes to the state; these

Theodore Roosevelt is often identified as the "trust-busting" president. As this cartoon notes, however, he was not against all trusts but favored those that made the United States more competitive internationally or led to lower prices. He chose to go after "bad trusts"—those that reduced competition.

during this period, but a significant portion was the result of the shifting landscape brought about by modifications in state and federal laws.

Antitrust Enforcement as Policy

Like any other policies, those that shape industries have changed over time. One constant has been that states have retained the authority to determine whether and how businesses can be incorporated.[9] Federal antitrust policy, however, has gone through many changes. Although the Sherman Act of 1890 is often regarded as a major development in this area, for nearly a decade it was rarely used, and then it was often used against labor unions rather than corporations. During the administrations of Theodore Roosevelt and William Howard Taft, however, enforcement picked up as the Department of Justice issued 120 lawsuits against companies in different industries. The results were mixed, as in each case the courts applied a "rule of reason" that focused on whether the alleged monopoly was acting in a way that damaged the competitive environment. The behavior of Standard Oil of New Jersey was found to violate that standard, and in 1911 the courts ordered the corporation to be broken up into smaller entities, thus creating Standard Oil of Indiana (later known as Amoco), of New York (Mobil Oil), and of California (Chevron Oil), while the New Jersey corporation (called Esso—created from *s* and *o*, the initials of Standard Oil) remained viable. In many other cases, however, federal lawsuits against trusts failed in court or were dropped.

In 1914, again riding a popular wave of antitrust sentiment, Congress passed two acts. The Clayton Antitrust Act included provisions focusing on corporate practices that tended to be monopolistic, whereas the Federal Trade Commission Act established a regulatory body (the Federal Trade Commission [FTC]) that would monitor business practices in general as well as scrutinizing how corporations were organized. In 1933, the antitrust work of the Department of Justice was consolidated under the newly organized Antitrust Division. Over the years, Congress has added or modified other provisions of antitrust policies, with states also playing a role under their own laws regarding anticompetitive practices.

included Rockefeller's Standard Oil, which then became Standard Oil of New Jersey.[7] Other states would follow New Jersey's lead in liberalizing their business chartering laws.[8]

At the federal level, in 1890 Congress passed (with near unanimous votes in both the House and Senate) the Sherman Antitrust Act, which outlawed trusts and any other "conspiracy" that fostered monopolistic behavior. The act was a reaction to public demands, but it did little more than put into statutory law what was already regarded as a basic legal standard under common law. For the major trusts that had already taken steps to incorporate, it closed off one major option for future competitors.

But most notable for our concern here is that these policy changes at the state and federal levels transformed the business landscape. Between 1895 and 1904, more than 1,800 businesses disappeared as the number of new corporations increased. We can attribute part of the change to market turmoil

The effectiveness of antitrust laws has depended, perhaps more than other policies, on their enforcement. The history of antitrust actions under the joint jurisdiction of the Antitrust Division of the Department of Justice and the FTC has often been characterized metaphorically as a pendulum pattern, with periods of active enforcement followed by periods of lax enforcement. But it has also been characterized as evolutionary, as enforcement has adapted to both the nature of legal interpretations and economic changes within specific industries. Still another view holds that antitrust policies are politically responsive to shifts in the priorities of Congress, the White House, and the courts.[10]

What these different views share is the conclusion that antitrust regulation plays a major role in shaping the corporate environment that is so central to our daily lives. How it does this depends on which industry we are focusing on and which government agencies have jurisdiction. Over the years, the FTC and the Antitrust Division of the Department of Justice have worked under the assumption that the commission would focus its attention on industries where consumer spending is a major factor—for example, health care, food, and energy—and the Department of Justice would typically focus on basic industries that play major roles in the general economy—for example, transportation (airlines and railroads), telecommunications, and banking. In addition, the Department of Justice assumes jurisdiction when the FTC determines that an antitrust case calls for criminal prosecution.

Although the media conglomerates are subject to the general antitrust policies of both the FTC and the Department of Justice, core parts of their holdings come under the jurisdiction of other government agencies, especially the Federal Communications Commission (FCC), which has regulated the nation's airwaves since its creation in 1934.

That's Entertainment!

Because a good deal of our daily lives is spent consuming various forms of information and entertainment generated by mass media corporations, we should be aware of how those giant organizations developed. Among the more fascinating characteristics of the six multimedia conglomerates is that each emerged through a very different path. Disney

Corporation, for example, traces its roots to Walt Disney's film animation studios in Hollywood, whereas 21st Century Fox developed through Rupert Murdoch's leverage of the Australia-based newspaper business owned by his father. Although Viacom was a prominent player in the television entertainment business (as part of CBS) through the 1970s and 1980s, it achieved its current status as one of the big six under the guidance of Sumner Redstone, an investor who used the resources of his family's movie-distribution business (National Amusements) to leverage the purchase of Viacom, which now includes Paramount Pictures, MTV, and more than 170 other cable and pay-TV networks. Redstone's family business also has a significant investment in another conglomerate, CBS Corporation, which has its roots in broadcast television.

Tracing the roots of Time Warner is complicated, because the media giant is a composite of companies with foundations in publishing (Time), movie production (Warner Brothers), and television (Turner Broadcasting and HBO). The same is true of Comcast, which includes not only a major cable TV and Internet service provider with its own news and sports stations but also the broadcasting and cable properties of the NBC network and the production and distribution operations of Universal Studios.

But knowing the details about the unique background of each of these major conglomerates does not explain how the industry went from fifty in 1983 to these six in 2014. Each made critical strategic decisions, and some succeeded while others did not. What is important is that many of those decisions were linked to government policies.

Among the success stories is that of Sumner Redstone. His family's National Amusements Company was a key player in the movie-distribution business through its ownership of movie theaters around the world. Convinced that content would prove to be more important than distribution in the long term, Redstone made significant investments in several movie studios during the 1960s, and he was on the lookout for other investments. The opportunity came in 1970, when the Federal Communications Commission issued a set of rules that prevented the major television networks from airing nonnews programming that they had a financial stake in. That rule revolutionized TV production by forcing the networks to go outside their companies to develop prime time shows, but it also led CBS to spin off its very successful production and syndication division—Viacom—into a separate corporation.[11] Redstone immediately took a major financial position in the new company. As FCC rules were relaxed, Redstone brought CBS under the control of Viacom in 1999, and several years later spun off a newly reconfigured CBS while retaining control over Viacom.

The relaxation of those FCC rules in the 1980s was actually part of the major shift in all antitrust enforcement that was part of a general trend favoring deregulation of the American economy. Policies aimed at deregulating various parts of the U.S. economy began under the Carter administration as a bipartisan effort led by consumer advocates (who believed regulation led to higher prices and poorer service in regulated markets) and conservative economists (who made the case for freer markets). Initially focused on the heavily regulated transport industries (e.g., airlines, buses), deregulation became a significant part of Ronald Reagan's effort to reduce the size of government and its role in the economy. Some antitrust efforts pursued at that time (e.g., the forced breakup of the AT&T monopoly in telecommunications) complemented the deregulation agenda, but in other areas, such an the entertainment industry, antitrust enforcement was eventually relaxed.[12] One result, according to historian Jennifer Holt, was that the "well-regulated borders" that kept the different parts of the entertainment and media industry apart were slowly eliminated, and as they were, the consolidation and integration of media properties began.[13]

The pivotal development was a 1983 decision by the Antitrust Division not to challenge the plans of three media companies—Columbia Pictures (at the time owned by Coca Cola), HBO, and CBS—to back the creation of a new Hollywood studio: Tri-Star Pictures. The arrangement effectively joined three segments of the media industry—movie production (Columbia), cable distribution (HBO) and TV broadcasting (CBS)—in a venture that would become the model for similar combinations. The logic at that time was that antitrust laws could be applied to mergers and other efforts that might reduce competition *within* media markets (e.g., movies, cable TV, and broadcast television) but not *across* markets. That logic opened the door to corporate decisions that eventually led to the consolidation and integration of media companies—and, as a result, the emergence of today's media industry giants, as the borders gave way to investment frontiers.[14]

Conclusion

How do government policies shape the media landscape?

Although this Policy Connection has highlighted how government antitrust policies helped shape today's media industry, we should also recognize the role of other factors. Copyright and patent laws have been crucial in the development of media technologies,[15] as have the regulatory rules regarding content and ownership of media properties that we discussed in Chapter 10. The growth of these media conglomerates has also been tied to the globalization of the economy, which has subjected these companies to the legal and political forces of other nations.

Ultimately, however, it is the decisions made by the top managers at these conglomerates that determine their form and future. The U.S. media landscape in 2014 was dominated by six conglomerates, but the form and number of these media giants remain in flux. For example, the number of media giants actually increases at times when their owners decide to "spin off" some of their holdings for business reasons. Thus, in 2013 Rupert Murdoch split NewsCorp from 21st Century Fox, and Time Warner put its publications division into a separate company, Time, Inc. Other moves indicate more consolidation. The media landscape is likely to change even more in the coming years.

In addition, the future of the media industry is increasingly linked to decisions made by technology and online giants such as Apple, Google, Amazon, and Netflix. Each has already made a difference in the various segments of the media industry, especially in music production, book publishing, and movie/TV distribution and production. Their decisions, as well as any further shifts in antitrust enforcement and other regulatory policies, will likely determine what the media industry looks like in five years.

QUESTIONS FOR DISCUSSION

1. Many observers have argued that the continued consolidation of media holdings poses a threat to American democracy because it puts more control over information and news in the hands of a small group of corporations. Others claim that these fears are unwarranted, because the media industry is so competitive and new technologies emerge that tend to limit control. How concerned are you about the trend toward the consolidation and concentration of media ownership in the hands of a few corporations?

2. The media industry is not the only segment of the American economy that has been subject to domination by a few corporations. Consider the roles that companies like Apple, Microsoft, and Google play in their markets. And despite many antitrust actions against it dating back over a hundred years, the oil industry remains dominated by a few companies. The pharmaceutical, telecommunications, and eyewear markets are also highly concentrated. What role should the government play in these markets? At what point and to what extent should antitrust policies be used to break up such concentration in different markets?

CHAPTER 11

MYTHS & REALITIES

Is Congress ineffective and buried under partisan bickering?

Congress

Filibustering One's Own Bill

In the midst of a 2012 congressional debate over the debt ceiling limit, minority leader Senator Mitch McConnell (R-KY) offered up a bill to end the stalemate. The bill would have authorized President Obama to simply lift the debt ceiling, unless two-thirds of Congress voted otherwise. Obviously, Obama would have welcomed this power, as he had long advocated just such a solution. But no one seriously thought that Congress would strip away its own power to manage fiscal affairs and give any president unilateral power. Indeed, when he requested a vote on the issue, Senator McConnell believed that a majority of Democrats would vote against the bill, demonstrating that they really did not want to end the debate over the budget ceiling.

When Senator McConnell brought his bill to the floor, Senate majority leader Harry Reid (D-NV) initially declined to hold a vote. Later that afternoon, Reid changed his mind, however. After talking with his fellow Democrats, the majority leader agreed to hold an up-or-down vote on the bill that afternoon. This time, Senator McConnell objected to having a vote. He argued that his bill needed sixty votes to pass; in other words, the senator was announcing his intention to **filibuster** the bill—that is to engage in prolonged debate in the Senate intended to kill a bill by preventing a vote on it. Observing that Senator McConnell was objecting to his own bill, Senator Reid said, "So I guess we have a filibuster of his own bill."[1]

To many Americans, Senator McConnell's actions were proof that Congress is paralyzed by its own internal partisan bickering and lacks effective leadership. Public approval of Congress is seldom high. Moreover, this view

Filibuster A prolonged debate in the Senate that is intended to kill a bill by preventing a vote on it.

< The U.S. Capitol Building, the meeting place for both houses of Congress, sits atop Capitol Hill in the District of Columbia. Pictured here is the building's most noteworthy architectural feature, the cast-iron dome. The dome and the statute, *Freedom*, were added to the building in the middle of the nineteenth century.

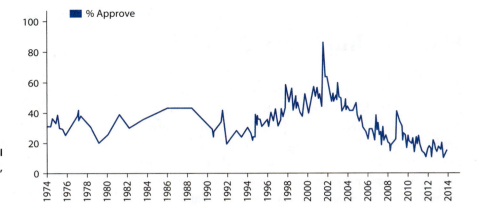

FIGURE 11.1 Congressional
Job Approval Ratings Trend,
1974–Present
Source: Gallup Poll, 2014.

of Congress is as old as the republic. Distrust of Congress is not the exception in American history; it is the rule (see Figure 11.1).

Consequently, a widely held *myth of Congress as the broken branch*, as an institution incapable of effective action, is hardly surprising. That image of Congress seems easy to support by listing the pressing national problems that remain unsolved. The huge national debt, homelessness, sagging educational performance, the troubled health care system, and the countless other problems plaguing U.S. society could be solved, so the myth assumes, if only Congress were more effective. However, putting aside the possibility that, in the short run at least, the problems may be insolvable, the myth does an injustice to the complex nature of Congress as an institution.

As we will see, the myth rests on the perception that Congress is solely a policymaking body. But this view ignores the full range of congressional responsibilities and their often contradictory nature. For instance, Congress is a representative institution as well as a policymaking one. Representation means more than policymaking; it also includes service to the constituents. Here Congress excels—a fact that partially explains why people disdain Congress but generally like its members.

Even when we look at the policymaking function, it is important to remember that Congress does not just make laws for the nation; its members are also expected to represent the interests of the states and districts that they serve. Congress must find ways to reconcile these different interests in the course of producing national policy. Moreover, Congress was designed as a deliberative body that would act to change the status quo only if a broad consensus favored change. Efficiency was never the goal. Our look at how Congress is organized should help illustrate these points.

The simple fact is, at various points in our history, members of Congress have found it hard to create consensus and represent the wishes of diverse constituencies at the same time. There is no denying that at times Congress does exemplify the myth of the broken branch. This is particularly true when the voters have chosen divided government, in which one party controls the White House and the other controls at least one of the legislative houses. Unfortunately, even good faith attempts to deal with our differences of opinion reflect badly on Congress. As political scientists John R. Hibbing and Elizabeth Theiss-Morse have noted, "People do not wish to see uncertainty, conflicting opinions, long debate, competing interests, confusion, bargaining, and compromised, imperfect solutions. They want government to do its job quietly and efficiently."[2] But, of course, people also want it done their way.

A Portrait of Congress

> **Who serves in Congress?**

Article I of the Constitution specifies only three criteria to qualify for membership in the U.S. Congress. To be eligible to serve as a senator, a person must have reached the age of thirty by the time he or she takes office, must have been a citizen of the United States for at least nine years, and must reside in the state from which he or she is elected. Representatives may enter office at the age of twenty-five and after only seven years of citizenship. Members of the House must also reside in the states from which they are chosen, but the Constitution does not require them to reside in the districts they represent.

Stability and Change in the Make-up of Congress

Despite these minimal requirements, a group portrait of Congress reveals an institution composed primarily of individuals drawn from the upper levels of American society. The typical member is a middle-aged, highly educated white male who was previously employed in a high-status occupation that earned him an income well above the national average.

Education and Occupation. As befits an elite, virtually all members of Congress hold a college degree, and a majority have completed some form of graduate work or professional study. Senators and representatives come from many different occupations, but lawyers outnumber the members of any other profession; they currently constitute about 40 percent of the membership. Next to law, business and banking are the most common occupations of legislators. Members of such occupational groups as manufacturing workers, farm laborers, and domestic servants are rarely found in Congress.

Race and Sex. In the period immediately after the Civil War, more than twenty African Americans (all of them Republicans) served in Congress. By the late nineteenth century, however, restrictions on the voting rights of African Americans

Members of the Congressional Black Caucus are committed to ensuring equal opportunity for everyone. Pictured here are the caucus members during the 113th Congress (2013–2014).

had eliminated their congressional representation entirely. No African Americans served in Congress from 1900 until 1928, when Oscar DePriest, a Republican from Chicago, was elected to the House of Representatives. During the next twenty-five years, only three more African Americans entered Congress.

Starting in the 1970s, the number of African American legislators increased significantly; after the 2014 midterm elections, forty-seven African Americans had seats in the House and two had seats in the Senate. Despite these recent gains, African Americans, who constitute about 11 percent of the population, are still underrepresented in Congress.

The Hispanic community is faring slightly better, with almost 7 percent of the seats in the House. This is a sevenfold increase since 1980, when the House contained only four Hispanics. The first woman to serve in Congress, Representative Jeannette Rankin, a Montana Republican, was elected in 1916, four years before the Nineteenth Amendment guaranteed women nationwide the right to vote. Although she was defeated in 1918 when she sought the Republican nomination for a Senate seat, she returned to Congress for one term in 1940. Since Rankin's election, more than 250 women have served in Congress.

During the 1970s and 1980s, women made only incremental gains in the number of congressional seats held. Between 1980 and 1991, for instance, women gained only seven seats. But in 1992, which many dubbed the "Year of the Woman," women won a record-breaking forty-seven House seats. Since then, the pace has slowed again, but women continue to make some gains. After the 2014 midterm elections, more than eighty women had seats in the House, and twenty were serving in the Senate. (For an international perspective on the number of women serving in legislatures, see Asked & Answered on page 357).

ASKED & ANSWERED

ASKED: *Why are there so few women serving in legislative bodies?*

ANSWERED: Globally, only about 18 percent of the world's legislators are women. It is easy to dismiss these global numbers by pointing to countries where culture, and even law, restricts the freedoms of women, but the underrepresentation of women is not limited to countries with these restrictions. Underrepresentation of women is also common in many older, affluent democratic nations, including our own. Consider the following statistics: Although some long-standing democracies post impressive numbers—in Sweden, for instance, women hold 45 percent of the parliamentary seats—the percentage of national legislative seats held by women in the United States only slightly exceeds the world average yet still tops the percentages in Japan, France, and Greece.

To equalize representation along gender lines, some nations have tried an active approach: implementing gender quotas. In 1991, for example, Argentina instituted a quota system for parties contesting elections. Thirty percent of each party's list, at minimum, must be women, and noncompliance results in disapproval of the entire list. A decade after the implementation of the quota system, women constituted almost 31 percent of the national assembly, up from less than 5 percent before implementation.

But comparable laws in other Latin American countries and in Europe have not produced such a dramatic effect; results vary, but on average the gains have been slight. In 1999, for example, France passed a parity law similar to Argentina's requiring that 50 percent of party nomination lists be women. Failure to reach parity now results in a loss of government financial support for party activities. Unlike the Argentine experience, however, the French law has produced only a small gain for women, less than a 2 percent increase in women legislators. Likewise, Belgium passed an act in 1994 requiring that no more than two-thirds of the candidates nominated by a party be of the same gender, but it produced only modest gains in the seats held by women.

Why is it that, even with legal quotas, gender parity in legislative seats is so difficult to achieve? The answer involves several characteristics of culture and politics, but the most important element seems to be the electoral system itself. Key to increasing the number of legislative seats held by women seems to be the use of multimember districts (elections in which voters choose multiple candidates to represent the district) as opposed to the typical U.S. single-member district election, in which only one candidate is selected. After controlling for cultural norms and laws mandating parity, the use of multimember districts is the most important factor increasing women's success in winning legislative seats. Evidence from the United States confirms this: The percentage of women holding legislative seats in states using multimember districts is higher than that in states using single-member districts, and states that have shifted from multimember to single-member districts have generally seen a decline in the percentage of women legislators.

Just why multimember districts promote more gender diversity is unclear, but there are some possible explanations. First of all, in single-member districts, elections tend to be candidate centered, with the personal qualities of the candidates playing a considerable role in the voters' decision, whereas voters in multimember districts cast their vote for a group of candidates from the same party, which usually includes women candidates. Second, single-member districts are notoriously advantageous for incumbents, allowing them, as the only representative from the district, to develop a personal relationship with constituents. Because most incumbents are men, the success of women candidates in single-member electoral systems is limited. Candidates, female or male, have considerable difficulty beating incumbents.

Source: Pippa Norris, Electoral Engineering: Voting Rules and Political Behavior *(Cambridge: Cambridge University Press, 2004).*

Getting Elected

Despite the myth of Congress as the broken branch, the American public demonstrates considerable faith in individual members by consistently reelecting incumbents—proving, as Albert Cover put it, that "one good term deserves another."[3] Since 1946, more than 90 percent of the House incumbents who have sought reelection have won, and slightly more than 80 percent of the incumbent senators seeking reelection have been victorious.

Remarkably, incumbents did well even in 1994. The 1994 election marked an historic change in Congress as the Republicans gained fifty-three seats and took control of the House for the first time in forty years. Several highly prominent members of the House were defeated, including Thomas S. Foley, the Speaker of the House in the 103rd Congress. (Foley became the first Speaker to be defeated in a reelection bid since 1860.) Subsequent elections trimmed the size of the Republican majority in both houses.

Nevertheless, the continued successes of Republicans lead pundits to talk about a "permanent majority," with Republicans entrenched by the advantages of incumbency and Democrats perpetually in the minority. As it turned out, however, there was no permanent majority. Instead, the parties have battled back and forth for control of Congress. In 2006, for instance, an increasingly unpopular war in Iraq and a series of congressional scandals enabled Democrats to gain thirty seats in the House and six in the Senate. In 2008, the Democrats picked up more seats in the House. Two years later, however, the Democrats' gains were reversed. Republicans took back the House and made gains in the Senate. Incumbents in 2010 did badly; only 86 percent of the House incumbents won their elections. Only two Republican incumbents lost their House races; the rest of the losses were absorbed by Democratic incumbents. Then in 2014 the Republicans added to their margins in the House and took control of the Senate for the first time in eight years. In an election in which more than 95 percent of the House incumbents won reelection, the Democrats lost ten incumbents and the Republicans only two. All of the losing Senate incumbents were Democrats. .

Just why incumbents do so well is the subject of much speculation. One frequent explanation is that House incumbents are "safe by design"—that is, that their districts have been drawn to maximize their party's strength among voters. The process of designing districts does, in fact, have a major impact on political power within Congress. Every ten years, in response to the U.S. census, House seats are redistributed among the states, and House districts are redrawn by state legislatures. The Supreme Court has held that, in drawing the new boundaries, state legislatures must create districts that are approximately equal in population.[4]

States are nominally constrained in that they may not create districts that dilute minority voting strength.[5] However, in *Miller v. Johnson* (1995), the Supreme Court ruled that so-called **majority-minority districts**, districts that create a political majority for a racial or ethnic minority, are unconstitutional if race was the "predominant factor" in drawing the boundaries. Thus, if districts are designed with the intent of giving a particular racial or ethnic group an advantage, they are likely to be unconstitutional.

Majority-minority districts Congressional districts that create a political majority for a racial or ethnic minority.

The few restraints that the Court has placed on state legislatures have left them considerable freedom to engage in the practice of **gerrymandering**—the drawing of district boundaries in ways that provide political advantage. Indeed, the Supreme Court has ruled that partisan gerrymandering is an acceptable practice. Justice Antonin Scalia, writing for the majority in *Vieth v. Jubelirer* (2004), reasoned that "political affiliation is not an immutable characteristic, but may shift from one election to the next." Moreover, four of the justices concluded that partisan gerrymandering could never be challenged in court, because there were no clear standards to defining partisan gerrymanders.[6] Consequently, state legislatures may design congressional districts with the intent of advantaging a political party, but they may not draw districts with the intent of advantaging a racial or ethnic group.

Partisan gerrymandering gained even more support as a result of the Supreme Court's 2006 ruling in *League of United Latin American Citizens v. Perry*.[7] The *Perry* case arose out of the failed effort of the Texas legislature to draw new districts following the 2000 census. With the state senate controlled by Republicans and the House controlled by the Democrats, Texas was unable to agree on a single plan. As a result, the Texas congressional districts were redrawn by a federal court. The court-imposed plan produced a congressional delegation composed of seventeen Democrats and fifteen Republicans. In 2002, however, Republicans took control of both houses of the state legislature and promptly set about redrawing the state's congressional districts. They produced a plan that eventually resulted in a seven-seat gain for the party. Opponents of the newly

Gerrymandering The practice by the party controlling the state legislature of drawing congressional and other district boundaries to maximize the number of seats it can win.

Gerrymandering is often invoked to explain the high rate of electoral success enjoyed by congressional incumbents. For many observers of politics, gerrymandering has become so prevalent that the states need to consider significant reform of the redistricting process.

drawn plan sued, claiming that a mid-decade redistricting of congressional seats out of a desire to increase partisan representation violated the Constitution. But the Supreme Court disagreed with that contention. Although the seven justices in the majority gave varying reasons for rejecting the challenge to the law, they agreed that a mid-decade redistricting plan, even one designed to increase the number of seats held by a party, did not violate the Constitution. It remains to be seen how many states will adopt the strategy, but the Court's decision is clearly an incitement to gerrymandering.

Over the last couple of decades gerrymandering has become much easier and considerably more accurate. Sophisticated mapping programs combined with a variety of data sources matching people to their political preferences allows political leaders to run multiple models until they find the one plan that will maximize the number of House seats that the party can win. There are two basic approaches to creating a partisan advantage. One strategy, called *packing*, tries to concentrate the other party's supporters in the fewest possible districts. The minority party then wins a few districts by very large margins—much larger than they need to win the district. Concentrating its opponents in a few districts leaves the party that controls the redistricting a secure although not commanding majority in multiple districts. Alternatively, the party in power may engage in *cracking*; according to this practice, the party in power tries to spread the other party's supporters over several districts, making them the minority party in each of those districts.[8]

Clearly, incumbents benefit from these practices, and in many cases districts are configured to practically guarantee that the incumbents will be successful. But gerrymandering alone cannot explain the success of incumbents. Incumbents have been receiving larger percentages of the vote, even in states that did not redistrict.[9] There is some evidence that the competitiveness or lack of competitiveness of congressional elections is also shaped by demography. As one commentator observed, "The problem is not who draws the lines—it's where people live."[10] "More people are choosing where to live based on demographic factors that now align with political party. In effect, voters themselves are largely responsible for tipping the balance in many districts by moving to where they can find neighbors of like mind."[11] Even without gerrymandering, congressional districts are likely to become less competitive as people sort themselves in ways that mirror their political views.

With or without gerrymandering, incumbents have a variety of resources on which to draw. They find it easy to get their names before the public, and they are almost always better known and viewed more favorably than their challengers. Former Speaker of the House Jim Wright may have been correct when he said that, outside their districts, members of the House are individuals of "widespread obscurity," but within their districts they are conspicuous.[12] This visibility is the result of hard work and the skillful use of the resources of office. As one observer noted, "When we say Congressman Smith is unbeatable, we mean Congressman Smith is unbeatable as long as he continues to do the things he is doing."[13]

Members of Congress have a wide array of official resources that they can use in pursuing reelection. For example, incumbents can mail newsletters or questionnaires free of charge. Using this **franking privilege** enables them to cultivate

Franking privilege The power of members of Congress to send out mail free of charge; this allows incumbents to cultivate a favorable image among their constituents.

a favorable image among constituents. Shared use of a completely equipped television studio, an allowance to maintain district offices, a well-funded staff dedicated solely to constituent service, and a travel allowance sufficient to permit weekly visits to their districts further help incumbents enhance their name recognition. The dollar value of these services and privileges is conservatively estimated at well more than $1.5 million over a two-year House term. And senators receive much more than do representatives. Just how much more depends on the size of their states, as their allowances vary by state populations.

Sitting members of Congress also have opportunities to engage in "credit claiming"— taking credit for benefits that their constituents receive from the national government.[14] When a representative or senator announces an award of federal money for a new dam, a highway extension, or an important defense contract, the effect is to portray him or her as someone who is working hard for the district and getting results.

Closely linked to credit claiming is legislation appropriating funds for local projects—an activity often referred to as **pork-barrel legislation**. Securing such benefits for one's district is "bringing home the bacon." Most often the bacon comes in the form an **earmark**. There is no precise definition of earmarks. The House and the Senate, for instance, have different definitions, but in general an earmark is a proposal to provide spending or favorable tax treatment for specific projects in the sponsor's district or state. A provision in a bill to build a new highway or a bridge in a specific congressional district is a classic example.

Although earmarks have been around a long time, in recent years they have come under attack. Earmarks were never a large part of national expenditures, but they were visible and often easily ridiculed. Foremost among the examples of earmarks gone bad is the 2005 Alaskan bridge earmark. Members of both the Left and the Right criticized Congress for considering an earmark from Senator Ted Stevens of Alaska to build a bridge from the small town of Ketchikan, Alaska (population 8,900), to the island of Gravina (population 50). The estimated cost of the bridge, dubbed by its critics as the "Bridge to Nowhere," was $223 million, and many considered it proof that Congress was fiscally irresponsible.[15] Prompted by the pandemonium surrounding the Bridge to Nowhere and other projects, Congress chose to restrict the use of earmarks. The 113th Congress placed a moratorium on all spending earmarks. Of course, members of Congress have found ways around the moratorium, but "securing the bacon" has become more difficult.

Finally, incumbents' success depends on what political scientist Richard Fenno has called their **home style**, or the way they present themselves to their constituents. As Fenno observed, "It is the style, not the issue content, that counts most in the reelection constituency."[16] Although incumbents may differ in how they present themselves, their purpose is the same: to win the voters' trust. This kind of bond does not develop overnight; it takes time and constant attention, but the rewards can be great. An incumbent who is trusted by the voters is relatively safe from political attack and is likely to find constituents understanding of occasional political mistakes. In the brief time span of a campaign, challengers find it difficult to establish this kind of relationship.

Pork-barrel legislation Legislation that appropriates funds for local projects in an area that a member of Congress represents.

Earmark A legislative proposal to provide spending or favorable tax treatment for specific projects in the sponsor's district or state.

Home style The way in which incumbent members of Congress present themselves to their constituents in an attempt to win the voters' trust.

Although incumbents have a strong advantage, they are not invincible. Challengers can win, but they generally have to spend a great deal of money; just how much varies from race to race. As we mentioned in Chapter 8, on campaigns and elections, money does not buy elections, but it may buy the name recognition that is essential for competing against well-known incumbents.[17]

Unfortunately for challengers, incumbents have a decided advantage in attracting campaign contributions. First of all, as already noted, they are better known than the challengers. Moreover, large campaign donors tend to see contributions as investments: These donors want access to policymakers. Because the odds are heavily in favor of incumbents, those seeking access will see incumbents as the best investment.

Despite their advantages, many incumbents worry a great deal about their reelection chances. As political scientist Gary Jacobson notes, "Members tend to exaggerate electoral threats and overreact to them. They are inspired by worst-case scenarios—what would they have to do to win if everything went wrong?—rather than the objective probabilities."[18] It takes only one or two losses by established incumbents to elevate the sense of uncertainty and risk of the others. Since the elections of 2010, many Republicans have expressed great apprehension over the possibility that they will be *primaried*—a new term in the political lexicon, used to describe being defeated in a primary. What Jacobson would call the "objective probabilities" point to continued success for incumbents, but many of them, even those in safe districts, are working overtime to see to it that they win their primary.

The Work of Congress

> **What are the major functions of Congress?**

Even though the Constitution established a government in which three branches share power, the Framers were united in the belief that the legislature should play the central role in governing. As a result, Congress is charged with several different kinds of duties.

Making Laws

Article I of the Constitution charges Congress with making laws. In addition, Section 8 of Article I lists a series of specific congressional powers, known as the *enumerated powers*—for example, the power to establish post offices and to coin money. Section 8 also gives Congress the power "to make all laws which shall be necessary and proper for carrying into Execution the foregoing Powers, and all other Powers vested by this Constitution in the Government of the United States." This "necessary and proper" clause has been interpreted by the Supreme Court in such sweeping terms that Congress can now legislate in nearly every aspect of American life.[19]

The Power to Tax

Foremost among the duties of Congress is the setting of taxing and spending policies for the nation. According to the Constitution, bills raising revenue (taxes) are to originate in the House; but, because the Senate may amend these bills, the distinction is not particularly significant.

It was evident that tax policies were a top priority early in President George W. Bush's tenure, when he proposed a $1.6 trillion tax cut. In 2001, the president got most of the tax cut that he wanted, but the cuts were spread out over several years, and most were designed to expire later in the decade. This time frame guaranteed that tax policies would remain a perennial issue of dispute. Faced with growing budget deficits, two wars, the collapse of numerous financial institutions, and the subsequent recession, the Obama administration was reluctant to renew some of the Bush-era tax cuts. But in 2010 Congress extended the tax cuts for two more years. Then again, in 2012, Congress returned to the Bush-era cuts. This time they were forced to negotiate with a president determined to extend the lower rates for everyone of low to moderate income but not for the wealthy. Months of negotiations led to an agreement to continue the lower rates for single individuals earning $400,000 or less and married couples making $450,000 or less. For those earning more than these cutoffs, the tax rate would go from 35 percent to 39.6 percent.

Few members of Congress have been happy with the current tax code. There is widespread consensus in Congress that it needs to dramatically reform the current tax system, not simply tweak the rates. The problem is that there is no consensus on the nature of that reform. On the one hand, most Republicans believe that any reform should be revenue neutral—that is, no one's taxes should increase as result of the new system. On the other hand, most Democrats see closing loopholes in the current tax code as a means of raising more revenue. It is obvious that Congress will not be able to make significant changes in taxes until its members can reach some kind of bipartisan consensus or until one party controls both houses and probably also the presidency.

Producing the Budget

Equally controversial are the spending decisions, or *appropriations*, that Congress makes each year and incorporates as the federal budget. Throughout most of the nation's history, Congress made no attempt to coordinate the federal budget. The budget was simply the total of the separate appropriations for each department of government. Over the past four decades, however, Congress has attempted to centralize the budget process and place restraints on overall spending levels.

With the 1974 passage of the Budget and Impoundment Control Act, Congress established a new budget committee in each house. These committees receive the president's budget and an analysis provided by the Congressional Budget Office (CBO), which was created to provide Congress with expertise equivalent to that possessed by the executive branch. The CBO analyzes the president's budget, identifies changes in spending levels, and estimates the expected revenue from taxes and other sources. It also projects the cost of **entitlement programs**, programs that commit the government to supplying funds or services to all citizens who meet specified eligibility requirements, Social Security benefits and military pensions are examples. On the basis of that information, the budget committees recommend to their respective houses spending ceilings for major funding categories. These recommendations constitute the **First Concurrent Budget Resolution,**

Entitlement programs Programs such as Social Security that commit the government to supplying funds or services to all citizens who meet specified eligibility requirements.

First Concurrent Budget Resolution The recommendation for spending ceilings in major funding categories. It is submitted to the House and Senate by their respective budget committees and must be passed by April 15.

which both the House of Representatives and the Senate must pass by April 15 each year.

Despite the law, the last time that Congress produced the First Concurrent Budget Resolution on time was 2003. In formulating the funding bills for specific departments and programs, the various appropriations committees of the two houses are expected to follow the overall spending guidelines set by the budget resolution. If these guidelines are exceeded, either the appropriations must be reduced or the House and Senate must agree to amend the amounts in the first budget resolution.[20] They must complete this process, known as *reconciliation*, by the passage of a second budget resolution in September.

The act gave the budgeting process a new sense of coherence, but it did not reduce the budget deficit. It was simply too easy for Congress to ignore the first budget resolution and pass a second one that merely totaled the various appropriations bills. Subsequent reform bills in the 1980s and 1990s also failed to reign in federal deficits.

Although in 2001 the government began predicting a surplus for the next decade, by the end of the year the surplus was gone, and the government had returned to deficit spending. The dramatic downturn in the economy, especially after the terrorist attacks of 2001 and the collapse of the high-tech bubble, substantially reduced government revenue, even as the wars in Afghanistan and Iraq drove spending ever higher. With the collapse of the nation's financial institutions in 2008 and the subsequent recession, the nation went from a surplus to record deficits in a few short years.

As the deficit climbed, the politics of budgeting became even more contentious. Year after year, Congress struggled to come up with a budget bill that could attract a majority. Failing to pass a budget bill or the various appropriations bills needed to make the government work, Congress turned to passing a series of **continuing resolutions**—bills that authorize the government to spend for a few months, usually at the previous year's rate. Debates over the 2014 fiscal year budget reached a stalemate, so, on October 1, 2013, the U.S. government, excepting several "essential services," was shut down. The shutdown lasted for sixteen days and was only resolved when, on October 16, the House and Senate agreed on another continuing resolution. In December 2013, the House and Senate finally agreed on a budget resolution, the first step in the budget process. Although it was a step forward, the budget resolution had to be followed by another continuing resolution keeping the government operating until the two houses could pass the necessary appropriation bills. In January, a single, all-encompassing appropriation bill was passed and signed by the president. It was three and a half months late, but, then again, it was the first budget actually passed in three years. Throughout the three previous years the government had operated on a series of continuing resolutions.

Continuing resolutions Bills that authorize the government to spend for a few months, usually at the previous year's rate.

Casework

In addition to representing constituents on policy questions, members of Congress are expected to provide their constituents with personal services, called **casework**. Senators, representatives, and their staffs spend a great deal of time and energy helping constituents through the maze of federal programs and

Casework Work done by members of Congress to provide constituents with personal services and help them through the maze of federal programs and benefits.

benefits. For instance, are you leaving the country and do you need a passport in a hurry? Contact your representative. Maybe you need help with a Small Business Administration official who will not return your phone calls. Or maybe you're having problems getting a Veterans Administration or Social Security check. Perhaps you have a son or daughter in the army who has not written home in several weeks. Call the district office of your representative or senator.

Many members of Congress complain that casework reduces them to errand runners, but few refuse to do the work. Instead, most members have accommodated the demand for casework by enlarging their district or state offices. Between 1972 and 1987, the total number of staff assigned by members of the House to their district offices more than doubled, and the number of Senate staffers located in the state offices more than tripled.[21] Since then, however, staff sizes have stabilized.

Although it may be tiresome, casework is good electoral politics. As Morris Fiorina has pointed out, "The nice thing about casework is that it is mostly profit; one makes many more friends than enemies."[22] But casework is more than simply good politics; it is also a form of representation. Richard Fenno reminds us that constituents may want "good access or the assurance of good access as much as they want good policy."[23] Contrary to the myth of Congress as the broken branch, members of both the House and the Senate are indeed effective at providing that access.

Congressional Oversight

The passage of a law rarely ends congressional involvement in the matter. Congress is responsible for overseeing the activities of the executive agencies that are charged with implementing policy. This process of legislative oversight, which has become a crucial aspect of congressional work, takes many forms. For instance, casework can sometimes bring the weakness or ineffective administration of a program to a member's attention.[24] Congress may also require executive officials to prepare periodic, detailed reports of their activities. In the 1996 Department of Defense appropriations act, for instance, Congress mandated so many reports that it took the Pentagon 111 pages just to list them. Often, however, the oversight function is performed as part of the appropriation process. The hearings that are held to consider agency budgets give members of both houses an opportunity to question executive officials extensively. As one member of the House Appropriations Committee remarked, "You keep asking questions just to let them know someone is watching them."[25]

More dramatically, Congress may exercise oversight by conducting committee investigations. A committee of either house can compel testimony and evidence from government officials and private citizens for the purpose of proposing new legislation. In 2010, Congress used this committee oversight function to investigate BP's responsibility for the Gulf of Mexico oil spill and the performance of the government agencies that were responsible for regulating offshore drilling.

For decades, Congress relied for oversight on the **legislative veto**—a device in a bill that allowed Congress or a committee of Congress to veto the actions of an executive agency or the president in an area covered by the bill. To establish the legislative veto, Congress would pass a statute granting the president or an

Legislative veto A device in a bill that allowed Congress or a congressional committee to veto the actions of an executive agency or the president in an area covered by the bill. It was declared unconstitutional by the Supreme Court in 1983.

In performing its oversight function, Congress often requires officials to come before it to report on administration activities. Here, Kathleen Sebelius, former Secretary of Health and Human Services, acquiesces to photographers prior to her testimony before the House Energy and Commerce Committee. Secretary Sebelius was there to answer questions regarding the botched rollout of HealthCare.gov.

administrative agency wide discretion in formulating specific policies, but these policies would be subject to congressional approval. Thus, in the War Powers Resolution of 1973, Congress gave the president the authority to send troops into a hostile situation for sixty days. The troops would have to leave at the end of that period unless Congress declared war or provided specific statutory authorization.

In 1983, the Supreme Court declared the legislative veto unconstitutional.[26] Nevertheless, Congress has been reluctant to give up this form of oversight. Because the language of the Supreme Court opinion is not entirely clear, Congress has continued to include the legislative veto in statutes. Whether federal courts will declare these laws unconstitutional remains to be seen.[27] Even if the laws are declared unconstitutional, Congress has devised other informal means of holding agencies accountable. The most popular of these methods is to provide only short-term appropriations, so that the agency has to come back to Congress again and again.

The Organization of Congress

> **What role do the parties play in organizing Congress?**

Bicameral Refers to a legislature that is divided into two separate houses, such as the U.S. Congress.

The U.S. Congress is a **bicameral** legislature—a legislature that is divided into two separate houses. Our Congress, however, differs markedly from most bicameral legislatures in other countries in that the two houses have nearly equal power. That arrangement was set up to divide power and to strike a balance between the large and the small states. Furthermore, Congress is "an assembly of equals,"[28] in which each senator or representative has his or her own constituency to represent, and consequently each member of Congress has an equal claim to legitimacy. The effect of this egalitarianism in Congress is to fragment and decentralize power, which must then be structured in some other manner if the institution is to make policy.

Bicameralism

The founders designed the two houses to represent different elements in American society. The House of Representatives, with its membership based on frequent and popular elections, was to be the voice of current public opinion. James Madison considered the House "the grand repository of the democratic principles of government." In contrast, senators, who were originally chosen by state legislatures, were expected to curb the radical tendencies of House members. George Washington gave what may be the best description of the purpose of the Senate. When asked by Thomas Jefferson why the Constitutional Convention had agreed to the second body, Washington replied, "Why did you pour that coffee into your saucer?" "To cool it," responded Jefferson. "Even so," said Washington, "we pour legislation into the senatorial saucer to cool it."[29]

The Seventeenth Amendment, ratified in 1913, changed the method of electing senators, making it so that they are chosen, as are representatives, directly by the electorate. Although the founders' expectations for the two bodies may not have been completely fulfilled, the bicameral structure is still an important feature of the American legislative system. Because the two houses are nearly equal in power, public policies are the product of two distinct legislative processes, with two sets of rules, politics, and internal dynamics. These differences fragment power and give Congress a decentralized organization.

Congressional Leadership

Although the Constitution does not mention political parties, congressional leadership is party leadership, because the political parties organize Congress.

Leadership in the House. The **Speaker of the House** is the presiding officer of the House, the leader of its majority party, and second in line, behind the vice president, to succeed the president. The only House position created by the Constitution, the Speaker was supposed to be elected by the entire body but is actually chosen by a vote of the majority party. Not since 1923 has there been a floor battle over the Speaker, because, on this matter, the members of the House vote along straight party lines.

Because the Speaker serves as leader of the majority party and presides over the House, the position is the most powerful in Congress. Nevertheless, the Speaker's power has greatly diminished since the early 1900s, when Speakers dominated the business of the House. The last of the truly powerful Speakers, Joseph "Uncle Joe" Cannon, assigned members of both parties to committees, appointed and removed committee chairs at will, controlled the flow of bills to the floor, and exercised complete authority over which members were recognized to speak on the floor. Cannon's almost dictatorial control of the House precipitated the 1910 "revolt against the Speaker," which stripped the office of all committee-assignment powers and drastically limited the power of recognition. Modern Speakers have regained a great deal of power, but their power falls far short of that possessed by Speaker Cannon.

Speaker of the House The only House position created by the Constitution. The Speaker is chosen by a vote of the majority party and is the presiding officer of the House, the leader of its majority party, and second in line to succeed the president.

Whenever the majority in the House of Representatives changes from one party to the other, the leadership in the House changes. Pictured here is Nancy Pelosi (D-CA), the first woman to serve as Speaker of the House, surrendering the gavel to John Boehner (R-OH). Democrats lost control of the House as a result of the 2010 elections and therefore lost control of the speakership.

Majority leader The second-ranking party position in the House (and the first in the Senate). The majority leader schedules floor action on bills and guides the party's legislative program through the House.

Minority leader The head of the minority party in the Senate. This term also refers to the leader of the minority party in the House, who represents its interests by consulting with the Speaker and the majority leader on the scheduling of bills and rules for floor action.

Party whips Members of Congress who support the party leaders in the House and Senate by communicating the party's positions to the membership and keeping the leaders informed of members' views.

The holder of the second-ranking position in the majority party, the **majority leader**, schedules floor action on bills and guides the party's legislative program through the House. The majority leader also works with the Speaker and other party leaders to develop the party's legislative agenda.

The **minority leader**, chosen by a vote of the minority party, heads the opposition party in the House and represents its interests. The minority leader also consults with the Speaker and the majority leader on the scheduling of bills and rules for floor action. The most important job of the minority leader is to work to win back control of the House. Like their counterparts in the majority party, minority leaders are generally seasoned legislators. The majority and minority leaders have the assistance of the **party whips**, who support the party leaders by communicating the party's positions to the membership and keeping the leaders informed of members' views. In recent years, both parties have expanded their whip system by creating the positions of deputy and regional whips. Expanding the whip system allows the parties to bring more members into the leadership ranks and thus to give more members an incentive to support the party leadership.

Leadership in the Senate. Article I of the Constitution makes the vice president of the United States president of the Senate. This is mostly a ceremonial position. The Constitution specifies that the vice president presides over the Senate, but, unlike the Speaker of the House, the Senate's presiding officer has very little power. The Constitution does, however, provide that the vice president can vote to break a tie. Not surprisingly, vice presidents spend very little time officiating over the Senate, but they are always ready to take the role should a close vote occur. In addition to the Senate president, the Constitution also provides for a president pro tempore to preside over the Senate in the vice president's absence.

Traditionally, the president pro tempore is the majority party senator with the longest continuous service. Despite the existence of these other officers, it is the majority and minority leaders who exercise the most power in the Senate.

Much like their counterparts in the House, the majority and minority leaders of the Senate are expected to organize support for party initiatives. Furthermore, the majority leader is expected to manage floor activity, whereas the minority leader represents the "loyal opposition." When the majority leader is a Democrat, he or she heads the party in the Senate and chairs the committees that assign members to committees and that schedule floor debates. When the Republicans are in the majority, these tasks are assigned to three different senators. The Senate also has whips, although they have fewer responsibilities than House whips.

The Committee System

Party leaders in both houses struggle to bring organization to a fragmented institution. In their efforts to manage the Congress, they must contend with a committee system that distributes power to many others, because it is committees and subcommittees that mostly carry out the work in the modern Congress. These "little legislatures," as Woodrow Wilson referred to them, screen the thousands of bills that are introduced during each session and decide which should be recommended for consideration by the larger body. The few bills that the committees recommend for floor action define the congressional agenda. Bills that are passed over by committees rarely reach the floor.

This arrangement has not always been the practice. In the early days of Congress, temporary committees considered specific legislative proposals and then disbanded.[30] These committees had little independent power and could not withhold a bill from floor consideration. Only gradually did Congress come to rely on permanent committees.

Types of Committees. The most important committees in Congress are the **standing committees**. These permanently established committees consider proposed legislation in specified policy areas and decide whether to refer it to the larger body. It is to the standing committees that nearly all legislation is sent. Table 11.1 lists the standing committees of the 113th Congress.

Most of the standing committees also have subcommittees, each of which covers a portion of the policy area controlled by the larger committee. Throughout the 1980s, the number and power of subcommittees grew to the point that congressional scholars began to describe the policy process as being dominated by subcommittees. The number of subcommittees in the House was reduced. All committees except those responsible for appropriations and government reform are limited to six subcommittees. House rules also limit members to serving on no more than four subcommittees.

Select, or special, committees are temporary committees established by the House or the Senate to study particular problems. For instance, in 1986, both the House and the Senate created select committees to investigate the Reagan administration's sale of arms to Iran and the diversion of funds from the sale to forces seeking the overthrow of the government of Nicaragua. Select or special committees usually last for no more than two years and are disbanded at the end

Standing committees
Permanently established committees that consider proposed legislation in specified policy areas and decide whether to recommend its passage by the larger body.

Select, or special, committees Temporary committees established by the House or Senate to study particular problems.

TABLE 11.1 Standing Committees of the House and Senate, 113th Congress (2013–2014)

Almost all of these committees have subcommittees. The number of members ranges from ten to sixty-one.

House	Number of Subcommittees	Senate	Number of Subcommittees
Agriculture	5	Agriculture, Nutrition, and Forestry	5
Appropriations	12	Appropriations	12
Armed Services	7	Armed Services	6
		Banking, Housing, and Urban Affairs	5
Budget	None	Budget	None
Education and the Workforces	4	Commerce, Science, and Transportation	4
Energy and Commerce	6	Energy and Natural Resources	7
		Environment and Public Works	6
Ethics	None		
Financial Services	5	Finance	6
Foreign Affairs	6	Foreign Relations	7
		Health, Education, Labor, and Pensions	3
Homeland Security	6	Homeland Security and Governmental Affairs	4
House Administration	None		
Intelligence	3		
Judiciary	5	Judiciary	7
Natural Resources	5		
Oversight and Government Reform	5		
Rules	2	Rules and Administration	None
Science, Space, and Technology	5		
Small Business	5	Small Business and Entrepreneurship	None
Transportation and Infrastructure	6		
Veterans Affairs	4	Veterans Affairs	None
Ways and Means	6		

Source: http://www.congress.gov/.

of the congressional session. Unlike the standing committees, select or special committees generally have no authority to receive bills and are primarily investigative bodies, although in extraordinary circumstances they may be empowered to initiate legislation. There are also four permanent **joint committees**, composed of an equal number of members from each house. During each congressional session, the leadership of these committees rotates between the House and the Senate. One of these joint committees is the Joint Library Committee, which oversees the activities of the Library of Congress. In addition, temporary **conference committees** are formed to reconcile differences between the House and Senate versions of a bill. Sometimes called the "third house of Congress," conference committees are composed of members of both bodies. Because a bill may be sent to the president only if it has been passed in identical form by both houses, the conference committees often take on great importance in giving legislation its final form.

Committee Size and Membership. Party leaders settle by negotiation questions concerning the size of a committee and the number of Democratic and Republican members it has. Each house can adjust the size of its committees from session to session.

The ratio of majority to minority party members on each committee causes far more controversy than does the size of the committee. Generally, the allocations reflect the strength of each party in the full House or Senate. The question of the partisan ratio of committees briefly took on added importance after the 2000 elections. With the Senate tied at fifty Republicans and fifty Democrats, the Republicans technically controlled the body, because the Constitution gives the vice president—at that time, Republican Dick Cheney—the power to break ties. However, the split gave the Democrats substantial power to deadlock the Senate. After weeks of negotiations, the two parties agreed to allocate an equal number of seats on committees to each party and to share the staff resources of the committees evenly. Under this unprecedented power-sharing agreement, the Republicans were allowed

Joint committees
Congressional committees that are usually permanent and consist of an equal number of members from each house.

Conference committees
Temporary joint committees that are formed to reconcile differences between the House and Senate versions of a bill. Such committees often play a critical role in shaping legislation.

Pictured here is Vice President Joe Biden presiding over the Senate.

to retain the committee chairs, but in the event of a tie vote on a bill or nomination, either party leader could move the decision in question to the floor for a vote. This agreement ended in June 2001, when Senator James Jeffords resigned from the Republican Party, declaring himself an Independent but caucusing with the Democrats. Jeffords's defection made the Democrats the majority party in the Senate, and the Democrats then took over the leadership of all the committees in the Senate.

Committee Assignments. The House and Senate rules specify that the full membership is responsible for electing individuals to committees. By custom, however, the parties make the assignments, and the chambers simply ratify their choices.

Because of the key role that standing committees play in controlling the flow of bills to the floor of Congress, competition for places on these committees is often keen. Junior members struggling for a desirable assignment seek allies among the senior members and among outsiders who have an interest in the committee's area. Members will often mount intense campaigns to win what for them is a desirable committee assignment. For instance, House Democrats who are desirous of a seat on the Education and Workforce Committee often entreat leaders of organized labor to intervene on their behalf.

Individual goals also play an important part in committee assignments. Legislators worried about reelection and focused on prioritizing constituent service choose committees that serve their districts' interests. Not surprisingly, for example, representatives from rural districts are usually desirous of a seat on the Agriculture Committee. Members who want to acquire influence in the House or Senate have a different set of committee preferences. They may prefer appointment to the Rules Committee in the House or one of the budget committees. Still others may pick committees that allow them to pursue certain policy objectives.[31] Of course, these goals are not necessarily contradictory, and each member's preferences may result from a mix of goals.

Committee Leadership. Following the principle that the parties organize Congress, chairs of committees and subcommittees are always members of the majority party in the body. Generally, committee leadership reflects the **seniority system**, a tradition that provides that the member of the majority party with the longest continuous service on a committee becomes its chair. Similarly, the most senior member of the minority party is generally the ranking minority member. Senate Republicans observe this rule strictly. A Republican chair is always the party member with the longest continuous service on the committee. Similarly, if the Republicans are in the minority, the ranking minority member on a committee is always the one with the most seniority. In the House, neither party applies seniority as strictly as the Senate Republicans do. Although seniority remains an important criterion, it is not the sole standard.

A series of Republican Party reforms in 1995 shifted the locus of control over House committee assignments, giving the party leadership more power over the selection of committee chairs. The reforms also put a six-year term limit on committee and subcommittee chairs. Although seniority remained a factor in the selection of chairs, other characteristics, especially a history of raising campaign

Seniority system The tradition that provides that the member of the majority party with the longest continuous service on a committee automatically becomes its chair.

The work of Congress takes place in its standing committees, which means that the chairs of the committees possess significant power. Here, Dave Camp (R-MI), chair of the powerful House Ways and Means Committee, presides over a committee work session.

contributions for the party, became important. Because these rules applied only to Republicans, the Democrats were not bound by them.

In their treatment of seniority, the parties—in the House—have struck different versions of a necessary balance. Republicans, with their term limits and devaluing of seniority in awarding committee posts, have sought to instill greater party discipline. Seniority is a buffer against control by the party leadership. On the one hand, when committee leadership positions are determined by criteria other than seniority, the party leadership has more discretion and can demand more partisan loyalty from those appointed. On the other hand, when the most important criterion for a position as committee chair is the length of service on the committee, members are far freer of party leaders. Their committee leadership positions are defined only by the voters' willingness to return them to Congress. The advantage to the institution, however, is that lengthy service on a standing committee encourages members to develop an expertise in the subject matter of the committee.

The Congressional Staff

At the beginning of the twentieth century, representatives had no personal staff, and all the senators collectively had only 39 personal assistants. By 1987, however, the number of personal assistants allocated to members had mushroomed to more than 11,000, a number that has seems to have stabilized.[32] Although most of these assistants spend their time providing constituent service and attending to casework, staffers also participate in the legislative process. Members of both the House and the Senate have come to rely heavily on their personal staff to conduct research, write questions to be posed to witnesses in committee hearings, write speeches, draft bills and amendments to bills, and prepare briefs on pending legislation. Moreover, much of the negotiation among members is conducted not by the members themselves but by staff assistants representing their respective employers.

In addition to the members' personal staff, more than 2,000 staffers are assigned to the various committees and subcommittees of Congress. With little, if any, responsibility for constituent service, committee staffers are involved purely in drafting legislation and conducting committee investigations. Because they provide needed technical expertise, committee staffers often play a vital role in forming policy. In fact, they often act as policy entrepreneurs, developing new initiatives and then persuading the committee to accept them.

Congress has also created three major support agencies to furnish technical advice. The staffs of the Congressional Research Service, the General Accountability Office, and the Congressional Budget Office are responsible for providing detailed policy analysis.

With all these staff resources, Congress has become better informed on technical matters and far less dependent on the expertise of the executive branch. Moreover, individual members, faced with more complex issues and busier schedules, naturally find their staffs invaluable. But the growing size of the staffs also has a cost. As the pool of politically relevant participants grows larger, Congress becomes further decentralized. As former Senator Fritz Hollings, a South Carolina Democrat, put it, "Everybody is working for staff, staff, staff, driving you nutty, in fact. It has gotten to the point where the senators never actually sit down and exchange ideas and learn from the experience of others and listen."[33]

How a Bill Becomes Law

> **How do the procedures for passing legislation in the House and Senate differ from each other?**

The most obvious congressional function, lawmaking, is also the function that Congress has the most difficulty performing. For those who wish to pass legislation, the congressional process is an obstacle course.[34] The maze of complex rules and multiple points of power overwhelmingly favors the opponents of legislation. Ignoring the old saying that the public should never see the making of sausages or legislation, we now look at the making of laws. Figure 11.2 shows the process schematically.

Any member of Congress—but only a member—may introduce legislation. To aid in this important task, each house has an Office of Legislative Counsel that assists in the actual drafting of legislation; members need only present their ideas to this office. Some of the bills that are introduced may in fact have been drafted elsewhere—by constituents, interest groups, or the presidential administration.

Regardless of a proposal's source, the formal process of introduction is the same. Representatives simply drop the proposal into a box called the "hopper." Senators hand the proposed law to a clerk for publication in the *Congressional Record*. After the initial action is taken, the bill is numbered (by order of introduction) and sent to the Government Printing Office, which makes multiple copies. An "HR" preceding the number identifies bills introduced in the House; Senate bills are marked with an "S."

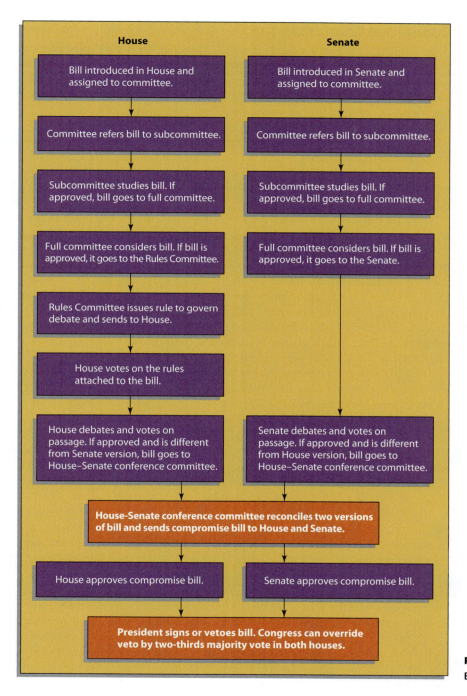

FIGURE 11.2 How a Bill
Becomes a Law

Committee Consideration

After a bill has been appropriately introduced, the Speaker of the House or the Senate's presiding officer refers it to a committee. Because both houses have elaborate rules that restrain the leaders' choice of committee, most proposed bills automatically go to the committee that specializes in the area the bill deals with. On occasion, however, the presiding officer may be able to choose among rival committees. Perhaps the most notable example of the exercise of this option occurred in 1963, when the Kennedy administration's civil rights bill was referred to the Senate's Commerce Committee rather than to the Judiciary Committee, which had a predominantly southern membership. In the House, however, the bill was given to the House Judiciary Committee, whose chair strongly supported civil rights legislation.

If the subject is broad enough, proposed bills may need to be referred to more than one committee. Under the rules, the Speaker may refer a bill to only one committee at a time. However, on rare occasions, a special or select committee may be created to deal with a single bill. This is what happened in the House when, in 2001, President George W. Bush asked for the authority to create the Department of Homeland Security. Because the president proposed consolidating employees from many different agencies, the bill would have had to be referred to the several committees overseeing all the agencies affected. Sequential assignment of the bill to so many committees would have delayed action on it interminably. To speed up the process, in 2002 the House passed a resolution creating the Select Committee on Homeland Security. The resolution directed the committee to propose comprehensive legislation establishing the Department of Homeland Security, after which it was to dissolve.

When a bill reaches a committee, it is usually referred to the subcommittee that has jurisdiction in the matter. For the vast majority of bills, that is the final resting place. Woodrow Wilson best described the fate of bills in committee when he said, "As a rule, a bill committed [to committee] is a bill doomed. When it goes from the clerk's desk to a committee room, it crosses a parliamentary bridge of sighs and dim dungeons of silence whence it will never return."[35]

If the subcommittee chooses to hold hearings, members of the president's administration, congressional colleagues, representatives of interest groups, and (time permitting) private citizens are invited to testify. Afterward, the subcommittee meets in what is called a *markup session*, in which it votes on amendments to the bill and settles on the bill's precise language. Sometimes that process involves a line-by-line analysis of the bill, with debate on the language or intent of virtually every sentence. In other cases, the subcommittee may substitute an entirely new version of the bill. Subsequently, most bills go to the full committee; at this point, the process of hearings and markup may begin again, or the full committee may accept the subcommittee version. The full committee may also take no action, thus killing the bill, or may send the bill back to the subcommittee for further work.

If the committee orders the bill reported—that is, votes to approve it—the bill is sent for consideration to the full originating body (the House or the Senate). A committee report explaining the bill and justifying the committee's action accompanies it. These reports are crucial, because, for some members of Congress, they are the main source of information about a bill. Senators and representatives who are not on the committee that approved the bill are unlikely to have a great deal of expertise in the subject matter. Thus, they often look to the committee reports for guidance.

Floor Action

When a committee orders a bill reported, it is placed on a calendar. The next steps are different in the House and in the Senate.[36]

The House Floor. In the House, the Rules Committee determines the scheduling of controversial bills that are unlikely to receive unanimous consent from the floor and bills that require the expenditure of public funds. This committee specifies the time allocated for debate and may set limitations on amendments. The committee may, for instance, attach a rule prohibiting amendments from the floor; such a rule is known as a *closed rule*. In formulating the rules for a bill, the committee may conduct hearings of its own or may kill the bill by doing nothing.

The actions of the Rules Committee with regard to a particular bill are stated in a resolution that must be approved on the House floor before the bill can be considered. Often the battle over this resolution is the most important floor action. In 1981, for instance, a fierce struggle developed over the rule for Reagan's budget cuts. A Democratic-sponsored rule would have required the House to vote on individual spending cuts separately. Republican leaders opposed it, fearing that a majority would not vote to cut popular social programs if they were separated from the larger package. With the help of conservative Democrats, Republicans managed to defeat the resolution and substitute one that permitted the cuts to be voted up or down as a whole.

Once a rule is accepted, the House can begin debate, which is strictly limited by the rules adopted. The time allotted for debate ranges from an hour or two for a noncontroversial bill to ten hours for difficult legislation. Votes on amendments, if these are permitted under the rules, are crucial, because they can alter the bill sufficiently to attract or lose supporters. Once debate is over, the full House votes on the bill and any amendments that have been attached to it.

The Senate Floor. Because the Senate is a smaller body than the House, the floor procedures are considerably more casual. The Senate has no counterpart to the House Rules Committee. Bills come off the Senate's calendar when the majority leader schedules them. The Senate also allows its members to engage in unlimited debate. This privilege of unlimited debate can lead to a filibuster—prolonged debate that is intended to prevent a vote on a bill and thus kill it. Filibusters can be broken, but only with difficulty, because the rule for **cloture**, or ending of debate, requires that at least sixty senators vote to cut off the discussion.

Whereas once filibusters were used by a minority holding strong beliefs on important issues, nowadays filibusters and threats to filibuster are common occurrences. The days of filibustering by delivering long floor speeches are gone. Senator Strom Thurman's record of commanding the Senate floor for twenty-four

Cloture The rule for ending debate in the Senate; it requires that at least sixty senators vote to cut off discussion.

hours and eighteen minutes to protest the majority's impending passage of a civil rights bill is most likely safe. Today's filibuster seldom requires any floor action.

Even threats to filibuster a bill can effectively kill it. Indeed, threats to filibuster have become routine. A small band of senators or even an individual senator need only announce the intention to filibuster to delay and obstruct the passage of legislation. The reality is that if the sponsors cannot get the support of sixty senators, there is no point in bringing it to the floor. Even a bill supported by a majority of the Senate will die, because as long as there is even the possibility of a filibuster, supporters of the bill will need sixty votes to move the bill to the floor.[37] Little gets through the modern Senate with a simple majority vote. Indeed, in late 2013, Senate Democrats used an arcane rule to exempt executive branch appointments and federal judicial nominees (excluding appointments to the Supreme Court) from filibusters by setting the number needed to invoke at fifty-one.

POLITICS & POPULAR CULTURE: Visit the book's companion website at **www.oup.com/us/gitelson** to read the special feature *Good and Evil in the U.S. Senate.*

Conference Work

Before a bill can be sent to the president, both houses of Congress must pass it in identical form. Usually this requirement poses little difficulty. If the last house to act on the bill makes only slight changes, the bill is generally sent back to the originating house for approval. Often the two houses will engage in what is called ping-pong amending—sending a bill back and forth to each other until both chambers are satisfied with the wording. When the two versions differ significantly, however, a conference committee is appointed to work out the differences.

If the members of this committee cannot reach agreement, the legislation may die in conference. More commonly, the committee reports a compromise bill, which must then be accepted by both houses. The compromise may, however, include provisions not in any previous version of the bill. Conference committee members may add or delete anything from the two bills in order to produce a single bill. Thus, conference committees are sometimes referred to as the "third house of Congress." So much work has gone into producing the legislation that rejection of the bill and the committee report is rare. The bill is then sent to the president, who either signs or vetoes it.

As we discussed earlier, the lawmaking process is an obstacle course studded with complex rules and multiple points of power. In fact, many of these rules reflect the original intent of the founders, which was to create a legislative system that works slowly and is not unduly influenced by the passions of a few. As it has evolved, the system is best designed for preventing the passage of legislation and so has reinforced the myth of Congress as the broken branch. Yet Congress does make the system work, and not just in small matters. Congress can and does respond when a consensus forms in society.

Congressional Voting

> **What are the important influences on members' voting decisions?**

Members of Congress cast thousands of votes every year on a staggering array of issues. Understanding how they vote and why they vote as they do has long been a preoccupation of students of Congress. This task is a difficult one, because each vote represents not a single choice but a set of choices. As one observer noted, "The predicament of the legislator is that every vote is a dozen votes upon as many issues all wrapped together, tied in a verbal package, and given a number of this bill or that."[38] In addition, legislators must routinely vote on bills covering an incredibly broad range of subjects.

A member's party remains the single best predictor of how that member will vote. Over the past three decades, Congress has become increasingly polarized, and party voting has increased considerably. In 2012, for instance, 75.8 percent of the votes in the House were party-unity votes—votes in which a majority of Democrats oppose a majority of Republicans.[39] Given the extensive party organizations within Congress, this outcome is not surprising. Party leaders have several resources they can use to induce party unity in voting. Of course, because the members of a party are likely to attract the same kinds of supporters, they may be voting alike more because of loyalty to these constituents than because of party loyalty.

Do the members' constituencies influence legislative decision making? The answer is difficult to determine, in part because constituents do not clearly express their views. When an issue arouses deep feelings, the constituency may well sway a senator's or representative's decision. In most instances, however, members of Congress receive little or no instruction from their districts. In such cases, members of Congress often work to shape or rally public opinion, rather than simply reacting to what they think the public wants.[40] Nonetheless, a district's majority usually exerts at least an indirect influence, because most members of Congress share their constituents' views. In fact, that is why they were elected.

The threat of electoral defeat also ensures a measure of constituency influence. A single vote in Congress rarely ends a senator's or representative's career. In general, a representative or senator who has cultivated an effective home style can now and then take a position that is at odds with constituents' views. But some issues are a danger for every member. Few members of Congress relish votes on particularly controversial issues, because such issues may in fact be very costly to their reelection efforts. Issues such as abortion and gun control may well spell defeat for members who go against the views of their constituency, or at least those of the organized elements in their constituency. Moreover, members are constantly concerned with what use future opponents may make of their floor votes. As former senator Thomas Daschle, a Democrat from South Dakota, said, "I dare say the first thing that comes to my mind in a vote is: Can it [the issue] pass the thirty-second test, [and] how successful will my opponent be in applying it to a thirty-second ad? It's a screen that comes up whenever there is a vote."[41] Hence few members of Congress frequently vote against the wishes of their districts.

Given the time constraints under which senators and representatives operate, no member can be fully informed on every issue. Therefore, members turn to one another for information and guidance on how to vote. Most members develop a set of colleagues with whom they are in general agreement and whom they can trust to provide honest and knowledgeable advice. These experts are often members of the subcommittee or committee in charge of the area in question. Thus, members are usually extremely well informed on the narrow range of issues with which they are familiar but heavily dependent on trusted colleagues with regard to other legislation.

Conclusion

We began this chapter by noting that Congress is generally perceived as the broken branch. This is not a recent perception but rather a long-standing complaint. For instance, the nineteenth House of Representatives struck President Woodrow Wilson as "a disintegrated mass of jarring elements."[42]

Yet individual members of Congress seem to satisfy their constituents. Although they bemoan the condition of Congress in general, voters return the same members to that institution election after election. Thus, despite the myth of Congress as the broken branch, voters seem satisfied with the incumbents. That situation is no accident. Most incumbent members of Congress are safe because they work hard at carrying out their constituents' wishes for personal services. In that area of activity, Congress surely cannot be deemed a failure.

Part of the reason that Congress works slowly is that the founders designed it that way. They set up its complex rules and maze of procedural hurdles to frustrate immediate responses. George Washington's talk of cooling legislation in the Senate might well describe the entire legislative process. But the lawmaking function of Congress is also filtered through the representational function. Responding to the demands of constituents enhances the representative nature of Congress, but it also diminishes the ability of members to engage in policymaking. Moreover, the representative function encourages members to view policy in local rather than national terms. Nevertheless, Congress is capable of fomenting great change when a nationwide consensus develops.

Key Terms

Bicameral p. 366
Budget deficit p. 383
Budget sequestration p. 387
Budget surplus p. 383
Casework p. 364
Cloture p. 377
Conference committees p. 371
Continuing resolutions p. 364
Discretionary spending p. 386
Earmarks p. 361
Entitlement programs p. 386

Entitlement programs p. 363
Filibuster p. 353
First Concurrent Budget
    Resolution p. 363
Franking privilege p. 360
Gerrymandering p. 359
Home style p. 361
Joint committees p. 371
Legislative veto p. 365
Majority leader p. 368
Majority-minority districts p. 358

Mandatory spending p. 386
Minority leader p. 368
National debt p. 383
Party whips p. 368
Pork-barrel legislation p. 361
Select, or special, committees
    p. 369
Seniority system p. 372
Speaker of the House p. 367
Standing committees p. 369
Tax expenditures p. 385

Focus Questions Review

1. **Who serves in Congress?** > > >
    *   Members of Congress tend to be wealthier and better educated than the public they represent. Furthermore, Congress includes proportionately fewer members of minority

groups and women than in the general population.
*   Despite the public's seeming dissatisfaction with Congress, incumbents are greatly favored in congressional elections. Incumbents use the

opportunities and resources available to them to win the voters' trust.

2. **What are the major functions of Congress?** > > >
   - Members of Congress perform many roles. For example, Congress is responsible for the creation of taxing and spending policies for the nation. The members are also expected to represent the interests of their constituents and oversee the actions of the executive branch.

3. **What role do the parties play in organizing Congress?** > > >
   - The political parties organize Congress and staff the leadership positions.
   - The most powerful position in the House of Representatives is that of the Speaker of the House. Elected by the majority party, the Speaker is assisted by the majority leader and the majority party whip. Leadership of the minority party in the House falls to the minority leader and the minority party whip.
   - Although the Constitution makes the vice president the presiding officer of the Senate, the majority and minority party leaders are of greater importance.
   - Most of the work of Congress is done in its committees and subcommittees. This reliance on committees and subcommittees results in decision making by highly specialized members.
   - Committee leaders are generally those members of the majority party who have the greatest seniority on the committee. The reforms of 1994 gave the leadership more power in selecting committee chairs and displaced the seniority rule for selection of chairs. Although seniority remained a factor in the selection of chairs, a history of providing

support for the party and a record of raising campaign contributions for the party also became important criteria in the selection of committee chairs. Because these rules applied to Republican Party procedures, the Democrats were not bound by them in organizing the 110th Congress. The Republicans, however, reinstated the rules when they took back the House in 2010. Those rules continue to be applied as long the Republicans are the majority party.

4. **How do the procedures for passing legislation in the House and Senate differ from each other?** > > >
   - As a bicameral institution, Congress is highly decentralized. The two houses of Congress have developed their own rules and internal dynamics.
   - A bill becomes law only after it has passed through a maze of complex procedures. Although they resemble an obstacle course, these rules and procedures are in keeping with the founders' intent that Congress not act in haste.
   - Because the Senate is a smaller body than the House, the floor procedures are more casual.
   - The Senate has no counterpart to the House Rules Committee. Moreover, the Senate allows its members to engage in unlimited debate, creating the possibility of filibusters.

5. **What are the important influences on members' voting decisions?** > > >
   - Members of Congress make decisions on a broad range of issues. In doing so, they take into account the desires of party leaders and those of their constituents. The members also accept and seek out the advice of trusted colleagues who have expertise in the subjects under consideration.

Review Questions

1. Why are incumbents so successful at gaining reelection?
2. Do the views of constituents influence members' voting behavior, or is their voting determined by party loyalty?

 For more information and access to study materials, visit the book's companion website at www.oup.com/us/gitelson.

Policy Connection

What policies are responsible for the national debt?

The Policy Challenge

In Policy Connection 7 we focused on the long-standing basic debate between Democrats and Republicans over how to manage the economy, and at the heart of that debate was the question of the **national debt**—that is, the total amount of money the federal government owes as a result of having spent more funds than it has received in revenues. Each year the federal government accumulates either a **budget surplus** (when its revenues, or receipts, exceed spending, or expenditures) or a **budget deficit** (when expenditures exceed revenues, or receipts). Over the past few decades, the government has generated a budget surplus only in 1998 and 1999; as a result, the national debt has increased almost every year since at least the 1970s.

As we learned in Chapter 11, debates over the annual budget deficit and the national debt are commonplace in Congress. In fact, in recent years they have become headline news, as members of both chambers have threatened not to pass a *debt ceiling increase*—a step that likely would create a crisis in financial markets given the importance of the U.S. government's debt on credit markets.

Debates over the national debt or the annual budget deficits that add to it involve a good deal of finger-pointing, as politicians attempt to blame one another for the perceived problems associated with the debt. In this Policy Connection, we avoid the issue of who creates the national debt and, rather, focus on what policies tend to sustain the debt at its seemingly astronomical levels.

The Debt Itself

We begin by noting that the very existence of the U.S. national debt was the result of a policy decision made by the Constitution's Framers as they met in Philadelphia.[1] During the American Revolution, the Continental Congress accumulated a substantial debt, and by 1781 the collective debt of the rebellious colonies was already a concern. The congress under the Articles of Confederation had no power to tax; thus it could not make much headway in paying off that debt other than by selling the western lands under its control and pleading for the states to assume responsibility for a portion of the debt. Although those efforts did reduce the debt somewhat, the nation's poor credit and the constant threat of bankruptcy were key factors leading to calls in 1787 for the Philadelphia convention that was to address the problem.[2] It is not surprising, therefore, that payment of the public debt was among the first in the list of powers granted Congress in Article I, Section 8, of the Constitution.[3]

In fact, one of the first actions of the secretary of the treasury, Alexander Hamilton, was to put that provision to work by requesting that Congress allow his office to assume responsibility for all outstanding state and national debts at face value and by paying them off from customs revenues at a low interest rate over time. He argued that it was a matter not just of paying the nation's debts but of establishing the credibility and "public credit" of the United States. The proposal met with strong opposition, led by James Madison (at the time a member of the House from Virginia) and Thomas Jefferson (then secretary of state), who believed that, although Hamilton's goal

383

was correct, his plan to establish the creditworthiness of the country would reward speculators who had purchased the outstanding debt below its face value as well as those states that had been slow to pay their outstanding loans. The issue divided the Congress and the country;[4] eventually a deal was struck that allowed Hamilton to implement his plan, but only after he agreed to support the location of the new national capital near Virginia in what is now the District of Columbia. And thus maintaining an ongoing national debt—and the creditworthiness of the United States—became a formal policy.

That policy decision, however, has always drawn criticism from those who believe that debts should be paid off as soon as possible and budgets balanced each year. Besides regarding debt as an inherently bad thing—an indicator of wasteful or frivolous spending—they argue that the government's debts compete for credit with private debt that could be more productively used for investments and consumer purchases that energize the economy. Given the assumption that there is a limit to the amount of money that can be borrowed, the national debt ends up increasing the interest rate demanded by lenders.[5] Moreover, as a commitment to pay later for current expenditures, the national debt imposes a burden on future generations who might not benefit from today's spending.

Supporters of policies that maintain the national debt counter that the federal government's debt (called U.S. "sovereign debt" in global financial markets) is very different from personal or household debt, and that a longer-term perspective is necessary. As a form of debt, U.S government bonds are perceived as the global standard for a safe investment—so safe, in fact, that even after partisan bickering in Congress over raising the debt ceiling in 2011 led one rating agency to lower its credit rating of U.S. bonds to AA+ from AAA, they remain very attractive to both domestic and foreign investors.[6] Supporters also note that, each year, the government—directly or indirectly—provides funding for programs that can have significant payoffs in the future (e.g., spending on research in health care and space technology and support for education, including subsidizing student loans) and are therefore investments that will benefit, rather than burden, future generations.

Another concern about the national debt is the fact that it makes us vulnerable to decisions by the country's creditors, especially foreign creditors such as the Chinese government. Although foreign and private creditors hold a substantial portion of America's national debt ($17 trillion by October 2013), the major creditor is actually the U.S. government itself, which borrows from various trust funds and other pools of government money (see Figure 11PC.1). For example,

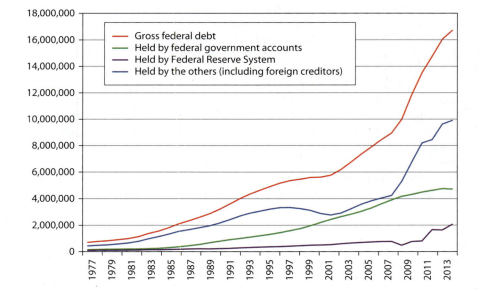

FIGURE 11PC.1 The Gross U.S. National Debt and Its Major Creditors (FY 1977–FY 2013)

Source: U.S. Department of the Treasury, Bureau of the Fiscal Service, Daily Treasury Statements, http://www.fms.treas.gov/dts/index.html.

around $2.65 trillion was owed to the Social Security Trust Fund, whereas Federal Reserve banks (technically not a part of government) held just more than $2 trillion. More than 225 other federal agencies also have their special fund surpluses invested in U.S. bonds (called *intragovernmental holdings*), whereas state and local governments are owed a little more than $700 billion. Although $5.9 trillion is owed to foreign sources, clearly much more of the debt is held domestically.[7]

Tax Expenditures

Putting aside the question of whether there ought to be a policy that favors a sustained national debt, we turn our attention to policies related to taxing and spending that add to annual deficits. Many of us think of the deficits as the result of government spending too much, but there is also the fact that government does not generate enough revenues or fees to pay for all public programs and services. In short, deficits and the national debt grow because we don't tax ourselves enough.

The idea of reducing deficits and the debt by raising taxes would likely meet considerable resistance in the U.S. Congress, especially in recent years, when many members have signed no-tax-increase pledges.[8] Another approach would be to reduce or eliminate those tax breaks that provide government support for certain types of activities by partially or completely exempting such activities from taxation. Economists do not see these tax breaks as merely an act of relief from the burdens of taxation; they regard them as an indirect means for government to support some private-sector activity— or **tax expenditures**. In other words, certain provisions of the U.S. tax code are really spending programs masquerading as tax breaks (see Table 11PC.1).[9] In 2014, tax expenditures amounted to an estimated $1.8 trillion— more than the amount of money spent by the federal government through discretionary expenditures (see the following discussion).

TABLE 11PC.1 Exceptions to the Normal Tax Structure

Tax Expenditure*	Description	Examples
Exclusion	Excludes income that would otherwise constitute part of a taxpayer's gross income.	Employees generally pay no income taxes on contributions their employers make on their behalf for medical insurance premiums.
Exemption	Reduces gross income for taxpayers because of their status or circumstances.	Taxpayers may be able to reduce their tax liability if they have a dependent who is a child aged 19 through 23 and is a full-time student.
Deduction	Reduces gross income due to expenses taxpayers incur.	Taxpayers may be able to deduct state and local income taxes and property taxes.
Credit	Reduces tax liability dollar for dollar. Additionally, some credits are refundable, meaning that a credit in excess of tax liability results in a cash refund.	Taxpayers with children under age 17 potentially can qualify for a partially refundable, per-child credit of up to $1,000, provided their income does not exceed a certain level.
Preferential tax rate	Reduces tax rates on some forms of income.	Capital gains on certain types of income are subject to lower tax rates under the individual income tax.
Deferral	Delays the recognition of income or accelerates some deductions otherwise attributable to future years.	Taxpayers may defer paying tax on interest earned on certain U.S. savings bonds until the bonds are redeemed.

Source: U.S. Government Accountability Office.

*This includes the types of tax expenditures that are identified in the Congressional Budget and Impoundment Act of 1974.

The best-known tax expenditures are those dealing with homeownership. There are a number of rationales for promoting homeownership, including the role it plays in enhancing a family's wealth and status and in facilitating the market for new home construction and all the economic activity associated with it. The government has a number of policies to promote homeownership, including direct assistance to those who qualify for public subsidies and low-interest loan programs through various government agencies (the best know being FHA loans from the Federal Housing Administration). But by far the most significant program involves allowing tax deductions for mortgage interest and property taxes, as well as special tax treatment for those who rent their properties or use them to conduct business. Just the home mortgage interest deduction cost the federal government an estimated $82 billion in foregone revenues in 2012 alone, and it is projected to rise to more than $126 billion by 2016.[10]

Although most Americans are familiar with the tax deductions they receive when they file personal income taxes each April, there are many other tax expenditures, some involving tax credits (e.g., credits for biodiesel producers and energy-efficient appliances), tax exclusions (e.g., for scholarship and fellowship income and self-employment medical insurance premiums), or tax deferrals (e.g., deferrals of interest on U.S. savings bonds or income on life insurance annuities). The bottom line is that these many (literally hundreds) of tax breaks have a major impact on the annual deficit and therefore the national debt.

Mandatory Spending and Entitlements

Mandatory spending includes both **entitlement programs** and government spending obligations that are not subject to the annual government appropriations process.[11] As we discussed in Chapter 11, entitlement programs, such as Social Security and unemployment benefits, commit the government to supplying funds or services to all citizens who meet specified eligibility requirements set in law. Because the amount of money spent depends on the number of people who meet those standards, this spending is

uncontrollable from year to year unless the requirements change. For example, as more people reach retirement age or as more become unemployed during a recession, government spending increases without any congressional or executive action.

The same mandates are true for obligatory spending, such as payments to veterans and federal government retirees and obligations assumed under guaranteed loan or other federal insurance programs (e.g., claims made under bank deposit insurance, crop insurance, and student loan defaults). Interest payments on the national debt are also regarded as mandatory obligations. The government has no choice but to spend the required amount.

Most mandatory expenditures are related to government receipts. For example, Social Security and unemployment insurance payouts are offset by payroll deductions taken directly from our paychecks in the form of FICA (Federal Insurance Contributions Act) taxes. But as Figure 11PC.2 shows, mandatory spending (which in this case does not include interest on the national debt) typically exceeds those receipts and thus regularly contributes to the annual deficit and national debt.

Discretionary Spending

Another component of government spending adding to the national debt are those programs and policies that are subject to funding through the annual appropriations process, in which Congress sets the level of funding—what policymakers in Washington call **discretionary spending**. After we take into account mandatory spending (including interest on the federal debt), less than one-third of the annual federal budget—about $1.1 trillion estimated for fiscal year 2014—falls under the discretionary category.

Those critics who are anxious about the growing national debt—sometimes called "deficit hawks"—frequently call for reductions in tax expenditures and entitlement programs, but because these are politically difficult to change, discussions often turn to reducing the federal budget by cutting back on discretionary spending. But cuts in these programs can also be difficult. Nearly two-thirds of discretionary funding is appropriated for defense and national

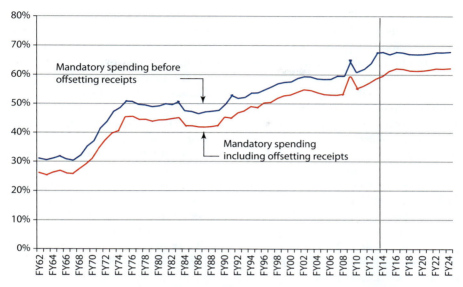

FIGURE 11PC.2 **Mandatory Spending and Offsetting Receipts as a Percentage of Total Outlays (FY 1962–FY 2024)**

Source: Mindy R. Levit and D. Andrew Austin, Mandatory Spending Since 1962 *(Washington, DC: Congressional Research Service, 2014), p. 6, http://www.senate.gov/CRSReports/crs-publish.cfm?pid='0E%2C *P%3C%5B%3C%23P++%0A. The data for FY 1962–FY 1973 are taken from the Office of Management and Budget (OMB),* Budget for Fiscal Year 2014, Historical Tables, *Tables 1.3 and 8.5; the data for FY 1974–FY 2024 are taken from the Congressional Budget Office (CBO)* Historical Tables *and the CBO* Budget Projections *data.*

security programs that are rarely subjected to major cuts. Given the historical choice between guns and butter, it is defense spending that typically wins out (see Policy Connection 12).[12] The rest is distributed among hundreds of different programs, from the National Parks and the Forest Service to the Centers for Disease Control and Prevention and the Bureau of Labor Statistics. Cutting back on the services of these agencies is never popular among those who benefit from their operations—a fact that became clear during those episodes when congressional inaction on the budget led to extended government shutdowns in 1995 (twenty-one days) and 2013 (sixteen days).[13] Discretionary spending cuts also affect government grants to states and localities, as well as federal funding for research.

One recent approach to reduce discretionary spending is **budget sequestration**, a process in which Congress agrees to cap expenditures within a broadly defined category of spending. In the Budget Control Act of 2011, automatic sequestration was to be triggered unless members of Congress agreed on a significant deficit-reduction plan. Because no agreement was reached by March 2013, $42 billion in sequestration cuts were implemented across many discretionary-funded programs.

It's Complicated . . .

Attempts to reduce discretionary spending raise the question of why these government programs exist— that is, why Congress decided to spend money on these programs to begin with. The answer is complicated, for each government program is the product of many historical and political factors. Major crises such as wars or severe economic recessions produce demands for government action; although many of the programs created in response disappear after the crisis passes, others do not.

For example, during World War II, the federal government expanded its reach into almost every aspect of domestic life, for example, establishing rationing for critical resources, taking over the production operations of several major companies, developing "manpower" policies that effectively determined working conditions throughout the economy, and creating agencies devoted to propaganda and to monitoring the behavior of certain segments of the population. At the end of the war, many of these programs were quickly dismantled, but some survived. Parts of the Federal Emergency Management Agency (FEMA), for example, can be traced to the Office of Civilian Defense (OCD), created in 1941 to help coordinate federal, state, and local responses to war emergencies. The Civilian Air Patrol (CAP), an official civilian auxiliary of the U.S. Air Force created as part of the OCD just prior to the U.S. entry into World War II, still receives government funding to carry out some of the missions it assumed when it was chartered by Congress as a nonprofit organization. Today's National Security Agency (NSA) and other intelligence agencies can also be traced back to agencies and functions established during the war.

The most notable legacy of World War II spending was the Servicemen's Readjustment Act of 1944, most often called the GI Bill. Constantly renewed and expanded after the war, it is rarely regarded as a target for discretionary-spending cuts. When the 2013 sequestrations were announced, for example, the GI Bill's provisions were exempted.

Major economic crises can have the same impact as wars on long-term discretionary spending. In response to the Great Recession of 2008, in 2009 Congress approved a $787 billion economic stimulus package (the American Recovery and Reinvestment Act) that included $357 billion to be spent on discretionary-funded programs.[14] Almost all of that spending was applied to ongoing programs, and by 2014 only a few of the non-spending provisions of the package were still in place.

Another source of discretionary spending is pork-barrel legislation and earmarking, discussed in Chapter 11. After Hurricane Sandy devastated communities along the New Jersey and New York coast in 2012, for example, a bill to provide more than $60 billion in emergency funding made its way to final passage in early 2013. By the time the measure was ready for a vote, it contained provisions to fund road-improvement projects in states not impacted by the storm as well as subsidies for Alaskan fisheries and funding for repairs of the roof at Washington's Smithsonian Institution, construction work at the Guantanamo Bay prison facilities in Cuba, and repairs at the Kennedy Space Center in Florida—all probably worthy expenditures, but not germane to the rationale for the Sandy relief bill. "Every disaster," commented the *Wall Street Journal*, "has become a political opportunity,"[15] and in Congress that has meant an opportunity to add funding for one's pet project.

Most discretionary funding, however, provides for the bulk of public goods and services that have been given due consideration through the legislative process. Many of these emerge during periods when a particular problem or issue captures the attention of some group or individual lawmaker who is able to put the topic on the agenda and follow through the often lengthy process of congressional authorization and appropriations. The need for a local post office or funds to help construct science classrooms or support a homeless shelter—these too are part of what adds to government expenditures, and often to increases in the national debt.

Conclusion

What policies are responsible for the national debt?

The debate over America's national debt is as old as the country itself, and it is unlikely to disappear from the halls of Congress or the media in the foreseeable future. It does help, however, if we understand what the debate is about. As we have seen from this general overview of the policy sources of the debt, the challenge may be not to reduce or eliminate the debt (or the annual deficits that feed it) but rather to establish a policy for managing the debt that fulfills Hamilton's goal of using it for positive purposes.

QUESTIONS FOR DISCUSSION

1. It is obvious to those calling themselves "deficit hawks" that the main challenge in the effort to reduce the national debt is to control mandatory entitlement spending. But major entitlements such as Social Security and Medicare make up nearly half the annual budget and are politically difficult to change. If you were in a position to decide where to cut spending, which programs would you focus on? National defense? Social services and income-security programs such as school lunch programs? Support for K–12 education programs? Support for higher education?

2. "It's a good thing our grandparents didn't worry about burdening their grandchildren with government debt. If they didn't spend all that money on highways, schools and hospitals we'd be in pretty sad shape right now." Do you agree or disagree with that statement? Should our grandparents have been more concerned about the debt they have passed on to us? How concerned should we be about the government debts we are leaving for our grandchildren?

CHAPTER 12

MYTHS & REALITIES

Is the president all-powerful?

The Presidency

They Are All Mine

After concluding a brief review of a group of U.S. Marines bound for the conflict in Vietnam, President Lyndon B. Johnson headed for a helicopter that would take him away. Before the president reached the helicopter, he was intercepted by a marine officer. The young officer, pointing to another helicopter, said "That's your helicopter over there sir." "Son," said the president, "they are all my helicopters." Although it is tempting to pass this off as an idle boast, the fact is that President Johnson was expressing a general conception of the American president's power.[1] Presidents are set apart not only from average citizens but also from other leaders in our society because, for many citizens, the president *is* American government. When things go well, they do so because the president is exercising leadership; when they go badly, the president is weak or incapable. If we could just get the right president— perhaps another Lincoln or Roosevelt—all would somehow be well. As presidential scholar Thomas Cronin noted, "There exists some element in the American mind . . . that it is possible to find a savior-hero who will deliver us to an era of greener grass and a land of milk and honey."[2]

Whether it is called the "textbook presidency,"[3] the "imagined presidency,"[4] or the "savior" model of the presidency,[5] this view of the president as a savior-hero projects the *myth of the all-powerful president*. Its imagination fueled by legends of great presidents, the public has come to believe that all of the country's problems—social, economic, and international—can be solved by the immense power available to the president. Even presidents themselves can

< The seal of the president of the United States adorns the presidential podium and appears on the floor of the Oval Office. Notice that the eagle, which holds thirteen arrows in one claw and an olive branch with thirteen leaves in the other, is surrounded by fifty stars. President Harry Truman made the seal official in 1945, and in the process he ordered that the eagle's head be turned toward the olive branch of peace rather than the arrows of war.

succumb to this myth. Jimmy Carter once contended that "the president is the only person who can speak with a clear voice to the American people and set a standard of ethics and morality, excellence and greatness."[6]

In this chapter, we consider the expectations placed on presidents and the powers at their disposal. We begin by examining the evolution of the presidency, for even though the Constitution has changed little with respect to presidential power, the modern presidency is a far different institution from that in the eighteenth century.

The Growth of the Presidency

> **How has the presidency evolved into a powerful office?**

On April 30, 1789, General George Washington stood before the assembled Congress and repeated the oath of office, administered by Robert Livingston. The oath completed, Washington lifted the Bible to his lips as Livingston cried out, "It is done." But just what had been done must have been a mystery to all that were present, for no one could be sure what shape the presidency would take or what influence presidents would have. Nor did the character of the modern presidency develop in an instant. Rather, the office has evolved over the course of two centuries, and during that period the balance of power has moved back and forth between the presidency and Congress.

First Presidents

As the first president, Washington was keenly aware that he was building a new institution and that his every act created a precedent. Although he respected the need to cooperate with others, he was careful to protect the dignity and strength of the office. During his presidency, Washington developed a notably broad interpretation of executive power. Although he stayed aloof from congressional politics, he was indeed active in formulating legislation. Using his secretary of the treasury, Alexander Hamilton, to build congressional support, Washington successfully steered his program of economic development through Congress.

Washington also established a number of presidential roles and customs, including the practice of meeting with the heads of his executive departments as a cabinet. His response to international threats established a dominant role in foreign affairs for the president. Finally, by refusing to seek a third term, Washington eased fears that the presidency would become a monarchy.

Thomas Jefferson advocated restrictions on the national government. Yet, as president, he enlarged the powers of the office and skillfully used his political party in Congress. During his presidency, he planned his party's legislative strategy and worked diligently to elect party faithful to Congress. By these actions, he greatly enhanced the president's effectiveness as a legislative leader. Furthermore, without consulting Congress, he doubled the landmass of the United States through the Louisiana Purchase of 1803.

With the election of Andrew Jackson in 1828, the United States had its first president who was truly elected by the people. Until then, the state legislatures had appointed most members of the Electoral College, but by 1828 only Delaware and South Carolina refused to select delegates by popular vote. At the same time, the elimination of the requirement that only property owners could vote had significantly expanded the eligible electorate.

Capitalizing on his personal popularity, Jackson established a popular base for the presidency and strengthened the executive's role. He styled himself as the only representative of all the people and went over the heads of congressional leaders to appeal directly to the public, which supported him in his confrontations with Congress. He vetoed twelve acts of Congress, more than all his predecessors combined. More important, he claimed the right to veto legislation simply because he disagreed with Congress; previous presidents had vetoed bills only when they thought them unconstitutional.

In Abraham Lincoln (1861–1865), the nation found a president of immense influence who used the powers of the presidency in new and extraordinary ways. He blockaded southern ports, called up the militia, closed opposition newspapers, ordered the arrest of suspected traitors, closed the mail to "treasonable correspondence," and issued the Emancipation Proclamation—all without prior congressional approval. Throughout the Civil War, Lincoln did whatever he thought was necessary in order to win the war. In doing so, he demonstrated that in times of national emergency the American presidency possessed virtually unlimited powers.

Prior to becoming president, Andrew Jackson was famous as the general who defeated the British at the Battle of New Orleans. His aggressive style of leadership earned him the nickname "Old Hickory."

Among these presidents was a series of weak and unsuccessful presidents whose administrations, in most cases, were dominated by Congress. Only the vigorous administrations of Theodore Roosevelt and Woodrow Wilson briefly interrupted the era of congressional government. Viewing the presidency as a "bully pulpit" from which he could appeal to and educate the American public, Roosevelt skillfully used public opinion to build support for his actions. He articulated the "stewardship theory" of presidential power: that the president, as the only official elected by the entire nation, has the duty to take whatever action is necessary so long as it is not specifically forbidden by the Constitution or by law. Taking a similar view of the presidency, Wilson was the first president to propose a comprehensive legislative program.

The Modern Presidency

Theodore Roosevelt argued for a strong presidency, but it was Franklin D. Roosevelt who gave the office the power it now has. Confronting the Great Depression and then World War II, the second Roosevelt rallied the American people to accept his leadership and, in the process, the legitimacy of the powerful presidency. Immediately after his inauguration in 1933, Roosevelt called Congress into special session and in the first one hundred days introduced fifteen major pieces of legislation. A willing Congress passed all of them.

Franklin D. Roosevelt pioneered the use of radio to reach the American public. Here, Roosevelt prepares to deliver one of his famous fireside chats. The president was set to announce the 1944 liberation of Rome.

World War II helped to expand Roosevelt's power still further. The mobilization effort needed to fight a total war led to such spectacular growth in the size and authority of the federal government that the government became involved in every aspect of life. The heroic image of Roosevelt rescuing the nation so changed the presidency that the nation came to expect action from a vigorous president as the norm.

Opposite this image were Lyndon B. Johnson and Richard M. Nixon, who used their power to prosecute an increasingly unpopular war in Southeast Asia. Revelations of secret bombings of Cambodia, the Watergate scandal, and Nixon's resignation led to a general disenchantment with the presidency. Arthur M. Schlesinger Jr., whose biographies of Andrew Jackson, Franklin D. Roosevelt, and John F. Kennedy had done so much to build myths around the presidency, began to warn of the dangers of the *imperial presidency*—the increased authority and decreased accountability of the presidency in the 1960s.[7] In the wake of these concerns, leadership passed to two successive presidents who were anything but imperial. Gerald Ford and Jimmy Carter sought to reduce the pomp surrounding the president. Failing to project the image of a strong leader, both were rejected by the voters at the polls, and presidential observers began to worry about the *tethered presidency*—a presidency that was too constrained to be effective.[8]

The election of Ronald Reagan in 1980 seemed to confirm the concern over the tethered presidency. Elected on the promise to dismantle much of the federal government, the former actor seemed unlikely to manifest the characteristics of a strong president. His first term saw major legislative victories on tax and budget reductions, but deepening economic problems soon overshadowed these triumphs. Midway through Reagan's first term, the number of unemployed reached 11 million.

Yet those who wrote off Reagan as one-term president misjudged the situation. Riding the wave of an economic recovery, Reagan scored a landslide victory in 1984. However, his second term was also marred by the Iran-Contra affair—which resulted in the forced resignation and criminal conviction of some of the president's closest advisers—and by a much-enlarged federal deficit.

Vice President George H. W. Bush benefited directly from Reagan's popularity in his campaign for the presidency. But, unlike Reagan, Bush was forced to begin his administration with both houses of Congress controlled by the Democrats. Recognizing this as a potential problem, Bush called for a "new engagement" between the president and Congress, one characterized by cooperation and mutual respect. The public perceived both the invasion of Panama and the war with Iraq as great successes, and Bush's popularity soared. In his fourth year, however, his popular approval dropped below 40 percent as the economy suffered a recession. As a result, Bush became another one-term president.

Since the recession that began in 2008, electoral politics in America has focused on growing the economy. Both parties agree that expanding the economy is the top priority, but they disagree on how to create a more prosperous economy.

President Bill Clinton initially had the advantage of taking office with his party controlling both houses of Congress. That advantage was more apparent than real, however. The administration had some early success in Congress, most notably the passage of the North American Free Trade Agreement (NAFTA), but after the 1994 elections, Clinton had to cope with a Republican-controlled Congress. Clinton won reelection in 1996, and, despite the scandals that resulted in his impeachment, he left office with an unprecedented 65 percent approval rating.

With the elongated election of 2000, decided only when the Supreme Court barred further recounts in Florida, the Republicans recaptured the office with the election of George W. Bush. Given the fact that George W. Bush received fewer votes than Al Gore, many people expected the new Bush administration to be weak and timid in its approach to governing. That was not the case, however. George W. Bush began his tenure with a quick congressional victory on tax cuts, but the real change for the administration came in the wake of the terrorist attacks of September 11, 2001. His response to the events, including the wars in Afghanistan and Iraq, elevated his public approval ratings and strengthened his leadership.

Riding the wave of strong public approval, George W. Bush won reelection in 2004. But the lengthy wars in Afghanistan and Iraq, the flawed relief efforts following Hurricane Katrina, the collapse of the housing finance market, and the takeover of both houses of Congress by the Democrats following the 2006 elections stalled action on his agenda. Despite a strong push from the White House,

Nothing confirms Americans' expectations of the presidency as does the leader in times of crisis. Pictured here is President George W. Bush addressing the workers amid the rubble of the World Trade Center in New York after 9/11.

the president's efforts at immigration reform failed to pass the Senate in 2007, and by his last year in office his public approval ratings had slipped below 30 percent.

The perception by an overwhelming majority of the American public that the nation was headed in the wrong direction propelled Senator Barack Obama to victory in 2008. Once elected, Obama had to contend with two wars and an economy already in a deep recession. His protracted, but ultimately successful, battle to pass a health care bill along with a continuously high unemployment rate extracted a substantial cost to his approval ratings. Republicans made the 2010 midterm elections a referendum on the president and his policies and took back the House.

In the weeks before the new Congress convened, President Obama was able to strike a series of deals with the incoming Republican congressional leadership.[9] In exchange for a two-year extension of the Bush-era tax cuts and a reduction of estate taxes, Republican leaders accepted the president's plan to temporarily reduce payroll taxes. The president also got enough Senate Republican votes to ratify the Strategic Arms Reduction Treaty (STARTII)—a pact with Russia to reduce the number of strategic arms possessed by both countries—and enough support to repeal "don't ask, don't tell" (see Chapter 5). These deals were the exception, however. Executive-congressional relations deteriorated very quickly in the new Congress. Against this background, however, Obama won a second term.

As reaffirming as the election was, the first year of the president's second term was plagued with problems. Two major policy initiatives—a proposal requiring background checks for the purchase of firearms and a comprehensive immigration bill—failed to generate much support in Congress. Congressional Republicans and the White House deadlocked on a budget bill, leading to a sixteen-day shutdown of the national government. At the same time, the website for the president's signature legislation, the Affordable Care Act (also known as Obamacare), failed to work properly.

All of these events occurred amid Edward Snowden's release of thousands of pages of National Security Agency (NSA) materials. The leaked documents revealed surveillance programs that collected the telephone and Internet records of millions of Americans, and revelations of the NSA's spying on our allies created serious domestic and diplomatic problems for the administration.

For Democrats, the 2014 elections were destined to be difficult. It was a year in which several incumbent Democratic senators, in states that Romney had carried, were seeking reelection. Moreover the president's approval ratings were so low that most candidates did not want to be seen with him. In the end, the Republicans increased their majority in the House and took control of the Senate. President Obama, like Presidents Dwight Eisenhower, Ronald Reagan, and George W. Bush was forced, for the remainder of his second term, to accept a congress controlled by the opposition party.

Presidential Roles

> **What are the various roles we expect presidents to play, and what are the constitutional foundations for these roles?**

Tethered or free, Americans perceive presidents as being central to the country's politics. Perhaps the strongest evidence of their eminence is the variety of roles we expect them to play. Taken together, these roles create the appearance of what has been called "the awesome burden" of the presidency.

Chief of State

Americans look to the president to symbolize their government. In their role as chief of state, presidents entertain foreign dignitaries and prominent Americans, throw out the first baseball of the season, review parades, issue proclamations, and carry out other ceremonial duties. To some people, these activities may seem like a waste of valuable time, but presidents view them as enhancing their prestige. Ever mindful of the value of pageantry, George Washington regularly rode through the streets of Manhattan (New York then being the nation's capital) in an elaborate carriage pulled by six cream-colored horses.

Chief Executive

Article II of the Constitution clearly specifies that "the executive power shall be vested in a President of the United States of America" and that the president shall "take care that the laws be faithfully executed." Thus, on the surface, the president appears all-powerful as a chief executive. After all, no other official shares executive authority. Yet the notion that one person can manage an executive branch that has grown to more than 2 million civilian employees is an illusion. Modern presidents quickly discover that management is a considerably more difficult and time-consuming function than they had imagined. Indeed, they often neglect management functions in favor of more immediate and rewarding political concerns.

Powers to Appoint and Remove. Given the president's role as chief executive, it stands to reason that he would possess enormous power to staff the executive branch. Such is not the case, however. Because the vast majority of federal employees are protected by the civil service (see Chapter 13), the president can fill fewer than 2,000 positions by appointment. Moreover, many of these appointments require senatorial approval.

Senatorial approval of presidential nominees has, in recent years, become difficult to secure, because the minority party has been aggressive, blocking nominees for purely partisan reasons. Nominations to executive branch positions have often been obstructed and delayed by threats to filibuster and, on occasion, actual filibusters. In late 2013, however, the Senate voted to change the filibuster rules. Under the new rules, a filibuster of executive branch appointees can be broken by a cloture petition of only fifty-one votes. A simple majority, not the sixty votes required for actions on most bills, suffices to end a filibuster on presidential nominees. Obviously, if the president's party controls the Senate, confirmations are easier, but it does not mean that the president can simply ignore the minority party.

The new rule has made it easier to invoke cloture, but the minority still has several sources of obstruction. For instance, once cloture is invoked, the minority is allowed thirty hours of debate before the final vote on the nomination can occur. The opposition may not be able to block the nomination, but it can bring the Senate to a virtual halt, impairing the Senate's ability to govern.[10]

Whereas the Constitution provides for the appointment of executive branch officials, it is strangely silent on the issue of presidential removal powers. May presidential appointees be fired by the president? Over the years, the question of who may and who may not be removed from executive branch offices has been decided by the Supreme Court. According to Supreme Court decisions, the president can hire and fire agency heads and others who perform purely executive functions. Officials who perform quasi-legislative or quasi-judicial functions, however, are protected by Congress from presidential discharge, although the line between purely executive functions and those that are quasi-legislative or quasi-judicial is somewhat unclear.[11]

Power to Pardon. The president's power to grant pardons and reprieves is one of the few executive powers that Congress may not limit. This power may be used to correct what the president sees as mistaken convictions or, as Alexander Hamilton put it, to "restore the tranquility of the commonwealth."[12] President Bush demonstrated the first of these uses when, in 2007, he granted clemency to I. Lewis (Scooter) Libby, the former chief of staff to Vice President Cheney. Convicted of perjury and obstruction of justice in the federal investigation into the leaking of the identity of a CIA agent, Libby had received a thirty-month jail

Believing that impending trials involving the recently resigned President Richard Nixon would prolong a period of divisiveness and would threaten the credibility of government at home and abroad, President Gerald Ford issued a full pardon to the former president. Here, President Ford addresses the nation with a brief statement announcing his decision to issue the pardon.

sentence and a $250,000 fine; President Bush commuted the jail sentence but let the fine stand. In issuing the clemency statement, Bush contended that although he respected the jury's verdict, he believed that the prison sentence was excessive. In the second category, President Ford justified his pardoning of Richard Nixon as necessary to end what he termed "our long national nightmare." As controversial as these and other pardons have been, the president's power to pardon is such that Congress has no meaningful way of limiting presidential actions in this area.

Executive Privilege. Even though the Constitution makes no mention of it, presidents from George Washington onward have claimed **executive privilege**—the right to withhold information from the legislature. Justifying their claims either by the need for secrecy in foreign affairs or by the necessity of keeping advice confidential, presidents have exercised this power sparingly without serious congressional challenge for almost two hundred years.

Executive privilege The right, claimed by presidents from Washington onward, to withhold information from Congress.

The use of executive privilege became an issue, however, when the Nixon administration attempted to greatly expand the meaning of the term. As the events of Watergate began to unfold, Nixon tried to deflect inquiry by claiming that executive privilege applied to all executive officials. At one point, he even claimed executive privilege for all those who had previously worked for the executive branch.

The confrontation arose when the Watergate special prosecutor requested tape recordings of White House conversations. The president, citing executive privilege, refused to turn over the tapes, and the special prosecutor pursued the matter in federal court. In the case of *United States v. Nixon* (1974), the Supreme Court ruled that presidents could rightfully claim executive privilege, but not when facing a criminal investigation.[13] In the Clinton administration, the courts further limited executive privilege by ruling that it could not be invoked to avoid or delay civil proceedings for actions taken prior to assuming the presidency.[14] Moreover, the courts made it more difficult for presidential aides to invoke executive privilege.[15] Even the president's Secret Service protectors can, in the future, be compelled to testify.[16] Thus, although the Court has recognized the need for executive privilege, it has also set limits on this power.

Intent on reinvigorating presidential powers, the George W. Bush administration invoked executive privilege in several high-profile situations. As a presidential candidate, Barack Obama criticized President Bush for invoking executive privilege. Indeed, candidate Obama promised "the most transparent administration in history." Nonetheless, President Obama found executive privilege useful when his administration was shaken by a Bureau of Alcohol, Tobacco, Firearms, and Explosives operation gone bad. The operation, known as "fast and furious," had allowed illegal purchases of guns to proceed in the hope that the agents could track the purchases to high-ranking cartel members. Unfortunately, the operation lost a lot of guns, one of which was used in the killing of a U.S. Border Patrol agent.[17] On learning of the operation, the House Oversight and Government Reform Committee began investigative hearings—hearings that implicated high-ranking Department of Justice officials. The committee's chair demanded e-mails and handwritten notes from twelve department officials. President Obama quickly invoked executive privilege, noting that to turn over the documents "would be inconsistent with the separation of powers established by the Constitution and would potentially create an imbalance in the relationship between these two co-equal branches."[18]

Chief Diplomat

According to Article II of the Constitution, the president is authorized to make treaties with the advice and consent of the Senate; to receive foreign ambassadors and ministers; and, with the advice and consent of the Senate, to nominate and appoint ambassadors, ministers, and consuls. As chief diplomat, the president plays a leading role in shaping U.S. foreign policy, although he is seldom free to do as he wishes. Presidents have found their role as chief diplomat far more constrained than the constitutional provision suggests.

Treaties. The power to make treaties illustrates the limits of the role. A literal reading of the Constitution suggests that both the president and the Senate are to take part in all phases of the treaty process. Such was President Washington's initial understanding, but he soon changed his mind. While negotiating a treaty with an Indian tribe, Washington appeared before the Senate and requested advice on certain provisions. The Senate, however, withdrew to discuss the matter without Washington. Angered by the Senate's refusal to engage in face-to-face discussions, Washington reversed his position.

Since Washington's time, no president has appeared before the entire Senate seeking advice on treaty provisions. Nevertheless, presidents routinely consult prominent senators. At times, individual senators are even included in the delegation appointed by the president to negotiate a treaty. For example, the 1963 nuclear test ban treaty was negotiated in the presence of a panel of senators. In contrast, at the end of World War I, President Woodrow Wilson did not include senators in the delegation to the conference that created the League of Nations, and many analysts believe that this oversight angered members of both his own and the opposition party and led the Senate to reject U.S. membership in the new international organization.

Consulting leading senators is imperative because every treaty must be approved by two-thirds of the Senate before it can take effect. Even if the Senate does not reject the treaty, it can modify it in ways that the president may find hard to accept.

Executive agreements
Agreements with other nations that are made by the president without the Senate's consent. They have all the legal force of treaties but, unlike treaties, are not binding on succeeding presidents.

Executive Agreements. To avoid the uncertainties associated with treaty ratification, presidents frequently turn to **executive agreements**, agreements with other nations that are made by the president without the Senate's consent. Such accords have all the legal force of treaties while they are in effect but, unlike treaties, are not binding on succeeding presidents.

Even though the Constitution does not provide for executive agreements, presidents from Washington onward have used them for both trivial and important matters. Because they can make executive agreements quickly and secretly, presidents use them to avoid rejection by the Senate. Thus, in 1905, when Senate Democrats, fearful of foreign commitments, blocked consideration of a proposal for American operation of customhouses on the Caribbean island of Santo Domingo, Theodore Roosevelt implemented the proposal as an executive agreement.[19]

Legally, anything that the president and the Senate can do through treaties the president can do alone through executive agreements. The political reality is sometimes quite different, however, because the implementation of an executive agreement often requires congressional action. For instance, executive agreements generally need appropriated money—thus, both the House and the Senate become involved in the implementation.

Congressional-Executive Agreements. Presidents have also started using a method known as the **congressional-executive agreement**—an agreement (usually a trade pact) with a foreign nation that the president negotiates and then submits to both houses of Congress for approval. By submitting the agreement to both houses, the president can win assent for the agreement while avoiding the constitutional requirement of a two-thirds vote in the Senate for treaty ratification. (Congressional-executive agreements need only a majority vote in each house for approval.) President Clinton successfully used this procedure to win approval for the NAFTA, which probably would not have received the necessary votes in the Senate had it been submitted as a treaty. Moreover, Clinton was able to fast-track the agreement—that is, the agreement negotiated by the president and submitted to Congress could not be amended nor filibustered. Fast-track authority expired in 2007, and President Obama has been urging Congress to restore that authority prior to his submission of the Trans-Pacific Strategic Economic Partnership (TPP). Congress, however, has been reluctant to yield its power to amend the agreement.

Congressional-executive agreement An agreement with a foreign nation that is negotiated by the president and then submitted to both houses of Congress for approval.

Power of Recognition. As an element of their constitutional power to receive foreign ambassadors and ministers, presidents possess the power of recognition. The simple act of receiving a foreign diplomat signifies the official recognition of the sponsoring government. Thus, President Washington granted recognition to the new French republic without consulting Congress. Similarly, in 2011, President Obama was quick to recognize the new Republic of South Sudan as a sovereign nation.

Diplomatic Appointments. A final aspect of the president's role as chief diplomat is the power to make diplomatic appointments. According to Article II of the Constitution, the president "shall nominate, and by and with the advice and consent of the Senate, shall appoint ambassadors, other public ministers and consuls." By and large, the Senate automatically approves such nominations, allowing the president to fill diplomatic posts with people who share his views. On occasion, however, members of the Senate delay and even obstruct a confirmation as a way of expressing displeasure with administration policy.

Commander in Chief

Of all the president's roles, the most controversial is that of commander in chief. Under the provisions of Article II of the Constitution, the president is the "Commander in Chief of the Army and Navy of the United States, and of the Militia of the several States, when called in the actual service of the United States."

Harry S. Truman, pictured here addressing the nation on the Korean crisis, relying on his broad interpretation of the president's constitutional powers, committed troops to the conflict without consulting Congress. Claiming that the U.S. involvement in Korea was a police action, not a war, Truman refused to seek any declaration from Congress.

The Constitution, however, clearly assigns the power to declare war to Congress, not to the president. The president was to command the troops once they were committed to battle, but Congress was to make the decision to wage war. Although the founders restricted the role of commander in chief, presidents have come to view this power expansively.

President Harry S. Truman, for instance, ordered U.S. troops to repel an attack on South Korea by North Korean troops without seeking a declaration of war. On learning of the North Korean assault, he immediately committed thousands of American soldiers to combat in what was called a "police action." Later, the administration justified this action as necessary to fulfill the U.S. commitment to the United Nations. However, a State Department publication noted at the time that the dispatching of military forces was really based on the "traditional power of the president to use the Armed Forces of the United States without consulting Congress."[20]

Presidents took over the power to make war because Congress and the public, particularly in the face of the perceived Soviet threat during the Cold War, let them do so. Not until the U.S. involvement in Vietnam divided the nation did Congress begin to reassess its own role.

Although the initial commitment of American military forces to Vietnam had followed a familiar pattern of executive leadership and congressional docility, Johnson's and Nixon's continuation of the Vietnam War led Congress and the public to question presidential power in this area. In August 1964, Johnson reported to Congress that the USS *Maddox* had been attacked while patrolling in international waters off the coast of North Vietnam. At the president's request, Congress passed the Gulf of Tonkin Resolution, which authorized the president "to take all necessary measures to repel any armed attack against the forces of the United States and to prevent further aggression." Thus, Congress provided the president with a blank check to increase American involvement as he saw fit.

Nine years after the Gulf of Tonkin Resolution, Congress moved to limit the president's war-making powers by passing the War Powers Resolution of 1973, which provided that the president could send troops into hostile territory for a period not to exceed sixty days (Congress can provide a thirty-day extension). If Congress did not approve the actions within that time or if by resolution it voted to withdraw the troops, they must be removed.

Years after the enactment of the War Powers Resolution, its effectiveness remains questionable. Following the Iraqi invasion of Kuwait, President George H. W. Bush deployed troops to Saudi Arabia without informing Congress. As the mission changed from defending Saudi Arabia to driving Iraq out of Kuwait, some members of Congress began to protest. Bush eventually requested and received congressional authorization for his actions, but only after he became convinced that he had strong support in Congress. By joint resolution in January 1991, Congress approved what amounted to a declaration of war when it authorized the president to use "all means necessary" to force Iraq out of Kuwait. Neither Congress nor the president, however, invoked the War Powers Resolution. For some analysts, the minor role played by the War Powers Resolution in the Gulf War suggests that it is no longer viable.[21]

Prior to the invasion of Afghanistan, George W. Bush requested action from Congress. The joint resolution, known as the Authorization for Use of Military Force, empowered the president to use all necessary and appropriate force against nations, organizations, or person(s) that planned, aided, authorized, or committed the terrorist acts of September 11, 2001. The resolution made clear that it was intended to constitute specific authorization as defined by the War Powers Resolution. Nevertheless, in 2002, even as the president was asking Congress to authorize the invasion of Iraq, the administration released a legal opinion prepared by the Department of State that dismissed entirely any need to consult with Congress.

President Obama has followed the path of his predecessors in believing that the office possesses unilateral power to deploy military force. In 2011, the president—without consulting Congress—approved missile strikes on Libya. Additionally, the administration has repeatedly used drones to strike at al-Qaeda operatives, without seeking any consultation with Congress. During the summer of 2013, the president announced he was going to seek congressional approval before attacking Syria but also made it clear that he didn't need anyone's permission by saying, "While I believe I have the authority to carry out this military action without specific congressional authorization, I know that the country will be strong . . . and our actions will be even more effective" if Congress authorizes the actions.[22]

Chief Legislator

These days, the mass media, the public, and even members of Congress look to the president as a kind of grand legislator who initiates public policy and then guides it through Congress. As soon as they take office, presidents are expected to formulate and present a well-defined legislative program.

These assumptions would suggest that the president possesses broad legislative powers, but such is not the case. Article II of the Constitution gives the president only these four rather narrow legislative duties:

1. To "convene both Houses, or either of them" in special sessions

2. To adjourn Congress if the two houses cannot agree on adjournment

3. To "from time to time give to the Congress Information of the State of the Union"

4. To recommend such measures "as he shall judge necessary and expedient"

In addition, Article I arms the president with a veto.

The president no longer uses his powers to convene and adjourn Congress, mostly because of the extended length of the legislative year.

Recommending Legislation. The weak presidents of the 1800s, for fear of appearing to meddle with the legislative process, offered Congress few specific policy proposals. Modern presidents show no such reluctance, and this attitude certainly contributes to the myth of their unlimited power. The State of the Union message delivered each January illustrates the change in presidential dealings with Congress. Today this message is a major political statement that the president addresses to the entire nation, in which he exalts the administration's achievements and presents legislative goals for the coming year. The contemporary State of the Union message gives the president an opportunity to mobilize congressional and public support.

The president presents legislative proposals in less conspicuous ways as well. Numerous statutes require the president to submit detailed reports and even specific legislation. Each year, for instance, the president, as directed by the Budget and Accounting Act of 1921, presents a proposed federal budget for congressional consideration. Similarly, the president reports annually on the nation's economic condition, as required by the Employment Act of 1946. Initiating legislation and mobilizing sufficient support to secure passage are two different matters. Members of Congress expect presidential initiatives; they even demand them. That does not mean, however, that they will approve the president's program.

The Veto Power. The president's ultimate weapon is the veto. After passing both houses of Congress, bills are submitted to the White House for the president's signature. A presidential signature is not necessary for a bill to become law, however. If the president fails to act within ten days of receiving the bill (Sundays excepted), it becomes law without presidential approval.

During the last ten days of a congressional session, however, the president's failure to sign has the opposite effect: It kills the bill. This action, known as a

Article II, Section 3, of the Constitution requires that the president shall "from time to time give to the Congress Information of the state of the Union." Pictured here is President Obama fulfilling the constitutional mandate by delivering the 2014 State of the Union address.

pocket veto, is particularly effective because Congress, having gone out of session, has no way to fight back. When presidents exercise their ordinary veto power by sending bills back to the originating house, these vetoes can be overridden by a vote of two-thirds of those present in both houses. In practice, Congress overrides few vetoes, giving presidents a substantial advantage.

Because Congress so rarely succeeds in overriding vetoes, presidents can wring concessions from it through the threat of a veto. In such instances, the House and Senate may drop provisions that run counter to White House priorities and will sometimes even withhold entire bills rather than face a certain veto. But to make the threat credible, the president must occasionally use the veto.

In recent years, presidents have complained that the veto power is too blunt an instrument to prevent wasteful spending. Because the president must sign or veto the entire bill, Congress has often attached **riders** (provisions, usually unrelated to the main purpose of the bill) that are opposed by the administration to a bill that the president wants. The president must then either accept the objectionable parts or veto the entire bill. In most cases, the president signs the bill.

The Line-Item Veto. Congress passed the Line Item Veto Act of 1996, giving the president a **line-item veto**: the power to veto certain portions of a bill but to sign the rest. Under the terms of the act, the president was empowered to sign a bill but to strike out individual spending provisions. The president was also given the authority to cancel any tax breaks that applied to a hundred or fewer taxpayers. Congress could restore these provisions by passing a bill disapproving the cuts, but the president was allowed to veto that legislation, forcing Congress to override that veto by a two-thirds vote.

Two months after the bill became effective, President Clinton used the line-item veto to cancel a spending provision and two portions of a tax bill giving special relief to small groups of taxpayers. But Clinton's use of the line-item veto was challenged in court. In the 1998 case of *Clinton v. City of New York*, the Supreme Court ruled the act unconstitutional. According to the Court, the act violated the presentment clause of the Constitution, which requires that a bill be passed by both houses of Congress in exactly the same language and then be sent to the president for signature or veto. The Court reasoned that allowing the president to veto a portion of a bill was to allow the president to create a different law, one that had not been passed by either the House or the Senate. (Another method of bypassing Congress, the signing statement, is discussed in Asked & Answered on page 406) If Congress wanted to create a new procedure, the Court said, it must do so by constitutional amendment.

Impoundment. Because the Line Item Veto Act did not pass constitutional muster, presidents are left to fashion a weak version of the line-item veto by **impounding** (withholding) funds appropriated by Congress. Traditionally, presidents have used impoundment cautiously to avoid confrontation with Congress; in most cases the money was eventually released. The Budget and Impoundment Control Act of 1974 allows Congress to limit the president's impoundment power: It set forty-five days as the maximum time that funds could be impounded. If, during that time, Congress did not pass a new act—a

Pocket veto A decision by the president not to sign a bill during the last ten days of a congressional session, effectively killing the bill.

Riders Provisions, usually unrelated to the main purpose of the bill, that Congress attaches to a bill; in general, these are provisions that it knows the president opposes, but Congress is counting on the fact that the president wants the bill to pass.

Line-item veto The power to veto portions of a bill but sign the rest of it. The president was given this power in 1997, but the act giving him this power was ruled unconstitutional.

Impounding Withholding by a president of funds that have been appropriated by Congress. This tactic is used in place of a line-item veto.

ASKED & ANSWERED

ASKED: What is a signing statement?

ANSWERED: When presidents are presented with a bill passed by both houses of Congress, they have the option of either signing it or vetoing it. Vetoed bills are sent back to the house that originated the legislation with a statement explaining the president's objections, whereas the signing of approved bills is frequently marked by a public ceremony. Often, however, the signing and ceremony mask the reality of the president's intentions for the bill and just how willing he is to implement its provisions. To make these intentions clearer, over the past several years presidents have taken the opportunity to add to their formal approval a *signing statement*, a document explaining the administration's interpretation of and concerns about the new law.

These signing statements are not simply a president's general musings on the law in question; they are calculated efforts to enhance presidential powers. By providing an alternative interpretation of a law, the president may in effect rewrite the law according to his own specifications. Signing statements also routinely instruct executive branch officials on how the administration wants the new law implemented.

Although several presidents have used signing statements, President George W. Bush has been the most aggressive to date. Ironically, although the president issued no vetoes in his first term, he produced a record-breaking 107 signing statements in those four years, and he continued that trend into his second term. In 2006, for instance, the president signed the extension of the Patriot Act, praising Congress for its work. Nonetheless, he then released a signing statement indicating that his administration felt free to ignore important provisions of the law, specifically those requiring that the president disclose to Congress how several of its powers were being used. The president's signing statement simply noted that, despite the congressional mandates that he provide reports, the president retained the right to withhold information when, in his judgment, it was in the national interest to do so. Likewise, the president signed the Defense Authorization Act, which included a controversial provision forbidding the torture of anyone in the government's custody. Although the president publicly applauded the provision, and its sponsor, Senator John McCain, his signing statement asserted that he could and would circumvent the law to protect national security.

What makes signing statements so attractive to presidents is that they are difficult to challenge. These presidential objections are frequently justified on the vague grounds that the legislation interferes with the executive's constitutional obligation to faithfully execute the laws. The vagueness of such justifications makes it difficult to challenge the president's interpretation as a violation of presidential authority. Moreover, unless the implementation instructions to executive officials are exact, it is often impossible to link the signing statement to specific problems that may result from the law's application. This is especially problematic because implementation of a law's provision may come long after passage of the law itself.

In summary, signing statements constitute a form of line-item veto, but without any procedures for congressional override. Whether future presidents will continue the vigorous use of the signing statement remains to be seen. However, the effectiveness of signing statements in challenging Congress suggests that their popularity will continue.

Source: Phillip J. Cooper, "George W. Bush, Edgar Allan Poe, and the Use and Abuse of Presidential Signing Statements," Presidential Studies Quarterly *35 (September 2005).*

rescission bill (as in *rescind*, or repeal)—to cancel the spending, the funds must be spent.

The Seamless Web

For the sake of easier discussion, we have considered presidential responsibilities as distinct roles. Yet presidential activity is not so neatly divided. In fact, the various roles form a seamless web of endless combinations, and doing well in one role may be helpful, or indeed essential, to performing another.[23] For instance, successful performance as chief of state can often benefit a president in other roles. Similarly, when diplomatic actions involve the threat or use of force, the distinction between chief diplomat and commander in chief may all but disappear.

The Institutional Presidency

> **Who are the president's most important advisers?**

According to the standard organizational charts, the president is the boss of more than 2 million civilian employees—the largest administrative organization in the country. Obviously, no single person can control an organization of that size, yet that is exactly what presidents are expected to do. But the president does not perform the task alone, for the modern president is surrounded by layers of advisers, known collectively as the institutional presidency.[24] Included in that group are members of the cabinet and of the Executive Office of the President, the White House staff, and the vice president.

The Cabinet

The original advisory group is the cabinet. Not provided for in the Constitution, the cabinet by tradition comprises the heads of the major executive departments and other officials whom the president designates. George Washington created the cabinet by meeting frequently with his attorney general and the secretaries of state, treasury, and war. (James Madison gave those meetings with Washington the title of the "president's cabinet.") By law, the modern cabinet consists of the fifteen department heads. In addition, the vice president is accorded a place in the cabinet. Presidents may also elevate others within their administration to cabinet-level rank. In 2012, for instance, President Obama elevated his White House chief of staff, the administrator of the Environmental Protection Agency, the director of the Office of Management and Budget, the U.S. trade representative, the ambassador to the United Nations, the chairman of the Council of Economic Advisors, and the administrator of the Small Business Administration to cabinet-level rank.[25]

As a unit, the cabinet has seldom functioned as an effective advisory body for the president. Many presidents have undoubtedly found themselves in the position of Lincoln when he asked his assembled cabinet for advice. As Lincoln went around the table, each member voted against the president's position. Undisturbed, Lincoln announced, "Seven nays and one aye; the ayes have it."[26]

Even though, collectively, the cabinet does not often act as an effective advisory body to the president, individual members may perform important advisory functions. In any cabinet, there are likely to be individuals who are close to the president. By virtue of the departments they head, members of what Thomas Cronin calls the "inner cabinet" (the attorney general and the secretaries of state, defense, and the treasury) are most likely to serve as important counselors to the president. The secretaries of the clientele-oriented agencies (that is, health and human services, education, labor, housing and urban development, the interior, agriculture, commerce, transportation, energy, and veterans affairs) generally constitute a kind of "outer cabinet" whose members often have little direct contact with the president.[27]

The Executive Office of the President

Executive order A rule or regulation issued by the president that has the effect of law.

In 1939, the President's Commission on Administrative Management reported: "The president needs help." Acting on the commission's recommendations, Franklin D. Roosevelt issued an **executive order**—a rule or regulation that has the effect of law—creating the Executive Office of the President (EOP). The EOP is not so much an office as an umbrella for a hodgepodge of organizations performing a wide variety of tasks for the president. Currently, the EOP is composed of ten separate organizations, the most important of which are the Office of Management and Budget, the Council of Economic Advisers, and the National Security Council.

The Office of Management and Budget. The Office of Management and Budget (OMB) is the largest of the organizations within the Executive Office of the President. Originally viewed as a professional organization producing independent analysis, in recent years it has become an institutional advocate for the president's initiatives, a status that often puts it in direct conflict with other departments, particularly those that compose the outer cabinet. The OMB's primary function in recent years has been to prepare the president's budget for presentation to Congress each January. Each of the departments and agencies of the executive branch submits its budget request to the OMB, which screens these requests for fidelity to the president's spending priorities and impact on the economy. Because no agency can request appropriations from Congress without clearance from the OMB, the director of the office, who is appointed by the president with senatorial confirmation, serves as an important means of controlling the budget and making policy through budgetary power.

In addition to its budgetary responsibilities, the OMB routinely reviews all legislation proposed by the executive departments and agencies to make sure that the proposals are consistent with the president's program.[28] Agencies proposing laws and regulations with projected costs of $100 million or more must justify the expense. The OMB cannot reject a proposal on the basis of such a cost-benefit analysis, but it can recommend that the president do so. Increasingly, the OMB even conducts cost-benefit analyses on its own. Although these procedures may help the president gain information, they heighten the tension between the departments and the Executive Office of the President.

The Council of Economic Advisers. Legislated into existence by the Employment Act of 1946, the Council of Economic Advisers (CEA) consists of three members, generally professional economists, who are appointed by the president with senatorial confirmation. Its small but highly qualified staff advises the president on the full range of economic issues: unemployment, inflation, taxes, federal spending levels, and the value of the dollar abroad. The CEA also prepares an annual report that contains analyses of current economic data and economic forecasts. Given its wide-ranging responsibilities, the CEA often finds itself competing for influence in economic policymaking with the director of the Office of Management and Budget, the chairman of the Federal Reserve Board, and the secretaries of the treasury, commerce, and labor.

The National Security Council. Created by the National Security Act of 1947, the National Security Council (NSC) advises the president on foreign and defense policy. The NSC consists of the president, the vice president, and the secretaries of state, defense, and treasury. In addition, the chair of the Joint Chiefs of Staff, the director of national intelligence, and the assistant to the president for national security affairs are statutory advisers. The president may also request the attendance of other officials.

The White House Office: Two Management Styles

> **How do presidents differ from one another in their management styles?**

Technically, the White House Office is part of the Executive Office of the President, but in an important sense the two organizations are separate. The White House Office is composed of staff members who are located in the White House and serve the president's political needs. Smaller than the Executive Office of the President, it is nevertheless a sizable organization in its own right—for example, during the Obama administration, it employed more than 480 people.[29] The White House Office includes assistants, special assistants, counselors, special counselors, and consultants with varying titles who function almost totally in the service of the president. Originally, the staff's function was limited to coordinating executive branch activities, but presidents, frustrated by their inability to control the bureaucracy, including the ever-expanding Executive Office of the President, have increasingly come to rely on the White House Office to develop and implement policy initiatives.

The structure of the office depends on the president's organizational preferences. Some presidents have favored a loose structure in which several aides report directly to the president. Sometimes referred to as the "wheel," this highly personalized approach is designed to ensure the president access to information. The downside for presidents is that competing advisers may clash and create the appearance of an administration in disarray.

Most modern presidents, including Obama and George W. Bush, have favored a tight structure, with staff responsibilities and reporting procedures clearly detailed, and subordinates reporting to a chief of staff. Under this organizational style, which resembles a pyramid, only one or two key aides have access to the president. Pyramid structures can reduce the president's burden, allowing him to concentrate on issues that truly require his time. But the relief may come at some cost. The top aides may limit their communications to what the president wants to hear, cutting off dissenting viewpoints. And they may make important decisions before the questions reach the president. As two critics have observed, "presidential assistants can become assistant presidents."[30]

The Vice President

Benjamin Franklin once suggested that the vice president be called "His Superfluous Majesty," and Daniel Webster, saying that "he did not propose to be buried until he was already dead," refused to accept nomination for the office.[31] Although fourteen vice presidents have later become president, esteem for the office has never been high. The reason rests with the Constitution, which provides the vice president with little to do. The vice president's only constitutionally prescribed task—presiding over the Senate—offers little real power, except in the rare case of a tied vote. The vice president has no role in the day-to-day business of that body.

The vice president does, of course, become president if the president dies in office, resigns, or is impeached and removed from office. Furthermore, since the adoption of the Twenty-Fifth Amendment, the vice president can assume the presidency if the president decides that he is disabled, or if the vice president and a majority of the cabinet declare the president to be disabled.

Because the Constitution does not specify the vice president's duties, they are determined by the president. Typically, presidents send their vice presidents to advisory panels and ceremonial occasions. In part, presidents have been reluctant to delegate too much power to their vice presidents for fear of creating a political rival. Generally, a vice-presidential candidate is chosen with an eye to drawing additional supporters to the ticket; thus, the vice president is a potential competitor for the limelight.

Recently, however, presidents have given their vice presidents expanded responsibilities and greater visibility. No vice president has matched the power and presidential access possessed by Vice President Dick Cheney. Vice President Joe Biden has become a valuable asset in dealing with his old Senate colleagues. Obama has, on several occasions, relied on Biden to negotiate deals in Congress in the name of the administration.

Presidential Influence

> **What tools does the president have to influence other decision makers?**

To those outside the office, the myth of the all-powerful president seems compelling. Yet presidents themselves stress the frustrations of holding office. Truman, describing what it was going to be like for his successor, Eisenhower, said, "He'll sit here, and he'll say, Do this! Do that! And nothing will happen. Poor Ike—it won't be a bit like the army."[32] Similarly, Lyndon Johnson once complained that the only power he had was nuclear, and he could not use it.

The point of these remarks is that the president's desires are not automatically translated into government policy. In the American system, power is shared. Congress, with its different constituency interests, often checks presidential initiatives. The bureaucracy has endless opportunities to circumvent presidential directives. According to political scientist and former presidential adviser Richard Neustadt, for a president to be effective, he must become adept at persuasion, convincing others that what he wants of them is in their own interest.[33]

Persuading Congress

Perhaps the greatest and most persistent problem facing any president is working with Congress. As you may recall from Chapter 11, presidential initiatives are only a starting point for congressional action. Obtaining congressional support is crucial. In pursuing this goal, presidents have four primary resources:

1. Party loyalty

2. Staff lobbyists

3. Personal appeal

4. Public opinion

Party Loyalty. At the heart of a successful strategy for dealing with Congress is the political party. Presidents must retain the support of members of their own party while gaining the support of as many members of the opposition party as possible. Presidents cannot take members of their own party for granted, but they must assume that most members of the opposition party will oppose them. Having a majority of seats in Congress is therefore no guarantee of an administration's success, but it is easier than dealing with a Congress controlled by the opposition.

Staff Lobbyists. Before 1953, contacts between the president and Congress were informal and largely based on personal relationships. Some presidents relied on frequent social events to discuss their concerns with members of Congress. Jefferson used that tactic with particular success. His elaborate dinner parties were planned as much for their lively talk as for their superb cuisine. In 1953, however, Eisenhower created the Office of Congressional Relations to formalize the administration's lobbying efforts, which provided the president with a structure for coordinating lobbying activities.

The office was initially small and mostly concerned with heading off the passage of legislation that the president opposed. Over the years, however, the office began to grow substantially, as later administrations took a more aggressive legislative posture. Johnson, in particular, used the office to inform members of Congress of the administration's position on issues and to solicit congressional support. More important, Johnson expanded the role of the office by instructing its staffers to help members of Congress with personal services for constituents.

Although talented lobbyists can be quite effective in persuading members of Congress to support administration proposals, they must be close to the president if they are to succeed.

Personal Appeal. A president's ability to appeal to members of Congress can be vital to his success. For example, Reagan used this approach to great advantage, offering frequent invitations to breakfast at the White House and gifts to cultivate relations with members of Congress. On important bills, the president often made phone calls to wavering members, personally soliciting their support. But even Reagan's personal appeal had its limits. Although he had success in securing congressional support early in his first term, his success rate declined markedly after 1982. A little flattery may go a long way, but too much dilutes its effectiveness.

Public Opinion

Lincoln once said, "Public sentiment is everything. With public sentiment nothing can fail, without it nothing can succeed."[34] Although Lincoln overstated the importance of public approval, popularity is an important tool of persuasion. One political scientist has argued that members of Congress try to predict the public's reaction to their behavior toward the president and often decide what tack they should take on that basis.[35] Lacking precise information about public attitudes, they look to the president's popularity as a guide. Popularity does not guarantee that a president will be successful, however. As Douglas Rivers and Nancy Rose point out, "When [a member of Congress] is confronted by a choice between supporting a popular president and the clear interests of his constituents, the president's public prestige is a poor match for his or her constituents' interests."[36]

POLITICS & POPULAR CULTURE: Visit the book's companion website at **www.oup.com/us/gitelson** to read the special feature *A Hero for President*.

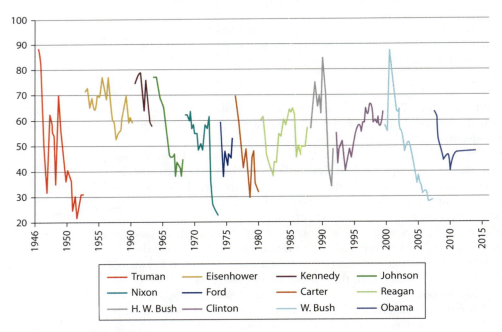

FIGURE 12.1 How the Presidents Stack Up
This chart illustrates U.S. presidents' job approval ratings from Truman to Obama.
Sources: Gallup and WSJ Research.

Naturally, presidents are well aware of the importance of public popularity. Lyndon Johnson used to carry the results of good polls in his breast pocket, ready to show anyone who needed convincing. George W. Bush demonstrated a keen awareness of the role of public opinion when, shortly after his reelection in 2004, he announced that the public had given him some capital that he was going to spend pursuing his policy agenda. Unfortunately for presidents, presidential popularity tends to decline during a president's term of office (see Figure 12.1).

At the beginning of a term, presidents traditionally enjoy a honeymoon period of broad public support and favorable media coverage. By a president's third year in office, however, public approval declines significantly.

The existence of this decline in presidential popularity is part of what political scientist Paul Light calls the "cycle of decreasing influence." According to Light, as a president's term progresses, his political capital (that is, public approval and partisan support), time, and energy diminish, seriously eroding his influence over public policy.[37] Given this cycle, presidents may even suffer from these initially high ratings. When the inflated ratings drop, as they inevitably will, "the fall can be all the more devastating."[38]

High levels of public approval may also be a trap for modern presidents. As a president's popularity surges, expectations of successful leadership also escalate. Indeed, the more popular the president, the more the myth of the all-powerful president seems a reality. But, as we have seen, presidents are not the government, and although high public approval ratings may give presidents some leeway, they do not automatically translate into power. A highly popular president who does not translate high approval ratings into visible legislative successes runs the risk of looking like a failure.

Conclusion

According to the myth of the all-powerful president, modern presidents possess awesome powers that, if mobilized, would enable them to solve all of the country's problems. Although that myth has not always prevailed, it colored what the public expected of the presidency in the latter half of the twentieth century. As the office evolved to its current state, the course of change has not been smooth. Presidential power has increased at times of grave emergency and great stress. In calmer periods, Congress has generally reasserted its role by reining in the president.

The broad range of roles ascribed to the president further enhances the myth of presidential power. Yet presidents often find that the duties associated with these roles are more difficult than they imagined. And Congress is hardly a silent spectator in the process of governing.

To give him support in his various roles, the president has acquired a multitude of advisers—in the cabinet, the Executive Office of the President, and the White House Office. In fact, presidents are surrounded by a bureaucracy of advisers who constitute the institutional presidency. Thus the president does not lack counsel; instead, the problem has become one of managing the advisers.

Finally, we have examined presidential power as persuasion. Although the office itself is generally seen as all-powerful, presidents find that their wishes do not automatically become policy. In this system of shared powers, the president must convince others that what he wants is in their interest as well. The invoking of party loyalty, effective lobbying, and personal appeal are all potential means of persuasion, but the support of the public is particularly useful. Although popular approval does not guarantee presidential success, it makes it more likely.

Key Terms

Balance of power p. 417
Congressional-executive
   agreement p. 401
Containment p. 416
Détente p. 417
Executive agreements p. 400

Executive order p. 408
Executive privilege p. 399
Flexible response p. 417
Impounding p. 405
Isolationism p. 416
Line-item veto p. 405

Marshall Plan p. 417
Massive retaliation p. 417
Pocket veto p. 405
Riders p. 405
Unilateralism p. 416

Focus Questions Review

1. **How has the presidency evolved into a powerful office?** > > >
   - The powers of the presidency have expanded significantly since the adoption of the Constitution. American history has witnessed periods of presidential dominance, usually in times of emergency, followed by congressional efforts to reassert the power of Congress by placing limits on the powers of the office. Over the years, however, the ebb and flow of power have generally benefited the presidency. As new problems and threats have emerged, Americans have perceived presidents as the most effective source of relief.

2. **What are the various roles we expect presidents to play, and what are the constitutional foundations for these roles?** > > >
   - The importance of the modern presidency is most apparent in the variety of roles that the incumbent is now expected to play:
     Chief of state
     Chief executive
     Chief diplomat
     Commander in chief
     Chief legislator
   - As chief of state, the president is the ceremonial head of the government.

   - As chief executive, the president must "take care that the laws be faithfully executed" and manage an executive branch composed of some 3 million employees. To perform the duties of chief executive, the president has the power of appointment, the power to grant pardons, and the power of executive privilege, but none of these is unlimited.
   - As chief diplomat, the president, with the advice and consent of the Senate, can negotiate treaties and make diplomatic appointments. The president also has the power to extend diplomatic recognition to other countries and can make executive agreements with other nations without Senate approval.
   - As commander in chief, the president is supreme commander of the nation's military forces. Presidents have also used that role to claim the power to make war.
   - As chief legislator, the president can convene special sessions of Congress and adjourn Congress if the two houses cannot agree on a date of adjournment. The president must also give Congress, "from time to time," information on the "State of the Union" and recommend measures for congressional action. Furthermore, the president has the power to veto acts of Congress, although the veto is subject to override.

3. **Who are the president's most important advisers? > > >**
   - The modern president is assisted by several advisory groups—the cabinet, the Executive Office of the President, and the White House Office—and by the vice president. These advisers constitute the institutional presidency.
   - The cabinet—consisting of the fifteen department heads, the ambassador to the United Nations, and other officials whom the president designates—is the original presidential advisory group. But the cabinet does not often function effectively, and most presidents hold cabinet meetings purely for ceremonial purposes.
   - Created by an executive order of Franklin D. Roosevelt, the Executive Office of the President (EOP) contains ten separate organizations, including the Office of Management and Budget, the Council of Economic Advisers, and the National Security Council.
   - Also within the EOP is the smaller White House Office, which includes assistants, special assistants, counselors, special counselors, and consultants who perform a wide variety of personal and political duties for the president.
   - The vice president presides over the Senate but votes only to break a tie. The vice president assumes the presidency if the president dies, resigns, is removed by impeachment, or is unable to function because of a disability.

4. **How do presidents differ from one another in their management styles? > > >**
   - In managing the White House Office, presidents demonstrate different styles.
   - Some presidents have preferred what is called the "wheel." The wheel is a loose organizational structure in which several aides report directly to the president. This structure guarantees that the president has access to a wide variety of views.
   - Most presidents, however, prefer the pyramidal style, requiring aides to report to a chief of staff. The advantage of the pyramid style of management is that it reduces the president's burden, allowing him to concentrate on what is truly important.

5. **What tools does the president have to influence other decision makers? > > >**
   - To be effective, presidents must be skilled at persuasion. In dealing with Congress, presidents can rely to some extent on party loyalty, but they must also assemble an effective lobbying staff and use it well. Skillful use of personal appeals to legislators is often effective and necessary.
   - Presidents are more successful at persuasion when their public popularity is high, but popularity often eludes them as their term progresses.

Review Questions

1. Write an essay in which you discuss the ways in which the various roles that a president is expected to play reinforce the myth of the all-powerful president.
2. What is meant by the phrase *the institutional presidency*, and why is it important to understand the term?

For more information and access to study materials, visit the book's companion website at www.oup.com/us/gitelson.

Policy Connection

Does the president really control American foreign policy?

The Policy Challenge

As noted in Chapter 12, it was George Washington who established the president's dominant role in foreign affairs, and few of us would question the assertion that, as chief diplomat, the presidents have played a leading role in shaping foreign policy throughout the nation's history. This was especially true at the height of the Cold War; by the mid-1960s, presidential power in foreign and defense policy matters had become so significant that one prominent observer, Aaron Wildavsky, was able to claim that

> The United States has one president, but it has two presidencies; one presidency is for domestic affairs, and the other is concerned with defense and foreign policy....
>
> In the realm of foreign policy [since World War II] there has not been a single major issue on which presidents, when they were serious and determined, have failed. The list of their victories is impressive.... Serious setbacks to the president in controlling foreign policy are extraordinary and unusual.[1]

For Wildavsky, the major problem facing the president in the foreign affairs arena was finding a "viable policy" for dealing with the realities of the Cold War. The challenge in this Policy Connection is that we consider the validity of Wildavsky's claim about the pivotal role of foreign policy to the presidency—in both the past and the present.

Containment Approaches

For most of the post–World War II period,[2] one overarching perspective dominated presidential foreign-policy strategies—that of containment.[3] As discussed in Policy Connection 5, **containment** emerged as a middle ground between doing nothing in the face of growing Soviet influence and directly confronting the USSR and its allies on the battlefield. Instead, it called for diplomatically, economically, and militarily countering the expansionist tendencies of the USSR and its allies in Eastern Europe and Asia, especially China.

Inherent in the containment approach when it was first articulated by U.S. diplomat George F. Kennan were two complementary beliefs:

1. There was no need for the United States and its allies to offer a universalistic alternative to the Soviet model; instead, they should pragmatically promote diversity among nations.

2. "A long-term, patient but firm and vigilant containment of Russian expansive tendencies" would eventually result in the regime's "break up or the gradual mellowing of Soviet power."[4]

Containment led to significant changes in American foreign policy. It involved an historic break with two major themes that had driven U.S. foreign policy until then: isolationism and unilateralism. Built on George Washington's advice for the United States to avoid any "political connection" with other nations while engaging in "commercial relations" with all, **isolationism** called for avoiding what Thomas Jefferson called "entangling alliances" (and was later extended to call for neutrality and nonintervention in world affairs), whereas **unilateralism** called for favoring a go-it-alone approach when confronted with the necessity of dealing with international crises or issues.

United States involvement in the two world wars would alter those two positions, but it was the country's major post–World War II role in establishing the United Nations and the creation of the North Atlantic Treaty Organization (NATO) in 1949 that formalized the break with both isolationism and unilateralism. Nevertheless, both themes have retained their power to influence U.S. foreign-policy choices, as the American public is often quick to question whether a given policy is in the country's national interest or whether some treaty obligation allows a foreign power to control the use of American military forces.

The Cold War also resulted in greater U.S. expenditures of foreign aid to countries that were vulnerable to Soviet influence. For example, the **Marshall Plan** (1948–1952), which involved a U.S. commitment to support the rebuilding of a war-devastated Europe, is often cited as a major U.S. foreign-policy success. The policy of containment took on more obvious military dimensions in 1950, when President Truman ordered American forces to South Korea after that country was invaded by North Korean troops.

Under Truman's successor, Dwight D. Eisenhower, the containment policy took on a slightly different form, as he and his secretary of state, John Foster Dulles, pursued a buildup of U.S. nuclear capabilities (to assure the USSR that it risked **massive retaliation** for any aggressive actions) while avoiding military interventions—what they termed "maximum force at minimal cost." As a result, by 1960 the United States was committed to the defense of nations in almost every region of the world, especially those bordering on Soviet bloc states.

Containment policy took a slightly different and perhaps more assertive form under Presidents Kennedy and Johnson. Just prior to his assassination in 1963, Kennedy declared that U.S. interests were best served "by preserving and protecting a world of diversity in which no one power or no one combination of powers can threaten the security of the United States." Achieving this goal, Kennedy contended, involved actively supporting "the independence of nations so that one bloc cannot gain sufficient power to finally overcome us."[5] The emphasis on active support meant that the United States would no longer wait for a crisis to arise before engaging in operations to strengthen pro-U.S. forces, and there was an inclination to assist the causes of those whose interests coincided with U.S. interests, even if they proved to be autocratic rulers. Moreover, having made commitments to anticommunist, pro-U.S. forces, the United States could not afford to have its resolve doubted—a view that led both Johnson and his successor, Richard Nixon, to hold firm on positions in the Vietnam conflict that would eventually lead to failure.

The Kennedy-Johnson shift on containment was also evident in U.S. defense policies, for although the Eisenhower administration invested heavily in building the U.S. nuclear arsenal, the 1960s saw a reorientation toward developing the military's capabilities to engage in a **flexible response** to crises. This approach meant investing heavily in the capacity of U.S. forces to take limited conventional and counterinsurgency (unconventional and covert) measures in response to all forms of aggression. In many respects it required a transformation of the U.S. defense establishment.

Nixon's contribution to the containment policy approach was to foster **détente**—or the relaxation of tensions—with the Soviet bloc, and especially with China. Nixon's secretary of state, Henry Kissinger, regarded détente as part of a broader strategy stressing an international **balance of power** (implied in Kennedy's 1963 speech) in which no nation could be permitted to put itself in a preeminent position in world affairs. It was a period of negotiations with the Soviets, bringing an end to direct American involvement in the Vietnam conflict, establishing diplomatic relations with the People's Republic of China, strengthening NATO and other alliances, and providing indirect assistance to nations threatened by communist takeovers. Kissinger continued to follow the Nixon agenda as secretary of state under Gerald Ford.

For President Jimmy Carter, the problem with the Nixonian version of containment was its disconnect from basic American values. American foreign policy, he believed, must be "rooted in our moral values" as a nation. Carter entered the presidency determined to abandon containment in favor of a policy less preoccupied with the communist threat. "It is a new world that calls for a new American foreign policy," he argued, "a policy based on constant decency in its values and on optimism in our historical vision." During this early period, he formalized relations with China and made adherence to human rights a key factor in determining how the United

Richard Nixon's 1972 visit to China was one of the most dramatic events during the Cold War and marked a major shift in U.S. foreign policy. A year earlier, he sent Secretary of State Henry Kissinger to China on a secret mission that would eventually reestablish diplomatic relations between the two nations.

Postcontainment Approaches

Policymakers in George H. W. Bush's administration were extremely pleased with the events that unfolded between 1989 and 1991, but they found it difficult to establish a viable policy response in lieu of containment. Major changes were clearly in the wind. American-Soviet relations had been the pivotal feature shaping U.S. foreign policy since World War II; significant changes in those relations were bound to affect other foreign-policy areas. America's NATO allies were especially eager to build on these improved relationships. By May 1990, most Eastern European nations had new, more liberal leadership or policies. Relations with China continued to improve, despite events such as the 1989 suppression of student protests in Beijing's Tiananmen Square. A more cooperative Soviet posture in Latin America, the Middle East, Africa, and other potential regional hot spots provided additional proof that real changes were taking place in the context in which U.S. foreign policy operated.

States related to other nations. Three years into his presidency, however, Carter focused on the Soviet threat to world peace and overseeing a foreign policy that was an extension of containment, but without détente.[6] Reacting to the Soviet invasion of Afghanistan, Carter imposed sanctions on trade with the USSR and prohibited U.S. participation in the 1980 Moscow Olympics.

Initially, Ronald Reagan's approach to containment was a return to pre-détente days. Articulating his view as "peace through strength," he supported the expansion of defense spending and engaged in rhetorical attacks on the Soviet Union as an "evil empire." By the time he left office, however, containment had become closer to détente, as he responded to the initiatives of Mikhail Gorbachev, the reform-oriented leader of the USSR.

As George H. W. Bush took office in 1989, events in Russia and elsewhere were rendering the very idea of containment irrelevant. In what many analysts regard as a vindication of the containment strategy articulated by Kennan in the late 1940s, the mellowing of the Russian threat to the West was followed by the collapse of the Soviet bloc.

Conditions started to take a turn for the worse as early as August 1990. The new governments of Eastern Europe were beginning to face the hard realities of making the transition to democracy and free-market economies. In the Soviet Union, Gorbachev became anxious about the rapid pace of the changes he had initiated and began to turn his back on the reform movement. Equally ominous was the successful Iraqi invasion of Kuwait early that month. The outlook for the post–Cold War era suddenly seemed bleaker.

In 1991, however, hope returned in regard to several political arenas. The Persian Gulf War against Iraq, launched by a U.S.-led alliance, was quickly concluded. In August, several hard-liners in the Soviet regime staged an abortive coup against Gorbachev, and by December of that year the Soviet Union was no more. In its place were the various republics that had once made up the USSR, each seeking to establish itself as an independent actor on the international stage. Foremost among these was Russia, which was still a powerful force to be reckoned with. There were other positive developments as well: In the Middle East, a U.S. initiative on peace talks began to take hold; in South Africa, progress was being made toward ending apartheid and establishing a majority-rule regime under Nelson Mandela; and in Central America, peace talks in El Salvador were being brought to a successful conclusion. But this newly regained sense of hope was now tempered by the realization that the post–Cold War era was not without its uncertainties, despite the many positive changes that had occurred.

In an attempt to define what was taking place, President Bush spoke of a "new world order" in which the United States would focus its efforts on assuring that the "rule of law" governed the conduct of nations.[7] The country was now in the precarious position of being the only superpower left, and Bush's actions in the Persian Gulf War indicated a willingness to take on the role of the world's police force, ready to take military action against those who would threaten the peaceful status quo. But, as other crises arose, especially in the former Yugoslavia, the United States under both Bush and President Bill Clinton proved to be a "reluctant sheriff," unwilling to use its military resources to deal with disturbances that did not seem to involve U.S. interests.[8]

In fact, for Clinton the biggest threat to America's security was economic, not military, and early in his administration he gave top priority to policies that would enhance the U.S. position in the global economy. In Clinton's first term, trade policies, especially the implementation of the North American Free Trade Agreement (NAFTA) and the establishment of the World Trade Organization (WTO), took center stage as national security were relegated to the second tier of foreign policy concerns.

On a more general level, the Clinton administration developed policies that would help Americans compete in the emerging global economy, in which physical boundaries and traditional national economic controls were becoming increasingly irrelevant. The trend toward globalization presented American policymakers with a new set of challenges beyond those related to economics. The administration found itself dealing with transnational issues, including new forms of environmental degradation and organized criminal activity that knew no borders. Although it did not ignore questions related to nuclear proliferation and the continuing crises in the Middle East, those seemed more like legacy issues carried over from the Cold War era.

Foreign-policy actions taken during the first months of George W. Bush's presidency seemed to indicate a turn in the direction of isolationism and unilateralism, as the administration began to signal its intent to withdraw from several international initiatives and to cut back on its military presence overseas. Whatever policy might have been emerging was soon put aside after the attacks of September 11, 2001, as Bush declared his position to the world community in blunt terms: "Every nation, in every region, now has a decision to make. Either you are with us, or you are with the terrorists."[9]

In a sense, war policy replaced foreign policy during the Bush presidency, and securing the country from another terrorist attack became an "overarching objective [that] allowed him to spin any U.S. policy as a righteous one."[10] To give his policy some focus after the initial 9/11 military action in Afghanistan to attempt to deal with al-Qaeda, Bush highlighted the threats coming from the countries that harbored or supported terrorists, with special attention to three countries—Iraq, Iran, and North Korea—that he termed the "axis of evil." Ultimately, the invasion of Iraq in 2003 and the drawn-out occupation that followed defined the Bush presidency, despite some efforts during his second term in office to follow other policy initiatives in the Middle East and Europe.

When he assumed the presidency, Barack Obama made it clear that he did not want the War on Terror to define and drive U.S. foreign policy. When asked about the administration's foreign-policy strategy, a key advisor summarized the strategy as ending the wars in Iraq and Afghanistan, reestablishing America's "standing and leadership" in the world, and refocusing on a "broader set of priorities" than those that had preoccupied the country in recent years. There was little or no emphasis on idealistic objectives such as promoting human rights, spreading democracy, or extolling the virtues of the free market, and rather than playing diplomatic hardball (such as threatening to sanction other countries), there was an inclination to rely on persuasion and other soft-power tactics that focus on getting others to want what the United States wants.[11]

The Myth of the Grand Strategy

In Policy Connection 5 we considered two myths that helped most Americans make sense of the country's foreign and defense policies: the myth of vulnerability and the myth of America exceptionalism. To those two myths we now must add a third, which Aaron Wildavsky implied in his claims about the two presidencies. It is the *myth of the grand strategy*— a belief that each American president must, and eventually does, develop a core viable policy approach to dealing with other nations and carrying out the U.S. agenda in world affairs.[12] The power and substance of this myth come from two sources: those who write the histories of U.S. foreign policy and those who offer critiques of current policies.

The contribution of historians derives from the fact that their projects often require using clear narratives that tell the story of a given period. At times, help comes from their examination of specific speeches, such as George H. W. Bush's references to a new world order in September 1991 or Barack Obama's comments as he accepted the Nobel Peace Prize in December 2009. At other times they focus on a particular policy initiative or major event—for example, the Monroe Doctrine issued in 1823 or the 1978 Camp David Accords between Israel and Egypt brokered by Jimmy Carter—and use it to imply the existence of a grand strategy. In the case of most pre–Cold War presidencies, historians have often pictured them through the lens of isolationism and unilateralism.

The contribution of contemporary foreign-policy critics also plays an important role. This was always the case for those who were in political opposition to the president. From the efforts of George Washington to negotiate a treaty with the British in 1794 (the Jay Treaty) to the Obama administration's initiation of talks with Iran to deal with its access to nuclear arms, presidents have been subject to critiques that focus on either the lack of a coherent strategic policy or the pursuit of a flawed strategy. In addition to criticisms by political opponents, the observations of many foreign-policy experts and media commentators also feed the myth. "The root cause of America's troubles," argued political scientist John Mearsheimer

in a widely cited article, "is that it adopted a flawed grand strategy after the Cold War."[13]

As with other myths, there is some truth to the fact that presidential policy choices are a major factor in shaping and directing U.S. foreign policy. But the myth itself begs the question of just how much leeway any president has in articulating or carrying out some strategic vision of America's policies abroad. The answer is that other factors also play important roles in the foreign- and defense-policy arenas, and these regard historical context, structural setting, and the presence of uncertainty.

In assuming the role of foreign-policy maker, every president knows that he or she must deal with the immediate past as well as the legacy of U.S. foreign policies tracing back to the founding. No one starts with a clean slate, and in the case of the Cold War presidents from Truman to George H. W. Bush, that history was closely tied to the relatively ambiguous idea of containment that emerged after World War II. Each of these presidents contributed his own variation of what containment entailed, but the actions of his predecessors—and their successes and failures—were always a factor. To some extent, each benefited from the constancy of a general strategic notion such as containment, and perhaps no one appreciated that more than George H. W. Bush, as he sought to make sense of the new world order he was attempting to shape in the early 1990s.

Another major factor is the structural setting of foreign- and defense-policy making. Any president who attempts to make decisions related to foreign or defense matters without at least consulting Congress is likely to regret not doing so, and in many cases the White House depends on explicit congressional authorization (as well as appropriations) to tackle even the most trivial of diplomatic defense-related tasks. And perhaps no one appreciates the questionable nature of the all-powerful-president myth more than the president's national security policy team as they attempt to bring about changes in the operations of the vast bureaucracy of which they are part. Even the most well-articulated strategic policy emanating from the Oval Office will be perceived differently at the Pentagon from the way it will be perceived at the State Department. Add the Central Intelligence Agency and other parts of the intelligence community to the mix, and what was initiated as a coherent approach to foreign and defense matters from within the White House might seem like a presidency in disarray to even the most casual observer.

The final factor—the existence of uncertainty—poses the most significant challenge to presidential efforts to control and direct America's foreign policy. Crises have been a constant feature of the history of American foreign policy since World War II. Some events, such as North Korea's invasion of South Korea in 1950 and the terrorist attacks of 9/11, might have been predicted with better intelligence, and to some extent the United States should have been better prepared to contend with the Cuban missile crisis in 1962 or the collapse of global financial markets in 2008. But, no matter how much effort presidents put into reducing uncertainties, it is not possible to develop or hold onto a strategic position that takes into account all possible scenarios and contingencies in world affairs. Things happen—and when they do, we are once again reminded of the limits to the development of a grand strategy that can guide U.S. foreign policy.

American foreign policy is constantly adjusting to international crises. In 2014, Russia "reclaimed" Crimea, a part of the former Soviet Union that had been part of Ukraine since the collapse of the USSR in 1991. Here, Russian troops stand guard in front of the Crimean parliament building after the annexation. The ensuing crisis led to the imposition of sanctions against Russia as well as a deterioration of U.S.-Russian relationships.

Conclusion

Does the president really control American foreign policy?

When we consider all these aspects, claims about the power and influence of the president in shaping and directing U.S. foreign policy seem overstated. To Wildavsky's credit, his initial claim was more nuanced and qualified. He spoke of the president's "dominant" role in foreign affairs relative to the more limited role he plays in the domestic policy arena. In addition, his goal was to characterize that role during a specific time in the history of the Cold War when tensions with the Soviets were especially high. Unfortunately, the widespread belief in the myth of the grand strategy rarely takes into account the realities that should inform the public's

understanding and appreciation of the nation's foreign and defense policies.

QUESTIONS FOR DISCUSSION

1. Russia's Vladimir Putin took military action against the countries of Georgia (2008) and Ukraine (2014). These actions generated strong diplomatic responses from the United States and raised questions as to whether the Cold War was really over. Some analysts have argued that the United States ought to reconsider its abandonment of Cold War policies such as containment. Considering how different the world is in the post–Cold War era, would containment be the best American foreign-policy response to such crises?

2. Given the complex and often dangerous nature of world affairs today, some would argue that decisions about American foreign policy should be concentrated in the hands of the president. Others argue for more involvement by Congress, especially because issues are often more focused on economic questions than military crises. Is it possible to conduct a coherent foreign policy when policymaking is shared?

CHAPTER 13

MYTHS & REALITIES

Are Washington bureaucrats unresponsive and incompetent?

Bureaucracy

Cries for Help—and Shattered Expectations

September 1, 2005: It had been three days since Hurricane Katrina had reached New Orleans and damaged the levies that protected the city. Entire sections of the city were underwater, and many residents were still trapped in their homes or unaccounted for. Approximately 20,000 individuals had sought shelter in the Louisiana Superdome, but the supplies on hand to handle that number were running low. When Mayor Ray Nagin went on a local radio program that evening, the sense of anger was palpable as he made his plea to the public:

> Organize people to write letters and make calls to their congressmen, to the president, to the governor. Flood their doggone offices with requests to do something. This is ridiculous.
>
> I don't want to see anybody do anymore goddamn press conferences. Put a moratorium on press conferences. Don't do another press conference until the resources are in this city. And then come down to this city and stand with us when there are military trucks and troops that we can't even count.
>
> Don't tell me 40,000 people are coming here. They're not here. It's too doggone late. Now get off your asses and do something, and let's fix the biggest goddamn crisis in the history of this country.[1]

The lack of a quick and effective response to Hurricane Katrina in 2005 raised major questions about the competence of one particular federal agency: the Federal Emergency Management Agency, or FEMA.[2] Created under an executive order issued by President Carter in 1979, it was a response to calls from governors and mayors for greater

CHAPTER OUTLINE AND FOCUS QUESTIONS

A Profile of the Federal Bureaucracy

> Who works in the bureaucracy? What do these people do? Where do they work?

The Growth of the American Bureaucracy

> What factors have led to the growth of the federal bureaucracy?

Bureaucratic Power

> What are the sources of (and limits on) bureaucratic power?

Bureaucratic Problems and Reforms

> What are the major problems with bureaucratic behavior, and what steps have been taken to control them?

< Although Americans deal with different bureaucracies each and every day, it is the Internal Revenue Service that stands out as the symbol of government's role in their lives.

coordination among the dozens of federal agencies and programs designed to provide assistance after disasters struck their states and communities. But the cries for help from Nagin and others in the aftermath of Katrina involved much more than attacks on FEMA or other government officials. They were pleas for assistance that came from public officials who were themselves expected to respond to these emergencies. They involved calls for mobilizing all available human and material resources to deal with immediate emergencies, and what Nagin expressed in his outrage was the sense that government in general—and FEMA in particular—was just not living up to expectations.

Expectations play a critical and complicated role in how we view government. For present purposes, we can distinguish between two types of expectations—those related to policies and those related to performance. Policy expectations reflect our opinions about what laws, regulations, and programs government ought to establish to deal with public problems. We expect our local government to put up traffic signals at dangerous intersections, just as we expect Congress to respond to severe economic downturns with stimulus packages that lower taxes or temporarily increase government spending. We typically express these policy expectations through elections, lobbying, public opinion polls, and debates and discussions about what ought to be done.

Performance expectations, in contrast, focus on whether and how those policies are being carried out. We expect that those traffic signals will reduce the number of accidents, just as we expect the economic stimulus package to get the economy back on track. In the case of dealing with disasters and other emergencies, the creation of FEMA met the policy expectations of state and local officials, but the agency's performance has sometimes been far below expectations.

Of course, the situation is actually more complicated than we have described. Once FEMA was created, it had its own set of policy expectations. It needed Congress and the White House to do their job by providing FEMA with the authority and resources needed to carry out the agency's job.[3] Within the agency, FEMA's mangers had performance expectations that applied to those at the street level of the government's emergency response network—people like mayors, who, in turn, expected FEMA to help them meet the performance expectations of the communities they served.

In this chapter we turn our attention to those institutions and individuals whose primary job it is to carry out the "business" of government—that is, to meet the performance expectations established by policymakers and demanded by the public they serve.

During the 1990s, FEMA was transformed into one of the federal government's most effective agencies, and it played a major role in dealing with disasters such as the devastation from the September 11, 2001, attack on the World Trade Center

As mayor of New Orleans, Ray Nagin was outspoken in his criticism of FEMA's response to Hurricane Katrina in 2005. Reelected in 2006, he played a major role in the city's recovery, but in 2009 evidence of corruption in the mayor's office surfaced. In July 2014, Nagin was sentenced to ten years in federal prison after being convicted of taking bribes from businesses seeking city contracts

We use the collective label *the bureaucracy* for these actors, but the term does not do justice to the complex arrangements of agencies and people who engage in enforcing law and implementing policies and programs in the United States. Technically, as described by sociologist Max

Bureaucracy Any large, complex organization in which employees have specific job responsibilities and work within a hierarchy. The term often refers to both government agencies and the people who work in them.

Weber,[4] a **bureaucracy** is a type of modern organization that has the following characteristics:

- It has a clearly defined jurisdiction that establishes what the organization can do, as well as how and where it can act.

- It operates in accordance with hierarchical principles; that is, a bureaucrat follows the orders handed down from a person at the next-higher level of authority.

- It relies on stable and clear rules; ideally, all decisions and actions must be based on clearly stated rules.

- It empowers its officials but locates power in the position (office), not the person who holds the office; the individual bureaucrat cannot exercise that official power outside the confines of his or her office.

- It is composed of career-oriented professionals appointed on the basis of competence, skill, and merit, who are paid a salary; they cannot personally benefit from the actions they take in office and should not be subject to political pressure.

Although there may be parts of the U.S. bureaucracy that have these Weberian features, we more often use the label to cover the wide range of organizations and persons who work for government. As important as the term, however, is the public image of the bureaucracy, which runs the gamut from very positive ("government by professionals") to very negative ("government by power-hungry incompetents"). In recent years, it has been the negative view that has prevailed, supported by two popular myths that have taken root in today's American political culture: the *myth of bureaucratic incompetence* and the *myth of the unresponsive bureaucracy*.

Behind the myth of bureaucratic incompetence is a widely held belief that governments ought to be as efficient and effective as businesses. The myth of bureaucratic incompetence has emerged because most government programs do not seem to measure up to private-sector standards. To most Americans, the federal bureaucracy seems too large and cumbersome, bloated by wasteful practices and inefficiencies.

Public opinion polls illustrate the popularity of this myth. Forty-three percent of those surveyed in 1958 said they believed government wasted "a lot" of the money they paid in taxes, and by 2008 that figure reached 72 percent.[5] Asked by an Associated Press-NORC poll what issues need to be addressed in 2014, 70 percent supported giving more attention to "improving the way the government functions"[6] (see Policy Connection 13). The myth of an unresponsive bureaucracy is also reflected in public opinion survey results. In one poll conducted by the Pew Research Center in September 2013, 77 percent of respondents indicated that they were either "frustrated" or "angry" with the federal government. As notable was the fact that although the sense of anger and frustration was highest (90 percent) among those identifying themselves as conservative Republicans, it was still evident among self-identifying liberal Democrats (68 percent).[7]

This negative view had been building over the past half century, as a growing number of Americans came to believe the government was listening more to special interests than to the general public. One well-respected exit poll conducted on Election Day in 1964 found that only 29 percent of respondents felt that the government was run by a "few big interests," whereas 64 percent thought that the government was run for the "benefit of all people"; in 2008, the same Election Day survey found the numbers completely reversed, with 69 percent agreeing that the government operated for the benefit of the few big interests and only 29 percent regarding it as run for the benefit of all.

Public concerns about the competence and responsiveness of government agencies also reflect a more general distrust of American government that has reached historically high levels in recent years. As reflected in Figure 13.1, the level of public trust in government has gone

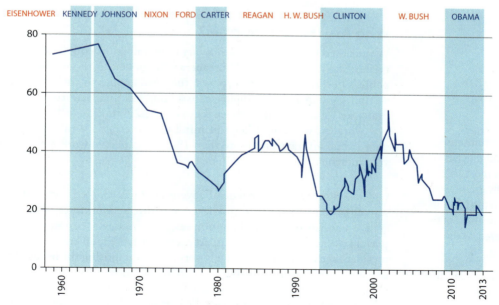

FIGURE 13.1 How Much of the Time Do You Trust the Government in Washington?

Sources: Pew Research Center, National Election Studies, Gallup, ABC/Washington Post, CBS/New York Times, and CNN polls. From 1976 to 2013, the trend represents a three-survey moving average. For party analysis, selected data sets were obtained from searches of the iPOLL Databank provided by the Roper Center for Public Opinion Research at the University of Connecticut.

from 73 percent in 1958 to 19 percent in 2013, whereas explicit distrust has ranged from 23 to 80 percent for the same years.

Despite the popularity of these myths, studies that test some of the basic assumptions underlying the case against bureaucracy indicate there is little evidence to support them.[8] The reality is that government agencies are reasonably efficient and effective, and although most Americans have little good to say about "bureaucracy" in general, they typically give good marks to those public services they have regular contact with.[9] Much of the problem, it seems, is that Americans lack a basic understanding of what government does and how it does it.

A Profile of the Federal Bureaucracy

> **Who works in the bureaucracy? What do these people do? Where do they work?**

The myths of an incompetent and unresponsive federal bureaucracy result in part from a lack of knowledge about the agencies and the people who make up the administrative machinery of our government. We often hear complaints about the bureaucracy as though it were a monolithic entity that could be found in a particular location in the middle of Washington, D.C.—just like Congress or the White House or the Supreme Court. As we shall see, the facts offer an entirely different picture.

Who Are the Bureaucrats?

We've noted that the term *bureaucracy* is an ambiguous one, and it is even more misleading when the term "bureaucrat" is applied to those who carry out the public's business. For our purposes, the term applies to the 2.85 million non-elected civilian federal employees working full and part time in the United States and abroad. Although we focus on the 2.6 million full-time civilian federal workers, we should keep in mind that another 1.4 million are on active duty in the military and more than 19 million people work for state and local governments.[10]

Political appointees
Government officials who occupy the most strategically important positions in the federal government; most of them are appointed by the president.

Cabinet An official advisory board to the president, made up of the heads (secretaries) of the major departments in the federal government.

Political Appointees. The federal government has adopted several different personnel systems to manage this large and diverse workforce. The most visible system consists of **political appointees**, who occupy the most strategically important positions in government. At the top of this group are the members of the president's, **cabinet**, an official advisory board comprising the heads of the fifteen major departments responsible for carrying out most of the federal government's policies and programs (see Chapter 12). The heads of these departments have the title of secretary, except at the U.S. Department of Justice, where the chief officer is called the attorney general. Below them are assistant and deputy department secretaries, deputy assistant secretaries, counselors, and a variety of other appointive positions (see Asked & Answered, p. 429).

ASKED & ANSWERED

ASKED: What are the plum jobs in the federal government?

ANSWERED: There are many ways to find out about employment opportunities in the federal government. You can visit the U.S. Office of Personnel Management's official job-listing website (www.usajobs.gov), try the *Federal Jobs Digest* website (www.jobsfed.com), or look for listings at the *Federal Times* site (www.federaltimes.com). But what if you are interested in aiming high—that is, looking for one of those plum jobs in Washington?

According to the *Oxford English Dictionary*, one of the figurative definitions of *plum* is "'a good thing' ... one of the best or choicest things among situations or appointments." Since 1960, in Washington, D.C., a "plum job" has been one listed in a plum-colored book issued every four years, alternatively by the U.S. House of Representative's Committee on Oversight and Governmental Reform or by the Senate's Committee on Homeland Security and Governmental Affairs.

Under the rather boring title of *United States Government Policy and Supporting Positions*, the 2012 Plum Book,* as it is known, is one of the most informative documents on the shelves of those who keep track of who's who in the government. It contains the names and positions of all those who hold the "noncompetitive" appointment positions in every agency at the time of publication. Do you want to know who sits on the Advisory Council on Historic Preservation? Turn to page 139. Or how about the executive director of the Harry S. Truman Scholarship Foundation? See page 161. Want to know what pay plan the White House chief of staff is compensated under (page 2), or when the term of the comptroller general of the United States expires

(his term is up in 2025 [page 1])? All this information is found in the Plum Book. The Plum Book is updated every four years immediately following a presidential election; the next edition is due out right after the 2016 election.

For those who succeed in getting one of the plum jobs, there is another available resource to make their transition to their new position a bit easier. The Political Appointee Project of the National Academy of Public Administration (http://politicalappointeeproject.org/welcome-political-appointee-project) is an online resource that focuses on the toughest positions in the federal government, and at times the toughest positions in specific areas of government. Originally issued in 1988 as the Prune Book[†] by the Council for Excellence in Government, it profiles and offers advice[‡] to potential appointees based on the premise that a "thick skin is essential armament in the politically charged environment in which you will be working." The site is filled with practical lessons drawn from experienced plum job veterans as well as general insights into the major programs and trends that new appointees can expect in their positions.

---

* To see online versions of the Plum Book for 1996 and later, visit www.gpoaccess.gov/plumbook/index.html.

[†] "A prune," the book's authors explained in their 2004 edition, "in our lexicon, is a plum seasoned by wisdom and experience, with a much thicker skin." The 2004 Prune Book: Top Management Challenges for Presidential Appointees, by John H. Trattner with Patricia McGinnis, was published by the Brookings Institution; you can read about it (and read the first chapter) at www.brookings.edu/press/Books/2004/2004prunebook.aspx.

[‡] See "A Survivor's Guide for Presidential Nominees" at http://www.napawash.org/wp-content/uploads/2013/05/SurvivorsGuide2013.pdf.

Beyond these presidential appointments, several thousand others can be filled by noncareer appointees. For example, every year the Office of Personnel Management designates a certain number of executive and managerial "spaces" for each agency based on an assessment of the agency's needs. During the two-term

Patronage A system of filling government positions in which individuals receive positions through noncompetitive means. It is used as a means both to reward supporters and to bridge divisions within the country through access to positions of power.

Spoils system Taken from the phrase "to the victor go the spoils," a patronage system in which government jobs at all levels are given to members of the party that has won the top political office.

presidency of George W. Bush, there were more than 3,800 such general spaces, and agency heads could fill these spaces with either career or noncareer personnel within certain limits set out in federal personnel policies. Still another 2,000 appointments fell under rules that made temporary exceptions to the appointments process. In short, although the number of political appointees in the federal government is a relatively small portion of the total civilian workforce, the complex rules of government employment give the White House considerable leverage to make strategic appointments.[11]

The fact that the White House can make thousands of political appointments may seem significant today, but at one time in our history, political appointees made up a vast majority of the federal bureaucracy. **Patronage**—the term generally given to systems in which individuals received government positions through noncompetitive means—was commonplace. Presidents often used patronage to reward their supporters, but just as often they used it to help offset political divisions within the country and to provide access to positions of power in government. George Washington, for instance, included both Alexander Hamilton and Thomas Jefferson in his first cabinet, despite the deep divisions between them. Thomas Jefferson used patronage in 1801 when he replaced many government workers who were loyal to John Adams and the Federalist Party with individuals who would be committed to his political objectives.

However, the first wholesale application of patronage appointments followed Andrew Jackson's election nearly three decades later. Jackson was committed to opening up government positions to ordinary American citizens, and the political appointment process was his means of promoting democracy. Others in the Jackson administration, however, regarded such appointments as a way to reward those who supported him in the election. For them, patronage was not a tool for democracy, but instead a reward for electoral victory. "To the victor go the spoils" was the phrase used by one defender of this system, and thus the idea of the **spoils system** was born.

The Jacksonian spoils system influenced the design and operation of the federal government for several decades. Under this system, the federal bureaucracy was probably more than usually responsive to the president's wishes, because loyalty to the White House was the key to getting the job in the first place. But there was another important outgrowth of this patronage approach. Because no one stayed in any position for very long, government jobs had to be redesigned and standardized so that anyone could step in to perform the tasks the position required. Thus, the job of being a postal clerk or a customs tax collector was made much simpler and less demanding. Instead of seeking people with special skills for special jobs, government agencies hired less skilled people

Andrew Jackson regarded patronage as a means for opening up government jobs to everyone, not just the elite few. By the 1870s, however, the system for giving out government jobs and contracts had become corrupt. In this 1877 political cartoon, Jackson's spoils system was ridiculed by those seeking reforms.

and then trained them to do the tasks demanded by the simply designed positions.[12]

Merit Systems. Patronage and the spoils system it bred inevitably led to undesirable outcomes, such as widespread political corruption in the administration of Ulysses S. Grant and the assassination of President James Garfield in 1881 by a disgruntled office seeker. These events led to calls for reform, and in 1883 Congress passed the **Pendleton Act**, which reduced the number of political appointments a president could make and established a merit system for about 10 percent of the existing federal jobs. A **merit system** stresses employees' ability, education, experience, and job performance; political factors are not supposed to be considered. Hiring and promotion depend on competitive examinations or job performance evaluations, usually overseen by a civil service commission or a professional personnel office.

The national government's merit system now applies to almost all federal civilian jobs. More than two-thirds of federal civilian employees come under the **General Schedule (GS) civil service system**, which covers government positions from weather forecasters to financial analysts and from librarians to civil engineers. Many of these federal workers obtain their jobs through a competitive process, and most are ranked according to a schedule that presently runs from GS-1 through GS-15 (see Table 13.1).

At the top of the general civil service and sitting astride the political appointee system is the **Senior Executive Service (SES)**, a select group of career federal public administrators who specialize in managing public agencies. Most of the

Pendleton Act A law passed in 1883 that established the first merit-based personnel system for the federal government.

Merit system A system that stresses the ability, education, and job performance of government employees rather than their political backgrounds.

General Schedule (GS) civil service system The merit-based system that covers most white-collar and technical positions in the federal government.

Senior Executive Service (SES) The highest category of senior-level federal employees, most of whom form a select group of career public administrators who specialize in agency management.

TABLE 13.1 Pay for Meritorious Service: The Salary Scale for White-Collar Federal Employees

Standard salaries for federal workers generally reflect the pay earned by their counterparts in private industry, except at the higher levels, at which ceilings on compensation are imposed by Congress.

Grade: Salary Range for 2014 (General Civil Service)	
1: $17,981–22,494	9: $41,979–54,570
2: $20,217–25,439	10: $46,229–60,098
3: $22,058–28,673	11: $50,790–66,027
4: $24,763–32,188	12: $60,877–79,138
5: $27,705–36,021	13: $72,391–94,108
6: $30,883–40,144	14: $85,544–111,203
7: $34,319–44,615	15: $100,624–130,810
8: $38,007–49,410	

Source: OPM website, http://www.opm.gov/oca/12tables/index.asp.

career (permanent) civil servants in the elite SES have made their mark as effective managers within the particular agency at which they have spent most of their career.

Career service personnel systems Separate personnel systems for highly specialized agencies like the Coast Guard and the Foreign Service.

Besides the general civil service and the SES, there are **career service personnel systems** for highly specialized agencies, such as the Forest Service and the Coast Guard; approximately 15 percent of nonpostal federal civilian employees fall into this category. Perhaps the best known of these career service systems is the Foreign Service, which includes more than 13,000 State Department officials who serve in American embassies throughout the world. The Department of Veterans Affairs (formerly the Veterans Administration) operates the largest career service system, employing more than 36,000 physicians and surgeons. Altogether, approximately 125,000 federal civilian employees occupy positions in these career service systems.

Wage systems Federal personnel systems covering more than a million federal workers who perform blue-collar and related jobs and are largely represented by unions or other associations with limited bargaining rights.

Wage Systems. Finally, a little less than a million workers can be classified as part of the federal government's **wage systems**. Included in this group are those with blue-collar and related jobs, ranging from pipefitting to janitorial work. More than 764,000 career and noncareer postal workers make up the largest single organized group in this category. Many of the workers in these wage systems are paid by the hour, and a great many are represented by unions or other associations that have limited bargaining rights under current civil service laws.

What Do Federal Bureaucrats Do?

The primary role of the national bureaucracy is to implement the policies of the federal government. In that sense, the work of federal agencies touches almost every aspect of American life. Sometimes these agencies carry out the policies themselves. For example, the Federal Aviation Administration (FAA) employs air traffic controllers to oversee the growing volume of aviation in America's skies, and federal rangers protect and manage national parks and forests throughout the country. We also deal directly with federal employees when the U.S. Postal Service delivers our mail, when we have questions about social security benefits, or when we have problems with our federal taxes.[13]

Proxy administration The government's use of indirect means to deliver public goods and services, such as contracting, grants-in-aid, loan guarantees, and government-sponsored enterprises.

At other times, the federal bureaucracy carries out its implementation tasks indirectly, through a variety of arrangements that one analyst has termed "government by proxy." **Proxy administration** of government programs includes such things as government contracts, grants-in-aid, loan guarantees, and the establishment of government-sponsored enterprises to carry out government programs.[14]

Many government activities are carried out through *government contracts* with private firms. The U.S. Department of Defense makes use of this approach when it hires private companies to build weapons systems or supply food for the troops. In fiscal year 2011, for example, Lockheed Martin Corporation earned more than $42.9 billion from contracts with the federal government, mostly with the Defense Department. Although that is a significant amount of business for one company, we should view it with the knowledge that the federal government purchased more than $536 billion in goods and services from more than 141,000 private companies during that same year, and the top two hundred contractors got two-thirds of the total.[15]

The role of contractors is looming ever larger in the federal government's budget. According to one estimate, if you consider only those federal funds spent on providing public-sector goods and services (that is, excluding grants, loans, entitlement payments such as Social Security, and so on), approximately 60 percent of the federal budget is spent through contracted agencies. Much of the budget of the National Aeronautics and Space Administration is spent through contracting, as is a good portion of the Department of Energy's annual budget. Three-fourths of the national government's spending on research and development is done through contracts to think tanks, university labs, and private industry. The idea of outsourcing work to the private and nonprofit sectors is nothing new in Washington, but it has increasingly become the preferred way of doing the government's business.[16]

Perhaps the most significant use of contractors in recent years has been the reliance on private firms by the Defense Department in its conduct of the post–September 11 war efforts in Iraq and Afghanistan. In 2006, for example, one contractor, Kellogg Brown and Root (KBR), had approximately 50,000 employees stationed in Iraq and Kuwait to provide logistical support and services for the U.S. military. KBR's contract has brought in more than $12 billion to the company since 2002, when the first contracts for the Iraq war operation were initiated.[17] More often than not, today's federal bureaucrat is dealing with contractors rather than directly with the public.

The federal government also uses other indirect means to carry out some of its policies. Through bank *loan guarantees*, for example, some federal agencies are able to get local financial institutions to lend money to home buyers, small business enterprises, or farmers who might not otherwise qualify. These guarantees cost the taxpayers nothing until and unless the borrower defaults on the loan.

Among the most controversial examples of government use of contractors was the use of private firms to provide "security" for some United States operations during the occupation of Iraq. Violent incidents involving one firm, Blackwater, led to investigations highlighting the risks and costs of relying on private companies for jobs that would have otherwise been carried out by military units.

Government-sponsored enterprises (GSEs) Federally initiated organizations designed to operate as if they were privately owned and operated, usually established for specific functions that serve targeted populations, such as helping to support inexpensive student loans. Many eventually are privatized.

Executive Office of the President (EOP) The collective name for several agencies, councils, and groups of staff members that advise the president and help manage the federal bureaucracy. The EOP was established in the 1930s; the number and type of agencies that constitute it change with each presidential administration.

Office of Management and Budget (OMB) An EOP agency that acts as the president's principal link to most federal agencies. The agency supervises matters relating to program and budget requests.

White House Office An EOP agency that includes the president's key advisers and assistants, who help him with the daily requirements of the presidency.

In some cases, the federal government has established special **government-sponsored enterprises (GSEs)**, which, among other functions, make credit for specific purposes more easily available to special populations without relying on loan guarantees. Although created by the government, these organizations often operate as if they were privately owned and operated, and in some cases they eventually are turned into investor-owned organizations; that is, they are *privatized*. For example, in 1972, the federal government created the Student Loan Marketing Association (known as "Sallie Mae") as a government-sponsored enterprise designed to promote low-cost loans to students by arranging to "buy" student bank loans from lending institutions and then selling them to investors. The success of Sallie Mae and the desire to have it expand its programs eventually led Congress to convert it into a private corporation in 2004, and today it is a publicly traded company operating under the name SLM Corporation.

But GSEs have not always been trouble-free. In 2004, Congress privatized two GSEs established to provide government backing for home mortgages: the Federal National Mortgage Association (known as "Fannie Mae") and the Federal Home Loan Mortgage Corporation ("Freddie Mac"). Both were successful as private enterprises until the housing market collapsed in 2008, and the federal government stepped in to establish management control over the firms.

Over the next few years, the financial condition of both firms stabilized, and by 2013 they were actually generating a surplus that went into the U.S. Treasury to repay the bailout of funding and loan guarantees that had saved them from closure.

Beyond their role as the implementers of policies and programs, some federal agencies provide expert advice to policymakers, especially in the design of special policies and highly technical programs. Agencies such as the Bureau of Reclamation and the Army Corps of Engineers develop plans for water diversion and storage projects, which then go to the White House and Congress for revision and adoption as official government programs; those agencies often oversee these programs after their approval. At other times Congress and the president establish the general outlines of policies and leave specific policy decisions to designated agencies. That approach is common with defense policies, in which program details are left to civilian and military experts at the Pentagon.

Where Do Civil Servants Work?

Federal civil servants work in hundreds of agencies, ranging from those closest to the president to agencies with a great deal of independence from the White House.

Executive Office of the President. Faced with the task of managing the federal bureaucracy, the president relies on several agencies that collectively make up the **Executive Office of the President (EOP)** (see Chapter 12).[18] Among the most important of the EOP agencies is the **Office of Management and Budget (OMB)**. The OMB is the president's principal link to most federal agencies. Almost all federal agencies report to the OMB on matters relating to program and budget requests. A smaller (but no less important) group of EOP employees is located in a variety of offices known collectively as the **White House Office**. These staff members include the president's key advisers, as well as those who help the chief executive deal with the day-to-day business of the presidency.

Also found in the EOP[19] are various councils and staff members specializing in particular policy areas. These agencies include the Council of Economic Advisers, the National Security Council, the Domestic Policy Council, the Council on Environmental Quality, and the Office of National Drug Control Policy. The number of these agencies changes with each presidential administration.

The Cabinet Departments. The most visible agencies in the executive branch are the fifteen *cabinet departments* (see Chapter 12 and Figure 13.2). Each cabinet department is composed of smaller units, called bureaus, offices, services, administrations, or divisions. For example, among the major units in the U.S. Department of the Treasury are the Internal Revenue Service (IRS), the Bureau of the Public Debt, the Financial Management Division, the U.S. Mint, the Bureau of Engraving and Printing, the Office of the Comptroller of the Currency, the U.S. Secret Service, and the Bureau of Alcohol, Tobacco, and Firearms. Many of these units are divided into even smaller subunits.

Historically, there has been no particular logic underlying the way in which cabinet departments are organized. The best way to understand their design is to realize that politics plays an important role in determining the organizational form, status, and location of any agency or function of government.

Independent Executive Branch Agencies. A great many federal bureaucrats work for the more than two hundred **independent agencies** that exist outside both the EOP and the cabinet departments. Many of these agencies carry out important government functions. The Environmental Protection Agency (EPA), for example, regulates air and water quality, as well as the use of pesticides, disposal of hazardous wastes, and other challenges to the environment. The National Aeronautics and Space Administration (NASA) runs the civilian space program. The General Services Administration (GSA) is essentially the government's all-purpose "housekeeping" agency, dealing with everything from paper clips to real estate and building management for many federal agencies. The independent Office of Personnel Management (OPM) oversees the human resource functions of the federal government. The administrators who head these independent executive branch agencies report directly to the president and do not have to work through a cabinet department bureaucracy.

Here, too, there is no overall rationale for the organization of these agencies. Some are independent, whereas others are part of cabinet departments. Sometimes the nature of what an agency does calls for this special status. In other instances, the political importance of an agency's programs at the time it was created made the difference.

Regulatory Commissions. Employing large professional staffs, **regulatory commissions** make policies affecting various sectors of the American economy. Although their members are appointed by the president, regulatory commissions are formally independent of the White House; that is, they exist independent of the cabinet departments and have a special legal status (provided by Congress

Independent agencies
More than two hundred agencies that exist outside the EOP and the cabinet departments. Reporting directly to the president, they perform a wide range of functions, from environmental protection (EPA) and managing social programs (SSA) to conducting the nation's space policy (NASA) and helping the president manage the federal government (GSA and OPM).

Regulatory commissions
Federal agencies led by presidentially appointed boards that make and enforce policies affecting various sectors of the U.S. economy. Formally independent of the White House to avoid presidential interference, these agencies employ large professional staffs to help them carry out their many functions.

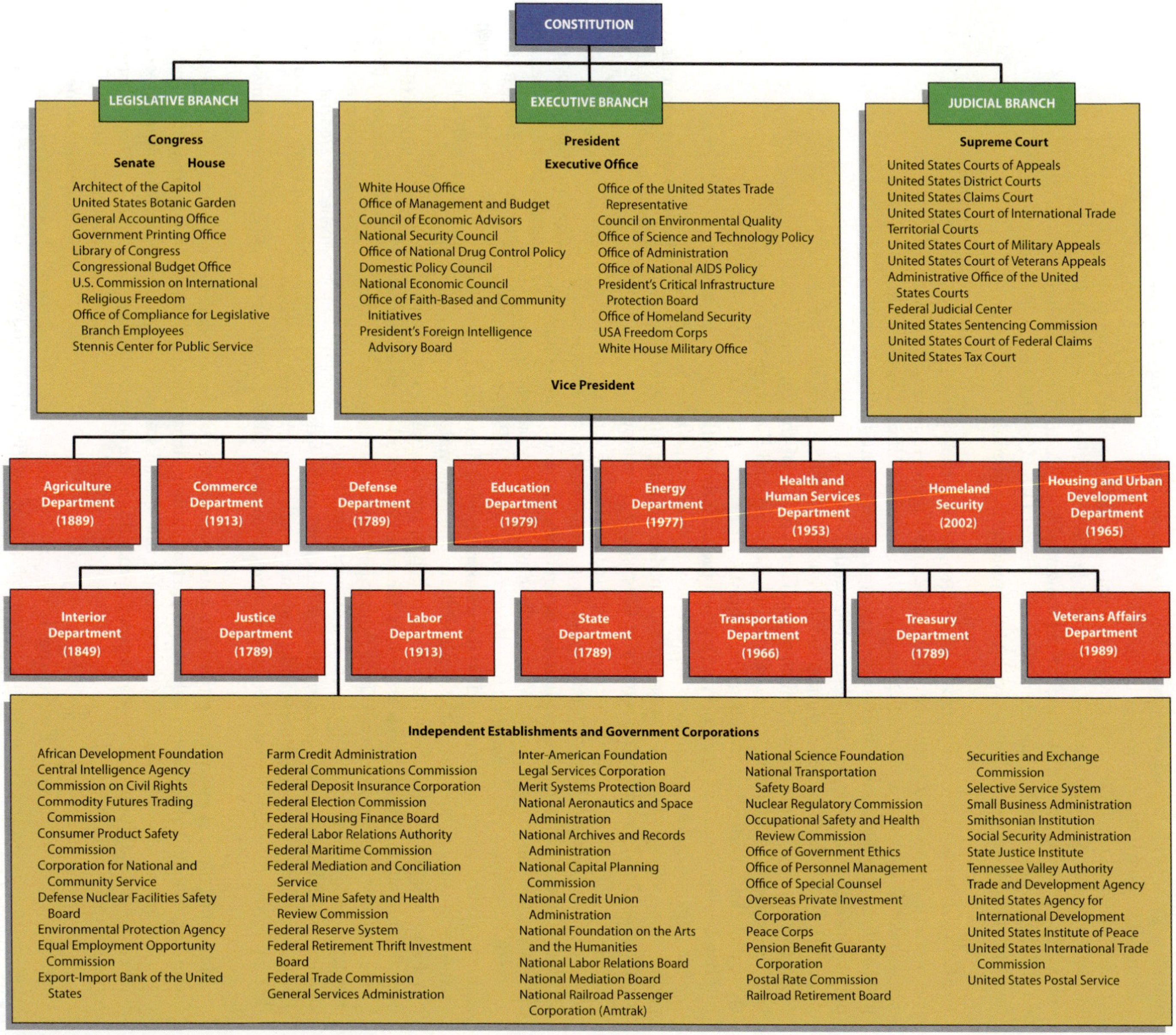

CONSTITUTION

LEGISLATIVE BRANCH

Congress

Senate **House**

Architect of the Capitol
United States Botanic Garden
Government Accounting Office
Government Printing Office
Library of Congress
Congressional Budget Office
U.S. Commission on International
Religious Freedom
Office of Compliance for Legislative
Branch Employees
Stennis Center for Public Service

EXECUTIVE BRANCH

President

Executive Office

White House Office
Office of Management and Budget
Council of Economic Advisors
National Security Council
Office of National Drug Control Policy
Domestic Policy Council
National Economic Council
Office of Faith-Based and Community
Initiatives
President's Foreign Intelligence
Advisory Board

Office of the United States Trade
Representative
Council on Environmental Quality
Office of Science and Technology Policy
Office of Administration
Office of National AIDS Policy
President's Critical Infrastructure
Protection Board
Office of Homeland Security
USA Freedom Corps
White House Military Office

Vice President

JUDICIAL BRANCH

Supreme Court

United States Courts of Appeals
United States District Courts
United States Claims Court
United States Court of International Trade
Territorial Courts
United States Court of Military Appeals
United States Court of Veterans Appeals
Administrative Office of the United
States Courts
Federal Judicial Center
United States Sentencing Commission
United States Court of Federal Claims
United States Tax Court

Agriculture Department (1889)
Interior Department (1849)
Commerce Department (1913)
Justice Department (1789)
Defense Department (1789)
Labor Department (1913)
Education Department (1979)
State Department (1789)
Energy Department (1977)
Transportation Department (1966)
Health and Human Services Department (1953)
Treasury Department (1789)
Homeland Security (2002)
Veterans Affairs Department (1989)
Housing and Urban Development Department (1965)

Independent Establishments and Government Corporations

African Development Foundation
Central Intelligence Agency
Commission on Civil Rights
Commodity Futures Trading
Commission
Consumer Product Safety
Commission
Corporation for National and
Community Service
Defense Nuclear Facilities Safety
Board
Environmental Protection Agency
Equal Employment Opportunity
Commission
Export-Import Bank of the United
States

Farm Credit Administration
Federal Communications Commission
Federal Deposit Insurance Corporation
Federal Election Commission
Federal Housing Finance Board
Federal Labor Relations Authority
Federal Maritime Commission
Federal Mediation and Conciliation
Service
Federal Mine Safety and Health
Review Commission
Federal Reserve System
Federal Retirement Thrift Investment
Board
Federal Trade Commission
General Services Administration

Inter-American Foundation
Legal Services Corporation
Merit Systems Protection Board
National Aeronautics and Space
Administration
National Archives and Records
Administration
National Capital Planning
Commission
National Credit Union
Administration
National Foundation on the Arts
and the Humanities
National Labor Relations Board
National Mediation Board
National Railroad Passenger
Corporation (Amtrak)

National Science Foundation
National Transportation
Safety Board
Nuclear Regulatory Commission
Occupational Safety and Health
Review Commission
Office of Government Ethics
Office of Personnel Management
Office of Special Counsel
Overseas Private Investment
Corporation
Peace Corps
Pension Benefit Guaranty
Corporation
Postal Rate Commission
Railroad Retirement Board

Securities and Exchange
Commission
Selective Service System
Small Business Administration
Smithsonian Institution
Social Security Administration
State Justice Institute
Tennessee Valley Authority
Trade and Development Agency
United States Agency for
International Development
United States Institute of Peace
United States International Trade
Commission
United States Postal Service

FIGURE 13.2 Government of the United States

436

and supported by the Supreme Court) that protects them from excessive presidential interference. For example, the president cannot fire commission members for political reasons—only for corruption or a similar cause. Of course, the president has considerable influence over many of the commissions; he appoints their members and designates their chairpersons, and so he can choose individuals whose views are likely to be in accord with his own.

Regulatory commissions have a special legal status in the federal bureaucracy because they are empowered to do more than enforce the law or implement public policy. Most of them have the authority to formulate rules that regulated companies or individuals must adhere to. In this sense, regulatory agencies are performing lawmaking, or **quasi-legislative functions**.[20] For example, in 1972 the *Federal Trade Commission (FTC)* issued regulations requiring that all billboard and magazine advertisements for cigarettes contain a warning from the surgeon general's office about the health hazards of smoking.

Along with enforcing and making rules, these commissions also have **quasi-judicial functions** because they sit in judgment on companies or individuals that are accused of violating the regulations. Violators of commission rules get their first court-like hearing before commission officials. For example, between 1990 and 2004, the Federal Communications Commission (FCC) levied $2.5 million in fines against Infinity Broadcasting and other stations who had broadcast segments of "shock jock" Howard Stern's show, which the FCC determined had violated the commission's regulations against indecency. Each fine was the result of hearings held after complaints were filed, and the broadcast companies were given the opportunity to appeal to the federal courts. In the end, however, they paid or settled the fines, and Stern eventually left the regulated airwaves for satellite radio, which is not subject to FCC regulations.[21]

Quasi-legislative functions
Lawmaking functions performed by regulatory commissions as authorized by Congress.

Quasi-judicial functions
Judicial functions performed by regulatory commissions. Agencies can hold hearings for companies or individuals accused of violating agency regulations. Commission decisions can be appealed to the federal courts.

Radio "shock jock" Howard Stern moved his popular talk show to unregulated satellite radio in 2005 after fines imposed on his former employers by the FCC made it difficult for him to broadcast on commercial (regulated) stations.

Government corporations
Public agencies that carry out specific economic or service functions (such as the Corporation for Public Broadcasting and the U.S. Postal Service) and are organized in the same way as private corporations.

Government Corporations. A unique form of bureaucracy, the **government corporation** is designed to act more like a private business than like a part of government. As we have already noted, some of these government corporations are actually *government-sponsored enterprises (GSEs)*. What is distinctive about GSEs is that despite the role of government in their creation and financing, they are treated as private enterprises under the law and are therefore subject to the same rules and regulations as other private corporations. The label of "government corporation," however, also applies to a number of federal agencies that remain under the executive branch of government but are explicitly designed to operate as if they were independent corporate entities. Some of these are actually located within cabinet departments. For example, the Commodity Credit Corporation—the organization through which farm subsidy programs are funded—is part of the Department of Agriculture. Still other government corporations—such as the Tennessee Valley Authority (TVA) and the U.S. Postal Service (USPS)—exist separately from other federal agencies. Each is run by a chief executive officer who reports to a board of directors and is expected to operate as if it were a private corporation. In fact, however, these agencies remain part of government and retain some of the special authority and legal immunities that all public agencies possess.

Most government corporations carry out specific functions, such as generating electric power or delivering the mail. Most are intended to be self-financing, but that does not always work out as planned. The Corporation for Public Broadcasting (CPB) helps promote and fund the Public Broadcasting System (PBS) and National Public Radio (NPR). In the past, the CPB has provided significant subsidies for public radio and television, either through government grants or by raising funds privately. That support has decreased in recent years both for financial and for conservative-pressure reasons, leaving PBS- and NPR-affiliate stations with the task of raising money through donations and sponsorships.

Other Agencies. Besides these five types of federal agencies, there are hundreds of boards, commissions, institutes, foundations, endowments, councils, and other organizations in the federal bureaucracy. They range in importance from the Federal Reserve System (better known as the "Fed") and the National Science Foundation (NSF) to the National Telecommunications Information Administration and the U.S. Metric Board.

A Diverse Institution

This profile of the federal bureaucracy makes clear that we are not discussing a single-minded, monolithic institution. Instead, we can see that the federal bureaucracy consists of hundreds of distinct organizations employing millions of individuals—a powerful institution that is so large and complex that to the uninformed citizen it seems to be a maze of shadowy structures to be viewed with sharp suspicion. Typically, Americans' suspicions regarding public agencies take the form of concerns about both the growth and the power of the federal bureaucracy. As we will see in the sections that follow, those concerns are also built on myths.

The Growth of the American Bureaucracy

> **What factors have led to the growth of the federal bureaucracy?**

Many Americans believe that the government bureaucracy has grown too large and has become a burden on the American public. They see bureaucratic growth as being an inevitable result of the incompetence and unresponsiveness of government agencies. An incompetent bureaucracy wastes resources. If government workers were more productive, they would use fewer resources, and the result would be smaller but more efficient public agencies. To many Americans, excessive bureaucratic growth is also related to unresponsive government agencies. Unresponsive agencies are more likely to serve their own needs—including the need to grow and expand. A truly responsive bureaucracy would aim to serve the general public's wishes for less, not more, government intrusion.

Has bureaucratic growth been excessive? Is that growth a result of bureaucratic incompetence and unresponsiveness?

Overview of Bureaucratic Growth

The Framers of the Constitution said little about how they thought the policies of the newly established republic should be administered. The Constitution makes the president responsible for ensuring that the laws and policies of the national government are carried out. The tasks that the Framers foresaw for the national government were relatively few and easy to implement. Executing the law meant keeping the peace, defending the country from foreign intruders, collecting import duties and other taxes, and delivering the mail. To the Framers, charging a single individual with overseeing the administration of government did not seem unreasonable. Consequently, in Section 2 of Article II, they made the president both commander in chief of the armed forces and the chief executive officer to whom the heads of all administrative departments would report.

Initially, the Framers' assumptions about the administration of the government were correct. The federal bureaucracy was small, and its functions were simple enough to permit the president to oversee most of the national government's tasks.[22] In 1802, for example, there were fewer than 10,000 civilian and military federal employees, and almost all the civilian employees were tax collectors or postal workers.

Of course, the number of federal workers grew during these early years. By the 1820s, the national government's civilian bureaucracy had more than doubled. However, that growth did not represent a major expansion of governmental activities. No major new agencies were created during this early period. Most of the growth in federal government jobs took place in the Post Office Department, in which nearly 75 percent of the federal workforce was employed.

A different pattern began to emerge after the Civil War, as Americans demanded more and better government services from elected officials at all levels. During the last half of the nineteenth century, the number of federal agencies doubled. The major agencies established during that period included the Department of Agriculture and the Interstate Commerce Commission. Federal workers were being hired to regulate railroads, assist farmers, manage the federal government's vast land holdings, survey and help settle newly acquired territories in the West, and promote American commerce overseas. The changing nature of government is evident when the relative size of the post office is considered. In 1861, the post office accounted for 80 percent of all federal civilian jobs; by 1901, post office positions made up only 58 percent of such jobs.[23]

Rapid bureaucratic expansion continued through the first decades of the twentieth century. Between 1901 and 1933, the number of major federal agencies increased from 90 to 170. Then, responding to the economic and social problems of the Great Depression, President Franklin D. Roosevelt proposed, and Congress enacted, many new federal programs and agencies, especially in the areas of employment and business regulation. Federal employment jumped under Roosevelt's New Deal, and the demands of World War II led to further growth in the bureaucracy and the expansion of government responsibilities in domestic and foreign affairs.

It is important to put that growth in perspective: although the federal civilian workforce numbers in the millions, it constitutes a relatively small—and shrinking—part of the total U.S. labor force. When we view it as part of the U.S. labor force, the federal bureaucracy does not look quite so big and is in fact shrinking in size each year. For example, the number of civilians employed in the federal executive branch was as high as 15 federal employees for every 1,000 Americans in 1968; by 2005, that figure was 8.9 per 1,000, and in 2012 it was about 8.4 per 1,000.[24] Nor does the federal bureaucracy seem too big when we compare its workforce with the number of civilian workers employed by state and local governments (see Figure 13.3). In relative terms the federal bureaucracy is not as big as it appears to be at first glance.

Another indicator of bureaucratic expansion is the growing federal budget. George Washington ran the government for about $1.5 million a year. By the time Andrew Jackson took office in 1829, the federal budget had increased tenfold, to more than $15 million. By 1940 the budget had climbed to $9.5 billion, and in 1960 the U.S. government spent a little more than $92 billion. The greatest growth in federal expenditures, however, took place over the next quarter century. In January 1987, President Reagan submitted the first trillion-dollar budget proposal to Congress, and federal government spending continued to climb under Presidents George H. W. Bush, Bill Clinton, and George W. Bush. In February 2014, the Obama administration submitted a proposed budget of $3.9 trillion for fiscal year 2015, and it projected that spending would reach nearly $4.7 trillion by the year 2019.

Explaining the Growth of the Bureaucracy

What accounts for the growth of the bureaucracy and of the number of bureaucrats since the late 1800s? Many observers believe that the growth can be attributed directly to the expansion of the nation itself. Not only do the residents of cities and suburbs require more services than did the predominantly rural

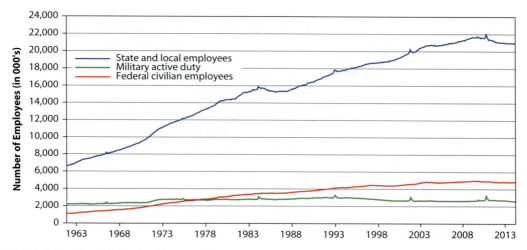

FIGURE 13.3 Relative Size of the Federal Bureaucracy

Contrary to conventional wisdom, the size of the federal bureaucracy has been shrinking, especially in comparison to the growth of state and local government employment.

Source: Federal Reserve Bank of St. Louis, Economic Research Division, http://research.stlouisfed.org/fred2/categories/32325.

dwellers of the early 1800s, but the challenges of urban and industrial life have intensified, outstripping the capacity of families or local and state governments to cope with them. Thus, the American people have increasingly turned to the national government for help.

The federal bureaucracy has also expanded in response to sudden changes in economic, social, cultural, and political conditions. During the Great Depression and World War II, for example, the federal bureaucracy grew to meet the challenges these situations created. It increased its regulation of important industries, and during the war it imposed controls on much of the American economy. When these crises ended, the public was reluctant to give up many of the federal welfare and economic programs that the government had implemented.

Political leaders, too, foster bureaucratic growth. Presidents running for re-election often enlarge government bureaucracies so that they can leave their mark on history. We have noted the large expansion of the federal bureaucracy that occurred under Franklin D. Roosevelt's New Deal. There is also considerable evidence that the bureaucracy itself plays a role in developing and expanding government programs.[25] Some analysts point out that expansion of their agency's programs and budgets is among the few personal rewards that bureaucrats can seek, because compensation for public employees is limited, and opportunities are very limited. Thus, a number of factors have contributed to the growth of the federal bureaucracy.

Bureaucratic Power

> **What are the sources of (and limits on) bureaucratic power?**

To operate effectively, government must employ qualified personnel and must have the financial resources to enable these employees to carry out their jobs. Another critical ingredient, however, is **bureaucratic power**. Government agencies require power if they are to be competent. This requirement is so great that one student of American public administration has called power the "lifeblood of administration."[26] Without sufficient power, government agencies would certainly live up to the myth of bureaucratic incompetence, for they would not be able to accomplish their tasks effectively or efficiently.

Bureaucratic power The power of government agencies, derived from law, external support, expertise, discretion, longevity in office, skill, leadership, and a variety of other sources.

In spite of the importance of bureaucratic power, the public is very suspicious of the role that this power plays in American government. Inherent in the myth of an unresponsive bureaucracy is a fear of bureaucratic power and a widespread belief that federal bureaucrats are misusing or even abusing this power. The U.S. constitutional system is rooted in the idea that the people should govern, if not directly then at least indirectly, through their elected representatives. Yet over the past two centuries, more and more governmental power has been placed in the hands of bureaucrats. Those who believe in the myth of an unresponsive bureaucracy are likely to worry about the existence and use of bureaucratic power.

The Sources of Bureaucratic Power

Where do bureaucracies get the power they need in order to function? Some of it is derived from the legitimacy of the laws they are required to enforce or the policies they are asked to implement (see Chapter 2). But often the legitimacy of these laws or these policies is not enough. We must consider other key factors.[27]

Policy subgovernments Alliances and relationships among specific agencies, interest groups, and relevant members of Congress that have been capable of effectively exercising authority in a narrowly defined policy area, such as transportation and farm price supports. Powerful alliances often form iron triangles, like the tobacco subgovernment; looser alliances involving a wide range of actors are called issue networks.

External Support. A major source of bureaucratic power is the support that government agencies receive from the general public, special-interest groups, the media, Congress, or the White House. The greater an agency's external support, the more power it is likely to wield. For example, the *Federal Bureau of Investigation (FBI)* came under severe scrutiny in the post–September 11 period, when questions were raised about its intelligence-gathering operations and how it missed indications that such an attack was being planned.[28] Over the next decade, it undertook major reforms of its operations to help regain public support.

Another form of external support comes from coalitions among bureaucracies and other actors in the American political arena. Thus, agencies sometimes participate in political alliances that might include their clientele group, other agencies, lobbyists for special interests, and members of Congress who preside over relevant committees and subcommittees.[29] Analysts call these alliances **policy subgovernments**, because the actors effectively exercise authority in a narrowly defined policy area.

In their most extreme forms, often called *iron triangles*, these subgovernments can be powerful coalitions (see Chapter 9). The success of any iron triangle coalition depends on its members' ability to limit participation to a few insiders and to maintain a low public profile. Until recently, one of Washington's most successful iron triangles was the tobacco subgovernment, which focused on policies related to promoting the consumption of tobacco products. The three main sets of actors in that subgovernment were members of Congress from tobacco-growing states who sat on the agriculture and appropriations committees; lobbyists representing tobacco growers and cigarette companies; and bureaucrats from tobacco-related programs at the agriculture and commerce departments. These actors created programs that helped tobacco farmers and the giant tobacco industry to fend off attacks from those who sought policies contrary to their interests. But in 1964, the cozy world of the tobacco subgovernment began to fall apart. That year, the surgeon general of the United States issued a report linking cigarette smoking to lung cancer, heart disease, and emphysema. The report was followed by a Federal Trade Commission proposal that cigarette packages and advertising carry health warnings. The tobacco subgovernment no longer had the low visibility that had made it so effective before the surgeon general's announcement.[30]

At the opposite extreme from iron triangles are subgovernments organized as issue networks. *Issue networks* involve a large number of participants with different degrees of interest in and commitment to the policies and problems that bring them together. An issue network is an open and at times highly visible subgovernment. The individuals taking part in it may come and go, and often members of these networks have neither the time nor the leadership resources to develop consistent shared attitudes toward policy. Bureaucrats also play a role in issue network subgovernments, but that role often depends on their grasp of the issues and their willingness to dive into the open policymaking process.[31]

Environmental policymaking is a classic example of an issue network in action. The challenge of environmental protection has attracted a multitude of actors, including dozens of members of Congress, hundreds of interest groups with varying points of view, and a host of media and academic observers. In the middle of that issue network sits the Environmental Protection Agency (EPA), created in 1970 to coordinate the implementation of federal environmental policy. The EPA maintained a leading role in the environmental issue network quite successfully during the 1970s. Beginning in 1981, however, the agency's situation changed.

The Reagan administration came to office intent on changing the direction of environmental policy through deregulation and reform. It planned to use the EPA to implement these changes by instituting new agency policies and by radically altering the way in which environmental regulations were enforced in established program areas. The administration's strategy ignored the interests of some of the major actors in the existing environmental policy issue network. Incensed at the EPA's new positions, environmental interest groups formed alliances to defeat Reagan's initiatives in a variety of program areas. In 1983, the administration acknowledged defeat and replaced the controversial head of the EPA with William Ruckelshaus, who was highly regarded by environmental interest groups and who had been the first administrator of the agency when it was created.[32]

Whether it takes the form of public support or coalitions with special-interest groups, external support plays an important role in shaping and directing bureaucratic power. The cases of the tobacco and environmental policy subgovernments indicate just how significant that support can be for individual agencies.

Expertise. An agency's power can also stem from its expertise. In matters of national defense, America's top policymakers often turn to experts at the Pentagon for advice. On issues involving public health, they ask the opinion of the surgeon general or the *Centers for Disease Control and Prevention (CDC)*. On international subjects, the *Central Intelligence Agency (CIA)* is regarded as the primary source of expert information. As long as such expert information is deemed accurate and reliable by those who use it, it enhances the power of the agency. But if the credibility of that information is brought into question—as happened to the CIA both in the late 1980s, when it failed to accurately predict the collapse of the Soviet bloc, and again in 2003 and 2004, when its intelligence on Iraq was brought into question—the public immediately questions the competence of the agency and its officials. Once the credibility of a bureaucracy's expertise is put in doubt, that bureaucracy's influence and power are likely to deteriorate.

Administrative Discretion. Bureaucrats are often permitted to use their own judgment in implementing public policies and programs. Congress and the White House frequently formulate policies in ambiguous and vague terms. When President John F. Kennedy issued a mandate to the National Aeronautics and Space Administration to land an American on the moon by 1970, he could not tell the agency exactly when and how to do it; those details were left to the discretion of NASA officials. Discretion can be an important source of power, for it gives some individuals within a bureaucracy considerable flexibility in deciding how to do their jobs.

Longevity in Office. The merit system, which protects most federal employees from being fired for political reasons, provides still another source of bureaucratic power. Because it is extremely difficult to dismiss a federal civil servant without a good, nonpolitical cause, civil servants usually stay in their jobs for a long time. The average bureaucrat serves through several presidential and congressional terms in office. As a result, elected officials and their appointees often find themselves relying on career civil servants to keep the agencies functioning. Thus, longevity in office can mean considerable power for the experienced bureaucrat.

Skill and Leadership. External support, expertise, discretion, and longevity in office will not accomplish much by themselves. Potential wielders of bureaucratic power must have the talents and the will to use those resources. This criterion is as true for agencies as it is for individuals. Without skill and leadership, even the most resource-rich federal agency will not be able to accomplish its objectives.

In short, power is the fuel that gives bureaucracies the energy to carry out their missions. A bureaucracy without power or the potential to exercise power is truly a waste of public resources. The question is not whether bureaucratic power exists or should exist but whether that power is responsive to the wishes of the American public and its elected representatives.

The Limits on Bureaucratic Power

The American political system does provide effective means of limiting bureau-cratic power and keeping it responsive. It offers a variety of internal and external checks designed to contain bureaucratic influence and authority within accept-able bounds.

Self-Restraint and Limited Resources. Some of the curbs come from bureaucratic self-restraint. In the mid-1970s, certain regulatory commissions took the initia-tive to relax the controls they had previously exercised over sectors of the American economy. For example, the *Civil Aeronautics Board (CAB)* intentionally eliminated many barriers to competition among the nation's major airlines. That initiative proved so popular that Congress formally deregulated the airline industry in 1978 and eliminated the CAB altogether in 1985. Although no other major regulatory commission has been abolished, most exercised similar self-restraint during the late 1970s and throughout the 1980s.

The quantity and quality of available resources also put limits on bureaucratic power. The *Internal Revenue Service (IRS)*, for example, does not have enough auditors and agents to review everyone's tax return and to investigate all sus-pected cases of tax fraud. In fact, the IRS is able to investigate only a small per-centage of the returns filed each year. Therefore, the competence of its auditors and agents determines how effectively the IRS collects taxes, as does the agency's increasing use of computers to process tax returns. Ultimately, however, the IRS's best tool is the individual taxpayer's fear that his or her return might be one of the few that the service may subject to a detailed audit.

The White House. The president today is often perceived as the head bureaucrat, who, like the chief executive of a large corporation, is responsible for overseeing and coordinating the day-to-day operations and decisions of his firm. In the language used by constitutional scholars, this view, called the **unitary executive theory**, reflects the idea that the work of federal agencies must be consistent with the priorities of the White House and the president's views regarding existing laws and policies. Advocates of this view see it as rooted in provisions of Article II of the Constitution, which states that executive power is "vested" in the presi-dent, who is also given the responsibility to ensure that the laws and policies of the country are being "faithfully executed." Some observers have been critical of this approach and the emergence of what is often termed the "imperial presi-dency" (see Chapter 12). They argue that those constitutional provisions do not empower the president to act as if he were heading a corporation but rather give the White House the task of making sure that federal bureaucrats are carrying out their duties under the law and not abusing their authority.

Unitary executive theory The idea that the Constitution gives the president the authority to oversee and manage the work of federal agencies to ensure that their priorities and actions are consistent with the views of the White House regarding existing laws and policies.

Congress. Congress can also impose limitations on the power of federal agen-cies. The Constitution authorizes Congress to establish public programs and to arrange for their implementation. Yet Congress has not always been detailed and explicit in its instructions to federal agencies. Vague legislation has led many critics to argue that Congress is not working hard enough to limit or control bureaucratic power, and bureaucrats themselves have complained about the lack of specificity. In 1979, one administrator openly criticized a congressional act that, in a single line of statutory language, required his agency to establish a program to protect the rights of the handicapped—with no details or guidance. "They're frequently very unhappy with what we do after they give us a mandate like that," he noted. "But the trouble is, the mandate is broad, they deliberately are ambiguous where there is conflict on details, and they leave it to us to try to resolve the ambiguities."[33]

Implied in such criticism is the belief that Congress has a right to exercise much more legislative control than it does today by expanding or narrowing an agency's authority to take action. When the secretary of the treasury asked Congress for broad, sweeping powers to deal with the emerging financial crisis in September 2008, Congress responded instead by imposing a system of checks and controls over the rescue effort. By contrast, provisions of two laws passed in 2010—the Patient Protection and Affordable Care Act (Obamacare) and the Wall Street Reform and Consumer Protection Act (also known as Dodd-Frank)—have been criticized for allowing agencies too much authority to fill in the details left out by Congress.[34]

Although Congress finds it difficult to control or limit bureaucratic power through detailed legislation, it has other tools with which to accomplish these ends.[35] Congress reviews agency budget requests each year, and it can use that opportunity to scrutinize agency operations. Almost every congressional committee has jurisdiction over a group of federal agencies, and these committees sometimes exercise their oversight responsibilities by holding public hearings on agency operations.[36] The Internal Revenue Service, for example, has been subject to oversight by House committees for three decades. In the late 1990s, one hearing focused on making the IRS more "customer-friendly" in its treatment of taxpayers. In 2013, an internal report that raised questions about the treatment of certain applications for nonprofit status led to congressional hearings that focused on accusations of political bias in the IRS, resulting in a number of personnel changes and a criminal investigation by the Department of Justice.[37]

Individual members of Congress often intercede with specific agencies on behalf of their constituents. Members of Congress can also order the Government Accountability Office to conduct an audit or investigation of any federal program. Finally, the role of the U.S. Senate in confirming political appointments provides that chamber with a unique opportunity to review bureaucratic actions.

The Courts. The courts also play a role in limiting the power of the federal bureaucracy.[38] In the period before 1937, the judiciary often agreed to hear cases challenging the authority given to federal agencies by Congress. Today the courts are much less likely to entertain such cases; nevertheless, they pay considerable attention to complaints that a federal agency has exceeded its authority or acted in an arbitrary or unreasonable way when carrying out its duties.

Some of the courts' power over the federal bureaucracy stems from specific provisions of the U.S. Constitution, such as the prohibition against "unreasonable searches and seizures" or the guarantee that citizens shall not be deprived of "life, liberty, or property without due process of law." These powers were reinforced by the Federal Tort Claims Act of 1946, which permits (with a few specified exceptions) Americans to sue the federal government for damages incurred through governmental actions. Congress has even made special provisions for taking legal action against specific agencies. Under provisions of the 1988 tax laws, for example, a taxpayer may sue an IRS employee for damages if the agent seeks to collect taxes in a reckless way or with intentional disregard of tax laws. The possibility of being challenged in court has proved to be an effective means of control.

The courts also play a role in shaping the relationships between the bureaucracy and the other branches of government. From time to time in our history, controversies have arisen about whether government agencies were subject to presidential or congressional control. Sometimes these have taken the form of court cases. In some of these cases the courts have sided with Congress, and in others they have deferred to the White House. The Supreme Court has tended to favor the presidency in recent years,[39] but over the past two hundred years there has been no consistent answer to the question of who runs the bureaucracy. Thus, the courts remain a major factor in the life of the federal bureaucracy.

Restraints. Competition among federal agencies is another source of limits on bureaucratic power. Many agencies have competitors in the federal government—other agencies that vie for the same set of authorizations or appropriations. The different branches of the armed forces, for instance, compete with one another for a bigger slice of the defense budget. Although such competition may seem inefficient, it does help impose restraints on the power of the military bureaucracies by leading each of them to keep an eye on the activities of the others.

A strong sense of professionalism and responsibility on the part of public-sector employees can also act as a brake on bureaucratic power, especially when someone within an agency exposes inappropriate, unethical, or questionable activities. Often called **whistle-blowers**, these government employees put their careers at risk, and for many years their efforts frequently led to reprimands and even the loss of their jobs. This changed in 1968, when a Pentagon employee in charge of monitoring the costs of a major defense contract went public with his concerns after being ignored by his superiors for three years. In addition to being made notorious in the press, A. Ernest Fitzgerald was demoted and transferred to another position, and his career was effectively sidetracked for the next few years. Unlike previous whistle-blowers, however, Fitzgerald took legal action and eventually won reinstatement. He also led efforts to have Congress provide legal protections for whistle-blowers and is still regarded as the classic model for this internal check on potential waste and abuses of agency power.[40]

Despite the legal protections now in place, whistle-blowers usually pay a high price for their honesty and candor. In many instances, blowing the whistle on an agency can make one an outcast in the organization and can end one's career. And in some cases in which blowing the whistle is regarded as a security violation, it can result in criminal action.[41] Each agency also has an office of the

Whistle-blowers
Employees who risk their careers by reporting corruption or waste in their agencies to oversight officials.

Daniel Ellsberg, a Defense Department contractor with access to a classified study that undermined the government's claims of success in the Vietnam War, copied and released the report to the *New York Times* in 1971. Ellsberg thought he would go to jail for his whistle-blowing act, but charges were dismissed because of government misconduct in its investigation of Ellsberg.

Inspector general An official in a government agency who is assigned the task of investigating complaints or suspicious behavior.

Freedom of Information Act (FOIA) A public disclosure law that requires federal agencies to release information on written request.

inspector general, which can investigate complaints by whistle-blowers and others as well as suspicious behavior.[42]

By investigating leads that might uncover major problems, an alert press corps can also restrain bureaucratic power. The **Freedom of Information Act (FOIA)** and other public disclosure laws restrain bureaucratic power as well.[43] Under the FOIA, agencies are required to provide citizens with public records on written request. The law does allow certain material to remain secret and does not apply to the courts or to Congress.

Limits and Responsiveness. As we have seen, although it is impossible to guarantee that bureaucratic power will not be misused or abused, mechanisms for limiting that power do exist. Because of these potential and actual restraints, bureaucratic power in the federal government has a good chance of being controlled.

In many respects, these limits work to make government agencies more, rather than less, responsive. The problem is that being responsive to one constituency group often means being perceived as unresponsive by others. Consumer groups, for example, often criticize the Department of Agriculture for being too supportive of farming interests and not sufficiently attentive to the needs of consumers. Similarly, many businesses complain that the Environmental Protection Agency and other regulatory agencies fail to take their interests and needs into account, whereas those who support regulation believe that the regulators are on the right track.

Bureaucratic Problems and Reforms

> **What are the major problems with bureaucratic behavior, and what steps have been taken to control them?**

If the myths of bureaucratic incompetence and unresponsiveness do not reflect the reality of government administration, why do so many Americans continue to complain about the way government operates? That they do is somewhat mysterious, for students of public administration find that many citizens are quite satisfied with most of their routine encounters with the bureaucracy.[44] The complaints that most Americans have about the federal bureaucracy may reflect what they hear about others' ordeals rather than what they have experienced themselves. Problems with the bureaucracy, however, do help keep the myths alive. At its best, the federal bureaucracy serves the public interest. At its worst, it seems to conduct itself in ways that feed the myths of incompetence and unresponsiveness. Students of American government describe these behaviors as **bureaucratic pathologies**—or *bureaupathologies*, for short.[45]

Bureaucratic Pathologies

Clientelism. In very general terms, public agencies attempt to work on behalf of the public interest. On a day-to-day basis, however, bureaucrats must deal with those who are served by the programs they implement—the agency's clientele. The Department of Agriculture works with farmers, the Department of Education with educators, and so on. This daily contact with their clientele is an absolute necessity for employees of these agencies if they are to be responsive to the needs of those they serve. But this constant contact can become pathological when bureaucrats begin to display favoritism toward their clientele's interests, especially when those interests seem not to serve the public good.

The tobacco subgovernment we discussed earlier is a classic example of clientelism at work. Bureaucrats within the Department of Agriculture who had worked with tobacco farmers for decades supported their clients' interests, even though they were contrary to emerging government policies to discourage smoking.

Pathological Incrementalism. Federal agencies exist to administer programs, and we expect them to do so with consistency and fairness. But the conditions under which agencies operate competently are not stagnant. Conditions and circumstances change—sometimes swiftly. One would expect public-sector agencies to adapt to those changes as quickly as possible, but often they resist change or make only small, incremental adjustments. At times this response may be intentional. For example, then-secretary of defense Dick Cheney and others in the first Bush administration resisted calls for radical reductions in the Pentagon's 1991 federal budget, despite the major changes that were taking place in the former Soviet Union and Eastern Europe.

However, incrementalist behavior can become pathological when it threatens the very program or service that the agency is supposedly providing. The U.S. military has often been plagued by pathological incrementalism. The navy was

Bureaucratic pathologies
Behaviors by bureaucrats that feed the idea that the bureaucracy is incompetent and unresponsive. They include clientelism, incrementalism, arbitrariness, parochialism, and imperialism.

slow to recognize the importance of air power in the 1920s until, in a widely publicized demonstration of the point, a maverick army general, Billy Mitchell, sank a warship. During that same period, it was equally difficult to convince many army leaders to abandon horse cavalry units. Bureaucracies tend to move cautiously and slowly, and sometimes that snail's pace can prove both dangerous and costly.

Arbitrariness. A competent bureaucracy is one that does its job effectively and efficiently. To achieve this condition, an agency often must adopt **standard operating procedures**, often called SOPs. At times, however, the use of regularized procedures can interfere with responsiveness or replace common sense, and then arbitrariness becomes a factor. For example, there are stories about people losing their welfare or unemployment benefits because they failed to show up for an appointment with a social worker or forgot to file a certain form on time. A bureaucrat who is unwilling to listen to excuses or explanations can hardly be faulted for sticking to the rules, but he or she can be faulted for being too arbitrary and losing sight of why a program or procedure exists. Bureaucracies often serve people with special needs or individuals facing special circumstances. Even if the aim is efficiency, arbitrary behavior can prove harmful under such conditions.

For instance, in the post–September 11 era, some agencies have adopted and strictly enforced rules and regulations that many Americans regard as poorly designed and arbitrary. One example is the new Transportation Security Administration (TSA), which is responsible for protecting the nation's transportation systems. Although the TSA deals with various transportation modes (e.g., rail, passenger ferries, etc.), it is best known for its work at airport checkpoints. Its policies and procedures, no matter how well intended, have drawn much criticism over the years. In response, the agency has invested heavily in communicating with the public. At the center of its campaign are a website (www.tsa.gov) and blog (www.tsa.gov/blog) that many regard as models for other agencies to follow. Not only do they provide information, but they also attempt to enter into a dialogue with those who are the most critical. In short, the TSA is reaching out to the public to change the perception that it is being arbitrary or abusing its authority.

Arbitrariness also arises when a bureaucrat acts without legal authority. Although a police officer has the authority to stop a driver whose vehicle is swerving dangerously, he or she cannot use a nightstick to beat the car's driver or occupants without cause.[46]

Parochialism. To perform their functions effectively, some government agencies believe that it is necessary to focus attention on the job at hand. Such concentration on getting the job done can result in another pathological behavior—parochialism.

For example, the job of the U.S. Army's Rocky Mountain Arsenal was to produce and store chemical and biological weapons, and for most of its thirty-year existence that organization carried out its work without paying much attention to the damage it was doing to its surroundings. That parochial attitude had both short-term and long-term effects. During the early 1970s, one geologist traced a series of earth tremors to a weapons disposal process being used at the arsenal located just outside Denver. After months of denying any link between its activities

Standard operating procedures (SOPs) Regularized procedures used in public agencies to help the agencies conduct administrative business effectively and efficiently.

and the disturbances, the arsenal temporarily halted the operation. The tremors came to an end, and the army finally agreed to discontinue the process permanently. Years later, when the army closed the arsenal, state and federal environmental protection investigators found that the land in and around the weapons facility was so contaminated that it might remain unusable for hundreds of years. Taken to its extreme, this type of pathological behavior can prove deadly.

Imperialism. As we noted earlier, bureaucracies need power in one form or another in order to do their jobs. Therefore, bureaucrats seek to obtain the resources they need if they are to carry out their assignments. At times, this goal means expanding agency operations and taking on more responsibilities and personnel. In some agencies, this drive for expansion becomes an end in itself—a key sign of the pathological behavior called *bureaucratic imperialism.*

Imperialism may involve getting a bigger slice of the federal budget pie, or it may mean starting new programs or even taking over another agency's functions. Whatever form it takes, most Americans do not regard expansion for its own sake as a desirable feature of bureaucratic operations.

POLITICS & POPULAR CULTURE: Visit the book's companion website at **www.oup.com/us/gitelson** to read the special feature *Hollywood Bureaucrats and Other Myths.*

Calls for Reform

These bureaupathological behaviors help to explain why the myths of incompetent and unresponsive bureaucracies remain popular today. Americans perceive these problems as the rule rather than the exception. It is not surprising, therefore, to hear calls for bureaucratic reform.

Often those reforms take place within the agencies and reflect a change in leadership or the adoption of some new or innovative managerial approach. This occurred in the Federal Emergency Management Agency after Hurricane Andrew in 1992.

The poor response to Hurricane Andrew was widely covered in the press and showed that FEMA was not up to the task of dealing with major disasters. When President Clinton took office in early 1993, he asked James Lee Witt, an experienced emergency management director, to take over FEMA. Under Witt's leadership, FEMA emerged as a model agency. Witt made changes in FEMA's personnel, giving more authority and responsibility to the most competent employees and boosting agency morale. He took the agency beyond its coordination role by creating rapid-response capabilities so that FEMA would be in touch with state officials and would be on the ground as soon as word of a major disaster reached the Washington office. He also made the agency more proactive by having it take the lead in pushing for states and localities to engage in more emergency preparedness activities, as well as working on programs that would help prevent or mitigate the impact of future disasters.

FEMA during the 1990s became a much-cited example of how government bureaucracies can be made more effective, efficient, and responsive. After the 2000 presidential election, George W. Bush replaced Witt with a political appointee (his former campaign manager). The agency continued to function well, and FEMA was a major presence at the site of the collapse of the World Trade Center after September 11. But, over time, the improvements made by Witt and others were altered, and the result was the well-publicized problems of the federal government's response to Hurricane Katrina.[47]

The dramatic turnaround of FEMA under James Lee Witt is just one example of the reform-from-within approach in the federal bureaucracy,[48] but few of those efforts get the attention they deserve from a media that feeds on stories of failures and scandals. With media attention focused primarily on the negative stories about bureaucracy, it is not surprising that policymakers attempt to bring about reforms from outside by seeking to radically alter the structure and operations of the entire bureaucratic complex. As discussed in Policy Connection 13, these changes in administrative policies have ranged from reorganizing government agencies and changing personnel systems to privatizing public services and imposing high-stakes performance measurement regimes.

Although efforts to reform the federal bureaucracy are well meaning, most of them are based on the two myths we have examined in this chapter. The reforms aim at making government agencies either more competent or more responsive, or both. Yet there is little evidence to support the contention that bureaucratic incompetence and unresponsiveness are as pervasive as many believe them to be. Instead, the problems of our national bureaucracy may be rooted in the constant effort of federal employees to respond competently to the diverse, changing, and often conflicting expectations of politicians, clients, taxpayers, and so on. Closer examination of the day-to-day operations of American bureaucracies reveals that they are not inherently incompetent or unresponsive. Rather, their performance is often the result of a desire to be effective and competent in the face of outside forces—some political, some nonpolitical—that they cannot control.

Conclusion

Americans are demanding citizens. They want government to be efficient and to keep costs to a minimum, while at the same time they insist that agencies spare no resources to get the job done. They want government workers to treat everyone equally, but they believe that bureaucrats should consider the special needs of individual citizens. They want public officials to increase the quantity and quality of public services, but they insist that program budgets be cut back. To put it bluntly, the principal problems facing our national bureaucracy lie in what the American people expect from it.

Expectations are important for bureaucrats because they spend most of their time trying to live up to the expectations of others—expectations that are as varied and diverse as the programs they administer.[49] We can trace many of the problems surrounding bureaucratic institutions to those efforts. If we are going to criticize the performance of our bureaucrats and accuse them of being wasteful or unresponsive, we must remember that federal employees are often responding to our demands.

Key Terms

Bureaucracy p. 426
Bureaucratic
    pathologies p. 449
Bureaucratic power p. 442

Cabinet p. 428
Career service personnel
    systems p. 432
Deregulation p. 457

Executive Office of the President
    (EOP) p. 434
Freedom of Information Act
    (FOIA) p. 448

Focus Questions Review

1. **Who works in the bureaucracy? What do these people do? Where do they work? > > >**
   - The federal bureaucracy comprises diverse groups of people who occupy a variety of white-collar and blue-collar positions. They are organized under several personnel systems, including the following:
       - The ranks of political appointees
       - The general civil service system
       - Wage systems
   - Much of what federal bureaucrats do is hidden from public view. Nevertheless, they play important roles in the policymaking process—roles that go beyond merely administering government programs.
   - Organizationally, federal bureaucrats work in hundreds of agencies, including the following:
       - The Executive Office of the President
       - Cabinet departments
       - Independent executive branch agencies
       - Regulatory commissions
       - Government corporations
       - Other types of agencies

2. **What factors have led to the growth of the federal bureaucracy? > > >**
   - The federal bureaucracy has grown in size and changed in nature over the past two centuries, mostly because of increasing demands by the public and changing conditions in American society.

3. **What are the sources of (and limits on) bureaucratic power? > > >**
   - Bureaucracies need power in order to function in the American political system. They derive that

power from a variety of sources, such as the following:
   - External support
   - Expertise
   - Bureaucratic discretion
   - Longevity
   - Skill
   - Leadership
   - There are many limits to bureaucratic power. These limits come from the legal and political controls exercised by the presidency, Congress, the courts, and various other groups.

4. **What are the major problems with bureaucratic behavior, and what steps have been taken to control them? > > >**
   - In their operation, bureaucracies sometimes develop pathological behavior patterns. They may
       - Give excessive attention to the interests of those they serve (clientelism)
       - Oppose change (incrementalism)
       - Be arbitrary and capricious (arbitrariness)
       - Take an overly narrow view of the world (parochialism)
       - Yield to an urge to expand (imperialism)
   - Pathological behaviors have stimulated a variety of reform efforts, many of which have focused on reorganizations and changes in personnel policies. Ultimately, however, bureaucracies must meet the expectations of the public in carrying out their responsibilities. In many instances, those expectations are in direct conflict with the standards of businesslike performance.

Review Questions

1. What are the different sources of bureaucratic power? What are the factors that limit or restrain the exercise of bureaucratic power?
2. Describe the various efforts made by U.S. presidents to bring about administrative reform.

For more information and access to study materials, visit the book's companion website at www.oup.com/us/gitelson.

Policy Connection

Have policymakers addressed the problems of incompetent and unresponsive government?

The Policy Challenge

As we discussed in Chapter 13, performance expectations play a central role in the work of government agencies and those who carry on the business of government. In many cases, improvements come about as a result of changes in leadership and internal management adjustments within the agencies themselves—as was the case when James Lee Witt took over as head of the Federal Emergency Management Agency in 1993.

At other times, however, improving the operations of government becomes a matter of public policy. This typically occurs as a byproduct of an election campaign promise made by a candidate who attempts to respond to the issues generated by the myths of incompetent and unresponsive bureaucracies. Often this promise is little more than a verbal commitment to get rid of waste, fraud, and abuse in government. But there are instances when the candidate articulates a particular plan or approach for improving the way government operates. As we will see in the pages that follow, the source of these administrative reform policy proposals varies.

These reform policies may reflect ideas drawn from the best practices of business firms or from some successful approach undertaken by foreign, state, or local governments. They can also emerge from reform movements that generate ideas for reducing corruption, enhancing accountability, improving agency efficiency, and achieving other objectives that fall in line with the reformers' view of good governance. Whatever their source, administrative reform policies have played a major role in shaping the way government carries out policies.

The Progressive Obsession

It is difficult to pinpoint exactly when the federal government first adopted administrative reform policies. Some historians would point to the efforts by President Jackson to democratize government by implementing a rotation-in-office policy for appointing individuals to public positions—a policy eventually associated with the patronage-based spoils system that would itself be the subject of reform a few decades later. Although subject to corrupt practices, the Jacksonian reforms led to a major redesign of the few federal jobs in post offices and customs houses, so that any citizen could take on any position with minimal difficulty.[1]

Most historians, however, would highlight the Progressive Era (1880–1920) as the launching point for modern administrative reform efforts. Many of the political and electoral reforms discussed earlier in this book emerged from this period, including the secret ballot, the use of primaries, initiative and referendum elections, and so on. The reformers of this period often regarded these electoral changes as necessary in order to bring about more fundamental changes in the administrative operations of government. Many of the first administrative reforms took place at the local level, especially with the widespread adoption of city management and county commission forms of government. Civil service reform and the elimination of partisan patronage were critical to their efforts.

The early reformers had several objectives, but the goal of taking politics out of the administration of government was central, a position summed up in an 1887 article by a young visiting lecturer of politics at Cornell University and future president, Woodrow Wilson, who argued that "administration lies outside the proper

455

sphere of *politics*. Administration questions are not political questions. Although politics sets the tasks for administration, it should not be suffered to manipulate its offices."[2] Once the political factors are cordoned off, the reformers argued, the work of government can be taken care of in a businesslike fashion.

A Call for Economy and Efficiency

Although initially focused at the state and local levels, the Progressive reform obsession with bringing businesslike practices to federal government agencies led to the appointment of the Committee on Department Methods (called the Keep Commission, after its chair, Charles Keep) in 1905. Reacting to news stories about inefficiencies in the military's procurement process that prevented soldiers from getting winter clothing, President Theodore Roosevelt asked the commission not to focus on scandals but to consider and recommend what changes ought to be made in the standard practices used by government agencies.[3] Covering everything from purchasing practices and agency sick leave policies to records management, the major reports and suggestions issued by the commission were submitted to Congress by Roosevelt in 1908 and 1909. Congressional reaction to the recommendations was initially hostile, for at the time the operations of specific government agencies came under the purview of congressional committees rather than the White House, and Congress regarded the reports and their recommendations as a form of presidential encroachment. Over time, however, they adopted many of the reforms as congressional policies,[4] and these set a precedent for future administrative reform policy initiatives.

The Keep Commission efforts reflected a subtle but important shift in the focus of reform policy advocates. Whereas civil service reform was designed to keep partisan politics out of government administration, the goal now was to make government operations more economical and effective. This theme continued under President Taft, who established the Commission on Economy and Efficiency (1910–1913), as well as throughout President Wilson's administration (1913–1921), which was preoccupied with the war effort. Although presidents played a role during this period, it was Congress that was ultimately responsible for any major administrative policy changes, a fact reflected in the work of the special Joint Committee on the Reorganization of the Administrative Branch of the Government (1920–1923), which attempted to follow through on earlier recommendations, especially in the area of improved budgeting and accounting practices.

Toward Executive Empowerment

Issues related to how best to manage government agencies came to the fore once again as policies and programs developed to deal with the Great Depression proliferated and expanded. In 1936, Franklin Roosevelt asked Louis Brownlow, a well-known and highly respected advocate of administrative reform, to chair the Committee on Administrative Management, which made the case for a more president-centered approach to coordinating government actions. The Brownlow Committee report (with an accompanying legislative proposal) was forwarded to Congress in 1937, where it was not well received. Opponents of the proposal labeled it the "dictator bill" and instead supported a report generated by the Senate Select Committee to Investigate the Executive Agencies of Government, which sought to limit presidential authority over the operations of government agencies.

The policy debate over the different approaches was heated, but in 1939 Congress eventually passed legislation that gave the White House considerable power over the organization and operations of government agencies.[5] Administrative policies enacted during World War II reinforced the empowering of the presidency, and postwar efforts by Congress to regain its influence over agencies ultimately failed to stop the trend.[6] What became known as the "unitary theory" of government placed primary authority over administrative matters in the hands of the president.

The issue over whether Congress or the White House ought to "control" the federal bureaucracy continued to define administrative policy debates through the 1970s, although the rhetoric often turned on the older issues of keeping politics out of administration and making government operations more efficient and economical. Two presidential commissions chaired by former president Herbert Hoover (one under President Truman and the other under President Eisenhower) called for the reorganization of the federal bureaucracy and led to recommendations that eliminated or consolidated some agencies and even created new ones.[7] During the Eisenhower, Kennedy, and Johnson administrations, various advisory committees and task forces on administrative organization came and went, all focused on how to enhance the role of the president as chief executive of the federal bureaucracy.

In 1969, President Nixon appointed the Advisory Council on Executive Organizations, headed by businessman Roy Ash. The Ash Council report, combined with presidential authority (granted by Congress) allowing Nixon to reorganize through executive orders, led to still more changes in the federal bureaucracy, including the creation of the National Oceanic and Atmospheric Administration, the Nuclear Regulatory Commission, and the Environmental Protection Agency. Most important, it led to the creation of the Office of Management and Budget to deal with both management and budgetary issues—and Nixon appointed Roy Ash to head that agency.[8] Nixon was also committed to making additional changes requiring explicit congressional approval that would completely reorganize the cabinet and establish what one insider has called an "administrative presidency,"[9] but his plans were put on hold by the Watergate investigations and his eventual resignation.

Post-Watergate Retreat from Bureaucracy

In addition to the Watergate scandal, which raised questions about the potential for the misuse of presidential authority over law enforcement and regulatory agencies, there emerged a growing sense that the problem with bureaucracy may not be how it was organized or controlled but whether government agencies and programs were in fact the best means for dealing with public problems. From the mid-1970s through the 1990s, administrative reform policy became associated with deregulation, privatization, and contracting out (or outsourcing).

Whereas the Ash Council report had addressed the value of having so many regulatory agencies be "independent" of presidential control, many leading economists and policymakers on both the left and the right began questioning whether there was too much regulation and whether it might not be better to allow the marketplace to deal with airlines, energy costs, banking, and other areas.[10] Thus began what one author has called the "war against regulation," which was reflected in legislative and executive actions over the next three decades.[11]

Deregulation involved a loosening of government controls over activities and economic sectors previously subject to government rules and regulations. In some instances, the policy led to the dismantling of regulatory bodies such as the Civil Aeronautics Board. Some regulations were changed by law, as when, in 1996, Congress lifted the forty-station cap on the number of radio stations one company can own. At other times, changes concerned regulations issued by agencies, such as the decision by the Department of Justice Antitrust Division not to take action against certain types of media acquisitions (see Policy Connection 10). There were also instances when agencies such as the Securities and Exchange Commission made clear that certain rules would not be strictly enforced.

Alternatively, privatization and outsourcing reforms are administrative policies that seek to turn over government functions and services to private enterprises or nonprofit organizations based on the assumption that they can operate more efficiently and effectively than public bureaucracies. These efforts were compatible with the antigovernment agenda set by the Reagan administration.

In its most extreme form, privatization involves the government's relinquishing its role in a government enterprise, as when the federal government withdrew from its major stake in COMSAT, the Communications Satellite Corporation, which it helped start in the 1960s. More often, **privatization** involves either turning over a government enterprise to a private company or giving a nongovernmental firm a franchise or license to provide what was previously a government function.[12] Perhaps the most controversial example of this practice has been local, state, and federal use of private prison facilities. In the case of the U.S. Bureau of Prisons, once a private correctional facility has been approved, prisoners can be incarcerated there for an agreed-upon per-diem fee. This approach differs from **outsourcing** or contracting out, which involves arranging for private or nonprofit firms to provide specific services on behalf of the government. For example, in some cities, the operation of public transportation such as buses or commuter rail is carried out by private companies under contract; at the federal level, government increasingly relies on private security services to monitor and protect many of its courthouses and other facilities.

Analysts have severely criticized these reform arrangements on a number of grounds. Some question whether privatization or outsourcing is truly cost-effective, and the experience of relying on contractors to provide some basic services to support military operations in war zones has been brought into question after a number of audits. Analysts have also raised questions about the use of private firms for some critical functions. After the 9/11 attacks, for example, the federal government formed the Transportation Security Agency to take control of airport security when they found that the private firms hired by individual airports had failed to live up to expectations.

Emphasis on Performance

During the late 1980s and early 1990s, the **reinventing government** movement emerged as an alternative approach to deregulation/privatization reforms. Based on the assumption that those working for government would be more competent and responsive if they were freed of bureaucratic and arbitrary constraints, this administrative policy movement had its start in state and local governments and soon became a major part of Bill Clinton's campaign for the presidency. Once elected, Clinton put his vice president, Al Gore, in charge of the effort, called the National Performance Review (NPR). Influenced by the writings of David Osborne and Ted Gaebler,[13] the NPR called for the agencies to "put people first" by cutting unnecessary spending, focusing on "customer service," empowering their employees, and helping communities to solve their own problems while fostering excellence in public service.

The NPR effort differed from past presidential reform initiatives in several important ways. First, it did not stress increased presidential power over the bureaucracy. In fact, its emphasis on empowering government employees and communities seemed contrary to past efforts at centralization. Nor did the NPR focus obsessively on cutting the size of government; instead, it sought to improve the government's performance. Furthermore, the NPR's strategy was to push reform from the inside—to make government employees a force for reform instead of trying to impose changes from outside or from the top.

To accomplish these objectives required establishing a general policy to "deregulate government"[14]— that is, to allow agency managers to take initiatives that sometimes broke with traditional operating rules. Procurement rules for minor purchases (e.g., office supplies) were relaxed, and an effort was made to reduce red tape throughout government.[15] It also meant creating an agency **ombudsman office** to hear citizen complaints concerning the agency's programs.

One byproduct of the efforts to reinvent government was the passage of the Government Performance and Results Act of 1993, in which Congress, starting in 1999, required each agency to issue annual performance plans and reports. It believed that regular reporting and the growing use of performance measures in the federal government would likely have a long-term impact, but many critics feel it failed to generate any significant improvements in the operations of the federal bureaucracy.[16]

With the election of George W. Bush, White House support for reinventing government was replaced by other priorities, such as the push for making greater use of faith-based

President Clinton gave Vice President Al Gore the task of heading up the National Performance Review—an effort to reinvent and streamline government.

TABLE 13PC.1 Major Reform Policies, from the 1880s to the 2010s

Theme	Period	Major Events	Key Ideas
Progressive Era	1880s–1920	Civil service reform	A focus on getting politics out of administration and making government more businesslike
Economy and efficiency	1900s–1920s	Keep, Taft, and the Joint Committee	A focus on operations, budgeting, and accounting
Executive empowerment	1930s–1970s	The Brownlow Committee, Hoover commissions, and Ash Council	Increasing the role of the presidency; developing an "administrative presidency"
Retreat from bureaucracy	1975–1990s	Deregulation, privatization, and outsourcing; the Reagan revolution	Relying on markets and shrinking government
Performance and transparency	1990s–2010s	An emphasis on accountability and openness	Performance measurement tied to incentives; more access to information and feedback

organizations in delivering public services (see the discussion in Chapter 3). However, the post–9/11 reorganization of the federal government to focus on homeland security provided a major opportunity to bring about other changes, and the Bush White House responded with an approach to performance assessment it called Program Assessment Rating Tool (PART). The primary objective of PART was to make certain that the aims and operations of federal programs were brought in line with the overall priorities of the president's program.[17]

Conclusion

Have policymakers addressed the problems of incompetent and unresponsive government?

Performance-focused reforms remained important under the Obama administration, but there has been no widely articulated policy to match Clinton's effort to establish a governmentwide administrative reform policy. During Obama's first term, certain themes, such as accountability and transparency, became increasingly important in the operations of government, but the sharp political divisions that have defined the Obama years have not allowed for a positive administrative policy agenda to emerge. Issues related to contracting out, government surveillance and secrecy, and the implementation of homeland security policies by federal law enforcement officials are highlighted in the

media almost daily, but a new plan for reforming how government operates has yet to emerge. (Table 13PC.1 summarizes the major reform policies we have discussed in this Policy Connection.)

After reviewing the history of administrative reform policies, some students of administrative reform have expressed concern about whether truly significant change is possible. That is, public-sector agencies have legal and constitutional obligations that they must fulfill, and some reforms—no matter how sensible, well designed, or well intentioned—might not fit well into the American political and legal framework.[18]

QUESTIONS FOR DISCUSSION

1. Some reformers emphasize the need for managerial changes that will make the government more efficient, whereas others argue for reforms that would have government rely on private firms that are able to perform more like businesses. Still others argue that it all depends on what the nature of the service is. Consider the following services and discuss which approach to reform is the best one: airport security, trash collection, and operating federal prisons.

2. Think of your own experience in dealing with a government agency such as the Internal Revenue Service or the Department of Motor Vehicles. Were you satisfied or dissatisfied with the service or the treatment you received? What changes, if any, would you suggest to improve the service?

CHAPTER 14

MYTHS & REALITIES
Are judicial decisions completely objective and final?

Courts, Judges, and the Law

The Supreme Court Chooses a President

By now, the story of the presidential election of 2000 is a well-known tale of unparalleled drama. It was an election so close that the outcome of the Electoral College vote came down to a handful of contested votes in Florida. But the 2000 presidential election also demonstrated the importance of courts in American society. In the thirty-six days that followed the November 7 election, the candidates and their supporters filed more than fifty lawsuits. In the end, it was the U.S. Supreme Court that ended the election, when it ordered a halt to the manual recounting of votes in Florida. With the recount stopped, Al Gore conceded the election, and George W. Bush called for national unity. In the early 1800s, the French observer Alexis de Tocqueville noted that in America, all political questions become legal questions. If ever this observation needed verification, the 2000 election provided it.

In large measure, the uniqueness of the American political system stems from the role played by the courts. No other nation grants so much authority and political power to the judiciary, nor are citizens of other nations quite as willing to entrust their fate to courts as are Americans. Yet, for all their faith in courts, most Americans know very little about the legal system. They may have had a brush with the local traffic court, have been entertained by Judge Judy, or be frequent viewers of cable television's truTV channel. Nevertheless, when pressed to elaborate on what courts do and why they do it, most

< Although the Supreme Court is one of the three branches of government provided for in the Constitution, it was not until 1935, 146 years after it was created, that the Court procured a building of its own. After the federal government moved to the District of Columbia, the Court changed its meeting place six times before it finally moved into the stately building you see here.

people revert to some vague notions about the law. Most often, John Adams's famous adage that we are a "government of laws and not of men" comes to mind.[1]

Courts are shrouded in symbolism and myth. Pomp and circumstance surround even the lowliest of courts. Only in a courtroom will you find a black-robed individual looking down from a raised platform. No other U.S. public official is allowed such trappings. In fact, a mayor or senator decked out in a black robe would seem a pompous fool. Yet when a judge puts on those same robes, no one laughs or even thinks it odd; instead, the robes evoke respect. The same is true of the myths that surround the American court system: If they were attributed to any other political institution, they would seem preposterous.

Perhaps the most widespread of the illusions surrounding the courts is the idea that they are above politics. In contrast to the compromise and partisanship of the political world, the *myth of the nonpolitical courts* represents the judiciary as operating with the certainty that comes from the neutral application of a body of specialized knowledge. Presidents and members of Congress may act out of self-interest; judges simply apply the law. It is the fate of courts to be characterized as the defenders of the rule of law as opposed to the rule of ordinary men and women.

As comforting as this myth may be, it distorts reality. In the pages that follow, you will see that even the act of creating the federal courts was fraught with political conflict. Similarly, not only is the process of selecting judges mired in political controversy, but those chosen are often active participants in politics. The idea that courts have special powers also gives rise to the *myth of finality*, which assumes that once a court—especially the Supreme Court—has spoken, implementation of the decision automatically takes place. This tendency to view court decisions as an endpoint in the political process makes courts seem more powerful than they actually are. But courts cannot compel anyone to comply with their decisions. Their orders become effective only with the aid of others—aid that they do not always provide. Final authority does not rest with the Supreme Court, nor should it in a representative democracy.

We begin our discussion of the role of courts in American society by distinguishing the various sources of law. Then we look at the structure of the court system and the way in which judges are appointed and removed. We conclude the chapter with an examination of the workings of the Supreme Court and the question of compliance.

The Origins and Types of American Law

> **How does civil law differ from criminal law?**

As you may recall from Chapter 2, on constitutional foundations, the oldest source of law applied by U.S. courts is *common*, or *judge-made*, *law*, which dates from medieval England. A comparatively modern and increasingly important source of law is *statutory law*, which originates from specifically designated lawmaking bodies—for example, Congress and state legislatures.

The distinction between civil and criminal actions is also important for our understanding of the legal process. **Civil actions** involve a conflict between private persons and/or organizations. Typical cases involve disputes over contracts, claims for damages resulting from a personal injury, and divorce petitions. In a civil case, the person bringing the suit is called the plaintiff, and the person being sued is the defendant.

Criminal law applies to offenses against the public order and entails a specified range of punishments. Acts that are in violation of criminal law are specifically detailed in governmental statutes. The party demanding legal action (the national, state, or other government) is called the prosecution, and the person being prosecuted is called the defendant. Most of these cases arise in state courts, although there is a growing body of federal criminal law cases dealing with such issues as kidnapping, tax evasion, and the sale of narcotics that have taken place in federal courts.

Civil actions Suits arising out of conflicts between private persons and/or organizations; they typically include disputes over contracts, claims for damages, and divorce petitions.

Criminal law The branch of the law dealing with offenses against the public order and providing for a specified punishment. Most criminal law cases arise in state courts.

The Structure of the Court Systems

> **How do trial courts differ from appellate courts?**

When most Americans think about courts, the U.S. Supreme Court immediately comes to mind. As the highest court in the land, the Supreme Court symbolizes the American judiciary. Yet it is only one of more than 18,000 American courts, most of which are the creations of the various states. The District of Columbia and the Commonwealth of Puerto Rico have their own independent court systems. Because state laws govern most criminal prosecutions and civil actions, these are the courts that most affect the average citizen. For example, a motorist who is accused of driving under the influence of alcohol must appear before a court in the state in which the violation occurred.

Obviously, with so many court systems, there is a great deal of variability; in fact, no two of these systems are exactly alike. Nevertheless, two types of courts exist in all systems.

Trial courts, the lowest level of a court system, are the courts of first instance, possessing **original jurisdiction** (the power to be the first court to hear a case). These courts take evidence, listen to witnesses, and decide what is true and what is not. Trial courts handle both criminal and civil cases.

Trial court decisions may be made by a single judge (a procedure known as a *bench trial*) or by a jury made up of citizens selected from the community. The

Trial courts Courts at the lowest level of the system. They possess original jurisdiction.

Original jurisdiction The authority to hear a case before any other court does.

In the spring of 2013, the nation was briefly captivated by the trial of Ariel Castro. Castro kidnapped three women and held them prisoner for more than a decade. He pled guilty to more than nine hundred counts of rape, to kidnapping, and to aggravated murder for the suspected termination of a pregnancy of one of the captives. The deal allowed him to evade the death penalty, but he was sentenced to life in prison plus 1,000 years. During his first month in prison, Castro committed suicide.

Appellate courts Courts that reconsider the decisions rendered by trial courts if the losing party requests such reconsideration and demonstrates grounds for it.

Constitution provides for jury trials in all criminal cases and in civil cases in which the value contested exceeds $20. Most state constitutions contain similar provisions for jury trials. Nevertheless, jury trials tend to be the exception rather than the rule. The desire for a quick decision encourages many defendants to waive the time-consuming jury-selection process in favor of a faster decision by a judge. Parties to particularly complicated civil litigation may also assume that members of a jury will be less capable of following the detailed arguments than a judge. In criminal cases, a high percentage of defendants enter into plea-bargaining agreements, in which the accused, with the consent of the prosecutor, avoids a trial by pleading guilty to a lesser crime or accepting a less severe punishment.

In contrast, **appellate courts** are charged with the responsibility of reviewing decisions made by trial courts when the losing party requests it. The appellate review is designed to ensure that there is no error in judicial procedures or interpretations of the law. Because appellate courts simply review the written record of lower courts, they do not use juries.

The Federal and State Court Systems

>   **What are the major components of the federal and state court systems?**

On paper, the federal court structure appears to be relatively simple and eminently rational. After all, the system is composed of a single supreme court, several appellate and trial courts, and a limited number of specialized trial courts (see Figure 14.1). But behind the judicial system's facade of orderliness is a history of intense political struggle that contradicts the myth of the nonpolitical courts.

Lower Courts

Article III of the Constitution creates only one court, the Supreme Court, giving Congress the power to create such "inferior courts" as it deems necessary. This peculiar approach to court structure was the direct result of the bitter struggle between the Federalists and the Anti-Federalists at the Constitutional Convention. The Anti-Federalists, in order to protect the power of the states, wanted a system in which all cases, even those involving the national government, would be heard by the state courts. The Federalists argued for a national court system, which would establish the supremacy of the central government and limit the biases of the local courts.[2] Unable to reach agreement, the delegates finally compromised by creating the Supreme Court and leaving the responsibility for filling in the details of the system to Congress.

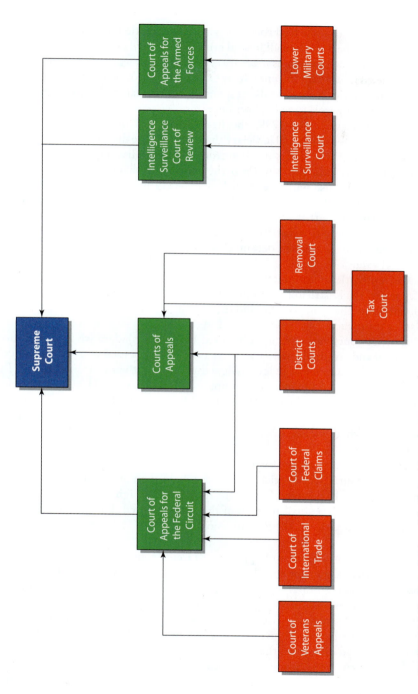

FIGURE 14.1 The Organization of the Federal Court System

The lines and arrows show the routes of cases through appeals and Supreme Court grants of hearings.

Source: Lawrence Baum, American Courts: Process and Policy, 2nd ed. (Boston: Houghton Mifflin, 1998), p. 28.

U.S. District Courts. As trial courts of general jurisdiction for the federal system, district courts hear trials in all federal criminal and civil cases. The district courts also hear what are known as *diversity cases*: suits between parties from different states when the amount in controversy exceeds $75,000. In addition to their trial duties, the district courts are also responsible for the naturalization of aliens and the granting of parole to federal prisoners.

The Judiciary Act of 1789, the first Senate bill introduced in the First Congress, created a national judiciary that included the district courts. Although the creation of these courts resulted from the Federalist impulse to establish a strong national judiciary, the form they took was shaped by the Federalists' need to compromise with the Anti-Federalists. Thus, the Federalist forces attained their goal of a national court system, but the Anti-Federalists insisted on district boundaries that were contained within state borders—a structure that remains in place to this day. By limiting each district court to a single state, the Anti-Federalists achieved a decentralized structure that was committed to local political values.

Currently, there are ninety-four U.S. district courts distributed among the fifty states, the District of Columbia, and the four territories. Twenty-four states contain more than one district, and the remaining states and territories have one district court each.

District court cases are usually heard by a single judge, who presides over both civil and criminal trials. The district courts have a total of 678 judicial positions, but the number of judges assigned to a district varies from 1 to 28. The federal territory of Guam, for example, constitutes a single judicial district, staffed by one judge. Among the states, Idaho, North Dakota, and Vermont each contain one district with two judges. In contrast, the Southern District of New York, which includes Manhattan and the Bronx, has twenty-eight judges assigned to it.

To most Americans, the district courts may seem to be the least important of the federal courts. Yet district courts hear more than 300,000 cases each year, and fewer than 10 percent of them are appealed to a higher court. Of those that are appealed, only a small fraction of them are reversed. For most litigants, the district court decision is the final decision.

Circuit courts Federal courts of appeals that rank above the district courts and serve as the major appellate courts for the federal system. They review all cases, both civil and criminal, and the decisions of independent regulatory agencies and departments.

Courts of Appeals. Courts of appeals, or **circuit courts**, as they are sometimes called, serve as the major appellate courts for the federal system. They review all cases—civil and criminal—that are appealed from the district courts. Moreover, on occasion, these courts review decisions of the independent regulatory agencies and executive branch departments. For example, decisions of the Federal Communications Commission involving the renewal of radio and television licenses can be appealed directly to the District of Columbia Circuit.

There are twelve U.S. courts of appeals, one for the District of Columbia and eleven others covering regional groupings of states (see Figure 14.2). Although the circuits include more than one state, no state is divided among circuits. A thirteenth court of appeals, the U.S. Court of Appeals for the Federal Circuit, is an appellate court charged with hearing patent and trademark cases.

Not shown are Puerto Rico (first circuit), Virgin Islands (third circuit), and Guam and the Northern Mariana Islands (ninth circuit).

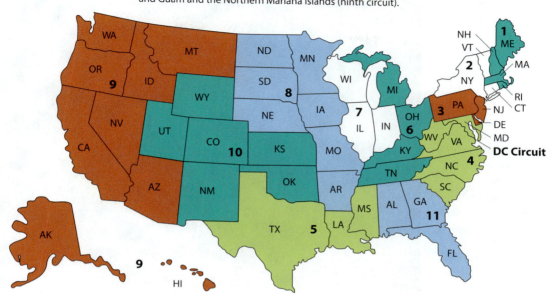

FIGURE 14.2 U.S. Circuit Courts of Appeals

The twelve courts of appeals of general jurisdiction have 179 authorized judgeships. As in the district courts, however, these judges are unevenly distributed among the circuits. Individual circuits have anywhere from 6 to 28 judges assigned to them. The number is determined by Congress and is supposed to reflect the workload of the circuit. Ordinarily, the courts of appeals hear cases in panels of three judges, and the membership of these panels varies from case to case.

The Supreme Court

The Constitution is remarkably vague even with regard to the Supreme Court. It is worth comparing Article I with Article III and noticing how detailed Article I is concerning the makeup and duties of Congress, and how lacking in such details about the Court Article III is.

How many justices serve on the Supreme Court? The answer is currently nine, but you will not discover that number from reading the Constitution; the size of the Court is left up to Congress. Since 1869, the Court has been staffed by a chief justice and eight associate justices. Until 1869, however, Congress made frequent changes in the size of the Court. Often these changes were thinly disguised efforts to promote partisan political objectives. During the Civil War, for instance, Congress created a tenth seat on the Supreme Court, assuring President Abraham Lincoln a solid majority in the Court.

The Supreme Court consists of eight associate justices and the chief justice. Seated, from the left: Clarence Thomas, Antonin Scalia, John G. Roberts (chief justice), Anthony Kennedy, and Ruth Bader Ginsburg. Standing, from the left: Sonia Sotomayor, Stephen Breyer, Samuel Alito Jr., and Elena Kagan.

According to the Constitution, the Supreme Court has both original and appellate jurisdiction. Original jurisdiction, as stated earlier, means that a court is empowered to make the first decision in a particular kind of dispute; it is the court of first instance. Article III limits the Supreme Court's original jurisdiction to cases involving foreign ambassadors and those in which a state is a party. Suits under original jurisdiction account for a very small portion of the Supreme Court's workload—usually only one or two cases a year.

The chief labor of the Supreme Court is appellate. For much of the nation's history, Congress required the Court to hear all cases that came to it. The justices' complaints that the workload was unmanageable finally led Congress to pass the Judiciary Act of 1925. Under the provisions of this act, the Court has tremendous latitude in selecting the cases it wants to hear.

Of the more than 10,000 cases brought to the Supreme Court each year, more than 90 percent come by way of a request for a **writ of certiorari**—a request that the Supreme Court order the lower court to send up the record of the case. Cases are accepted for review by means of the *rule of four*; that is, four justices must vote to consider the case. More than 95 percent of requests for writs of certiorari are denied, normally without explanation. The Court simply notes that certiorari is denied and that the decision of the lower court stands. Cases can also come to the Court by **appeal**, in which the litigants have some right under the law to have their cases reviewed. In practice, appeals are treated in the same discretionary way as requests for certiorari—that is, most are denied.

Because the Court receives many more petitions each year than it can possibly process, the freedom to accept only a limited number of cases is essential to its

Writ of certiorari An order by the Supreme Court that a lower court send up the record of a case.

Appeal A route by which cases can reach the Supreme Court. In such cases, litigants have some right under the law to have their cases reviewed.

effective operation. But there are also political advantages to the screening process. By carefully selecting cases for review, the justices can and do advance their policy preferences. Moreover, they can use the ability to deny review without explanation to avoid particularly controversial political issues. Initially, for instance, the Court refused to hear appeals concerning the rights of detainees at Guantanamo, but, in a highly unusual move at the end of the 2006 term, the Court announced that it would grant certiorari.

Specialized Courts

In addition to the federal courts that we have discussed, Congress has also created a few specialized courts. One of them is the U.S. Court of Federal Claims, created to litigate disputes involving government contracts. Other special courts include the U.S. Court of Military Appeals, the U.S. Court of International Trade, the Court of Veterans Appeals, and the U.S. Tax Court. Staffed by judges with expertise in a particular area, these courts reduce the workload of the general courts.

Usually these specialized courts attract little public attention, but in recent years the U.S. Foreign Intelligence Surveillance Court (FISA Court) has been thrust into the limelight. Created in 1978, the FISA Court was established as a secret court authorized to adjudicate, or give a ruling on, government applications for surveillance warrants (known as FISA warrants) to conduct electronic and physical searches. The court is staffed by eleven U.S. District Court judges, appointed by the chief justice of the Supreme Court. (The chief justice has the sole power of appointment and needs no approval from any other person or body.) Judges serve seven-year, staggered terms, and they may not be reappointed. Congress has directed that the judges must come from at least six different district courts, but to guarantee that the court can convene quickly, at least three of the judges must reside within twenty miles of the District of Columbia.

Requests for warrants are presented to a single judge, in what is known as an ex parte proceeding—the only party before the court is the government. Based on the case presented by the government and advice from the court's staff attorneys, the judge decides whether to grant or deny the warrant. In most cases, these decisions are rendered within seven days of the filing. We know very little about the decisions, because few opinions are published and because those that are published are heavily redacted. We know with certainly, however, that the government seldom loses. In 2012, for instance, the U.S. government made 1,789 requests for warrants authorizing electronic searches. Only one of these was withdrawn, although we do not know why. Thus, 1,788 of the warrants were granted. The court did, however, require modifications in forty cases.[3]

Just in case the court should turn down a government application for a warrant, the Department of Justice may appeal to the U.S. Foreign Intelligence Surveillance Court of Review. This specialized appellate court is composed of three judges (district or appeals court) appointed by the chief justice of the Supreme Court. Like the FISA Court judges, the appellate judges serve seven-year terms. Unlike the FISA Court judges, however, the Court of Review judges have little to do, because the government seldom loses. In fact, although the Court of Review was also created in 1978, it did not meet until 2002, as it had no need to meet. The Department of Justice did not appeal a FISA Court decision until 2002.

As a result of Edward Snowden's leak of a secret FISA Court opinion, the court has been recognized as the body that authorized the collection and storage of the telephone records of millions of Americans, none of whom were named as relevant to an authorized investigation into terrorism or foreign intelligence activities. The court's sanctioning of the so-called metadata has led to calls for reform. Indeed, President Obama's Review Group on Intelligence and Communications Technologies recommended creating a public interest advocate to represent the privacy and civil liberties interests of Americans before the court. Members of the commission also recommended that the power to appoint judges be divided among the justices of the Supreme Court.[4] In January 2014, President Obama promised several changes in the intelligence-gathering activities of the government, but he recommended only one change to the FISA Court. In the speech, President Obama recognized the need for a public advocate to argue before the court. Of course, the creation of such a position requires congressional action.

State Court Systems

Each state has at least one appellate court that serves as its highest tribunal. These courts are not always identifiable by title, however. For example, in the state of New York, the highest court is called the court of appeals, and the trial courts are designated as the supreme courts. Whatever the name, nearly every state has one court that reviews the decisions of all other courts. (Both Texas and Oklahoma have two high courts—one for civil litigation and one that handles only criminal appeals.) Slightly more than half of the states also make use of an intermediate appellate court to hear appeals from trial court decisions. Such courts permit the parties to appeal without overburdening the highest court.

There are two types of trial courts, the most numerous state courts: those with limited jurisdiction and those with general jurisdiction. Trial courts of **limited jurisdiction** are empowered to hear only a narrowly defined class of cases. These specialized courts often process a large number of routine cases involving minor issues. Among the most common courts in this category are traffic courts and small-claims courts.

Trial courts of **general jurisdiction** have authority over a much broader range of issues. Ordinarily, such courts hear all civil cases involving nontrivial monetary value and all cases involving serious criminal matters. Although the courts of general jurisdiction are not as specialized as the courts of limited jurisdiction, it is not unusual to find courts of general jurisdiction divided further into criminal and civil courts, especially in metropolitan areas with heavy caseloads.

Interactions Among Court Systems

The existence of so many court systems obviously complicates the interactions among them. Often the litigants (parties involved in a suit) can choose among several different courts. Indeed, it is common for the plaintiff (the party bringing suit) to shop around for a court, hoping to find one that will be favorable to his or her side.

Limited jurisdiction The power of certain trial courts that are allowed to hear only a narrowly defined class of cases.

General jurisdiction The power of trial courts to hear cases on a broad range of issues, ordinarily including all civil cases involving nontrivial monetary value and all cases involving serious criminal matters.

Court complexity is heightened by the fact that both state and national courts may have jurisdiction over the same issues—a situation known as *concurrent jurisdiction*. For example, Congress has granted to the federal district courts the right to hear so-called diversity cases—cases involving citizens of different states contesting a sum greater than $75,000. In doing so, however, Congress has not denied the state courts the right to hear such cases; it merely established an additional forum for resolving them.[5]

Although the complex network of multiple court systems gives plaintiffs the opportunity to seek a favorable court before bringing an action, once the case has been tried, appeals must be made within the same court system. Occasionally, decisions of a state's highest court are successfully appealed to the U.S. Supreme Court, but this step can occur only when the state's highest court has rendered a decision interpreting provisions of the U.S. Constitution, a treaty, or a federal law. Decisions of a court in one state may never be appealed to a court in another state, nor is it possible to appeal a federal court decision to a state court.

POLITICS & POPULAR CULTURE: Visit the book's companion website at **www.oup.com/us/gitelson** to read the special feature *Law & Order*.

Recruiting and Removing Judges

> **How are judges selected in the United States?**

In contrast to nations such as Italy, the United States does not have a career judiciary; judges do not have to undergo special training. In fact, the U.S. Constitution does not even require legal training as a qualification for service on the Supreme Court. All 112 justices who have served on the Supreme Court have been lawyers, but it was not until 1957 that all members of the Court had earned law degrees.

There is an old adage in American politics that a judge is a lawyer who knew a senator or governor. Although something of an overstatement, this saying indicates that beyond the formal requirements of constitutions and statutes lies a selection process that is highly political. The myth of the nonpolitical courts suggests that judicial selections are or should be based solely on merit. The reality is that the choices are always political.

Federal Judges

According to Article II of the Constitution, the president shall nominate and, with the "advice and consent of the Senate," appoint justices of the Supreme Court. The president proposes a candidate to the Senate; if a majority of the Senate approves, the nominee takes office. Of course, these nominations, like any legislative act in the Senate, may be blocked by a filibuster, requiring sixty votes to invoke cloture. This same formal method is used to appoint judges to the courts of appeals and district courts, but for these appointments a filibuster may be overcome by a simple majority vote of the Senate. Constitutional provisions alone do not describe the political complexity of the selection process, nor do they take into account informal methods of selection that have evolved alongside the formal process. (To see how state judges are selected, see Asked & Answered, page 472.)

ASKED & ANSWERED

ASKED: *Are all judges selected the same way?*

ANSWERED: Although all major courts in the U.S. federal system are staffed by judges appointed by the president, with the advice and consent of the Senate, the fifty states use a variety of selection systems. Indeed, many states have established different selection methods for different levels of courts. Nevertheless, five methods dominate.

1. *Gubernatorial appointment.* This holdover from the colonial experience allows the governor to make the appointment, but in virtually all instances such appointments must gain legislative confirmation—usually by the state senate. Confined largely to northeastern states, this system attempts to ensure a judiciary independent of popular sentiment or political pressure.

2. *Legislative election.* Two states—South Carolina and Virginia—authorize the legislature to elect judges. Like the gubernatorial system, legislative election stresses a politically independent judiciary.

3. *Partisan election.* In this system, judicial candidates run on a partisan ballot, after winning nomination, usually by way of a partisan primary. A product of the Jacksonian era's emphasis on democratic accountability, partisan elections are intended to ensure that judges are not insulated from popular opinion. Partisan election systems most commonly occur in southern and lower Midwestern states—states that entered the union during the Jacksonian era.

4. *Nonpartisan elections.* When states use this system, candidates' names appear on the ballot without party labels. This method of selection aims to create a judiciary that is responsive to the people. A product of the Populist and Progressive movements' reaction to partisan abuses of power, the nonpartisan election system occurs most often in the upper Midwestern and western states.

5. *Merit selection.* Also known as the Missouri Plan, named for the state that first adopted it, merit selection attempts to blend independence and accountability. There are several nuances, but in general the following procedure applies: a nominating commission composed of three lawyers selected by a state bar association, three non-lawyers selected by the governor, and an incumbent judge submits a short list of candidates (usually three) to the governor. The governor makes the appointment from the list. After a brief term of service, the new judge faces the electorate in a retention election. There is no opponent; the electorate simply chooses whether or not to retain the judge. If the electorate prefers not to retain the judge, the process starts over again. Since 1940, when Missouri adopted the system, most states that have altered their selection system have adopted some version of merit selection.

Does it matter which system a state adopts? Most political scientists who have looked at judicial recruitment have found no substantial differences in the personal characteristics of judges that can be attributed to the selection method. Merit systems tend to produce slightly higher proportions of Protestant judges than other selection systems, and women and minorities are somewhat favored by gubernatorial systems. Even the length of service varies little. Judges in partisan election states have slightly shorter careers than those in states using gubernatorial selection, but again the differences are small.

Appointments to the District Courts. The president has the power to make nominations to the district courts. Most administrations establish guidelines detailing the qualities the president expects in a nominee and then leave the search for candidates to the U.S. Department of Justice.

In nominating candidates for the district courts, however, the executive branch must always be mindful of the power of individual senators. Under the unwritten rule of senatorial courtesy, if a senator from a nominee's state opposes the nomination of a candidate, the Senate as a whole will reject the nomination. In recent years, senatorial courtesy has been exercised at the committee stage by use of the "blue slip." When the Senate Judiciary Committee receives a nomination to a federal court, it notifies the senators by means of a blue slip. If a senator from the nominee's state fails to return the blue slip, it kills the appointment. The committee will simply refuse to take any action until the nomination is withdrawn.[6]

Rather than provoke confrontations with the Senate, presidents have, as a rule, accepted advice from the relevant senators. Often this practice translates into formal nomination by the president but informal nomination by a senator. In fact, the prominence of senatorial courtesy led one former assistant attorney general to remark, "The Constitution is backwards. Article II, Section 2, should read: 'the Senators shall nominate, and by and with the consent of the President, shall appoint.'"[7]

Appointments to the Courts of Appeals. The president and the Justice Department have a freer hand in making appointments to the courts of appeals than they do in making appointments to district courts. Because each circuit contains more than one state, no senator can unambiguously claim senatorial courtesy. However, because it is generally assumed that each state in a circuit should have at least one judge on that circuit's appellate bench, the president is constrained by having to maintain the proper balance of state representation.

Over the past decade, judicial appointments, especially those to courts of appeals, have become more controversial and thus more difficult for presidents. During the Clinton administration, Republicans refused even to give a hearing to several Clinton nominees, thus dooming any possibility of their nomination. With George W. Bush in the White House, the Democrats replied by obstructing committee action and, in 2005, filibustering five nominees. The Republicans in turn threatened to use an arcane rule to cut off Senate debate and end the filibuster. This so-called nuclear option would have allowed the Senate to end the debate on judicial nominees with a simple majority vote rather than the sixty votes needed to invoke cloture. A showdown was avoided when fourteen senators (seven Republicans and seven Democrats) agreed to allow three of the nominations to go forward on the condition that none of the participating senators would support the filibuster of a future nominee except under "extraordinary circumstances." But that agreement fell apart in President Obama's second term. Frustrated by the Republicans' use of the filibuster to block judicial nominees, the Democrats did what the Republicans had threatened to do in 2005. They used the nuclear option and changed the rules by allowing cloture to be invoked with a simple majority vote. The change does not, however, apply to Supreme Court appointments.

Appointments to the Supreme Court. The Supreme Court is a national institution, with no special ties to states or regions. Thus, the president need not worry that individual senators will exercise senatorial courtesy, although the senators from the nominee's state are asked to serve as sponsors. The Senate is far from irrelevant to the nomination process, however, and it has considered itself free to reject candidates for a variety of reasons. Reagan's nomination of Judge Robert Bork, for instance, failed in the Senate because of widespread opposition to his restrictive views on the right to privacy and equal rights for women.

In the nineteenth century, the Senate was more likely to disapprove a presidential nomination on purely partisan grounds than it is today. Before the Bork nomination, the two most recent nominations to fail in the Senate, those of Judges Clement Haynsworth and G. Harrold Carswell, were opposed by Senate liberals for ideological reasons, but both candidates had other serious disadvantages. Haynsworth came under attack for having purchased stock in a company that had been a party in a case before him; he had bought the stock after the decision had been made, but before it was announced. Carswell was criticized for lacking the professional qualifications expected of a Supreme Court justice. His fate was probably sealed when one of his defenders, Republican senator Roman Hruska from Nebraska, argued that "there are a lot of mediocre judges and people and lawyers. They are entitled to a little representation, aren't they, and a little chance?"[8]

Because justices of the Supreme Court are appointed for life and occupy such a prominent position in the American system of government, presidents are careful to choose justices whose ideological views seem to be in harmony with theirs. If fate provides enough vacancies, a president's appointments can reshape the judiciary to reflect his views, perpetuating the president's philosophical positions long after the administration has left office (see Table 14.1).[9]

TABLE 14.1 The Roberts Court

Justice	Year Born	Year Appointed	Appointing President	Political Party
John Roberts	1955	2005	George W. Bush	Republican
Antonin Scalia	1936	1986	Reagan	Republican
Anthony Kennedy	1936	1988	Reagan	Republican
Clarence Thomas	1948	1991	George H. W. Bush	Republican
Ruth Bader Ginsburg	1933	1993	Clinton	Democratic
Stephen G. Breyer	1938	1994	Clinton	Democratic
Samuel Alito	1950	2006	George W. Bush	Republican
Sonia Sotomayor	1954	2009	Obama	Democratic
Elena Kagan	1960	2010	Obama	Democratic

In both the 2000 and 2004 presidential elections, George W. Bush promised that he would transform the Supreme Court by appointing individuals similar to Justice Antonin Scalia, perhaps the Court's most conservative justice. During the president's first term, however, the Court membership remained stable, but in July 2005 the Court's makeup began to change, when Justice Sandra Day O'Connor notified the president that she intended to retire once her successor was confirmed by the Senate. Shortly thereafter, President Bush nominated Judge John Roberts to fill the O'Connor vacancy. Then, on September 3, 2005, as Judge Roberts was preparing for his Senate confirmation hearings, Chief Justice William Rehnquist died. Three days later, the president withdrew the Roberts nomination to fill O'Connor's seat and nominated him to be the new chief justice instead. Given his record as a conservative appeals court judge, Democrats were wary of the nomination. Nevertheless, Roberts was confirmed by a vote of 78 to 22, with every Republican voting for him and the Democrats evenly divided.

Roberts's confirmation left the O'Connor seat still to be filled. Initially, the president, at the urging of Senate minority leader Harry Reid, nominated Harriet Miers, his White House counsel and, prior to that, his personal attorney. Interestingly, Miers had chaired the committee that recommended Judge Roberts for the O'Connor seat. From the beginning, the Miers nomination was controversial. Her lack of judicial experience led senators from both parties to question her suitability for the job. Additionally, conservatives in the president's own party expressed strong concerns about her level of commitment to basic conservative beliefs. After three contentious weeks, Miers asked the president to withdraw her nomination.

The president then nominated Judge Samuel Alito, known to his critics as "Scalito" for his similarity to Justice Scalia. Unlike the Roberts nomination, which was—after all—an appointment of a conservative to replace a conservative, the Alito nomination, which appeared to replace a moderate justice with a conservative justice, stirred up significant partisanship. The nominee was confirmed by a highly partisan vote of 58–42. Only four Democrats supported his nomination, whereas only one Republican voted against confirmation.

Although President George W. Bush had to wait until the start of his second term to appoint anyone to the Supreme Court, President Obama made two appointments in his first eighteen months in office. The president's first nominee was Judge Sonia Sotomayor; the Court's first Hispanic Justice was appointed to fill the vacancy created by the retirement of Justice David Souter. Justice Sotomayor was confirmed by a Senate vote of 68–31. Elena Kagan was President Obama's choice to replace Justice John Paul Stevens. Although the Senate confirmed Justice Kagan, the vote was divided, with few Republicans supporting her

Only four women have served on the Supreme Court. Pictured here is a portrait of the four. Seated, from the left: Sandra Day O'Connor (the first woman appointed to the court) and Ruth Bader Ginsburg. Standing, from the left: Sonia Sotomayor and Elena Kagan.

After an extraordinary career as a leader in the civil rights movement, a career that included arguing *Brown v. Board of Education* before the Supreme Court, Thurgood Marshall became Justice Thurgood Marshall. Marshall was the first African American to serve on the nation's highest court.

appointment. The appointments of Sotomayor and Kagan, however, did little to change the ideological balance of the Court.

Of course, presidents are not always successful in predicting what a candidate will do once she or he is in office. Perhaps the most famous example of a president who was frustrated by his own appointment is Theodore Roosevelt, who nominated Oliver Wendell Holmes. Before forwarding the nomination of Holmes to the Senate, Roosevelt had assured himself that the candidate shared his views on the antitrust statutes. When Holmes immediately voted against the president's view in an antitrust case, Roosevelt quipped that he could "make a judge with a stronger backbone out of a banana."[10] Similarly, President Dwight D. Eisenhower came to regret his appointment of Earl Warren as chief justice. Eisenhower had made the appointment expecting Warren to adhere to the president's own middle-of-the-road political views. Instead, the Warren Court (1953–1969) became known as the most liberal Supreme Court in U.S. history. Eisenhower referred to the appointment as "the biggest damned-fool mistake I ever made."[11]

Nominations to the Supreme Court also give presidents a chance to recognize important constituent groups, especially social groups that have previously been unrepresented. President Lyndon B. Johnson broke the Supreme Court's color barrier by appointing Thurgood Marshall, the first African American justice. President Reagan appointed Sandra Day O'Connor, the first woman to serve on the Court. Obviously, the appointment of a woman or a member of a minority group to the Court is unlikely to have a substantive impact on decisions, but representation for a group that has traditionally been excluded from the process has great symbolic value.

Who Becomes a Federal Judge?

No recruitment system is ever neutral. Any system will favor certain skills and characteristics and downplay others. The process of selecting Supreme Court justices favors individuals from socially advantaged families. As an observer has noted, "The typical Supreme Court Justice has generally been white, Protestant (with a penchant for a high social status denomination), usually of ethnic stock originating in the British Isles, and born in comfortable circumstances in an urban or small-town environment."[12] In addition, almost two-thirds of the justices have come from politically active families. And those appointed to the Court have by and large been politically active themselves, with the vast majority having previously held political office.

When we examine the judiciary in the lower federal courts, we see a similar, although less pronounced, pattern of upper- and middle-class appointees. Compared with Supreme Court justices, judges on the courts of appeals, for instance, are slightly less likely to come from politically active families and more likely to have been educated at less prestigious law schools.

Because appointments are for life, the federal courts are an especially rich source of political patronage, and presidents are under some pressure to reward the party faithful with such appointments. Although presidents occasionally nominate a member of the opposition party, most have selected at least 90 percent of their appointees from their own party. Staffing the courts with partisans ensures a party a foothold in the government even when the party is out of favor with the voters. Aside from patronage questions, relying on members of their own party allows presidents to choose judges who are more likely to share their political outlook. Thus the bias toward fellow party members serves two goals, both of which clearly contradict the myth of nonpolitical courts.

Removing Judges

In the early days of the republic, one of the most important problems facing the federal courts was attracting and retaining judges. As strange as it may seem, President George Washington had problems filling positions on the Supreme Court. John Jay, the nation's first chief justice, resigned to become governor of New York, and John Rutledge, one of Washington's first appointees, resigned before the Court ever met to become the chief justice of the South Carolina Supreme Court—a position he apparently found more attractive.[13] As the prestige of the federal courts increased, recruitment problems diminished, although attracting and retaining lower-court judges is sometimes difficult, because the salaries are low compared with what many potential appointees could earn in private law practice.

Because the prestige and power of a judgeship are understandably hard to give up, it is occasionally necessary to remove an ill or incompetent judge who refuses to retire. This problem is particularly thorny in the federal courts, because the only means for removing federal judges is the impeachment process, which, according to the constitution, requires evidence of "Treason, Bribery, or other high Crimes and Misdemeanors."

Over the years there have been few impeachment trials. In 1989, however, Congress impeached and convicted two district court judges. Judge Walter Nixon of Mississippi was removed from the bench on the grounds that he had committed perjury. At the time of his Senate conviction, he was serving a five-year prison sentence for knowingly making false statements to a grand jury. More controversial was the impeachment and conviction of Judge Alcee L. Hastings of Florida. Hastings was removed for accepting a bribe in a criminal case. Unlike Nixon, Hastings had been acquitted of related charges in a criminal trial, but the Senate concluded that he had lied and presented false evidence at the criminal trial. These two impeachment trials in a single year prompted several members of Congress to seek alternatives to the time-consuming process. Suggested constitutional amendments to provide for an easy removal procedure were introduced in 1990, but no action has been taken on them.

Even if impeachment were easier, it would probably not be deemed appropriate for judges who suffer from illness or senility. A case in point is that of Utah District Court judge Willis Ritter. Ritter first drew national attention when he ordered court officials to arrest noisy plumbers who were making repairs near his courtroom.[14] He also engaged in such eccentric behavior as hissing throughout an attorney's presentation to the court. Although this behavior is clearly odd, it nevertheless does not seem to fit the definition of an impeachable offense: "Treason, Bribery, or other high Crimes and Misdemeanors."

Lacking an effective means of removing judges, Congress has turned to providing pension programs as an incentive for them to step down. Under a 1954 act of Congress, a judge can opt for the status of senior judge. Senior judges receive a pension equal to full pay and may participate, where needed, in as many cases as they choose. This option allows a judge to enjoy a reduced workload without completely retiring. Senior judges have become essential to the operation of many of the overworked lower federal courts. Senior judges typically handle about 20 percent of the appellate and district court cases.

Because judges do not have to accept senior status, Congress has also provided a mechanism for denying case assignments to sitting judges on the lower federal courts.[15] The judge retains the post and the salary but receives no work.

The Supreme Court at Work

> **What are the major steps in Supreme Court decision making?**

The Supreme Court term begins the first Monday in October and runs through June or into early July, depending on the workload. Court terms are designated by the year in which they begin, even though very few decisions will actually be handed down in October, November, or December of that year. Throughout the term, the Court alternates between two weeks of open court, called sessions, and two weeks of recess, the time when the justices read petitions and write opinions.

Oral Argument

During the weeks that the Court is in session, the justices meet Monday through Wednesday to hear oral arguments. These sessions begin at 10 a.m. and last until 3 p.m., with a one-hour break for lunch. Ordinary cases are allotted one hour for arguments, and the time is evenly divided between the parties. If the case is especially important or involves multiple parties raising a variety of issues, the Court may permit longer presentations.

The attorneys presenting oral arguments are reminded of their time limitations by two lights on the lectern. When the white light appears, they know that they have five minutes left. The flash of the red light signals that their time is up, and they must cease speaking unless the chief justice grants an extension. Most often the parties are held strictly to their allotted time. Chief Justice Charles E. Hughes (1930–1941) was so rigid in enforcing the time limit that he is said to have stopped an attorney in the middle of the word *if*.

Briefs Documents submitted to a court by attorneys that contain a summary of the issues and the laws applying to the case and arguments supporting counsel's position.

Because all parties have prepared written **briefs** (documents containing a summary of the issues, the laws applying to the case, and arguments supporting counsel's position), the Court discourages attorneys from reading prepared statements. Indeed, the Court's rules state that "the Court looks with disfavor on any oral argument that is read from a prepared text." Generally, the justices expect the attorneys to discuss the case, not to deliver a lecture. Often the attorneys spend their allotted time answering questions posed by the justices, and the justices frequently use these questions as a means of debating with one another. On one occasion, as Justice Felix Frankfurter repeatedly questioned a nervous attorney, Justice William O. Douglas repeatedly responded with answers helpful to the attorney. Finally, a frustrated Frankfurter, directing his remarks to the attorney, said, "I thought you were arguing this case." The attorney responded, "I am, but I can use all the help I can get."[16]

In addition to the arguments of the lawyers representing the parties to the case, the Court may also consider the positions taken by interested third parties. Any individual or organization, with the consent of the parties involved in the case or by Court permission, may submit written arguments known as **amicus curiae** (friend of the court) briefs. Occasionally, amicus participation may even include the offering of oral arguments. For instance, in the 1989 abortion case *Webster v. Reproductive Health Services*, seventy-eight amicus briefs were filed, and the Court allowed the federal government, acting as amicus, ten minutes of oral argument.[17] Amicus participation has become an important means of interest-group lobbying before the courts.

Amicus curiae A Latin phrase meaning "friend of the court." Amicus curiae briefs are written briefs submitted to the Supreme Court by third-party individuals or organizations that want their opinions to be considered in a case.

Conference Work

Although oral argument may be dramatic, the crucial work of the Court is done in conference. When the Court is in session, the justices gather in the conference room twice a week to discuss and decide cases. No one else is admitted—not even secretaries or law clerks to help the justices. If a justice needs anything from outside the room, the junior justice (the least senior in terms of service, not the youngest) must go to the door and summon a messenger. In the past, the junior justice was even responsible for pouring the coffee, a practice rumored to have ended with the appointment of Justice Sandra Day O'Connor.

Generally, the justices first decide which petitions should be accepted. Before the conference, the chief justice, with the aid of law clerks, prepares and circulates to the other justices a "discuss list": a list of cases that the chief justice thinks worthy of discussion. Any case that is not on the list will be automatically denied review unless another justice requests that it be added to the list. Apparently, as many as 70 percent of the requests for review are denied without any discussion.[18]

Cases that make the list are not automatically accepted for review, however. Instead, each case is considered and voted on by the justices. Only those cases that receive four votes (the rule of four) are accepted and scheduled for further action, and the number of such cases is usually quite small. In recent years the Court has accepted for review only about eighty cases a term.

After deciding which cases to accept for review, the Court moves on to the cases being argued that week. The chief justice begins the discussion of each case by outlining and commenting on the main issues. Then each justice, in order of seniority, comments on the case. If the votes of the justices are not clear from the discussion, the chief justice calls for a formal vote. Most questions, however, require no vote, because the justices' positions will be clear from their initial comments. These conference votes are only tentative votes, however. As Justice John Harlan explained, "The books on voting are never closed until the decision actually comes down."[19]

After the vote, the chief justice, if in the majority, assigns the writing of the opinion. If the chief justice is not in the majority, then the majority's most senior justice makes the assignment. The assignment of an opinion writer is important because it will determine the grounds for the Court's decision and perhaps even the size of the majority, because the conference vote was tentative. The justice who assigns the writing of the opinion may decide to write the opinion himself or herself or may give the task to the member of the majority whose views are closest to his or her views. As rumor has it, when Warren Burger was chief justice, he frequently let his turn in the discussion of important cases pass so that he could remain free to join the majority at the end and therefore pick the opinion writer. This practice reportedly became so common that Justice Potter Stewart is said to have drawn a tombstone for Burger with the words, "I'll Pass for the Moment."[20]

Writing and Announcing the Opinion

Once the writing of the opinion has been assigned, the justice who was given this task begins work on a draft that expresses his or her own ideas and also takes into account opinions expressed by others in the conference. At the same time, other justices may be drafting separate **concurring opinions** (opinions that agree with the conclusion but not with the reasoning of the majority) or **dissenting opinions** (opinions that disagree with the majority conclusion).

As the drafts are completed, they are circulated so that all justices can see them and have an opportunity to comment on them. As justices suggest changes in wording and reasoning, negotiations begin. The justice who has drafted the majority opinion, as well as any justices working on concurring or dissenting opinions, may have to make changes to satisfy the others. Sometimes conflicting views among the justices make this process extremely difficult and time-consuming. More important, the need to compromise may produce vague decisions that offer little guidance to lower courts. For instance, many Court observers have attributed the extraordinarily vague command of *Brown v. Board of Education II* (1955) to desegregate with "all deliberate speed" to the chief justice's desire for a unanimous decision.[21]

Occasionally, the justice assigned to write the majority opinion will change her or his position and become a dissenter, or vice versa. Justice William Brennan described the process when he noted, "I have had to convert more than one of my proposed majority opinions into a dissent before the final opinion was announced. I have also, however, had the more satisfying experience of rewriting a dissent as a majority opinion of the Court."[22]

The opinion-writing stage does not end until all the justices have decided which opinion to join. Once they do so, the Court announces the opinion. Throughout much of the Court's history, the justices read their opinions—majority, concurring, and dissenting—publicly. Currently, the opinion writers read only short statements describing the issues and the disposition.

Concurring opinions Opinions written by Supreme Court justices that agree with the conclusion but not with the reasoning of the majority opinion.

Dissenting opinions Legal opinions written by Supreme Court justices that disagree with the majority conclusion.

During the last few years, major Supreme Court decisions have often drawn large crowds outside the building in anticipation of a decision. Here, supporters of same-sex marriage gather outside the Supreme Court, anticipating the opinion on the constitutionality of Section 3 of DOMA. The Court's decision that Section 3 was unconstitutional allowed for federal recognition of the rights and benefits of all legally married gays.

Interpreting the Constitution

Chief Justice Hughes once quipped, "We are under a Constitution, but the Constitution is what the judges say it is."[23] Of course, as we discussed in Chapter 2, on constitutional foundations, judges are not the sole interpreters of that document. Nevertheless, judges, and particularly justices of the Supreme Court, do play a leading role in interpreting the Constitution, largely because of the power of **judicial review**: the power of the courts to declare acts of Congress to be in conflict with the Constitution.

Nowhere in the Constitution is the U.S. Supreme Court specifically granted such authority. Instead, judicial review was inferred by the Court in the 1803 case of *Marbury v. Madison*. [24] After the election of 1800, in which Thomas Jefferson and members of his party won control of the White House and both chambers of Congress, the incumbent president, John Adams, and the Federalist Party attempted to maintain a foothold in government by using the time between the election and the inauguration to fill the judiciary with Federalists. First, John Marshall, secretary of state in the Adams administration, was named the new chief justice of the Supreme Court. Congress then created fifty-eight additional judgeships, to be filled by loyal Federalists. (Because these appointments came in the last days of the Adams administration, they became known as the "midnight appointments.")

So great was the Adams administration's haste that it failed to deliver the commissions of four newly appointed justices of the peace for the District of Columbia. The four undelivered commissions were returned to the secretary of state's office, where James Madison, the new secretary of state, found them.

Judicial review The power of the courts to declare acts of Congress to be in conflict with the Constitution.

Although he was the fourth chief justice of the Supreme Court, John Marshall, more than any other individual, was responsible for elevating the Court to the level of a respected third branch. During his thirty-four years as chief justice, Marshall introduced the principle of judicial review and established the Court as the interpreter of the Constitution.

On orders of President Jefferson, Madison refused to deliver the commissions, prompting William Marbury, one of the four whose papers were withheld, to bring suit in the Supreme Court. Marbury requested that the Court issue a writ of mandamus (an order to a government official to carry out a duty of his or her office) compelling Madison to deliver the commission. The case was filed with the Supreme Court directly because a congressional statute, the Judiciary Act of 1789, empowered the Supreme Court to issue such writs as an act of original jurisdiction.

Marbury's suit placed the Court in a difficult and politically charged situation. Congress had given the Court a warning by canceling its 1802 term; thus, Marbury's case had to be postponed until 1803. The Court appeared to be faced with two choices, neither of them attractive. The justices could have issued the writ and ordered Madison to deliver the commission, but that would have been to no avail. Madison would most certainly have defied the writ, making the Court look powerless. On the other hand, the Court could have refused to issue the writ, but that action would have amounted to an admission of impotence.

Chief Justice Marshall, however, devised a third alternative. He wrote an opinion that attacked the administration for neglecting constitutional duties, but he ruled that the Court could not constitutionally issue the writ of mandamus. The Court was powerless in this instance, Marshall argued, because the provision of the Judiciary Act of 1789 that granted it original jurisdiction to issue such writs was unconstitutional. Article III of the Constitution specifies the circumstances under which the Court possesses original jurisdiction, and the issuance of writs of mandamus is not included. Therefore, argued Marshall, the Judiciary Act of 1789, by adding such writs to the Court's original jurisdiction, was actually attempting to alter the Constitution by simple statute rather than by the prescribed method of amendment. Because Congress may not do this, Marshall concluded that the act was null and void and the Court was without power to grant Marbury a writ of mandamus.

As a political document, Marshall's decision was a masterpiece. By arguing that Madison was obligated to deliver the commission, Marshall attacked the Jefferson administration. Yet, by refusing to issue the writ, he avoided a confrontation with the president that the Court would have been sure to lose. More important, Marshall created for the Court the power of judicial review and insulated that power from attack. The only loser in the case was Marbury, who was sacrificed to Marshall's larger political design.

The political brilliance of Marshall's opinion is unquestionable, but to this day the legal reasoning employed remains subject to debate. In a straightforward manner, Marshall simply stated that

1. The Constitution is superior to any statute.

2. The Judiciary Act of 1789 contradicted the Constitution.

3. Therefore, the Judiciary Act of 1789 must be unconstitutional.

As an exercise in logic, the conclusion seems inescapable.

To many critics, however, Marshall's logic misses the point. Why is it the job of the Court, composed of life-tenured appointees, to decide whether an act conflicts with the Constitution? Why, ask Marshall's critics, should this power not belong to elected officials?[25]

Although judicial review has become a standard element of American politics, it remains controversial. Those judges and legal scholars who find Marshall's reasoning unconvincing advocate **judicial restraint**—the limited and infrequent use of judicial review. Advocates of judicial restraint argue that the frequent use of judicial review substitutes the judgment of unelected, life-tenured officials for that of elected representatives and is therefore undemocratic. Indeed, the frequent use of judicial review, according to some critics, creates an "imperial judiciary," which makes decisions that are best left to the elected branches of a democratic government.[26] Opposing judicial restraint are those judges and legal scholars who believe in **judicial activism**: that the Court has a right, and even an obligation, to exercise judicial review. Today, activism is usually justified by liberals as necessary for the defense of political minorities, but the frequent use of judicial review and the numerous precedents overturned by the Roberts Court demonstrate that conservatives may also be activists.

A more recent judicial argument concerns how the Constitution is to be interpreted. One perspective on its interpretation demands that justices adhere to a literal reading of the Constitution or, if the language is not specific, to the intent of the provisions' authors. During the 1980s, this view, known as *original intent*, was forcefully advocated by President Reagan's attorney general, Edwin Meese. Meese repeatedly argued that the justices should restrict themselves to the Constitution's original intent and not its spirit. Original intent assumes that judges do not make law but rather find it ready-made by others—those who authored the Constitution.

Opponents of that view—a loose collection of scholars and judges, conservatives and liberals—contend that many of the Constitution's most important provisions are "deliberate models of ambiguity."[27] Although these opponents often disagree among themselves on the preferred interpretation of constitutional provisions, they are united in their belief that judging involves choosing among competing values and not simply finding the law.[28]

Judicial restraint Limited and infrequent use of judicial review. It is advocated on the grounds that unelected judges should not overrule laws passed by elected representatives.

Judicial activism The concept that the Court has both a right and an obligation to engage in judicial review; today it is usually justified as necessary for the defense of political minorities.

The Implementation of Court Decisions

> **Why is it that Court decisions are not simply self-executing?**

The pomp and circumstance surrounding the announcement of a Supreme Court decision lends credibility to the myth of finality. Yet this ceremony seldom settles the matter. Rather than being the end of the case, the Court's announcement is only the beginning of a long process of implementation.

Court orders are not self-executing, and the Court needs the cooperation of others to carry out the announced policy. It cannot force compliance; it cannot call on an army or police force to carry out its orders, nor can it levy taxes to fund their implementation. Furthermore, if a particular decision is not being implemented, the Court cannot act until someone brings suit in a lower court. Unlike the other agencies of government, courts must await cases; they cannot seek them out. Their only recourse is to signal their willingness to consider cases involving particular issues by the language that they use in deciding cases before them.

Compliance by Other Courts

Compliance is not just a matter of getting the parties in a case to go along with the decision. When the Supreme Court overturns the decision of a lower court, it generally sends (remands) the case back to the lower court for a decision "not inconsistent" with its opinion. But lower courts do not always follow the Supreme Court's wishes.

In some cases, lower courts may find it difficult to carry out an ambiguous Supreme Court decision. If multiple concurring and dissenting opinions accompany a decision, the lower court may find the decision difficult to interpret. In *Furman v. Georgia* (1972), for example, five justices ruled that the death penalty as it was applied in that particular case was unconstitutional, but they could not agree on the reason.[29] Consequently, each justice wrote a separate opinion. Lower courts cannot interpret such a decision easily, and in such situations, lower-court judges find it easier to substitute their own values and beliefs.

Because lower federal and state courts are independent of the Supreme Court, they can—and occasionally do—defy the Court's rulings. There is little that the Court can do in such cases. The judges of these lower courts are sworn to uphold the U.S. Constitution, but not the opinions of the Supreme Court, and the Court lacks the power to fire even the most disobedient judge. Thus the Supreme Court's power to reverse lower-court decisions is limited both by its inability to police lower courts and by time constraints (it cannot review every lower-court decision).

Reversal sometimes causes difficulties for lower-court judges. Judges who are caught between the mandates of the Supreme Court, located in far-off Washington, and the strong, contradictory desires of their neighbors may find the displeasure of the Supreme Court easier to bear than the anger of their community. Elected state judges may be especially reluctant to enforce Court orders that might anger voters, even if they personally agree with the Court. In the 1950s, federal district court judges were deeply embroiled in the school desegregation issue—a conflict of national versus local values. Many communities resisted Court-ordered desegregation, often vehemently. Those district judges who enforced *Brown v. Board of Education* (1954) found themselves cut off from their own communities, with old friends and colleagues falling away. Many were threatened, and some were even physically harmed.[30]

The Role of Congress and the President in Implementing Court Decisions

Just as the Supreme Court must depend on the so-called inferior courts to implement decisions, so too must it rely on the cooperation of Congress and the president. Both institutions have the power to aid or hinder the implementation of Supreme Court decisions.

The most important power that Congress has is its control of public funds. By providing or withholding the funds necessary to carry out Court policy, Congress can significantly affect implementation, as the history of school desegregation amply illustrates. During Lyndon Johnson's administration, Congress authorized the U.S. Department of Health, Education, and Welfare to withhold federal funds from school systems that refused to desegregate—giving communities a strong incentive to comply with the Supreme Court's 1954 ruling. In 1975, however, Congress, disturbed by court-ordered busing, diminished the incentive by prohibiting the withholding of funds from school districts that refused to implement busing.

The actions of individual members of Congress may also advance or impede Court policy. Whether important political leaders defend or attack a Court decision may have much to do with the willingness of others to accept that decision. Clearly, the cause of school desegregation was not helped when, in 1956, ninety-six members of Congress signed the Southern Manifesto, a document attacking the *Brown* decision. Those who believed that the Supreme Court was wrong could always point to distinguished members of Congress who shared their view. Furthermore, the support of so many in Congress undoubtedly gave opponents of desegregation hope that the decision would someday be overturned.

Congress may also use its powers to directly counteract Court decisions. Decisions interpreting the Constitution, for example, may be overturned by a congressionally initiated constitutional amendment. Although the process is cumbersome and difficult, it has been used on five occasions. Most recently, the Twenty-Sixth Amendment, which lowered the voting age to eighteen, overturned the decision in *Oregon v. Mitchell* (1970).[31] (In the *Mitchell* decision, the Court had ruled that Congress could, by statute, lower the voting age to eighteen in national but not state elections.) The Court's decision prohibiting prayer in public schools has generated hundreds of proposals for constitutional amendments. To date, none of these proposals has passed both houses of Congress.

Occasionally, Congress tries to pressure the Court into reversing a decision. In 1964, for instance, angered by a series of Warren Court rulings that required reapportionment of state legislatures solely on the basis of population, Congress gave the justices a smaller pay raise than that for other top-level officials. To underscore the point, Republican Representative Robert Dole of Kansas proposed that the pay increase be contingent on reversal of the decision.[32]

The president and the executive branch can also vitally affect the fate of Supreme Court decisions. On average, a president appoints a new justice every twenty-two months. Thus, a two-term president has the potential to reshape the Court, and it can then negate a troublesome policy. Richard Nixon certainly intended to do just that when, in 1968, he campaigned for the presidency on the promise to appoint justices who would be tough on criminal defendants. Much of Nixon's 1968 presidential campaign was an attack on the liberal Warren Court.

His four appointments to the Supreme Court, including a new chief justice (Warren Burger), managed to modify the liberal trend set by the Warren Court and even to reverse some previous liberal decisions.

As the most visible public official, the president may influence public opinion by his willingness to accept a decision. His silence, on the other hand, may encourage disobedience or delay implementation. President Eisenhower's initial refusal to endorse the *Brown* decision gave support to those who opposed the Court. Although in 1957 Eisenhower dispatched troops to enforce court-ordered desegregation of the schools in Little Rock, Arkansas, many commentators have argued that his initial reluctance to support the decision had encouraged the avoidance of court orders. Indeed, a Supreme Court justice of that period, Tom C. Clark, observed that "if Mr. Eisenhower had come through, it would have changed things a lot."[33]

As the head of the executive branch, the president may also order the U.S. Department of Justice to prosecute noncompliance vigorously or to make only a token effort. On the one hand, President Johnson's vigorous use of the department to prosecute segregated school districts was very important in implementing *Brown*. President Nixon, on the other hand, slowed the process of desegregation by curtailing the department's prosecutorial activities.

Conclusion

This brief discussion of the American legal system demonstrates that, no matter how much we may wish it were otherwise, the courts are political institutions. As soothing as it may be, the myth of the nonpolitical courts simply does not reflect the American legal system. Although the conflict that produced the basic structure of the federal courts occurred long ago, the potential for political discord still exists, and we should not be blind to this fact. Nor can we ignore the link between partisan politics and the courts that is inherent in the system of judicial selection. Because judicial positions go to those who demonstrate faithful service to the party, individuals with considerable political experience staff the courts.

The myth of finality likewise fails to capture the reality of American courts. The implementation of court decisions requires the participation and cooperation of many in the political system. A simple pronouncement from a court does not suffice.

Key Terms

Amicus curiae p. 479
Appeal p. 468
Appellate courts p. 464
Briefs p. 478
Circuit courts p. 466
Civil actions p. 463

Concurring opinions p. 480
Criminal law p. 463
Dissenting opinions p. 480
General jurisdiction p. 470
Judicial activism p. 483
Judicial restraint p. 483

Judicial review p. 481
Limited jurisdiction p. 470
Original jurisdiction p. 463
Plea bargain p. 491
Trial courts p. 463
Writ of certiorari p. 468

Focus Questions Review

1. How does civil law differ from criminal law? > > >
- Civil actions cover conflicts between private individuals or organizations.
- Criminal law concerns wrongs done to the public.

2. How do trial courts differ from appellate courts? > > >
- Trial courts are courts of first instance—the first courts to hear cases. These courts take evidence, hear witnesses, and make determinations of fact.
- Appellate courts, on the other hand, are responsible for reviewing the decisions of trial courts. Appellate review is designed to ensure that there was no error in judicial procedures or interpretations of the law.

3. What are the major components of the federal and state court systems? > > >
- The United States has fifty-two court systems, one for the national government, one for each state, and a separate system for the Commonwealth of Puerto Rico.
- The ninety-four U.S. district courts are the trial courts for the federal system. Approximately 200,000 cases a year are heard by the district courts, and fewer than 10 percent of their decisions are appealed.
- The twelve U.S. courts of appeals handle most of the appellate work in the federal system. Organized into state groupings known as circuits, the courts of appeals hear all appeals from the federal district courts and some independent regulatory agencies and departments.
- Cases are appealed to the Supreme Court primarily either by an appeal or by a writ of certiorari. The Court has great latitude in deciding which cases it wants to hear.
- Each state has at least one appellate court that serves as its highest tribunal, reviewing the decisions of all other courts in the state. (Texas and Oklahoma have two high courts—one for civil litigation and one that handles only criminal cases.) Slightly more than half of the states also make use

of intermediate appellate courts to hear appeals from the trial courts.
- The most numerous courts in the states are the trial courts. Trial courts at the state level tend to be divided into two types: those with limited jurisdiction and those with general jurisdiction.

4. How are judges selected in the United States? > > >
- The Constitution requires that federal judges be nominated by the president and appointed with the advice and consent of the Senate. Appointment procedures vary considerably, however, depending on the level of the court involved. The nomination of district court judges often originates with the senator or senators of the president's party from the nominee's state. These senators may exercise senatorial courtesy. Because courts of appeals are organized into circuits that cross state boundaries, no senator is entitled to exercise senatorial courtesy over these appointments.
- Because federal judges are appointed for life, the need to remove an ill or incompetent judge occasionally arises. Because the Constitution provides for removal only by impeachment, Congress has created the position of senior judge as a means of encouraging judges to retire.

5. What are the major steps in Supreme Court decision making? > > >
- The public phase of the Supreme Court's business consists of oral arguments presented before the justices. These are formalized procedures conducted under tight time constraints.
- The most important part of the Court's work takes place in its conferences, which are closed to all but the justices themselves. Here, the justices discuss and vote on the cases.
- Once a vote has been taken on a case, the chief justice, if in the majority, or the senior justice in the majority assigns the writing of the opinion. The justice assigned to write the opinion must then circulate drafts of the decision to the other justices. No opinion is final until at least a majority of the Court agrees on it.

- Justices who disagree with the majority opinion are free to write dissenting opinions explaining why they cannot accept the majority decision. Justices who agree with the majority opinion but not its reasoning may write concurring opinions.
- Judges are often involved in interpreting the Constitution, although controversy exists over how aggressively the courts should pursue such judicial review.

6. **Why is it that Court decisions are not simply self-executing?** > > >
  - Lower courts do not necessarily comply with Supreme Court decisions. Often they find the decisions sufficiently ambiguous to make compliance extremely difficult. When Supreme Court decisions conflict with locally held values, lower-court judges may be reluctant to displease their communities by enforcing the Supreme Court's rulings.
  - Congress also possesses a great deal of power over the implementation of Supreme Court decisions, because implementation often requires the appropriation of public funds, a function controlled by Congress. Congress can also propose constitutional amendments to overturn Supreme Court decisions.
  - The successful implementation of Supreme Court decisions also requires the cooperation of the president, or at least his acceptance of the policy. A president's willingness to accept a particular Court opinion can influence public opinion. More important, a president may seek to reshape the Court through the appointment process.

Review Questions

1. In an essay describe the difference between trial and appellate courts.
2. Write an essay in which you examine the contending views of the proper use of judicial review.

For more information and access to study materials, visit the book's companion website at www.oup.com/us/gitelson.

Policy Connection

What role does discretion play in our criminal justice system?

The Policy Challenge

It is easy to fall into the trap of believing that the policymaking process is complete once the votes take place in Congress, the president issues an order, or the courts hand down a decision. However, more detail is involved in enforcing and implementing policies, and many more decision makers are engaged in filling in the blanks as they put laws into effect. To the extent that they are doing so, people who implement and enforce policies are said to be exercising "policy discretion." Our goal in this Policy Connection is to provide a general picture of the role policy discretion plays in filling out the judicial function of government.[1]

Specifically, we focus our attention on the role that discretion plays in shaping the outcomes—the policy impacts—of our criminal justice system. When it comes to basic law enforcement, discretion is important because there are so many points in the legal process at which the application of laws and policies is left up to the people in the field—from the police to the prosecutors, to the judges, and to those who impose whatever punishment or sanctions the courts require.

The Four Stages of Discretion in Criminal Justice

Ask anyone who has become directly caught up in the American criminal justice system, and that person will tell you that he or she came away knowing a good deal more about how government really operates—perhaps more than he or she wanted to know. This individual likely had to deal with a reality that most of us know only indirectly by watching one of the many versions of TV's popular *Law & Order* series.[2]

What those shows highlight in dramatic fashion is the work of the police and the prosecutors, but in doing so they typically cover only half the story of the criminal justice process—the work of the police and the government prosecution team. Because some of the action takes place in courtrooms, we do get a limited exposure to the trial itself and the work of judges and those who run the courts. However, only in a rare episode or two among the hundreds associated with that popular TV franchise do we get a glimpse of the work that takes place after a trial has concluded with a conviction—the punishment or postsentencing stage.

To make sense of the role that discretion plays in shaping our criminal justice system, we must consider all four stages in which it plays a role: policing, prosecution, the trial, and punishment (see Table 14PC.1). Decisions are being made at each stage by officials in positions that by their very nature require them to make choices—hard choices. These are choices with impacts and implications not only for those subject to suspicion, arrest, prosecution, and possible incarceration but for the victims of crimes and the community as a whole. For those who study criminal justice, those choices are public policy at the street level.

TABLE 14PC.1 The Four Stages of Discretion

Type of Discretion	Who Is Involved?	Functions Performed
Police discretion (policing stage)	Police and others involved in investigations—e.g., forensic experts and crime lab personnel	Crime-related functions (investigation, apprehension, interrogation, and incarceration), order maintenance, and provision of community services (emergency services, educational services, and crime prevention)
Prosecutorial discretion (prosecution stage)	Prosecutors and others involved in pretrial activities	Administrative (processing), quasi-judicial (ensuring due process and proper police behavior), and adversarial (advocating for state cases) functions
Judicial discretion (trial stage)	Judges and court administrators	Administrative (court management), procedural (upholding legal requirements and standards), instructional (managing juries), and judgmental (deciding cases and assessing jury verdicts) functions
Postsentencing discretion (punishment stage)	Agencies in charge of corrections, prison managers and personnel, and parole managers	Administrative (processing prisoners and handling fines), incarceration (managing prisons), parole-related functions, and rehabilitative and social service functions and law enforcement

The Aaron Swartz Case

Aaron Swartz was widely known as a hacker—an individual revered for his programming skills within the IT community but regarded with suspicion by others. Swartz (at age 14!) played a key role in the development of the widely used RSS feed program and later had leading roles in a number of projects (e.g., Reddit, Infogami, and Jottit) that expanded the interactive and social media capacity of the Internet.

Swartz was also a leading advocate for reforming copyright laws he regarded as overly protective and an advocate and activist for open access. For example, he had openly (and successfully) challenged two government agencies that attempted to charge for access to public information by hacking into their systems and downloading many gigabytes of material. In one case, Swartz downloaded and posted for free public use the entire bibliographic database of the Library of Congress. In another case, he downloaded and released millions of federal court documents that were located behind a paywall. In both instances no charges were brought because the

material involved was determined to be in the public domain.

In 2011, however, Swartz seemed to cross the line and was arrested near the Harvard University campus (where he worked as a research Fellow).[3] The local charges concerned "breaking and entering" an unlocked closet on the nearby MIT campus with the intent of stealing information from the university's computer system. The closet housed wiring that gave Swartz access to the MIT computer system, and he had set up a laptop that was programmed to download the entire content of JSTOR—a digital collection of academic journals accessible only to those with library privileges at the more than 8,000 institutional subscribers. Access to JSTOR is typically limited to current students and faculty at those institutions. MIT had a more open policy, however, allowing access to anyone on campus—even visitors. At the time Swartz initiated his download (October 2010), there were no explicit restrictions on how or where campus visitors could access online library collections, and technically Swartz was taking advantage of that policy. JSTOR eventually discovered the hack and notified MIT of the problem. It is at that juncture in the Aaron Swartz case that we begin to see the role that discretion plays in the policy-making process.

The first point of discretion came when authorities decided to arrest the then unknown hacker on criminal charges. But on what grounds? After all, he was not violating any campus policy, because MIT allowed open access to JSTOR to anyone on campus. But he had gained that access through questionable means—that is, by entering a nonpublic access area (the unlocked closet) and tapping into the network through the system's wiring. It was decided that his methods constituted breaking and entering; the campus police were notified and eventually Swartz was arrested after he was seen entering the closet to check on his equipment.

Local and federal prosecutors then made a number of other decisions over the subsequent months as the case entered the next stages of the criminal justice system. In July 2011, the federal court (at the request of the U.S. attorney's office) formally issued four criminal charges against Swartz, and in November a local grand jury charged him with grand larceny and unauthorized access to a computer system in addition to the original breaking and entering charges. A month later, the local district attorney's office announced that it had decided not to pursue the original breaking and entering charges, and in March 2012 the district attorneys decided to drop the local grand jury charges altogether. "In the interest of justice," they announced, "we agreed to let the federal cases have precedence." Swartz's attorney reacted to the decision by calling it an "*exercise of proper discretion* by a wise and experienced prosecutor's office."[4]

With full control over the case, prosecutors at the U.S. attorney's office in Boston had the discretionary authority to pursue a number of options. Typically, a hacking case like this would lead to a **plea bargain**, in which the hacker would plead guilty or no contest to the charges. As a result, an arrangement is made for reduced sanctions, including a fine and no imprisonment if the hacker agrees to adhere to specific conditions—for example, avoiding the use of computers for a given period. In this instance, however,

federal prosecutors decided to make an example of Swartz by indicting him on nine additional charges and exposing him to a possible jail term of up to fifty years and a $1 million fine.

Why treat Swartz so differently from other cases? The federal prosecutors were probably influenced by the fact that he had engaged in this kind of activity earlier and gotten away with it. In comments he made to friends, however, Swartz suggested that well-known public statements he had made about the "moral imperative" to engage in these hacking projects[5] had a lot to do with the prosecutor's decision to go after him with such determination. The fact that both JSTOR and MIT had told prosecutors that they had "no further interest" in pressing charges in the case, or that the state of Massachusetts had dropped its indictments, made no difference; and whatever negotiations were taking place between Swartz's attorneys and the U.S. attorney's office in Boston seemed (at least to Swartz) to be going nowhere.

On January 11, 2013, news of Aaron Swartz's suicide was greeted with shock and dismay by everyone familiar with the case. And there was anger as well. Whatever other factors might have led him to take his own life, it was clear that the pressure brought to bear was a major contributing cause. Supporters of Swartz immediately raised questions about the decisions made by federal prosecutors, and among the most articulate critics was Lawrence Lessig, a Harvard law professor who had worked closely with Swartz. Although he noted that he disagreed with Swartz's tactics, Lessig was more outraged with the prosecutor's decisions, which he characterized as "absurd" and shameful. What Lessig found most difficult to comprehend was why the prosecutors used their discretion in such an extreme manner. "I get wrong. But I also get proportionality. And if you don't get both, you don't deserve to have the power of the United States government behind you."[6]

The Aaron Swartz case is unique in terms of the attention it generated and its tragic outcome, but in other respects it reflects the sequence of policy decisions made in the criminal justice system each day.

Police discretion has many dimensions. Determining whether an act is a violation sufficient to warrant arresting an individual is discretionary. A state trooper monitoring the highways must decide whether to pull you over for driving five or ten or fifteen miles per hour over the speed limit. Similarly, university security personnel at MIT could have taken different steps when they discovered the laptop in the unlocked closet. They could have disconnected and removed the computer at that point, but rather than shut down the breach, officials made a decision to set up surveillance in the hope of capturing the hacker as he entered the still-unlocked closet. Given the sensitivity to issues related to hacking, they also decided to contact the U.S. Secret Service, thus expanding the involvement of legal authorities. Each of these decisions involved an exercise of discretion on the part of law enforcement officers, and each would play a role in the tragedy that followed.

Prosecutorial discretion came into play when law enforcement consulted with local prosecutors to determine whether an arrest was warranted in this case and what charges would be brought. The decision was made that entering the closet would constitute the basis for a charge of breaking and entering, and this was the primary basis for arresting Swartz two days later. As Swartz was being arraigned in the local court on those initial charges, both the local district attorney and the U.S. attorney's office were making decisions regarding the range of charges to be filed later and the prosecutorial process that would be followed. The events that followed—the grand jury indictments, the decision by local authorities not to prosecute, and the decision by federal prosecutors to make an example of Swartz—reflect a policy-implementation process based on the discretionary authority given to those decision makers who operate the American criminal justice system.

We can only speculate about what would have followed had Swartz not taken his life and had the case had gone to court as scheduled in April 2013. Once a trial is scheduled, judicial discretion becomes a factor, as the trial judge now has an interest in making certain that all parties to the case follow due process and other legal standards. It is possible that Swartz's lawyers and federal prosecutors might have negotiated a plea bargain, or that the U.S. attorney might have decided to limit or reduce the indictment. In both cases, the lawyers or prosecutors must notify the trial judge, who has the discretion to accept or reject such pleas. Once a trial is underway, the discretionary authority of the presiding judge would become a factor in determining such things as the admissibility of evidence or the relevance of testimony. If Swartz were determined by a jury to be guilty, federal judges would have some leeway (within sentencing guidelines) in determining the punishment and fines to be imposed. If punishment included imprisonment, we enter the postsentencing phase, and an entirely different set of authorities and agencies becomes involved, from those who assign prisoners to different facilities, to the wardens who manage those prisons, and to those who manage the parole process. At each step along the way, the criminal justice system allows some degree of discretion in regard to implementing public policies.

The Necessary Evil (?) of Discretion

As the Swartz case demonstrates, the exercise of discretionary authority to make decisions can prove extremely controversial, and yet one cannot imagine how the criminal justice system could operate without empowering officials to make decisions at each stage of the process. Given the fact that no two crimes (or those accused of committing them) are alike, there is no way to develop a system of uniform procedures to deal with all arrests, prosecutions, trials, and incarcerations. Discretion—and the potential abuse of discretionary authority—may be the necessary evil we have to accept for a functional criminal justice system.

Although we rely on law enforcement to prevent crime or arrest those suspected of criminal acts, we all too often hear complaints about abusive police practices or the excessive use of force.[7] Stories about what Lessig has called "prosecutorial bullying"[8] are also widely circulated, and in recent years there has been increasing evidence that past convictions may have been the result of questionable police and prosecutorial practices.[9] Critics have questioned the fairness of some court proceedings, and many focus on either the leniency or the harshness of decisions by judges in various cases.[10] As for the work of prisons and parole systems, both the news media and popular culture outlets are filled with negative reports and narratives related to the way government officials conduct the postsentencing functions of the criminal justice system.[11]

Less widely known or reported are those instances when discretionary authority has been applied wisely or as a corrective to possible injustices. Problems associated with the misuse of police discretion have been addressed in a variety of ways, ranging from court decisions related to constitutional protections (see Chapter 4) to changes in the operating procedures of law enforcement agencies and the professionalization of policing and related fields. Most important have been efforts to rein in the possibility of discriminatory behavior, especially those practices based on racial and ethnic profiling.[12]

Prosecutorial discretion has also been subjected to reform efforts, as examples such as the Swartz case make front-page news. The major push has been to change the prosecutorial norms in order to emphasize the need for justice and to check the tendency to engage in the overzealous pursuit of convictions by any means possible.[13] In 1940, Justice Robert H. Jackson had set the standard by arguing that "the citizen's safety lies in the prosecutor who tempers zeal with human kindness, who seeks truth and not victims, who serves the law and not factional purposes, and who approaches his task with humility."[14] Altering the operational norms of prosecutors has its limitations in a world in which performance and winning cases is the measure of success for prosecutors.

The disparities in sentencing among judges as well as the perception that many judges were too lenient in their sentences led to the passage of federal and state laws in the 1970s and 1980s that were designed to limit judicial discretion in that specific area. The U.S. Sentencing Reform Act of 1984 has been particularly controversial,[15] although studies have indicated that it had some impact in increasing jail terms for federal crimes (see Figure 14PC.1). Nevertheless, over time, the provisions of the act have been loosened through Supreme Court decisions and efforts by judges to have the guidelines themselves loosened to allow for greater discretion. Those who carry out judicial functions in administrative agencies have also taken discretionary initiatives to assure that the work of others adheres to basic due process guarantees. This has been especially true in recent years, as immigration policy enforcement has become increasingly important.

The exercise of postsentencing discretion has also undergone a number of reforms. Public policies related to the management of American prisons have been the subject of study and change since the early 1800s,[16] and over the decades a range of approaches have been developed to deal with the treatment of prisoners, most of them relying on giving prison administrators considerable authority to manage their facilities.[17] In recent years, the emphasis on rights and rehabilitation has been offset by budget cuts and overcrowding in many facilities, and these trends have had an impact on the options available to those who run prison facilities at local, state, and federal levels. Similarly, the management of parole services has been reformed and transformed over the decades, sometimes resulting in the expansion of discretion and at other times leading to the imposition of limits.

Conclusion

What role does discretion play in our criminal justice system?

The answer to the central question posed in this Policy Connection is that discretion plays an important role in our criminal justice system. We cannot make sense of America's criminal justice policy—and the system that implements it—unless we focus

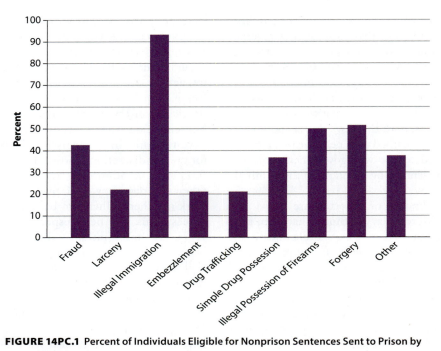

FIGURE 14PC.1 Percent of Individuals Eligible for Nonprison Sentences Sent to Prison by U.S. Federal Judges, FY 2012

More than 13,300 individuals convicted of a range of legal violations in fiscal year 2012 were eligible for "nonprison" sentences under federal sentencing guidelines. Given the discretion to determine whether or not an individual would face incarceration, federal judges were more likely to order imprisonment for some crimes than for others.

Source: U.S. Sentencing Commission, Interactive Sourcebook of Federal Sentencing Statistics, Fiscal Year 2012, Figure F; compiled at isb.ussc.gov using the Commission's fiscal year 2012 Datafile.

attention on those who are engaged in making significant decisions at each of the four stages outlined here.

As important is a more general observation about the role of discretionary authority in other public policy arenas. As we have seen in earlier chapters and Policy Connections, antitrust policies and the efforts to regulate key sectors of the economy (e.g., banking) depend on how those who work in the relevant agencies use their authority to monitor, investigate, and pursue legal remedies against those who may cross the legal line.[18] For example, in recent years, the amount of discretion given to those in command positions to deal with charges of sexual abuse in the military has been brought into question.[19] In 2013, a managerial decision within one Internal Revenue

Service (IRS) office about how to handle applications for tax-exempt status led to a major scandal that cost several officials their jobs.[20]

In summary, to make sense of American policy means making sense of discretion and how it is used in the everyday operations of our government.

QUESTIONS FOR DISCUSSION

1. **Judges operating under federal and state sentencing guidelines often complain that they ought to be allowed more discretion in determining the punishment handed down for someone convicted of a crime. Others believe in strict adherence to the guidelines in order to avoid sentencing that is either too harsh or too lenient. Which position do you think has more merit?**

2. This Policy Connection focused on the role policy discretion plays in the criminal justice system, but there are many other areas of our lives that are impacted by decisions made by public officials who administer government programs. School officials, for example, decide on whether or not to hold classes when warned of an approaching snowstorm. Social workers in a state agency must determine whether a family is eligible for some government benefit or service. Someone at the IRS is making a decision about whose tax return will be subject to an audit. What has been your experience with the exercise of policy discretion? Do you believe the exercise of discretion in your case was handled well or poorly?

The Declaration of Independence

When in the course of human events, it becomes necessary for one people to dissolve the political bands which have connected them with another, and to assume, among the powers of the earth, the separate and equal station to which the Laws of Nature and of Nature's God entitle them, a decent respect to the opinions of mankind requires that they should declare the causes which impel them to the separation.

We hold these truths to be self-evident, that all men are created equal, that they are endowed by their Creator with certain unalienable Rights, that among these are life, liberty and the pursuit of happiness. That to secure these rights, governments are instituted among men, deriving their just powers from the consent of the governed; that whenever any form of government becomes destructive of these ends, it is the right of the people to alter or to abolish it, and to institute new Government, laying its foundation on such principles and organizing its powers in such form, as to them shall seem most likely to effect their safety and happiness. Prudence, indeed, will dictate that Governments long established should not be changed for light and transient causes; and, accordingly, all experience hath shown, that mankind are more disposed to suffer, while evils are sufferable, than to right themselves by abolishing the forms to which they are accustomed. But when a long train of abuses and usurpations, pursuing invariably the same object evinces a design to reduce them under absolute despotism, it is their right, it is their duty, to throw off such government, and to provide new guards for their future security. Such has been the patient sufferance of these colonies; and such is now the necessity which constrains them to alter their former systems of government. The history of the present King of Great Britain is a history of repeated injuries and usurpations, all having in direct object the establishment of an absolute tyranny over these States. To prove this, let facts be submitted to a candid world:

He has refused his assent to laws, the most wholesome and necessary for the public good.

He has forbidden his governors to pass laws of immediate and pressing importance, unless suspended in their operation till his assent should be obtained; and, when so suspended, he has utterly neglected to attend to them.

He has refused to pass other laws for the accommodation of large districts of people, unless those people would relinquish the right of representation in the legislature, a right inestimable to them and formidable to tyrants only.

He has called together legislative bodies at places unusual, uncomfortable, and distant from the depository of their public records, for the sole purpose of fatiguing them into compliance with his measures.

He has dissolved representative houses repeatedly, for opposing with manly firmness his invasions on the rights of the people.

He has refused for a long time, after such dissolutions, to cause others to be elected; whereby the legislative powers, incapable of annihilation, have returned to the People at large for their exercise; the State remaining in the mean time exposed to all the dangers of invasion from without, and convulsions within.

He has endeavored to prevent the population of these States; for that purpose obstructing the laws for naturalization of foreigners; refusing to pass others to encourage their migrations hither, and raising the conditions of new appropriations of lands.

He has obstructed the administration of justice, by refusing his assent to laws for establishing judiciary powers.

He has made judges dependent on his will alone, for the tenure of their offices, and the amount and payment of their salaries.

He has erected a multitude of new offices, and sent hither swarms of officers to harass our people, and eat out their substance.

He has kept among us, in times of peace, standing armies without the consent of our legislatures.

He has affected to render the Military independent of, and superior to, the civil power.

He has combined with others to subject us to a jurisdiction foreign to our constitution and unacknowledged by our laws; giving his assent to their acts of pretended legislation:

For quartering large bodies of armed troops among us;

For protecting them, by a mock trial, from punishment for any murders which they should commit on the inhabitants of these States;

For cutting off our trade with all parts of the world;

For imposing taxes on us without our Consent;

For depriving us, in many cases, of the benefits of Trial by Jury;

For transporting us beyond Seas to be tried for pretended offences;

For abolishing the free System of English Laws in a neighbouring Province, establishing therein an Arbitrary government, and enlarging its Boundaries so as to render it at once an example and fit instrument for introducing the same absolute rule into these colonies;

For taking away our charters, abolishing our most valuable laws, and altering fundamentally the forms of our governments;

For suspending our own legislatures, and declaring themselves invested with power to legislate for us in all cases whatsoever.

He has abdicated government here, by declaring us out of his protection and waging war against us.

He has plundered our seas, ravaged our coasts, burnt our towns, and destroyed the lives of our people.

He is at this time transporting large armies of foreign mercenaries to complete the works of death, desolation and tyranny, already begun with circumstances of cruelty and perfidy scarcely paralleled in the most barbarous ages, and totally unworthy the head of a civilized nation.

He has constrained our fellow citizens taken captive on the high seas to bear arms against their country, to become the executioners of their friends and brethren, or to fall themselves by their hands.

He has excited domestic insurrections amongst us, and has endeavored to bring on the inhabitants of our frontiers, the merciless Indian savages, whose known rule of warfare, is an undistinguished destruction of all ages, sexes and conditions.

In every stage of these oppressions we have petitioned for redress in the most humble terms; our repeated petitions have been answered only by repeated injury. A prince whose character is thus marked by every act which may define a tyrant, is unfit to be the ruler of a free people.

Nor have we been wanting in attentions to our British brethren. We have warned them from time to time of attempts by their legislature to extend an unwarrantable jurisdiction over us. We have reminded them of the circumstances of our emigration and settlement here. We have appealed to their native justice and magnanimity, and we have conjured them by the ties of our common kindred to disavow these usurpations, which, would inevitably interrupt our connections and correspondence. They, too, have been deaf to the voice of justice and of consanguinity. We must, therefore, acquiesce in the necessity, which denounces our separation, and hold them, as we hold the rest of mankind, enemies in war, in peace friends.

We, therefore, the representatives of the United States of America, in general Congress, assembled, appealing to the Supreme Judge of the world for the rectitude of our intentions, do, in the name, and by the authority of the good people of these colonies, solemnly publish and declare, that these united colonies are, and of right ought to be free and independent states; that they are absolved from all allegiance to the British Crown, and that all political connection between them and the state of Great Britain, is and ought to be totally dissolved; and that, as free and independent states, they have full power to levy war, conclude peace, contract alliances, establish commerce, and to do all other acts and things which independent states may of right do. And for the support of this declaration, with a firm reliance on the protection of Divine Providence, we mutually pledge to each other our lives, our fortunes and our sacred honor.

The Constitution of the United States of America

We the People of the United States, in Order to form a more perfect Union, establish Justice, insure domestic Tranquility, provide for the common defence, promote the general Welfare, and secure the Blessings of Liberty to ourselves and our Posterity, do ordain and establish this Constitution for the United States of America.

Article I

Section 1

All legislative Powers herein granted shall be vested in a Congress of the United States, which shall consist of a Senate and House of Representatives.

Section 2

The House of Representatives shall be composed of Members chosen every second Year by the People of the several States, and the Electors in each State shall have the Qualifications requisite for Electors of the most numerous Branch of the State Legislature.

No Person shall be a Representative who shall not have attained to the Age of twenty five Years, and been seven Years a Citizen of the United States, and who shall not, when elected, be an Inhabitant of that State in which he shall be chosen.

Representatives [and direct Taxes]* shall be apportioned among the several States [which may be included within this Union, according to their respective Numbers, which shall be determined by adding to the whole Number of free Persons, including those bound to Service for a Term of Years, and excluding Indians not taxed, three fifths of all other Persons].** The actual Enumeration shall be made within three Years after the first Meeting of the Congress of the United States, and within every subsequent Term of ten Years, in such Manner as they shall by Law direct. The Number of Representatives shall not exceed one for every thirty Thousand, but each State shall have at Least one Representative; and until such enumeration shall be made, the State of New Hampshire shall be

Modified by the Sixteenth Amendment.
Negated by the Fourteenth Amendment.

entitled to choose three, Massachusetts eight, Rhode-Island and Providence Plantations one, Connecticut five, New York six, New Jersey four, Pennsylvania eight, Delaware one, Maryland six, Virginia ten, North Carolina five, South Carolina five, and Georgia three.

When vacancies happen in the Representation from any State, the Executive Authority thereof shall issue Writs of Election to fill such Vacancies.

The House of Representatives shall choose their Speaker and other Officers; and shall have the sole Power of Impeachment.

Section 3

The Senate of the United States shall be composed of two Senators from each State, chosen [by the Legislature thereof]* for six Years; and each Senator shall have one Vote.

Immediately after they shall be assembled in Consequence of the first Election, they shall be divided as equally as may be into three Classes. The Seats of the Senators of the first Class shall be vacated at the Expiration of the second Year, of the second Class at the Expiration of the fourth Year, and of the third Class at the Expiration of the sixth Year, so that one third may be chosen every second Year, [and if Vacancies happen by Resignation, or otherwise, during the Recess of the Legislature of any State, the Executive thereof may make temporary Appointments until the next Meeting of the Legislature, which shall then fill such Vacancies].**

No Person shall be a Senator who shall not have attained to the Age of thirty Years, and been nine Years a Citizen of the United States, and who shall not, when elected, be an Inhabitant of that State for which he shall be chosen.

The Vice President of the United States shall be President of the Senate, but shall have no Vote, unless they be equally divided.

The Senate shall choose their other Officers, and also a President pro tempore, in the Absence of the Vice President, or when he shall exercise the Office of President of the United States.

The Senate shall have the sole Power to try all Impeachments. When sitting for that Purpose, they shall be on Oath or Affirmation. When the President of the United States is tried, the Chief Justice shall preside: And no Person shall be convicted without the Concurrence of two thirds of the Members present.

Judgment in Cases of Impeachment shall not extend further than to removal from Office, and disqualification to hold and enjoy any Office of honor, Trust or Profit under the United States: but the Party convicted shall nevertheless be liable and subject to Indictment, Trial, Judgment and Punishment, according to Law.

Section 4

The Times, Places and Manner of holding Elections for Senators and Representatives, shall be prescribed in each State by the Legislature thereof; but the

---

Changed by the Seventeenth Amendment.

**Modified by the Seventeenth Amendment.*

Congress may at any time by Law make or alter such Regulations, except as to the Places of chusing Senators.

[The Congress shall assemble at least once in every Year, and such Meeting shall be on the first Monday in December, unless they shall by Law appoint a different Day.]*

Section 5

Each House shall be the Judge of the Elections, Returns and Qualifications of its own Members, and a Majority of each shall constitute a Quorum to do Business; but a smaller Number may adjourn from day to day, and may be authorized to compel the Attendance of absent Members, in such Manner, and under such Penalties as each House may provide.

Each House may determine the Rules of its Proceedings, punish its Members for disorderly Behaviour, and, with the Concurrence of two thirds, expel a Member.

Each House shall keep a Journal of its Proceedings, and from time to time publish the same, excepting such Parts as may in their Judgment require Secrecy; and the Yeas and Nays of the Members of either House on any question shall, at the Desire of one fifth of those Present, be entered on the Journal.

Neither House, during the Session of Congress, shall, without the Consent of the other, adjourn for more than three days, nor to any other Place than that in which the two Houses shall be sitting.

Section 6

The Senators and Representatives shall receive a Compensation for their Services, to be ascertained by Law, and paid out of the Treasury of the United States. They shall in all Cases, except Treason, Felony and Breach of the Peace, be privileged from Arrest during their Attendance at the Session of their respective Houses, and in going to and returning from the same; and for any Speech or Debate in either House, they shall not be questioned in any other Place.

No Senator or Representative shall, during the Time for which he was elected, be appointed to any civil Office under the Authority of the United States, which shall have been created, or the Emoluments whereof shall have been increased during such time; and no Person holding any Office under the United States, shall be a Member of either House during his Continuance in Office.

Section 7

All Bills for raising Revenue shall originate in the House of Representatives; but the Senate may propose or concur with Amendments as on other Bills.

Every Bill which shall have passed the House of Representatives and the Senate, shall, before it become a Law, be presented to the President of the United States: If he approve he shall sign it, but if not he shall return it, with his Objections to that House in which it shall have originated, who shall enter the Objections at large on their Journal, and proceed to reconsider it. If after such Reconsideration two thirds

---

Changed to January 3 by the Twentieth Amendment.

of that House shall agree to pass the Bill, it shall be sent, together with the Objections, to the other House, by which it shall likewise be reconsidered, and if approved by two thirds of that House, it shall become a Law. But in all such Cases the Votes of both Houses shall be determined by yeas and Nays, and the Names of the Persons voting for and against the Bill shall be entered on the Journal of each House respectively. If any Bill shall not be returned by the President within ten Days (Sundays excepted) after it shall have been presented to him, the Same shall be a Law, in like Manner as if he had signed it, unless the Congress by their Adjournment prevent its Return, in which Case it shall not be a Law.

Every Order, Resolution, or Vote to which the Concurrence of the Senate and House of Representatives may be necessary (except on a question of Adjournment) shall be presented to the President of the United States; and before the Same shall take Effect, shall be approved by him, or being disapproved by him, shall be repassed by two thirds of the Senate and House of Representatives, according to the Rules and Limitations prescribed in the Case of a Bill.

Section 8

The Congress shall have Power

To lay and collect Taxes, Duties, Imposts and Excises, to pay the Debts and provide for the common Defence and general Welfare of the United States; but all Duties, Imposts and Excises shall be uniform throughout the United States;

To borrow Money on the credit of the United States;

To regulate Commerce with foreign Nations, and among the several States, and with the Indian Tribes;

To establish an uniform Rule of Naturalization, and uniform Laws on the subject of Bankruptcies throughout the United States;

To coin Money, regulate the Value thereof, and of foreign Coin, and fix the Standard of Weights and Measures;

To provide for the Punishment of counterfeiting the Securities and current Coin of the United States;

To establish Post Offices and post Roads;

To promote the Progress of Science and useful Arts, by securing for limited Times to Authors and Inventors the exclusive Right to their respective Writings and Discoveries;

To constitute Tribunals inferior to the supreme Court;

To define and punish Piracies and Felonies committed on the high Seas, and Offences against the Law of Nations;

To declare War, grant Letters of Marque and Reprisal, and make Rules concerning Captures on Land and Water;

To raise and support Armies, but no Appropriation of Money to that Use shall be for a longer Term than two Years;

To provide and maintain a Navy;

To make Rules for the Government and Regulation of the land and naval Forces;

To provide for calling forth the Militia to execute the Laws of the Union, suppress Insurrections and repel Invasions;

To provide for organizing, arming, and disciplining the Militia, and for governing such Part of them as may be employed in the Service of the United States, reserving to the States respectively, the Appointment of the Officers, and the Authority of training the Militia according to the discipline prescribed by Congress;

To exercise exclusive Legislation in all Cases whatsoever, over such District (not exceeding ten Miles square) as may, by Cession of particular States, and the Acceptance of Congress, become the Seat of the Government of the United States, and to exercise like Authority over all Places purchased by the Consent of the Legislature of the State in which the Same shall be, for the Erection of Forts, Magazines, Arsenals, dock-Yards, and other needful Buildings;—And

To make all Laws which shall be necessary and proper for carrying into Execution the foregoing Powers, and all other Powers vested by this Constitution in the Government of the United States, or in any Department or Officer thereof.

Section 9

The Migration or Importation of such Persons as any of the States now existing shall think proper to admit, shall not be prohibited by the Congress prior to the Year one thousand eight hundred and eight, but a Tax or duty may be imposed on such Importation, not exceeding ten dollars for each Person.

The Privilege of the Writ of Habeas Corpus shall not be suspended, unless when in Cases of Rebellion or Invasion the public Safety may require it.

No Bill of Attainder or ex post facto Law shall be passed.

[No Capitation, or other direct, Tax shall be laid, unless in Proportion to the Census or enumeration herein before directed to be taken.]*

No Tax or Duty shall be laid on Articles exported from any State.

No Preference shall be given by any Regulation of Commerce or Revenue to the Ports of one State over those of another; nor shall Vessels bound to, or from, one State, be obliged to enter, clear, or pay Duties in another.

No Money shall be drawn from the Treasury, but in Consequence of Appropriations made by Law; and a regular Statement and Account of the Receipts and Expenditures of all public Money shall be published from time to time.

No Title of Nobility shall be granted by the United States: And no Person holding any Office of Profit or Trust under them, shall, without the Consent of the Congress, accept of any present, Emolument, Office, or Title, of any kind whatever, from any King, Prince, or foreign State.

Section 10

No State shall enter into any Treaty, Alliance, or Confederation; grant Letters of Marque and Reprisal; coin Money; emit Bills of Credit; make any Thing but gold and silver Coin a Tender in Payment of Debts; pass any Bill of Attainder, ex post facto Law, or Law impairing the Obligation of Contracts, or grant any Title of Nobility.

Modified by the Sixteenth Amendment.

No State shall, without the Consent of the Congress, lay any Imposts or Duties on Imports or Exports, except what may be absolutely necessary for executing it's inspection Laws: and the net Produce of all Duties and Imposts, laid by any State on Imports or Exports, shall be for the Use of the Treasury of the United States; and all such Laws shall be subject to the Revision and Control of the Congress.

No State shall, without the Consent of Congress, lay any Duty of Tonnage, keep Troops, or Ships of War in time of Peace, enter into any Agreement or Compact with another State, or with a foreign Power, or engage in War, unless actually invaded, or in such imminent Danger as will not admit of delay.

Article II

Section 1

The executive Power shall be vested in a President of the United States of America. He shall hold his Office during the Term of four Years, and, together with the Vice President, chosen for the same Term, be elected, as follows:

Each State shall appoint, in such Manner as the Legislature thereof may direct, a Number of Electors, equal to the whole Number of Senators and Representatives to which the State may be entitled in the Congress: but no Senator or Representative, or Person holding an Office of Trust or Profit under the United States, shall be appointed an Elector.

[The Electors shall meet in their respective States, and vote by Ballot for two Persons, of whom one at least shall not be an Inhabitant of the same State with themselves. And they shall make a List of all the Persons voted for, and of the Number of Votes for each; which List they shall sign and certify, and transmit sealed to the Seat of the Government of the United States, directed to the President of the Senate. The President of the Senate shall, in the Presence of the Senate and House of Representatives, open all the Certificates, and the Votes shall then be counted. The Person having the greatest Number of Votes shall be the President, if such Number be a Majority of the whole Number of Electors appointed; and if there be more than one who have such Majority, and have an equal Number of Votes, then the House of Representatives shall immediately choose by Ballot one of them for President; and if no Person have a Majority, then from the five highest on the List the said House shall in like Manner choose the President. But in choosing the President, the Votes shall be taken by States, the Representation from each State having one Vote; a quorum for this purpose shall consist of a Member or Members from two thirds of the States, and a Majority of all the States shall be necessary to a Choice. In every Case, after the Choice of the President, the Person having the greatest Number of Votes of the Electors shall be the Vice President. But if there should remain two or more who have equal Votes, the Senate shall choose from them by Ballot the Vice President.]*

Changed by the Twelfth and Twentieth Amendments.

The Congress may determine the Time of choosing the Electors, and the Day on which they shall give their Votes; which Day shall be the same throughout the United States.

No Person except a natural born Citizen, or a Citizen of the United States, at the time of the Adoption of this Constitution, shall be eligible to the Office of President; neither shall any Person be eligible to that Office who shall not have attained to the Age of thirty five Years, and been fourteen Years a Resident within the United States.

In Case of the Removal of the President from Office, or of his Death, Resignation, or Inability to discharge the Powers and Duties of the said Office, the Same shall devolve on the Vice President, and the Congress may by Law provide for the Case of Removal, Death, Resignation or Inability, both of the President and Vice President, declaring what Officer shall then act as President, and such Officer shall act accordingly, until the Disability be removed, or a President shall be elected.

The President shall, at stated Times, receive for his Services, a Compensation, which shall neither be increased nor diminished during the Period for which he shall have been elected, and he shall not receive within that Period any other Emolument from the United States, or any of them.

Before he enter on the Execution of his Office, he shall take the following Oath or Affirmation:—"I do solemnly swear (or affirm) that I will faithfully execute the Office of President of the United States, and will to the best of my Ability, preserve, protect and defend the Constitution of the United States."

Section 2

The President shall be Commander in Chief of the Army and Navy of the United States, and of the Militia of the several States, when called into the actual Service of the United States; he may require the Opinion, in writing, of the principal Officer in each of the executive Departments, upon any Subject relating to the Duties of their respective Offices, and he shall have Power to grant Reprieves and Pardons for Offences against the United States, except in Cases of Impeachment.

He shall have Power, by and with the Advice and Consent of the Senate, to make Treaties, provided two thirds of the Senators present concur; and he shall nominate, and by and with the Advice and Consent of the Senate, shall appoint Ambassadors, other public Ministers and Consuls, Judges of the supreme Court, and all other Officers of the United States, whose Appointments are not herein otherwise provided for, and which shall be established by Law: but the Congress may by Law vest the Appointment of such inferior Officers, as they think proper, in the President alone, in the Courts of Law, or in the Heads of Departments.

The President shall have Power to fill up all Vacancies that may happen during the Recess of the Senate, by granting Commissions which shall expire at the End of their next Session.

Section 3

He shall from time to time give to the Congress Information of the State of the Union, and recommend to their Consideration such Measures as he shall judge necessary and expedient; he may, on extraordinary Occasions, convene both Houses, or either of them, and in Case of Disagreement between them, with

Respect to the Time of Adjournment, he may adjourn them to such Time as he shall think proper; he shall receive Ambassadors and other public Ministers; he shall take Care that the Laws be faithfully executed, and shall Commission all the Officers of the United States.

Section 4

The President, Vice President and all civil Officers of the United States, shall be removed from Office on Impeachment for, and Conviction of, Treason, Bribery, or other high Crimes and Misdemeanors.

Article III

Section 1

The judicial Power of the United States shall be vested in one supreme Court, and in such inferior Courts as the Congress may from time to time ordain and establish. The Judges, both of the supreme and inferior Courts, shall hold their Offices during good Behaviour, and shall, at stated Times, receive for their Services a Compensation, which shall not be diminished during their Continuance in Office.

Section 2

The judicial Power shall extend to all Cases, in Law and Equity, arising under this Constitution, the Laws of the United States, and Treaties made, or which shall be made, under their Authority;—to all Cases affecting Ambassadors, other public Ministers and Consuls;—to all Cases of admiralty and maritime Jurisdiction;—to Controversies to which the United States shall be a Party;—to Controversies between two or more States;—[between a State and Citizens of another State];—between Citizens of different States;—between Citizens of the same State claiming Lands under Grants of different States, [and between a State,] or the Citizens thereof, [and foreign States, Citizens or Subjects].*

In all Cases affecting Ambassadors, other public Ministers and Consuls, and those in which a State shall be Party, the supreme Court shall have original Jurisdiction. In all the other Cases before mentioned, the supreme Court shall have appellate Jurisdiction, both as to Law and Fact, with such Exceptions, and under such Regulations as the Congress shall make.

The Trial of all Crimes, except in Cases of Impeachment, shall be by Jury; and such Trial shall be held in the State where the said Crimes shall have been committed; but when not committed within any State, the Trial shall be at such Place or Places as the Congress may by Law have directed.

Section 3

Treason against the United States, shall consist only in levying War against them, or in adhering to their Enemies, giving them Aid and Comfort. No Person

*Altered by the Twelfth Amendment.

shall be convicted of Treason unless on the Testimony of two Witnesses to the same overt Act, or on Confession in open Court.

The Congress shall have Power to declare the Punishment of Treason, but no Attainder of Treason shall work Corruption of Blood, or Forfeiture except during the Life of the Person attainted.

Article IV

Section 1

Full Faith and Credit shall be given in each State to the public Acts, Records, and judicial Proceedings of every other State. And the Congress may by general Laws prescribe the Manner in which such Acts, Records and Proceedings shall be proved, and the Effect thereof.

Section 2

The Citizens of each State shall be entitled to all Privileges and Immunities of Citizens in the several States.

A Person charged in any State with Treason, Felony, or other Crime, who shall flee from Justice, and be found in another State, shall on Demand of the executive Authority of the State from which he fled, be delivered up, to be removed to the State having Jurisdiction of the Crime.

[No Person held to Service or Labour in one State, under the Laws thereof, escaping into another, shall, in Consequence of any Law or Regulation therein, be discharged from such Service or Labour, but shall be delivered up on Claim of the Party to whom such Service or Labour may be due.]*

Section 3

New States may be admitted by the Congress into this Union; but no new State shall be formed or erected within the Jurisdiction of any other State; nor any State be formed by the Junction of two or more States, or Parts of States, without the Consent of the Legislatures of the States concerned as well as of the Congress.

The Congress shall have Power to dispose of and make all needful Rules and Regulations respecting the Territory or other Property belonging to the United States; and nothing in this Constitution shall be so construed as to Prejudice any Claims of the United States, or of any particular State.

Section 4

The United States shall guarantee to every State in this Union a Republican Form of Government, and shall protect each of them against Invasion; and on Application of the Legislature, or of the Executive (when the Legislature cannot be convened), against domestic Violence.

Repealed by the Thirteenth Amendment.

Article V

The Congress, whenever two thirds of both Houses shall deem it necessary, shall propose Amendments to this Constitution, or, on the Application of the Legislatures of two thirds of the several States, shall call a Convention for proposing Amendments, which, in either Case, shall be valid to all Intents and Purposes, as Part of this Constitution, when ratified by the Legislatures of three fourths of the several States, or by Conventions in three fourths thereof, as the one or the other Mode of Ratification may be proposed by the Congress; Provided that no Amendment which may be made prior to the Year One thousand eight hundred and eight shall in any Manner affect the first and fourth Clauses in the Ninth Section of the first Article; and that no State, without its Consent, shall be deprived of its equal Suffrage in the Senate.

Article VI

All Debts contracted and Engagements entered into, before the Adoption of this Constitution, shall be as valid against the United States under this Constitution, as under the Confederation.

This Constitution, and the Laws of the United States which shall be made in Pursuance thereof; and all Treaties made, or which shall be made, under the Authority of the United States, shall be the supreme Law of the Land; and the Judges in every State shall be bound thereby, any Thing in the Constitution or Laws of any State to the Contrary notwithstanding.

The Senators and Representatives before mentioned, and the Members of the several State Legislatures, and all executive and judicial Officers, both of the United States and of the several States, shall be bound by Oath or Affirmation, to support this Constitution; but no religious Test shall ever be required as a Qualification to any Office or public Trust under the United States.

Article VII

The Ratification of the Conventions of nine States, shall be sufficient for the Establishment of this Constitution between the States so ratifying the Same.

The Word, "the," being interlined between the seventh and eighth Lines of the first Page, the Word "Thirty" being partly written on an Erazure in the fifteenth Line of the first Page, The Words "is tried" being interlined between the thirty second and thirty third Lines of the first Page and the Word "the" being interlined between the forty third and forty fourth Lines of the second Page.

Attest William Jackson Secretary

Done in Convention by the Unanimous Consent of the States present the Seventeenth Day of September in the Year of our Lord one thousand seven hundred and Eighty seven and of the Independence of the United States of America the Twelfth In witness whereof We have hereunto subscribed our Names,

G°. Washington
Presidt and deputy from Virginia

Delaware
Geo: Read
Gunning Bedford jun
John Dickinson
Richard Bassett
Jaco: Broom

Maryland
James McHenry
Dan of St Thos.
  Jenifer
Danl. Carroll

Virginia
John Blair
James Madison Jr.

North Carolina
Wm. Blount
Richd. Dobbs
  Spaight
Hu Williamson

South Carolina
J. Rutledge
Charles Cotesworth
  Pinckney
Charles Pinckney
Pierce Butler

Georgia
William Few
Abr Baldwin

New Hampshire
John Langdon
Nicholas Gilman

Massachusetts
Nathaniel Gorham
Rufus King

Connecticut
Wm. Saml. Johnson
Roger Sherman

New York
Alexander Hamilton

New Jersey
Wil: Livingston
David Brearley
Wm. Paterson
Jona: Dayton

Pennsylvania
B Franklin
Thomas Mifflin
Robt. Morris
Geo. Clymer
Thos. FitzSimons
Jared Ingersoll
James Wilson
Gouv Morris

Articles

In addition to, and Amendment of the Constitution of the United States of America, proposed by Congress, and ratified by the Legislatures of the several States, pursuant to the fifth Article of the original Constitution.

(The first ten amendments to the U.S. Constitution were ratified December 15, 1791, and form what is known as the "Bill of Rights.")

Amendment I

Congress shall make no law respecting an establishment of religion, or prohibiting the free exercise thereof; or abridging the freedom of speech, or of the press; or the right of the people peaceably to assemble, and to petition the Government for a redress of grievances.

Amendment II

A well regulated Militia, being necessary to the security of a free State, the right of the people to keep and bear Arms, shall not be infringed.

Amendment III

No Soldier shall, in time of peace be quartered in any house, without the consent of the Owner, nor in time of war, but in a manner to be prescribed by law.

Amendment IV

The right of the people to be secure in their persons, houses, papers, and effects, against unreasonable searches and seizures, shall not be violated, and no Warrants shall issue, but upon probable cause, supported by Oath or affirmation, and particularly describing the place to be searched, and the persons or things to be seized.

Amendment V

No person shall be held to answer for a capital, or otherwise infamous crime, unless on a presentment or indictment of a Grand Jury, except in cases arising in the land or naval forces, or in the Militia, when in actual service in time of War or public danger; nor shall any person be subject for the same offence to be twice put in jeopardy of life or limb; nor shall be compelled in any criminal case to be a witness against himself, nor be deprived of life, liberty, or property, without due process of law; nor shall private property be taken for public use, without just compensation.

Amendment VI

In all criminal prosecutions, the accused shall enjoy the right to a speedy and public trial, by an impartial jury of the State and district wherein the crime shall have been committed, which district shall have been previously ascertained by law, and to be informed of the nature and cause of the accusation; to be confronted with the witnesses against him; to have compulsory process for obtaining witnesses in his favor, and to have the Assistance of Counsel for his defence.

Amendment VII

In Suits at common law, where the value in controversy shall exceed twenty dollars, the right of trial by jury shall be preserved, and no fact tried by a jury, shall be otherwise re-examined in any Court of the United States, than according to the rules of the common law.

Amendment VIII

Excessive bail shall not be required, nor excessive fines imposed, nor cruel and unusual punishments inflicted.

Amendment IX

The enumeration in the Constitution, of certain rights, shall not be construed to deny or disparage others retained by the people.

Amendment X

The powers not delegated to the United States by the Constitution, nor prohibited by it to the States, are reserved to the States respectively, or to the people.

Amendment XI

Passed by Congress March 4, 1794. Ratified February 7, 1795.

Note: Article III, Section 2, of the Constitution was modified by Amendment XI.

The Judicial power of the United States shall not be construed to extend to any suit in law or equity, commenced or prosecuted against one of the United States by Citizens of another State, or by Citizens or Subjects of any Foreign State.

Amendment XII

Passed by Congress December 9, 1803. Ratified June 15, 1804.

Note: A portion of Article II, Section 1, of the Constitution was superseded by the Twelfth Amendment.

The Electors shall meet in their respective states and vote by ballot for President and Vice-President, one of whom, at least, shall not be an inhabitant of the same state with themselves; they shall name in their ballots the person voted for as President, and in distinct ballots the person voted for as Vice-President, and they shall make distinct lists of all persons voted for as President, and of all persons voted for as Vice-President, and of the number of votes for each, which lists they shall sign and certify, and transmit sealed to the seat of the government of the United States, directed to the President of the Senate;—the President of the Senate shall, in the presence of the Senate and House of Representatives, open all the certificates and the votes shall then be counted;—The person having the greatest number of votes for President, shall be the President, if such number be a majority of the whole number of Electors appointed; and if no person have such majority, then from the persons having the highest numbers not exceeding three on the list of those voted for as President, the House of Representatives shall choose immediately, by ballot, the President. But in choosing the President, the votes shall be taken by states, the representation from each state having one vote; a quorum for this purpose shall consist of a member or members from two-thirds of the states, and a majority of all the states shall be necessary to a choice. [And if the House of Representatives shall not choose a President whenever the right of choice shall devolve upon them, before the fourth day of March next following, then the Vice-President shall act as President, as in case of the death or other constitutional disability of the President.—]* The person having the greatest number of votes as Vice-President, shall be the Vice-President, if such number be a majority of the whole number of Electors appointed, and if no person have a majority, then from the two highest numbers on the list, the Senate shall choose the Vice-President; a quorum for the purpose shall consist of two-thirds of the whole number of Senators, and a majority of the whole number shall be necessary to a choice. But no person constitutionally ineligible to the office of President shall be eligible to that of Vice-President of the United States.

Amendment XIII

Passed by Congress January 31, 1865. Ratified December 6, 1865.

   Note: A portion of Article IV, Section 2, of the Constitution was superseded by the Thirteenth Amendment.

Section 1

Neither slavery nor involuntary servitude, except as a punishment for crime whereof the party shall have been duly convicted, shall exist within the United States, or any place subject to their jurisdiction.

Section 2

Congress shall have power to enforce this article by appropriate legislation.

Amendment XIV

Passed by Congress June 13, 1866. Ratified July 9, 1868.

   Note: Article I, Section 2, of the Constitution was modified by Section 2 of the Fourteenth Amendment.

Section 1

All persons born or naturalized in the United States, and subject to the jurisdiction thereof, are citizens of the United States and of the State wherein they reside. No State shall make or enforce any law which shall abridge the privileges or immunities of citizens of the United States; nor shall any State deprive any person of life, liberty, or property, without due process of law; nor deny to any person within its jurisdiction the equal protection of the laws.

Section 2

Representatives shall be apportioned among the several States according to their respective numbers, counting the whole number of persons in each State, excluding Indians not taxed. But when the right to vote at any election for the choice of electors for President and Vice-President of the United States, Representatives in Congress, the Executive and Judicial officers of a State, or the members of the

---

Superseded by Section 3 of the Twentieth Amendment.

Legislature thereof, is denied to any of the male inhabitants of such State, being twenty-one years of age,* and citizens of the United States, or in any way abridged, except for participation in rebellion, or other crime, the basis of representation therein shall be reduced in the proportion which the number of such male citizens shall bear to the whole number of male citizens twenty-one years of age in such State.

Section 3

No person shall be a Senator or Representative in Congress, or elector of President and Vice-President, or hold any office, civil or military, under the United States, or under any State, who, having previously taken an oath, as a member of Congress, or as an officer of the United States, or as a member of any State legislature, or as an executive or judicial officer of any State, to support the Constitution of the United States, shall have engaged in insurrection or rebellion against the same, or given aid or comfort to the enemies thereof. But Congress may by a vote of two-thirds of each House, remove such disability.

Section 4

The validity of the public debt of the United States, authorized by law, including debts incurred for payment of pensions and bounties for services in suppressing insurrection or rebellion, shall not be questioned. But neither the United States nor any State shall assume or pay any debt or obligation incurred in aid of insurrection or rebellion against the United States, or any claim for the loss or emancipation of any slave; but all such debts, obligations and claims shall be held illegal and void.

Section 5

The Congress shall have the power to enforce, by appropriate legislation, the provisions of this article.

Amendment XV

Passed by Congress February 26, 1869. Ratified February 3, 1870.

Section 1

The right of citizens of the United States to vote shall not be denied or abridged by the United States or by any State on account of race, color, or previous condition of servitude.

Section 2

The Congress shall have the power to enforce this article by appropriate legislation.

Changed by Section 1 of the Twenty-sixth Amendment.

Amendment XVI

Passed by Congress July 2, 1909. Ratified February 3, 1913.

Note: Article I, Section 9, of the Constitution was modified by Amendment XVI.

The Congress shall have power to lay and collect taxes on incomes, from whatever source derived, without apportionment among the several States, and without regard to any census or enumeration.

Amendment XVII

Passed by Congress May 13, 1912. Ratified April 8, 1913.

Note: Article I, Section 3, of the Constitution was modified by the Seventeenth Amendment.

The Senate of the United States shall be composed of two Senators from each State, elected by the people thereof, for six years; and each Senator shall have one vote. The electors in each State shall have the qualifications requisite for electors of the most numerous branch of the State legislatures.

When vacancies happen in the representation of any State in the Senate, the executive authority of such State shall issue writs of election to fill such vacancies: Provided, That the legislature of any State may empower the executive thereof to make temporary appointments until the people fill the vacancies by election as the legislature may direct.

This amendment shall not be so construed as to affect the election or term of any Senator chosen before it becomes valid as part of the Constitution.

Amendment XVIII

Passed by Congress December 18, 1917. Ratified January 16, 1919. Repealed by Amendment XXI.

Section 1

After one year from the ratification of this article the manufacture, sale, or transportation of intoxicating liquors within, the importation thereof into, or the exportation thereof from the United States and all territory subject to the jurisdiction thereof for beverage purposes is hereby prohibited.

Section 2

The Congress and the several States shall have concurrent power to enforce this article by appropriate legislation.

Section 3

This article shall be inoperative unless it shall have been ratified as an amendment to the Constitution by the legislatures of the several States, as provided in the Constitution, within seven years from the date of the submission hereof to the States by the Congress.

Amendment XIX

Passed by Congress June 4, 1919. Ratified August 18, 1920.

The right of citizens of the United States to vote shall not be denied or abridged by the United States or by any State on account of sex.

Congress shall have power to enforce this article by appropriate legislation.

Amendment XX

Passed by Congress March 2, 1932. Ratified January 23, 1933.

Note: Article I, Section 4, of the Constitution was modified by Section 2 of this amendment. In addition, a portion of the Twelfth Amendment was superseded by Section 3.

Section 1

The terms of the President and the Vice President shall end at noon on the 20th day of January, and the terms of Senators and Representatives at noon on the 3d day of January, of the years in which such terms would have ended if this article had not been ratified; and the terms of their successors shall then begin.

Section 2

The Congress shall assemble at least once in every year, and such meeting shall begin at noon on the 3d day of January, unless they shall by law appoint a different day.

Section 3

If, at the time fixed for the beginning of the term of the President, the President elect shall have died, the Vice President elect shall become President. If a President shall not have been chosen before the time fixed for the beginning of his term, or if the President elect shall have failed to qualify, then the Vice President elect shall act as President until a President shall have qualified; and the Congress may by law provide for the case wherein neither a President elect nor a Vice President shall have qualified, declaring who shall then act as President, or the manner in which one who is to act shall be selected, and such person shall act accordingly until a President or Vice President shall have qualified.

Section 4

The Congress may by law provide for the case of the death of any of the persons from whom the House of Representatives may choose a President whenever the right of choice shall have devolved upon them, and for the case of the death of any of the persons from whom the Senate may choose a Vice President whenever the right of choice shall have devolved upon them.

Section 5

Sections 1 and 2 shall take effect on the 15th day of October following the ratification of this article.

Section 6

This article shall be inoperative unless it shall have been ratified as an amendment to the Constitution by the legislatures of three-fourths of the several States within seven years from the date of its submission.

Amendment XXI

Passed by Congress February 20, 1933. Ratified December 5, 1933.

Section 1

The eighteenth article of amendment to the Constitution of the United States is hereby repealed.

Section 2

The transportation or importation into any State, Territory, or Possession of the United States for delivery or use therein of intoxicating liquors, in violation of the laws thereof, is hereby prohibited.

Section 3

This article shall be inoperative unless it shall have been ratified as an amendment to the Constitution by conventions in the several States, as provided in the Constitution, within seven years from the date of the submission hereof to the States by the Congress.

Amendment XXII

Passed by Congress March 21, 1947. Ratified February 27, 1951.

Section 1

No person shall be elected to the office of the President more than twice, and no person who has held the office of President, or acted as President, for more than two years of a term to which some other person was elected President shall be elected to the office of President more than once. But this Article shall not apply to any person holding the office of President when this Article was proposed by Congress, and shall not prevent any person who may be holding the office of President, or acting as President, during the term within which this Article becomes operative from holding the office of President or acting as President during the remainder of such term.

Section 2

This article shall be inoperative unless it shall have been ratified as an amendment to the Constitution by the legislatures of three-fourths of the several States within seven years from the date of its submission to the States by the Congress.

Amendment XXIII

Passed by Congress June 16, 1960. Ratified March 29, 1961.

Section 1

The District constituting the seat of Government of the United States shall appoint in such manner as Congress may direct:

A number of electors of President and Vice President equal to the whole number of Senators and Representatives in Congress to which the District would be entitled if it were a State, but in no event more than the least populous State; they shall be in addition to those appointed by the States, but they shall be considered, for the purposes of the election of President and Vice President, to be electors appointed by a State; and they shall meet in the District and perform such duties as provided by the twelfth article of amendment.

Section 2

The Congress shall have power to enforce this article by appropriate legislation.

Amendment XXIV

Passed by Congress August 27, 1962. Ratified January 23, 1964.

Section 1

The right of citizens of the United States to vote in any primary or other election for President or Vice President, for electors for President or Vice President, or for Senator or Representative in Congress, shall not be denied or abridged by the United States or any State by reason of failure to pay poll tax or other tax.

Section 2

The Congress shall have power to enforce this article by appropriate legislation.

Amendment XXV

Passed by Congress July 6, 1965. Ratified February 10, 1967.

Note: Article II, Section 1, of the Constitution was affected by the Twenty-Fifth Amendment.

Section 1

In case of the removal of the President from office or of his death or resignation, the Vice President shall become President.

Section 2

Whenever there is a vacancy in the office of the Vice President, the President shall nominate a Vice President who shall take office upon confirmation by a majority vote of both Houses of Congress.

Section 3

Whenever the President transmits to the President pro tempore of the Senate and the Speaker of the House of Representatives his written declaration that he is unable to discharge the powers and duties of his office, and until he transmits to them a written declaration to the contrary, such powers and duties shall be discharged by the Vice President as Acting President.

Section 4

Whenever the Vice President and a majority of either the principal officers of the executive departments or of such other body as Congress may by law provide, transmit to the President pro tempore of the Senate and the Speaker of the House of Representatives their written declaration that the President is unable to discharge the powers and duties of his office, the Vice President shall immediately assume the powers and duties of the office as Acting President.

Thereafter, when the President transmits to the President pro tempore of the Senate and the Speaker of the House of Representatives his written declaration that no inability exists, he shall resume the powers and duties of his office unless the Vice President and a majority of either the principal officers of the executive department or of such other body as Congress may by law provide, transmit within four days to the President pro tempore of the Senate and the Speaker of the House of Representatives their written declaration that the President is unable to discharge the powers and duties of his office. Thereupon Congress shall decide the issue, assembling within forty-eight hours for that purpose if not in session. If the Congress, within twenty-one days after receipt of the latter written declaration, or, if Congress is not in session, within twenty-one days after Congress is required to assemble, determines by two-thirds vote of both Houses that the President is unable to discharge the powers and duties of his office, the Vice President shall continue to discharge the same as Acting President; otherwise, the President shall resume the powers and duties of his office.

Amendment XXVI

Passed by Congress March 23, 1971. Ratified July 1, 1971.

Note: Amendment XIV, Section 2, of the Constitution was modified by Section 1 of the Twenty-Sixth Amendment.

Section 1

The right of citizens of the United States, who are eighteen years of age or older, to vote shall not be denied or abridged by the United States or by any State on account of age.

Section 2

The Congress shall have power to enforce this article by appropriate legislation.

Amendment XXVII

Originally proposed Sept. 25, 1789. Ratified May 7, 1992.

No law, varying the compensation for the services of the Senators and Representatives, shall take effect, until an election of representatives shall have intervened.

Glossary

Accommodationist interpretation A reading of the establishment clause that bars only the establishment by Congress of an official public church. Accommodationists agree with state support of religion as long as all religions are treated equally.

Affirmative action A set of procedures that attempts to correct the effects of past discrimination against minority groups. It can include specific goals and quotas for hiring minority applicants.

Agenda setting The second stage of policymaking, in which the issue or problem is seriously considered by the policymaking institution.

Amicus curiae A Latin phrase meaning "friend of the court." Amicus curiae briefs are written briefs submitted to the Supreme Court by third-party individuals or organizations that want their opinions to be considered in a case.

Anti-miscegenation laws State laws that made interracial marriage a criminal offence.

Appeal A route by which cases can reach the Supreme Court. In such cases, litigants have some right under the law to have their cases reviewed.

Appellate courts Courts that reconsider the decisions rendered by trial courts if the losing party requests such reconsideration and demonstrates grounds for it.

Appropriation of funds The actions taken by Congress to authorize the spending of funds.

Articles of Confederation The first constitution of the United States, ratified in 1781. They established a loose union of states and a congress with limited powers.

Authority The capacity to make and enforce public policies that is possessed by individuals who occupy formal governmental roles.

Bad tendency test The principle that the Supreme Court began to prefer, in First Amendment cases, over the clear and present danger test. It allowed the government to punish speech that might cause people to behave illegally.

Balance of power A realist's approach to foreign policy, based on the need to offset any imbalance in international relations that might lead to one nation becoming too powerful. Advocated by Secretary of State Henry Kissinger, it was the central premise of American foreign policy for most of the 1970s.

Balance of trade The net difference between the value of what Americans buy and what they sell overseas.

Beliefs Those strongly held assumptions and attitudes about politics and government we grow up with or develop over time. In contrast to reasoned analysis or myths, beliefs do not rely on empirical evidence or narratives.

Bicameral Refers to a legislature that is divided into two separate houses, such as the U.S. Congress.

Bill of attainder A legislative act declaring a person guilty of a crime and setting punishment without the benefit of a formal trial.

Bill of Rights In the United States, the first ten amendments to the Constitution, which collectively guarantee the fundamental liberties of citizens against abuse by the national government.

Block grants Money given to the states by Congress that can be used in broad areas and is not limited to specific purposes, as categorical grants are. They were introduced in the mid-1960s as a means of giving states greater freedom.

Briefs Documents submitted to a court by attorneys that contain a summary of the issues and the laws applying to the case and arguments supporting counsel's position.

Budget deficit The result when expenditures exceed revenues.

Budget sequestration A process in which Congress agrees to cap expenditures within a broadly defined category of spending.

Budget surplus The result when budget revenues exceed expenditures.

Bureaucracy Any large, complex organization in which employees have specific job responsibilities and work within a hierarchy. The term often refers to both government agencies and the people who work in them.

Bureaucratic pathologies Behaviors by bureaucrats that feed the idea that the bureaucracy is incompetent and unresponsive.

They include clientelism, incrementalism, arbitrariness, parochialism, and imperialism.

Bureaucratic power The power of government agencies, derived from law, external support, expertise, discretion, longevity in office, skill, leadership, and a variety of other sources.

Cabinet An official advisory board to the president, made up of the heads (secretaries) of the major departments in the federal government.

Candidate-centered campaign A campaign in which paid consultants or volunteers coordinate campaign activities, develop strategies, and raise funds. Parties play a secondary role.

Capital expenditures In the public sector, that part of a government budget allocated to the construction or major repairs of large, fixed assets such as roads, buildings, dams, and so on.

Career service personnel systems Separate personnel systems for highly specialized agencies like the Coast Guard and the Foreign Service.

Casework Work done by members of Congress to provide constituents with personal services and help them through the maze of federal programs and benefits.

Categorical, or conditional, grants-in-aid Money given to the states and localities by Congress to be used for limited purposes under specific rules.

Caucus A forum for choosing candidates that was closed to the public until the Progressive Era; contemporary caucuses are local party meetings, open to all who live in the precinct, in which citizens discuss and then vote for delegates to district and state conventions.

Checks and balances The principle that lets the executive, legislative, and judicial branches share some responsibilities and gives each branch some control over the others' activities. The major support for checks and balances comes from the Constitution's distribution of shared powers.

Circuit courts Federal courts of appeals that rank above the district courts and serve as the major appellate courts for the federal system. They review all cases, both civil and criminal, and the decisions of independent regulatory agencies and departments.

Civil actions Suits arising out of conflicts between private persons and/or organizations; they typically include disputes over contracts, claims for damages, and divorce petitions.

Civil disobedience A refusal to obey civil laws that are regarded as unjust. This may involve methods of passive resistance such as sit-ins and boycotts.

Civil liberties Freedoms, most of which are spelled out in the Bill of Rights, from excessive or arbitrary government interference.

Civil rights Guarantees of protection by the government against discrimination or unreasonable treatment by other individuals or groups.

Clear and present danger test The proposition, proclaimed by the Supreme Court in *Schenck v. United States* (1919), that the government has the right to punish speech if it can be shown to present a grave and immediate danger to the country's interests.

Closed primary A primary election in which a voter is allowed to obtain only a ballot of the party in which he or she is registered.

Cloture The rule for ending debate in the Senate; it requires that at least sixty senators vote to cut off discussion.

Coalition building The bringing together of diverse interest groups in a common lobbying effort.

Cold War The period dating from just after the end of World War II until the collapse of the Soviet Union in 1991, characterized in part by American efforts to win the support of those nations in Africa, Asia, and Latin America emerging from colonialism or dictatorship.

Concurrent powers Those powers that the Constitution grants to the national government but does not deny to the states—for example, the power to lay and collect taxes.

Concurring opinions Opinions written by Supreme Court justices that agree with the conclusion but not with the reasoning of the majority opinion.

Confederation An arrangement in which ultimate governmental authority is vested in the states that make up the union, with whatever power the national government has being derived from the states' willingness to give up some of their authority to a central government.

Conference committees Temporary joint committees that are formed to reconcile differences between the House and Senate versions of a bill. Such committees often play a critical role in shaping legislation.

Confirmation The power of the U.S. Senate to approve or disapprove a presidential nominee for an executive or judicial post.

Congressional authorization The power of Congress to provide the president with the right to carry out legislated policies.

Congressional-executive agreement An agreement with a foreign nation that is negotiated by the president and then submitted to both houses of Congress for approval.

Conservatism A set of ideological beliefs that tend to resist government interference in economic matters but favor government action to regulate private affairs for moral purposes.

Constitutional construction A form of constitutional change that occurs as public officials fill in the institutional "blank spaces" left by the Constitution.

Constitutional interpretation A process of constitutional change that involves attempts to discover the meaning of the words used in the different provisions of the Constitution as they might apply to specific situations.

Containment The U.S. commitment to diplomatically, economically, and militarily counter the expansionist tendencies of the Soviet Union and its allies in Eastern Europe and Asia.

Continuing resolutions Bills that authorize the government to spend for a few months, usually at the previous year's rate.

Cooperative federalism A period of cooperation between state and national governments that began during the Great Depression. The national government began to take on new responsibilities, and state and local officials accepted it as an ally, not an enemy.

Councils of governments Local and regional bodies created in the early 1970s with federal funds to help solve problems such as coordinating applications for federal grants.

Criminal law The branch of the law dealing with offenses against the public order and providing for a specified punishment. Most criminal law cases arise in state courts.

Decentralization A term that contends that many different individuals within the party share the decision-making power, with power dispersed. No single individual or organization controls the entire system (as compared, for example, with Great Britain, Germany, and Italy, which have highly centralized party organizations controlled by relatively few individuals or central committees). In effect, party organizations in the United States are fragmented and multilayered, often operating independently of each other.

Declaration of Independence A document declaring the colonies to be free and independent states, and also articulating the fundamental principles under which the new nation would be governed, which was adopted by the Second Continental Congress in July 1776.

Delegated powers The powers the Constitution gives to Congress that are specifically listed in the first seventeen clauses in Section 8 of Article I; they are sometimes referred to as "enumerated powers."

Democracy To Americans, a government in which authority is based on the consent and will of the majority.

Democratic model of policymaking The view that policymaking can and ought to be the product of public deliberation in which those whose lives are affected by a decision are given the opportunity to participate.

Deregulation Administrative reform policies initiated in the 1970s that emphasized a loosening of government controls over activities and economic sectors previously subject to government rules and regulations.

Détente The relaxation of tensions between nations. It became the name for President Nixon's policy of taking a more cooperative approach in dealing with Soviet bloc nations while enhancing U.S. security arrangements with its allies.

Devolution A term indicating the effort to give more functions and responsibilities to states and localities in the intergovernmental system.

Discretionary spending Those programs and policies that are subject to funding through the annual appropriations process, in which Congress sets the level of funding.

Dissenting opinions Legal opinions written by Supreme Court justices that disagree with the majority conclusion.

Dual federalism The perspective on federalism that emerged after the Civil War. It saw the national and state governments as equal but independent partners, with each responsible for distinct policy functions and each barred from interfering with the other's work.

Earmark A legislative proposal to provide spending or favorable tax treatment for specific projects in the sponsor's district or state.

Economic development policies Policies intended to promote and protect businesses to enhance overall economic growth.

Electioneering Participating in the election process by providing services or raising campaign contributions.

Electoral coalitions Groups of loyal supporters who agree with the party's stand on most issues and vote for its candidates for office.

Electoral College The constitutional body designed to select the president. This system is described in Article II of the Constitution

Elite model of policymaking The theory that public policies are made by a relatively small group of influential leaders who share common goals and points of view.

Elitist view of power The view that political power should be in the hands of a relatively small part of the general population that shares a common understanding about the fundamental issues facing society and government.

Eminent domain The right of a sovereign government to take property for public purposes for just compensation, even if the owner objects.

Enlightenment The period from the 1600s through the 1700s in European intellectual history. It was dominated by the idea that human reason, not religious tradition, was the primary source of knowledge and wisdom.

Entitlement programs Programs such as Social Security that commit the government to supplying funds or services to all citizens who meet specified eligibility requirements.

Equal-time rule A Federal Communications Commission rule that requires a broadcaster who permits one candidate to campaign on the station to provide all other candidates for the same office with equal time at identical rates.

Exclusionary rule The principle that evidence, no matter how incriminating, cannot be used to convict someone if it is gathered illegally. This concept was established by the Supreme Court in *Mapp v. Ohio* (1961).

Executive agreements Agreements with other nations that are made by the president without the Senate's consent. They have all the legal force of treaties but, unlike treaties, are not binding on succeeding presidents.

Executive Office of the President (EOP) The collective name for several agencies, councils, and groups of staff members that advise the president and help manage the federal bureaucracy. The EOP was established in the 1930s; the number and type of agencies that constitute it change with each presidential administration.

Executive order A rule or regulation issued by the president that has the effect of law.

Executive privilege The right, claimed by presidents from Washington onward, to withhold information from Congress.

Ex post facto law A law declaring an action criminal even if it was performed before the law making it illegal was passed.

Faith-based organizations (FBOs) Church-related social service organizations.

Federal Communications Commission (FCC) The agency created in 1934 to monitor and regulate the use of the airwaves.

Federal Poverty Level A standard set by the U.S. Census Bureau to indicate the level of income resources needed by an individual or family to meet the basic needs for healthy living; those who fall below this level have insufficient income to provide the food, shelter, and clothing needed to preserve health. This standard is often used in determining an individual or family's eligibility for the government welfare program.

The Federalist Papers A series of editorials written by James Madison, Alexander Hamilton, and John Jay in 1788 to support the ratification of the Constitution in New York State. This collection is now regarded as a major source of information on what the Framers were thinking when they wrote the Constitution.

Federation (federal system) A system in which the authority of government is shared by both national and state governments. In its ideal form, a federal constitution gives the national government exclusive authority over some governmental tasks, while giving the states exclusive authority over other governmental matters; in some areas the two levels of government share authority.

Filibuster A prolonged debate in the Senate that is intended to kill a bill by preventing a vote on it.

First Concurrent Budget Resolution The recommendation for spending ceilings in major funding categories. It is submitted to the House and Senate by their respective budget committees and must be passed by April 15.

Fiscal policy The management of government expenditures and tax rates as a means for conducting national economic policy. Policymakers raise or lower government spending and taxes to execute fiscal policy.

527 committees Tax-exempt groups that can raise unlimited soft money to be used to mobilize targeted voters and for issue advocacy if there is no expressed support for or against a specific candidate. These 527 committees are not regulated by the Federal Election Commission.

Flexible response The military strategy adopted by the United States during the 1960s, which shifted emphasis from solely nuclear weapons power to increasing the U.S. ability to engage in limited, conventional wars in order to make deterrence more credible.

Food stamps Now called the Supplemental Nutrition Assistance Program, or SNAP, it is a program that begun in 1961 as an experiment and continues to be the primary source of food assistance for the poor.

Formula grants Grants given to states and localities on the basis of population, the number of eligible persons, per capita income, or other factors.

Framing effect The effect that the wording of a question or the way the question is asked may have on the response by an individual in a survey. That wording may influence the response of the person being interviewed.

Franking privilege The power of members of Congress to send out mail free of charge; this allows incumbents to cultivate a favorable image among their constituents.

Freedom of Information Act (FOIA) A public disclosure law that requires federal agencies to release information on written request.

Free riders Those who benefit from the actions of interest groups without spending time or money to aid those groups

Free trade An international economic policy that calls for the abolition of tariffs and other barriers so that goods and services may be exchanged freely among nations.

Front-loading The scheduling of primaries very early in the campaign season by states eager to have an early influence on the Republican and Democratic nomination process.

Full faith and credit The requirement, found in Article IV of the Constitution, that each state respect in all ways the acts, records, and judicial proceedings of the other states.

General jurisdiction The power of trial courts to hear cases on a broad range of issues, ordinarily including all civil cases involving nontrivial monetary value and all cases involving serious criminal matters.

General revenue sharing A small but innovative grant-in-aid program, used in the 1970s and 1980s, that had no significant conditions attached to it. State and local governments received funds according to a formula based on population and related factors.

General Schedule (GS) civil service system The merit-based system that covers most white-collar and technical positions in the federal government.

General service governments Local governments, such as counties, municipalities, and townships, that provide a wide range of public services to those who live within their borders.

Gerrymandering The practice by the party controlling the state legislature of drawing congressional and other district boundaries to maximize the number of seats it can win.

Glass ceiling A phrase used to denote the subtle barriers preventing women and minorities from attaining the upper-level jobs in organizations.

Globalization The idea that an increasing amount of human activity and social interrelations are being conducted on a global scale, rather than at the local, regional, or national levels that have been predominant for the past several centuries.

Government Those institutions and officials whose purpose it is to write and enact laws and to execute and enforce public policy.

Government corporations Public agencies that carry out specific economic or service functions (such as the Corporation for Public Broadcasting and the U.S. Postal Service) and are organized in the same way as private corporations.

Government-sponsored enterprises (GSEs) Federally initiated organizations designed to operate as if they were privately owned and operated, usually established for specific functions that serve targeted populations, such as helping to support inexpensive student loans. Many eventually are privatized.

Grant-in-aid programs Federal appropriations that are given to states and localities to fund state policies and programs. The Morrill Act (1862) was the first instance of such a program.

Grassroots pressure Lobbying by rank-and-file members of an interest group who use such tactics as letter writing and public protests to influence government.

Great Compromise The proposal offered by the Connecticut delegation to the Constitutional Convention in 1787. It called for the establishment of a bicameral congress, consisting of a house, in which states were represented according to their population size, and a senate, in which each state had an equal voice.

Homeland security Domestic programs intended to prevent and, when necessary, deal with the consequences of terrorist attacks on U.S. soil.

Home style The way in which incumbent members of Congress present themselves to their constituents in an attempt to win the voters' trust.

Ideologies Conceptually coherent beliefs used to help us think about whether government is doing what it should be doing.

Impeachment A formal charge of misconduct brought against a federal public official by the House of Representatives. If found guilty of the charge by the Senate, the official is removed from office.

Implied powers Those powers given to Congress by Article I, Section 8, clause 18, of the Constitution that are not specifically named but are provided for by the necessary and proper clause.

Impounding Withholding by a president of funds that have been appropriated by Congress. This tactic is used in place of a line-item veto.

Incremental model of decision making A more realistic model of decision making that sees public policy as a process of making decisions at the margins of current policies by adding to or subtracting from those policies.

Incumbent A candidate who holds a contested office at the time of an election.

Independent agencies More than two hundred agencies that exist outside the EOP and the cabinet departments. Reporting directly to the president, they perform a wide range of functions, from environmental protection (EPA) and managing social programs (SSA) to conducting the nation's space policy (NASA) and helping the president manage the federal government (GSA and OPM).

Industrial policy A comprehensive strategy for using government policies to restructure the nation's economy.

Infrastructure In government, those basic physical and organizational structures that support the operations of a system or program. The term is typically applied to utilities such as water supply, waste disposal (sewers), electrical grids, information technology systems, and telecommunications, as well as bridges, tunnels, and other public assets.

Initiative A policy measure placed on an election ballot by members of the electorate through a prescribed petition process.

Initiative and referendum A method of democratic decision making that places questions of public policy on the ballot for voters to consider directly. Initiatives are placed on the ballot by citizen petition, whereas a referendum is generated by the legislature.

Inspector general An official in a government agency who is assigned the task of investigating complaints or suspicious behavior.

Interest group Any organized group of individuals who share common goals and who seek to influence government decision making.

Intergovernmental lobby The many individuals and groups that have a special interest in the policies and programs implemented through the growing intergovernmental relations systems. These lobbyists represent private, consumer, and business groups.

Intergovernmental relations The style of federalism that recognizes the interdependence of Washington and state and local governments. The various levels of government share functions, and each level is able to influence the others.

Interstate commerce Trade across state lines, in contrast to intrastate (within state boundaries) trade and foreign trade.

Interstate compacts A formal agreement among two or more states allowed under Article I, Section 10, of the Constitution with the consent of Congress.

Isolationism A basic tenet of American policy that advocated American neutrality and avoidance of direct involvement in European affairs. Isolationism was effectively abandoned as a policy option after World War II, although it is still a factor in American attitudes toward world affairs.

Issue identification The first of six stages in policymaking, in which some event, person, or group calls attention to a problem that needs government action.

Joint committees Congressional committees that are usually permanent and consist of an equal number of members from each house.

Judicial activism The concept that the Court has both a right and an obligation to engage in judicial review; today it is usually justified as necessary for the defense of political minorities.

Judicial restraint Limited and infrequent use of judicial review. It is advocated on the grounds that unelected judges should not overrule laws passed by elected representatives

Judicial review The power assumed by the courts in *Marbury v. Madison* to declare acts of Congress to be in conflict with the Constitution. This power makes the courts part of the system of checks and balances.

Judicial review (2) The power of the courts to declare acts of Congress to be in conflict with the Constitution.

Keynesians Followers of economist John Maynard Keynes. They advocate government spending when the economy is sluggish (even if a deficit results) in order to revive the economy.

Legislative veto A device in a bill that allowed Congress or a congressional committee to veto the actions of an executive agency or the president in an area covered by the bill. It was declared unconstitutional by the Supreme Court in 1983.

Libel The use of print or pictures to harm someone's reputation; it is punishable by criminal law and subject to civil suits for damages.

Liberalism A set of ideological beliefs that usually favor government intervention in the economy but oppose government interference in the private lives of individuals.

Libertarianism The ideological belief that government should do no more than what is minimally necessary in the areas of both economic affairs and personal freedom.

Limited jurisdiction The power of certain trial courts that are allowed to hear only a narrowly defined class of cases.

Line-item veto The power to veto portions of a bill but sign the rest of it. The president was given this power in 1997, but the act giving him this power was ruled unconstitutional.

Legitimacy The belief of citizens in a government's right to pass and enforce laws.

Lobbying The act of trying to influence government decision makers; it is named after the public rooms in which it first took place.

Lobbyist An individual who works for a specific interest group or who serves as the spokesperson for a specific set of interests.

Marshall Plan The popular name given to the European Recovery Program, which was initiated after World War II by the United States to help rebuild war-torn Europe. Announced by then–Secretary of State George C. Marshall in 1947, it covered the period of 1948–1952 and is regarded as the basis for today's European Union as well as a model for foreign assistance programs.

Massive resistance A practice in which some state and local governments routinely either ignored court-ordered desegregation or complied so slightly that they had to be dragged through each step. Many public officials believed that if they held off long enough, the rest of America would come to believe that desegregation would not work and would give up on the idea.

Massive retaliation The military strategy favored by the United States during the 1950s, which involved warning the Soviet Union and its allies that any military confrontation could produce an annihilating nuclear attack on Moscow and other Soviet cities.

Matching grants Programs in which the national government requires recipient governments to provide a certain percentage of the funds needed to implement the programs.

Majoritarian view of power The view that political power should be distributed as equally as possible in a political system to facilitate meaningful majority rule.

Majority leader The second-ranking party position in the House (and the first in the Senate). The majority leader schedules floor action on bills and guides the party's legislative program through the House.

Majority-minority districts Congressional districts that create a political majority for a racial or ethnic minority.

Mandatory spending Government expenditures, including both entitlement programs and long-term spending obligations, that are not subject to the annual government appropriations process.

Mayflower Compact A document, composed by the Pilgrims, that set forth major principles for the Plymouth Colony's government.

Medicaid A federal program formally established in 1965 that provides health care coverage for families and individuals with low incomes and minimal resources.

Medicaid (2) A program established in 1965 as part of the Social Security system that provides health care assistance to the poor.

Medicare Health care coverage for the elderly originally passed in 1965 as an amendment to Social Security. Originally, it included mandatory coverage for hospitalization and nursing care (Part A) and voluntary coverage for physician and outpatient services. The program has since been expanded to offer greater flexibility (Part C) as well as prescription drug coverage (Part D).

Merit system A system that stresses the ability, education, and job performance of government employees rather than their political backgrounds.

Minority leader The head of the minority party in the Senate. This term also refers to the leader of the minority party in the House, who represents its interests by consulting with the Speaker and the majority leader on the scheduling of bills and rules for floor action.

Monetarists A group of economists who reject the argument that constant government intervention in the economy can bring either sustained prosperity or stability.

Monetary policy The manipulation of the money supply to control the economy. The Federal Reserve System, or the "Fed," is the principle mechanism for making monetary policy.

Myths Those stories, proverbial sayings, pervasive attitudes, and other narratives that we use to help us think about the world around us.

National debt The total amount of money the government owes as a result of spending more than it has taken in.

National security policies The actions taken by government to safeguard the physical, economic, and social institutions that are deemed critical to our survival as a country.

National supremacy The principle—stated in Article VI, the "supremacy clause"—that makes the Constitution and those laws and treaties passed under it the "supreme Law of the Land."

Nation-centered federalism The view that the authority of the national government goes beyond the responsibilities listed in Article I, Section 8, of the Constitution; it is based on the necessary and proper clause and the principle of national supremacy.

Necessary and proper clause The eighteenth clause of Article I, Section 8, of the Constitution, which establishes "implied powers" for Congress that go beyond those powers listed elsewhere in the Constitution.

Nonpartisan primary A primary in which candidates are listed on a ballot with no party identification.

Office of Management and Budget (OMB) An EOP agency that acts as the president's principal link to most federal agencies. The agency supervises matters relating to program and budget requests.

Ombudsman office A special office created to hear citizen complaints concerning the agency's programs.

Open primary A primary election in which any qualified voter may participate, regardless of party affiliation. The voter chooses one party ballot at the polling place.

Open race An election in which there is no incumbent in the race.

Opinion direction One's position in favor of or against a particular issue. Much of the time there are various shades of support for an issue, with no clear and precise direction of public opinion.

Opinion intensity The strength of one's opinion about an issue.

Opinion saliency One's perception of the relevancy of an issue.

Opinion stability The degree to which public opinion on an issue changes over time.

Opportunity structure The political ladder of local, state, and national offices that results in greater prestige and power as one moves toward the presidency.

Originalism An approach to interpreting the Constitution that seeks to rely on the original understanding of its provisions by the Framers.

Original jurisdiction The authority to hear a case before any other court does.

Outsourcing Administrative reform policies that involve contracting with private or nonprofit firms to provide specific services on behalf of the government.

Partisan primary A primary in which candidates run for their own party's nomination.

Party-as-organization An entity with few members, primarily consisting of state and county chairpersons and local ward and precinct captains, who work for the party throughout the year, recruiting candidates and participating in fundraising activities.

Party-centered campaign A campaign in which the party coordinates activities, raises money, and develops strategies.

Party dealignment A period in which the public disassociates itself from both parties and splits its votes between them.

Party identification The tendency of citizens to think of themselves as Democrats, Republicans, or independents.

Party-in-government The individuals who have been elected or appointed to a governmental office under a party label. They play a major role in organizing government and in setting policy.

Party-in-the-electorate The coalition of everyone who identifies with a particular party and tends to vote for that party's candidates; these people may also contribute to and work on campaigns.

Party realignment A major shift by voters from one party to another that occurs when one party becomes dominant in the political system, controlling the presidency and Congress, and many state legislatures as well.

Party whips Members of Congress who support the party leaders in the House and Senate by communicating the party's positions to the membership and keeping the leaders informed of members' views.

Patronage The provision of jobs for party loyalists in return for their political support at election time.

Patronage (2) A system of filling government positions in which individuals receive positions through noncompetitive means. It is used as a means both to reward supporters and to bridge divisions within the country through access to positions of power.

Pendleton Act A law passed in 1883 that established the first merit-based personnel system for the federal government.

Penny press The term for the first generation of newspapers with mass popular appeal. The name comes from the New York *Sun*, which was sold for a penny a copy in the mid-1800s.

Platforms Statements of party goals and specific policy agendas that are taken seriously by the party's candidates but are not binding.

Plea bargain A process in which a person who is accused of a crime is allowed to say that he or she is guilty of a less serious crime in order to be given a less severe sentence.

Pluralist model of policymaking A theory that attributes policy outcomes to pressures exerted by different interest groups.

Pluralist view of power The view that political power should be dispersed among many elites who share a common acceptance of the rules of the game.

Pocket veto A decision by the president not to sign a bill during the last ten days of a congressional session, effectively killing the bill.

Police powers The powers of state governments over the regulation of behavior within their borders. These police powers were used to justify state jurisdiction over economic matters.

Policy adoption The fourth stage of policymaking, which is usually a fight to gain governmental support for a policy and demands much bargaining and compromise.

Policy evaluation The final stage in the policymaking process: looking at the government's actions and programs to see whether their goals have been achieved or to assess their effectiveness and efficiency.

Policy formulation The third stage of policymaking, in which policymakers and their staffs deliberate the pros and cons of different courses of action, a process that may take years to complete.

Policy implementation The carrying out of policy mandates through public programs and actions—the fifth stage in the policymaking process.

Policy subgovernments Alliances and relationships among specific agencies, interest groups, and relevant members of Congress that have been capable of effectively exercising authority in a narrowly defined policy area, such as transportation and farm price supports. Powerful alliances often form iron triangles, like the tobacco subgovernment; looser alliances involving a wide range of actors are called issue networks.

Political action committee (PAC) An independent organization that can be established by interest groups, officeholders, and political candidates for the sole purpose of contributing money to the campaigns of candidates who sympathize with its aims. PACs are the result of federal laws that prohibit most interest groups from donating money to federal political campaigns.

Political appointees Government officials who occupy the most strategically important positions in the federal government; most of them are appointed by the president.

Political consultant An individual, often trained in public relations, media, or polling techniques, who advises candidates on organizing their campaigns.

Political culture A set of values, beliefs, and traditions about politics and government that are shared by most members of society. Political culture in the United States includes faith in democracy, representative government, freedom of speech, and individual rights.

Political efficacy The perception of one's ability to have an impact on the political system.

Political ideology A pattern of complex political ideas presented in an understandable structure that inspires people to act to achieve certain goals.

Political participation Taking part in any of a broad range of activities, from involvement in learning about politics to engagement in efforts that directly affect the structure of government, the selection of government authorities, or the policies of government.

Political party In the United States, a coalition of people organized formally to recruit, nominate, and elect individuals to office and to use elected office to achieve shared political goals.

Political public opinion The collective preferences expressed by people on political issues, policies, institutions, and individuals.

Political socialization The process by which individuals acquire political values and knowledge about politics. It is strongly influenced by the people with whom an individual has come into contact with from early childhood through adulthood.

Politics Those activities aimed at influencing or controlling government for the purpose of formulating or guiding public policy.

Populism A set of ideological beliefs that favor government intervention in both economic and personal affairs.

Popular sovereignty The concept, first described by Jean-Jacques Rousseau around the time of the American Revolution, that the best form of government is one that reflects the general will of the people, which is the sum total of those interests that all citizens have in common.

Pork-barrel legislation Legislation that appropriates funds for local projects in an area that a member of Congress represents.

Power The capacity and ability to influence the behavior and choices of others through the use of politically relevant resources.

Precinct The bottom of the typical local party structure—a voting district, generally covering an area of several blocks.

Preferments The provision of services or contracts in return for political support. Party committee members use patronage and preferments to court voters and obtain campaign contributions.

Preferred freedoms test The principle that some freedoms—such as free speech—are so fundamental to a democracy that they merit special protection. The test was instituted by the Warren Court of the 1960s.

Primary An election in which party members select candidates to run for office under the party banner. (In some states, nonparty members and independents may participate).

Priming The capacity of the media to isolate particular issues, events, or themes in the news as the criteria for evaluating politicians.

Prior restraint The government's blocking of a publication before it can be made available to the public. The Supreme Court has repeatedly struck down laws that imposed prior restraint on publications.

Privatization Administrative reform policies involving either turning over a government enterprise to a private company or giving a nongovernmental firm a franchise or license to provide what was previously a government function.

Privileges and immunities A provision in Article IV of the Constitution requiring that the citizens of one state not be treated unreasonably by officials of another state.

Project grants Grants awarded to states and localities for a specific program or plan of action.

Proportional representation The electoral system used by many European nations, in which legislative seats are assigned to party candidates in proportion to the percentage of the vote that the party receives within a district.

Proxy administration The government's use of indirect means to deliver public goods and services, such as contracting, grants-in-aid, loan guarantees, and government-sponsored enterprises.

Pseudo-events Events, such as speeches, rallies, and personal appearances, that are staged by politicians simply to win maximum media coverage.

Public goods Also known as *collective goods*, these are goods or services that cannot be provided through normal marketplaces (e.g., national defense) or have been politically determined to be too important to be provided by the private sector (e.g., public education).

Public interest groups Citizen activist groups that try to represent what they deem to be the interests of the public at large.

Public policies The composite of decisions made and actions taken by government officials in response to problems identified and issues raised through the political system.

Public-sector interest groups A lobby that represents the interests of elected officials and other major governmental actors involved in the intergovernmental relations system. An example is the National Governors' Association.

Quasi-judicial functions Judicial functions performed by regulatory commissions. Agencies can hold hearings for companies or individuals accused of violating agency regulations. Commission decisions can be appealed to the federal courts.

Quasi-legislative functions Lawmaking functions performed by regulatory commissions as authorized by Congress.

Racial profiling A practice in which decisions about whether to enforce a law are based on the race or ethnicity of an individual rather than on any suspicious or illegal act.

Random probability sampling A method by which pollsters choose interviewees, based on the idea that the opinions of individuals selected by chance will be representative of the opinions of the population at large.

Rational model of decision making A model that assumes that the policymakers have a clear objective and all the information needed for a sound and reasoned decision, with the result being the selection of the policy alternative that offers the most efficient and effective way to achieve the desired goal.

Recall A form of initiative in many jurisdictions in which citizens petition to have a sitting elected public official leave office before her or his formal term is over. Technically, however, recalls are not votes on policies per se.

Referendum A policy measure placed on an election ballot so that voters can express their support for or opposition to a proposal made by or already passed by a legislative body.

Regulatory commissions Federal agencies led by presidentially appointed boards that make and enforce policies affecting various sectors of the U.S. economy. Formally independent of the White House to avoid presidential interference, these agencies employ large professional staffs to help them carry out their many functions.

Reinventing government The term given to administrative reform policies (also known as the National Performance Review) initiated by the Clinton administration based on the assumption that those working for government would be more competent and responsive if they were freed of bureaucratic and arbitrary constraints.

Representative democracy See Republic.

Republic A system in which people govern indirectly by electing certain individuals to make decisions on their behalf.

Republicanism A doctrine of government in which decisions are made by elected or appointed officials who are answerable to the people, not directly by the people themselves.

Reserved powers The powers that the Constitution provides for the states, although it does not list them specifically; they are sometimes called "residual powers." As stated in the Tenth Amendment, these include all powers not expressly given to the national government or denied to the states.

Retrospective voting When individuals base their votes on the candidates' or parties' past record of performance.

Riders Provisions, usually unrelated to the main purpose of the bill, that Congress attaches to a bill; in general, these are provisions that it knows the president opposes, but Congress is counting on the fact that the president wants the bill to pass.

Rule of law The principle that a standard of impartiality, fairness, and equality against which all governmental actions can be evaluated exists. More narrowly, this includes the concept that no individual stands above the law and that rulers, like those they rule, are answerable to the law.

Runoff primary An electoral contest between the top two vote getters in the primary that determines the party's candidate in a general election. Such primaries are held in the ten southern states in which a majority of the vote is needed to win the primary.

School vouchers Programs that provide state funds to parents who want to send their child to a private school rather than the assigned public school.

Search warrant A written grant of permission to conduct a search issued by a neutral magistrate to police authorities. Police must describe what they expect to find and must show probable cause.

Selective incorporation The Supreme Court's practice of making applicable to the states only those portions of the Bill of Rights that a majority of justices felt to be fundamental to a democratic society.

Select, or special, committees Temporary committees established by the House or Senate to study particular problems.

Separation of powers The division of the powers to make, execute, and judge the law among the three branches of American government: Congress, the presidency, and the courts. This principle was adopted by the Framers to prevent tyranny and factionalism in the government.

Senior Executive Service (SES) The highest category of senior-level federal employees, most of whom form a select group of career public administrators who specialize in agency management.

Seniority system The tradition that provides that the member of the majority party with the longest continuous service on a committee automatically becomes its chair.

Sexual harassment Unwelcome sexual advances, requests for sexual favors, or other verbal or physical conduct of a sexual nature by an employer or coworker.

Single-issue group An activist group that seeks to lobby Congress on a single issue or a narrow range of issues.

Single-member district, winner-take-all electoral system The system of election used in the United States in all national and state elections and in most local elections; officials are elected from districts that are served by only one legislator, and a candidate must win a plurality—the most votes.

Slander Injury by spoken word. Like libel, it is outside First Amendment protection and punishable by criminal law and civil suits.

Soft money Unrestricted contributions to political parties by individuals, corporations, and unions that can be spent on party-building activities such as voter registration drives and get-out-the-vote efforts. The problem is that loopholes in the law allow soft money also to be spent in support of party candidates so long as key words such as *elect*, *vote for*, or *vote against* do not appear in the ads.

Sovereignty The ultimate source of authority in any political system.

Speaker of the House The only House position created by the Constitution. The Speaker is chosen by a vote of the majority party and is the presiding officer of the House, the leader of its majority party, and second in line to succeed the president.

Special district governments Local governments that deal with one or two distinctive government functions, such as education, fire protection, public transportation, or sewage treatment.

Spoils system Taken from the phrase "to the victor go the spoils," a patronage system in which government jobs at all levels are given to members of the party that has won the top political office.

Standard operating procedures (SOPs) Regularized procedures used in public agencies to help the agencies conduct administrative business effectively and efficiently.

Standing committees Permanently established committees that consider proposed legislation in specified policy areas and decide whether to recommend its passage by the larger body.

State-centered federalism The view that the Constitution allowed the national government only limited powers and that the states could overrule national laws if they determined that those laws were in violation of the Constitution.

Straw polls Polls that rely on an unsystematic selection of respondents. The respondents in straw polls frequently are not representative of the public at large.

Superdelegates Individuals who automatically are designated delegates to the national party conventions because they are members of Congress or hold statewide offices or are prominent party leaders.

Super PACs Officially known as "independent-expenditure only committees," super PACs may raise unlimited contributions from corporations, unions, professional and business associations, and individuals for the purpose of making unlimited expenditures in favor of or against a candidate running for federal office. Like traditional PACs, a super PAC must report the names of all its donors to the Federal Election Commission. Unlike traditional PACs, super PACs are barred from making direct contributions to the campaigns of any political candidate.

Supplemental Security Income (SSI) A program created in 1972 to provide direct monthly benefits from the federal government to the aged, those with visual handicaps, and those with mental or physical disabilities, regardless of their level of assistance from other programs.

Supply-side economics An economic policy strategy popular during the Reagan administration that advocates increasing the production of goods by cutting taxes to help stimulate investment, lifting regulations in the marketplace, and eliminating other government restraints on private business incentives.

Supremacy clause A provision in Article VI declaring the Constitution to be the supreme law of the land, taking precedence over state laws.

Tariffs Taxes on goods brought into the country from abroad; they are often intended to protect growing industries from foreign competition.

Tax expenditures An indirect means for government to support some private-sector activity. Certain provisions of the U.S. tax code are really spending programs masquerading as tax breaks.

Tax incentives Tax breaks used to reward people for investing or spending in a way that promotes economic growth.

Textualism An approach to interpreting the Constitution that relies on a literal, "plain words" reading of the document.

Third World nations The designation given to those countries emerging from colonial rule during the Cold War era that fell outside the Western and Soviet alliances. Today they are more likely to be regarded as "developing" or "emerging" nations rather than "Third World" nations.

Treaty ratification The power of the U.S. Senate to approve or disapprove formal treaties negotiated by the president on behalf of the nation.

Trial courts Courts at the lowest level of the system. They possess original jurisdiction.

Unfunded mandates Required actions imposed on lower-level governments by federal (and state) governments that are not accompanied by money to pay for the activities being mandated.

Unicameral Refers to a legislature that has only one house.

Unilateralism The policy of taking action independently in foreign affairs, avoiding political or military alliances. As with isolationism, unilateralism was abandoned as a policy option after World War II, although it is still a factor in American attitudes toward world affairs.

Unitary executive theory The idea that the Constitution gives the president the authority to oversee and manage the work of federal agencies to ensure that their priorities and actions are consistent with the views of the White House regarding existing laws and policies.

Unitary system A form of government in which the ultimate authority rests with the national government, with whatever powers state or local governments have being given to them by the central government.

Veto The president's power to reject legislation passed by Congress. Vetoes can be overruled by a two-thirds vote of both chambers of Congress.

Wage systems Federal personnel systems covering more than a million federal workers who perform blue-collar and related jobs and are largely represented by unions or other associations with limited bargaining rights.

Wall of separation An interpretation of the establishment clause that requires a complete separation of government and religion.

Ward A city council district; in the party organization, this is the level below the citywide level.

Whistle-blowers Employees who risk their careers by reporting corruption or waste in their agencies to oversight officials.

White House Office An EOP agency that includes the president's key advisers and assistants, who help him with the daily requirements of the presidency.

Writ of certiorari An order by the Supreme Court that a lower court send up the record of a case.

Writ of habeas corpus A court order that protects people against arbitrary arrest and detention by requiring officials to bring the "body" (i.e., the person) before the court.

Yellow journalism A type of journalism that flourished in the late nineteenth century and whose popularity was based on sensationalized stories of scandal and corruption.

References

Chapter 1

1. See Jeffrey M. Jones, "Congress' Approval Rating Remains Near Historical Lows: Fourteen Percent Approve and 81% Disapprove," *Gallup Politics*, August 13, 2013, http://www.gallup.com/poll/163964/congress-approval-rating-remains-near-historical-lows.asp; Alyssa Brown, *Gallup Politics*, "U.S. Congress Approval Remains Dismal: Fifteen Percent of Americans Approve of Congress in July," July 17, 2013, http://www.gallup.com/poll/163550/congress-approval-remains-dismal.aspx; "Reelection Rates Over the Years," *Open Secrets.org/Center for Responsive Politics*, http://www.opensecrets.org/bigpicture/reelect.php.

2. In 2012, 91 percent were reelected. See Todd Phillips, "How Was 91 Percent of Congress Re-Elected Despite a 10 Percent Approval Rating?" *The Blog, Huffington Post: Politics*, November 13, 2012, http://www.huffingtonpost.com/todd-phillips/congress-election-results_b_2114947.html.

3. Mark Schorer, "The Necessity of Myth," *Daedalus* 88, no. 2 (1959): 360.

4. See Mary Midgley, *The Myths We Live By* (London: Routledge, 2003); see also Colin Grant, *Myths We Live By* (Ottawa: University of Ottawa Press, 1998).

5. Colbert used the term *truthiness* in a 2005 sketch; see http://www.colbertnation.com/the-colbert-report-videos/24039/october-17-2005/the-word—truthiness. The word went viral, eventually being selected as the "2006 Word of the Year" in the *Merriam-Webster Dictionary*; see http://www.merriam-webster.com/info/06words.htm.

6. See the work of L. S. Vygotsky, *Mind in Society: The Development of Higher Psychological Processes* (Cambridge, MA: Harvard University Press, 1978); see also Claude Lévi-Strauss, *Myth and Meaning* (New York: Schocken Books, 1979).

7. See the discussion in Peter Heehs, "Myth, History, and Theory," *History and Theory* 33, no. 1 (1994): 1–19.

8. For a general overview of the study of myths, see William G. Doty, *Mythography: The Study of Myths and Rituals*, 2nd ed. (Tuscaloosa: University of Alabama Press, 2000). Also see Joseph Campbell, *The Masks of Gods* (New York: Arkana, 1991).

9. Binyamin Appelbaum, "Employment Data May Be the Key to the President's Job," *New York Times*, June 1, 2011, A1, also found at http://www.nytimes.com/2011/06/02/business/economy/02jobs.html?partner=rss&emc=rss.

10. Robert S. Erikson and Christopher Wlezien, "The Objective and Subjective Economy and the Presidential Vote," *PS: Political Science & Politics* 45, no. 4 (2012): 620–624. In contrast, see Michael J. Berry and Kenneth N. Bickers, "Forecasting the 2012 Election with State- Level Economic Indicators: A Postmortem," *PS: Political Science & Politics* 46, no. 1 (2013): 46–47.

11. Arthur M. Schlesinger Jr., *The Cycles of American History* (Boston: Houghton Mifflin, 1986), p. 219.

12. See Stuart Bruchey, *The Roots of American Economic Growth, 1607–1861: An Essay in Social Causation* (New York: Harper Torchbooks, 1968); and Stuart Bruchey, *The Wealth of the Nation: An Economic History of the United States* (New York: Harper & Row, 1988); see also Frank Bourgin, *The Great Challenge: The Myth of Laissez-Faire in the Early Republic* (New York: George Braziller, 1989).

13. See Theda Skocpol, *Protecting Soldiers and Mothers: The Political Origins of Social Policy in the United States* (Cambridge, MA: Belknap Press, 1992); see also Michael B. Katz, *The Price of Citizenship: Redefining America's Welfare State* (New York: Metropolitan Books, 2001).

14. See Richard N. L. Andrews, *Managing the Environment, Managing Ourselves: A History of American Environmental Policy* (New Haven, CT: Yale University Press, 1999).

15. NBC/*Wall Street Journal* Poll, July 18–21, 2008, 13, http://s.wsj.net/public/resources/documents/WSJ_Poll_072308.pdf.

16. For an in-depth discussion of authority, see Richard Sennett, *Authority* (New York: Vintage Books, 1980).

17. Aristotle. *The Politics,* trans. Ernest Barker and R. F. Stalley. (Oxford: Oxford University Press, 2009).

18. For an extended analysis of power, see Dennis H. Wrong, *Power: Its Forms, Bases, and Uses* (New York: Harper & Row, 1979).

19. Stories about bureaucratic waste and inefficiency were so popular that they had their own weekly segment on nightly news broadcasts. For example, for decades *NBC Nightly News* had a regular feature called *The Fleecing of America* that often focused on government programs. While no longer a regular feature, NBC and other news channels often highlight stories of government waste, fraud and abuse.

20. See Geoffrey A. Hosking and George Schöpflin, eds., *Myths and Nationhood* (New York: Routledge, in association with the School of Slavonic and East European Studies, University of London, 1997); see also Richard Slotkin, *Regeneration Through Violence: The Mythology of the American Frontier, 1600–1860* (Norman: University of Oklahoma Press, 2000).

21. See Murray Edelman, *Politics as Symbolic Action: Mass Arousal and Quiescence* (Chicago: Markham, 1971); and Murray J. Edelman, *Constructing* the *Political Spectacle* (Chicago: University of Chicago Press, 1988).

22. Two popular examples of such stories are Clyde V. Prestowitz Jr., *Trading Places: How We Are Giving Our Future to Japan and How to Reclaim It* (New York: Basic Books, 1988); and Pat Choate, *Agents of Influence* (New York: Touchstone, 1990).

23. See Robert B. Reich, *The Work of Nations: Preparing Ourselves for 21st-Century Capitalism* (New York: Vintage Books, 1992).

24. According to H. Mark Roelofs, myths offer us a "nationally shared framework of political consciousness" by which we become aware of ourselves as "a people, as having an identity in history," and by which we are "prepared to recognize some governing regime . . . as legitimate." See H. Mark Roelofs, *Ideology and Myth in American Politics: A Critique of a National Political Mind* (Boston: Little, Brown, 1976), p. 4. Also see Christopher Flood, *Political Myth: A Theoretical Introduction* (New York: Routledge, 1996); and Andrew Delbanco, *The Real American Dream: A Meditation on Hope* (Cambridge, MA.: Harvard University Press, 1999).

25. Robert C. Tucker, *Political Culture and Leadership in Soviet Russia: From Lenin to Gorbachev* (New York: Norton, 1987), pp. 22–23.

26. James Oliver Robertson, *American Myth, American Reality* (New York: Hill and Wang, 1980), p. 17.

27. See Tucker, *Political Culture and Leadership in Soviet Russia.*

28. Murray Edelman, *The Symbolic Uses of Politics* (Urbana: University of Illinois Press, 1964), pp. 2–3.

29. See Walter Russell Mead, *Special Providence: American Foreign Policy and How It Changed the World* (New York: Knopf, 2001).

30. Christopher Lasch, *The True and Only Heaven: Progress and Its Critics* (New York: Norton, 1991), p. 93.

31. Quoted from Frances FitzGerald, *Fire in the Lake*, in Robertson, *American Myth, American Reality*, p. 5.

32. See Lawrence L. LeShan, *The Psychology of War: Comprehending Its*

Mystique and Its Madness, expanded ed. (New York: Helios Press, 2002) for a discussion of how people characterize their enemies in wartime.

33. Bob Woodward, *The Commanders* (New York: Simon & Schuster, 1991), pp. 306–307; see also James Kitfield, *Prodigal Soldiers: How the Generation of Officers Born of Vietnam Revolutionized the American Style of War* (Washington, DC: Brassey's, 1995).

34. Samuel L. Popkin, *The Reasoning Voter: Communication and Persuasion in Presidential Campaigns*, 2nd ed. (Chicago: University of Chicago Press, 1994).

35. For a classic introduction to legal reasoning, see Edward Hirsch Levi, *An Introduction to Legal Reasoning* (Chicago: University of Chicago Press, 1949).

36. On the relationship between myths and ideologies, see Flood, *Political Myth*; see also Roelofs, *Ideology and Myth in American Politics*, p. 4. On the concept of ideology, see David E. Apter, *Introduction to Political Analysis* (Cambridge, MA: Winthrop, 1977), chap. 8.

37. See Tucker, *Political Culture and Leadership in Soviet Russia*; see also Zbigniew Brzezinski and Samuel P. Huntington, *Political Power: USA/ USSR* (New York: Viking, 1964), pp. 45ff.

38. See Joel D. Aberbach, Robert D. Putnam, and Bert A. Rockman, *Bureaucrats and Politicians in 36 Western Democracies* (Cambridge, MA: Harvard University Press, 1981), chap. 5.

39. William S. Maddox and Stuart A. Lilie, *Beyond Liberal and Conservative: Reassessing the Political Spectrum* (Washington, DC: The Cato Institute, 1984).

40. E. J. Dionne Jr., *Why Americans Hate Politics* (New York: Simon & Schuster, 1991), p. 11.

41. Roelofs, *Ideology and Myth in American Politics*, pp. 4–5.

42. Daniel M. Shea and Alex Sproveri, "The Rise and Fall of Nasty Politics in America," *PS: Political Science and Politics* 45, no. 3 (2012): 416–421. See also Daniel M. Shea and Morris P. Fiorina,

Can We Talk? The Rise of Rude, Nasty, Stubborn Politics (New York: Pearson, 2013).

43. Morris P. Fiorina, Samuel J. Abrams, and Jeremy Pope, *Culture War? The Myth of a Polarized America*, 3rd ed. (Boston: Longman, 2011).

44. Alan Abramowitz, *The Polarized Public? Why Our Government Is So Dysfunctional* (Upper Saddle River, NJ: Pearson, 2013).

Chapter 2

1. See Christina Sterbenz, "New York City Used to Be a Terrifying Place," *Business Insider*, July 12, 2013, http://www.businessinsider.com/new-york-city-used-to-be-a-terrifying-place-photos-2013-7?op=1#ixzz2hGNyAZCl (accessed October 9, 2013).

2. Crime statistics for New York City can be accessed at http://ccrjustice .org/files/Floyd-Liability-Opinion-8-12-13.pdf.

3. *Floyd v. City of New York*, August 12, 2013, http://ccrjustice.org/files/Floyd-Liability-Opinion-8-12-13.pdf.

4. See Sanford Levinson, *Constitutional Faith* (Princeton, NJ: Princeton University Press, 1988), chap. 6. The three who refused to sign were George Mason and Edmund Randolph of Virginia and Elbridge Gerry of Massachusetts.

5. Shays led 1,000 ragtag insurgents against the arsenal, but the defeat of the uprising was made possible only after local merchants and bankers financed a defense of the weapons storehouse. The congress could not afford to do more than provide a few guards for the arsenal. See Gordon S. Wood, *The Creation of the American Republic, 1776–1787* (New York: Norton, 1972), p. 19.

6. A distinction should be made between those who were present at the Philadelphia convention—the "Framers"—and the better-known group whom Americans regard as the "founders." For a popular history of the founders, see Joseph J. Ellis, *Founding Brothers: The Revolutionary Generation* (New York: Alfred A. Knopf, 2000).

7. Martin Diamond, *The Founding of the Democratic Republic* (Itasca, IL: F. E. Peacock, 1981), p. 15. For an authoritative general overview of the convention, see Max Farrand, *The Framing of the Constitution of the United States* (New Haven, CT: Yale University Press, 1913). See also Robert G. Ferris and James H. Charleton, *The Signers of the Constitution* (Flagstaff, AZ: Interpretive Publications, 1986), pp. 35–36; and Catherine Drinker Bowen, *Miracle at Philadelphia: The Story of the Constitutional Convention, May to September 1787* (Boston: Atlantic–Little, Brown, 1966).

8. See Richard Brookhiser, *Founding Father: Rediscovering George Washington* (New York: Free Press, 1996).

9. See H. W. Brands, *The First American: The Life and Times of Benjamin Franklin* (New York: Doubleday, 2000).

10. "Speech in the Convention at the Conclusion of Its Deliberations," in *Benjamin Franklin: Writings*, ed. J. A. Leo Lemay (New York: Literary Classics of the United States, 1987), pp. 1139–1141. On Franklin's health, see Ferris and Charleton, *The Signers of the Constitution*, p. 35. For other supportive comments attributed to Franklin at the convention, see Farrand, *The Framing of the Constitution of the United States*, p. 194.

11. For an in-depth analysis of the roots of the Constitution, see Donald S. Lutz, *The Origins of American Constitutionalism* (Baton Rouge: Louisiana State University Press, 1988). Also see Jack P. Greene, *The Intellectual Heritage of the Constitutional Era: The Delegate's Library* (Philadelphia: The Library Company of Philadelphia, 1986).

12. For an excellent introduction to life and culture in the British colonies, see David Hackett Fischer, *Albion's Seed: Four British Folkways in America* (New York: Oxford University Press, 1989).

13. Lutz contends that this situation came about because, for most of the seventeenth century, the British were preoccupied with trying to settle their own constitutional problems. See Lutz, *The Origins of American Constitutionalism*, p. 63.

14. See Lawrence J. R. Herson, *The Politics of Ideas: Political Theory and American Public Policy* (Homewood, IL: Dorsey Press, 1984), pp. 28–29.

15. For example, see David Thomas Konig, "Constitutional Contexts: The Theory of History and the Process of Constitutional Change in Revolutionary America," in *Constitutionalism and American Culture: Writing the New Constitutional History*, ed. Sandra F. VanBurkleo, Kermit Hall, and Robert J. Kaczorowski (Lawrence: University Press of Kansas, 2002), pp. 3–28.

16. See Robert N. Bellah, *The Broken Covenant: American Civil Religion in Time of Trial*, 2nd ed. (Chicago: University of Chicago Press, 1992). Also see Isaac Kramnick and R. Laurence Moore, *The Godless Constitution: The Case Against Religious Correctness* (New York: Norton, 1997).

17. See Daniel Walker Howe, "Why the Scottish Enlightenment Was Useful to the Framers of the American Constitution," *Comparative Studies in Society and History* 31, no. 3 (1989): 572–587.

18. Vincent Ostrom, "The American Contribution to a Theory of Constitutional Choice," *Journal of Politics* 38, no. 3 (1976): 56–78. See also Walter Berns, "The New Pursuit of Happiness," *The Public Interest*, no. 86 (1987): 65–76.

19. See Greene, *The Intellectual Heritage of the Constitutional Era*, chap. 2. Also see Joshua Foa Dienstag, "Between History and Nature: Social Contract Theory in Locke and the Founders," *Journal of Politics* 58, no. 4 (1996): 985–1009.

20. In fact, of all the philosophers and authors cited by those who debated the Constitution, Montesquieu was mentioned most often. See Greene, *The Intellectual Heritage of the Constitutional Era*, pp. 43–44; see also Lutz, *The Origins of American Constitutionalism*, pp. 139–147.

21. See Diamond, *The Founding of the Democratic Republic*, pp. 3–6. For a controversial interpretation of the Declaration of Independence, see Garry Wills, *Inventing America: Jefferson's Declaration of Independence* (New York: Vintage Books, 1978).

22. For an interesting analysis of the Constitution based on a perspective that gives special standing to the constitutional mechanisms that support the legitimacy of "We the People," see Bruce A. Ackerman, *We the People*, vol. 1, *Foundations* (Cambridge, MA: Belknap/Harvard University Press, 1991). Also see Beard, *The Republic: Conversations on Fundamentals* (New York: Viking Compass Books, 1943), chap. 1.

23. See Preston King, *Federalism and Federation* (Baltimore, MD: Johns Hopkins University Press, 1982). Also see Ronald L. Watts, "Federalism, Federal Political Systems, and Federations," *Annual Review of Political Science* 1, no. 1 (1998): 117–137.

24. On the election of 1800 and its consequences, see Edward J. Larson, *A Magnificent Catastrophe: The Tumultuous Election of 1800, America's First Presidential Campaign* (New York: Free Press, 2007); see also Susan Dunn, *Jefferson's Second Revolution: The Election Crisis of 1800 and the Triumph of Republicanism* (Boston: Houghton Mifflin, 2004).

25. See Paul Schumaker and Burdett A. Loomis, eds., *Choosing a President: The Electoral College and Beyond* (New York: Chatham House, 2002).

26. McCulloch v. Maryland, 17 U.S. 316 (1819), 81.

27. The controversy over a national bank has a long history. For more details, see Bray Hammond, "The Bank Cases," in *Quarrels That Have Shaped the Constitution*, ed. John Arthur Garraty (New York: Perennial Library, 1987), pp 37–55. See also William Greider, *Secrets of the Temple: How the Federal Reserve Runs the Country* (New York: Simon & Schuster, 1987), chaps. 8–9.

28. James Madison, "Federalist No. 39," in *The Federalist*, ed. Jacob E. Cooke (Middletown, CT: Wesleyan University Press, 1961), p. 256.

29. The privilege was suspended most recently in the then territory of Hawaii, when it was placed under martial law immediately after the bombing of Pearl Harbor. The state of martial law lasted nearly three years and was eventually lifted and later declared unconstitutional. See Harry N. Scheiber and Jane L. Scheiber, "Bayonets in Paradise: A Half-Century Retrospect on Martial Law in Hawaii, 1941–1946," *University of Hawaii Law Review* 19 (1997): 477–648.

30. See Michael Allen Gillespie and Michael Lienesch, eds., *Ratifying the Constitution* (Lawrence: University Press of Kansas, 1989).

31. For a history of the amending process, see Richard B. Bernstein and Jerome Agel, *Amending America: If We Love the Constitution So Much, Why Do We Keep Trying to Change It?* (New York: New York Times Books, 1993).

32. See Stephen M. Griffin, *American Constitutionalism: From Theory to Politics* (Princeton, NJ: Princeton University Press, 1996).

33. Daniel N. Hoffman, *Our Elusive Constitution: Silences, Paradoxes, Priorities* (Albany: State University of New York Press, 1997).

34. From the transcript of Hamilton's remarks at the New York state convention convened to ratify the Constitution; found in Jonathan Elliot, editor, *The Debates in the Several State Conventions, on the Adoption of the Federal Constitution*, 2nd edition, Volume 2 (Washington, DC: Jonathan Elliot, 1836), p. 344.

35. See Keith E. Whittington, *Constitutional Construction: Divided Powers and Constitutional Meaning* (Cambridge, MA: Harvard University Press, 1999); and Keith E. Whittington, *Constitutional Interpretation: Textual Meaning, Original Intent, and Judicial Review* (Lawrence: University Press of Kansas, 1999).

36. This quote is taken from a transcription of remarks at a conference. See Pew Forum on Religion and Public Life, *A Call for Reckoning: Religion and the Death Penalty (January 25)—Session Three: Religion, Politics, and the Death Penalty*, E. J. Dionne Jr., Moderator, University of Chicago, 2002, http://features.pewforum.org/death-penalty/resources/transcript3.html (accessed July 10, 2002).

37. Political scientist Robert A. Dahl, for example, contends that the American Constitution is behind the times when compared with the constitutions of other advanced industrialized nations. When it comes to "protection of fundamental rights, fair representation," and the reliance on democratic consensus in making key policy decisions, Dahl believes the United States compares rather unfavorably to the world's other major democracies (p. 116). He places a good deal of the blame for this on the flaws in the American constitutional system, which he believes can be traced to institutional features that have not changed over the decades. See Robert A. Dahl, *How Democratic Is the American Constitution?* (New Haven, CT: Yale University Press, 2001).

38. Bruce A. Ackerman, *We the People*, vol. 2, *Transformations* (Cambridge, MA: Belknap Press of Harvard University Press, 1998).

39. Kermit L. Hall, *The Magic Mirror: Law in American History* (New York: Oxford University Press, 1989), p. 6; also see Cass R. Sunstein, *The Partial Constitution* (Cambridge, MA: Harvard University Press, 1993).

40. Sunstein, *The Partial Constitution*, pp. 32–37.

41. See "Federalist No. 10," in *The Federalist*, ed. Cooke, p. 61.

42. "Federalist No. 10," in *The Federalist*, ed. Cooke, pp. 57–58.

43. "Federalist No. 39," in *The Federalist*, ed. Cooke, p. 251.

44. Madison, "Federalist No. 51," in *The Federalist*, ed. Cooke, p. 3224.

45. Jack N. Rakove, *The Beginnings of National Politics: An Interpretive History of the Continental Congress* (Baltimore, MD: Johns Hopkins University Press, 1979), pp. 394–395.

46. Fortas would later resign his associate justice position after questions were raised about his personal finances that reflected badly on his role as a justice.

47. During the Cold War, several sitting members of Congress retained their high-ranking positions in the military reserve forces—a seeming violation of the prohibition against holding positions in more than one branch of the national government because the military is part of the executive branch.

48. See "Federalist No. 44," in *The Federalist*, ed. Cooke, p. 306.

49. Samuel P. Huntington, *American Politics: The Promise of Disharmony* (Cambridge, MA: Belknap/Harvard University Press, 1981), p. 30.

50. Levinson, *Constitutional Faith*, p. 4.

Chapter 2 Policy Connection

1. An informative and readable political biography of Bismarck was written by Henry A. Kissinger—an individual who (as national security advisor and secretary of state under Richard Nixon) demonstrated considerable skill in the "art of the possible"; see "The White Revolutionary: Reflections on Bismarck," *Daedalus* 97, no. 3 (1968): 888–924. On the history of the modern welfare state, see Peter Flora and Arnold J. Heidenheimer, eds., *The Development of Welfare States in Europe and America* (New Brunswick, NJ: Transaction Books, 1981).

2. See Randy Shilts, *And the Band Played On: Politics, People, and the AIDS Epidemic* (New York: Penguin Books, 1988).

3. Marion Nestle and Michael F. Jacobson, "Halting the Obesity Epidemic: A Public Health Policy Approach," *Public Health Reports* 115 (January/February, 2000): 12–24.

4. On the 1988 reforms, see Julie Rovner, "Welfare Reform: The Issue That Bubbled Up from the States to Capitol Hill," *Governing* 2, no. 2 (December 1988): 17–21. See background information on the passage of the 1996 act at http://www.ssa.gov/history/tally1996.html.

5. For the story of Dodd-Frank, see Robert G. Kaiser, *Act of Congress: How America's Essential Institution Works, and How It Doesn't* (New York: Alfred A. Knopf, 2013).

6. Jeffrey H. Birnbaum and Alan S. Murray, *Showdown at Gucci Gulch: Lawmakers, Lobbyists, and the Unlikely Triumph of Tax Reform* (New York: Vintage, 1987).

7. Paul C. Light, *Forging Legislation* (New York: Norton, 1992).
8. See Stephen Skowronek, *The Politics Presidents Make: Leadership from John Adams to George Bush* (Cambridge, MA: Belknap/Harvard, 1997).
9. The Court's decision-making process remains one of the mysteries of Washington. Whatever insights we have into the process come from the recollections of law clerks and others who served the justices. One popular effort to understand what takes place inside the Court is found in Bob Woodward and Scott Armstrong, *The Brethren: Inside the Supreme Court* (New York: Simon & Schuster, 1979).
10. See John W. Kingdon, *Agendas, Alternatives, and Public Policies*, 2nd ed. (New York: Longman, 1995).
11. The classic statement of this model is found in Anthony Downs, *An Economic Theory of Democracy* (New York: Harper and Row, 1957).
12. Perhaps the most famous critic of the rational choice model was Herbert Simon, a political scientist who was awarded the Nobel Prize in Economics in 1978 for his work, which focused on the "limited rationality" of human decision making. For a clearly written overview of his approach, see Herbert A. Simon, *Reason in Human Affairs* (Stanford, CA: Stanford University Press, 1983).
13. The classic statement of this model is found in Charles E. Lindblom, "The Science of 'Muddling Through,'" *Public Administration Review* 19, no. 2 (1959): 79–88.
14. Jacob E. Cooke, "The Compromise of 1790," *William & Mary Quarterly, Third Series* 27, no. 4 (1970): 523–545.
15. A leading advocate of this view is James S. Fishkin; see his *Democracy and Deliberation: New Directions for Democratic Reform* (New Haven, CT: Yale University Press, 1991).
16. See C. Wright Mills, *The Power Elite* (New York: Oxford University Press, 1956), for a classic expression of this model.
17. Robert A. Dahl, *Pluralist Democracy in the United States: Conflict and Consent* (Chicago: Rand McNally, 1967).
18. See Paul A. Sabatier, ed., *Theories of the Policy Process*, 2nd ed. (Boulder, CO: Westview Press, 2007).

Chapter 3

1. In recent years, North Korea and Iran have been of most concern in terms of the proliferation of nuclear weapons. As for meltdowns, the two major (Level 7, highest danger) events took place at the Soviet Union's Chernobyl Nuclear Plant in 1986 and in 2011, when the Fukushima Daiichi plant went into meltdown after a tsunami struck Japan's coastline. A less dangerous (Level 5) event took place in the United States at Three Mile Island in Pennsylvania in 1979. On the different levels of nuclear accidents, see http://en.wikipedia.org/wiki/International_Nuclear_Event_Scale.
2. For a general overview of the radioactive waste disposal problem, see http://www.epa.gov/rpdweb00/docs/radwaste/.
3. The government formally withdrew from the Yucca site in March 2010; see http://energy.gov/sites/prod/files/edg/media/DOE_Motion_to_Withdraw.pdf.
4. See Matthew Wald, "Nuclear Waste Solution Seen in Desert Salt Beds," *New York Times*, February 10, 2014, A9, also found at http://www.nytimes.com/2014/02/10/science/earth/nuclear-waste-solution-seen-in-desert-salt-beds.html?_r=0.
5. *New York v. United States*, 505 U.S. 144, at 175 (1992).
6. For a general overview of the conflicting theories of federalism, see Richard H. Leach, *American Federalism* (New York: Norton, 1970), chap.1. See also William H. Riker, *Federalism: Origin, Operation, Significance* (Boston: Little, Brown, 1964).
7. This view had its most direct expression in the Virginia and Kentucky resolutions of 1798. Written by Jefferson and Madison, the resolutions called for the "nullification" of the unpopular Alien and Sedition Acts—laws that had led to the conviction of several newspaper editors critical of American foreign policy decisions. The resolutions circulated among the states, but the election of Jefferson as president in 1800 seemed to end the controversy, because the new president was a leading advocate of this view.
8. The quote is from Justice Barbour's decision in *Miln v. New York* (1837); quoted in W. Brooke Graves, *American Intergovernmental Relations: Their Origin, Historical Development, and Current Status* (New York: Charles Scribner's Sons, 1964), pp. 319–320.
9. Charles Sumner of Massachusetts was severely beaten on the floor of the U.S. Senate by Representative Preston Brooks, a member of the House from South Carolina, who took exception to remarks made by the senator. Sumner did not return to the Senate chamber for three years and never really recovered from the attack. Brooks resigned from the House but was reelected by his constituents, who regarded him as a hero.
10. The quote is from the Supreme Court's 1871 decision in the *Table* case, quoted in Deil S. Wright, *Understanding Intergovernmental Relations*, 3rd ed. (Pacific Grove, CA: Brooks/Cole, 1988), p. 41. For a more general discussion, see Graves, *American Intergovernmental Relations*, pp. 321–324.
11. *Hammer v. Dagenhart* (1918).
12. McDonald, pp. 24–25.
13. The federal government had provided special funding for canals and similar projects earlier in the century, and the states had received parts of a national budget surplus into the 1830s. However, the first formal grant-in-aid program was the Morrill Act. See Graves, *American Intergovernmental Relations*, chap. 14.
14. See David B. Walker, *The Rebirth of Federalism: Slouching Toward Washington* (Chatham, NJ: Chatham House, 1995), pp. 82–83.
15. U.S. Bureau of the Census, *Historical Statistics of the United States, Colonial Times to 1970* (Washington, DC: U.S. Government Printing Office, 1975), Table Y638, p. 1125.

16. Walker, *The Rebirth of Federalism*, chap. 4; see also Wright, *Understanding Intergovernmental Relations*, pp. 71–72.

17. Roscoe C. Martin, *The Cities and the Federal System* (New York: Atherton Press, 1965), chaps. 4 and 5.

18. See Kenneth T. Palmer, "The Evolution of Grant Policies," in *The Changing Politics of Federal Grants*, ed. Lawrence D. Brown, James W. Fossett, and Kenneth T. Palmer (Washington, DC: The Brookings Institution, 1984).

19. For a general overview of how the national government used this strategy, see Advisory Commission on Intergovernmental Relations (ACIR), *Regulatory Federalism: Policy, Process, Impact and Reform: A Commission Report* (Washington, DC: ACIR, 1984).

20. For the story of how these cuts were accomplished, see David A. Stockman, *The Triumph of Politics: How the Reagan Revolution Failed* (New York: Harper & Row, 1986).

21. See George E. Peterson, "Federalism and the States: An Experiment in Decentralization," in *The Reagan Experiment: An Examination of Economic and Social Policies Under the Reagan Administration*, ed. John L. Palmer and Isabel V. Sawhill (Washington, DC: Urban Institute Press, 1982), p. 228.

22. Historical and up-to-date figures on federal grants to states and localities are included in the annual federal budget submitted by the president. This can be found at http://w3.access.gpo.gov/usbudget/.

23. Thomas R. Swartz and John E. Peck, "The Changing Face of Fiscal Federalism," *Challenge* (November/December 1990): 41–46.

24. The National Conference of State Legislatures maintains a "mandate monitor" at http://www.ncsl.org/ncsl-in-dc/standing-committees/budgets-and-revenue/mandate-monitor-overview.aspx.

25. Updated information on the Congressional Budget Office's tracking of unfunded mandates is found at http://www.cbo.gov/publication/44032.

26. Clinton was prominently featured in one book that addressed the strengths of state governments in the 1980s; see David Osborne, *Laboratories of Democracy* (Boston: Harvard Business School Press, 1988).

27. Ruben Barrales, "Federalism in the Bush Administration," *Spectrum: Journal of State Government* (Summer 2001): 5–6.

28. For background on this approach, see E. J. Dionne and John J. DiIulio, eds., *What's God Got to Do with the American Experiment?* (Washington, DC: Brookings Institution Press, 2000). Also see J. John DiIulio Jr., "Getting Faith-Based Programs Right," *Public Interest*, no. 155 (2004): 75–88; and John J. DiIulio, *Godly Republic: A Centrist Civic Blueprint for America's Faith-Based Future* (Berkeley: University of California Press, 2007). For a critical assessment of the Bush administration's efforts by an "insider," see J. David Kuo, *Tempting Faith: An Inside Story of Political Seduction* (New York: Free Press, 2006).

29. See the White House's "The Quiet Revolution: The President's Faith-Based and Community Initiative: A Seven-Year Progress Report," at http://www.whitehouse.gov/government/fbci/reports.html (accessed April 7, 2008). On the Obama administration's efforts, visit http://www.whitehouse.gov/administration/eop/ofbnp.

30. For a ten-year retrospective view of how the War on Terror impacted federalism, see Matthew C. Waxman, "National Security Federalism in the Age of Terror," *Stanford Law Review* 64, no. 2 (2012): 289–350.

31. Ultimately the Supreme Court struck down most of the major provisions of the Arizona law. See Christopher N. Lasch, "Preempting Immigration Detainer Enforcement Under *Arizona v. United States*." *Wake Forest Journal of Law and Policy* 3 (2013): 281–331.

32. Justice Thomas in *Federal Maritime Commission v. South Carolina State Ports Authority*, 122 U.S. 743 (2002), at 751; also see Justice Antonin Scalia's majority decision in *Blatchford v. Native Village of Noatak*, 501 U.S. 775 (1991), at 779.

33. On the ARRA, see Christopher Boone, Arindrajit Dube, and Ethan Kaplan, "The Political Economy of Discretionary Spending: Evidence from the American Recovery and Reinvestment Act." *Brookings Economic Studies* (2014).

34. On the aftermath of the 2010 election, see Shama Gamkhar and J. Mitchell Pickerill, "The State of American Federalism 2010–2011: The Economy, Healthcare Reform and Midterm Elections Shape the Intergovernmental Agenda," *Publius: The Journal of Federalism* 41, no. 3 (2011): 361–394. On the legal strategies behind the Tea Party movement (many of which were focused on federalism issues), see Barak Orbach, Kathleen Callahan, and Lisa Lindemenn, "Arming States' Rights: Federalism, Private Lawmakers, and the Battering Ram Strategy," *Arizona Law Review* 52 (2010): 1161–1206. On developments after the 2012 election, see Cynthia J. Bowling and J. Mitchell Pickerill, "Fragmented Federalism: The State of American Federalism 2012–13." *Publius: The Journal of Federalism* 43, no. 3 (2013): 315–46.

35. In *Baker v. Carr* (1962), for instance, the Court forced the states to reapportion their legislative seats to guarantee equal representation for all their citizens. In *Roe v. Wade* (1973), the Court limited the authority states have to regulate abortion (see Chapter 4). Finally, in *Garcia v. San Antonio Metropolitan Transit Authority* (1985), the Court held that federal wage and hour laws should apply to state and local governments.

36. David E. Satterfield III, representative from Richmond, Virginia, quoted in Rochelle L. Stanfield, "Federal Aid—Taking the Good with the Bad," *National Journal* (July 8, 1978): 1076. For more on the central role of Congress in shaping federalism and intergovernmental relations, see Morris P. Fiorina, *Congress: Keystone of the Washington Establishment* (New Haven, CT: Yale University Press, 1977).

37. See David B. Walker, "The Advent of an Ambiguous Federalism and the Emergence of New Federalism, III," *Public Administration Review* 56, no. 3 (1996): 271.

38. For an overview of Clinton's efforts in this regard, see R. Kent Weaver, *Ending Welfare as We Know It.* (Washington, D.C.: Brookings Institution Press, 2000).

39. Timothy J. Conlan and Paul L. Posner, "Inflection Point? Federalism and the Obama Administration," *Publius: The Journal of Federalism* 41, no. 3 (2011): 443.

40. See Advisory Commission on Intergovernmental Relations (ACIR), *State Laws Governing Local Government Structure and Administration* (Washington, DC: ACIR, 1993).

41. Ann O'M. Bowman and Richard C. Kearney, *The Resurgence of the States* (Englewood Cliffs, NJ: Prentice-Hall, 1986), p. 136.

42. P. Gillette Clayton, "Fiscal Federalism, Political Will, and Strategic Use of Municipal Bankruptcy," *The University of Chicago Law Review* 79, no. 1 (2012): 281–330.

43. See Osborne, *Laboratories of Democracy*; see also Bowman and Kearney, *The Resurgence of the States*, pp. 25–27. Each year, *Governing* magazine publishes numerous state and local "government success stories" that rarely make headlines elsewhere. Visit http://governing.com/.

44. Luther Gulick, quoted in Terry Sanford, *Storm over the States* (New York: McGraw-Hill, 1967), p. 21.

45. See John D. Donahue, *Disunited States* (New York: Basic Books, 1997) for a critical perspective; in contrast, see Bowman and Kearney, *The Resurgence of the States*.

46. See Richard L. Cole and John Kincaid, "Public Opinion and American Federalism: Perspectives on Taxes, Spending and Trust," *Spectrum: Journal of State Government* (Summer 2001): 14–18.

47. For an interesting perspective on how Americans have viewed their local governments, see Anwar Hussain Syed, *The Political Theory of American Local Government* (New York: Random House, 1966).

48. The U.S. Census Bureau conducts its Census of Government every five years. For the latest figures, visit http://www.census.gov/govs. For an overview of the 2012 census, see http://www2.census.gov/govs/cog/g12_org.pdf.

49. On the work of the Southern Poverty Law Center, see http://www.splcenter.org/; for more on the work of disability rights organizations, see http://www.ndrn.org/index.php; and for updates on efforts to deal with prison-related issues, see http://www.prisonlaw.com/events.php.

50. On the history and growth of public-sector interest groups, see Donald H. Haider, *When Governments Come to Washington: Governors, Mayors, and Intergovernmental Lobbying* (New York: Free Press, 1974). See also Alan Ehrenhalt, "As Interest in Its Agenda Wanes, a Shrinking Urban Bloc in Congress Plays Defense," *Governing* 2, no. 10 (July 1989): 21–25; and Jonathan Walters, "Lobbying for the Good Old Days," *Governing* 4, no. 9 (June 1991): 32–37.

51. Parris Glendening, "Pragmatic Federalism and State-Federal Partnerships," *Spectrum: Journal of State Government* (Summer 2001): 7–8.

Chapter 3 Policy Connection

1. For up-to-date data on poverty in the United States as well as informative policy "briefs," visit the U.S. Census Bureau site at http://www.census.gov/hhes/www/poverty/data/.

2. See Edward S. Corwin, "The Passing of Dual Federalism," *Virginia Law Review* 36 (1950): 1–24.

3. For a collection of documents relevant to federalism and education policy, see http://www.archives.nysed.gov/edpolicy/research/res_digitized.shtml. An historical overview is provided at the U.S. Department of Education website: http://www2.ed.gov/about/overview/fed/role.html.

4. You can access a copy of the Northwest Ordinance at www.yale.edu/lawweb/avalon/nworder.htm.

5. On the work of the Office of Civil Rights, see http://www2.ed.gov/about/offices/list/ocr/know.html.

6. For an overview of the NDEA, see Arthur S. Flemming, "The Philosophy and Objectives of the National Defense Education Act," *Annals of the American Academy of Political and Social Science* 327, no. 1 (1960): 132–138.

7. "Duncan Pushes Back on Attacks on Common Core Standards," press release, U.S. Department of Education, June 25, 2013, http://www.ed.gov/news/speeches/duncan-pushes-back-attacks-common-core-standards.

8. See Diane Ravitch, *Reign of Error: The Hoax of the Privatization Movement and the Danger to America's Public Schools* (New York: Alfred A. Knopf, 2013). Also see her *The Death and Life of the Great American School System: How Testing and Choice Are Undermining Education* (New York: Basic Books, 2010).

9. See Theda Skocpol, *Protecting Soldiers and Mothers: The Political Origins of Social Policy in the United States* (Cambridge, MA: Belknap/Harvard, 1992). See also Sidney Fine, *Laissez Faire and the General Welfare State: A Study in Conflict in American Thought, 1865–1901* (Ann Arbor, MI: Ann Arbor Paperbacks, 1969), pp. 22–23, 360–361; Clarke A. Chambers, *Seedtime of Reform: American Social Service and Social Action, 1918–1933* (Ann Arbor, MI: Ann Arbor Paperbacks, 1963); and Robert Morris, *Social Policy of the American Welfare State: An Introduction to Policy Analysis*, 2nd ed. (New York: Longman, 1985).

10. For a general discussion of contemporary social welfare policy, see Theodore R. Marmor, Jerry L. Mashaw, and Philip L. Harvey, *America's Misunderstood Welfare State: Persistent Myths, Enduring Realities* (New York: Basic Books, 1990).

11. For an overview of the "old" welfare system, see Thomas E. Patterson, *America's Struggle Against Poverty, 1900–1980* (Cambridge, MA: Harvard University Press, 1981); and U.S. House of Representatives, Committee on Ways and Means, *Overview of*

Entitlement Programs: 1994 Green Book (Washington, DC: U.S. Government Printing Office, July 15, 1994).
12. See Charles Murray, *Losing Ground: American Social Policy* (New York: Basic Books, 1984). See also Nathan Glazer, *The Limits of Social Policy* (Cambridge, MA: Harvard University Press, 1988). For a counterargument, refer to John E. Schwarz, *America's Hidden Success: A Reassessment of Twenty Years of Public Policy* (New York: Norton, 1983). See also William Julius Wilson, *The Truly Disadvantaged: The Inner City, the Underclass, and Public Policy* (Chicago: University of Chicago Press, 1987).
13. The Urban Institute has been tracking this reform from its passage. See its informative website at http://www.urban.org/welfare/tanf.cfm.
14. For monthly figures on SNAP, see http://www.fns.usda.gov/pd/34snapmonthly.htm.
15. For a critical assessment of the 1996 reforms, see Sandra Morgen, Joan Acker, and Jill Weigt, *Stretched Thin: Poor Families, Welfare Work, and Welfare Reform* (Ithaca, NY: Cornell University Press, 2013).
16. For an overview of Medicaid, see the Kaiser Family Foundation website at http://kff.org/medicaid/fact-sheet/the-medicaid-program-at-a-glance-update/.

Chapter 4

1. Letter from John Adams to Abigail Adams, July 7, 1775 [electronic edition], *Adams Family Papers: An Electronic Archive*, Massachusetts Historical Society, http://www.masshist.org/digitaladams/.
2. *Barron v. Baltimore*, 32 U.S. (7 Pet.) 243 (1833).
3. See Justice Black's concurring opinion in *Adamson v. California*, 332 U.S. 67 (1947).
4. *Palko v. Connecticut*, 302 U.S. 319 (1937).
5. *Milk Wagon Drivers Union v. Meadowmoor Dairies*, 312 U.S. 287 (1941).
6. *Schenck v. United States*, 249 U.S. 47 (1919).
7. *Gitlow v. New York*, 268 U.S. 652 (1925).

8. *Texas v. Johnson*, 491 U.S. 397 (1989).
9. Janet Cawley, "Bush Calls Flag-Burning Dead Wrong," *Chicago Tribune*, June 23, 1989, p 5.
10. *United States v. Eichman*, 496 U.S. 310 (1990).
11. *Madsen v. Women's Health Center Inc.*, 512 U.S. 753 (1994).
12. *Hill v. Colorado*, 120 S. Ct. 2480 (2000).
13. *West Virginia State Board of Education v. Barnette*, 319 U.S. 624 (1943).
14. "The War over Free Speech, Harassment and Trolls Hits Another Social-Media Site," *Mother Jones*, August 27, 2013, www.motherjones.com/media/2013/elevatorgates-storify-troll.
15. "U.S. Court Says 'Liking' Something on Facebook Is Free Speech," *CNN*, September 19, 2013, www.cnn.com/2013/09/18/tech/social-media/facebook-likes.
16. *Near v. Minnesota*, 283 U.S. 697 (1931).
17. *New York Times v. United States*, 403 U.S. 713 (1971).
18. *New York Times v. Sullivan*, 376 U.S. 254 (1964).
19. *Roth v. United States*, 354 U.S. 476 (1957).
20. *Memoirs of a Woman of Pleasure v. Massachusetts*, 382 U.S. 975 (1966).
21. *Miller v. California*, 413 U.S. 15 (1973).
22. C. Herman Pritchett, *Constitutional Civil Liberties* (Englewood Cliffs, NJ: Prentice-Hall, 1984), pp. 132–133.
23. *Everson v. Board of Education*, 330 U.S. 1 (1947).
24. *Zelman v. Simmons-Harris*, 122 S. Ct. 2460 (2002).
25. *Engel v. Vitale*, 370 U.S. 421 (1962).
26. *School District of Abington Township v. Schempp*, 374 U.S. 203 (1963).
27. *Santa Fe Independent School District v. Doe*, 168 F. 3d 806 (2000).
28. *Marsh v. Chambers*, 463 U.S. 783 (1983).
29. 559 U.S. 700 (2010).
30. *Reynolds v. United States*, 98 U.S. 145 (1879).

31. *Braunfeld v. Brown*, 366 U.S. 599 (1961).
32. *Jacobson v. Massachusetts*, 197 U.S. 11 (1905).
33. *Wisconsin v. Yoder*, 406 U.S. 215 (1972).
34. *Employment Division, Dept. of Human Resources of Oregon v. Smith*, 494 U.S. 872 (1990).
35. *City of Boerne v. Flores*, 521 U.S. 507 (1997).
36. *U.S. v. Miller*, 307 U.S. 174 (1939). For a full discussion of the history of Second Amendment case law, see Robert Spitzer, *Saving the Constitution from Lawyers: How Legal Training and Law Reviews Distort Constitutional Meaning* (New York: Cambridge University Press, 2008), chap. 5.
37. "Gun-Control Advocates Losing Ground Despite Recent Rampages," *Washington Post*, September 22, 2013, A13.
38. *Powell v. Alabama*, 287 U.S. 45 (1932).
39. *Gideon v. Wainwright*, 372 U.S. 335 (1963).
40. *Argersinger v. Hamlin*, 407 U.S. 25 (1972).
41. *Escobedo v. Illinois*, 378 U.S. 478 (1964).
42. *Miranda v. Arizona*, 384 U.S. 436 (1966).
43. *Duckworth v. Eagan*, 492 U.S. 195 (1989).
44. *New York v. Quarles*, 467 U.S. 649 (1984).
45. *Arizona v. Fuliminante*, 111 S. Ct. 1246 (1991).
46. *Schneckloth v. Bustamonte*, 412 U.S. 218 (1973).
47. *Mapp v. Ohio*, 367 U.S. 643 (1961).
48. *Nix v. Williams*, 476 U.S. 431 (1984).
49. *United States v. Leon*, 468 U.S. 897 (1984).
50. *Robinson v. California*, 370 U.S. 660 (1962).
51. *Hammelin v. Michigan*, 111 S. Ct. 2680 (1991).
52. *Furman v. Georgia*, 408 U.S. 238 (1972).
53. *Ring v. Arizona*, 122 S. Ct. 2428 (2002).

54. Charles Warren and Louis Brandeis, "The Right of Privacy," *Harvard Law Review* 4 (1890): 193–221.

55. *Griswold v. Connecticut*, 381 U.S. 479 (1965).

56. *Roe v. Wade*, 410 U.S. 113 (1973).

57. *Webster v. Reproductive Health Services*, 492 U.S. 490 (1989).

58. *Planned Parenthood of Southeastern Pennsylvania v. Casey*, 505 U.S. 833 (1992).

59. 550 U.S. 124 (2007).

60. *Washington v. Glucksberg*, 117 S. Ct. 2258 (1997).

61. *Vacco v. Quill*, 521 U.S. 793 (1997).

Chapter 4 Policy Connection

1. Bob Woodward, *Bush at War* (New York: Simon & Schuster, 2002), p. 15.

2. See Joseph J. Romm, *Defining National Security: The Nonmilitary Aspects* (New York: Council on Foreign Relations Press), 1993.

3. James Chace and Caleb Carr, *America Invulnerable: The Quest for Absolute Security from 1812 to Star Wars* (New York: Summit Books, 1988), p. 12.

4. See Patrick J. Buchanan, *A Republic, Not an Empire: Reclaiming America's Destiny* (Washington, DC: Regnery Publishers, 1999).

5. Walter Russell Mead, *Special Providence: American Foreign Policy and How It Changed the World* (New York: Knopf, 2001), pp. 57–66.

6. These results are from an *Esquire–NBC News* poll conducted in August 2013. The results were posted in October at *The Politics Blog* of *Esquire*, http://www.esquire.com/blogs/politics/new-american-center-1113.

7. See Melvin J. Dubnick, "Postscripts for a "state of War": Public Administration and Civil Liberties After September 11." *Public Administration Review* 62, no. Special Issue (2002): 86–91.

8. Harold D. Lasswell, "The Garrison State," *American Journal of Sociology* 46, no. 4 (1941): 455–468.

9. For more on this episode, visit the Densho website, which is dedicated to preserving the testimonies of those incarcerated as a result of that order, found at http://www.densho.org/.

10. See William L. Waugh Jr., "Terrorism, Homeland Security and the National Emergency Management Network," *Public Organization Review* 3, no. 4 (2003): 373–385. In the case of the Boston Marathon, law enforcement ordered the population of entire towns to stay indoors while they conducted their search for the bombers.

11. See the entire Moynihan Commission report at http://www.fas.org/sgp/library/moynihan/index.html; also see Donald Patrick Moynihan, "The Culture of Secrecy," *Public Interest* 128 (1997): 55–72.

12. David Cole and James X. Dempsey, *Terrorism and the Constitution: Sacrificing Civil Liberties in the Name of National Security*, 3rd ed. (New York: New Press, 2006).

13. See David Cole, "The Three Leakers and What to Do About Them," *New York Review of Books*, February 6, 2014, http://www.nybooks.com/articles/archives/2014/feb/06/three-leakers-and-what-do-about-them/?insrc=toc.

14. Matt Apuzzo and Adam Goldman, *Enemies Within: Inside the NYPD's Secret Spying Unit and Bin Laden's Final Plot Against America* (New York: Touchstone Books, 2013).

Chapter 5

1. The details of the two cases have been constructed from various news reports. On the court hearing for Charles Barkley, see Mike Shurman, "Barkley Car Search Was Illegal, Judge Rules," *Philly.com*, September 17, 1988, http://articles.philly.com/1988-09-17/sports/26232748_1_atlantic-city-expressway-atlantic-county-superior-court-passenger-seat (accessed November 6, 2013). The Barneys incident in 2013 was covered by a number of media outlets; see Julia Marsh, "Barneys Busted Student for 'Shopping While Black,'" *New York Post*, October 22, 2013, http://www.nydailynews.com/new-york/barneys-accused-stealing-black-teen-article-1.1493101.

2. See Shaun L. Gabbidon, "Racial Profiling by Store Clerks and Security Personnel in Retail Establishments: An Exploration of 'Shopping While Black,'" *Journal of Contemporary Criminal Justice* 19, no. 3 (2003): 345–364. See also Donald Tomaskovic-Devey, Marcinda Mason, and Matthew Zingraff, "Looking for the Driving While Black Phenomena: Conceptualizing Racial Bias Processes and Their Associated Distributions," *Police Quarterly* 7, no. 1 (2004): 3–29.

3. President Obama made these remarks following the news of the acquittal in the trial of George Zimmerman for the shooting death of Trayvon Martin in Sanford, Florida. Transcripts of his remarks appear at http://www.whitehouse.gov/the-press-office/2013/07/19/remarks-president-trayvon-martin.

4. C. Vann Woodward, *The Strange Career of Jim Crow* (New York: Oxford University Press, 1966).

5. Eric Foner, *Reconstruction: America's Unfinished Revolution 1863–1877* (New York: Harper & Row, 1988): 255.

6. The Civil Rights Cases, 109 U.S. 3 (1883).

7. *Plessy v. Ferguson*, 163 U.S. 537 (1896).

8. Paul Oberst, "The Strange Career of *Plessy v. Ferguson*," *Arizona Law Review* 15 (1973): 389–418.

9. *Cumming v. Richmond County Board of Education*, 175 U.S. 528 (1899).

10. *Missouri ex rel. Gaines v. Canada*, 305 U.S. 337 (1938).

11. *Sweatt v. Painter*, 339 U.S. 629 (1950).

12. *Brown v. Board of Education of Topeka*, 347 U.S. 483 (1954).

13. *Brown v. Board of Education II*, 349 U.S. 294 (1955).

14. *Alexander v. Holmes County Board of Education*, 396 U.S. 19 (1969).

15. *Milliken v. Bradley*, 418 U.S. 717 (1974).

16. C. Herman Pritchett, *Constitutional Civil Liberties* (Englewood Cliffs, NJ: Prentice-Hall, 1984), 345.

17. For a full account of the incident and much more about Susan B. Anthony, see N. E. H. Hull, *The*

Woman Who Dared to Vote: The Trial of Susan B. Anthony (Lawrence: University of Kansas Press, 2012).

18. *Goesaert v. Cleary*, 335 U.S. 464 (1948).

19. *Craig v. Boren*, 429 U.S. 190 (1976).

20. *Kahn v. Shevin*, 416 U.S. 351 (1974).

21. *United States v. Virginia*, 518 U.S. 515 (1996).

22. Quoted in Susan Gluck Mezey, *In Pursuit of Equality: Women, Public Policy, and the Federal Courts* (New York: St. Martin's Press, 1991), p. 97.

23. *General Electric Co. v. Gilbert*, 429 U.S. 125 (1976).

24. Sheryl May Stolberg, "Obama Signs Equal-Pay Legislation," *New York Times*, www.nytimes.com/2009/01/03/us/politics/30/ledbetter-web.html?_r=0 (accessed October 22, 2013).

25. Jacqueline E. King, "Gender Equality in Higher Education," *On Campus with Women*, Association of American Colleges and Universities, www.aacu.org/ocww/volume35_3/feature.cfm?section=2 (accessed October 29, 2013).

26. *Williams v. Saxbe*, 413 F. Supp. 654 (D.D.C. 1976).

27. *Meritor Savings Bank v. Vinson*, 477 U.S. 57 (1986).

28. *Harris v. Forklift*, 570 U.S. 17 (1993).

29. U.S. Equal Appointment Opportunity Commission, "Sexual Harassment," www.eeoc.gov/laws/types/sexual_harassment.cfm (accessed October 15, 2013).

30. *Bowers v. Hardwick*, 478 U.S. 186 (1986).

31. *Romer v. Evans*, 517 U.S. 620 (1996).

32. *Lawrence v. Texas*, 539 U.S. 123 (2003).

33. *U.S. v. Windsor* 570 U.S. 12 (2013).

34. *Hollingsworth* v. *Perry* 570 U.S. ___(2013)

35. Nate Silver, "How Opinion on Same-Sex Marriage Is Changing, and What It Means," *New York Times*, March 26, 2013, fivethirtyeight.blogs.nytimes.com/2013/03/26/how-opinion-on-same-sex-marriage-is-changing-and-what-it-means/?_r=0 (accessed October 25, 2013).

36. Brian J. McCabe, "Public Opinion on Don't Ask, Don't Tell," *New York Times*, November 30, 2010, fivethirtyeight.blogs.nytimes.com/2010/11/30/public-opinion-on-dont-ask-dont-tell/ (accessed November 15, 2013).

37. *Plyler v. Doe*, 457 U.S. 202 (1982).

38. Julia Preston and John H. Cushman Jr., "Obama to Permit Young Migrants to Remain in U.S.," *New York Times*, www.nytimes.com/2012/06/16/us/us-to-stop-deporting-some-illegal-immigrants.html?pagewanted=all&_r=0 (accessed October 23, 2013).

39. *Regents of the University of California v. Bakke*, 438 U.S. 265 (1978).

40. *Gutter v. Bollinger*, 539 U.S. 306 (2003).

Chapter 5 Policy Connection

1. Mary L. Dudziak, *Cold War Civil: Race and the Image of American Democracy* (Princeton, NJ: Princeton University Press, 2000), p. 80.

2. Dudziak, *Cold War Civil*, p. 77.

3. Dudziak, *Cold War Civil*, pp. 249–250.

4. Hans J. Morgenthau, "The Mainsprings of American Foreign Policy: The National Interest vs. Moral Abstractions," *The American Political Science Review* 44, no. 4 (1950): 833–854.

5. Henry Kissinger, *Diplomacy* (New York: Simon & Schuster, 1994).

6. The full address is found at http://www.ourdocuments.gov/doc.php?doc=15&page=transcript.

7. See Walter Russell Mead, *Special Providence: American Foreign Policy and How It Changed the World* (New York: Knopf, 2001).

8. In 1997, film director Spike Lee released *4 Little Girls*, a documentary about the 1963 bombing; for more information, see http://www.imdb.com/title/tt0118540/. For a brief remembrance of the bombing, visit http://www.npr.org/templates/story/story.php?storyId=1431932.

9. Quoted in Elaine Sciolino, "New U.S. Peacekeeping Policy De-Emphasizes Role of the U.N.," *New York Times*, May 6, 1994, http://www.nytimes.com/1994/05/06/world/new-us-peacekeeping-policy-de-emphasizes-role-of-the-un.html. Four years later, Bill Clinton visited Rwanda and made clear his sense that the United States failed to live up to its own values and vision, and he offered a commitment more in tune with America's public values: "We did not act quickly enough after the killing began. We should not have allowed the refugee camps to become safe havens for the killers. We did not immediately call these crimes by their rightful name: genocide. We cannot change the past. But we can and must do everything in our power to help you build a future without fear, and full of hope." The full text of Clinton's 1998 remarks to survivors of the Rwanda genocide are found at http://www.cbsnews.com/news/text-of-clintons-rwanda-speech/.

Chapter 6

1. Gallup Poll News Service, November 1, 2005; Gallup Poll News Service, October 31, 2000.

2. Pew Research Center for the People & the Press, "As Health Care Law Proceeds, Opposition and Uncertainty Persist," September 16, 2013; Pew Research Center/USA Today Poll, September 4–8, 2013.

3. V. O. Key Jr., *Public Opinion and American Democracy* (New York: Knopf, 1961), p. 2.

4. Pew Research Center for the People & the Press, *Trends in Political Values and Core Attitudes: 1987–2007*, press release, March 22, 2007; Gallup Poll News Service, February 17, 2014.

5. Gallup Poll News Service, January 9, 2013.

6. M. Margaret Conway, *Political Participation in the United States*, 3rd ed. (Washington, DC: Congressional Quarterly Press, 1999), pp. 25–29; Bernard Hennessy, *Public Opinion*, 5th ed. (Monterey, CA: Brooks/Cole, 1985), p. 200.

7. *New York Times*, November 16, 2009, p. B7.
8. Huff Post Media, "2012 Convention Coverage: Drastic Change Coming to Networks' Plans," August 22, 2012.
9. Pew Research Center, Project for Excellence in Journalism, "The State of the News Media 2013," March 26, 2013.
10. See Daniel Elazar, *American Federalism: A View from the States*, 2nd ed. (New York: Crowell, 1972); and Robert S. Erikson, Gerald C. Wright, and John P. McIver, *Statehouse Democracy* (New York: Cambridge University Press, 1993), for two excellent discussions of political culture, subculture, and public opinion.
11. For a systematic and readable review of polling and the measurement of public opinion, see Herbert Asher, *Polling and the Public*, 8th ed. (Washington, DC: Congressional Quarterly Press, 2011).
12. National Election Study, Center for Political Studies, University of Michigan, Ann Arbor, 2000.
13. Richard Morin, "The Public May Not Know Much, but It Knows What It Doesn't Like," *Washington Post National Weekly Edition*, January 23–29, 1989, p. 37.
14. National Opinion Research Center of International Studies, Princeton University, Princeton, NJ, March 1960.
15. Pew Research Center for the People & the Press, "Views of Government: Key Data Points," March 9, 2013.
16. Adam Clymer, "U.S. Attitudes Altered Little by September 11," *New York Times*, May 20, 2002.
17. Pew Research Center for the People & the Press, "State Governments Viewed Favorably as Federal Rating Hits New Low," April 15, 2013. See also Joy Wilke, "Americans' Satisfaction with U.S. Gov't. Drops to New Low," Gallup Poll Report, October 10, 2013; NBC/*Wall Street Journal* poll, October 10, 2013.
18. Gallup Poll, May 27, 2013.
19. Gallup Poll, "Americans Losing Confidence in All Branches of U.S. Gov't," Justin McCarthy, June 30,

2014; www.gallup.com/poll/171992/americans-losing-confidence-branches-gov.
20. Gallup Poll News Service, July 4, 2013.
21. Gallup Poll News Service, July 12, 2013.
22. Council on Foreign Relations Report, Andrew Kohut and Michael Dimock, "Resilient American Values: Optimism in an Era of Growing Inequality and Economic Difficulty," May18, 2013.
23. Pew Research Center for the People & the Press, "The Gender Gap: Three Decades Old, As Wide as Ever," March 29, 2012.
24. Pew Research Center for the People & the Press, "Trends in Political Values and Core Attitudes: 1987–2009," May 11, 2009.
25. John H. Pryor, Kevin Eagan, Laura Palucki Blake, Sylvia Hurtado, Jennifer Berdan, and Matthew H. Case, *The American Freshman: National Norms for Fall 2012* (Los Angeles: The Cooperative Institutional Research Program at the Higher Education Research Institute at UCLA, December 2012).
26. Ibid., p. 32.
27. Gallup Poll News Service, July 25, 2013.
28. Gallup Poll News Service, July 24, 2013.
29. ABC/*Washington Post* poll, October 10, 2013.
30. Gallup Poll News Service, August 16, 2013.
31. *Newsweek* poll, as reported by MSNBC, September 10, 2005.
32. Darryl Fears, "After Zimmerman Verdict, a Racial Divide Lingers," *Washington Post*, July 27, 2013; Aaron Blake, "Majority of Americans Approve of Stand Your Ground Laws," *Washington Post*, August 2, 2013.
33. Pew Research Center for the People & the Press, "The Black and White of Public Opinion," October 31, 2005.
34. Gallup Poll News Service, February 8, 2013.
35. Ibid.
36. Mark Hugo Lopez and Paul Taylor, "Latino Voters in the 2012

Election," Pew Research Hispanic Trend Project, November 7, 2012, www.pewhispanic.org/2012/11/07/latino-voters-in-the-2012-election/.
37. Ruy Teixeira, "When Will Your State Become Majority-Minority? *ThinkProgress*, May 8, 2013. www.thinkprogress.org.
38. "Hispanics' 'Majority-Minority' Status Increases," *Financial Times*, June 13, 2013.
39. "Trends in American Values: 1987-2012,", Pew Research Center for the People & the Press, June 4, 2012, p.97, www.people-press.org.
40. See evangelicalsforsocialaction.org.
41. Patricia Zapor, "End of the 'Catholic Vote'? Other Categories May Predict Election Better," *Catholic News Service*, November 9, 2004.
42. Gallup Poll News Service, May 29, 2013.
43. See David C. Leege and Lyman A. Kellstadt, eds., *Rediscovering the Religious Factor in American Politics* (Armonk, NY: M. E. Sharpe, 1993); John Green, *The Faith Factor* (Washington, DC: Potomac Books, 2011).
44. The latter part of the definition of participation, given in quotes, comes from Conway, *Political Participation in the United States*, pp. 3–4.
45. Max J. Skidmore, *Ideologies: Politics in Action* (New York: Harcourt Brace Jovanovich, 1989), p. 7. (Italics added.)
46. Quote from Everett Carll Ladd, "Citizens Participation," *Public Perspective* (March/April 1994), p. 36, based on a study by Sidney Verba, Kay L. Schlozman, Henry R. Brady, and Norman H. Nie, "The Citizen Participation Project: Summary Findings," a project supported by the National Science Foundation and the Spencer, Ford, and Hewlett Foundations, with survey work done in 1990 by the National Opinion Research Center.
47. Pew Research Center, Internet & American Life Project, August 1, 2008.
48. Pew Research Center, Internet & American Life Project, "Civic Engagement in the Digital Age," April 25, 2013.

49. Sidney Verba and Norman H. Nie, *Participation in America: Political Democracy and Social Equality* (New York: Harper & Row, 1972), pp. 95–101.

50. Harold W. Stanley and Richard N. Niemi, *Vital Statistics in American Politics 2013–2014* (Thousand Oaks, CA: Sage, 2013), p. 173.

51. International IDEA Annual Tabulation (most recent data, 2008–2010).

52. Michael McDonald, United States Elections Project, 2012 General Election Turnout Rates, July 22, 2013.

53. Pryor et al., *The American Freshman*, p. 32.

54. Center for the American Woman and Politics (CAWP), Eagleton Institute of Politics, "Gender Differences in Voter Turnout," Figure 2, Rutgers University, New Brunswick, NJ, 2007, www.cawp.rutgers.edu.

55. Kelly Dittmar, "Women Candidates in U.S. House Primaries," Center for American Women and Politics, October 3, 2013.

56. U.S. Census Bureau, Current Population Survey, Release, May 8, 2013.

57. Stanley and Niemi, *Vital Statistics in American Politics 2013–2014*, Table 1-22, pp. 54–55.

58. "Black, Latino Obama Vote Provokes Emergence of 'Pernicious Narrative' Among Conservative Pundits: Report," *Huffpost News*, November 9, 2012.

59. "Asian American Access to Democracy in the 2004 Elections," Asian American Legal Defense and Education Fund, August 2005, p. 3.

Chapter 6 Policy Connection

1. A copy of the 2007 report can be accessed at http://www.ipcc.ch/publications_and_data/publications_ipcc_fourth_assessment_report_synthesis_report.htm; information on the UN Framework Convention on Climate Change is found at http://unfccc.int/essential_background/convention/items/6036.php.

2. Myron Ebell, then head of the Competitive Enterprise Institute,

interviewed by John Hockenberry for the PBS *Frontline* documentary *Climate of Doubt*, originally aired October 23, 2012; see the transcript at http://www.pbs.org/wgbh/pages/frontline/environment/climate-of-doubt/transcript-31/.

3. V. O. Key Jr., *Public Opinion and American Democracy* (New York: Alfred A. Knopf, 1961), p. 547.

4. For example, see Paul Burstein, "The Impact of Public Opinion on Public Policy: A Review and an Agenda," *Political Research Quarterly* 56, no. 1 (2003): 29–40; and Benjamin I. Page and Robert Y. Shapiro, *The Rational Public: Fifty Years of Trends in Americans' Policy Preferences* (Chicago: University of Chicago Press, 1992).

5. Leonard Greenburg, Morris B. Jacobs, Bernadette M. Drolette, Franklyn Field, and M. M. Braverman, "Report of an Air Pollution Incident in New York City, November 1953," *Public Health Reports (1896–1970)* 77, no. 1 (1962): 7–16.

6. See Matthew A. Crenson, *The Un-Politics of Air Pollution: A Study of Non-Decisionmaking in the Cities* (Baltimore, MD: Johns Hopkins University Press, 1971), pp. 1–3.

7. Rachel Carson, *Silent Spring* (Boston: Houghton Mifflin, 1962).

8. For a general overview, see Michael E. Kraft and Norman J. Vig, "Environmental Policy over Four Decades: Achievements and New Directions," in *Environmental Policy: New Directions for the Twenty-First Century*, ed. Norman J. Vig and Michael E. Kraft (Thousand Oaks, CA: Congressional Quarterly Press, 2013), pp. 2–19.

9. See Hiram Martin Chittenden, *The Yellowstone National Park, Historical and Descriptive*, new and enl. ed. (Cincinnati, OH: Stewart & Kidd, 1918), chap. X.

10. Stephen R. Fox, *The American Conservation Movement: John Muir and His Legacy* (Madison: University of Wisconsin Press, 1985).

11. See Char Miller, *Gifford Pinchot and the Making of Modern Environmentalism* (Washington, DC: Island Press/Shearwater Books, 2001).

12. The EPA itself was the result of a presidential executive order (see Chapters 12 and 13 issued by President Nixon under authority granted by Congress.

13. Anthony Downs, "Up and Down with Ecology—the 'Issue-Attention Cycle,'" *The Public Interest* 28 (1972): 64–76.

Chapter 7

1. Gallup Poll News Service, July 5, 2013.

2. Also known as "Washington's Farewell Address," the letter can be viewed and downloaded at http://www.gpo.gov/fdsys/pkg/GPO-CDOC-106sdoc21/pdf/GPO-CDOC-106sdoc21.pdf.

3. Adams's often-cited comment is found in a letter to a friend written in 1780 related to the emergence of parties during the period under the Articles of Confederation. See Francis Hopkinson, spondence with les of Confederation. See Charles Francis Adams, ed., *The Works of John Adams, Second President, of the United States*, vol. 9 (Boston: Little, Brown, 1854), p. 511. Jefferson's comment is from a letter written while he was U.S. ambassador to Paris; see "From Thomas Jefferson to Francis Hopkinson, 13 March 1789," Founders Online, National Archives, http://founders.archives.gov/documents/Jefferson/01-14-02-0402, ver. 2013-09-28. Source: Julian P. Boyd, ed., *The Papers of Thomas Jefferson, 8 October 1788 – 26 March 1789*, vol. 14 (Princeton, NJ: Princeton University Press, 1958), pp. 649–651.

4. Marc J. Hetherington and William J. Keefe, *Parties, Politics, and Public Policy in America*, 10th ed. (Washington, DC: Congressional Quarterly Press, 2007), p. 12.

5. Alan R. Gitelson, M. Margaret Conway, and Frank B. Feigert, *American Political Parties: Stability and Change* (Boston: Houghton Mifflin, 1984), p. 4; Marjorie Randon Hershey, *Party Politics in America*, 15th ed. (New York: Pearson Longman, 2013).

6. For a brief comparative overview of select party systems around the world, see Mark Kesselman, Joel Krieger, and William A. Joseph, eds., *Introduction to Comparative Politics*, 3rd ed. (Boston: Houghton Mifflin, 2004). See also Kay Lawson, *Cleavages, Parties, and Voters: Studies from Bulgaria, the Czech Republic, Hungary, Poland, and Romania* (Westport, CT: Greenwood, 1999); and Kay Lawson and Thomas Poguntke, *How Political Parties Respond: Interest Aggregation Revisited* (New York: Routledge, 2004).

7. Reference to this term can be found in Paul Allen Beck and Frank J. Sorauf, *Party Politics in America*, 7th ed. (Glenview, IL: HarperCollins, 1992); and Hershey, *Party Politics in America*.

8. Gallup Poll News Service, August 7–11, 2013.

9. Adam Clymer, "U.S. Attitudes Altered Little by September 11," *New York Times*, May 20, 2002.

10. Gallup Poll News Service, May 7, 2013.

11. Rasmussen Reports, October 14, 2013. See also Gallup Poll News Service, "Public's Rating of Parties," for a discussion of the historically low public opinion of political parties. See www.poll.gallup.com for public polling on the Iraq War. For a discussion on the decline of parties from the early 1950s to the mid-1990s, see Martin P. Wattenberg, *The Decline of American Political Parties: 1952–1996* (Cambridge, MA: Harvard University Press, 1998). For a discussion on the decline or resurgence of parties, see Jeffrey E. Cohen, Richard Fleisher, and Paul Kantor, eds., *American Political Parties: Decline or Resurgence?* (Washington, DC: Congressional Quarterly Press, 2001).

12. See Alan R. Gitelson and Patricia Bayer Richard, "Ticket-Splitting: Aggregate Measures v. Actual Ballots," *Western Political Quarterly* 36 (September 1983): 410–419; and Frank B. Feigert, "Illusions of Ticket-Splitting," *American Politics Quarterly* 7 (October 1979): 470–488.

13. Gitelson, Conway, and Feigert, *American Political Parties*, p. 131;

Greenberg Quinlan Rosner Research Poll, February 20–24, 2010, p. 23; Gallup Poll Trend Polls, 2004–2013, August 2013.

14. For one of the classic defenses of the role of parties, see E. E. Schattschneider, *Party Government* (New York: Rinehart, 1942). For an equally compelling argument in support of parties by a leading proponent of the view that parties are in decline, see Walter Dean Burnham, "The Changing Shape of the American Political Universe," in *Controversies in Voting Behavior*, ed. Richard G. Niemi and Herbert F. Weisberg (San Francisco, W. H. Freeman and Company, 1976, 451–483.

15. Allan D. Monroe, "American Party Platforms and Public Opinion," *American Journal of Political Science* 27 (February 1983): 27–42; Gerald M. Pomper, with Susan S. Lederman, *Elections in America: Control and Influences in Democratic Politics*, 2nd ed. (New York: Longman, 1980).

16. Pomper and Lederman, *Elections in America*, pp. 173–174.

17. John P. Frendreis and Alan R. Gitelson, "Local Political Parties in an Age of Change," *American Review of Politics* 14 (Winter 1993): 533–548; John Frendreis and Alan R. Gitelson, "Local Parties in the 1990s: Spokes in a Candidate-Centered Wheel," in *The State of the Parties*, 3rd ed., ed. John C. Green and Daniel M. Shea (Lanham, MD: Rowman & Littlefield, 1999), pp. 135–153.

18. W. Stanley and Richard G. Niemi, *Vital Statistics on American Politics 2013–2014* (Washington, DC: Congressional Quarterly Press, 2013), p. 210; see also www.opencongress.org/people/votes_with_party/house/republican and www.opencongress.org/people/votes_ with_party/house/democrat.

19. Woodrow Wilson, *Constitutional Government in the United States* (New York: Columbia University Press, 1961), pp. 206, 217.

20. For the most comprehensive discussion of the realignment process, see V. O. Key Jr., "A Theory of Critical Elections," *Journal of Politics* 17

(February 1955): 3–18; Walter Dean Burnham, *Critical Elections and the Mainspring of American Politics* (New York: Norton, 1970); and James L. Sundquist, *Dynamics of the Party System: Alignment and Realignment of Political Parties in the United States*, rev. ed. (Washington, DC: The Brookings Institution, 1983).

21. See, for example, Paul Allen Beck, "The Dealignment Era in America," in *Electoral Change in Advanced Industrial Democracies: Realignment or Dealignment?*, ed. Russell J. Dalton, Scott C. Flanagan, and Paul Allen Beck (Princeton, NJ: Princeton University Press, 1984), pp. 240–266. For a brief but succinct discussion of realignment and dealignment, see Paul R. Abramson, John H. Aldrich, and David W. Rohde, *Change and Continuity in the 2012 and 2014 Elections* (Washington, DC: Congressional Quarterly Press, 2015).

22. For a review of the several theories that we discuss in this section, see Hershey, *Party Politics in America*, pp. 31–35.

23. Two proponents of the institutionalist explanation for the two-party system are Schattschneider and Maurice Duverger; see Schattschneider, *Party Government*, and Duverger, *Political Parties* (New York: Wiley, 1954).

24. V. O. Key Jr., *Politics, Parties, and Pressure Groups*, 5th ed. (New York: Crowell, 1964); Louis Hartz, *The Liberal Tradition in America* (New York: Harcourt, Brace and World, 1955).

25. For a discussion of reform club activities in the United States and their impact on the electoral system, see Alan R. Gitelson, "Reform Clubs," in *Political Parties & Elections in the United States: An Encyclopedia*, vol. II, ed. L. Sandy Maisel (New York: Garland, 1991), pp. 926–931.

26. See John Frendreis, Alan R. Gitelson, Gregory Flemming, and Anne Layzell, "Local Political Parties and the 1992 Campaign for the State Legislature," paper presented at the annual meeting of the American Political Science Association, Washington, DC, September 2–5,

1993; and Frendreis and Gitelson, "Local Political Parties in an Age of Change."

27. Abby Livingston, "The 7 Most Dysfunctional State Parties," *Roll Call*, July 23, 2013.

28. See John F. Bibby and Brian F. Schaefner, *Politics, Parties, and Elections in America*, 6th ed. (Belmont, CA: Thomson/Wadsworth, 2008), pp. 286–290; and Ann O'M. Bowman and Richard C. Kearney, *State and Local Government* (Boston: Houghton Mifflin, 2005), pp. 111–121.

29. For comprehensive reviews of party reform during the past two decades, see Robert L. Dudley and Alan R. Gitelson, *American Elections: The Rules Matter* (New York: Longman, 2002), pp. 38–42; William Crotty, *Political Reform and the American Experiment* (New York: Crowell, 1977); and William Crotty, *Party Reform* (New York: Longman, 1983).

30. See Burnham, *Critical Elections and the Mainspring of American Politics*; William Crotty, *American Parties in Decline* (Boston: Little, Brown, 1984); and Wattenberg. Also see Walter Dean Burnham, "The Changing Shape of the American Political Universe," in *Controversies in American Voting Behavior*, ed. Richard G. Niemi and Herbert F. Weisberg (San Francisco: Freeman, 1976), pp. 451–483; and Burnham, *Critical Elections and the Mainspring of American Politics*.

31. See Gitelson, Conway, and Feigert, *American Political Parties*, chap. 15, for a discussion of the transformation of political parties. See also Hershey, *Party Politics in America*, chap. 16.

Chapter 7 Policy Connection

1. E. E. Schattschneider saw this development as a natural outcome of the limited capacity of the mass electorate to deal with the complex issues facing government. "The people are a sovereign whose vocabulary is limited to two words, 'Yes' and 'No,'" he argued. "This sovereign, moreover, can speak only when spoken to. As interlocutors of the people the parties frame the question and elicit the answers." See his *Party Government: American Government in Action*, Library of Liberal Thought (New Brunswick, NJ: Transaction, 2004), p. 52.

2. For an overview, see Gary Miller and Norman Schofield, "The Transformation of the Republican and Democratic Party Coalitions in the U.S.," *Perspectives on Politics* 6, no. 3 (2008): 433–450.

3. For more on the early history of economic policy in the United States, see Carl Bridenbaugh, *Cities in the Wilderness: The First Century of Urban Life in America, 1625–1742*, 2nd ed. (New York: Knopf, 1955); Gerald D. Nash, *State Government and Economic Development: A History of Administrative Policies in California, 1849–1933* (Berkeley: Institute of Governmental Studies/University of California, 1964), pp. 10–26; and Stuart Bruchey, *The Roots of American Economic Growth, 1607–1861: An Essay in Social Causation* (New York: Harper Torchbooks, 1968). For an interesting study of Jefferson's views, see Frank Bourgin, *The Great Challenge: The Myth of Laissez-Faire in the Early Republic* (New York: George Braziller, 1989), chaps. 7 and 8.

4. Arthur M. Okun, *The Political Economy of Prosperity* (New York: Norton, 1970); Herbert Stein, *The Fiscal Revolution in America* (Chicago: University of Chicago Press, 1969).

5. See Alan S. Blinder, *Economic Policy and the Great Stagflation*, student ed. (New York: Academic Press, 1981).

6. The idea of an emerging "new economy" is most often attributed to management theorist Peter F. Drucker. See his *The New Realities: In Government and Politics/In Economics and Business/In Society and World View* (New York: Harper & Row, 1989) and *Management Challenges for the 21st Century* (New York: HarperBusiness, 1999).

7. See Richard A. Posner, *A Failure of Capitalism: The Crisis of '08 and the Descent into Depression* (Cambridge, MA: Harvard University Press, 2009).

8. See I. M. Destler, *American Trade Politics: System Under Stress* (Washington, DC: Institute for International Economics, 1986).

9. See Jan Aart Scholte, "Global Capitalism and the State," *International Affairs* 73, no. 3 (1997): 427–452.

10. Especially controversial has been U.S. involvement in the World Trade Organization (WTO). Formed in 1995 as an international organization designed to establish and enforce the rules of world trade, the WTO is a major facilitator of globalization, along with the International Monetary Fund (IMF) and the World Bank. The policies of all three have been regarded by some U.S. groups as a threat to American jobs, the environment, and the interests of many of the world's poorer nations. The WTO in particular has drawn protests. Among the most violent were the protests held when the organization met in Seattle in 1999. For information on the World Trade Organization, visit its website at www.wto.org/wto/.

11. On tax incentives as public policy at the state level, see the website of the Economic Development Tax Incentives Project at http://www.pewstates.org/projects/economic-development-tax-incentives-project-329163. Also see the discussion of tax expenditures in Policy Connection 11.

12. On industrial policy, see Otis L. Graham Jr., *Losing Time: The Industrial Policy Debate* (Cambridge, MA: Harvard University Press, 1992).

13. For a short overview of supply-side economics, see James D. Gwartney, "Supply-Side Economics," in *The Concise Encyclopedia of Economics*, ed. David R. Henderson (Liberty Fund, 2008), available at the Library of Economics and Liberty, http://www.econlib.org/library/Enc/SupplySideEconomics.html (accessed December 2, 2013). See also Barry Bosworth, *Tax Incentives and Economic Growth* (Washington, DC: Brookings Institution, 1984), chap. 1.

14. The Ford Motor Company was the only one of the major U.S. automakers that did not have to be rescued by the federal government. When the financial markets collapsed, Ford happened to be in the midst of a major reorganization of its finances and found itself in a solid position at the very moment when financial markets froze. It was able to weather the recession without turning for help from Washington.

Chapter 8

1. Chris Cillizza, "Kentucky Senate Race Could Top $100 million," *Washington Post*, August 11, 2013.
2. Pew Center for the People & the Press, October 18, 2013, www.people-press.org/2013/10/18trust-in-government-interactive/; see also G. Calvin Markenzie and Judith M. Labiner, "Opportunity Lost: The Rise and Fall of Trust and Confidence after September 11," Center for Public Service, The Brookings Institution, May 30, 2002, p. 8.
3. "Survey of Young Americans' Attitudes Toward Politics and Public Service: 23r Edition," Institute of Politics, Harvard University, April 30, 2013, p.18.
4. V. O. Key, *The Responsible Electorate: Rationality in Presidential Voting, 1936–1960* (Cambridge, MA: Belknap Press of Harvard University Press, 1966), pp. 2–3.
5. Michael J. Malbin, "1994 Vote: The Money Story," in *America at the Polls 1994*, ed. Everett Carll Ladd (Storrs, CT: The Roper Center for Public Opinion Research, 1995), p. 128.
6. See Joseph A. Schlesinger, *Ambition and Politics: Political Careers in the United States* (Chicago: Rand McNally, 1966), pp. 16–20; Gordon Black, "A Theory of Political Ambition: Career Choices and the Role of Structural Incentives," *American Political Science Review* 66 (March 1972): 144–159. For an excellent study on political ambition that points out the limitations of Schlesinger's opportunity structure theory, see Linda L. Fowler and Robert D. McClure, *Political Ambition: Who Decides to Run for Congress* (New Haven, CT: Yale University Press, 1989).
7. National Association of Secretaries of State, Presidential Primaries Guide, January 20, 2012.

8. Federal Election Commission, news release, April 19, 2013.
9. For a concise discussion of the presidential nomination process, see William Crotty and John S. Jackson III, *The Politics of Presidential Selection*, 2nd ed. (New York: Longman, 2001).
10. Barbara Farah, "Delegate Polls: 1944–1984," *Public Opinion* (August/September 1984): 44.
11. George Thayer, *Who Shakes the Money Tree?* (New York: Simon & Schuster, 1973), p. 150.
12. Federal Election Commission data released electronically on April 19, 2013.
13. Reid Wilson, "TV Ad Spending on Presidential Race Surpasses Two-Thirds of a Billion," *National Review*, September 21, 2012.
14. Kantar Media, 2013, www.kantar.com; www.publicopinionline.com; "Under Review: Is Super Bowl Worth $4 Million?," *Advertising Age*, November 4, 2013.
15. Trevor Potter and Kirk L. Jowers, "Summary Analysis of Bipartisan Campaign Finance Reform Act Passed by House and Senate and Sent to President," *The Brookings Institution*, March 2002, www.Brookings.edu; *New York Times*, February 15, 2002, A18.
16. "New Study Finds That State Parties Are Soft Money Conduits," Campaign and Media Legal Center, press release, June 25, 2002.
17. Richard A. Oppell, quoting Charles Lewis, "State Parties Adept at Raising Soft Money, Report Shows," *New York Times*, June 26, 2002, A19.
18. www.opensecrets.org/527s.
19. *Morning Edition*, National Public Radio, January 21, 2010. See also Stephen R. Weissman, "Campaign Finance Ruling's Likely Impact Overblown," *Los Angeles Times*, January 28, 2010, http://articles.latimes.com/2010/jan/28/opinion/la-oe-weissman28-2010jan28; Dan Eggen, "Democrats Suggest Ways to Curb Companies' Campaign Spending," *Washington Post*, February 11, 2010, http://www.washingtonpost.com/wp-dyn/content/article/2010/02/11/AR2010021102678.html.

20. For a discussion of the impact of spending by challengers in congressional races, see Paul R. Abramson, John H. Aldrich, and David W. Rohde, *Change and Continuity in the 2012–2014 Elections* (Washington, DC: Congressional Quarterly Press, 2015).
21. Alan R. Gitelson, M. Margaret Conway, and Frank B. Feigert, *American Political Parties: Stability and Change* (Boston: Houghton Mifflin, 1984), p. 242; for a contemporary examination of polling, see Herbert Asher, *Polling and the Public: What Every Citizen Should Know*, 8th ed. (Washington, DC: Congressional Quarterly Press, 2011).
22. For a comprehensive study of campaign consultants, see James A. Thurber and Candice J. Nelson, *Campaign Warriors: Political Consultants in Elections* (Washington, DC: The Brookings Institution, 2000).
23. Elise Hu, "Presidential Debates Can Be Great Theater, but How Much Do They Matter?," *Morning Edition*, National Public Radio, September 16, 2012.
24. *Medialife Magazine*, July 10, 2012, "Political Spending on Cable Will Double." See also Todd Blair and Garrett Biggs, "Cable Advertising: An Underrated Medium for Local Elections," *Campaigns & Elections* (September 2005): 40–41.
25. Bruce Campbell, *The American Electorate: Attitudes and Action* (New York: Holt, Rinehart and Winston, 1979), pp. 12–13.
26. See Raymond E. Wolfinger and Steven J. Rosenstone, *Who Votes?* (New Haven, CT: Yale University Press, 1980).
27. Ibid., p. 18.
28. Abramson, Aldrich, and Rohde, *Change and Continuity in the 2012–2014 Elections*, chap. 6.
29. For the most comprehensive discussion of retrospective voting, see Morris P. Fiorina, *Retrospective Voting in American National Elections* (New Haven, CT: Yale University Press, 1999).
30. For a discussion on the Electoral College and alternative plans for

electing the president, see Robert L. Dudley and Alan R. Gitelson, *American Elections: The Rules Matter* (New York: Longman, 2002), chap. 6.

31. See Gerald M. Pomper, with Susan S. Lederman, *Elections in America: Control and Influence in Democratic Politics*, 2nd ed. (New York: Longman, 1980).

32. See data from a project by Terry Royed and Steven Borrelli, Party Pledges and Policy Change in the UK and US, 1970s–1990s, funded by National Science Foundation grant #SBR-9730785.

Chapter 8 Policy Connection

1. A useful source of historical data on ballot measures is the Initiative and Referendum Institute, http://www.iandrinstitute.org/.

2. See Frank M. Bryan, *Real Democracy: The New England Town Meeting and How It Works* (Chicago: University of Chicago Press, 2004).

3. In some states and localities, the legislature body can decide that a proposal is controversial enough to warrant being sent to the voters for their approval or disapproval. At other times, the state constitution or city charter requires that some types of legislation, such as tax increases that exceed a certain amount or large (capital) expenditures—for example, providing financial support for building a new sports arena—be placed on the ballot. Others allow for the submission of a certain number of voter signatures on petitions in order to have a recently passed law be put up for a vote at the next election or in some special election.

4. Two years later, another draft of the constitution—developed by a special assembly convened for that purpose—passed a popular vote. That document remains the basic law of the commonwealth of Massachusetts and lays claim to being both the model for the U.S. Constitution and the world's oldest functioning written constitution. For a brief historical overview of the Massachusetts constitution, see "John Adams and the Massachusetts Constitution," http://www.mass.gov/courts/court-info/sjc/edu-res-center/jn-adams/mass-constitution-1-gen.html.

5. Delaware doesn't require voter approval.

6. For an overview and positive assessment of initiatives, see John G. Matsusaka, *For the Many or the Few: The Initiative, Public Policy, and American Democracy* (Chicago: University of Chicago Press, 2004). Many referenda are actually popularly initiated and fall under his analysis.

7. For an overview of Proposition 13 and its consequences, see Jack Citrin and Isaac William Martin, *After the Tax Revolt: California's Proposition 13 Turns 30* (Berkeley, CA: Berkeley Public Policy Press, 2009).

8. This is an example of history repeating itself, for in 1913 the Anti-Saloon League lost several popular votes and decided to invest its resources into winning the state houses in order to accomplish its goals through legislative bodies. See Daniel Okrent, *Last Call: The Rise and Fall of Prohibition* (New York: Scribner, 2010), p. 60.

9. Jeffrey M. Jones, "Americans in Favor of National Referenda on Key Issues," *Gallup Politics*, July 10, 2013, http://www.gallup.com/poll/163433/americans-favor-national-referenda-key-issues.aspx.

10. For a widely cited critique, see David S. Broder, *Direct Democracy: The Politics of Initiative, Referendum, and Recall* (New York: Harcourt, 2000).

Chapter 9

1. Franco Ordonez, McClatchy Washington Bureau, "Immigration Debate Attracts Wide Swath of Lobbyists," May 13, 2013, www.mcclatchydc.com; Jill Replogle, "Lobbying Dollars Fly in Immigration Reform Debate," *KPBS Public Broadcasting* (San Diego, CA), March 12, 2013.

2. Anupama Narayanswamy, "Immigration: Give Me Your Poor, Your Tired, . . . Your Lobbyists?," *Sunlight Foundation*, March 21, 2013, http://reporting.sunlightfoundation.com/2013/immigration/.

3. For up-to-date information on lobbying on a variety of issues, visit the Lobbying Database at http://www.opensecrets.org/lobby/. Data for immigration lobbying in 2013 is found at http://www.opensecrets.org/lobby/issuesum.php?id=IMM&year=2013.

4. Eric Lipton, "Some Countries Lobby for More in Race for Visas," *New York Times*, May 11, 2013.

5. http://www.opensecrets.org/lobby/.

6. Gallup Poll News Service,"Seven in 10 Americans Say Lobbyists Have Too Much Power,", April 11, 2011, and "Record 64% Rate Honesty, Ethics of Congress Low," December 12, 2011.

7. See Jeffrey M. Berry and Clyde Wilcox, *The Interest Group Society*, 5th ed. (New York: Longman, 2009); Kay Lehman Schlozman and John T. Tierney, *Organized Interests and American Democracy* (New York: Harper & Row, 1986); and Allan J. Cigler and Burdett A. Loomis, *Interest Group Politics*, 8th ed. (Washington, DC: Congressional Quarterly Press, 2011).

8. Alan R. Gitelson, M. Margaret Conway, and Frank B. Feigert, *American Political Parties: Stability and Change* (Boston: Houghton Mifflin, 1984), pp. 333–335.

9. Schlozman and Tierney, *Organized Interests and American Democracy*, p. 50.

10. For a discussion of public interest groups, see Berry and Wilcox, *The Interest Group Society*; and Jeffrey M. Berry, *Lobbying for the People* (Princeton, NJ: Princeton University Press, 1977). For an excellent study of the conflicts and contradictions in the practices of advocacy organizations as they fight for social and economic justice, see Dara Z. Strolovitch, *Affirmative Advocacy: Race, Class, and Gender in Interest Group Politics* (Chicago: University of Chicago Press, 2007).

11. These categories are drawn, in part, from Schlozman and Tierney's excellent study on interest-group politics, *Organized Interests and American Democracy*, pp. 45–49.

12. Ibid., pp. 45–46.

13. Berry and Wilcox, *The Interest Group Society*, pp. 139–161.
14. Federal Election Commission, www.fec.gov.
15. *Citizens United v. Federal Election Commission* (2010) and *Speechnow.org v. FEC* (2010).
16. See Mancur Olson, *The Logic of Collective Action* (Cambridge, MA: Harvard University Press, 1965).
17. Ibid. See also E. E. Schattschneider, *The Semisovereign People* (New York: Holt, Rinehart and Winston, 1960).
18. Schlozman and Tierney, *Organized Interests and American Democracy*, pp. 103–106.
19. Ibid., p. 106.
20. Berry and Wilcox, *The Interest Group Society*, pp. 40–42.
21. Schlozman and Tierney, *Organized Interests and American Democracy*, pp. 150–151.
22. *Current American Government: Fall 1991 Guide* (Washington, DC: Congressional Quarterly Press, 1991), p. 150.
23. Ronald Hrebenar, *Interest Group Politics in America*, 3rd ed. (Armonk, NY: M. E. Sharpe, 1997), pp. 279–281. See also David M. Herszenhorn, "Congressional Crackdown on Lobbying Is Already Showing Cracks," *New York Times*, January 3, 2008, www.nytimes.com.
24. *Guide to Current American Government, Spring 1983* (Washington, DC: Congressional Quarterly Press, 1983), p. 48.
25. Schlozman and Tierney, *Organized Interests and American Democracy*, p. 104.
26. Ibid., p. 150.
27. Jeffrey Taylor, "Accountants' Campaign Contributions Are About to Pay Off in Legislation on Lawsuit Protection," *Wall Street Journal*, March 8, 1995, p. 1; see also Berry and Wilcox, *The Interest Group Society*, pp. 154–160.
28. See U.S. Supreme Court case *Citizens United v. Federal Election Commission* (08-2050), decided on January 21, 2010.
29. Berry and Wilcox, *The Interest Group Society*, p. 120.
30. Quoted in David S. Broder, "News of the Week," *Washington Post*, National Weekly Edition, January 13–19, 1997, p. 21.
31. See Haynes Johnson and David S. Broder, *The System* (Boston: Little, Brown, 1996), p. 215.
32. For a review of the role that the courts play in the lobbying process, see Berry and Wilcox, *The Interest Group Society*, pp. 146–152.
33. Karen O'Connor, *Women's Organizations' Use of the Courts* (Lexington, MA: Lexington Books, 1980), p. 118.

Chapter 9 Policy Connection

1. For a classic case study of tax reform policymaking, see Jeffrey H. Birnbaum and Alan S. Murray, *Showdown at Gucci Gulch: Lawmakers, Lobbyists, and the Unlikely Triumph of Tax Reform* (New York: Vintage Books, 1987). On the various Commodities Credit Corporation programs, see Joseph W. Glauber, "The Growth of the Federal Crop Insurance Program, 1990–2011," *American Journal of Agricultural Economics* 95, no. 2 (2013): 482–488.
2. See A. Lee Fritschler and Catherine E. Rudder, *Smoking and Politics: Bureaucracy Centered Policymaking*, 6th ed. (Upper Saddle River, NJ: Pearson/Prentice Hall, 2007).
3. For an overview of the history of gun control legislation and the role of the NRA, see Adam Winkler, *Gunfight: The Battle over the Right to Bear Arms in America* (New York: W.W. Norton, 2011).
4. *Proceedings of the National Medical Conventions, New York, May 1846, and Philadelphia, May 1847.* (Philadelphia: Printed for the American Medical Association, T. K. & P. G. Collins, printers, 1847), p. 120.
5. See Forest A. Walker, "Compulsory Health Insurance: The Next Great Step in Social Legislation," *Journal of American History* 56, no. 2 (1969): 290–304; see also J. Dennis Chasse, "The American Association for Labor Legislation and the Institutionalist Tradition in National Health Insurance." *Journal of Economic Issues* 28, no. 4 (1994): 1063–1090.
6. The discussion of the early history of the AMA's consideration of social insurance legislation is drawn from the association's archives, found at http://ama.nmtvault.com/jsp/browse.jsp.
7. The minutes of the 1921 meeting of the AMA House of Delegates contains numerous hostile references to the practice of what it termed "state medicine," including the compulsory health insurance legislation. Most telling are portions of the minutes devoted to chastising Dr. Frank Billings, the AMA's executive secretary, for a published endorsement of the AALL social insurance legislation he offered in 1916. In response, Billings claimed that the endorsement was composed of transcriptions of comments he made at a conference that were clearly misstated. He was, in fact, adamantly opposed to any such plan.
8. For an overview of the development of private health care insurance in the United States, see Melissa A. Thomasson, "From Sickness to Health: The Twentieth-Century Development of U.S. Health Insurance," *Explorations in Economic History* 39, no. 3 (2002): 233–253.
9. This discussion of FDR's (and later) efforts is drawn from several sources: Paul Starr, *The Social Transformation of American Medicine* (New York: Basic Books, 1982); Rick Mayes, *Universal Coverage: The Elusive Quest for National Health Insurance* (Ann Arbor: University of Michigan Press, 2004); Jill S. Quadagno, *One Nation, Uninsured: Why the U.S. Has No National Health Insurance* (New York: Oxford University Press, 2006).
10. Quoted in Starr, *The Social Transformation of American Medicine*, p. 279.
11. For a detailed account of Truman's efforts, see Monte M. Poen, *Harry S. Truman Versus the Medical Lobby: The Genesis of Medicare* (Columbia: University of Missouri Press, 1979).
12. Robert D. Schremmer and Jane F. Knapp, "Harry Truman and Health Care Reform: The Debate Started Here," *Pediatrics* 127, no. 3 (2011): 399–401.
13. Republicans remained in the minority in both chambers, but they had

gained twenty-eight seats in the House and five in the Senate.

14. Quoted in Quadagno, *One Nation, Uninsured*, p. 46.

15. In addition to the previously noted sources (see note 8), see Theodor R. Marmor, *The Politics of Medicare*, 2nd ed. (New York: A. de Gruyter, 2000).

16. John Colombotos, "Physicians' Responses to Changes in Health Care: Some Projections," *Inquiry* 8, no. 1 (1971): 20–26.

17. J. S. Todd, S. V. Seekins, J. A. Krichbaum, and L. K. Harvey, "Health Access America—Strengthening the US Health Care System," *Journal of the American Medical Association* 265, no. 19 (1991): 2503.

18. Theda Skocpol, *Boomerang: Health Care Reform and the Turn Against Government* (New York: W. W. Norton, 1997).

19. A summary of the AMA's position on Obamacare as of 2013 appears at http://www.medicarenewsgroup.com/news/medicare-faqs/individual-faq?faqId=d7a04b02-28b7-47dd-a838-88561f629624.

Chapter 10

1. See "War of the Worlds," *American Experience*, PBS, aired October 10, 2013. You can view it at video.pbs.org/video/2365108972.

2. Jefferson Pooley and Michael Socolow, "The Myth of the War of the Worlds Panic," *Slate*, October 29, 2013, www.slate.com/articles/art/history/2013/10/orson_welles_war_of_the_worlds_panic_myth_the_infamous_radio_broadcast_did.html.

3. For a detailed discussion of this assumption, see Kevin Arceneaux and Martin Johnson, *Changing Minds or Changing Channels?* (Chicago: University Chicago Press, 2013).

4. Roan Conrad, "TV News and the 1976 Election: A Dialogue," *Wilson Quarterly* 1 (Spring 1977): 84.

5. Techlogon.com/2011/11/15 how-many-websites-are-there-in-the-world/ (accessed January 30, 2014).

6. http://www.thecultureist.com/2013/05/09/how-many-people-use-the-internet-more-than-2-billion-infographic/.

7. www.onehourpersecond.com (accessed January 30, 2014).

8. Ronald Berkman and Laura W. Kitch, *Politics in the Media Age* (New York: McGraw-Hill, 1986), p. 21.

9. Phillip Knightley, *The First Casualty* (New York: Harcourt Brace Jovanovich, 1975), p. 56.

10. Quoted in Berkman and Kitch, *Politics in the Media Age*, p. 25.

11. Doris A. Graber, *Mass Media and American Politics*, 8th ed. (Washington, DC: Congressional Quarterly Press, 2009), p. 39.

12. Kathleen Hall Jamieson and Karlyn Kohrs Campbell, *The Interplay of Influence* (Belmont, CA: Wadsworth, 1983), p. 10.

13. Thomas E. Mann, *It's Even Worse than It Looks: How the American Constitutional System Collided with the New Politics of Extremism* (New York: Basic Books, 2012), p. 60.

14. George F. Gilder, *Life After Television* (New York: Norton, 1994).

15. Quoted in Robert W. McChesney, *Rich Media, Poor Democracy* (Urbana: University of Illinois Press, 1999), p. 120.

16. Tim Wu, *The Master Switch: The Rise and Fall of Information Empires* (New York: Vintage Books, 2011), p. 6.

17. Jamieson and Campbell, *The Interplay of Influence*, p. 16.

18. Graber, *Mass Media and American Politics*, chapter 4.

19. Quoted in Ibid, p75.

20. Herbert J. Gans, *Deciding What's News: A Study of CBS Evening News, NBC Nightly News*, Newsweek *and* Time (New York: Vintage, 1980), p. 9.

21. John Fiske, *Television Culture* (New York: Routledge, 1995), p. 281.

22. Paul Lazarfeld, Bernard Berelson, and H. Gaudet, *The People's Choice* (New York: Columbia University Press, 1948).

23. Thomas E. Patterson, *The Mass Media Election: How Americans Choose Their President* (New York: Praeger, 1980), pp. 86–91.

24. Benjamin I. Page, Robert Y. Shapiro, and Glenn R. Dempsey, "What Moves Public Opinion," *American Political Science Review* 81 (March 1987): 23–43.

25. Arceneaux and Johnson, *Changing Minds or Changing Channels?*, p. 101.

26. Markus Prior, *Post-Broadcast Democracy: How Media Choice Increases Inequality in Political Involvement and Polarizes Elections* (New York: Cambridge University Press, 2007).

27. Austin Ranney, *Channels of Power: The Impact of Television on American Politics* (New York: Basic Books, 1983), p. 17.

28. Shanto Iyengar, Mark D. Peters, and Donald R. Kinder, "Experimental Demonstrations of the 'Not-So-Minimal' Consequences of Television News Programs," *American Political Science Review* 76 (December 1982): 848–858.

29. Stephen Ansolabehere, Roy Behr, and Shanto Iyengar, *The Media Game: American Politics in the Television Age* (New York: Macmillan, 1993), p. 148.

30. The Center for Media and Public Affairs, "Journalists Monopolize TV Election News," October 30, 2000, www.cmpa.com/wp-content/uploads/2013/10/prev_pres_elections/2000/2000.10.30.Journalists-Monopolize-TV-Election-News.pdf.

31. Stephen J. Farnsworth and S. Robert Lichter, *The Nightly News Nightmare: Media Coverage of U.S. Presidential Elections: 1988–2008* (Lanham, MD: Rowman & Littlefield, 2011), pp. 74–75.

32. Reid Wilson, "It's a Small World, After All," *National Journal*, September 10, 2011, p. 17.

33. President Obama gave several speeches to student audiences on this topic, each time he touted #dontdoublemyrate. The first occasion and the source of the quote here, was his address to the students at the University of North Carolina—Chapel Hill. You can view this entire speech at, www.youtube.com/watch?v=n4WPfgbd. Fok The reference to the hashtag can be viewed, beginning at the 53 minute mark into the speech.

34. Karen Tumulty, "140 Characters Say a Lot about Modern Politics," *Washington Post*, April 27, 2012, A4.

REFERENCES

551

35. Stephen Hess, "President Clinton and the White House Press Corps—Year One," *Media Studies Journal* 8 (Spring 1994): 4.

36. The Pew Research Center, Project for Excellence in Journalism, "The State of the News Media 2013," stateofthemedia.org/2013/special-reports-landing-page/the-media-and-campaign-2012/ (accessed February 10, 2014).

37. Dayton Duncan, *Press, Polls, and the 1988 Campaign: An Insider's Critique* (Cambridge, MA: Joan Shorenstein Barone Center for the Press and Public Policy, John F. Kennedy School of Government, Harvard University, April 1989), pp. 3, 5.

38. Quoted in Graber, *Mass Media and American Politics*, p. 235.

39. Fred Smoller, "The Six O'Clock Presidency: Patterns of Network News Coverage of the President," *Presidential Studies Quarterly* 16 (Winter 1986); 31–49.

40. David Wise, *The Politics of Lying: Government Deception, Secrecy, and Power* (New York: Vintage, 1973), p. 460.

41. Michael Baruch Grossman and Martha Joynt Kumar, *Portraying the President: The White House and the Media* (Baltimore, MD: Johns Hopkins University Press, 1981), p. 116.

42. Quoted in Charles Peters, "Why the White House Press Didn't Get the Watergate Story," *Washington Monthly* 4 (July/August 1973): 6.

43. Quoted in Joseph C. Spear, *Presidents and the Press: The Nixon Legacy* (Cambridge, MA: MIT Press, 1984), pp. 10–11.

44. For a complete discussion of going public, see Samuel Kernell, *Going Public: New Strategies of Presidential Leadership*, 3rd ed. (Washington, DC: Congressional Quarterly Press, 1997).

45. For a less optimistic view of the president's power to persuade people, see George C. Edwards III, *On Deaf Ears: The Limits of the Bully Pulpit* (New Haven, CT: Yale University Press, 2003).

46. Stephen Hess, *The Washington Reporters* (Washington, DC: The Brookings Institution, 1981), pp. 98–99.

47. Quoted in David M. O'Brien, *Storm Center: The Supreme Court in American Politics* (New York: Norton, 1986), p. 281.

Chapter 10 Policy Connection

1. Some analysts might come up with a different number, depending on how they conduct their count. For example, on a global level, they might include the Bertelsmann Corporation of Germany, which has significant U.S. media holdings but is not often regarded as one of the major players in the U.S. media market. Among publishers, Pearson (a British corporation) is regarded as a major player in education, economics reporting (under its Financial Times Group), and book publishing. Others might consider Viacom and CBS to be a single conglomerate because both are technically owned by National Amusements, a U.S.-based corporation. However, operationally, the two entities act as autonomous corporations. Still others might include Google and Apple, given their growing role in mass media markets, but the main thrust of their businesses remains computer based.

2. Adolph Berle and Gardiner Means, *The Modern Corporation and Private Property* (New Brunswick, NJ: Transaction, 1932), p. 4.

3. See Alfred D. Chandler Jr., *The Visible Hand: The Managerial Revolution in American Business* (Cambridge, MA: Belknap Press/Harvard University Press, 1977).

4. By 1850, only fourteen of the thirty-one states had laws related to incorporation per se. For an analytic overview of the historical patterns of incorporation in the United States and France, see Naomi R. Lamoreaux and Jean-Laurent Rosenthal, "Legal Regime and Contractual Flexibility: A Comparison of Business's Organizational Choices in France and the United States During the Era of Industrialization," *American Law and Economics Review* 7, no. 1 (2005): 28–61.

5. For a brief overview of the history or antitrust, see United States Department of Agriculture, Rural Business and Cooperative Development Service, *Antitrust Status of Farmer Cooperatives: The Story of the Capper-Volstead Act* (Washington, DC: United States Department of Agriculture, 2002), pp. 14–19, accessible at http://www.rurdev.usda.gov/rbs/pub/cir59.pdf.

6. In legal terms, a *trust* is a person or business that is given the authority to act on behalf of another actor. It can be used in many types of situations, as when someone might legally appoint another individual to be the trustee of some property or inheritance. As important, at the time, laws dealing with trusts were relatively standard among most of the states. By negotiating trust arrangements with others in the oil business (who were given shares of the Standard Oil Trust in exchange for entering into the agreement), Rockefeller was able to effectively assume control of their operations and make the necessary changes required to form a single business enterprise capable of operating more efficiently throughout the United States.

7. In 1999, Standard Oil of New Jersey (by then known as Exxon) merged with Standard Oil of New York (Mobil Oil) to become Exxon-Mobil, now headquartered in Irving, Texas, but it is still incorporated in New Jersey.

8. Although New Jersey led the way, the competition among the states for hosting the most corporations was eventually won by Delaware, which remains the legal home of most major U.S. corporations. Today, legal mavens regard the Delaware Court of Chancery, where disputes over corporate law are heard, as the most important venue for such cases.

9. From time to time, there has been debate about "federalizing" corporate law by requiring a national corporate charter, but for the most part Congress has limited itself to dealing with corporations through regulatory policies focused on their markets rather than the enterprises themselves. See

Jill E. Fisch, "Leave It to Delaware: Why Congress Should Stay out of Corporate Governance," *Delaware Journal of Corporate Law* 37 (2013): 731–929.

10. See William E. Kovacic, "The Modern Evolution of U.S. Competition Policy Enforcement Norms," *Antitrust Law Journal* 71, no. 2 (2003): 377–478; Robert Pitofsky, "Past, Present, and Future of Antitrust Enforcement at the Federal Trade Commission," *The University of Chicago Law Review* 72, no. 1 (2005): 209–227; Rudolph J. Peritz, "A Counter-History of Antitrust Law," *Duke Law Journal*, no. 2 (1990): 263–320; and B. Dan Wood and James E. Anderson, "The Politics of U.S. Antitrust Regulation," *American Journal of Political Science* 37, no. 1 (February 1993): 1–39.

11. Among the shows controlled by Viacom at the time were *I Love Lucy*, *The Cosby Show*, and other lucrative properties. Viacom also served as the distributor of syndicated programs owned by other companies, such as *All in the Family* and *The Mary Tyler Moore Show*.

12. Some analysts claim this was especially true for the entertainment industry, which had particularly close ties to Reagan.

13. For an informative and readable examination of the emergence of the media giants, see Jennifer Holt, *Empires of Entertainment: Media Industries and the Politics of Deregulation, 1980–1996* (New Brunswick, NJ: Rutgers University Press, 2011).

14. Holt, *Empires of Entertainment*, especially chaps. 1–2.

15. See Lawrence Lessig, *Free Culture: How Big Media Uses Technology and the Law to Lock Down Culture and Control Creativity* (New York: Penguin Press, 2004); see also Tim Wu, *The Master Switch: The Rise and Fall of Information Empires* (New York: Knopf, 2010).

Chapter 11

1. "Sen. Mitch McConnell Filibusters His Own Bill," *Real Clear Politics*, December 6, 2012, www.realclearpolitics .com/video/2012/12/06/mitch_ mcconnell_filibusters_his_own_bill .html (accessed December 5, 2013).

2. John R. Hibbing and Elizabeth Theiss-Morse, *Congress as Public Enemy* (Cambridge, MA: Cambridge University Press, 1995), p. 147.

3. Albert D. Cover, "One Good Term Deserves Another: The Advantage of Incumbency in Congressional Elections," *American Journal of Political Science* 21 (August 1977): 523–541.

4. *Wesberry v. Sanders*, 376 U.S. 1 (1964).

5. Gary C. Jacobson, *The Politics of Congressional Elections*, 6th ed. (Boston: Pearson, 2013), pp. 14–17.

6. *Vieth v. Jubelirer*, 541 U.S. 267 (2004).

7. *League of United Latin American Citizens v. Perry*, 548 U.S. 399 (2006).

8. For a full discussion of apportionment and gerrymandering, see Bruce Cain, *The Reapportionment Puzzle* (Berkeley: University of California Press, 1984).

9. Morris Fiorina, *Congress: Keystone of the Washington Establishment* (New Haven, CT: Yale University Press, 1977), pp. 17–19.

10. Bill Bishop, "You Can't Compete with Voter's Feet," *Washington Post*, May 15, 2005, www.washingtonpost .com/wp-dyn/content/article/2005/ 05/14/AR2005051400072.html (accessed December 3, 2013).

11. Ibid.

12. Jim Wright, *You and Your Congressman* (New York: Coward, McMann and Geoghegan, 1972), p. 22.

13. David R. Mayhew, *Congress: The Electoral Connection* (New Haven, CT: Yale University Press, 1974), p. 37.

14. Ibid., p. 61.

15. Ronald D. Utt, "The Bridge to Nowhere: A National Embarrassment," Heritage Foundation, October 20, 2005, www.heritage.org/research/ reports/2005/10/the-bridge-to-nowhere- a-national-embarrassment (accessed December 3, 2013).

16. Richard F. Fenno Jr., *Home Style: House Members in Their Districts* (Boston: Little, Brown, 1978), p. 61.

17. Jacobson, *The Politics of Congressional Elections*, p. 54.

18. Ibid., p. 113.

19. *McCulloch v. Maryland*, 17 U.S. (4 Wheat.) 316 (1819).

20. For a detailed account of the budget process, see Allen Schick, *Congress and Money* (Washington, DC: The Urban Institute, 1980). See also James P. Pfiffner, *The President, the Budget, and Congress: Impoundment and the 1974 Budget Act* (Boulder, CO: Westview Press, 1979).

21. Richard Shapiro, *Frontline Management: A Guide for Congressional District/State Offices* (Washington, DC: Congressional Management Foundation, 1989), pp. 1–7.

22. Morris P. Fiorina, "The Case of the Vanishing Marginals: The Bureaucracy Did It," *American Political Science Review* 71 (March 1977): 180.

23. Fenno, *Home Style*, p. 240.

24. See Mathew McCubbins and Thomas Schwartz, "Congressional Oversight Overlooked: Police Patrols Versus Fire Alarms," *American Journal of Political Science* 28 (February 1984): 165–179.

25. Quoted in Barbara Hinckley, *Stability and Change in Congress* (New York: Harper & Row, 1983), p. 243.

26. *Immigration and Naturalization Service v. Chadha*, 103 S. Ct. 2764 (1983).

27. For a general discussion of the legislative veto and its alternatives, see Joseph Cooper, "The Legislative Veto in the 1980s," in *Congress Reconsidered*, 3rd ed., ed. Lawrence C. Dodd and Bruce I. Oppenheimer (Washington, DC: Congressional Quarterly Press, 1985), pp. 364–389.

28. Hinckley, *Stability and Change in Congress*, p. 16.

29. Paul Boller, *Presidential Anecdotes* (New York: Penguin, 1981), p. 18.

30. See Steven S. Smith and Christopher J. Deering, *Committees in Congress*, 2nd ed. (Washington, DC: Congressional Quarterly Press, 1990).

31. Richard Fenno Jr., *Congressmen in Committees* (Boston: Little, Brown, 1973).

32. Norman J. Ornstein, Thomas E. Mann, and Michael J. Malbin, *Vital*

Statistics on Congress: 1989–1990 (Washington, DC: Congressional Quarterly Press, 1990).

33. Quoted in Hedrick Smith, *The Power Game: How Washington Works* (New York: Ballantine, 1989), p. 287.

34. Ibid., p. 266.

35. Quoted in Congressional Quarterly, *Origins and Development of Congress*, (Washington, D.C.: Congressional Quarterly Press, 1982), p. 122.

36. For an excellent discussion of House and Senate rules, see Walter J. Oleszek, *Congressional Procedures and the Policy Process* (Washington, DC: Congressional Quarterly Press, 1978).

37. Thomas E. Mann and Norman J. Ornstein, *It's Even Worse than It Looks: How the American Constitutional System Collided with the New Politics of Extremism* (New York: Basic Books, 2012), pp. 84–91.

38. Quoted in William J. Keefe and Morris S. Ogul, *The American Legislative Process: Congress and the States* (Englewood Cliffs, NJ: Prentice-Hall, 1981), pp. 259–260.

39. Roger Davidson, Walter Oleszek, Francis Lee, and Eric Schickler, *Congress and Its Members*, 14th ed. (Los Angeles: Sage, 2014), p. 255.

40. David R. Mayhew, *America's Congress: Actions in the Public Sphere, James Madison Through Newt Gingrich* (New Haven, CT: Yale University Press, 2000).

41. Quoted in Helen Dewar, "On Capitol Hill, Symbols Triumph," *Washington Post*, November 26, 1991, A4.

42. Woodrow Wilson, *Congressional Government*, rev. ed. (New York: Meridian Books, 1956), p. 210.

Chapter 11 Policy Connection

1. See Simon Johnson and James Kwak, *White House Burning: The Founding Fathers, Our National Debt, and Why It Matters to You* (New York: Pantheon Books, 2012).

2. Many historians—most famously Charles Beard—would argue that the Constitution reflects the fact that many of those who attended were creditors of the U.S. government and had an interest in making certain the national debt would be settled rather than abandoned.

3. Article I, Section 8, clause 1: "The Congress shall have Power To lay and collect Taxes, Duties, Imposts and Excises, *to pay the Debts* and provide for the common Defence and general Welfare of the United States."

4. Many historians see this debate as the source of the two-party system, with Hamilton and his federalist supporters on one side and Madison and Jefferson initiating an opposing caucus that eventually became the Democratic-Republican Party.

5. In 2010, economists Carmen Reinhart and Kenneth Rogoff presented a paper based on historical data contending that there were counterproductive impacts on the economy when a country's gross national debt exceeded 90 percent of its annual gross domestic product. See Carmen M. Reinhart and Kenneth S. Rogoff, "Growth in a Time of Debt," *National Bureau of Economic Research Working Paper Series*, no. 15639 (2010), http://www.nber.org/papers/w15639.pdf. At the time, it was projected that the debt-to-GDP ratio for the United States would reach 108 percent in 2014, and many deficit hawks use that paper to counter calls for more stimulus spending. In 2013, however, a team of economists from the University of Massachusetts found an error in the model used for the Reinhart-Rogoff thesis, and the hopes of those who favored more spending in light of the economic downturn (and thus were less concerned about increased deficits and the climbing national debt) were buoyed. See Paul Krugman, "The Excel Depression," *New York Times*, April 18, 2013.

6. The downgrade came from Standard and Poor's. Other rating agencies, for example, Fitch and Moody's, expressed concern but still regarded the possibility of a U.S. loan default to be highly unlikely.

7. For up-to-date tracking of who holds the national debt, visit http://www.treasurydirect.gov/NP/debt/current.

8. The leading promoter of this movement is Grover Nordquist, an antitax advocate who heads the influential Americans for Tax Reform (ATR) interest group. To get the support of ATR and its substantial resources, candidates for Congress and other elected offices (primarily Republicans) sign the Taxpayer Protection Pledge, which involves a "written commitment to their constituents to 'oppose and vote against tax increases.'" For a list of those in the 1113th Congress who sign the pledge, see http://s3.amazonaws.com/atrfiles/files/files/073013-113thCongress.pdf.

9. For an overview of tax expenditures, see U.S. Government Accountability Office, *Tax Expenditures: Background and Evaluation Criteria and Questions*, 2012, GAO-13-167SP, http://www.gao.gov/assets/660/650371.pdf.

10. Each year, the Office of Management and Budget issues estimates and projections for tax expenditures as part of the Analytic Perspectives report sent to Congress with the annual White House budget requests. For fiscal year 2014, see http://www.whitehouse.gov/sites/default/files/omb/budget/fy2014/assets/spec.pdf.

11. For a brief but concise overview, see Mindy R. Levit and D. Andrew Austin, *Mandatory Spending Since 1962* (Washington, DC: U.S. Congress, Congressional Research Service, 2013), RL33074.

12. For a study of how members of Congress deal with the guns-or-butter choice, see Jungkun Seo, "The Party Politics of 'Guns Versus Butter' in Post-Vietnam America," *Journal of American Studies* 45, no. 2 (2011): 317–336.

13. Technically there were other shutdowns as far back as 1981, but these were of short duration—typically one to five days. The 1995 shutdown lasted into 1996, but its impact was mitigated by the timing of the holiday season.

14. The rest involved tax incentives and fiscal relief grants to states and localities.

15. "The Outrageous Sandy Outrage," *Wall Street Journal*, January 3, 2013, http://online.wsj.com/news/articles/SB10001424127887323374504578219733538204830 (accessed January 2, 2014). Also see Thomas Husted and David Nickerson, "Political Economy of Presidential Disaster Declarations and Federal Disaster Assistance," *Public Finance Review* 42, no. 1 (2014): 35–57.

Chapter 12

1. Fred Greenstein, *The Presidential Difference: Leadership Style from FDR to Barack Obama* (Princeton, NJ: Princeton University Press, 2009), p. 6.
2. Thomas E. Cronin, *The State of the Presidency*, 2nd ed. (Boston: Little, Brown, 1975), p. 24.
3. Cronin, *The State of the Presidency*, pp. 76–84.
4. Louis W. Koenig, *The Chief Executive*, 3rd ed. (New York: Harcourt Brace Jovanovich, 1975), pp. 7–12.
5. Michael Nelson, "Evaluating the Presidency," in *The Presidency and the Political System*, ed. Michael Nelson (Washington, DC: Congressional Quarterly Press, 1984), pp. 5–28.
6. Quoted in Koenig, *The Chief Executive*, p. 8.
7. Arthur M. Schlesinger Jr., *The Imperial Presidency* (Boston: Houghton Mifflin, 1973).
8. Thomas Franck, ed., *The Tethered Presidency* (New York: New York University Press, 1981).
9. Bob Woodward, *The Price of Politics* (New York: Simon and Schuster Paperbacks, 2013), p. 80.
10. Roger H. Davidson, Walter J. Oleszek, Francis E. Lee, and Eric Schickler, *Congress and Its Members* (Los Angeles: Sage, 2014), pp. 234–240.
11. *Humphrey's Executor v. United States*, 295 U.S. 602 (1935).
12. Alexander Hamilton, "Federalist No. 74,"in *The Federalist Papers*, edited by Clinton Rossiter (New York: Penguin Putnam, 2003), p. 447.
13. *United States v. Nixon*, 418 U.S. 683 (1974).

14. See *Clinton v. Jones*, 520 U.S. 681 (1997).
15. See *In Re Sealed Case (Espy)*, 121 F.3d 729 (1997) and *In Re Lindsey*, 158 F.3d 1263 (1998).
16. See *In Re Sealed Case (Secret Service)*, 148 F.3d 1073 (1998).
17. Sari Horowitz, "A Gunrunning Gone Fatally Wrong," *Washington Post*, July 14, 2011, www.washingtonpost.com/investigations/us-anti-gunrunning-effort-turns-fatally-wrong/2011/07/14/gIQAH5d6YI_story.html (accessed December 20, 2013).
18. Conor Friedersdorf, "Obama Discovers the Convenience of Executive Privilege," *Atlantic*, June 21, 2012, www.theatlantic.com/politics/archive/2012/06/obama-discovers-the-convenence-of-executive-privilege/258766 (accessed December 20, 2013).
19. Richard M. Pious, *The American Presidency* (New York: Basic Books, 1979), p. 340.
20. Quoted in Pious, *The American Presidency*, p. 395.
21. For an excellent discussion of the Gulf War and the War Powers Resolution, see Marcia Lynn Whicker, Raymond A. Moore, and James P. Pfiffner, *The Presidency and the Persian Gulf War* (Lexington: University of Kentucky Press, 1996).
22. Patrick Reis, "Obama Says He Doesn't Need Congress' Permission to Strike Syria, So Why Is He Asking for it?," *National Journal*, December 30, 2013, 1www.nationaljournal.com/whitehouse/obama-says-he-doesn't-need-congress-permission-to-strike-syria-so-why-is-he-asking-for-it-2013083 (accessed December 21, 2013).
23. Clinton Rossiter, *The American Presidency* (New York: Harcourt, Brace, 1960).
24. For a concise but highly informative account of the institutional presidency, see James P. Pfiffner, *The Modern Presidency* (Boston: Wadsworth, 2011), pp. 97–125.
25. For a listing of the agencies and offices, see www.whitehouse.gov/administration/eop/.
26. Quoted in Thomas E. Cronin, *The State of the Presidency*, p. 11.

27. Cronin, *The State of the Presidency*, pp. 276–278.
28. For a history of such clearance procedures, see Andrew Rudalevige, *Managing the President's Program: Presidential Leadership and Legislative Policy Formulation* (Princeton, NJ: Princeton University Press, 2002), pp. 45–62.
29. For a list of those employed in the White House Office, see www.whitehouse.gov/briefing-room/disclosures/annual-records/2012.
30. George Edwards and Stephen Wayne, *Presidential Leadership: Politics and Policy Making* (New York: St. Martin's, 1985), p. 189. For an excellent discussion of the dilemmas faced by presidents surrounded by staff, see Hugh Heclo, "The Changing Presidential Office," in *Understanding the Presidency*, ed. James P. Pfiffner and Roger H. Davidson (New York: Addison-Wesley, 1997), pp. 169–180.
31. Barbara Hinckley, *Problems of the Presidency: A Text with Readings* (Glenview, IL: Scott, Foresman, 1985), p. 101.
32. Quoted in Richard E. Neustadt, *Presidential Power: The Politics of Leadership from FDR to Carter* (New York: Wiley, 1980), p. 9. For a discussion of the limits of presidential persuasion, see George C. Edwards, *The Strategic President: Persuasion and Opportunity in Presidential Leadership* (Princeton, NJ: Princeton University Press, 2009).
33. Neustadt, *Presidential Power*, chap. 3.
34. Quoted in Doris Kearns Goodwin, *Team of Rivals: The Political Genius of Abraham Lincoln* (NY: Simon & Schuster, 2005), p. 206.
35. George Edwards, *Presidential Influence in Congress* (San Francisco: Freeman, 1980), p. 89.
36. Douglas Rivers and Nancy L. Rose, "Passing the President's Program: Public Opinion and Presidential Influence in Congress," *American Journal of Political Science* 29 (1985): 187.
37. Paul C. Light, *The President's Agenda: Domestic Policy Choice from Kennedy to Clinton*, 3rd ed. (Baltimore: Johns Hopkins University Press, 1999).

38. Paul Brace and Barbara Hinckley, *Follow the Leader* (New York: Basic Books, 1994), p. 161.

Chapter 12 Policy Connection

1. Aaron Wildavsky, "The Two Presidencies," *Trans-Action*, December 4, 1966, 7.
2. For an excellent history of U.S. foreign policy during this period, see Stephen E. Ambrose and Douglas Brinkley, *Rise to Globalism: American Foreign Policy Since 1938*, 9th rev. ed. (New York: Penguin Books, 2011).
3. For an historical overview of containment policy in its various strategic forms, see John Lewis Gaddis, *Strategies of Containment: A Critical Appraisal of American National Security Policy During the Cold War*, 2nd rev. ed. (New York: Oxford University Press, 2005).
4. The policy of containment is most closely associated with George F. Kennan, an American diplomat and scholar who was very influential in shaping U.S. strategies during the Cold War. See his *American Diplomacy—Sixtieth-anniversary expanded edition*, (Chicago: University of Chicago Press, 2012), p. 125. The quotes are from his famous "X" article in *Foreign Affairs*, which is reprinted in that volume.
5. Quoted in Gaddis, *Strategies of Containment*, p. 200.
6. Quotes and analysis from Gaddis, *Strategies of Containment*, pp. 343–344.
7. Bush's new-world-order approach was the focus of his remarks in a speech to Congress in September 1991, after the end of the Persian Gulf War; the full text is found at http://en.wikisource.org/wiki/Toward_a_New_World_Order. The roots of the policy, however, were traced by Bush and his national security advisor, Brent Scowcroft, to a summit at Malta with the Soviet Union's Mikhail Gorbachev in December 1989. See George H. W. Bush and Brent Scowcroft, *A World Transformed* (New York: Knopf, 1998).
8. Richard Haass, *The Reluctant Sheriff: The United States After the Cold War*

(New York, Washington, DC: Council on Foreign Relations Press; distributed by Brookings Institution Press, 1997).
9. From Bush's "Address to a Joint Session of Congress and the American People," delivered on September 20, 2001; see www.georgewbush-whitehouse.archives.gov/news/releases/2001/09/20010920-8.html.
10. Ambrose and Brinkley, *Rise to Globalism*, p. 355.
11. See Ray Lizza, "The Consequentialist: How the Arab Spring Remade Obama's Foreign Policy," *The New Yorker*, May 2, 2011, 44–55.
12. Daniel W. Drezner, "Does Obama Have a Grand Strategy? Why We Need Doctrines in Uncertain Times," *Foreign Affairs* 90, no. 4 (2011): 57–68.
13. John J. Mearsheimer, "Imperial by Design," *The National Interest* (January/February 2011): p. 18.

Chapter 13

1. A transcript of the Ray Nagin interview is found at http://www.cnn.com/2005/US/09/02/nagin.transcript/index.html (accessed January 4, 2014).
2. Visit the FEMA history webpage at http://www.fema.gov/about/history.shtm.
3. See James Lee Witt and James Morgan, *Stronger in the Broken Places: Nine Lessons for Turning Crisis into Triumph* (New York: Times Books, 2002).
4. See Max Weber, *From Max Weber: Essays in Sociology*, ed. H. W. Gerth and C. W. Mills (New York: Oxford University Press, 1946).
5. Another 26 percent answered that government wasted at least "some" of their tax dollars, bringing the total to 98 percent. See American National Election Studies, Center for Political Studies, University of Michigan, "The ANES Guide to Public Opinion and Electoral Behavior: Do People in Government Waste Tax Money, 1958–2008," http://electionstudies.org/nesguide/toptable/tab5a_3.htm.
6. Only "reducing the federal budget deficit" received a higher rating, at 71 percent. See Jennifer Benz, Trevor

Thompson, and Jennifer Agiesta, "The People's Agenda: America's Priorities and Outlook for 2014" (Washington, DC: The Associated Press-NORC Center for Public Affairs Research, January 2014), p. 4. The report is accessible at http://www.apnorc.org/PDFs/Peoples%20Agenda/AP-NORC-The%20Public%20Agenda_FINAL.pdf.
7. The results of the poll by the Pew Research Center are found at http://www.people-press.org/files/legacy-pdf/09-30-13%20Views%20of%20Gov't%20Release.pdf. It should be noted that the survey was conducted as the deadline for a congressional debate over the budget was looming and as a threatened shutdown of the federal government was being highlighted in the news media.
8. See especially Charles T. Goodsell, *The Case for Bureaucracy: A Public Administration Polemic*, 4th ed. (Washington, DC: Congressional Quarterly Press, 2004).
9. There are some academic studies of "public satisfaction" for a few federal agencies, but most detailed surveys are in-house. Local governments have been using citizen satisfaction surveys more regularly. For an interesting overview of the surveys conducted for local governments by one firm, see Mike Maciag, "What Government Services Are Citizens Most, Least Satisfied With?," *Governing*, March 6, 2013, http://www.governing.com/blogs/by-the-numbers/citizen-satisfaction-surveys-transportation-ranks-lowest.html.
10. For general figures on civilian employees from the 2012 census of governments, see http://www.census.gov/govs/apes/.
11. For an overall summary of positions, see the Plum Book appendix at http://www.gpo.gov/fdsys/pkg/GPO-PLUM-BOOK-2012/content-detail.html.
12. See Matthew A. Crenson, *The Federal Machine: Beginnings of Bureaucracy in Jacksonian America* (Baltimore, MD: Johns Hopkins University Press, 1975).
13. For an historical perspective on federal agencies, see George Thomas

Kurian, ed., *A Historical Guide to the U.S. Government* (New York: Oxford University Press, 1998).

14. Donald D. Kettl, *Government by Proxy: (Mis?) Managing Federal Programs* (Washington, DC: Congressional Quarterly Press, 1988).

15. The federal government posts annual contractor information at https://www.fpds.gov/fpdsng_cms/index.php/en/reports/62-top-100-contractors-report.

16. Richard J. Stillman, *The American Bureaucracy: The Core of the Modern Government* (Belmont, CA: Wadsworth/Thomson Learning, 2004), pp. 180–188.

17. For a dramatic overview of the role of private contractors in the Iraq war, see the documentary *Private Warriors* at the Frontline/PBS site at www.pbs.org/wgbh/pages/frontline/shows/warriors/view/#lower (accessed April 7, 2008).

18. You can find information on the various offices in the EOP at the EOP White House website, www.whitehouse.gov/government/eop.html.

19. Technically, some of these more specialized policy units are located within the White House Office.

20. See Cornelius M. Kerwin and Scott R. Furlong. *Rulemaking: How Government Agencies Write Law and Make Policy*, 4th ed. (Washington, DC: Congressional Quarterly Press, 2011).

21. On Stern, see Howard Kurtz, "Stern on Satellite: A Bruised Flower, Blossoming Anew," *Washington Post*, December 11, 2005, at http://www.washingtonpost.com/wp-dyn/content/article/2005/12/10/AR2005121001432.html, accessed January 14, 2014.

22. Leonard D. White, *The Federalists* (New York: Macmillan, 1948); Leonard D. White, *The Jacksonians: A Study in Administrative History, 1829–1861* (New York: Macmillan, 1954); Leonard D. White, *The Jeffersonians* (New York: Macmillan, 1951).

23. Leonard D. White, *The Republican Era, 1869–1901: A Study in Administrative History* (New York: Macmillan, 1958).

24. Data on government employment are drawn from federal census and budgetary data posted at www.census.gov/ and http://gpo.gov/usbudget.

25. For example, see R. Douglas Arnold, *Congress and the Bureaucracy: A Theory of Influence* (New Haven, CT: Yale University Press, 1979).

26. Norton E. Long, "Power and Administration," *Public Administration Review* 9 (Autumn 1949): 257–264.

27. See Francis E. Rourke, *Bureaucracy, Politics, and Public Policy*, 3rd ed. (Boston: Little, Brown, 1984).

28. A detailed critique of the pre–9/11 failures of the FBI and other agencies is found in chapter 11 of *The 9/11 Commission Report*, which can be accessed at https://www.fas.org/irp/offdocs/911comm-sec11.pdf. Also see *The Man Who Knew*, a *Frontline* (PBS) documentary, http://www.pbs.org/wgbh/pages/frontline/shows/knew/.

29. See Arnold, *Congress and the Bureaucracy.*

30. A. Lee Fritschler and James M. Hoefler, *Smoking and Politics: Policy Making and the Federal Bureaucracy*, 5th ed. (Upper Saddle River, NJ: Prentice-Hall, 1996); Richard Kluger, *Ashes to Ashes: America's Hundred-Year Cigarette War, the Public Health, and the Unabashed Triumph of Philip Morris* (New York: Vintage Books, 1997).

31. The concept of issue networks was first described in detail in Hugh Heclo, "Issue Networks and the Executive Establishment," in *The New American Political System*, ed. Anthony King (Washington, DC: American Enterprise Institute, 1978).

32. For a general overview of EPA politics, see Michael E. Kraft and Norman J. Vig, "Environmental Policy over Four Decades: Achievements and New Directions," in *Environmental Policy: New Directions for the Twenty-First Century*, ed. Norman J. Vig and Michael E. Kraft (Thousand Oaks, CA: Congressional Quarterly Press, 2013), pp. 2–29.

33. Quoted in James L. Sundquist, *The Decline and Resurgence of Congress* (Washington, DC: The Brookings Institution, 1981), p. 320.

34. C. Boyden Gray, "Congressional Abdication: Delegation Without Detail and Without Waiver," *Harvard Journal of Law & Public Policy* 36, no. 1 (2013): 41–50.

35. See Joel D. Aberbach, *Keeping a Watchful Eye: The Politics of Congressional Oversight* (Washington, DC: The Brookings Institution, 1990).

36. For a study of how Congress has responded to the emergence of the administrative state, see David H. Rosenbloom, *Building a Legislative-Centered Public Administration: Congress and the Administrative State, 1946–1999* (Tuscaloosa: University of Alabama Press, 2000).

37. For information on the 1998 legislation and IRS efforts to meet congressional demands, visit the IRS website at www.irs.gov. The 2013 hearings by the House Committee on Oversight and Government Reform can be found at http://oversight.house.gov/hearing/the-irs-systematic-delay-and-scrutiny-of-tea-party-applications/. The criminal investigation determined there were no violations of law in the IRS's activities, but a wide range of managerial changes were put in place.

38. See David H. Rosenbloom, *Public Administration and Law: Bench v. Bureau in the United States* (New York: Marcel Dekker, 1983); see also David H. Rosenbloom, James D. Carroll, and Jonathan D. Carroll, *Constitutional Competence for Public Managers: Cases and Commentary* (Itasca, IL: F.E. Peacock, 2000).

39. See Louis Fisher, "The Administrative World of Chadha and Bowsher," *Public Administration Review* 47, no. 3 (May/June 1987): 213–219.

40. For more information on whistleblowing, see the website of the National Whistleblower Center at www.whistleblowers.org.

41. In 2013, for example, Pfc. Bradley Manning was sentenced to thirty-five years in prison for leaking intelligence documents to WikiLeaks. That same year, a private contractor working for the National Security Agency (NSA) turned over to reporters information about NSA activities he regarded as questionable and then sought asylum abroad because he would be charged with a crime in the United States. For more on the motivation of whistle-blowers and similar "dissenters," see Rosemary O'Leary, *The Ethics of Dissent: Managing Guerrilla Government*, 2nd ed. (Los Angeles: SAGE, 2014).

42. On the role of the inspector general (IG) in protecting whistleblowers, see Eric Kempen and Andrew P. Bakaj, "Marshalling Whistleblower Protection," *The Journal of Public Inquiry* (Spring/Summer 2009): 6–8. On the role of IGs in general, see Paul C. Light, *Monitoring Government: Inspectors General and the Search for Accountability* (Washington, DC: The Brookings Institution, 1993).

43. Susan Dudley Gold, *Freedom of Information Act* (New York: Marshall Cavendish Benchmark, 2012).

44. See Goodsell, *The Case for Bureaucracy.*

45. See Gerald E. Caiden, "What Is Maladministration?," *Public Administration Review* 51, no. 6 (November/December 1991): 486–493. See also William T. Gormley, *Taming the Bureaucracy: Muscles, Prayers, and Other Strategies* (Princeton, NJ: Princeton University Press, 1989).

46. James Q. Wilson, *Bureaucracy: What Government Agencies Do and Why They Do It* (New York: Basic Books, 1989), pp. 326–331.

47. See Witt and Morgan, *Stronger in the Broken Places.* Also see *Frontline*'s excellent documentary on Hurricane Katrina: *The Storm*, at www.pbs.org/wgbh/pages/frontline/storm/.

48. See Norma M. Riccucci, *Unsung Heroes: Federal Execucrats Making a Difference* (Washington, DC: Georgetown University Press, 1995).

49. See Melvin J. Dubnick and Barbara S. Romzek, *American Public Administration: Politics and the Management of Expectations* (New York: Macmillan, 1991), especially chap. 3; and Melvin J. Dubnick and Barbara S. Romzek, "Accountability and the Centrality of Expectations in American Public Administration," in *Research in Public Administration*, ed. James L. Perry (Greenwich, CT: JAI Press, 1993).

Chapter 13 Policy Connection

1. Matthew A. Crenson, *The Federal Machine: Beginnings of Bureaucracy in Jacksonian America* (Baltimore, MD: Johns Hopkins University Press, 1975).

2. Woodrow Wilson, "The Study of Administration," *Political Science Quarterly* 2, no. 2 (1887): 210. For more on Wilson's early views, see Brian J. Cook, "Efficiency, Responsibility, and Law: Public Administration in the Early Political Rhetoric of Woodrow Wilson," *Administrative Theory & Praxis* 20, no. 1 (1998): 43–54.

3. Harold T. Pinkett, "The Keep Commission, 1905–1909: A Rooseveltian Effort for Administrative Reform," *The Journal of American History* 52, no. 2 (1965): 297–312.

4. Among the long-term changes was the creation of the General Services Administration (to deal with procurement), the National Archives (to address records management issues), personnel and merit pay classification systems for federal employees (today's General Schedule salary system), and a pension system for government employees. See Richard D. White Jr., "Executive Reorganization, Theodore Roosevelt and the Keep Commission," *Administrative Theory & Praxis* 24, no. 3 (2002): 507–518.

5. David H. Rosenbloom, "History Lessons for Reinventors," *Public Administration Review* 61, no. 2 (2001): 161–165. Also see Peri E. Arnold, "Executive Reorganization and the Origins of the Managerial Presidency," *Polity* 13, no. 4 (1981): 568–599.

6. On this effort, see David H. Rosenbloom, *Building a Legislative-Centered Public Administration: Congress and the Administrative State, 1946–1999* (Tuscaloosa: University of Alabama Press, 2000).

7. To read the Hoover Commission Reports, go to http://www.archives.gov/research/guide-fed-records/groups/264.html. See Ronald C. Moe, *The Hoover Commissions Revisited* (Boulder, CO: Westview Press, 1982).

8. See Roger G. Noll, *Reforming Regulation: An Evaluation of the Ash Council Proposals* (Washington, DC:

Brookings, 1971). See also Roger C. Camton, "Regulatory Structure and Regulatory Performance: A Critique of the Ash Council Report," *Public Administration Review* 32, no. 4 (1972): 284–291.

9. Richard P. Nathan, *The Administrative Presidency* (New York: John Wiley and Sons, 1983).

10. See especially George J. Stigler, *The Citizen and the State: Essays on Regulation* (Chicago: University of Chicago Press, 1975).

11. For an overview, see Phillip J. Cooper, *The War Against Regulation: From Jimmy Carter to George W. Bush* (Lawrence: University Press of Kansas, 2009).

12. E. S. Savas, *Privatization: The Key to Better Government* (Chatham, NJ: Chatham House, 1987); John D. Donahue, *The Privatization Decision: Public Ends, Private Means* (New York: Basic Books, 1989), provides a more critical perspective. For an overview of worldwide privatization efforts, see Graeme A. Hodge, *Privatization: An International Review of Performance, Theoretical Lenses on Public Policy* (Boulder, CO: Westview Press, 1999).

13. David Osborne and Ted Gaebler, *Reinventing Government: How the Entrepreneurial Spirit Is Transforming the Public Sector* (Reading, MA: Addison-Wesley, 1992).

14. John J. DiIulio Jr., ed., *Deregulating the Public Service: Can Government Be Improved?* (Washington, DC: Brookings Institution, 1994). For a critical view of this approach, see Melvin J. Dubnick, "A Coup Against King Bureaucracy?" in that volume (pp. 249–287).

15. Steven Kelman, *Unleashing Change: A Study of Organizational Renewal in Government* (Washington, DC: Brookings Institution Press, 2005).

16. See Beryl A. Radin, "The Government Performance and Results Act and the Tradition of Federal Management Reform: Square Pegs in Round Holes?," *Journal of Public Administration Research and Theory* 10, no. 1 (January 2000): 111–135.

17. Information on PART is archived at http://web.archive.org/web/20080616222524/http://www.whitehouse.gov/omb/part/.

18. Beryl Radin, *Federal Management Reform in a World of Contradictions*, Public Management and Change Series (Washington, DC: Georgetown University Press, 2012).

Chapter 14

1. This adage, attributed to John Adams, is found in the "Novanglus" papers in the *Boston Gazette* (1774). The maxim was also imbedded in the 1780 Massachusetts Constitution. Adams always credited James Harrington, author of the 1656 book *The Commonwealth of Oceana*.

2. Richard J. Richardson and Kenneth N. Vines, *The Politics of Federal Courts: Lower Courts in the United States* (Boston: Little, Brown, 1970).

3. Department of Justice letter to the Honorable Harry Reid, majority leader of the U.S. Senate, April 2013, www.fas.org/irp/agency/doj/fisa/2012rept.pdf (accessed January 10, 2014).

4. "Liberty and Security in a Changing World: Report and Recommendations of the President's Review Group on Intelligence and Communications Technologies," www.whitehouse.gov/sites/default/files/docs/2013-12-12_rg_final_report.pdf (accessed January 20, 2014).

5. For a comprehensive discussion of the uses of diversity jurisdiction, see Victor E. Flango, "Attorney's Perspectives on Choice of Forum in Diversity Cases," *Akron Law Review* 25 (Summer 1991): 1–82.

6. For a full account of the appointment process, see Lee Epstein and Jeffrey A. Segal, *Advice and Consent: The Politics of Judicial Appointments* (New York: Oxford University Press, 2005).

7. Quoted in Howard Ball, *Courts and Politics: The Federal Judicial System* (Englewood Cliffs, NJ: Prentice-Hall, 1980), p. 176.

8. "CQ on the Floor," *Congressional Quarterly Weekly Report*, March 20, 1970, 776.

9. See Laurence H. Tribe, *God Save This Honorable Court: How the Choice of Supreme Court Justices Shapes Our History* (New York: Random House, 1985).

10. Quoted in Stephen Wasby, *The Supreme Court in the Federal System*, 2nd ed. (New York: Holt, Rinehart and Winston, 1984), p. 89.

11. Congressional Quarterly, *The Supreme Court: Justice and the Law* (Washington, DC: Congressional Quarterly Press, 1981), p. 163.

12. John Schmidauser, *Judges and Justices: The Federal Appellate Judiciary* (Boston: Little, Brown, 1979), p. 96.

13. Bernard Schwartz, *A History of the Supreme Court* (New York: Oxford University Press, 1993), p. 16.

14. Sheldon Goldman and Thomas P. Jahnige, *The Federal Courts as a Political System* (New York: Harper & Row, 1985), p. 250.

15. See Stephen Wasby, *The Supreme Court in the Federal System*, 3rd ed. (New York: Holt, Rinehart and Winston, 1984), pp. 91–97.

16. Quoted in Henry J. Abraham, *The Judicial Process* (New York: Oxford University Press, 1980), p. 203.

17. *Webster v. Reproductive Health Services*, 492 U.S. 490 (1989).

18. Doris Marie Provine, *Case Selection in the United States Supreme Court* (Chicago: University of Chicago Press, 1980).

19. Quoted in David M. O'Brien, *Storm Center: The Supreme Court in American Politics*, 2nd ed. (New York: Norton, 1990), p. 283.

20. Quoted in Bob Woodward and Scott Armstrong, *The Brethren: Inside the Supreme Court* (New York: Avon Books, 1979), p. 490.

21. *Brown v. Board of Education II*, 349 U.S. 294 (1955).

22. William J. Brennan, "Inside View of the High Court," *New York Times Magazine*, October 6, 1963, 22.

23. Quoted in James F. Simon, *FDR and Chief Justice Hughes: The President, the Supreme Court, and the Epic Battle Over the New Deal* (New York: Simon and Schuster, 2012), 39-40.

24. *Marbury v. Madison*, 5 U.S. (1 Cranch) 137 (1803).

25. For a complete discussion of the *Marbury* decision, see Craig R. Ducat, *Modes of Constitutional Interpretation* (St. Paul, MN: West, 1978), pp. 1–41.

26. See, in particular, Nathan Glazer, "Toward an Imperial Judiciary," *The Public Interest* 47 (Fall 1975): 104–123; and Raoul Berger, *Government by the Judiciary: The Transformation of the Fourteenth Amendment* (Cambridge, MA: Harvard University Press, 1977).

27. Tribe, *God Save This Honorable Court*, p. 42.

28. For a conservative critique of the original intent approach, see Richard A. Posner, "What Am I? A Potted Plant?," *New Republic*, September 28, 1987, 23–25.

29. *Furman v. Georgia*, 408 U.S. 238 (1972).

30. See Jack Peltason, *Fifty-Eight Lonely Men: Southern Federal Judges and School Desegregation* (Urbana: University of Illinois Press, 1971).

31. *Oregon v. Mitchell*, 400 U.S. 112 (1970).

32. Cited in O'Brien, *Storm Center*, p. 361.

33. Quoted in Richard Kluger, *Simple Justice: The History of* Brown v. Board of Education *and Black America's Struggle for Equality* (New York: Knopf, 1976), p. 753.

Chapter 14 Policy Connection

1. The classic work on discretion at the street level is Michael Lipsky, *Street-Level Bureaucracy: Dilemmas of the Individual in Public Services* (New York: Russell Sage Foundation, 1980).

2. The original *Law and Order* TV series was broadcast from 1990 to 2010. One reason for the popularity and success of the series (and its several spinoffs) was its reliance on storylines generated by recent headlines. Although inspired by headlines, the plots were fictional, and the writers took considerable liberties with real-world time frames. See http://www.imdb.com/title/tt0098844/ for an overview of that series.

3. Details about the arrest and prosecution of Swartz appear in a report to the president of MIT by a faculty-led committee. See http://swartz-report

.mit.edu/. Also see Larissa MacFarquhar, "Requiem for a Dream," *The New Yorker*, March 11, 2013, http://www.newyorker.com/reporting/2013/03/11/130311fa_fact_macfarquhar.

4. "State Drops Charges Against Swartz; Federal Charges Remain," *The Tech Online Edition*, March 16, 2012, http://tech.mit.edu/V132/N12/swartz.html (emphasis added).

5. The statement was part of Swartz's "Guerilla Open Access Manifesto"; see https://archive.org/details/GuerillaOpenAccessManifesto.

6. Lessig posted his eulogy to Swartz on his blog the day of his friend's funeral. See "Prosecutor as Bully," http://lessig.tumblr.com/post/40347463044/prosecutor-as-bully.

7. See Jerome H. Skolnick and James J. Fyfe, *Above the Law: Police and the Excessive Use of Force* (New York: Free Press, 1993).

8. See Lessig, "Prosecutor as Bully."

9. Daniel S. Medwed, *Prosecution Complex: America's Race to Convict, and Its Impact on the Innocent* (New York: New York University Press, 2012).

10. Maurice Rosenberg, "Judicial Discretion of the Trial Court, Viewed from Above," *Syracuse Law Review* 22, no. 3 (1970): 635–668; see also Cass R. Sunstein, *Radicals in Robes: Why Extreme Right-Wing Courts Are Wrong for America* (New York: Basic Books, 2006).

11. See John J. DiIulio Jr., *Barbed Wire Bureaucracy: Politics and Administration in the Federal Bureau of Prisons, 1930–1988* (New York: Oxford University Press, 1995).

12. See James Q. Wilson, *Varieties of Police Behavior: The Management of Law and Order in Eight Communities* (New York: Atheneum, 1973); see also Jerome H. Skolnick and David H. Bayley, *The New Blue Line: Police Innovation in Six American Cities* (New York: Free Press, 1986).

13. See Medwed, *Prosecution Complex*.

14. Robert H. Jackson, "The Federal Prosecutor," *Journal of the American Judicature Society* 24, no. 1 (1940): 18–20.

15. Charles J. Ogletree Jr., "The Death of Discretion? Reflections on the Federal Sentencing Guidelines," *Harvard Law Review* 101, no. 8 (1988): 1938–1960; Frank O. Bowman, "The Failure of the Federal Sentencing Guidelines: A Structural Analysis," *Columbia Law Review* 105, no. 4 (2005): 1315–1350. See also Rachel E. Barkow, "Sentencing Guidelines at the Crossroads of Politics and Expertise," *University of Pennsylvania Law Review* 160, no. 6 (2012): 1599–1630.

16. The original intent of Alexis De Tocqueville's travels to America was to report on the U.S. approach to incarceration. See Richard Reeves, *American Journey: Traveling with Tocqueville in Search of Democracy in America* (New York: Simon and Schuster, 1982).

17. John J. DiIulio Jr., *Governing Prisons: A Comparative Study of Correctional Management* (New York: Free Press, 1987).

18. See *The Untouchables*, a PBS *Frontline* documentary, accessible at http://www.pbs.org/wgbh/pages/frontline/untouchables/.

19. See the documentary *The Invisible War*, information posted at http://invisiblewarmovie.com/.

20. See Lily Kahng, "The IRS Tea Party Controversy and Administrative Discretion," *Cornell Law Review Online* 99 (2013): 41–55.

Credits

Photo Credits

J.B. Forbes; p. 298 (right): AP Photo/Tulsa World, Mike Simons; p. 302: Charley Gallay/Getty Images for Children's Defense Fund-California; p. 306: Christopher Gregory; p. 310: Harry Hamburg/AP Images; p. 317: LBJ Library Photo

CHAPTER 10

p. 320: Steve White/QMI Agency; p. 322: New York Daily News Archive via Getty Images; p. 325: Lewis Hine, National Child Labor Committee Collection (U.S.), Library of Congress Prints and Photographs Division; p. 328: MOHAMMED ABED/AFP/Getty Images; p. 330: Loic Le Meur; p. 332: © 247PapsTV/Splash News/Corbis; p. 336: AP Photo/Carolyn Kaster, File; p. 337: David Paul Morris/Bloomberg via Getty Images; p. 346: © Copyright 2014, Joe Heller, hellertoon.com; p. 348: Keppler & Schwarzmann, *Puck*, v. 55, no. 1421 (1904 May 25), cover/Library of Congress Prints and Photographs Division

CHAPTER 11

p. 352: © Dhuss/istock; p. 356: © Benjamin J. Myers/Corbis; p. ©Copyright 2010 Jeff Parker/Florida Today; p. 366: AP Photo/Evan Vucci; p. 368: AP Photo/Susan Walsh; p. 371: AP Photo/Susan Walsh; p. 373: AP Photo/Evan Vucci

CHAPTER 12

p. 390: JEWEL SAMAD/AFP/Getty Images; p. 393: Breuker & Kessler lith., Philada./Library of Congress Prints and Photographs Division; p. 394: AP Photo; p. 395: Wolf Grulkey; p. 396: AP Photo/Doug Mills; p. 398: © Bettmann/CORBIS; p. 402: Hank Walker/The LIFE Picture Collection/Getty Images; p. 404: Alex Wong/Getty Images; p. 418: AP Photo/File; p. 421: Sean Gallup/Getty Images

CHAPTER 13

p. 422: AP Photo/Susan Walsh, File; p. 425 (top): Michael Rieger/FEMA News Photo; p. 425 (bottom): AP Photo/Gerald Herbert; p. 430: Thomas Nast, Harper's weekly, 1877 April 28, p. 325/Library of Congress Prints and Photographs Division; p. 434: AHMAD AL-RUBAYE/AFP/Getty Images; p. 437: AP Photo/Gregory Bull; p. 448: AP Photo; p. 458: © North American Syndicate

CHAPTER 14

p. 460: Photographs in the Carol M. Highsmith Archive, Library of Congress, Prints and Photographs Division LC-DIG-highsm-13879. Carol M. Highsmith; 2011; p. 464: AP Photo/Tony Dejak; p. 468: The Collection of the Supreme Court of the United States/MCT via Getty Images; p. 475: AP Photo/Manuel Balce Ceneta; p. 476: AP Photo; p. 481: JEWEL SAMAD/AFP/Getty Images; p. 482: Thomas Marshall Smith, Baltimore, Md./Library of Congress Prints and Photographs Division

Figure Credits

CHAPTER 1

p. 16: Intercollegiate Studies Institute American Civic Literacy Program, "Our Fading Heritage: Americans Fail a Basic Test on Their History and Institutions," at http://www.americancivicliteracy.org/2008/report_card.html; p. 26: William S. Maddox and Stuart A. Lillie, *Beyond Liberal and Conservative: Reassessing the Political Spectrum* (Washington, D.C.: The Cato Institute, 1984)

CHAPTER 3

p. 92 (top and bottom): US Government Printing Office, Historical Tables, Budget of the United States Government, Fiscal Year 2015, Table 12.1 - Summary Comparison of Total Outlays for Grants to State and Local Governments, http://www.gpo.gov/fdsys/pkg/BUDGET-2015-TAB/xls/BUDGET-2015-TAB-12-1.xls (accessed 9/17/14); p. 97: National Association of State Budget Officers, State Expenditure Report National Association of State Budget Officers, State Expenditure Report, FY 2012 (Washington D.C., 2013), p. 4; p. 112: U.S. Census Bureau, 2012 American Community Survey, 2012 Puerto Rican Community Survey

CHAPTER 4

p. 139: ©2014 Death Penalty Information Center

CHAPTER 6

p. 184: Gallup Poll, 2013. Secondary source: http://fivethirtyeight.blogs.nytimes.com/2013/07/17/in-public-opinion-on-abortion-few-absolutes/?_r=0

CHAPTER 7

p. 223: The results are based on more than 18,000 interviews with Americans from 13 separate Gallup multiple-day polls conducted in 2013; p. 245: Figure created based on data from *U.S. News & World Report.*

CHAPTER 8

p. 279: Figure created based on data from U.S. National Archives and Records Administration, Washington, D.C.

CHAPTER 9

p. 300: Figure created based on data from Federal Election Commission press releases.

CHAPTER 10

p. 327: *PEW Research Center,* http://www.journalism.org/2013/11/14/news-use-across-social-media-platforms/; p. 340: Gerhard Peters, "Presidential News Conferences." *The American Presidency Project*, ed. John T. Wooley and Gerhard Peters (Santa Barbara: University of California,

1999-2014); see http://www.presidency.ucsb.edu/data/news-conferences.php.

CHAPTER 11
p. 354: Gallup Poll, 2014. Secondary source: Gallup/Newsweek; p. 384: US Department of the Treasury, Bureau of the Fiscal Service, Daily Treasury Statements, http://www.fms.treas.gov/dts/index.html; p. 387: Data for FY1962-FY1973 from OMB, Budget for Fiscal Year 2014, Historical Tables, Tables 1.3 and 8.5; Data for FY974-FY2024 from CBO Historical Tables and CBO Budget Projections data.

CHAPTER 12
p. 412: Line Graph by WSJ Research. Secondary source: Gallup Poll, 2014.

CHAPTER 13
p. 427: Pew Research Center, National Election Studies, Gallup, ABC/Washington Post, CBS/New York Times, and CNN polls. From 1976 to 2013 the trend represents a three-survey moving average. For party analysis, selected data sets obtained from searches of the iPOLL Databank provided by the Roper Center for Public Opinion Research, University of Connecticut; p. 436: US Government Printing Office, United States Government Manual, issued annually; http://www.gpo.gov/help/index.html#about_united_states_government_manual.htm; p. 441: Federal Reserve Bank of St. Louis, Economic Research Division, http://research.stlouis-fed.org/fred2/categories/32325

CHAPTER 14
p. 465: From Lawrence Baum, *American Courts: Process and Policy*, 2nd ed., p. 28. © 1998 by Houghton Mifflin Company; p. 467: Administrative Office of the U.S. Courts; p. 494: US Sentencing Commission, Interactive Sourcebook of Federal Sentencing Statistics, Fiscal Year 2012, Figure F; compiled at isb.ussc.gov using the Commission's fiscal year 2012 Datafile.

Index

Page numbers followed by *f* indicate a figure. Page numbers followed by *t* indicate a table. Page numbers in italic indicate photographs or illustrations.

A

AAA. *See* American Automobile Association
AALL. *See* American Association for Labor Legislation
Aaron Swartz Case, 490–92
AARP. *See* American Association of Retired People
ABC Network, 326, 327–28
abortion
    civil rights and, 287
    public opinion about, 184*f*
    rights, 287
    Supreme Court on, 140–41
ACA. *See* Affordable Care Act
accommodationist interpretation, 128
Acheson, Dean, 177
activists
    citizen activist interest groups, 297
    community, 203
    Keystone Pipeline demonstration, *298*
    Montgomery bus boycott, 158–59
    parochial, 203
    Social Networking Sites and, *328*
ACT UP, 311
Adams, Abigail, 115
Adams, John, 481
    on civil liberties, 115
    Constitution and, 42
    economy and, 244
    on government, 462
    on political parties, 220
administrative discretion, 444
adult socialization, 190–91
advertising
    campaign financing, 260, 263–64, 268
    campaign posters, *252*
    news and, 332
    television, 260, 263–64, 269, 326
Advisory Council on Executive Organizations (Ash Council), 457
affirmative action, 173–74, 198
Affordable Care Act (ACA, Obamacare), 446
    AMA and, 318
    constitutionality of, 94, 314

Massachusetts health care as model for, 98
    provisions of, 74, 112
    public opinion and, 183–84, 193
    religion and, 132
    website failure of, 396
Afghanistan war, 274
AFL-CIO. *See* American Federation of Labor and Congress of Industrial Organizations
African Americans. *See also* civil rights; discrimination
    affirmative action, 173–74, 198
    in Congress, 355–56
    in House of Representatives, 356
    Obama, B., as first president as, 207
    party identification of, 200
    political participation of, 206–7
    in Senate, 356
    in Supreme Court, *476*
    voting rights of, 154, 159–60, 206, 271, 355–56
AFSCME. *See* American Federation of State, County and Municipal Employees
age
    of citizens, 100
    discrimination, 94, 108
    groups of college students, 197
    political activism and, 205
    voter turnout and, 199
    voting, 188, 199, 272
    young people and political process, 199
Age Discrimination Act (1975), 108
agendas
    media and political, 334–35
    setting, 70
AHA. *See* American Hospital Association
AIDS, 70, 311
Air Force, U.S., 388
airline industry, 72–73, 296, 304, 349, 350, 445
Alaska, 286, 361
Alger, Horatio, Jr., 17
Alien and Sedition Acts (1797), 148–49
aliens, 147, *171*

Alito, Samuel, 133, 475
AMA. *See* American Medical Association
Amazon.com, 351
Amendment I, 90, 116, 117, 508
    accommodationist interpretation, 128
    bad tendency test, 121
    cell phones and, 125
    civil liberties, 120–32
    clear and present danger, 121
    establishment of, 128–29
    freedom of press, 125–27
    freedom of religion, 128–32
    freedom of speech, 121–25, 264–65
    libel, 126–27, 330
    obscenity, 127, 330
    preferred freedoms test, 122
    prior restraint, 126
    school vouchers, 129
    slander, 126–27
    social networks and, 124–25
    symbolic speech, 122, *123*, 124
    technology and free speech, 124–25
    wall of separation, 128
Amendment II, 118, 132–33, 508–9
Amendment III, 509
Amendment IV, 509
    searches and seizures, 135–38, 152
Amendment IX, 510
Amendments, 57*t*
    formal process of, 54, 55*f*, 56
    ratification of, 55*f*, 56
Amendment V, 60, 117, 118, 134, 509
Amendment VI, 509
    right to counsel, 134–35
Amendment VII, 509
Amendment VIII, 509
Amendment X, 51, 83, 107, 510
Amendment XI, 510
Amendment XII, 510–11
Amendment XIII, 153, 154, 511
    cruel and unusual punishment, 137–40
Amendment XIV, 60, 117–18, 511–12
    doctor-assisted suicide, 141–42, 285
    equal protection of the laws clause, 153–54, 159, 167–68, 174
    public education and, 156
    Section 5, 131–32

TSA. *See* Transportation Security
Administration
Turner Broadcasting, 349
Tweed, Boss (William M.), *236*
Twelfth Amendment.
See Amendment XII
Twentieth Amendment.
See Amendment XX
Twenty-Fifth Amendment.
See Amendment XXV
Twenty-First Amendment.
See Amendment XXI
Twenty-Fourth Amendment.
See Amendment XXIV
Twenty-Second Amendment.
See Amendment XXII
Twenty-Seventh Amendment.
See Amendment XXVII
Twenty-Sixth Amendment.
See Amendment XXVI
Twenty-Third Amendment.
See Amendment XXIII
Twitter, 124–25, *190*, 268, 326, 327*f*,
329, 337
two-party system, 229–34, 243–49
Two Treaties on Government (Locke), 44
tyranny, 61–62

U

unalienable rights, 45
undue burden, 141
unemployment, 246
benefits, 11
Great Recession and, 274
insurance, 315–16
rate, elections and, 7–8
UN Framework Convention on Climate
Change, 212
unfunded mandates, 89
unicameral, 48
unilateralism, 416
unions, 299
unitary executive theory, 445, 456
unitary system, 47
United Nations, 402
United States (U.S.). *See also* Colonial
America; *specific institutions*
civic literacy in, 21, 22*f*, 23
debt, 384*f*
Japan and, 18
Louisiana Territory, *10*, 11
Mexican border, *172*
origins and types of law in, 463
political participation in, 202*t*, 204,
208–9

political parties in, 221–22
poverty in, 112*f*
public and campaigns, 251–53
public opinion of, 194
Soviet Union and, 421
third parties in, 232–33, 234*t*
two-party system of, 229–34
*United States Government Policy
and Supporting Positions*, 429
United States Student Association
(USSA), 294
United States v. Banks (2003), 138
United States v. Eichman (1990), 122
United States v. Nixon (1974), 399
United States v. Terry (1968), 136
United States v. Virginia, 162
United States v. Windsor, 94, 168, 170
Universal Studios, 349
universities, 293*t*, 294
Univision, *336*
unstable government coalitions, 235
USA Today, 327
U.S. Conference of Mayors, *102*
USSA. *See* United States Student
Association
USS *Maddox*, 402
Utah, 286

V

values, civil liberties and, 116
veto
congressional legislative, 365–66
line-item, 405–6
pocket, 405
power of president, 62–63, 393, 404–6
Viacom, 346, 349, 350
vice-presidency
Article I, 368
in Constitution, 371, 410
Franklin, B., on, 410
Senate and, 368–69, 410
video news release (VNR), 335–36
Vieth v. Jubelirer (2004), 359
Vietnam War, 20, 126, 178, 204, 214, 402
violence, 155
Virginia Military Institute (VMI), 162
Virginia Plan, 48
Virginia Women's Institute for
Leadership (VWIL), 162
VMI. *See* Virginia Military Institute
VNR. *See* video news release
volunteering, 204
voter turnout
age and, 199
in Great Britain, 272
in other nations, 272

in presidential elections, 199, 204, 271
2008 elections, 204
2014 elections, 271
voting, 21–22
ages, 188, 199, 272
candidate image and, 275
candidate information and, 226
in Congress, 378–79
in Constitution, 271
demographics, 271–72
education and, 272
eligibility for, 271
in Europe, 272
group influences and, 275
issues, 274–75
motivation for, 274–75
for Obama, B., 275
parliamentary systems and, 235
party dealignment, 230–31
party identification and, 275
party realignment, 230–31
polls and, 192
population size and campaign
financing, 263
reasons for not, 272, 273*t*, 274
registration, 199, 207
retrospective, 275
for Romney, M., 275
simplification through political
parties, 226, 231–32
specialists, 203
women and, 161
voting rights, 198, 205
of African Americans, 154, 159–60,
206, 271, 355–56
civil rights, 159–60
property ownership and, 271
residency and, 271
Supreme Court on, 160, 271
for women in amendment XIX, 356
Voting Rights Act (1965), 159–60, 272
vulnerability, myth of, 17, 19, 34–35,
146–49, 179–80
VWIL. *See* Virginia Women's Institute
for Leadership

W

wage systems, 432
wall of separation, 128
Wall Street Journal, *320*
Wall Street Reform and Consumer
Protection Act, 446
wards, 236
Warner Brothers, 349
War of the Worlds (Wells, H. G.), 321, *322*
War on Drugs, 89